W. JOHN ALLISON JR.
ATTORNEY AT LAW
SUITE ONE, THE KATY BUILDING
701 COMMERCE STREET.
DALLAS, TEXAS 75202

Trial Practice Series

CONSTITUTIONAL LIMITATIONS ON CRIMINAL PROCEDURE

1986 Cumulative Supplement
Current through July 15, 1986

Richard B. McNamara
Partner
Wiggin & Nourie
Manchester, New Hampshire

Insert in the pocket at the back
of the bound volume. Discard
supplement dated 1985.

SHEPARD'S/McGRAW-HILL, INC.
P.O. Box 1235
Colorado Springs, Colorado 80901

Bound book ISBN 0–07–045674–7
Supplement ISBN 0–07–045677–1

Preface to the Supplement

The 1985 term of the United States Supreme Court did not result in the sweeping changes which characterized the 1982 and 1983 terms. The Court did deal with the issue of warrantless aerial surveillance for the first time. However, there were few search and seizure decisions of great importance. Rather, the Court seemed to focus on the mechanics of trial and the right to counsel. In a number of cases, the Court expounded upon the standard for determining when counsel for a defendant may be said to be ineffective. The Court dealt with the difficult problem raised when counsel in a criminal case believes his or her client may commit perjury. The Court reaffirmed its traditional rule barring surreptitious interrogation of a defendant once the right to counsel has attached. In several cases, the Court discussed the scope of the right to cross-examine and confront witnesses.

State courts of last resort in even larger numbers have begun to consider whether to adopt some of the more significant federal decisions, such as the good faith exception to the exclusionary rule and the totality of the circumstances test for establishing the reliability of an informer's tips. Numerous states have adopted laws providing for the admission of out of court statements of infant victims of sexual assault; such laws have provided grist for the judicial mill.

This supplement includes significant cases decided through July 30, 1986 and includes all decisions of the October 1985 term of the United States Supreme Court.

RBM

iii

New sections appearing in this supplement

1

The Constitution and Criminal Procedure

§1.02 Interpretation of Constitutional Guarantees

Page 3, note 13, at end of note add:

See also Connecticut v Johnson, 460 US 73 (1983).

Page 3, note 15, at end of note add:

See also Connecticut v Johnson, 460 US 73, 81 n 9 (1983) ("State courts, of course, are free to interpret their own constitutions and laws to permit fewer applications of the harmless error rule than does the Federal Constitution").

§1.04 Retroactivity of Constitutional Decisions

Page 5, note 24, at end of note add:

Solem v Stumes, 104 S Ct 1338, 1341 (1984).

Page 5, text, add at end of section:

In *United States v Johnson*, 457 US 537 (1982), a five-judge majority reconsidered its prior analysis of retroactivity, and held that a decision of the Court construing the Fourth Amendment is to be applied retroactively to all convictions that were not final at the time the decision was made. In so holding, the Court was careful to note that in areas apart from the Fourth Amendment, its precedents were left undisturbed. *Id* 562.

In *Johnson,* the defendant sought reversal of his conviction on the ground that evidence obtained in violation of *Payton v New York,* 445 US 573 (1980) (which prohibits the police from making a warrantless and nonconsensual entry into a suspect's home to make a routine felony arrest) was admitted at his trial, which occurred before *Payton* was decided. While his appeal was pending, the United States Supreme Court decided *Payton.* The Court held that the retroactivity issue raised by this particular case was not controlled by the prior precedents of the Court, because *Payton* did not simply apply settled law to a new set of facts, did not announce a new and entirely unanticipated principle of law, and did not overturn any long-standing practice approved by a near-unanimous body of lower court authority. *Id* 2588-89. At least with respect to the Fourth Amendment, the Court embraced the retroactivity rationale expounded by Justice Harlan in *Desist v United States,* 394 US 244, 256 (1969) (dissenting opinion), and *Mackey v United States,* 401 US 667, 675 (1971) (separate opinion). Justice Harlan had rejected the view that the Court could apply a new constitutional rule entirely prospectively, while making an exception only for the particular litigant whose case was chosen as the vehicle for establishing that rule, reasoning that:

> [A] proper perception of our duties as a court of law, charged with applying the Constitution to resolve every legal dispute within our jurisdiction on direct review, mandates that we apply the law as it is at the time, not as it once was.

Mackey v United States, 401 US at 681, *quoted with approval in United States v Johnson,* 102 S Ct 2579, 2586 (1982). The majority opinion delivered by Justice Blackmun was joined in by four other justices, and four justices dissented. Justice Brennan concurred in the majority opinion "on [the] understanding that the decision leaves undisturbed our retroactivity precedents as applied to convictions final at the time of decision." *United States v Johnson,* 102 S Ct at 2595 (Brennan, J, concurring). Because Justice Blackmun's majority opinion purported to leave undisturbed retroactivity precedents in other areas, and expressly left open the retroactive reach of the Court's decisions to those cases which raise Fourth Amendment issues on collateral attack, it is likely that further litigation of the issue of retroactivity will occur. *Id* 2594 n 20.

The traditional retroactivity standards outlined in *Linkletter,* however, were applied by the Court in *Solem v Stumes,* 104 S Ct 1338 (1984), to hold that *Edwards v Arizona,* 451 US 477 (1981), which established a prophylactic rule to safeguard the right to fair interrogation, should not be given retroactive effect.

However, in *Shea v Louisiana,* 105 S Ct 1065 (1985), the Court stated "there is nothing about a Fourth Amendment rule that suggests that

... it should be given greater retroactive effect than a Fifth Amendment rule," and specifically held that the Court's analysis of retroactivity in *United States v Johnson,* should be applied to the case before it, in which the defendant, whose conviction was pending on direct appeal to a state court at the time *Edwards v Arizona,* 451 US 477 (1981), was decided, was entitled to the benefit of the rule announced in *Edwards.* Justice Blackmun wrote for a five-judge majority:

> ... a Fifth Amendment violation may be more likely to effect the truth finding process then a Fourth Amendment violation. And Justice Harlan's reasoning—that principled decisionmaking and fairness to similarly situation petitioners requires application of a new rule to all cases pending on direct review—is applicable with equal force to the situation presently before us. We hold that our analysis in Johnson is relevant for petitioner's direct-review Fifth Amendment claim under *Edwards.* Id 1070.

It appears that *Shea* may signal a significant departure for the Court. Justice White, dissenting, stated that:

> ... the majority apparently adopts a rule long advocated by a shifting minority of justices, and endorsed in limited circumstances by the majority in *United States v. Johnson:* namely, the rule that any new constitutional decision—except perhaps one that constitutes a 'clear break with the past'—must be applied to all cases pending on direct appeal at the time it is handed down. Id 1071 (White, J. dissenting).

§1.09 The Void for Vagueness Doctrine

Page 11, note 68, at end of note add:

See also Kolender v Lawson, 461 US 352, 357-58 (1983).

Page 12, note 73, at end of note add:

See also Kolender v Lawson, 461 US 352 (1983):

> Although the doctrine focuses both on actual notice to citizens and arbitrary enforcement, we have recognized recently that the more important aspect of the vagueness doctrine "is not actual notice, but the other principal element of the doctrine—the requirement that a legislature establish minimal guidelines to govern law enforcement" [citation omitted]. Where the legislature fails to provide such minimal guidelines, a criminal statute

may permit "a standardless sweep [that] allows policemen, prosecutors and juries to pursue their personal predilections."

2

Police-Citizen Contact and Extraordinary Investigative Techniques

§2.01 Police-Citizen Contact and the Fourth Amendment

Page 15, note 2, at end of note add:

Florida v Royer, 460 US 491 (1983). *See also* Tennessee v Garner, 105 S Ct 1694, 1699 (1985) ("Whenever an officer restrains the freedom of a person to walk away, he has seized that person.").

Page 15, note 3, at end of note add:

INS v Delgado, 104 S Ct 1758 (1984).

Page 15, note 4, at end of note add:

INS v Delgado, 104 S Ct 1758 (1984); Florida v Royer, 460 US 491 (1983). *See also* United States v Villamonte-Marquez, 462 US 579 (1983).

§2.02 Questioning by Police Officers

Page 17, text, add at end of section:

The right of policemen to question and the right of citizens to refuse to answer was addressed by the plurality in *Florida v Royer*, 460 US 491 (1983):

> [L]aw enforcement officers do not violate the Fourth Amendment by merely approaching an individual on the street or in a public place, by asking him if he is willing to answer some questions, by putting questions to him if the person is willing to listen, or by

offering in evidence in a criminal prosecution his voluntary answers to such questions [citation omitted]. Nor would the fact that the officer identifies himself as a police officer, without more, convert the encounter into a seizure requiring some level of objective justification [citation omitted]. The person approached, however, need not answer any question put to him; indeed, he may decline to listen to the questions at all and may go on his way [citation omitted]. He may not be detained even momentarily without reasonable objective grounds for doing so; and his refusal to listen or answer does not, without more, furnish those grounds.

Id 497-98. *See also* INS v Delgado, 104 S Ct 1758 (1984).

§2.03   Investigative Stops

Page 17, note 16, at end of note add:

See also Florida v Royer, 460 US 491 (1983).

Page 17, note 17, at end of note add:

See also Florida v Royer, 460 US 491 (1983).

Page 18, note 19, at end of note add:

Florida v Royer, 460 US 491 (1983).

Page 18, text, add at end of section:

In *Florida v Royer*, 460 US 491 (1983), the four-judge plurality concluded that seizures on less than probable cause may be permissible in some circumstances because law enforcement interests warrant a limited intrusion on the personal security of the suspect. Justice White wrote:

> The scope of the intrusion permitted will vary to some extent with the particular facts and circumstances of each case. This much, however, is clear: an investigative detention must be temporary and last no longer than is necessary to effectuate the purpose of the stop. Similarly, the investigative methods employed should be the least intrusive means reasonably available to verify or dispel the officer's suspicion in a short period of time.

Id 500.

The Supreme Court has held that use of a trained dog to sniff luggage to determine whether it contains illicit drugs is not a search within the meaning of the Fourth Amendment. *United States v Place*, 462 US 696 (1983). The Court has made explicitly clear, however, that the line between arrest and investigative stops "is crossed when the police, without probable cause or a warrant, forceably remove a person from his home or other place in which he is entitled to be and transport him to the police station where he is detained, although briefly, for investigative purposes." *Hayes v Florida*, 105 S Ct 1643, 1647 (1985). The Court has held that police officers may not, without a warrant, take a person to a police station against his or her will so that fingerprints may be taken based upon reasonable suspicion that he or she was involved in a crime. *Id; Davis v Mississippi*, 394 US 721 (1969). However, the Court has stated that "there is support in our cases for the view that the Fourth Amendment would permit seizures for the purpose of fingerprinting, if there is a reasonable basis for believing that fingerprinting will establish or negate the suspects' connection with the crime, and if the procedure is carried out with dispatch." *Hayes v Florida*, 105 S Ct 1643, 1647 (1985). The Court has also suggested that "under circumscribed procedures, the Fourth Amendment might permit the judiciary to authorize the seizure of a person on less than probable cause and his removal to the police station for the purpose of fingerprinting." *Id.* State courts have reached different results about the validity of such procedures. *Compare People v Madson*, 196 Colo 507, 638 P2d 18, 31-32 (1981) *with State v Evans*, 215 Neb 433, 438-39, 338 NW2d 788, 792-93 (1983) *and In re An Investigation into the Death of Abe A*, 56 NY2d 288, 295-96, 437 NE2d 265, 269, 452 NYS2d 6, 10 (1982).

Page 18, note 21, at end of note add:

In New York v Class, 106 S Ct 960 (1986), the Court held that a police officer who had stopped the defendant's vehicle for traffic offenses and asked him to exit the vehicle had the right to reach into the passenger compartment to move papers obscuring the Vehicle Identification Number (VIN), so that a gun he observed while doing so could be admitted into evidence.

However, the Hawaii Supreme Court has, based on the Hawaii constitution, rejected Pennsylvania v Mimms, and held that a lawful traffic stop is not, of itself, a sufficient basis for a police officer to order a motorist to get out of a car. State v Kim, 711 P2d 1291 (Hawaii 1985).

§2.04 Regulatory Checks

Page 18, note 23, at end of note add:

People v John BB, 56 NY2d 482, 438 NE2d 864, 453 NYS2d 158 (1982). However, the spot checks must be conducted in such a manner as to minimize the discretion of officers in the field. In Ekstrom v Justice

Court, 136 Ariz 1, 663 P2d 992 (1983), the Arizona Supreme Court held that roadblocks, set up at the discretion of local highway patrolmen and operated without specific directions or guidelines, were violative of the Fourth Amendment.

Page 18, text, at end of section add:

While the United States Supreme Court has never specifically ruled on the issue of whether roadblocks to apprehend drunk drivers are violative of the constitutional prohibition of unreasonable search and seizure, numerous state courts have considered the issue with varying results. Such roadblocks were upheld in *People v Bartley*, 109 Ill 2d 273, 486 NE2d 880 (1985), *cert denied sub nom Bartley v Illinois*, 106 S CT 1384 (1986); *Little v State*, 300 Md 485, 479 A2d 903 (1984); *State v Deskins*, 234 Kan 529, 673 P2d 1174 (1983) and *State v Marchand*, 104 Wash 2d 434, 706 P2d 225 (1985). Police roadblocks were invalidated as "close to a police state tactic" in *State v Koppel*, 127 NH 286, 499 A2d 995 (1985) and *State v Smith*, 674 P2d 562 (Okla Crim App 1984).

§2.05   Stop and Frisk

Page 18, note 26, at end of note add:

See also Florida v Royer, 460 US 491 (1983). When police seize luggage on less than probable cause, the luggage may not be held longer than a person could be held during a *Terry*-type investigative stop. United States v Place, 462 US 696 (1983).

Page 18, note 27, at end of note add:

See also Florida v Royer, 460 US 491 (1983).

Page 20, text, add at end of section:

Because of the hazardous nature of a roadside encounter, the need for protection of police can justify protective searches of automobile passenger compartments, limited to those areas in which a weapon may be concealed. *Michigan v Long*, 463 US 1032 (1983).

§2.07   —After Person Has Been Charged with Crime

Page 21 note 47, at end of note add:

Maine v Moulton, 106 S Ct 477 (1985).

Page 21, note 48, at end of note add:

Maine v Moulton, 106 S Ct 477 (1985).

Page 22, text, add at end of section:

In *United States v Mastroianni,* 749 F2d 900 (1st Cir 1984) as in *Weatherford v Bursey,* 429 US 545 (1977), a defendant invited the state's informant to a meeting with his counsel. Despite this fact, the court stated "without proof of exceptional circumstances, the state cannot intrude into a defense meeting" and held that the government holds the burden of proving the necessity for its representative to attend meetings between the defendant and his counsel. *Id* 905. The mere recitation of the need to protect the informant will not do; "the government's burden to prove the necessity for an informant's presence at a defense meeting is high." *Id* 906 n 2.

In *Maine v Moulton,* 106 S Ct 477 (1986), the Court reaffirmed its holdings in *Massiah* and *Henry,* and held that an indicted defendant's Sixth Amendment rights are violated when the state arranges to record conversations between co-defendants, even though it is the target defendant, and not the police, who arranges the meeting. Similarly, the fact that the police had other legitimate reasons for listening to the conversation, namely to investigate the target defendant's plan for killing a witness, does not justify admission of the evidence. Such evidence could, of course, be admitted if relevant to crimes to which the Sixth Amendment has not attached. *Id* 489.

However, the Court has made clear that the sixth Amendment is not violated when, by luck or happenstance, the state obtains incriminating statements from an accused after the right to counsel has attached. In *Kuhlman v Wilson,* 106 S Ct 2616 (1986), the Court held that merely placing the defendant in a cell occupied by a police informer, who made no attempt to elicit incriminating remarks, did not violate the Sixth Amendment. Distinguishing *United States v Henry,* 447 US 264 (1980), since in that case the government created a situation likely to induce the defendant to make inculpatory statements, the Court held that "a defendant does not make out a violation of [his Sixth Amendment] right simply by showing that an informant either through prior arrangement or voluntarily, reported his incriminating statements to the police." *Id,* 2630.

§2.09 Electronic Surveillance

Page 23, note 57, at end of note add:

See also United States v Knotts, 460 US 276 (1983).

Page 24, note 66, at end of note add:

The New Jersey Supreme Court has declined to follow Smith v Maryland, 442 US 735 (1979) and has held that the New Jersey Constitution establishes a protected right of privacy in telephone toll records. State v Hunt, 91 NJ 338, 450 A2d 952 (1982).

§2.09A Use of Concealed Radio Transmitters (New)

In *United States v Knotts*, 460 US 276 (1983), the defendant was suspected by law enforcement officers of manufacturing drugs. They arranged with the seller of a chemical which could be used to manufacture illegal drugs to put a so-called beeper inside the container which would be purchased by the defendant. When the defendant purchased the container, the police followed him, maintaining visual contact, and monitoring the beeper. Finally, the officers lost sight of the defendant's car, but it was located, through use of the beeper, at a secluded cabin. After three days of surveillance, the officers obtained a search warrant and discovered the container and facilities for manufacturing illicit drugs. The defendant moved to suppress the fruits of the search. The United States Supreme Court held that the search was lawful, because monitoring the beeper signals did not invade any legitimate expectation of privacy on the part of the defendant, and since it did not, there was neither a search nor seizure within the contemplation of the Fourth Amendment. *Id* 285. In so holding, the Court emphasized that all the police did was what they could have done lawfully—follow the defendant on public thoroughfares to his dwelling. Justice Rehnquist pointed out:

> A person travelling in an automobile on public thoroughfares has no reasonable expectation of privacy in his movements from one place to another. When [the defendant] travelled over the public streets, he voluntarily conveyed to anyone who wanted to look the fact that he was travelling over particular roads in a particular direction, the fact of whatever stops he made, and the fact of his final destination when he exited from public roads onto private property.

Id 281-282. Since visual surveillance of the defendant from public places along his route or adjoining the cabin would have revealed the same information revealed by the beeper, the Court found no constitutional infirmity: "Nothing in the Fourth Amendment prohibited the police from augmenting the sensory faculties bestowed upon them at birth with such enhancement as science and technology afforded them in this case." *Id* 282.

In *United States v Karo,* 104 S Ct 3296 (1984), the court considered two questions left unresolved in *Knotts:* whether installation of a beeper in a container of chemicals, with the consent of the owner, constitutes a search or seizure when the container is to be delivered to a buyer having no knowledge of the presence of the beeper, and whether the monitoring of a beeper falls within the ambit of the Fourth Amendment when it reveals information that could not have been obtained through visual surveillance.

In holding that installation of a beeper in a container, with the owner's consent, even though the government is aware that the owner intends to sell the container to a target, does not violate the Fourth Amendment, the Court rejected the lower court's premise that "all individuals have a legitimate expectation of privacy that objects coming into their rightful ownership do not have electronic devices attached to them, devices that would give law enforcement agents the opportunity to monitor the location of the objects at all times and in every place that the objects are taken, including inside private residences and other areas where the right to be free from warrantless governmental intrusion is unquestioned." *Id* 3302.

The Court considered placement of a beeper neither a search nor a seizure, because until it is transmitting, it conveys no information, and placement of the beeper does not interfere with anyone's possessory interest.

However, in holding that monitoring of a beeper *does* fall within the ambit of the Fourth Amendment, and that a warrant is required for such activity, Justice White wrote: "Indiscriminate monitoring of property that has been withdrawn from public view would present far too serious a threat to privacy interests in the home to escape entirely some sort of Fourth Amendment oversight." *Id* 3304. The Court emphasized, as it had in *Knotts,* the distinction between monitoring movements which occur in public and monitoring concealed movements. Monitoring the former is permissible, since a person conducting public activity can have no reasonable expectation of privacy regarding that activity, but monitoring the latter without a warrant is impermissible.

§2.10 Government Manufacture of Crime

Page 25, text, add at end of section:

In a fragmented opinion, the United States Court of Appeals for the District of Columbia reversed the district court's opinion in *United States v Kelly,* 707 F2d 1460 (DC Cir 1983). The majority of the court held that the guarantee of fundamental fairness had not been violated on the facts before it. While the majority referred to the district court's opinion as thoughtful, and stated that it "might be attracted" to an approach similar to the district court's, "were the slate clean," it felt constrained by the decisions of the Supreme Court to limit application of the doctrine that courts may dismiss criminal prosecutions if the government is deeply involved in the criminal activity:

> We may not alter the contours of the entrapment defense under a Due Process cloak, and we lack authority, where no specific constitutional right of the defendant has been violated, to dismiss indictments as an exercise of supervisory power over the conduct of federal law enforcement agents [citation omitted]. Precedent dictates that we refrain from applying the general Due Process constraint to bar a conviction except in the rare instance of "police overinvolvement in crime" that reaches a demonstrable level of outrageousness. . . . [The] broad fundamental fairness guarantee, it appears from High Court decisions, is not transgressed absent coercion, violence or brutality to the person [citation omitted]. Without further Supreme Court elaboration, we have no guide to a more dynamic definition of the outrageousness concept, and no warrant, as lower court judges, to devise such a definition in advance of any signal to do so from higher authority.

Id 1475-76. The other Abscam defendants have been equally unsuccessful in attacking the techniques employed by the government. *United States v Williams*, 705 F2d 603 (2d Cir 1983), *cert denied*, 104 S Ct 524 (1984); *United States v Myers*, 692 F2d 823 (2d Cir 1982), *cert denied*, 103 S Ct 2437 (1983); *United States v Jannotti*, 673 F2d 578 (3d Cir), *cert denied*, 102 S Ct 2906 (1982); *United States v Alexandro*, 674 F2d 34, 39-42 (2d Cir), *cert denied*, 103 S Ct 78 (1982); *cf United States v Hastings*, 461 US 499 (1983).

One of the rare cases in which indictments were actually dismissed by a court as a result of prosecutorial misconduct is *State v Glosson*, 462 So 2d 1085 (Fla 1985). In that case, the sheriff and one Willson entered into an agreement whereby Willson would receive 10 per cent of all civil forfeitures arising out of successful criminal investigations he completed in Levy County, Florida. Willson agreed to sell the defendants several hundred pounds of cannabis. The defendants moved to dismiss and the government objected, asserting that the due process defense is not available in a case "which did not involve acts or threats of violence by government agents." *Id* 1064. Explicitly rejecting the approach taken in *United States v Kelley*, 707 F2d 1460 (DC Cir 1983), Justice McDonald wrote:

> We reject the narrow application of the due process defense found in the federal cases. Based upon the due process provision of article 1, section 9 of the Florida Constitution . . . we agree

> ... that governmental misconduct which violates the constitutional due process rights of a defendant, regardless of that defendants predisposition, requires dismissal of criminal charges.

Id 1085.

3 Search

§3.02 Areas Protected from Government Search

Page 29, note 9, at end of note add:

A person has no legitimate expectation of privacy when a bailee of property opens a sealed package and then turns the opened package over to a government agent. United States v Jacobson, 104 S Ct 1652 (1984). *See also* Maryland v Macon, 105 S Ct 2778 (1985), holding that an undercover police officer's entry of an adult bookstore is not a search, and his purchase of an allegedly obscene publication is not a seizure.

Page 29, note 10, at end of note add:

See also Michigan v Clifford, 104 S Ct 641 (1984), in which a plurality of the Court held that the expectation of privacy a person possesses in his or her fire-damaged home requires that police or firemen secure an administrative warrant if the primary object of the search is to determine the cause and origin of the fire, and that a criminal search warrant is to be obtained if the primary object of the search is to gather evidence of criminal activity.

In Hudson v Palmer, 104 S Ct 3194 (1984), the Court held that a prisoner has no expectation of privacy in his prison cell entitling him to the protection of the Fourth Amendment against unreasonable searches.

See, e.g., New Jersey v TLO, 105 S Ct 733 (1985), holding that schoolchildren have legitimate expectations of privacy in property brought onto school grounds.

Page 29, note 11, at end of note add:

See United States v Knotts, 460 US 276 (1983), in which the Court held that no violation of the Fourth Amendment occurred when police officers arranged with the seller of chemicals to a suspected illicit drug manufacturer to place a beeper (a radio transmitter) in the drum sold to the illicit drug manufacturer so that the police could follow his automobile, and the police located his cabin as the result of the beeper. The Court emphasized that a person travelling in an automobile has "no reasonable expectation of privacy in his movements from one place to another." *Id* 281. While the defendant would have had the traditional expectation of privacy within his cabin, the Court reasoned that "no such expectation of privacy extended to the visual observation of [the defendant's] automobile arriving on the premises after leaving a public highway, nor to movements of objects such as the drum [containing the beeper] outside the cabin in the open fields." *Id* 282.

A warrantless viewing of the inside of an opaque greenhouse, located on brushy, rural property a mile from the nearest road, and at least 100 yards from the nearest vantage point on neighboring property, by using a telephoto lens to look through ventilation louvers was held to violate the defendant's Fourth Amendment rights. Wheeler v State, 659 SW2d 381 (Tex Crim App 1983).

Page 29, note 12, at end of note add:

The rule that the "special protection accorded by the Fourth Amendment to the people in their persons, houses, paper, and effects" is not extended to open fields was reaffirmed in Oliver v United States, 104 S Ct 1735 (1984). In *Oliver*, the Court considered two different cases in which police officers, without warrants, entered upon private land, upon which "no trespassing" signs had been placed, and located contraband property not visible from adjacent property. The Court held that there was no constitutionally protected expectation of privacy in an open field, since open fields are accessible to the public in a way that a building is not. Also, the common law, by implying that only the land immediately surrounded by the home warrants the Fourth Amendment protections that attach to the home, conversely implies that no expectation of privacy attaches to open fields. The fact that the officers' action was a trespass at common law did not make it a search in the constitutional sense.

The Nebraska Supreme Court has declined to adopt a more narrow open field exception to the warrant requirement of the Nebraska Constitution and has held that the open field exception articulated in *Oliver* is applicable to warrantless searches challenged on the basis of the Nebraska Constitution. State v Havlatt, 222 Neb 554, NW2d 436 (1986).

Page 29, note 13, at end of note add:

California v Ciraolo, 106 S Ct 1809 (1986).

The open area of an industrial plant complex with numerous plant structures spread over an area of 2,000 acres is not analogous to the curtilage of a dwelling, but is more comparable to an open field and as such it is open to the view and observation of persons in aircraft lawfully in the public airspace immediatley above or sufficiently near the area for the reach of cameras. Dow Chem Co v United States, 106 S Ct 1819 (1986).

§3.03   Abandoned Property

Page 30, text, add at end of section:

To abandon property, however, a person must take some affirmative step. A person who leaves an airport without his or her luggage does not necessarily relinquish ownership over that property. *United States v Sanders*, 719 F2d 882 (6th Cir 1983).

Moreover, there is a distinction between lost and abandoned property. While lost property may be inventoried by the police for identification, safekeeping, and safety purposes, an owner does not give up all expectation of privacy in lost property. In *State v Ching*, 67 Hawaii 911, 678 P2d 1008 (1984), for example, the court held that an illegal search was conducted by a police officer who, after recovering a lost leather pouch, inventoried the contents of the pouch, found the defendant's identification and an opaque brass cylinder, and opened the cylinder to find a white powder.

§3.04   Search by Private Individuals

Page 31, note 22, at end of note add:

The Fifth Circuit has held that a search conducted by private citizens is a search pursuant to governmental authority, and therefore subject to the constraints of the Fourth Amendment, when the government has so far insinuated itself into a position of interdependence with a private entity that it must be considered a joint participant in the challenged activity, or the private parties are exercising powers traditionally reserved by the government and delegated to private parties, or in the case of a regulated private entity where there is so close a nexus between the challenged action of the regulated private party and the state that the action of the private entity may be treated as the action of the state. Dobyns v E-Systems, 667 F2d 1219 (5th Cir 1982).

All public school teachers and school administrators are said to act in loco parentis in their dealing with students; the United States Supreme Court has held that they exercise public authority in searching students and that therefore the Fourth Amendment governs their actions. New Jersey v TLO, 105 S Ct 733 (1985). See also **§3.27B.**

Page 31, note 23, at end of note add:

Similary, in United States v Jacobson, 104 S Ct 1652 (1984), the Court held that no Fourth Amendment violation occurred when a damaged package was opened by employees at a private parcel express service office, pursuant to company policy, and was found to contain white powder. The company employees called the Drug Enforcement Administration, an agent arrived and did a field test, and determined that the powder was cocaine. The Court reasoned that the owner of the package could have no reasonable expectation of privacy in the opened container, and that the agent's inspection of the contents of the package enabled him to learn nothing that had not been learned during the private search. *Id* 1660.

§3.05   What May Be Searched For—The Mere Evidence Rule

Page 32, note 28, at end of note add:

See also Texas v Brown, 460 US 730, 742 (1983).

§3.06   Subpoenas and the Right to Be Free from Unreasonable Seizures

Page 33, note 32, at end of note add:

In United States v Doe, 104 S Ct 1237 (1984), the Court affirmed motions to quash subpoenas for business records of a sole proprietorship (except as to records required by law to be kept) where the respondent had asserted his Fifth Amendment privilege. The Court held that the act of producing the documents in question would be privileged. The court of appeals had, in affirming the district court's grant of the motion to quash, held that business records of a sole proprietor are no different from individual-owner personal papers, and both are privileged. The Court seemingly rejected the notion that the Fifth Amendment protects the privacy of papers which originated in Boyd v United States, 116 US 616, 630 (1886). 104 S Ct at 1245 (O'Connor, J., concurring).

§3.07 The Requirement of Probable Cause

Page 34, note 37, at end of note add:

Illinois v Gates, 462 US 213 (1983). *See also* Texas v Brown, 460 US 730, 742 (1983):

> [P]robable cause is a flexible common-sense standard. It merely requires that the facts available to the officer would "warrant a man of reasonable caution in the belief " [citation omitted] that certain items may be contraband or stolen or useful as evidence of a crime; it does not demand any showing that such a belief be correct or more likely true than false. A "practical, nontechnical" probability that incriminating evidence is involved is all that is required.

Id 1543.

Page 34, note 38, at end of note add:

In Illinois v Gates, 462 US 213, 235 (1983), the Court noted:

> Finely tuned standards such as proof beyond a reasonable doubt or by preponderance of the evidence, useful in formal trials, have no place in the magistrate's decision. While an effort to fix some general, numerically precise degree of certainty corresponding to "probable cause" may not be helpful, it is clear that only the probability, and not a prima facie showing, of criminal activity is the standard of probable cause.

See also Texas v Brown, 460 US 730, 742 (1983):

> [P]robable cause is a flexible common-sense standard. It merely requires that the facts available to the officer would "warrant a man of reasonable caution in the belief " [citation omitted] that certain items may be contraband or stolen or useful as evidence of a crime; it does not demand any showing that such a belief be correct or more likely true than false. A "practical, nontechnical" probability that incriminating evidence is involved is all that is required.

Page 34, note 39, at end of note add:

See also Texas v Brown, 460 US 730, 742 (1983):

> [P]robable cause is a flexible common-sense standard. It merely requires that the facts available to the officer would "warrant a man of reasonable caution in the belief " [citation omitted] that

certain items may be contraband or stolen or useful as evidence of a crime; it does not demand any showing that such a belief be correct or more likely true than false. A "practical, nontechnical" probability that incriminating evidence is involved is all that is required.

Page 35, note 43, at end of note add:

Texas v Brown, 460 US 730 (1983).

Page 35, text, add to end of section:

No higher probable cause standard is required to obtain a warrant to seize materials presumptively protected by the First Amendment. *New York v PJ Video, Inc,* 106 S Ct 1610 (1986). An application for a warrant to seize material presumptively protected by the First Amendment should be evaluated under the same probable cause standard used to review warrant applications generally, namely that there is a fair probability that evidence of a crime will be found in the particular place to be searched. *Id.*

§3.08 Information from Informers

Page 35, text, delete section and substitute:

In *Illinois v Gates,* 462 US 213 (1983), the United States Supreme Court drastically altered the law concerning sufficiency of information supplied by informers, rejecting the *two-prong* test of *Aguilar v Texas,* 378 US 108 (1964), and adopting a *totality of the circumstances* test to determine whether or not information received from an anonymous informant establishes probable cause.

The factual record upon which the Court acted was complex. The Bloomington, Illinois police department received an anonymous letter on May 3rd stating that the defendant wife would drive to Florida on May 3rd to be loaded with drugs, and the defendant husband would fly to Florida a few days later to drive their car, loaded with drugs, back. The letter stated that the trunk would be loaded with drugs, and that the defendants had over $100,000 worth of drugs in their basement. A police officer, acting on the tip, obtained the defendant husband's address and learned he had made a reservation for a May 5th flight to Florida. Surveillance disclosed that the husband made the flight, stayed overnight in a motel room registered in his wife's name, and left the following morning with a woman in a car bearing an Illinois license plate issued to him. A search warrant for their residence and automobile was obtained by the police, based upon an affidavit setting forth the facts in the letter, and the facts learned by the police. When the defendants arrived home, the police were waiting. They searched the automobile and the house pursuant to warrant.

The Illinois Courts suppressed the evidence obtained, holding that the affidavit was inadequate to establish probable cause under *Aguilar v Texas* and *Spinelli v United States,* 393 US 410 (1969), because there was no basis for concluding that the person who wrote the letter was credible and because the letter gave no hint of the basis of the writer's knowledge. The Supreme Court reversed. Justice Rehnquist, writing for a five-judge majority, concluded that the two-prong test established in *Aguilar* and *Spinelli* should be abandoned:

> [T]he "two pronged test" directs analysis into two largely independent channels—the informant's "veracity" or reliability and his "basis of knowledge." There are persuasive arguments against according these two elements such independent status. Instead, they are better understood as relevant considerations in the totality of circumstances analysis that traditionally has guided probable cause determinations: a deficiency in one may be compensated for, in determining the overall reliability of a tip, by a strong showing as to the other, or by some other indicia of reliability.

Illinois v Gates, 462 US 213, 232 (1983). The Court emphasized that while an informer's veracity, reliability, and basis of knowledge are all highly relevant in determining the value of his or her information, they should not "be understood as entirely separate and independent tests to be rigidly exacted in each case. . . . Rather, . . . they should be understood simply as closely intertwined issues that may usefully illuminate the commonsense, practical question whether there is probable cause to believe that contraband or evidence is located in a particular place." *Id* 229-30.

Turning to the facts of the case before it, the Court emphasized that it had "consistently recognized the value of corroboration of details of an informant tip by independent police work." *Id* 241. Referring to *Draper v United States,* 358 US 307 (1959), as the *classic* case on the value of corroboration, the Court concluded that "[the] showing of probable cause in the present case was fully as compelling as that in *Draper."* *Id* 2334. The Court emphasized that even standing alone, the facts of the Gates' trip was suggestive of a drug transaction; the letter's prediction that the Gates' car would be in Florida, that Mr. Gates would fly to Florida in the next day or so, and that he would drive the car north all suggested that the informer's other information might be true. Moreover, the Court thought that the letter writer's accurate information about the Gates' travel plans was likely to be obtained only from the Gates themselves, or from someone familiar with their plans. If an informant had access to accurate information of this type, a magistrate might properly conclude that the informer had access to reliable information of the Gates' illegal activities.

The Supreme Court of Washington has held that the Washington Constitution requires that in evaluating the existence of probable cause in relation to informer's tips, the affidavit in support of the warrant must establish the basis of information and credibility of the informant, and has thus declined to abandon the *Aguilar-Spinelli* "two prong test." *State v Jackson*, 102 Wash 2d 432, 688 P2d 136 (1984). The Alaska Supreme Court has retained the *Aguilar-Spinelli* test as a matter of Alaska constitutional law. *State v Jones*, 706 P2d 317 (Alaska 1985). Similarly, the New York Court of Appeals has, relying on the New York Constitution, declined to follow *Gates* and has instead adhered to the "predictable, structured analysis of the quality of evidence needed to support intrusive searches and seizures" of *Aguilar-Spinelli*. *People v Johnson,,* 66 NY2d 398, 488 NE2d 439, 497 NYS2d 618 (1985). Similarly, the Massachusetts Supreme Judicial Court has held that article 14 of the Declaration of Rights of the Commonwealth's Constitution provides more substantive protection to criminal defendants than does the Fourth Amendment in the determination of probable cause. That court has rejected the *Gates* rule as well, and held that the principles developed under *Aguilar* and *Spinelli* "if not applied hypertechnically, provide a more appropriate structure for probable cause inquires under article 14." *Commonwealth v Upton*, 394 Mass 363, 476 NE2d 548, 556 (1985). Numerous other courts have embraced *Gates* as a matter of state constitutional or common law. *See, e.g., Thompson v State*, 280 Ark 265, 658 SW2d 350 (1983); *State v Lang*, 105 Idaho 683, 672 P2d 561 (1983); *People v Tisler*, 103 Ill 2d 226, 469 NE2d 147 (1984); *State v Rose*, 8 Kan App 2d 659, 665 P2d 1111 (1983), approved in *State v Walter*, 234 Kan 78, 670 P2d 1354 (1983); *Beemer v Commonwealth*, 665 SW2d 912 (Ky 1984); *Potts v State*, 300 Md 567, 479 A2d 1335 (1984); *State v Arrington*, 311 NC 633, 319 SE2d 254 (1984); *Bonsness v State*, 672 P2d 1291 (Wyo 1983). A few courts have explicitly left the issue open. *People v Stark*, 691 P2d 334, 338 n 3 (Colo 1984); *State v Ronngren*, 361 NW2d 224, 230 (ND 1985); *Commonwealth v Jones* 313 Pa Super 602, 484 A2d 1383, 1388-89 (1984).

§3.09 Probable Cause for Warrantless Search

Page 37, text, add at end of section:

However, the Court has specifically held that school officials may search public school students without a warrant whenever there are reasonable grounds to suspect the search will turn up evidence that the student has violated or is violating either the law or the rules of the school. *New Jersey v TLO*, 105 S Ct 733 (1985). See also **§3.27B.**

§3.13 Who May Issue Warrants

Page 39, note 71, at end of note add:

See also Illinois v Gates, 462 US 213 (1983).

Page 39, note 72, at end of note add:

See also Illinois v Gates, 462 US 213 (1983).

§3.14 Effect of Misrepresentation in Supporting Affidavit

Page 40, note 75, at end of note add:

Failure of federal agents to discover an informant's prior perjury conviction was held to be "no more than negligence, if that" in United States v Miller, 753 F2d 1475, 1478 (9th Cir 1985).

Page 40, text, add at end of section:

The Illinois courts have held that under Illinois law, deliberate inclusion of a false statement in a search warrant affidavit invalidates the warrant, without regard to whether the remainder of the affidavit would establish probable cause. *People v Garcia,* 109 Ill App 3d 142, 440 NE2d 269 (1982).

§3.17A The "Good Faith" Exception to the Exclusionary Rule in Searches Pursuant to Warrant (New)

The preference for search warrants, which had been expressed by the Court in many prior cases, took on particular significance in *United States v Leon,* 104 S Ct 3405 (1984). The Court characterized the issue before it as

> whether the Fourth Amendment exclusionary rule should be modified so as not to bar the use in the prosecution's case in chief of evidence obtained by officers acting in reasonable reliance on a search warrant issued by a neutral and detached magistrate but ultimately found to be unsupported by probable cause.

Id 3409.

The facts of the particular case were straightforward. An experienced and well-trained narcotics investigator prepared a warrant application, which was reviewed by several deputy district attorneys, and a facially sufficient warrant was issued by a state superior court judge. Drugs were discovered in the search, and the defendants were indicted in federal court. The defendants filed motions to suppress, which were granted in part by the district court, which found that the affidavit was insufficient to establish probable cause, but that not all of the defendants had standing to challenge all of the searches. The district court, in response to the government's request, made clear that the officer had acted in good faith, but rejected the government's argument that the exclusionary rule should not apply. The court of appeals affirmed.

Recognizing the the court of appeals had acted with "commendable self-restraint" in applying the existing law, the Supreme Court "re-examined the purposes of the exclusionary rule and the propriety of its application in cases where officers have relied on a subsequently invalidated search warrant," and concluded that "the rule's purposes will only rarely be served by applying it in such circumstances." *Id* 3423. The Court emphasized the "substantial social costs exacted by the exclusionary rule," and reasoned that the rule should be limited to those areas "where its remedial objectives are thought most efficaciously served." *Id* 3413.

The Court reasoned that the exclusionary rule existed to deter police misconduct rather than to punish the errors of judges and magistrates, and stated that there exists no evidence that judges and magistrates are inclined to ignore or subvert the Fourth Amendment. Moreover, there is no basis for assuming that exclusion of evidence will have any deterrent effect on the issuing judge or magistrate.

Similarly, the Court rejected arguments that applying the exclusionary rule in cases where the police did not establish probable cause would deter "magistrate shopping" or require policemen to scrutinize their warrants more carefully, finding such arguments "speculative." *Id* 3419.

The Court stated that suppressing evidence cannot deter an officer when, acting with objective good faith, he or she has obtained a search warrant from a judge or magistrate and acted within its scope:

> In the ordinary case, an officer cannot be expected to question the magistrate's probable cause determination or his judgment that the form of the warrant is technically sufficient . . . . Penalizing the officer for the magistrate's error rather than his own cannot logically contribute to the deterrence of Fourth Amendment violations.

Id 3420. The Court emphasized that in order to act with objective good faith, officers must "have a reasonable knowledge of what the law prohibits." *Id* 3420 n 20.

The Court made clear that exclusion is not always inappropriate even in cases where a police officer has obtained a warrant and abided by its terms:

> Suppression . . . remains an appropriate remedy if the magistrate or judge in issuing a warrant was misled by information in an affidavit that the affiant knew was false or would have known was false except for his reckless disregard of the truth [citation omitted]. The exception we recognize today will not apply in cases where the issuing magistrate wholly abandoned his judicial role in the manner condemned in *Lo-Ji Sales, Inc v New York*, 442 US 319 (1979); in such circumstances, no reasonably well trained officer should rely on the warrant. Nor would an officer manifest objective good faith in relying on a warrant based on an affidavit "so lacking in indicia of probable cause as to render official belief in its existence entirely unreasonable" [citation omitted]. Finally, depending upon the circumstances of the particular case, a warrant may be so facially deficient—i.e., failing to particularize the place to be searched or the things to be seized—that the executing officers cannot reasonably presume it to be valid.

Id 3421-22.

While Justice Brennan, dissenting, stated that "the Court's victory over the Fourth Amendment is complete" (*id* 3430 (Brennan, J., dissenting)), Justice White, writing for a six-judge majority, stated:

> In so limiting the suppression remedy, we leave untouched the probable cause standard and the various requirements for a valid warrant. Other objections to the modification of the Fourth Amendment exclusionary rule we consider to be insubstantial. The good faith exception for searches conducted pursuant to warrants is not intended to signal our unwillingness strictly to enforce the requirements of the Fourth Amendment and we do not believe it will have this effect.

Id 3422.

In a companion case, *Massachusetts v Sheppard*, 104 S Ct 3424 (1984), the Court held that suppression of evidence obtained was not required where a police officer drafted an affidavit supporting an arrest and search warrant, which was reviewed by the district attorney and then presented to a judge. Because it was a Sunday, the officer had a difficult time finding a form, and finally used a form for search warrants for controlled drugs from another district. After making some changes in the form, the officer presented it to the judge, telling him further changes might be necessary. The judge made some changes but did not correct the form to incorporate the affidavit or change the substantive portion, which continued to authorize a search for controlled drugs. The ensuing search was limited to the items requested.

In holding that the fruits of the search need not be suppressed, Justice White noted:

> In sum, the police conduct in this case clearly was objectively reasonable and largely error free. An error of constitutional dimensions may have been committed with respect to the issuance of the warrant but it was the judge, not the police officers, who made the critical mistake. . . . Suppressing evidence because the judge failed to make all the necessary clerical corrections despite his assurance that such changes would be made will not serve the deterrent function that the exclusionary rule was designed to achieve.

Id 3429-30.

There can be little doubt that *Leon* and *Sheppard* are landmark decisions. It is impossible to say whether the "good faith" exception in searches conducted with a warrant will be extended to searches conducted without a warrant. What is clear is that the rules established by *Leon* and *Sheppard* will engender much litigation, as lawyers come to grips with terms such as "objective good faith," "reasonable knowledge of what the law prohibits," and "affidavits so lacking in indicia of probable cause as to render official belief in its existence entirely unreasonable."

The good faith exception does not, of course, authorize searches outside the scope of the warrant. Thus, for example, seizure of household items pursuant to a warrant authorizing seizure of "stolen mail" could not be upheld on the basis of the good faith exception. *United States v Strand,* 716 F2d 449 (8th Cir 1985).

The Mississippi Supreme Court has declined to follow *United States v Leon* and has held that there is no good faith exception to the exclusionary rule required by the Mississippi Constitution. *Stringer v State,* 477 So 2d 1335, (Miss Feb 27, 1985).

Similarly, in *State v Novembrino,* 200 NJ Super 229, 491 A2d 37 (App Div 1985) the Appellate Division of the New Jersey Superior Court held that the New Jersey Constitution precludes a good faith exception to the exclusionary rule. The court reasoned that article 1, paragraph 7, of the New Jersey Constitution which requires that no warrant shall issue except upon probable cause would be violated if the state were permitted to introduce in its case-in-chief evidence seized without probable cause. Judge Coleman wrote:

> The *Leon* good faith exception eliminates any meaningful review of probable cause determinations. Long experience with the suppression rule leaves us with the settled conviction that once the police act under cover of a warrant, even though issued

without probable cause, as a practical matter their good faith is immune to attack. The Leon good faith exception contemplates that appellate courts defer to trial courts and trial courts defer to the police. It fosters a careless attitude towards details by the police and issuing judicial officers and it even encourages them to get away with conduct which is heretofore viewed as unconstitutional.

The most compelling reason to exclude from the state's case-in-chief evidence seized without probable cause is to protect the integrity of our State criminal trials. The integrity of the criminal justice process is vital in this state. (Citation omitted). By admitting evidence unconstitutionally seized, the Courts' condone this lawlessness and in the process dirty their hands with the unconstitutional spoils. *Id* at ____, 491 A2d at 45-46.

Other courts have begun to consider, in the words of Justice Hays of the Arkansas Supreme Court, "how far below the standard of probable cause or a constitutionally valid warrant the Supreme Court is willing to go and still find good faith on the part of the police." *State v Anderson*, 286 Ark 58, 688 SW2d 947, 949 (1985). In *Anderson*, the court held that a search warrant obtained without an affidavit or recorded testimony under oath so far deviated from standard practice that such a deficiency could not be considered good faith error. *See also Collins v State*, 465 So 2d 1266 (Fla Dist Ct App 1985).

The New York Court of Appeals has declined to recognize a good faith exception to the exclusionary rule based on the New York Constitution. *People v Bigelow*, 66 NY2d 417, 488 NE2d 451, 497 NYS2d 630 (1985). A divided Ohio Supreme Court has embraced the good faith exception to the exclusionary rule. *State v Wilmoth*, 22 Ohio St 3d 251, 490 NE2d 1236 (1986).

§3.21   Warrantless Searches in General

Page 44, text, add at end of section:

The United States Supreme Court has expressly declined to establish a "murder scene exception" to the warrant requirements of the Fourth and Fourteenth Amendments. *Thompson v Louisiana*, 105 S Ct 409 (1985).

§3.22   Exceptions—Plain View

Page 44, note 102, at end of note add:

Texas v Brown, 460 US 730 (1983).

Page 44, note 103, at end of note add:

Texas v Brown, 460 US 730 (1983).

Page 45, note 104, at end of note add:

United States v Villamonte-Marquez, 462 US 579 (1983) (warrantless boarding of a sailboat to check documentation; officers smelled burning marijuana, and observed bales of marijuana through an open hatch); *see also* Texas v Brown, 460 US 730, (1983).

Page 45, text, add to end of runover paragraph:

In *California v Ciraolo,* 106 S Ct 1809 (1986), the Court held that no Fourth Amendment violation occurred when the police, believing that the defendant was cultivating marijuana in the fenced-in back yard within the curtilage of his home, secured a private plane, and from an altitude of 1,000 feet observed marijuana plants. In holding the police activity did not violate the Fourth Amendment, Chief Justice Burger stated:

> In an age where private and commercial flight in the public airways is routine, it is unreasonable for respondent to expect that his marijuana plants were constitutionally protected from being observed with the naked eye from an altitude of 1,000 feet. The Fourth Amendment simply does not require the police traveling in the public airways at this altitude to obtain a warrant to observe what is visible to the naked eye. *Id* 1813.

In *Dow Chemical Co v United States,* 106 S Ct 1819 (1986), the held that the EPA did not violate the Fourth Amendment whe having been refused access to Dow's 2,000-acre chemical pla without obtaining an administrative warrant, it employed a com aerial photographer, using a standard precision mapping can take photos of the plant from various altitudes, all within na airspace.

Page 45, text, add at end of section:

The plain view exception does not require that it be immediately apparent to the officer that the object to be seized is contraband. Rather, the officer need only have probable cause to believe the object in plain view is contraband. *Texas v Brown,* 460 US 730, 735-38 (1983).

§3.23 —Exigent Circumstances

Page 46, note 114, at end of note add:

See also Michigan v Clifford, 104 S Ct 641 (1984).

§3.24 Hot Pursuit

Page 47, note 118, at end of note add:

See also United States v Irizarry, 673 F2d 554 (1st Cir 1982).

§3.25 Automobile

Page 47, note 121, at end of note add:

See also Michigan v Thomas, 458 US 259 (1982), in which the Court held that when police officers have probable cause to believe that there is contraband in an automobile that has been stopped on the road, the officers may conduct a warrantless search of the vehicle even after it has been impounded and is in police custody.

Page 48, note 123, at end of note add:

Michigan v Thomas, 458 US 259 (1982) (if police officers have probable cause to believe that an automobile stopped on the road, which has been impounded, contains contraband, it may be searched without a warrant); *see also* United States v Knotts, 460 US 276 (1983), pointing out that a person travelling in an automobile on public thoroughfares has no reasonable expectation of privacy in his or her movements from one place to another.

Page 48, note 126, at end of note add:

See also Michigan v Thomas, 458 US 259 (1982).

Page 48, note 127, at end of note add:

The California Supreme Court held that it would follow United States v Ross in People v Chavers, 33 Cal 3d 462, 658 P2d 96, 189 Cal Rptr 169 (1983).

Page 49, text, add at end of section:

The Washington Supreme Court has, based upon analysis of its own constitution, seemingly rejected a separate automobile exception to the warrant requirement of the Washington State Constitution, holding that warrantless searches of automobiles must be justified by exigent circumstances. *State v Ringer*, 100 Wash 2d 686, 674 P2d 1240 (1983).

In *United States v Johns*, 105 S Ct 881 (1985) the Court considered whether *Ross* authorized a warrantless search of packages three days after they had been removed from vehicles that police officers had probable cause to believe contained contraband. In holding the search lawful, the Court rejected the lower courts view that *Ross* only allows warrantless searches of containers within an automobile if the search occurs immediately as part of the vehicle inspection or soon thereafter, stating that such a rule failed to further the privacy interests protected by the Fourth Amendment. *Id* 886. However, the Court made clear that packages may not be held indefinitely before a search is conducted:

> We do not suggest that police officers may indefinitely retain possession of a vehicle and its contents before they complete a vehicle search. [Citation omitted.] Nor do we foreclose the possibility that the owner of a vehicle or its contents might attempt to prove that delay in the completion of a vehicle search was unreasonable because it adversely affected a privacy or possessory interest.

Id 887.

The Court pointed out that in the case before it, the defendants had never sought return of the property or challenged the legitimacy of the searches, or even alleged that the delay in searching adversely affected any interest protected by the Fourth Amendment. Thus, the Court found no constitutional infirmative in the three-day delay.

The Court has held that the automobile exception to the warrant requirement is applicable to motor homes located in public places. *California v Carney*, 105 S Ct 2066 (1985). Chief Justice Burger reasoned:

> When a vehicle is being used on the highways, or if it is readily capable of such use and is found stationary in a place not used for residential purposes—temporary or otherwise—the two justifications for the vehicle exception come into play. First, the vehicle is obviously readily mobile by the turn of a switch key, if not actually moving. Second, there is a reduced expectation of privacy stemming from its use as a licensed motor vehicle subject to a range of police regulations inapplicable to a fixed dwelling. At least in these circumstances, the overriding societal interests in effective law enforcement justify an immediate search before the vehicle and its occupants become unavailable.

Id 2070. *Compare Commonwealth v Upton,* ___ Mass ___, 376 NE2d 548 (1985).

§3.26 —Search Incident to Arrest

Page 50, text, add at end of section:

The Oregon Supreme Court has, based upon the Oregon Constitution, adopted a standard for searches incident to arrest more narrow than the federal standard. The Oregon court has held that "a valid custodial arrest does not alone give rise to a unique right to search." Rather, such a search must be justified by the circumstances surrounding the arrest. The validity of the search depends upon whether the search is related to the offense for which the defendant has been arrested, and whether the search is reasonable. *State v Caraher,* 293 Or 741, 653 P2d 942 (1982).

Like Oregon, New York has interpreted its constitution to provide a narrower standard for searches of containers in the control of an arrested person. In *People v Gokey,* 60 NY2d 309, 457 NE2d 723, 469 NYS2d 618 (1983), the court held that a duffel bag which is in the immediate control or "grabbable area" of a suspect at the time of his or her arrest may not be subjected to a warrantless search incident to the arrest, unless the circumstances leading to the arrest support a reasonable belief that the suspect may gain possession of a weapon or be able to destroy evidence located in the bag.

The United States Supreme Court has held that neither a warrant nor probable cause is necessary to conduct an inventory search prior to incarcerating a person, since the practical necessities of securing persons and property in a jailhouse setting justify an inventory search as part of the standard procedure prior to incarceration. *Illinois v Lafayette,* 462 US 640 (1983).

§3.27 Border Searches

Page 50, text, add at end of section:

A warrantless opening of a container at an international border is, of course, proper. If, at an international border, a container is opened, and drugs are found, the container may be resealed, and delivered. If it has been kept under surveillance, or if there is no substantial likelihood that the contents have changed, the container may be reopened without a warrant, since there is no legitimate expectation of privacy in the contents of a container previously opened under lawful authority. *Illinois v Andreas,* 463 US 765 (1983).

The Court has emphasized that the Fourth Amendment balance of reasonableness is qualitatively different at the international border than in the interior. Routine searches of the person and effects of entrants are not subject to any requirement of reasonable suspicion, probable cause or warrant, and detention of a traveler at the border, beyond the scope of a routine customs search and inspection, is justified at its inception of customs agents, considering all of the facts surrounding the traveler and his or her trip, reasonably suspect that the traveler is smuggling contraband in his or her alimentary canal. *United States v Montoya De Hernandez*, 105 S Ct 3304 (1985). The Court has upheld a 16-hour detention of an individual reasonably suspected of narcotic smuggling, while law enforcement officers awaited a bowel movement, when the defendant declined to permit X-rays of her person. *Id.*

§3.27A   Ships and Vessels (New)

A new exception to the warrant requirement was seemingly recognized in *United States v Villamonte-Marquez*, 462 US 579 (1983). In the case before the Court, customs officers, patrolling a ship channel which leads to the Gulf of Mexico, observed an anchored 40-foot sailing vessel rock violently because of the wake made by a huge freighter. The customs patrolboat approached the sailboat and asked a crewman if the boat and crew were all right. The crewman shrugged his shoulders in an unresponsive manner. The customs officers, accompanied by a Louisiana State Policeman, then boarded the vessel, and asked to see its documentation. While on board, the customs officer smelled burning marijuana, looked through an open hatch, and observed marijuana. The defendants were convicted of various offenses relating to possession and distribution of controlled drugs.

Prior to trial, the defendants had unsuccessfully moved to suppress the evidence obtained from them, on the ground that it was illegally obtained. The Court of Appeals for the Fifth Circuit reversed their convictions, finding that the officers' boarding of the vessel was not *reasonable* under the Fourth Amendment, because the boarding occurred in the absence of a reasonable suspicion of a violation of law. The government relied upon 15 USC §1581(a) which provides that:

> any officer of the customs may at any time go on board of any vessel . . . at any place in the United States . . . and examine the manifest and other documents and papers . . . and to this end may hail and stop such vessel . . . and use all necessary force to compel compliance.

The United States Supreme Court reversed, holding that the action of the customs officers in boarding the vessel was reasonable, and thus consistent with the Fourth Amendment. The Court recognized that 15

USC §1581(a), in substance, authorized random stops of vessels, and that such random stops of automobiles at any point except an international border or its functional equivalent would be impermissable. However, the Court reasoned that "no reasonable claim can be made that permanent checkpoints would be practical on waters such as these where vessels can move in any direction at any time and need not follow established 'avenues' as automobiles must do." *United States v Villamonte-Marquez*, 462 US 579, 589 (1983). Permanent checkpoints cannot be established at harbors, because vessels having ready access to the open sea need never come to harbor; persons engaged in illegal activity may simply anchor at some obscure location on the shoreline. Moreover, the documentation requirements of vessels are significantly different and more complex than those required by the system of automobile registration which prevails throughout the United States. A policeman patrolling a highway can usually determine whether a vehicle is in compliance with state law by observing its license plates and other outward markings. No comparable license plates are issued by the federal government to vessels. Rather, a "panoply of statutes and regulations governing marine documentation" require vessels to carry numerous certificates, licenses, and other documents. The Court concluded that the documentation requirements serve the public interest, and the need to make document checks is great. The Court also found that the intrusion on Fourth Amendment interests caused by such checks was quite limited. *Id* 592. Justice Rehnquist wrote:

> While [a document check] does intrude on one's ability to make free passage without interruption [citation omitted], it involves only a brief detention where officials come on board, visit public areas of the vessel and inspect documents [citation omitted]. "Neither [the vessel] nor its occupants are searched, and visual inspection of the [vessel] is limited to what can be seen without a search" [citation omitted]. Any interference with interests protected by the Fourth Amendment is of course, intrusive to some degree. But in this case, the interference created only a modest intrusion.

Id 592.

Balancing these factors, the Court concluded that the stopping and boarding of the vehicle in the case before it was reasonable.

Applying the balancing test of *Villamonte-Marquez*, to a daytime boarding of a pleasure craft 2000 miles from the continental United States and more than 700 miles from the closest landfall in the Aleutian Islands, the Ninth Circuit held in *United States v Humphrey*, 759 F2d 743, 746 (9th Cir 1985) that a daytime boarding by the Coast Guard for the purpose of conducting a document check did not violate the constitution, notwithstanding that the boarding was conducted without a warrant, without probable cause or even reasonable suspicion that the vessel was carrying contraband or was in violation of safety or document regulations, and without an administrative plan limiting the discretion of Coast Guard officers.

§3.27B   Searches of Public Schoolchildren (New)

The United States Supreme Court has long held that the requirements of the Fourth and Fourteenth Amendment govern the activities of both civil and criminal authorities. In *New Jersey v TLO,* 105 S Ct 733 (1985), the Court applied this traditional rule to public school teachers, and held that the Fourth Amendment governs searches of students by public school teachers. However, while recognizing that schoolchildren have legitimate expectations of privacy, the Court held that the schools need to maintain an environment in which learning can take place and that this interest requires relaxation of the strictures of the Fourth Amendment. Justice White, writing for the majority, held that school officials need not obtain a warrant before searching a child suspected of infraction of school rules or of the criminal law since requiring a teacher to obtain a warrant would unduly interfere with the maintenance of swift and informal disciplinary proceedings needed in the schools. Moreover, such searches need not be based on probable cause; the legality of a search depends upon the reasonableness under all of the circumstances of the case:

> Determining the reasonableness of any search involves a twofold inquiry: first, one must consider whether the . . . action was justified at its inception [citation omitted]; second, one must determine whether the search as actually conducted was reasonably related in scope to the circumstances which justified the interference in the first place. [Citation omitted.] Under ordinary circumstances, a search of a student by a teacher or other school official will be "justified at its inception" when there are reasonable grounds for suspecting that the search will turn up evidence that the student has violated or is violating either the law or the rules of the school. Such a search will be permissible in its scope when the measures adopted are reasonably related to the objectives of the search and not excessively intrusive in light of the age and sex of the student and the nature of the infraction.

Id 744.

In the case before it, a teacher had observed the 14-year-old defendant smoking cigarettes in a school lavatory in violation of school rules. The teacher took the student to the principal's office, where the student denied smoking. The principal then demanded to see her purse, and found a pack of cigarettes and rolling papers commonly associated with the use of marijuana. After a more thorough search, the principal found evidence which implicated the defendant in marijuana dealing. In holding the search reasonable under the circumstances, the Court emphasized that discovery of the rolling papers gave rise to a reasonable suspicion that the defendant was carrying marijuana, thus allowing a more thorough search of her purse.

§3.29   Standard for Valid Consent

Page 51, note 145, at end of note add:

See also Florida v Royer, 460 US 491 (1983). Of course, an illegal arrest taints consent to search. *Id.*

Page 51, note 146, at end of note add:

See also Florida v Royer, 460 US 491 (1983). Of course, an illegal arrest taints consent to search. *Id.*

4 Arrest

§4.01 Constitutional Significance of Arrest

Page 56, note 5, at end of note add:

Florida v Royer, 460 US 491 (1983) (consent to search luggage tainted by illegal arrest); *see also* Taylor v Alabama, 457 US 687 (1982).

§4.02 When Arrest Occurs

Page 57, note 10, at end of note add:

State v Bruzzese, 94 NJ 210, 463 A2d 320 (1983).

Page 57, note 11, at end of note add:

State v Freeman, 307 NC 357, 298 SE2d 331 (1983).

Page 57, note 12, at end of note add:

See also Florida v Royer, 460 US 491 (1983). The defendant, who fit a "drug courier profile," was accosted by police in an airport and asked for identification. When he produced a driver's license inconsistent with his airline ticket, the officers told him he was suspected of transporting narcotics, and asked him to accompany them to a small room, retaining his ticket and driver's license, without indicating he was in any way free to depart. The Court held that as a practical matter, a "reasonable person would have believed he was not free to leave," and that the defendant had been arrested.

§4.04   —Arrest in a Person's Home

Page 59, text, at end of first paragraph add:

The *Payton* decision has been applied retroactively to all convictions which were not yet final at the time the *Payton* decision was rendered. *United States v Johnson,* 457 US 537 (1982).

   The *Payton* rule was reaffirmed in *Welsh v Wisconsin,* 104 S Ct 2091 (1984), in which the Court held a warrantless entry into a person's home to arrest a person for operating a motor vehicle while under the influence of an intoxicant violated the Fourth Amendment. The Court noted that before government agents may make such a warrantless arrest, the government must demonstrate exigent circumstances which overcome the presumption of unreasonableness. Justice Brennan emphasized that "when the government's interest is only to arrest for a minor offense, th[e] presumption of unreasonableness is difficult to rebut, and the government usually should be allowed to make such arrests only with a warrant. . . ." *Id* 2098. Noting that "it is difficult to conceive of a warrantless home arrest which would not be unreasonable under the Fourth Amendment when the underlying offense is extremely minor," *id* 2099, the Court held that even a claim of exigent circumstances, because evidence of the defendant's blood alcohol level might have dissipated while the police obtained a warrant, would not justify the arrest in the case before it.

§4.05   Probable Cause for Arrest

Page 61, note 40, at end of note add:

   See also United States v Hensley, 105 S Ct 675 (1985), holding an investigative stop based upon a "wanted flyer" constitutionally permissible where the officer who issued the flyer had reasonable suspicion based upon articulable facts sufficient to justify a *Terry*-type stop.

Page 61, text, add at end of section:

In *Florida v Royer,* 460 US 491 (1983), the defendant was accosted by drug agents at Miami Airport because his appearance, mannerisms, luggage, and actions fit the so called "drug courier profile." The agents' attention was attracted by the facts that the defendant was carrying American Tourister luggage which appeared to be heavy; he was young, between 25 and 35; he was casually dressed; he appeared pale and nervous, looking around at other people; he paid for his ticket in cash; and rather than completing the airline identification tag for his luggage, he wrote only a name and destination. After the agents accosted him, they learned he had purchased his ticket under an

assumed name. The Cou   were insufficient to
establish probable cause:

> We cannot agree with the State . . . that every nervous young man
> paying cash for a ticket to New York City under an assumed name
> and carrying two heavy American Tourister bags may be arrested
> and held to answer for a serious felony charge.

Id 1329.

An arrest cannot, of course, be justified by what it produces. The fact
that the police obtained evidence sufficient to obtain a warrant as the
result of fingerprints taken after the defendant's arrest on less than
probable cause cannot render the arrest lawful. *Taylor v Alabama*, 457
US 687 (1982).

§4.06   Force Used to Effect Arrest (New)

At common law, the general rule was that any force necessary,
including deadly force, could be used to effectuate the arrest of a
suspected felon. While there has not been a constant, or overwhelming
trend away from the common law rule, "the long term movement has
been away from the rule that deadly force may be used against any
fleeing felon." *Tennessee v Garner*, 105 S Ct 1694, 1705 (1985).

While the point at which minimal police interference becomes a
seizure is not precise, the Court has held that apprehension by the use
of deadly force is a seizure subject to the reasonableness requirement
of the Fourth Amendment. *Id* 1699. In *Tennessee v Garner* the Court held
that: "The use of deadly force to prevent the escape of all felony
suspects, whatever the circumstances, is constitutionally unreasonable.
It is not better that all felony suspects die than that they escape." *Id*
1701.

The use of deadly force is not forbidden under all circumstances,
however. Such force may be used if the officer has probable cause to
believe that the suspected felon poses a significant threat of death or
serious physical injury to the officer or other persons. *Id* 1697.

The Eleventh Circuit has held that the Court's holding in *Tennessee
v Garner* is retroactive. *Acoff v Abston*, 762 F2d 1543 (11th Cir 1985).

5

Rights of Persons in Custody

§5.02 Right to Counsel During Police Investigation of Crime

Page 65, note 14, at end of note add:

See also Mealer v Jones, 741 F2d 1451 (2d Cir 1984) holding that incriminating statements made by one arrested for and charged with murder, obtained by a police informer investigating the defendant's attempt to suborn perjury, may not be introduced at the defendant's murder trial, although they may be introduced at a trial on subsequent charges. The opposite result was reached in United States v DeWolf, 696 F2d 1 (1st Cir 1982).

§5.03 Waiver of Right to Counsel by Arrestee

Page 68, note 28, at end of note add:

The *Hobson* rule was rejected by the Montana Supreme Court in State v Norgaard, 653 P2d 483 (1982).

Page 68, note 31, at end of note add:

The New York rule was explicitly rejected by the Georgia Supreme Court in Blanks v State, 254 Ga 420, 330 SE2d 575 (1985).

Page 68, text, add at end of section:

The Delaware Supreme Court has held that when a suspect's attorney is at a police station during interrogation but the police do not inform the suspect of the presence of the attorney, the suspect cannot intelligently and knowingly waive counsel. *Weber v State*, 457 A2d 674 (Del 1983).

In *Moran v Burbine*, 106 S Ct 1135 (1986), the Court considered whether a pre-arraignment confession preceded by an otherwise valid waiver must be suppressed because the police misinformed an inquiring attorney who had been retained by the defendant's sister to represent him about their plans to interrogate the defendant, or because they failed to inform the defendant of the attorney's attempt to reach him. The Court held that police deception of the attorney was irrelevant to the issue of a valid waiver of *Miranda* rights:

> Granting that the 'deliberate or reckless' withholding of information is objectionable as a matter of ethics, such conduct is only relevant to the constitutional validity of a waiver if it deprives a defendant of knowledge essential to his ability to understand the nature of his rights and the consequences of abandoning them. Because respondent's voluntary decision to speak was made with full awareness and comprehension of all the information *Miranda* requires the police to convey, the waivers were valid.

Id 1142.

The Court further held that the defendant's Sixth Amendment rights were not violated since the right had not attached, as the events that led to the inculpatory statements preceded the formal initiation of adversary judicial proceedings. *Id* 1147. While recognizing that a number of state courts had reached contrary conclusions, Justice O'Connor wrote . . . "while we share respondent's distaste for the deliberate misleading of an attorney, reading *Miranda* to forbid police deception of an attorney would cut the decision completely loose from its own explicitly stated rationale." *Id* 1143.

The Court did, however, note that on facts more egregious, police deception might rise to the level of a due process violation. *Id* 1147.

§5.06 When Privilege against Self-Incrimination Is Applicable

Page 71, text, add at end of section:

A defendant's refusal to take a blood test, after a police officer has lawfully requested him or her to take the test, may be admitted into evidence without violation of the Fifth Amendment. A refusal to take the test is not an act coerced by the officer, and thus the communication is not *compelled* in violation of the Fifth Amendment. *South Dakota v Neville*, 459 US 553 (1983).

Moreover, even if the police fail to warn the defendant that his or her failure to take the test will be introduced at trial, it is not fundamentally unfair to allow the evidence, since the failure to warn is not the sort of implicit promise that would unfairly trick the defendant if the evidence were introduced. Further, *Miranda* does not bar use of the refusal since in the context of an arrest for driving while intoxicated, a police inquiry of whether the suspect will take a blood alcohol test is not an interrogation within the meaning of *Miranda*. *Id* 564 n 15.

§5.07 Procedural Requirements of *Miranda v Arizona*

Page 72, text, add at end of section:

The Court has held that initial failure of police officers to administer Miranda warnings does not necessarily taint subsequent admissions made after the suspect has been fully advised of his or her Miranda rights. *Oregon v Elstad,* 105 S Ct 1285 (1985). Rather, the admissibility of such statements turns upon whether the subsequent statement was knowingly and voluntarily made. *Id* 1293-94. The Court has stated:

> It is an unwarranted extension of Miranda, to hold that a simple failure to administer the warnings unaccompanied by any actual coercion or other circumstances calculated to undermine the suspects ability to exercise his free will so taints the investigatory process that a subsequent voluntary and informed waiver is ineffective for some indeterminate period.

Id 1293.

§5.08 When Person Is in Custody within Meaning of *Miranda*

Page 73, note 51, at end of note add:

A probationer attending a routine interview with his probation officer is not "in custody" for purposes of *Miranda.* Minnesota v Murphy, 104 S Ct 1136 (1984).

Page 74, text, add at end of section:

The roadside questioning of a motorist detained pursuant to a routine traffic stop was held not to be custodial interrogation in *Berkemer v McCarty,* 104 S Ct 3138 (1984). While recognizing that a stop significantly curtails a driver's freedom of action, the Court found substantial differences between such a stop and an arrest, because such a stop does not "exert upon a detained person pressures that sufficiently impair his free exercise of his privilege against self incrimination to require he be warned of his constitutional rights." *Id* 3149. The Court reasoned that such detention is presumptively brief and temporary, and occurs in public. The atmosphere surrounding a traffic stop is "substantially less police dominated than that surrounding the kinds of interrogation at issue in *Miranda* itself. . . ." *Id* 3150.

Justice Marshall noted that the Court's opinion did not eliminate a need for *Miranda* until a person is taken to a police station:

> It is settled that the safeguards prescribed by *Miranda* become applicable as soon as a suspect's freedom of action is curtailed to a degree associated with formal arrest [citation omitted]. If a motorist who has been detained pursuant to a traffic stop thereafter is subjected to treatment that renders him "in custody" for practical purposes, he will be entitled to the full panoply of protections prescribed by *Miranda.*

Id 3151.

§5.09   Applicability of *Miranda* to Minor Offenses

Page 74, note 58, at end of note add:

In Berkemer v McCarty, 104 S Ct 3138 (1984), the Court explicitly held that there is no "traffic offense" exception to *Miranda,* and that a person subjected to custodial interrogation is entitled to the benefit of the procedural safeguards outlined in *Miranda* regardless of the severity of the offense charged. However, a person merely stopped for a routine traffic offense is not in custody for purposes of *Miranda.* The Court reasoned that such a stop is different from a formal arrest because such detention is presumptively temporary and brief, and a motorist's expectations are quite different from those of an arrestee undergoing interrogation. Moreover, such a stop occurs in public, which eliminates the element of coercion which attends a stationhouse interrogation.

§5.10   When Person Is Interrogated within Meaning of *Miranda*

Page 75, note 63, at end of note add:

See also State v Grisby, 97 Wash 2d 493, 647 P2d 6 (1982) (no *interrogation* where police exhibited physical evidence to accused, who then spontaneously made a statement).

Page 76, text, add at end of section:

In *South Dakota v Neville*, 459 US 553 (1983), the Court held that a defendant's refusal to take a blood test in accordance with a state implied consent law, after his arrest for driving while intoxicated, could be admitted at trial without violation of the Fifth Amendment. Justice O'Connor, in dicta, rejected any suggestion that *Miranda* would bar such evidence:

> In the context of an arrest for driving while intoxicated, a police inquiry of whether the suspect will take a blood alcohol test is not an interrogation within the meaning of *Miranda*. As we stated in *Rhode Island v Innis*, 446 US 291, 301 (1980), police words or actions "normally attendant to arrest and custody" do not constitute interrogation. The police inquiry here is highly regulated by State law, and is presented in virtually the same words to all suspects. It is similar to a police request to submit to fingerprinting or photography. Respondent's choice of refusal thus enjoys no prophylactic *Miranda* protection outside the basic Fifth Amendment protection.

Id 564 n 15.

§5.11 Interrogation After Invocation of Fifth Amendment Rights

Page 77, note 68, at end of note add:

In State v Johnson,____ P2d ____ (Mont 1986) the Court held that the Montana privilege against self incrimination is broader than the federal privilege, and that a request by an arrested person to talk to *someone* after his or her arrest constituted a request for counsel.

§5.12A Permissible Violation of *Miranda:* Public Safety Exception (New)

In *New York v Quarles*, 104 S Ct 2626 (1984), the United States Supreme Court for the first time recognized an exception to the *Miranda* rule that requires a person in custody to be advised of his or her rights. In the case before the Court, a woman approached two police officers on patrol and told them that she had been raped, and that the rapist had entered a nearby supermarket and was carrying a gun. One of the officers went into the supermarket and saw the defendant, who ran toward the rear of the store. The officer pursued him, but lost sight of him for several seconds. On locating him, the officer ordered the defendant to stop and put his hands over his head. The officer then frisked the defendant and discovered that he was wearing a shoulder holster, which was empty. The officer handcuffed the defendant and then asked where the gun was. The defendant nodded in the direction of some cartons, and said "The gun is over there." The officer retrieved a loaded revolver from the cartons, then formally placed the defendant under arrest, and read him his rights under *Miranda*.

The New York courts suppressed the defendant's statement because the defendant was in police custody at the time of the interrogation. The New York Court of Appeals observed that there was nothing to suggest that any of the police officers were concerned for their own safety, and declined to express an opinion on whether there might be a public safety exception to *Miranda*, because the lower courts had made no factual determination that the police acted with that motive. *Id* 2631-32.

Justice Rehnquist, writing for a five-judge majority, admitted that "the New York Court of Appeals was undoubtedly correct in deciding that the facts of this case come within the ambit of *Miranda* as we have subsequently interpreted it." *Id* 2626. However, he went on to say:

> We decline to place [police] officers . . . in the untenable position of having to consider, often in a matter of seconds, whether it best serves society for them to ask the necessary questions without the *Miranda* warnings and render whatever probative evidence they uncover inadmissible, or for them to give the warnings in order to preserve the admissibility of evidence they might uncover but possibly damage or destroy their ability to obtain that evidence and neutralize the volatile situation confronting them.

Id 2633.

Although formulating no bright-line test for application of the privilege, Justice Rehnquist thought:

> The exception will not be difficult for police officers to apply because in each case it will be circumscribed by the exigency which justifies it. We think police officers can and will distinguish almost instinctively between questions necessary to secure their own safety or the safety of the public and questions designed solely to elicit testimonial evidence from a suspect.

Id 2633.

§5.13   Interrogation After Invocation of Right to Counsel

Page 79, text, add at end of section:

Whether or not a waiver of counsel has occurred after invocation appears to depend upon the totality of the circumstances. In *Wyrick v Fields*, 459 US 42 (1982), the defendant, a soldier charged with rape, was released on bail, consulted with a civilian and a military attorney, and then requested a polygraph examination. An Army criminal investigator gave him the test, fully advising the defendant before it began of his *Miranda* rights, and of his right to stop answering questions at any time if he wanted to speak to a lawyer. After the test, the investigator told him there had been some deceit, and asked the defendant if he could explain why his answers were bothering him. The defendant then admitted having intercourse, but said the intercourse was consensual; these statements were admitted at his trial.

The Court held that by requesting a polygraph test, the defendant had "initiated interrogation," waiving his right to be free of contact with the authorities in the absence of an attorney, and his right to be free of interrogation about the crime of which he was suspected. The Court stated that the post-polygraph questioning would have been inadmissible only if the circumstances changed so seriously that his answers no longer were voluntary, or if the defendant was no longer making a knowing and intelligent relinquishment or abandonment of his rights.

Similarly, in *Oregon v Bradshaw*, 462 US 1039 (1983), where the defendant was arrested, advised of *Miranda*, asserted his right to counsel, but then asked "what was going to happen," and a police officer followed up by readvising him of his rights, and then suggested a polygraph, which led to the defendant making admissions, four judges held that there was no error because the defendant had initiated the further conversations, and the statements made were voluntary. Justice Powell, concurring in the result, thought that a two-step analysis of who initiated the conversations and whether the waiver was knowing and intelligent, was unnecessary, and that the only necessary inquiry was the voluntariness of the waiver. Justice Powell noted that lower courts continue to be badly split over whether invocation of the right to counsel imposes a per se prohibition of further interrogation.

Oregon v Bradshaw reflects the inability of the United States Supreme Court to formulate a clear definition of initiation within the meaning of *Edwards v Arizona*. However, in *Solem v Stumes*, 104 S Ct 1338 (1984), the Court seemed to establish a per se rule that, once the right to counsel has been invoked, a waiver of that right can never be valid if made in response to further police questioning. *Id* 1346 (Powell, J, concurring).

Page 79, note 80, at end of note add:

Edwards v Arizona, 451 US 477 (1981), was held to be nonretroactive in Solem v Stumes, 104 S Ct 1338 (1984). However, in Shea v Louisiana, 105 S Ct 1065 (1985), the United States Supreme Court held that the ruling in *Edwards v Arizona* applies to cases pending on direct appeal at the time *Edwards* was decided.

The rigid prophylactic rule, that an accused having expressed a desire to deal with the police only through counsel is not subject to further interrogation until counsel has been made available to him or her, has been said by the United States Supreme Court to embody two distinct inquiries. First, courts must determine whether the accused actually invoked the right to counsel. Second, if the accused invoked his or her right to counsel, courts may admit the responses to further questioning only upon a finding that he or she (1) initiated further discussions with the police and (2) knowingly and intelligently waived the right he or she had invoked. Smith v Illinois, 105 S Ct 490 (1984). While a request for counsel may be ambiguous, postrequest responses to further interrogation may not be used to cast retrospective doubt on the clarity of the initial request. Such statements are relevant only to the question of whether the defendant has waived his or her right to counsel. *Id.*

The rule of *Edwards v Arizona* that once a suspect has invoked his or her right to counsel during questioning, the police may not initiate interrogation until counsel has been made available, also applies when an accused requests counsel at his or her arraignment. Michigan v Jackson, 106 S Ct 1404 (1986).

§5.16 Requirement That Confession Be Voluntarily Made

Page 82, text, add at end of section:

If a trial judge determines that a confession was voluntarily made and denies a motion to suppress, alleging that the confession was involuntary, a defendant is still entitled, as a matter of federal constitutional law, to introduce competent, reliable evidence bearing on the credibility of the confession at trial. *Crane v Kentucky,* 106 S Ct 2142 (1986).

Page 82, note 100, at end of note add:

A promise made to a suspect by a detective with apparent authority, to the effect that if she confessed she would not be prosecuted, rendered the subsequent confession involuntary; use immunity of the involuntary statement was constitutionally required. People v Manning, 672 P2d 499 (Colo 1983).

§5.18   Comment on Silence of Defendant

Page 84, note 116, at end of note add:

Similarly, a prosecutor's use of evidence of the defendant's silence after being advised of his or her Miranda rights to establish the defendant's sanity in a case in which the defendant had pleaded not guilty by reason of insanity is violative of the due process clause of the Fourteenth Amendment. Wainwright v Greenfield, 106 S Ct 634 (1986).

Page 84, text, add at end of section:

The California Supreme Court has held that the California Constitution forbids a prosecutor from cross-examining a defendant about his or her silence before or after arrest. *People v Jacobs*, 158 Cal App 3d 740, 204 Cal Rptr 849 (1984).

§5.19   Physical Testing and Privilege against Self-Incrimination

Page 85, note 120, at end of note add:

A defendant's refusal to take a blood test, after a police officer has lawfully requested him or her to take the test, may be admitted into evidence without violation of the Fifth Amendment. A refusal to take the test is not an act coerced by the officer, and thus the communication is not *compelled* in violation of the Fifth Amendment. South Dakota v Neville, 459 US 553 (1983).

On remand, the South Dakota Supreme Court determined that the due process provision of the South Dakota Constitution requires that a person be fully advised of the consequences of his or her failing to consent to a chemical test, and that since the record disclosed that defendant had not been so advised, the results of the test must be suppressed. State v Neville, 346 NW2d 425 (SD 1984).

§5.20   Right to Counsel During Physical Testing

Page 87, note 135, at end of note add:

See also Copelin v State, 659 P2d 1206 (Alaska 1983) (based on Alaska statute).

Page 87, note 137, at end of note add:

See also Sites v State, 300 Md 702, 481 A2d 192 (1984) (holding that the due process clause of the Fourteenth Amendment as well as article 24 of the Maryland Declaration of Rights, requires that a person under detention for drunk driving must, on request, be permitted a reasonable opportunity to communicate with counsel before being required to submitted to a chemical sobriety test, as long as such attempted communication will not substantially interfere with the timely and efficacious administration of the testing process.)

§5.21 Physical Testing and Right of Person Arrested to Be Free from Unreasonable Searches

Page 89, text, at end of carryover paragraph add:

A compelled surgical intrusion into an individual's body implicates expectations of privacy and security of such magnitude that the intrusion may be unreasonable, within the meaning of the Fourth Amendment, even if likely to produce evidence of a crime. In *Winston v Lee,* 105 S Ct 1611 (1985), the defendant was charged with armed robbery. The perpetrator of the robbery of which he was accused had been shot by the victim, but had fled; the defendant had been found suffering from a gunshot wound in the same area 20 minutes later. The victim of the robbery identified the defendant as the robber shortly after the robbery. After the defendant was charged with the robbery, the state sought a court order directing the defendant to undergo surgery to remove an object believed to be a bullet lodged under his left collarbone. Expert testimony established that the surgery would require a general anesthetic, but conflicted on the time of the operation; one surgeon testified that the difficulty of discovering the exact location of the bullet could require extensive probing with attendant risks, and testified that the operation could take up to two and one-half hours.

The Court held that the reasonableness of surgical intrusion beneath the skin depends upon a case-by-case approach, in which the individual's privacy and security interests are weighed against society's interests in conducting the procedure. *Id* 1616. The threshold inquiry is, of course, probable cause. Other factors in analyzing the magnitude of the intrusion are the risk to the safety or health of the person and the extent of the intrusion on the individual's personal privacy and bodily integrity. *Id* 1617. Weighed against these interests is the community's interest in fairly and accurately determining guilt or innocence, an interest the Court has characterized as "of great importance." *Id* 1618.

Considering the facts of the case before it, the Court held that the search sought by the state was impermissible, since there was uncertainty about the medical risks posed by the operation, the intrusion on the defendant's privacy interests and bodily integrity could only be characterized as severe, and the state's need for the evidence was not compelling, since it had substantial other evidence available to establish the defendant's guilt. *Id* 1620.

7 Institution of Charges

§7.01 Decision to Charge a Crime

Page 108, note 9, at end of note add:

See also United States v Chagra, 669 F2d 241 (5th Cir 1982); Wayte v United States, 105 S Ct 1524, 1531 (1985).

Page 108, text, at end of carryover paragraph add:

The United States Supreme Court held that the Justice Department's so-called passive enforcement policy of prosecuting only those selective service violators who reported themselves, or were reported by others, and refused after the government attempted to persuade them to register voluntarily, did not violate the Constitution in *Wayte v United States*, 105 S Ct 1524 (1985). The Court began its inquiry by noting the broad discretion prosecutors have in deciding whether to institute charges at all:

> This broad discretion rests largely on the recognition that the decision to prosecute is particularly ill-suited to judicial review. Such factors as the strength of the case, the prosecution's general deterrence value, the government's enforcement priorities and the case's relationship to the government's overall enforcement plan are not readily susceptible to the kind of analysis the courts are competent to undertake.

Id 1531.

While recognizing the decision to prosecute may not be based upon an unjustifiable standard such as race, religion, or other arbitrary classification, or the exercise of protected statuatory or constitutional rights, *Id* 1531, the Court stated that "it is appropriate to judge selective prosecution claims according to ordinary equal protection standards." *Id.* The Court held that the defendant in the case before it was therefore required to "show both that the passive enforcement system had a discriminatory effect and that it was motivated by a discriminatory purpose." *Id.*

Since "all [the defendant was able to show was] that all those eventually prosecuted, along with many not prosecuted, reported themselves as having violated the law," *Id* 1532, the defendant could not establish that the government had prosecuted him because of his protest activities. The Court therefore rejected his selective prosecution claim.

The Court also rejected the defendant's First Amendment claim, since the government's regulation was within proper governmental power, furthered an important governmental interest, the interest was unrelated to the suppression of free speech, and the restriction on First Amendment freedom was no greater than is essential to the furtherance of the interest.

Page 109, note 14, at end of note add:

See also United States v Goodwin, 457 US 368 (1982). Although such action is not per se illegal, a prima facie case of prosecutorial vindictiveness is made when a defendant is indicted on new charges, arising out of the same set of facts, following a successful appeal. United States v Krezdorn, 718 F2d 1360 (5th Cir 1983). *See also* Thigpen v Roberts, 104 S Ct 2916 (1984) (leaving open the question of whether a narrower rule would apply if the new charges were instituted by a different prosecutor).

Page 108, note 16, at end of note add:

See also Wayte v United States, 105 S Ct 1524, 1531 n 9 (1985).

Page 109, note 15, at end of note add:

See also Thigpen v Roberts, 104 S Ct 2916 (1984) (leaving open the question of whether a narrower rule would apply if the new charges were instituted by a different prosecutor).

§7.02   Specificity of Charges

Page 113, note 41, at end of note add:

See also United States v Berardi, 675 F2d 894, 897 (7th Cir 1982).

§7.03   Nature of the Grand Jury

Page 115, note 55, at end of note add:

See also United States v Sells Engg, 463 US 418 (1983).

§7.04   Invocation of the Fifth Amendment in the Grand Jury Room

Page 117, note 60, at end of note add:

See also Pillsbury Co v Conboy, 459 US 248 (1983).

§7.05   Invocation of Privileges Other Than the Fifth Amendment Before a Grand Jury

Page 119, note 78, at end of note add:

See also In re Sealed Case, 676 F2d 793, 808-09 (DC Cir 1982); *In re* Grand Jury Proceedings, 674 F2d 309, 310 (4th Cir), *cert denied,* 102 S Ct 1632 (1982).

§7.11   Composition of Grand Juries

Page 124, text, add at end of carryover paragraph:

A five-judge majority of the Court declined to overrule *Strauder v West Virginia* in *Vasquez v Hillery,* 106 S Ct 617 (1986). Justice White joined in the opinion of the Court except for that portion of the opinion which stated that such error can never be harmless. *Id* 624 n 6.

Page 125, text, add at end of section:

In *Hobby v United States,* 104 S Ct 3093 (1984), the Court refused to reverse the conviction of a white male despite the defendant's claim that there was discrimination in the grand jury selection process, which had resulted in significant underrepresentation of women and blacks as grand jury foremen. The Court reasoned that the responsibilities of a federal grand jury foreman are essentially clerical in nature, and that "given the ministerial nature of the position, discrimination in the selection of one person from among the members of a properly constituted grand jury can have little, if indeed any, appreciable effect upon the defendant's due process right to fundamental fairness." *Id* 3097. Moreover, the due process concern that no large and identifiable segment of the community be excluded from grand jury service does not arise when the discrimination pertains only to selection of a foreman from among the members of a properly constituted grand jury. The Court did note that such a claim made in state systems in which a foreman has different power could lead to different results.

§7.12   Prosecutor's Duty to Present Exculpatory Evidence to Grand Jury

Page 127, note 123, at end of note add:

United States v Hyder, 732 F2d 841 (11th Cir 1984); People v Valles, 62 NY2d 36, 464 NE2d 418, 476 NYS2d 50 (1984).

Page 127, note 125, at end of note add:

A state prosecutor's failure to inform a grand jury of highly material and exculpatory evidence was held to be error of constitutional dimension requiring relief on habeus corpus, despite the fact that the defendant was subsequently found guilty of the crime charged in Kudish v Overbeck, 618 F Supp 196 (DNJ 1985).

8 | Bail and Pretrial Restraint

§8.02 Constitutional Necessity for Bail

Page 131, note 12, at end of note add:

See also Younder v Hubbard, 673 F2d 132, 134 (5th Cir 1982) (no absolute right to bail pending appeal; but the Eighth and Fourteenth Amendments require that bail pending appeal not be denied arbitrarily or unreasonably if the state makes provision for such bail).

§8.04 Excessive Bail

Page 133, note 26, at end of note add:

See also United States v James, 674 F2d 886, 891 (11th Cir 1982).

Page 134, text, add at end of section:

The Federal Bail Reform Act of 1984, 18 USC §3141 *et seq*, made a number of significant changes in bail procedures in the federal courts. The act "makes it in one respect harder and in another respect, easier for judicial officers to order pre-trial detention of those accused of crimes." *United States v Jessup*, 757 F2d 378 (1st Cir 1985). It "makes it harder by a specifying explicitly what was implicit in prior law, namely that magistrates and judges cannot impose any financial condition that will result in detention"; *Id* 379-80. High-money bail cannot be used as a device to keep a defendant in custody before trial. *Id* 380. However, the act makes detention easier, by broadening the category of persons whom the officer can order detained. In addition, the act requires that a judicial officer shall order detention if he "finds that no condition or combination of conditions [attaching to release] will reasonably assure

53

the appearance of the person as required and the safety of any other person and the community." 18 USC §3142(e).

The act also establishes several "rebuttable presumptions" for any officer to use in applying this basic standard. 18 USC §3142(e) provides in relevant part that:

> Subject to rebuttal by the person, it shall be presumed that no condition or combination of conditions will reasonably assure the appearance of the person as required and the safety of the community if the judicial officer finds that there is probable cause to believe that the person committed an offense for which a maximum term of imprisonment of 10 years or more is prescribed in the Controlled Substances Act. (21 USC §801 et seq.)

The First Circuit has ruled that this section shifts only the burden of production and not the burden of persuasion to the defendant. 757 F2d at 381. However, the presumption does not disappear, once conflicting evidence is introduced; rather, it is to be considered by the magistrate as one factor among many. *Id* 384. The court has further held that the use of this presumption does not render bail proceedings "constitutionally unfair." *Id* 385.

§8.05   Preventive Detention

Page 135, note 36, at end of note add:

The constitutionality of the District of Columbia statute was upheld in United States v Edwards, 430 A2d 1321 (DC App 1981) (en banc).

Page 135, text, after third paragraph add:

A divided Second Circuit Court of Appeals held that an eight-month pretrial detention based upon a finding that no combination of release condition could ensure the safety of the community was violative of the Constitution in *United States v Melendez Carrion,* 790 F2d 984 (2d Cir 1986).

Judge Newman concluded that preventive detention violates the Eighth Amendment's prohibition of excessive bail. Chief Judge Feinberg did not find it necessary to reach conclusions as broad as Judge Newman's, reasoning that the eight-month delay before the Court constituted punishment without an adjudication of guilt. Judge Timbers dissented. A majority of the same Court, however, concluded in *United States v Salerno,* No 86-1197 (2d Cir July 3, 1986) that pretrial detention imposed on the ground that no combination of release conditions will reasonably assure the safety of the community or a person constitutes a substantive due process violation regardless of the length of the detention.

Page 136, text, add at end of section:

While expressing no opinion on whether any governmental objective other than assuring an accused's presence at trial can constitutionally justify pretrial detention of adults accused of crime, the Court in *Schall v Martin*, 104 S Ct 2403 (1984), upheld a New York statute which authorizes pretrial detention of an accused juvenile based on a finding that there is a serious risk that the juvenile may before the return date commit an act which, if committed by an adult, would constitute a crime. Preventive detention under the statute, the Court found, serves a legitimate state purpose, protection of the juvenile and protection of society from harm. The Court pointed out that while a juvenile's interest in liberty is "undoubtedly substantial," that interest "must be qualified by the recognition that juveniles, unlike adults, are always in some form of custody." *Id* 2410. The Court noted that every state permitted preventive detention of children accused of crime. Under the statute in question, before a juvenile could be detained, significant procedural protections were afforded him or her. Notice, a hearing, and a statement of facts and reasons were given prior to any detention. A formal probable cause hearing was to be held within a short time thereafter, if the fact-finding hearing could not be scheduled within three days. The Court thus held the procedures adequate under the Fourth Amendment and under the due process clause.

Perhaps more importantly, the Court rejected the claim that detention based on a finding that there is a "serious risk" that the juvenile will commit a crime if released is unconstitutional because it is virtually impossible to predict future criminal conduct with any degree of accuracy:

> Our cases indicate . . . that from a legal point of view, there is nothing inherently unattainable about a prediction of future criminal conduct. Such a judgment forms an important element in many decisions, and we have specifically rejected the contention, based upon the same sort of sociological data relied upon by appellees and the district court that it is impossible to predict future behavior and that the question is so vague as to be meaningless.

Id 2417-18.

§8.07 Bail of Witnesses

Page 137, text, add at end of section:

In *United States v Valenzuela-Bernal*, 458 US 858 (1982), the Court pointed out that during fiscal year 1979, almost one-half of the more than 11,000 inmates incarcerated in federal facilities in the Southern District of California were material witnesses who had neither been charged with nor convicted of a criminal offense. *Id* 865.

§8.08 Bail Pending Appeal

Page 138, add at end of section:

The Federal Bail Reform Act of 1984 made significant changes in the procedures governing bail pending appeal in federal courts. The statute requires in substance that a judicial officer shall order that a person found guilty of an offense, who has filed an appeal or petition for certiorari be detained unless the judicial officer finds (1) by clear and convincing evidence that the person is not likely to flee or pose a danger to the safety of any person of the community if released and (2) that the appeal is not for purpose of delay and raises a substantial question of law or fact likely to result in a new trial. 18 USC §3143. The defendant has the burden of establishing these factors. *United States v Giancola*, 754 F2d 898, 901 (11th Cir 1985). The language of the statute requiring the judicial officer to find the appeal "raise[s] a substantial question of law or fact likely to result in reversal or a new trial," has been interpreted to require only that the court find that an appeal raise a substantial issue of law or fact and second, that if the substantial question is determined favorably to the defendant on appeal, the decision is likely to result in reversal or a new trial. *Id* 900; *United States v Miller*, 753 F2d 19, 24 (3d Cir 1985). As so interpreted, the statute's provisions have been upheld by at least two circuit courts of appeal. *Id.*

A *substantial question* for purposes of 18 USC §3142(b) has been held to be "one that is fairly debatable among jurists of reason." *United States v Smith*, 793 F2d 85 (3d Cir 1986).

§8.09 Bail and Indigents

Page 139, note 68, at end of note add:

The prohibition of such discrimination appears to be premised upon a due process analysis although due process and equal protection principles converge in the Court's analysis in these cases. Bearden v Georgia, 103 S Ct 2064 (1983).

9

The Prosecutor as Adversary

§9.01 Duties of the Prosecutor

Page 143, note 2, at end of note add:

Quoted with approval in United States v Bagley, 105 S Ct 3375, 3380 n 7 (1985).

§9.02 Duty to Protect the Integrity of the Criminal Process

Page 145, note 12, at end of note add:

See also United States v Allain, 671 F2d 248, 255 (7th Cir 1982).

Page 145, note 13, at end of note add:

But see United States v Sanzo, 673 F2d 64, 68 (2d Cir 1982).

Page 145, note 17, at end of note add:

However, the presentation of false evidence may be harmless error. United States v Widgery, 674 F2d 710, 713 (8th Cir 1982).

§9.03 *False Testimony* Which May Not Be Presented to a Jury

Page 146, text, add at end of section:

The Eighth Circuit has held that a contingency agreement between a witness and a prosecutor, under the terms of which the witness's sentence would be reduced if the witness's testimony led to the accomplice's conviction, created such a risk of perjury that even the jury's full knowledge of the agreement was insufficient to protect the defendant's right to due process. *United States v Waterman,* 732 F2d 1527 (8th Cir 1984), *cert denied,* 105 S Ct 2138 (1985).

§9.04   Duty to Provide Exculpatory Evidence—Upon Request

Page 147, note 26, at end of note add:

United States v Bledsoe, 674 F2d 647, 670 (8th Cir 1982).

Page 147, note 27, at end of note add:

Chaney v Brown, 730 F2d 1334 (10th Cir 1984).

Page 147, note 28, at end of note add:

Chaney v Brown, 730 F2d 1334 (10th Cir 1984).

Page 147, note 30, at end of note add:

Chaney v Brown, 730 F2d 1334 (10th Cir 1984).

Page 148, text, at end of section add:

In *United States v Bagley,* 105 S Ct 3375 (1985), the Court affirmed the rule of *Brady v Maryland* that the prosecution's suppression of evidence favorable to the accused violated due process where the evidence before it is material either to guilt or punishment. The Court rejected the rule adopted by the Ninth Circuit that the prosecutor's failure to disclose evidence which could have been used to impeach government witnesses requires automatic reversal.

The opinion of the court was delivered by Justice Blackmun, with Justice O'Connor, Chief Justice Burger, and Justices White and Rehnquist joining. Justice Powell did not participate, and Justices Brennan, Marshal and Stevens dissented. Justice Blackmun, joined only by Justice O'Connor in Part III of the opinion concluded that nondisclosed evidence is material only if that evidence creates a reasonable probability that had the evidence been disclosed, the results of the proceeding would have been different, and that this standard is sufficiently flexible to cover all cases of prosecutorial failure to disclose, whether the defendant makes a general, specific or no request for exculpatory evidence. Chief Justice Burger, and Justices White and Rehnquist declined to join Part III of Justice Blackmun's opinion, concluding that while they agreed with Justice Blackmun's formulation of the standard of materiality, and that the standards is sufficiently flexible to cover all instances of prosecutorial failure to disclose, there was no reason to attempt to elaborate on the relevance to the inquiry of the specificity of the request either generally or with respect to the case before the Court.

§9.05 —When No Request for Exculpatory Evidence or a Nonspecific Request Is Made by the Defendant

Page 148, note 36, at end of note add:

A careful analysis of the many cases concerning specificity of requests is contained in Chaney v Brown, 730 F2d 1334 (10th Cir 1984).

Page 149, note 40, at end of note add:

While the Fifth Circuit has continued to adhere to its rule that with respect to impeaching evidence, the defendant seeking a new trial must demonstrate that the new evidence probably would have resulted in acquittal, *see, e.g.,* United States v Mesa, 660 F2d 1070, 1076 (5th Cir 1981), the other circuits continue to apply the "reasonable doubt that did not otherwise exist" standard. *See, e.g.,* Hicks v Scurr, 671 F2d 255, 261-62 (8th Cir 1982); Mains v Butterworth, 619 F2d 83, 86 (1st Cir), *cert denied,* 449 US 864 (1980).

§9.06   Duty To Avoid Intimidating Defense Witnesses

Page 150, text, at end of carryover paragraph add:

A prosecutor may not enter into a plea bargain that requires a defendant not to testify on behalf of co-defendants. *State v Fort,* 107 NJ 123, 501 A2d 140 (1985).

§9.07   Duty of Prosecutor to Act Fairly

Page 151, note 58, at end of note add:

See also United States v Hastings, 461 US 499 (1983) in which the Court held that while federal courts have authority under their supervisory power to reverse convictions, such reversals "must be approached with some caution," and with a view toward balancing the interests involved. The interests enumerated by the Court in *Hastings* were prejudicial to the defendant, the effect of retrial on the victims, and the practical problems of retrial long after a first trial, as well as the nature of the prosecutorial overreaching which led the Court to consider exercise of the supervisory power.

Page 151, text, add at end of section:

The Court has recognized that to comport with the Fourteenth Amendment's requirement of fundamental fairness, it has developed "what might loosely be called the area of constitutionally guaranteed access to evidence." *United States v Valenzuela-Bernal,* 458 US 858, 867 (1982). However, in *California v Trombetta,* 104 S Ct 2528 (1984), the Court held that in drunken driving prosecutions, the Constitution does not require that law enforcement agencies preserve breath samples taken from arrested persons to be tested by the police. The fact that the actual breath samples are destroyed by the test is constitutionally irrelevant, since the evidence to be presented in such circumstances at trial is not the *breath itself,* but the test results. Moreover, the government does not destroy the samples in bad faith.

Most importantly, the Court held that the constitutional duty of the state to preserve evidence is limited to evidence which possesses an exculpatory value which was apparent before the evidence was destroyed, and which is of a nature such that the defendant would be unable to obtain comparable evidence by other reasonably available means. A unanimous Court found that since "a dispassionate review of the Intoxilyzer and the California testing procedures can only lead one to conclude that the chances are extremely low that preserved samples would have been exculpatory," and since the defendants could press their claim that the state test results were inaccurate by examining and challenging the machine and the testing officer, preservation was not constitutionally required. *Id* 2534.

On remand, the California Court of Appeal, First District, found no state due process right to have a sample for retesting preserved. *People v Trombetta,* 173 Cal App 3d 1093, 219 Cal Rptr 637 (1985).

10 Discovery

§10.01 The Constitution and Discovery

Page 154, note 2, at end of note add:

United States v Bagley, 105 S Ct 3375, 3380 n 7 (1985).

Page 154, note 7, at end of note add:

Gallagher v District Court, 656 P2d 287 (Colo 1983) (holding that police refusal to perform certain chemical tests on murder victim's body, or to make the body available to the defendant for testing, violated due process); *see also* People v Garries, 645 P2d 1306 (Colo 1982) (holding that due process requires suppression of evidence of blood testing procedures which destroyed the samples, and lacked safeguards to permit defense verification of the results).

§10.03 Constitutional Right to Obtain and Use Evidence Privileged on State Law Grounds from a Witness

Page 157, note 23, at end of note add:

Courts have generally found that a child has no constitutional right to refuse to testify about a parent. Three Juveniles v Commonwealth, 390 Mass 357, 455 NE2d 1203 (1983).

Page 158, text, after first full paragraph add:

The Connecticut Supreme Court has held that records protected by a state statutory privilege for communications between rape victims and counselors must yield to the defendant's right to confrontation at least in some cases. *In re Robert H,* 196 Conn 693, 509 A2d 475 (1986). The Connecticut Court has established a scheme which requires the defendant to make a showing of reasonable ground to believe failure to produce the records would violate the defendant's right of confrontation. If such a showing is made, the court must ask the victim for consent to in camera review of the material. If there is impeaching evidence it will, with the victim's consent, be turned over to the defendant. However, should the victim fail to consent to either procedure, the court will strike the victim's trial testimony.

In contrast, the Colorado Supreme Court has held that a sex offense defendant may not examine a victim's post-assault psychotherapy records unless the victim voluntarily waives the statutory privilege. *People v District Court,* P2d (Colo June 2, 1986). The court reasoned that the statutory privilege represents a public policy so important that no balancing of the privilege against the defendant's confrontation clause rights is required. *Id.*

§10.08 Government Discovery Right in General

Page 167 text, after carryover paragraph add:

The California Supreme Court, construing the California Constitution, declined to follow *Nobles,* and held that a California statute which permitted the prosecution to discover from the defendant or his counsel, following testimony on direct examination of defense witnesses other than the defendant, prior statements made by those witnesses, violated the defendant's rights. In *In re Misener,* 38 Cal 3d 543, 698 P2d 637, 213 Cal Rptr 569 (1985), the court reasoned that the statute violated that aspect of the defendant's privilege against self-incrimination, requiring the prosecution to carry the entire burden of proving the defendant's guilt, by compelling the defendant to supply the prosecution with evidence that could impeach his defense witnesses and thereby tend to incriminate him.

11 Time of Trial

§11.01 Constitutional Limits on Grant or Denial of Continuance

Page 170, note 5, at end of note add:

Morris v Slappy, 461 US 1 (1983).

Page 171, note 10, at end of note add:

Morris v Slappy, 461 US 1 (1983).

Page 171, note 14, at end of note add:

Compare Morris v Slappy, 461 US 1 (1983).

Page 171, text, add at end of section:

In *Morris v Slappy*, 461 US 1 (1983), the public defender who had been assigned to represent the defendant, and who had investigated his case, became ill shortly before the defendant's trial. A different public defender was assigned to represent the defendant six days before trial. On the morning of the trial, the defendant made a pro se motion for a continuance, asserting that the second, new public defender had not had enough time to investigate and prepare the case. The public defender told the court he had studied the investigation made by his predecessor, and did not believe that more time was necessary to prepare the case. Emphasizing that broad discretion must be given trial judges on matters of continuances, the Court held that it was "far from an abuse of discretion to deny a continuance." *Id* 12.

§11.03   When Right To Speedy Trial Attaches

Page 173, note 25, at end of note add:

See also United States v Loud Hawk, 106 S Ct 648 (1986) (time during which no indictment was outstanding against defendants should not weigh toward defendants' speedy trial claims and they were free of all restraints on their liberty).

§11.04   Effect of Delay in Bringing Charges

Page 174, note 32, at end of note add:

See also United States v Brown, 667 F2d 566, 568 (5th Cir 1982) (*held*, dismissal for preindictment delay necessary only when defendant shows right to fair trial substantially prejudiced).

Page 175, note 36, at end of note add:

See also United States v Brown, 667 F2d 566, 568 (5th Cir 1982).

§11.05   Standard for Determining When Right to Speedy Trial Has Been Denied

Page 176, note 43, at end of note add:

See also Jameson v Estelle, 666 F2d 241, 243 (5th Cir 1982); United States v Arkus, 675 F2d 245 (9th Cir 1982); United States v Gonzalez, 671 F2d 441 (11th Cir), *cert denied,* 102 S Ct 2279 (1982); United States v Loud Hawk, 106 S Ct 648 (1986).

Page 176, note 45, at end of note add:

Delay resulting from interlocutory appeals by the government "ordinarily is a valid reason for delay." United States v Loud Hawk, 106 S Ct 648, 656 (1986). In assessing the purpose and reasonableness of such an appeal, courts may consider the strength of the government's position on the appealed issue, the importance of the issue in the posture of the case, and in some cases, the seriousness of the crime. *Id.* Delay due to defendant's interlocutory appeals does not count toward their speedy trial claims. *Id.*

§11.07   Delay in Instituting Forfeiture Proceedings (New)

Statutes in most jurisdictions permit the government to institute civil proceedings to obtain forfeiture of property used in unlawful activity. In *United States v Eight Thousand Eight Hundred & Fifty Dollars in United States Currency*, 461 US 555 (1983), the United States Supreme Court considered a claim that an 18-month delay by the federal government in instituting civil proceedings to recover money transported in violation of 31 USC §1101 violated the claimant's right to due process of law. The Court recognized that the claimant had no right to a hearing prior to seizure of her property, since extraordinary circumstances justifying prehearing seizure exist when the government seizes property subject to forfeiture. Because a person whose property has been seized is entirely deprived of the use of his or her property until the government decides to initiate forfeiture proceedings, the Court analogized the owner's interests to those of a criminal defendant seeking a speedy trial. The Court therefore held that the balancing test developed in *Barker v Wingo*, 407 US 514 (1972), to determine whether the Sixth Amendment right to speedy trial has been violated, is appropriate to determine whether the Fifth Amendment right against deprivation of property without due process of law has been violated by delay. As in the speedy trial context, a court reviewing a claim that the institution of forfeiture proceedings has occurred an unconstitutionally long period of time after seizure of the property must consider the length of the delay, the reason for the delay, the claimant's assertion of his or her right to a hearing, and whether the claimant has been prejudiced by the delay.

In the case before it, the Court held that while the 18-month delay was significant, it was justified by the government's diligent efforts in processing the claimant's petition for remission, and in pursuing related criminal proceedings. The claimant had not asserted her right to an early forfeiture hearing by bringing a civil action, and did not show that the delay prejudiced her ability to defend against the forfeiture. Thus, the Court found no violation of due process. 103 S Ct at 569-70.

Because the Court found no violation of due process, it did not decide whether dismissal of the forfeiture action with prejudice would be an appropriate remedy for undue delay. Id at 561.

12 Guilty Plea

§12.03 Interpretation and Enforcement of Plea Bargain Agreements

Page 182, text, add at end of second paragraph:

Thus, a prosecutor may not enter into a plea bargain with a defendant which requires the defendant to agree not to testify for any co-defendants. *State v Fort*, 101 NJ 123, 501 A2d 140 (1985).

Page 183, note 27, at end of note add:

Of course, if a defendant reneges on a promise to cooperate made as part of a plea bargain, the government is no longer bound by the agreement. United States v Brooks, 670 F2d 625, 627 (5th Cir), *cert denied*, 102 S Ct 2943 (1982).

§12.04 General Requirements of Plea

Page 184, text, after carryover paragraph add:

Because an admission of facts sufficient to warrant a finding of delinquency may, like a plea of guilty to a criminal charge, entail serious loss of liberty, before a juvenile may knowingly and intelligently make such an admission, a court must explain in language understandable to the juvenile the rights he or she has and which will be waived by admission. *In re John D*, ____ RI ____, 479 A2d 1173 (1984).

§12.05   Voluntariness Requirement

Page 185, note 44, at end of note add:

A defendant who alleges that his or her plea was involuntary because he or she was denied the effective assistance of counsel must show that his or her attorney's representation fell below an objective standard of reasonableness, and that there was a reasonable probability that but for counsel's unprofessional errors, he or she would not have pleaded guilty and would have insisted on going to trial. Hill v Lockhart, 106 S Ct 366 (1985).

§12.06   —Threat by Prosecutor to Charge a More Serious Crime

Page 186, text, add at end of section:

While the Court has not departed from the proposition that it is a due process violation to punish a person for doing something he or she has a constitutional right to do, and that a prosecutor cannot bring more serious charges against an accused merely because he or she refused to plead guilty to less serious charges, in *United States v Goodwin*, 457 US 368 (1982), the Court refused to create a presumption that a prosecutor acts vindictively merely because felony charges are brought after a defendant refuses to plead guilty to misdemeanor charges and asserts his or her right to trial. In the case before it, the Court noted that there was no evidence that could give rise to a claim of *actual* vindictiveness, and refused to adopt what it called "an inflexible presumption of prosecutorial vindictiveness in a pretrial setting." *Id* 381. Distinguishing *Blackledge v Perry*, 417 US 21 (1974) (which held that the likelihood of vindictiveness when a prosecutor institutes felony charges against a misdemeanant who appeals for trial de novo justifies a presumption of vindictiveness, the Court emphasized that at the preliminary stages of the proceedings, the prosecutor's assessment of the proper extent of prosecution "may not have crystalized."*Id* 381. In contrast, once a trial has begun, and certainly by the time a conviction has been obtained, it is much more likely that the state has discovered and assessed all the information relevant. *Id* 381. Justice Stevens was, however, careful to note:

> In declining to apply a presumption of vindictiveness, we do not, of course, foreclose the possibility that a defendant in an appropriate case might prove objectively that the prosecutor's charging decision was motivated by a desire to punish him for doing something that the law plainly allowed him to do.

Id at 384.

§12.07   —Threat to Impose a More Serious Penalty

Page 186, note 49, at end of note add:

See also United States v Goodwin, 457 US 368 (1982).

§12.09   —Offers of Leniency to or Threats to Relatives

Page 189, note 66, at end of note add:

In re Ibarra, 34 Cal 3d 277, 666 P2d 980, 193 Cal Rptr 538 (1983).

§12.09A   —"Package Deal" Plea Bargains (New)

A prosecutor may offer a defendant the opportunity to plead guilty to a lesser charge and receive a lesser sentence, contingent upon a guilty plea by all co-defendants. In such an offer, factors unrelated to the government's interest vis-a-vis the particular defendant may become an important part of the plea bargain. Such a plea bargain offer may be disadvantageous to a defendant for several reasons. A defendant may lose the chance to accept a favorable plea bargain because of a co-defendant's intransigent unwillingness to plead guilty, or a defendant may be forced into an involuntary plea because of a threat to a co-defendant with whom he or she has an emotional relationship.

While courts have recognized the difficulties inherent in such bargaining techniques, they have not been willing to forbid prosecutors to make such contingent offers. However, the California Supreme Court held in *In re Ibarra*, 34 Cal 3d 277, 666 P2d 980, 193 Cal Rptr 538 (1983), that whenever a plea is taken pursuant to a package deal plea bargain, the court *must* inquire into the totality of the circumstances. The court must determine whether the inducement for the plea is proper, and must be satisfied that "the substance of the inducement is within the proper scope of the prosecutor's business" and determine whether the prosecutor has a "reasonable and good faith case" against the third parties to whom leniency is promised. The factual basis for the plea, the nature and degree of coerciveness, the degree of motivation to plead based on leniency to a third party, and other relevant factors must be examined by the court under the California scheme.

§12.09B   —Impermissible Plea Bargains (New)

The Eighth Circuit has held that a contingency agreement between a witness and a prosecutor, under the terms of which the witness's sentence would be reduced if the witness's testimony led to the accomplice's conviction, created such a risk of perjury that even the jury's full knowledge of the agreement was insufficient to protect the defendant's right to due process. *United States v Waterman*, 732 F2d 1527 (8th Cir 1984), *cert denied*, 105 S Ct 2138 (1985). On rehearing, the opinion was vacated and the district court order denying relief was affirmed by an equally divided panel. See **§13.09A.**

§12.13   Duty of Prosecutor When Plea Bargain Is Made

Page 191, note 82, at end of note add:

See also Mabry v Johnson, 104 S Ct 2543 (1984).

Page 192, text, at end of second full paragraph add:

In *Mabry v Johnson,* 104 S Ct 2543 (1984), the Supreme Court expressly faced the issue of when a defendant's acceptance of a prosecutor's proposed plea bargain creates a right to have the bargain specifically enforced. In the case before the Court, the prosecutor offered the defendant's attorney a recommendation of 21 years to be served concurrently with sentences the defendant was already serving. The defendant's attorney conveyed the offer to his client, who agreed to accept it, and the attorney called the prosecutor and communicated his client's acceptance of the offer. The prosecutor withdrew the offer, stating that a mistake had been made, and told the defendant's attorney he would recommend a sentence of 21 years to be served consecutively. The defendant, following a mistrial, accepted the state's offer, and in accordance with the plea bargain, the court imposed a 21-year sentence to be served consecutively.

The defendant sought habeas corpus relief in federal court. The Supreme Court held that the defendant was not in custody in violation of the federal constitution. The defendant did not challenge the district court's finding that he pleaded guilty with the advice of competent counsel and full awareness of the consequences. Judge Stevens wrote:

> Thus, because it did not impair the voluntariness or intelligence of his guilty plea, respondent's inability to enforce the prosecutor's offer is without constitutional significance. Neither is the question whether the prosecutor was negligent or otherwise culpable in first making and then withdrawing his offer relevant.

> The Due Process Clause is not a code of ethics for prosecutors; its concern is with the manner in which persons are deprived of their liberty. Here respondent was not deprived of his liberty in any fundamentally unfair way. Respondent was fully aware of the likely consequences when he pleaded guilty; it is not unfair to expect him to live with those circumstances now.

Id 2548.

The Court relegated to a footnote the defendant's claim that the prosecutor's withdrawal of the plea undermined his confidence in defense counsel, stating it could not "see how a defendant could reasonably attribute a prosecutor's change of heart to his counsel." *Id* 2548 n 11.

§12.14 Remedy for Prosecutor's Failure to Comply with Plea Bargain

Page 193, note 94, at end of note add:

The remedy for breach by the government will vary according to the facts of the case. *See, e.g.,* United States v Wilson, 669 F2d 922, 923 (4th Cir 1982) (resentencing before different judge proper remedy); United States v Cook, 668 F2d 317, 321 (7th Cir 1982) (post-sentence motion to withdraw plea proper remedy).

Page 193, text, add at end of section:

While dictum in *Mabry v Johnson,* 104 S Ct 2543, 2547 (1984), might be construed to require withdrawal of a plea where the prosecutor has breached the plea bargain agreement, some courts have adhered to the view that specific performance of the agreement is the chosen remedy. *In re Meunier,* ____ Vt ____, 491 A2d 1019 (1985). Where the agreement is not capable of being specifically enforced, an opportunity to withdraw the plea is necessary to remove all taint of false inducement. *Id.* A major factor in choosing the appropriate remedy is the prejudice caused to the defendant by the breach.

§12.15 Remedy for Breach of Plea Bargain by Defendant

Page 193, text, at end of section add:

A difficult consitutional question is raised when a defendant pleads guilty pursuant to a plea bargain which requires him or her to perform some act after pleading guilty, and he or she then declines to do the act. In *Adamson v Ricketts*, 789 F2d 722 (9th Cir 1986) (en banc), Adamson, a defendant in a murder case, agreed to testify against two co-defendants in exchange for being allowed to plead to second-degree murder. Adamson did testify against his co-defendants, and they were convicted, but their convictions were reversed on appeal. When the state sought to retry the co-defendants, Adamson declined to testify; the state then filed an information charging him with first-degree murder. The trial court vacated the second-degree murder plea and the state supreme court held that the defendant had breached the plea agreement and waived his double jeopardy rights by refusing to testify.

On habeas corpus, the Ninth Circuit held that jeopardy attached when the judge entered a judgment of conviction on the second-degree murder plea. Because the plea agreement was reasonably open to the interpretation the defendant advanced that he was only required to testify at the first trial, the court held that he could not be said to have knowingly and intelligently waived his double jeopardy rights "even if double jeopardy protection is waivable." Id at 727.

Page 193, note 95, at end of note add:

Of course, if a defendant reneges on a promise to cooperate made as part of a plea bargain, the government is no longer bound by the agreement. United States v Brooks, 670 F2d 625, 627 (5th Cir), *cert denied*, 102 S Ct 2943 (1982).

§12.16   Duty of Court When Plea Bargain Is Made

Page 195, note 100, at end of note add:

See also People v Killibrew, 416 Mich 189, 330 NW2d 834 (1982).

13 Witnesses

§13.02 Scope of Right to Compel Attendance

Page 200, text, add at end of section:

In *United States v Valenzuela-Bernal*, 458 US 858 (1982), the Court stated that "more than the mere absence of testimony is necessary to establish a violation of the right." *Id* 867. Justice Rehnquist, for a five-judge majority, wrote that a defendant:

> cannot establish a violation of his constitutional right to compulsory process merely by showing that deportation of [potential witnesses] deprived him of their testimony. He must at least make some plausible showing of how their testimony would have been both material and favorable to his defense.

Id 867. In the case before it, the Court held that the fact that the government deported illegal aliens the defendant was charged with transporting, before his attorney had an opportunity to interview them, did not violate the defendant's rights, where the government had made a good faith determination that the aliens possessed no evidence favorable to the defendant. *Id* 873-74.

In its opinion, the Court emphasized that the executive branch had a responsibility to faithfully execute the immigration policies adopted by Congress, and the Court referred to the practical considerations of detaining illegal aliens until trial, which included overcrowding in jails, and a great "human cost to potential witnesses who are incarcerated though charged with no crime." *Id* 865. Because of these considerations, extension of the *Valenzuela-Bernal* rationale to cases which do not involve deportation of illegal aliens is doubtful.

§13.03 Infringement by Government Right to Compel Attendance

Page 201, text, at end of first full paragraph add:

The state may not enter into a plea bargain with a defendant which is conditioned upon his or her agreement not to testify on behalf of co-defendants. Such a plea bargain violates the defendant's right to due process and to present witnesses in his or her favor. *State v Fort,* 107 NJ 123, 501 A2d 140 (1985).

Page 201, text, add at end of section:

In *United States v Valenzuela-Bernal,* 458 US 858 (1982), the Court stated that "more than the mere absence of testimony is necessary to establish a violation of the right." *Id* 867. Justice Rehnquist, for a five-judge majority, wrote that a defendant:

> cannot establish a violation of his constitutional right to compulsory process merely by showing that deportation of [potential witnesses] deprived him of their testimony. He must at least make some plausible showing of how their testimony would have been both material and favorable to his defense.

Id 867. In the case before it, the Court held that the fact that the government deported illegal aliens the defendant was charged with transporting, before his attorney has an opportunity to interview them, did not violate the defendant's rights, where the government had made a good faith determination that the aliens possessed no evidence favorable to the defendant. *Id* 873-74.

In its opinion, the Court emphasized that the executive branch had a responsibility faithfully to execute the immigration policies adopted by Congress, and the Court referred to the practical considerations of detaining illegal aliens until trial, which included overcrowding in jails, and a great "human cost to potential witnesses who are incarcerated though charged with no crime." *Id* 865. Because of these considerations, extension of the *Valenzuela-Bernal* rationale to cases which do not involve deportation of illegal aliens is doubtful.

§13.04   Nature and Source of Right to Confront

Page 201, note 25, at end of note add:

The confrontation clause does not require that testimony of an expert witness employed by the government be excluded if the witness cannot recall the precise method by which he or she came to his or her conclusion; "the Confrontation Clause is generally satisfied when the defense is given a full and fair opportunity to probe and expose these infirmities through cross-examination thereby calling to the attention of the fact finder the reasons for giving scant weight to the witness testimony." Delaware v Fensterer, 106 S Ct 292, 296 (1985).

Page 202, text, add at end of section:

A defendant waives his or her right to confront the witnesses against him, and the trial may proceed in absentia if he or she voluntarily absents him or herself after trial begins. *United States v Lochan,* 674 F2d 960, 967 (1st Cir 1982); *United States v Raper,* 676 US F2d 841, 846 (DC Cir 1982); *Brewer v Raines,* 670 F2d 117, 120 (9th Cir 1982).

§13.05   Hearsay and the Confrontation Clause

Page 202, note 33, at end of note add:

In United States v Inadi, 106 S Ct 1121 (1986), the Court specifically held that Fed R Evid 801 which allows declarations of coconspirators made during the course of and in furtherance of the conspiracy to be admitted into evidence, does not violate the Sixth Amendment.

Page 203, note 36, at end of note add:

See United States v Thevis, 665 F2d 616, 630 (5th Cir), *cert denied,* 456 US 1008 (1982) (admission of statements of deceased not violative of confrontation clause where defendant was responsible for the witness's death prior to trial).

Page 203, note 38, at end of note add:

Lee v Illinois, 106 S Ct 2056 (1986).

Page 203, text, add at end of section:

The Court has made clear that the confrontation clause analysis in *Roberts* focuses on those factors which come into play when the prosecution seeks to admit testimony from a prior judicial proceeding in place of live testimony at trial; it does not stand "for the radical proposition that no out of Court statement can be introduced by the government without a showing that the declarant is unavailable." *United States v Inadi,* 106 S Ct 1121, 1126 (1986). However, the Court has recognized that the confrontation clause "[c]ountenances only hearsay marked with such trustworthiness that there is no material departure from the reason of the general rule." *Lee v Illinios,* 106 S Ct 2056, 2064 (1986). In *Lee,* the Court reaffirmed the traditional rule that the confession of a co-defendant is presumptively unreliable and may only be admitted against a defendant if the presumption of unreliability has been rebutted. The fact that the confession may be found to be voluntary for Fifth Amendment purposes does not bear on the question of whether the confession was also free from any desire, motive, or impulse the co-defendant may have had to either mitigate the appearance of his own culpability by spreading the blame or to overstate the co-defendant's involvement in retaliation for his or her having implicated him in the crime. *Id.* The court noted that the record before it "documents a reality of the criminal process, namely that once partners in a crime recognize that the 'jig is up', they tend to lose any identity of interest and immediately become antagonists." *Id* 2064.

The Court also rejected that state's claim that the co-defendant's confession was admissible because it "interlocked" with the defendants confession on some points. Justice Brennan wrote:

> As we have consistently recognized a co-defendant's confession is presumptively unreliable as to the passages detailing the defendant's conduct or capability because those passages may well be the product of the co-defendant's desire to shift or spread blame, curry favor, avenge himself, or divert attention to another. If those portions of the co-defendant's purportedly 'interlocking' statement which bear to any significant degree on the defendant's participation in the crime are not thoroughly substantiated by the defendant's own confession, the admission of the statement poses too serious a threat to the accuracy of the verdict to be countenanced by the Sixth Amendment. In other words, when the discrepancies between the statements are not insignificant, the co-defendant's confession may not be admitted. *Id* 2064-65.

§13.05A   Right to Confront Infant Witnesses (New)

A few states have begun to enact statutes which allow out-of-court statements made by child victims of sexual assault to be admitted in court. *See, e.g.,* Wash Rev Code Ann §9A.44.120 (Supp 1985); Colo Rev Stat §13-25-129 (Supp 1984); Utah Code Ann §76-5-411 (Supp 1983);

Ariz Rev Stat Ann §13-1416 (1984). Such statutes are generally justified on the ground that (1) often the child victim's out-of-court statements constitute the only proof of the crime, (2) the child may be unable to testify at trial due to fading memory, retraction of earlier statements due to his or her guilt or fear, tender age or inability to appreciate the proceedings in which he or she is a participant, and (3) such statements are inherently reliable. *See, e.g., State v Myatt,* 237 Kan 17, 697 P2d 836 (1985).

The Kansas Supreme Court has held that Kan Stat Ann §60-460(dd) which allows for the admission of a child victim's hearsay statement if the child witness is unavailable or incompetent to testify, and the trial judge determines that the statement is "apparently reliable" and the child was not induced to make the statement falsely by use of threat or promise, does not violate the Sixth Amendment right of confrontation. A similar Washington statute, which allows out-of-court statements of a child victim who is incompetent because of his or her age, where the trial judge, in a hearing outside the jury's presence finds that the statement contains indicia of reliability and there is corroborative evidence of the act, was held not violative of either the federal or state constitutional rights to confrontation in *State v Ryan,* 103 Wash 2d 165, 691 P2d 197 (1984).

However, a majority of the Pennsylvania Superior Court has declined to recognize a tender years exception to the hearsay rule, which would allow admission into evidence of our of court assertions of children relating to sexual abuse. The court reasoned that it "did not believe that the out of court assertions of children, particularly four and five year-old children, are substantially more trustworthy than the out of court assertions of adults."*Commonwealth v Haber,*___ Pa Super___ 505 A2d 273 (1986).

An Arkansas statute which allows an infant sex abuse victim to give testimony by video deposition was held not to violate the Arkansas constitution in *McGuire v State,* 288 Ark 388, 706 SW2d 360 (1985).

§13.07 Extent of Cross-Examination

Page 206, note 51, at end of note add:

See also United States v Tracy, 675 F2d 433, 437 (1st Cir 1982) (holding that cross-examination can be limited only after the defendant has had a constitutionally required threshold level of inquiry); United States v Andrew, 666 F2d 915, 922 (5th Cir 1982); United States v Tolliver, 665 F2d 1005, 1008 (11th Cir), *cert denied,* 102 S Ct 1991 (1982).

Page 206, text, add at end of section:

In *Reese v State*, 458 A2d 492 (Md Ct App 1983), the Maryland Court of Special Appeals held that while a trial judge has discretion to limit cross-examination to protect a witness from embarrassment and humiliation, the trial judge erred in refusing to allow a robbery defendant to cross-examine the complaining witness about his psychological stability.

In *Delaware v Van Arsdall*, 106 S Ct 1431 (1986), the Court specifically held that a trial court's refusal to allow defense counsel to cross-examine a prosecution witness about an agreement he had made to speak to the prosecutor in exchange for dismissal of an unrelated criminal charge violated the defendant's rights under the confrontation clause of the Sixth Amendment. While recognizing that "trial judges retain wide latitude insofar as the Confrontation Clause is concerned to impose reasonable limits on . . . cross-examination based on concerns about, among other things, harassment, prejudice, confusion of the issues, the witness' safety or interrogation that is only marginally relevant," the Court held that by "cutting off all questioning about an event that the State had conceded had taken place and that jury might reasonably have found furnished the witness a motive for favoring the prosecution in his testimony, the Court's ruling violated [the defendant's] rights secured by the Confrontation Clause." *Id* 1435. Justice Rehnquist wrote:

> We think that a criminal defendant states a violation of the Confrontation Clause by showing that he was prohibited from engaging in otherwise appropriate cross-examination designed to show a prototypical form of bias on the part of the witness and thereby to expose to jury the facts from which jurors . . . could appropriately draw inferences relating to the reliability of the witness.

[citation omitted]. *Id* 1436.

However, the constitutionally improper denial of a defendant's opportunity to impeach a witness of bias, like other confrontation clause errors, is subject to harmless error analysis. *Id* 1438. Whether such an error is harmless depends upon the importance of the witness' testimony in the prosecution's case, whether the testimony was cumulative, the presence or absence of evidence corroborating or contradicting the testimony of the witness on material points, the extent of cross-examination otherwise permitted and the overall strength of the prosecution's case. *Id.*

§13.09 —Witness's Invocation of Fifth Amendment Privilege

Page 208, note 59, at end of note add:

See also United States v Hirst, 668 F2d 1180, 1182-83 (11th Cir 1982).

§13.09A Testimony of a Witness Having Entered Into Contingent Plea Bargain (New)

In United States v Waterman, 732 F2d 1527, 1531 (8th Cir 1984), *cert denied,* 105 S Ct 2138 (1985), the court held that a plea agreement made contingent upon the return of further indictments constituted a violation of the due process rights of any defendant against whom the witness may testify. On rehearing, however, the opinion was vacated and the district court order denying relief, was affirmed by an equally divided panel.

The First Circuit has held that a plea agreement which was contingent because it provided that the government's recommendation for a witness' sentence would depend "principally upon the value to the government of the defendant's cooperation" did not create such a risk of perjury that a defendant against whom such a witness testified would suffer violation of his or her due process rights. *United States v Dailey,* 759 F2d 192, 196 (1st Cir 1985). However, Judge Coffin stated that:

> ...We can think of no instance in which the government would be justified in making a promised benefit contingent upon the return of an indictment or a guilty verdict. Finally, we note that contingency agreements should be reserved for exceptional certain cases such as this one, where the value and extent of the accomplice's knowledge is uncertain, but very likely to be great.

Id 201.

§13.12 Scope of Immunity Required by Constitution

Page 211, note 76, at end of note add:

In Pillsbury Co v Conboy, 459 US 248 (1983), the Court held that a witness who had been granted use immunity in accordance with 18 USC §6002, and testified before a grand jury investigating criminal antitrust violations, could not be compelled to answer questions repeating verbatim or tracking closely his grand jury testimony at a civil deposition.

§13.13 Permitted Use of Testimony Given under a Grant of Immunity

Page 212, text, add at end of section:

In *Pillsbury Co v Conboy,* 459 US 248 (1983), the Court held that a witness who had been granted use immunity in accordance with 18 USC §6002, and testified before a grand jury investigating criminal antitrust violations, could not be compelled to answer questions repeating verbatim or tracking closely his grand jury testimony at a civil deposition.

The Court reasoned that even if the direct examination of the witness were limited to the questions and answers in the immunized transcript, cross-examination would likely produce information not elicited on direct, and that the scope of cross-examination could not easily be limited to the immunized testimony. In the case before it, the witness had refused to testify, although the district court had ordered him to do so. The Court stated that the witness acted properly in maintaining his silence, in part because "no court has authority to immunize a witness. That responsibility, as we have noted, is peculiarly an executive one." *Id* 261.

§13.14 Right to Have Immunity Granted to Defense Witnesses

Page 212, note 87, at end of note add:

United States v Drape, 668 F2d 22, 27 (1st Cir 1982).

Page 212, note 88, at end of note add:

Cf United States v Hunter, 672 F2d 815, 818 (10th Cir 1982).

Page 212, note 89, at end of note add:

In Pillsbury Co v Conboy, 459 US 248 (1983), in holding that a witness given use immunity at a grand jury could not be compelled to answer questions tracking his testimony in a subsequent civil deposition over a claim of Fifth Amendment privilege, the Court stated in dicta that: "No court has authority to immunize a witness. That responsibility, as we have noted, is peculiarly an executive one, and only the Attorney General, or a designated officer of the Department of Justice has authority to grant use immunity." *Id* 216. *See also* United States v Doe, 104 S Ct 1237 (1984), in which the Court declined to extend the jurisdiction of courts to include prospective grants of use immunity in the absence of the formal request that the statute requires.

14

Right to Counsel

§14.01 Nature and Source of Right of Indigents

Page 215, note 6, at end of note add:

The North Dakota Supreme Court, indicating that the right to counsel contained in the North Dakota Constitution may be broader than the federal right, has held that an uncounseled conviction of an offense for which counsel was not required by the federal constitution, may not be used to enhance a subsequent conviction. State v Orr, 375 NW2d 171 (ND 1985).

Page 215, note 7, at end of note add:

See also Bearden v Georgia, 103 S Ct 2064 (1983), discussing the development of the right to counsel.

§14.02 When Right Attaches

Page 216, note 10, at end of note add:

Maine v Moulton, 106 S Ct 477, 484 (1985).

Page 216, note 12, at end of note add:

In holding that a lawyer's "woefully inadequate" advice to a client to confess to a crime for which the defendant had not been arrested or charged did not violate the defendant's right to counsel, the New York Court of Appeals stated that "it is not irrational to draw a line at the commencement of criminal proceedings," but added it bears emphasis that this line does not blindly decree that the Sixth

Amendment right to counsel begins at the courthouse door. People v Claudio, 59 NY2d 556, 453 NE2d 500, 466 NYS2d 301 (1983).

Once the right to counsel has attached and the accused requests counsel, police may not initiate interogation until counsel has been made available unless the accused initiates further communication, exchanges, or conversations with the police. Michigan v Jackson, 106 S Ct 1404 (1986); Maine v Moulton, 106 S Ct 477, 484 (1985).

Page 217, note 17, at end of note add:

See also United States v Vasquez, 675 F2d 16, 17 (2d Cir 1982) (per curiam) (holding Sixth Amendment right to counsel not triggered when subpoenaed witness testifies before the grand jury.).

Page 217, note 19, at end of note add:

The New Jersey Supreme Court has held that a court-imposed restriction on a defendant's right to communicate with counsel during an overnight recess, whether the restriction is total or limited only to the defendant's testimony, constitutes the deprivation of a right so fundamental that it is reversible error, and prejudice need not be shown. State v Fusco, 93 NJ 578, 461 A2d 1169 (1983).

Page 217, note 21, at end of note add:

While an indigent has a constitutional right to counsel for at least one appeal, he or she has no right to compel the court-appointed attorney to present all the arguments which could be made in his or her behalf, even if the arguments are nonfrivolous, if the attorney, as a matter of professional judgment believes pressing those issues would be unwise. Jones v Barnes, 463 US 745 (1983); Evitts v Lucey, 105 S Ct 830 (1985).

Page 217, text, add at end of section:

In *United States v Gouveia,* 104 S Ct 2292 (1984), the defendant, an inmate of a federal prison, was placed in administrative segregation during the investigaiton of the murder of a fellow inmate. The defendant remained in administrative segregation for 19 months before being indicted for the murder, at which time counsel was appointed. The defendant was arraigned, but asserted that the indictment should be dismissed, since no counsel had been appointed until then. In rejecting the defendant's claim, the Court emphasized the dictum in *Kirby v Illinois* to the effect that the right to counsel does not attach until the time of or after the institution of formal charges, pointing out that the purpose of the guarantee is to protect the unaided layman during critical confrontations with his adversary, the state.

§14.03 Proceedings in Which Right Is Applicable

Page 218, text, add after carryover paragraph:

Despite the fact that the right to counsel under the Alaska constitution is more expansive than the right to counsel under the federal constitution, the Alaska Supreme Court has held that an indigent claimant, charged with narcotics offenses, has no right to counsel in forfeiture proceedings since such proceedings are not *criminal prosecutions* within the meaning of the Alaska Constitution. *Resek v State,* 706 P2d 288 (Alaska 1985).

§14.04 Indigent's Right to Expert Services

Page 219, note 31, at end of note add:

State v Anaya, 456 A2d 1255 (Me 1983).

Page 219, note 32, at end of note add:

State v Anaya, 456 A2d 1255 (Me 1983).

Page 219, note 35, at end of note add:

State v Anaya, 456 A2d 1255 (Me 1983).

Page 219, note 36, at end of note add:

State v Anaya, 456 A2d 1255 (Me 1983).

Page 220, text, at end of second paragraph add:

In *Ake v Oklahoma,* 105 S Ct 1087 (1985), the Court specifically held that when a defendant makes a preliminary showing that his or her sanity at the time of the offense is likely to be a significant factor at trial, the constitution requires the state to provide access to a psychiatrist's assistance if the defendant cannot otherwise afford one. The Court noted that in a number of cases concerning the right to counsel or appeal, transcripts, and filing fees, it had reaffirmed the rule that fundamental fairness entitles indigent defendants to "an adequate opportunity to present their claims fairly within the adversary system." *Id* 1094 (quoting *Ross v Moffitt,* 417 US 600, 612 (1974).) Noting that in many jurisdictions, statutes and state court rules require psychiatric assistance be provided indigent defendants when insanity is an issue, Justice Marshall wrote:

These statutes and court decisions reflect a reality that we recognize today, namely, that when the State has made the defendant's mental condition relevant to his criminal culpability and to the punishment he might suffer, the assistance of a psychiatrist might well be crucial to the defendant's ability to marshall his defense.

Id 1095.

The Court recognized that a defendant's mental condition is not necessarily at issue in every criminal proceeding and it is unlikely that psychiatric assistance would be of value in cases where it is not. Thus, Justice Marshall wrote:

We therefore hold that when a defendant demonstrates to the trial judge that his sanity at the time of the offense is to be a significant factor at trial, the State must, at a minimum, assure the defendant access to a competent psychiatrist who will conduct an appropriate examination and assist in evaluation, preparation and presentation of the defense. This is not to say, of course, that the indigent defendant has a constitutional right to choose a psychiatrist of his personal liking or to receive funds to hire his own. Our concern is that the indigent defendant have access to a competent psychiatrist for the purpose we have discussed, and as in the case of the provision of counsel, we leave to the State the decision on how to implement this right.

Id 1097.

In the case before the Court, after the defendant's conviction, a psychiatrist who had examined him on behalf of the state testified as to the defendant's dangerousness at the sentencing aspect of the case, which was a capital one. Since without a psychiatrist's assistance the defendant cannot offer a well-informed expert's opposing view, and therefore loses a significant opportunity to raise in the jurors' minds questions about the state's proof of an aggravating factor, the Court held that due process requires access to a psychiatric examination on relevant issues, to the testimony of the psychiatrist, and to assistance and preparation at the sentencing phase of the proceedings. *Id* 1097.

§14.05 Indigent's Right to Choose Appointed Counsel

Page 221, text, add at end of section:

In *Morris v Slappy*, 461 US 1 (1983), the Court rejected the Ninth Circuit's conclusion that a state trial judge had arbitrarily violated the defendant's right to counsel by refusing to grant a continuance which would have allowed a public defender, who had been representing the defendant until being hospitalized, to try the case. The Supreme Court held that the Ninth Circuit had misread the record, and that the record did not reveal that the defendant had sought a continuance in order to be represented by the public defender who had been representing him until he was hospitalized, until the trial had gone on for three days. At that point, the trial court was "abundantly justified" in denying the motion to continue, since "[the trial court] could reasonably have concluded that respondent's belated requests to be represented by [the hospitalized public defender] were not made in good faith but were a transparent ploy for delay." *Id* 13. More important than the holding was the dicta, rejecting the court of appeal's conclusion that the Sixth Amendment right to counsel "would be without substance if it did not include the right to a meaningful attorney-client relationship." *Id* 13. Chief Justice Burger wrote for a five-judge majority:

> No court could possibly guarantee that a defendant will develop the kind of rapport with his attorney-privately retained or provided by the public-that the Court of Appeals thought part of the Sixth Amendment guarantee of counsel. Accordingly, we reject the claim that the Sixth Amendment guarantees a "meaningful relationship" between an accused and his counsel."

Id 13-14. As a criminal defendant has no right to choose the particular attorney who will represent him or her, he or she has no right to compel appointed counsel to press points in appellate argument which, as a matter of professional judgment, the attorney believes should not be argued, even if those arguments may be characterized as "non-frivolous." *Jones v Barnes*, 463 US 745 (1983).

§14.06 Waiver of Counsel and Right to Proceed Pro Se

Page 222, note 54, at end of note add:

See also McKasle v Wiggins, 104 S Ct 944 (1984).

Page 222, text, add at end of section:

As the Court explicitly stated in *Faretta*, a trial judge may appoint standby counsel over the defendant's objection, to relieve the judge of the need to explain and enforce basic rules of courtroom procedure and assist the defendant in overcoming routine obstacles to his or her self-representation. In *McKasle v Wiggins*, 104 S Ct 944 (1984), the defendant objected to standby counsel's unsolicited participation in the trial, claiming that standby counsel's conduct deprived him of the right to conduct his own defense. The Court began its analysis by stating that "[i]n determining whether a defendant's *Faretta* rights have been respected, the primary focus must be on whether the defendant had a fair chance to present his case in his own way." *Id* 950. In beginning its analysis, the Court recognized:

> First, the pro se defendant is entitled to preserve actual control over the case he chooses to present to the jury. This is the core of the *Faretta* right . . .
>
> Second, participation by standby counsel without defendant's consent should not be allowed to destroy the jury's perception that the defendant is representing himself. . . .

Id 951.

The Court distinguished between proceedings held within and without the presence of the jury, and held that *Faretta* rights are adequately preserved in proceedings outside the presence of the jury if the pro se defendant is allowed to address the court freely on his own behalf, and if disagreements between counsel and the pro se defendant are resolved in the defendant's favor whenever the matter is one that would normally be left to the discretion of counsel. *Id* 952.

The Court held that even in the presence of the jury, a "categorical ban on participation by standby counsel" is "unnecessary." *Id* 953. The issue is whether standby counsel's actions undermine the defendant's appearance before the jury of maintaining the status of a pro se defendant. *Id* 954. In the case before it, apart from instances in which the standby counsel's participation before the jury was either approved by the defendant or was attendant to routine clerical matters, the court held that the lawyer's unsolicited comments were not substantial or serious enough to violate the defendant's *Faretta* rights.

A defendant is not constitutionally entitled to proceed as cocounsel with his or her attorney. *State v Gethers,* 197 Conn 369, 497 A2d 408 (1985).

§14.08 Effective Assistance of Retained and Appointed Counsel

Page 223, note 61, at end of note add:

See also Evitts v Lucey, 105 S Ct 830 (1985).

§14.09   Standard for Determining When Defendant Has Been Deprived of Counsel

Page 225, note 66, at end of note add:

See also United States v Talavera, 668 F2d 625, 634 (1st Cir 1982) (performance within the range of competence expected from attorneys to criminal cases); Mylar v Alabama, 671 F2d 1299, 1300-01 (11th Cir 1982).

The Second Circuit abandoned the sham and mockery test in Trapnell v United States, 725 F2d 149, 151-52 (2d Cir 1983).

Page 225, note 67, at end of note add:

See also People v Fosselman, 33 Cal 3d 572, 659 P2d 144, 189 Cal Rptr 159 (1983).

Page 225, note 70, at end of note add:

See also United States *ex rel* Edwards v Warden, 676 F2d 254, 258 (7th Cir 1982) (within reasonable range of professional competence); United States v DeRosa, 670 F2d 889, 896 (9th Cir 1982).

Page 225, note 71, at end of note add:

Maxwell v Mabry, 672 F2d 683, 685-86 (8th Cir 1982); United States v Sanford, 673 F2d 1070, 1073 (9th Cir 1982); United States v Ranieri, 670 F2d 702, 711-12 (7th Cir 1982).

Page 226, text, add at end of section:

The standard to be applied when a defendant claims that he or she was denied his or her constitutionally guaranteed right to counsel was carefully delineated at length by the United States Supreme Court in *United States v Cronic,* 104 S Ct 2039 (1984), and *Strickland v Washington,* 104 S Ct 2052 (1984). *Cronic* concerned a claim by convicted defendant that his lawyer's trial performance was so inadequate as to deprive him of his Sixth Amendment right to counsel; *Washington* concerned a claim by a defendant, who had pleaded guilty to murder, but after an adversarial sentencing hearing had been sentenced to death, that his lawyer's performance was similarly inadequate. The Court held that a capital sentencing hearing is sufficiently like a trial that counsel's role in the hearing is comparable to counsel's role at trial. *Washington,* 104 S Ct at 2064.

The Court noted in *Washington* that it had not expanded at length upon the requirement of a "reasonably competent attorney" providing advice "within the range of compliance demanded of attorneys in criminal cases" outlined in *McMann v Richardson*. Justice O'Connor stated:

> More specific guidelines are not appropriate. The Sixth Amendment refers simply to counsel, not specifying particular requirements of effective assistance. It relies instead on the legal profession's maintenance of standards sufficient to justify the law's presumption that counsel will fullfill the role in the adversary process that the Amendment envisions.

Strickland v Washington, 104 S Ct at 2065.

The Court determined that where an effective assistance claim is made,

> we must take [the Sixth Amendment's] purpose—to ensure a fair trial—as the guide. The benchmark for judging any claim of ineffective assistance must be whether counsel's conduct so undermined the proper functioning of the adversarial process that the trial cannot be relied upon as having produced a fair result.

Id 2064. A defendant raising such a claim must overcome the presumption that the lawyer is competent to provide the guiding hand the amendment requires. *United States v Cronic*, 104 S Ct at 2046. There are circumstances which are so likely to prejudice a defendant that the cost of litigating their effect in a particular case is unjustified: if the defendant is actually denied counsel at a critical stage of the trial; if counsel entirely fails to subject the prosecution case to meaningful adversarial testing; or if the circumstances are such that no lawyer, no matter how effective, could provide effective assistance. *Id* 2047. Similarly, while "not quite the per se rule of prejudice" which exists in the cases outlined above, prejudice is presumed if a defendant's lawyer actively represents conflicting interests at trial, and the conflict of interest adversely affects the lawyer's performance. *Strickland v Washington*, 104 S Ct at 2067.

In all other cases, however, the defendant who claims that his or her lawyer was constitutionally ineffective bears the burden of establishing the claim. The claim has two components. First, the defendant must show that counsel's performance was deficient. This requires showing that counsel made errors so serious that he or she was not functioning as the counsel guaranteed by the Sixth Amendment. *Id* 2064. Second, the defendant must establish that the deficient performance prejudiced the defendant. *Id.* This requires showing that counsel's errors were so serious as to deprive the defendant of a fair trial, a trial whose result is reliable. *Id.* Analogizing a claim of ineffective assistance to the test for the materiality of exculpatory evidence, the Court held that the defendant "must show that there is a reasonable probability that but for counsel's unprofessional errors, the result of the proceeding would have been different. A reasonable probability is a probability sufficient to undermine confidence in the result." Id 2068.

In *Cronic*, the lower court held simply, without determining whether the defendant had suffered prejudice, that the defendant had been deprived of effective assistance of counsel, where the defendant received a court-appointed attorney 25 days before trial, the government had investigated its case for four and one-half years, two co-defendants had decided to testify against the defendant, and the defendant's attorney was inexperienced, and normally carried on a real estate practice. The Supreme Court reversed and remanded the case for findings consistent with the opinion.

In *Washington*, the facts had been developed at greater length. In that case, against counsel's advice, the defendant, charged with one murder, admitted to two others. Also against counsel's advice, he pleaded guilty to capital murder, and refused an advisory jury. In a plea colloquy, the defendant told the judge he had no significant prior record and was under extreme stress at the time of his crimes.

Counsel did not seek character witnesses for nor request a psychiatric evaluation of the defendant, since he determined it was advisable not to allow the defendant to be examined by a state psychiatrist. Because he knew that a presentence report would disclose that the defendant had a lengthy prior record, he did not request one. Because the sentencing judge had a reputation as a judge who thought it important that a defendant admit to his crime, counsel emphasized that aspect of the case in the sentencing hearing. The judge found numerous aggravating circumstances, no mitigating circumstances, and sentenced the defendant to death.

On these facts, the Supreme Court held "even without . . . the presumption of adequate performance, that trial counsel's defense, although unsuccessful, was the result of reasonable professional judgment." *Id* 2071. Moreover, the character evidence the defendant claimed his lawyer should have offered would "barely have altered the sentencing profile presented to the sentencing judge." *Id.* The Court thus held that the defendant had not been denied effective assistance of counsel.

The two-part standard of *Strickland* for evaluating claims of ineffective assistance of counsel applies to guilty plea challenges. In order to satisfy this requirement, a defendant seeking to have his or her guilty plea set aside on the ground that his or her right to effective assistance of counsel was denied must show that counsel's representation fell below an objective standard of reasonableness and that there was a reasonable probability that, but for counsel's errors, he or she would not have pleaded guilty and would have insisted on going to trial. *Hill v Lockhart,* 106 S Ct 366 (1985).

§14.10   Denial of Effective Assistance of Counsel

Page 227, note 80, at end of note add:

See also Kimmelman v Morrison, 106 S Ct 2574 (1986), holding that defense counsel's failure to file a timely suppression motion because he had sought no discovery constituted performance below the level of reasonable professional assistance.

Page 228, text, add at end of section:

The Supreme Court has held that there is a presumption that counsel acts competently in any case. There are, however, three circumstances in which a court may find a denial of effective assistance of counsel without requiring any specific showing of prejudice. These circumstances are ones so likely to prejudice the accused that the cost of litigating their effect in a particular case is unjustified, i.e., when the defendant is actually denied counsel at a critical stage of the proceedings, when counsel entirely fails to subject the prosecution case to meaningful adversarial testing, or when the surrounding circumstances of the case are such that no lawyer could provide effective assistance. *United States v Cronic,* 104 S Ct 2047 (1984).

While not quite the "per se" rule that exists in the cases outlined above, prejudice is presumed if a defendant's lawyer actively represented conflicting interests at trial, and the conflict of interest adversely affected the lawyer's performance. *Strickland v Washington,* 104 S Ct 2067.

When a defendant claims that his or her lawyer's performance at trial was so ineffective as to deprive him or her of the counsel guaranteed by the Sixth Amendment, he or she bears the burden of establishing the claim. First, he or she must show that counsel made errors so serious that he or she was not functioning as the counsel guaranteed by the Constitution. *Id* 2064. Second, the defendant must establish that the deficient performance prejudiced him or her. *Id.* The defendant must show "that there is a reasonable probability that but for counsel's unprofessional errors, the result of the proceeding would have been different. A reasonable probability is a probability sufficient to undermine confidence in the result." *Id* 2068.

Any error may be harmless. The Court emphasized the "wide latitude counsel must have in making decisions," *id,* and stated that "judicial scrutiny of counsel's performance must be highly deferential." *Id* 2065. As a practical matter, it appears that if counsel made a reasoned choice of a trial tactic, that choice, no matter how disastrous, is unlikely to be considered ineffective assistance. Justice O'Connor noted: "There are countless ways to provide effective assistance in any case. Even the best criminal defense attorneys could not defend a particular client in the same way." Id 2066.

An illustration of representation falling below the wide range of professional assistance standard established in *Strickland* is *Kimmelman v Morrison*, 106 S Ct 2574 (1986), in which defense counsel did not file a timely suppression motion because he had requested no discovery from the prosecutor and was thus unaware of the existence of evidence which was arguably suppressible. In holding defense counsel's performance deficient, the Court noted:

> Respondent's lawyer neither investigated, nor made a reasonable decision not to investigate, the State's case through discovery. Such a complete lack of pretrial preparation puts at risk both the defendant's right to an 'ample opportunity to meet the case of the prosecution' [cit. omitted] and the reliability of the adversarial testing process. *Id* at 2589.

§14.10A Right to Counsel and Defendant's Right to Testify (New)

A defendant's right to testify in his or her own behalf, is, of course, unquestioned. Similarly, the ABA Model Rules of Professional Conduct and the Rules of Conduct in effect in most jurisdictions forbid a lawyer from "failing to disclose a material fact to a tribunal when disclosure is necessary to avoid assisting a criminal or fraudulent act by the client." ABA Model Rules of Professional Conduct Rule 3.3 (1983). In *Whiteside v Scurr*, 744 F2d 1323 (8th Cir 1984), *rehearing en banc denied by a 5-4 vote*, 750 F2d 713 (8th Cir 1984), defense counsel, convinced that his client would commit perjury, told him that if he did so he "would move to withdraw, advise the state trial judge the testimony was perjurious, and testify against him." *Id* 1326. On habeas corpus, the defendant alleged he had been denied the effective assistance of counsel.

While recognizing that a defendant's privilege to testify in his or her own defense does not create a right to commit perjury, the court, for purposes of its analysis, presumed the defendant would have done so if able but stated "the fact that appellant would have committed perjury does not mean that appellant has waived his right to a fair trial, due process or effective assistance of counsel." *Id* 1328. While stating that it expressed "no view on the Sixth Amendment implications of a lawyer's simply moving to withdraw without informing the trial court of the reason", the court held that "a lawyer who actively testified against his client could not be said to be rendering effective assistance. The same is true, we think of a lawyer who threatens to testify against his own client." *Id* 1331.

Thus, the court held that the defendant's right to the effective assistance of counsel had been violated. *Id.*

The United States Supreme Court, however, held that the defendant's Sixth Amendment right to counsel had not been violated since his attorney's conduct fell within the wide range of professional responses to threatened client perjury acceptable under the Sixth Amendment. *Nix v Whiteside,* 106 S Ct 988, 999 (1986). Moreover, as a matter of law, the attorney's conduct could not establish the prejudice required for relief since "whether he was persuaded or compelled to desist from perjury, Whiteside has no valid claim that confidence in the result of his trial has been diminished by his desistance from the contemplated perjury." *Id.*

§14.11   Joint Representation of Defendants

Page 229, note 93, at end of note add:

The Second Circuit has held that an attorney-defendant may validly waive a conflict of interest. United States v Cunningham, 672 F2d 1064 (2d Cir 1982).

15

Motions to Suppress Evidence or Bar Prosecution

§15.02 What Evidence May be Suppressed

Page 232, note 9, at end of note add:

The Massachusetts Supreme Judicial Court, with little discussion, adopted a state rule barring evidence, at least in some circumstances, obtained in violation of article 14 of the Massachusetts Constitution (which forbids unreasonable searches and seizures), overruling almost 150 years of contrary precedent in Commonwealth v Ford, 394 Mass 421, 476 NE2d 560 (1985).

Page 233, text, add at end of section:

The United States Supreme Court has held that an incriminating statement made by the accused, after police officers failed to provide *Miranda* warnings required by the circumstances of the case, does not necessarily require that a subsequent admission, made after proper *Miranda* warnings were given, must be suppressed. *Oregon v Elstad*, 105 S Ct 1285 (1985). The admissibility of such a subsequent statement turns "solely on whether it is knowingly and voluntarily made." *Id* 1293-94.

§15.03 Exceptions to Exclusionary Rule—Independent Source

Page 234, note 19, at end of note add:

See Segura v United States, 104 S Ct 3380 (1984) (holding illegal "securing" of apartment for 19 hours while police attempted to obtain warrant did not require exclusion of evidence obtained with warrant, since the information on which the warrant was secured came from sources wholly unrelated to the illegal entry, and was known to the officers prior to the illegal entry).

§15.04   —Purged Taint

Page 236, note 33, at end of note add:

See also Taylor v Alabama, 102 S Ct 2664 (1982).

Page 236, text, add at end of section:

In *Taylor v Alabama*, 457 US 687 (1982), the defendant was illegally arrested, taken to a police station, given his *Miranda* rights, fingerprinted, readvised of his *Miranda* rights, questioned, and placed in a line-up. The victim of the robbery in question was unable to identify him, but the police told him that his fingerprints matched those on some grocery items that had been handled by one of the participants in the robbery. After a short visit with his girlfriend and a male companion, the defendant signed a waiver of rights form, and executed a written confession. The Court held that the facts that six hours had elapsed between the arrest and the confession, that the confession may have been voluntary for Fifth Amendment purposes, that the defendant had been permitted a visit with his girlfriend, that the police did not abuse the defendant, and that the police did obtain a warrant, while interrogating the defendant (based upon the fingerprint evidence), were not sufficient to purge the taint of the illegal arrest.

§15.05   —Inevitable Discovery

Page 237, text, at end of second paragraph, add:

In *Nix v Williams*, 104 S Ct 2501 (1984), the Court specifically held that evidence obtained by unlawful means may be admitted at trial if the prosecution can establish, by a preponderance of the evidence, that the evidence ultimately or inevitably would have been discovered by lawful means. In the case before the Court, the defendant, arrested for murder, was interrogated by a police officer during a trip in a police car, after the police assured his attorney that they would not do so. The defendant thereupon led the police to the victim's body. The statements and evidence relating to the body were offered into evidence at the defendant's first trial, but his conviction was reversed on Sixth Amendment grounds in *Brewer v Williams*, 430 US 387 (1977). At the defendant's second trial, evidence of the condition of the victim's body was admitted, because the trial court concluded that the state had proved that if the defendant's admissions had not been obtained, a search which was already under way would have found the body in a short time in essentially the same condition in which it was found. The defendant's conviction was affirmed on appeal, and habeas corpus was denied by the district court. However, the Eighth Circuit reversed, holding that the prosecution must prove the absence of bad faith to take advantage of the inevitable discovery rule.

In reversing, the Supreme Court expressly rejected the Eighth Circuit's view that the absence of bad faith must be proved, holding that such a rule "would put the police in a worse position than they would have been in if no unlawful conduct had transpired." 104 S Ct at 2510.

§15.05A —Good Faith (New)

In the landmark cases of *United States v Leon,* 104 S Ct 3405 (1984), and *Massachusetts v Sheppard,* 104 S Ct 3424 (1984), the Supreme Court for the first time explicitly recognized a "good faith" exception to the exclusionary rule for searches conducted under the authority of a warrant which is subsequently invalidated. Noting that the exclusionary rule exists to deter police misconduct rather than to punish the errors of judges and magistrates, the Court declined to bar evidence obtained in good faith "by officers acting in reasonable reliance on a search warrant issued by a neutral and detached magistrate but ultimately found to be unsupported by probable cause." *United States v Leon,* 104 S Ct at 3409.

The Court also emphasized that the probable cause standard and the various requirements for valid warrants remain unchanged, and that to rely upon the good faith exception, an officer must reasonably presume the warrant to be valid.

For a full discussion of these two cases, see **§3.17A** of this supplement.

§15.07 —Exclusion of Press

Page 239, note 50, at end of note add:

See also Globe Newspaper Co v Superior Court, 457 US 596 (1982).

Page 239, note 51, at end of note add:

Such a right was explicitly found in United States v Brooklier, 685 F2d 1162 (9th Cir 1982).

Page 239, text, add at end of section:

The New Jersey Supreme Court has held, based upon both the federal and New Jersey Constitutions, that the public and press have a protectible constitutional interest in access to all pretrial proceedings in the prosecution of a criminal case. Thus, in New Jersey, pretrial proceedings must be open to the public and to the press. The only exception to this rule will arise in cases where the trial court is clearly satisfied that if the pretrial proceeding is conducted in open court, there is a realistic likelihood of prejudice to a fair trial by an impartial jury as a result of adverse publicity, and further, that such prejudice cannot be overcome by resort to various methods relating to the selection of jurors that will be available to the court at the time of trial. *State v Williams,* 93 NJ 39, 459 A2d 64 (1983).

The Ninth Circuit has held that there is a First Amendment right to access to pretrial proceedings and to the documents filed in such proceedings. *Associated Press v United States, District Court for Central District of California,* 705 F2d 1143 (9th Cir 1983).

Although most of the reported decisions have concerned the First Amendment right of the public and press to attend pretrial suppression hearings, in *Waller v Georgia,* 104 S Ct 2210 (1984), the Court held that the defendant's Sixth Amendment right to a public trial extends to such hearings. Such hearings may be closed, over defense objection, only if the party seeking closure advances an overridding interest that is likely to be prejudiced by publicity, closure is no broader than necessary to protect that interest, reasonable alternatives to closure have been considered, and the trial court makes findings adequate to support closure.

In the case before it, the Court found closure of a seven-day suppression hearing to avoid publication of two and one-half hours of unrelated tapes unjustified. However, while recognizing that the general rule is that a defendant should not be required to show prejudice in order to obtain relief for a violation of the public trial guarantee, the Court declined to order a new trial in the case before it. The Court remanded to the state court to determine what portions of the hearing, if any, should have be be closed. A new trial would be required only if the new hearing resulted in some "material change in the positions of the parties." *Id* 2217.

§15.10 Automatic Standing

Page 242, note 72, at end of note add:

In Commonwealth v Sell, 504 Pa 46, 470 A2d 457 (1983), the Court held that under the Pennsylvania Constitution, a defendant accused of a possessory crime will have automatic standing to challenge the admissibility of evidence alleged to be the fruit of an illegal search or seizure. State v Settle, 122 NH 214, 447 A2d 1284 (1982).

§15.13 Constitutional Prohibition against Double Jeopardy

Page 245, note 90, at end of note add:

See also Tibbs v Florida, 457 US 31, 47 (1982) (White, J, dissenting): "As our cases in this area indicate, the meaning of the Double Jeopardy Clause is not always readily apparent."

Page 245, text, at end of second full paragraph add:

However, simply because two criminal statutes may be construed to proscribe the same conduct does not mean that the double jeopardy clause precludes the imposition, in a single trial, of cumulative punishments pursuant to those statutes. Where the legislature specifically authorizes cumulative punishment under two statutes, regardless of whether those two statutes proscribe the same conduct, the prosecution may seek, and the court may impose, cumulative punishment under such statutes in a criminal trial. In *Missouri v Hunter,* 459 US 359 (1983), one Missouri statute provided that any person who commits any felony while armed with a deadly weapon is guilty of a separate felony, and another Missouri statute provided that a person convicted of the felony of first degree robbery by means of a dangerous weapon shall be punished by imprisonment for not less than five years. The defendant, as a result of an armed robbery, was sentenced under both statutes. The Court held that the double jeopardy clause did not forbid imposition, in a single trial, of cumulative punishments pursuant to those statutes. *Id* 368-69.

If a defendant is tried for two offenses and an appellate court determines that one of the offenses is jeopardy-barred, the court may reduce the greater offense to a lesser included offense. In such a case, however, the defendant may complain that he or she was prejudiced because the jury which convicted him or her heard evidence relating to a crime he or she should not have been charged with. The United States Supreme Court has held that when a jeopardy-barred conviction is reduced to a conviction for a lesser included offense which is not jeopardy-barred, the burden shifts to the defendant to demonstrate a *reasonable probability* that he or she would not have been convicted of the non-jeopardy-barred offense absent the presence of the jeopardy-barred offense. *Morris v Matthews,* 106 S Ct 1032, 1038 (1986). A "reasonable probability is a probability sufficient to undermine confidence in the outcome." *Id* To prevail in such a case, a defendant must show that but for the inclusion of the jeopardy-barred charge, the result of the proceeding probably would have been different. *Id* 1038.

Page 245, note 100, at end of note add:

The double jeopardy clause, of course, does not prohibit a state from charging a person with a greater and lesser offense based upon the same act. In Ohio v Johnson, 104 S Ct 2536 (1984), the defendant, charged in one indictment with murder and involuntary manslaughter, aggravated robbery and grand theft, all arising out of the same transaction, pleaded guilty over the state's objection to involuntary manslaughter and grand theft. On the defendant's motion, the trial court dismissed the remaining charges. In holding that the double jeopardy clause did not require dismissal, the Court emphasized that in this case, unlike *Brown v Ohio*, the state proceeded against the defendant with alternative charges in one proceeding.

Page 246, note 104, at end of note add:

A person convicted in a bench trial, in a state which retains a de novo system, may be retried de novo without any judicial determination that the evidence was sufficient at his or her prior bench trial. Justices of Boston Mun Court v Lydon, 104 S Ct 1805 (1984).

§15.14   When Jeopardy Attaches

Page 246, text, at end of section add:

However, double jeopardy does not bar the prosecution of a defendant whose plea of not guilty by reason of insanity to a crime was accepted, when it was later learned that the plea was fraudulent. *Lockett v Montemango*, 784 F2d 78 (2d Cir 1986). While recognizing that if the defendant "had managed to continue his fraud at trial and dupe a jury" into acquitting him by reason of insanity, the consitutional prohibition of double jeopardy would forclose the state from attacking the acquittal, the Court reasoned that since the plea was entered with the state's consent and the court's only options were to accept it or to let the criminal proceedings continue, the defendant had never been tried for his crimes and this had never been placed in jeopardy. *Id.*

§15.15 Appeal by Government

Page 247, note 111, at end of note add:

In Smalis v Pennsylvania, 106 S Ct 1745 (1986), a unanimous court held that double jeopardy barred an appeal by the Commonwealth from the granting of a demurrer, made at the close of the State's case, challenging the suffuciency of the evidence.

Page 247, note 112, at end of note add:

The Court has recognized a distinction between reversal by an appellate court due to insufficient evidence, and reversal by an appellate court because the verdict was against the weight of the evidence. In the first instance, the double jeopardy clause bars retrial; in the second it does not, because a reversal on the ground that the verdict was against the weight of the evidence does not mean that acquittal was the only proper verdict. Tibbs v Florida, 457 US 31 (1982). In such a case, the appellate court sits as a thirteenth juror and disagrees with the jury's resolution of the conflicting testimony. The appellate court's disagreement no more signifies acquittal than does disagreement among the jurors, and since the Court has consistently held that a deadlocked jury does not result in acquittal barring retrial under the double jeopardy clause, it has reasoned that the "appellate court's disagreement with the jurors' weighing of the evidence does not require the special deference accorded verdicts of acquittal." *Id* 42.

§15.17 Retrial After Mistrial

Page 249, note 130, at end of note add:

In Oregon v Kennedy, 456 US 667 (1982), a four-judge Court held that prosecutorial conduct which might be viewed as harrassment or overreaching, even if sufficient to justify a mistrial on the defendant's motion, does not bar retrial absent intent on the part of the prosecutor to subvert the protections afforded by the double jeopardy clause. Justice Powell, joining the Court's holding that the intention of the prosecutor determines whether retrial is barred, in a separate opinion emphasized that because subjective intent may often be unknowable, a court considering such a motion should rely primarily upon the objective facts and circumstances of the particular case.

On remand, the Oregon Supreme Court concluded that the federal rule established by the Supreme Court in *Oregon v Kennedy* was insufficient to protect a defendant's rights under the Oregon Constitution. The Oregon court held that a retrial is barred by Art I, §12 of the Oregon Constitution when improper official conduct is so prejudicial to the defendant that it cannot be cured by means short of a mistrial, and if the official knows that the conduct is improper and prejudicial and either intends or is indifferent to the resulting mistrial or reversal. State v Kennedy, 295 Or 260, 666 P2d 1316 (1983).

The Arizona Supreme Court, based on its own constitution, declined to follow *Oregon v Kennedy,* and held that jeopardy attaches when a mistrial is declared on motion of the defendant or by the court because of improper actions by the prosecutor, if "such conduct is not merely the result of legal error, negligence, mistake or insignificant impropriety, but, taken as a whole, amounts to intentional conduct which the prosecutor knows to be improper and prejudicial and which he pursues for any improper purpose with indifference to a significant resulting danger of mistrial or reversal" and the conduct causes prejudice to the defendant which cannot be cured by means short of a mistrial. Pool v Superior Court, 139 Ariz 97, 677 P2d 261 (1984).

Page 250, text, at end of carryover paragraph add:

While it is settled that the double jeopardy clause of the federal Constitution does not prohibit retrial of the defendant when a prior prosecution has ended in mistrial attributed to the jury's inability to reach a verdict, the New Jersey Supreme Court has held that precepts of fundamental fairness, together with the court's need to create appropriate and just remedies, confirm an inherent power in a trial court to dismiss an indictment with prejudice after successive juries have failed to agree on a verdict, and the state's chances of obtaining a conviction on further retrial are highly unlikly. *State v Abbati,* 99 NJ 418, 493 A2d 513 (1985); *see also State v Moriwake,* 65 Hawaii 47, 647 P2d 705 (1982).

§15.18   Prosecution by Two Sovereigns for Same Act

Page 250, note 137, at end of note add:

Heath v Alabama, 106 S Ct 433 (1985), (holding that the double jeopardy clause of the Fifth Amendment did not bar Alabama from trying the defendant for the capital offense of murder during a homicide after Georgia had convicted him of murder based upon the same homicide.)

16

Mode and Conduct of Trial

§16.01 Right to an Impartial Judge

Page 255, note 6, at end of note add:

See also Meachum v Longval, 693 F2d 236 (1st Cir 1982), *cert denied*, 103 S Ct 1799 (1983) (statement by judge, to defense attorney, during trial that "I strongly suggest that you ask your client to consider a plea, because if a jury returns a verdict of guilty, I might be disposed to impose a substantial prison sentence" led to a "reasonable apprehension of vindictiveness" that required resentencing before another judge). 693 F2d at 237.

§16.05 Rule of *Bruton v United States*

Page 260, text, at end of first full paragraph add:

Similarly, the Court held in *Tennessee v Street*, 105 S Ct 2078 (1985), that where a defendant testified that his confession had been coerced by a sheriff who had read an accomplice's confession to him and told him to say the same thing, the defendant's rights were not violated when the prosecutor was allowed on rebuttal to present the co-defendant's confession for the limited purpose of allowing the jury to compare the two confessions. The Court pointed out that:

> The *non-hearsay* aspect of [the accomplice's] confession—not to prove what happened at the murder scene, but to prove what happened when [defendant] confessed—raises no confrontation clause concerns. . . . The jury was pointedly instructed by the trial court not to consider the truthfullness of [the accomplice's] statement in any way.

Id 2081-82.

Page 261, note 40, at end of note add:

In Lee v Illinois, 106 S Ct 2056 (1986), the Court considered the issue of when a co-defendant's confession so interlocks with a defendant's confession that it may be admitted as substantive evidence against the defendant. See **§13.05.** Although the Illinois Court had admitted the confession on the theory that the defendant's confessions were interlocking, and this did not fall within the *Bruton* rule, Justice Brennan noted that the case before it was "not strictly speaking a *Bruton* case because we are not here concerned with the effectiveness of limiting instructions in preventing spill-over prejudice to a defendant when his co-defendant's confession is admitted against his co-defendant at a joint trial." *Id* 2063.

§16.06   Alternatives To Severance

Page 262, note 44, at end of note add:

State v Beam. 109 Idaho 616, 710 P2d 526 (1985).

§16.11   Right to a Public Trial

Page 264, note 59, at end of note add:

In holding that the defendant's Sixth Amendment right to a public trial extends to pretrial suppression hearings in Waller v Georgia, 104 S Ct 2210 (1984), the Court noted that it "agreed with the view" of the lower federal courts "that the defendant should not be required to prove prejudice in order to obtain relief for violation of the public trial guarantee." *Id* 2217.

Page 264, text, add at end of section:

In *Douglas v Wainwright*, 714 F2d 1532 (5th Cir 1983), *cert granted & vacated & remanded*, 104 S Ct 3580 (1984) the Court upheld a partial closure order in a Florida murder case. On the prosecutor's motion, the Court ordered that during the testimony of the state's chief witness, a 20-year-old woman who testified that she had been forced to engage in sexual intercourse just prior to the murder to which she was an eyewitness, only the families of the deceased, the victim, the witness, and representatives of the press would be allowed in the courtroom. The Court held that the purpose of the closure order, protection of the witness, was sufficiently compelling to justify the closure, where the partial closure did not undermine the purposes underlying the public trial right.

§16.12 Role of Press at Trial

Page 265, note 61, at end of note add:

Press-Enterprise Co v Superior Court, 104 S Ct 819 (1984).

The Court has held that the First Amendment right of the public applies to preliminary hearings and thus, such hearings may not be closed unless the trial court finds the closure is essential to preserve higher interests. Press-Enterprise Co v Superior Court, 106 S Ct 2735 (1986). Closure is permitted only to protect the defendant's right to a fair trial and in order to justify closure, the court must find that there is a substantial probability that the defendant's right to a fair trial will be prejudiced by publicity that closure would prevent and second, that reasonable alternatives to closure cannot adequately protect the defendant's fair trial right. *Id.*

Page 265, note 62, at end of note add:

Press-Enterprise Co v Superior Court, 104 S Ct 819 (1984).

Page 265, note 63, at end of note add:

See also Globe Newspaper Co v Superior Court, 457 US 596 (1982).

Page 265, note 65, at end of note add:

See also Globe Newspaper Co v Superior Court, 457 US 596 (1982).

Page 265, note 66, at end of note add:

A court must apply the same standards when a defendant seeks closure of voir dire proceedings. Press-Enterprise Co v Superior Court, 104 S Ct 819 (1984).

Page 265, text, add at end of section:

In *Globe Newspaper Co v Superior Court,* 457 US 596 (1982), the court held that a Massachusetts statute which *required* trial judges, at trials for specified sexual offenses involving a victim under the age of 18, to exclude the press and general public from the courtroom during the testimony of the victim was unconstitutional. The Court stated that the decision in *Richmond Newspapers, Inc v Virginia,* 448 US 555 (1980), firmly established that the press and the public have a constitutional right of access to criminal trials, which is embodied in the First

Amendment, and is applied to the states by the Fourteenth Amendment. *Id* at 603. While recognizing that the right of access was not absolute, the Court stated that:

> Where, as in the present case, the State attempts to deny the right of access in order to inhibit the disclosure of sensitive information, it must be shown that the denial is necessitated by a compelling governmental interest, and is narrowly tailored to serve that interest.

Id at 606-07.

While recognizing that the state's interest in safeguarding the physical and psychological wellbeing of a minor is compelling, the Court held that it did not justify a *mandatory* closure rule, since the circumstances of the particular case may affect the significance of the government's interest. The Court emphasized that its holding was a "narrow one: that a rule of mandatory closure respecting the testimony of minor sex victims is constitutionally infirm." *Id* at 611 n 27. The Court was careful to point out that in individual cases, and under appropriate circumstances, the First Amendment does not necessarily stand as a bar to the exclusion from the courtroom of the press and general public during the testimony of minor sex-offense victims.

§16.14   Source of Right to Be Present

Page 267, text, at end of first paragraph add:

While the constitutional right to presence at trial is rooted in the confrontation clause of the Sixth Amendment, the Court has recognized that the right to be present is protected by the due process clause in situations where the defendant is not actually confronting witnesses or evidence against him. *United States v Gagnon,* 105 S Ct 1482, 1484 (1985). The defendant has a due process right to be present at a proceeding whenever a fair and just hearing would be thwarted by his absence. *Id.* In *United States v Gagnon,* the Court held that the defendant's due process rights were not violated when the trial judge met in camera with a juror and a lawyer for one of four defendants to assess the juror's impartiality during the course of trial. *Id* 1484. The Court noted that:

> The encounter between the judge, the juror and [the defendants] lawyer was a short interlude in a complex trial; the conference was not the sort of event which every defendant had a right personally to attend under the Fifth Amendment. Respondents could have done nothing had they been at the conference, nor would they have gained anything by attending.

Id 1484-85.

Page 267, note 78, at end of note add:

United States v Gagnon, 105 S Ct 1482 (1985) (failure to object to in camera conference of judge with jurors constituted waiver of whatever rights defendant had to be present).

§16.15 Waiver of Defendant's Right to Attend Trial—Voluntary Absence

Page 268, note 81, at end of note add:

See also People v Parker, 57 NY2d 136, 440 NE2d 1313, 454 NY2d 967 (1982).

§16.16 —Disruptive Conduct

Page 268, note 85, at end of note add:

See also Wilson v McCarthy, 770 F2d 1482 (9th Cir 1985) (shackling of disruptive witness).

Page 268, text, add at end of section:

The Oklahoma Court of Criminal Appeals has held that a forceable injection of drugs, to restore a defendant to a condition of normality, violated none of his constitutional rights. In *Ake v State,* 663 P2d 1 (Okla Crim App 1983), the Court reasoned that if a defendant may be rendered competent to assist in his defense through the use of medication, it is in the "best interests of justice" to afford him a speedy trial. The Court rejected the defendant's argument that the trial court was under a duty first to cite him for contempt, and then secondly, to bind and gag him, prior to allowing the use of drugs to sedate him during his trial.

§16.17 Proof Beyond a Reasonable Doubt

Page 269, note 90, at end of note add:

The due process clause forbids any conviction based upon evidence insufficient to persuade a rational factfinder of proof beyond a reasonable doubt. Tibbs v Florida, 457 US 31 (1982).

§16.18   Proof Beyond a Reasonable Doubt and Use of Presumptions

Page 270, note 99, at end of note add:

See also Francis v Franklin, 105 S Ct 1965 (1985), holding that instructions that (1) the act of a person of sound mind and discretion are presumed to be the product of a person's will but the presumption may be rebutted and (2) a person of sound mind and discretion is presumed to intend the natural and probable consequences of his or her act, but the presumption may be rebutted, coupled with instructions that the defendant was presumed innocent and the state must prove each element of the offense beyond a reasonable doubt violated the Fourteenth Amendment requirement that the state prove every element of an offense beyond a reasonable doubt.

Page 271, text, add at end of section:

In *Connecticut v Johnson*, 460 US 73 (1983), the Court affirmed a decision of the Connecticut Supreme Court which had reversed a conviction obtained in violation of *Sandstrom v Montana*, 442 US 510 (1979) (which held that the due process clause of the Fourteenth Amendment was violated by a jury instruction that "the law presumes that a person intends the ordinary consequences of his voluntary acts"), without discussing whether the violation of *Sandstrom* was harmless error. Four Justices agreed with the state that a violation of *Sandstrom* may, in rare situations where the defendant is acquitted of an offense requiring specific intent, and the instruction had no bearing on the offense for which the defendant was convicted, or where the defendant's intent is not an issue, be harmless error, but found that the case before it was not one of those rare situations. Justice Stevens concurred only in the result, believing that the Connecticut decision rested upon adequate state grounds. Justice Powell, joined by three other justices, in a vigorous dissent, took the view that violation of *Sandstrom* may be harmless error even if the defendant does not concede intent, if the case against the defendant is strong enough.

The Court has expressly left open the question of whether an erroneous charge that shifts the burden of persuasion to the defendant on an essential element of an offense can be harmless. *Francis v Franklin*, 105 S Ct 1965, 1977 (1985).

§16.20 —Trial of Defendant in Prison Garb

Page 271, note 106, at end of note add:

Confinement in a prisoner's dock is only permissible when the trial judge has found such restraint reasonably necessary to maintain order, and when the jurors are instructed that they may not infer guilt therefrom. Young v Callahan, 700 F2d 32 (1st Cir 1983).

§16.20A Presence of Armed Court Officers At Trial (New)

The presence of guards in a courtroom during trial is not the sort of inherently prejudicial practice that should be permitted only where justified by an essential state interest. *Holbrook v Flynn,* 106 S Ct 1340 (1986). While shackling and prison clothes are unmistakable indications of the need to separate a defendant from the community at large, the presence of guards at a defendant's trial need not be interpreted as a sign that he or she is particularly dangerous or culpable. *Id.* Jurors may just as easily believe that the officers are there to guard against disruptions emanating from outside the courtroom, or to ensure that tense courtroom exchanges do not erupt into violence. *Id* 1346.

A defendant who claims that the deployment of security personnel during his or her trial violated the right to a fair trial bears the burden of establishing prejudice. *Id.*

§16.21 Constitutional Nature of Right to Argue

Page 272, note 108, at end of note add:

The United States Court of Appeals for the Second Circuit has held that there is no constitutional right to make an opening statement. United States v Salovitz, 701 F2d 17 (2d Cir 1983).

Page 272, text, add at end of section:

The opportunity to make a closing argument is a basic constitutional right, guaranteed by the Sixth Amendment to the United States Constitution. The Maryland Court of Appeals has held that the opportunity to argue, in a nonjury trial, after the court had rendered its verdict, and the verdict had been striken to allow counsel to argue, was insufficient to satisfy the right to counsel guaranteed by the Sixth Amendment and the Maryland Constitution. *Spence v State,* 296 Md 416, 463 A2d 808 (1983).

§16.22   Verdict

Page 272, note 112, at end of note add:

United States v Powell, 105 S Ct 471 (1984) (affirming the vitality of the *Dunn* rule, and holding that there is no exception to the *Dunn* rule where the jury acquits a defendant of a predicate felony, but convicts on the compound felony).

Page 272, note 113, at end of note add:

The United States Supreme Court has held that the fact that the *Dunn* rule may have been based in part on the view that there is no collateral estoppel in criminal cases, a view correct in 1932 and obviously incorrect at present, does not effect the vitality of the rule. The fact that inconsistency may be the result of lenity, coupled with the government's inability to appeal, suggest that inconsistent verdicts should not be reviewable at the defendant's behest, particularly since a criminal defendant is afforded protection against jury irrationality by the independent review of the sufficiency of the evidence undertaken by the trial and appellate courts. United States v Powell, 105 S Ct 471 (1984).

17 Trial by Jury

§17.02 Right Guaranteed by United States Constitution

Page 277, note 9, at end of note add:

Justices of Boston Mun Court v Lydon, 104 S Ct 1805 (1984).

Page 277, note 10, at end of note add:

Justices of Boston Mun Court v Lydon, 104 S Ct 1805 (1984).

Page 277, note 11, at end of note add:

Justices of Boston Mun Court v Lydon, 104 S Ct 1805 (1984).

§17.03 Cases in Which Jury Trial Is Constitutionally Required

Page 277, note 13, at end of note add:

The Washington Supreme Court has held that its constitution requires that a person be afforded a jury trial for any offense which constitutes a crime. City of Pasco v Mace, 98 Wash 2d 87, 653 P2d 618 (1982).

§17.05 Constitutional Requirement of a Fair Tribunal

Page 279, note 27, at end of note add:

See also Patton v Yount, 104 S Ct 2885 (1984).

Page 279, note 28, at end of note add:

See also Patton v Yount, 104 S Ct 2885 (1984).

Page 279, note 30, at end of note add:

Wainwright v Witt, 105 S Ct 844, 852 (1985).

Page 280, note 35, at end of note add:

See also Patton v Yount, 104 S Ct 2885 (1984).

Page 280, note 36, at end of note add:

See also Patton v Yount, 104 S Ct 2885 (1984).

Page 280, note 37, at end of note add:

See also Patton v Yount, 104 S Ct 2885 (1984).

§17.07 Fair Cross-Section of the Community Requirement

Page 283, note 50, at end of note add:

  The United States Court of Appeals for the First Circuit has
specifically held that young adults do not constitute a *distinctive group*
for purposes of the fair cross-section of the community requirement.
Barber v Ponte, 772 F2d 982 (1st Cir 1985). The court has also held
that *blue collar workers* do not constitute a distinct or cognizable group
for purposes of the fair cross-section requirement. Anaya v Hansen,
781 F2d 1 (1st Cir 1986).

§17.08 Use of Peremptory Challenges to Exclude Members of a Minority Group

Page 284, text, add at end of second paragraph:

  In *Batson v Kentucky*, 106 S Ct 1712 (1986), the Court reexamined its
holding in *Swain*, and held that a defendant in a criminal case may
establish a prima facie case of purposeful discrimination in selection
of the petit jury solely on evidence concerning the exercise of
peremptory challenges at the defendant's trial. Justice Powell wrote:

To establish such a case, the defendant first must show that he is a member of a cognizable racial group, [cit. omitted] and that the prosecutor has exercised peremptory challanges to remove from the venire members of the defendant's race. Second, the defendant is entitled to rely on the fact, as to which there can be no dispute, that peremptory challenges constitute a jury selection practice that permits 'those to discriminate who are of a mind to discriminate' [cit. omitted]. Finally, the defendant must show that these facts and any other relevant circumstances raise an inference that the prosecutor used that practice to exclude the veniremen from the petit jury on account of their race.

Id 1723.

Once the defendant makes a prima facie showing, the burden shifts to the state to come forward with a neutral explanation for challenging certain jurors. *Id* 1723. The Court emphasized that "the prosecutor's explanation need not rise to the level justifying exercise of a challenge for cause." *Id* 1723. But the prosecutor may not rebut the defendant's prima facie case of discrimination by stating merely that he or she challenged jurors of the defendant's race on the assumption of intuitive judgement that they would be partial to the defendant because of the shared race. *Id* 1723. The prosecutor must "articulate a neutral explanation related to the particular case to be tried." *Id* 1723.

Page 284, note 59, at end of note add:

The Illinois Supreme Court refused to go beyond *Swain* in People v Davis, 93 Ill 2d 155, 442 NE2d 855 (1982). *See also* People v Hall 35 Cal 3d 161, 672 P2d 854, 197 Cal Rptr 71 (1983).

Page 285, text, add at end of section:

While not embracing *Wheeler* or *Soares*, the Florida Supreme Court has held that the Florida constitution provides a defendant more protection than *Swain v Alabama*. In *State v Neil*, 457 So 2d 481 (Fla 1984), the court, embracing the reasoning of *People v Thompson*, 79 AD2d 87, 435 NYS2d 739 (1981) established a framework for determining when peremptory challenges are used unfairly. The court held that a party concerned about the other side's use of peremptory challenges must make a timely objection and demonstrate on the record that the challenged persons are members of a distinct racial group and that there is a strong likelihood they have been challenged solely because of their race. If a party accomplishes this, the trial court must decide if there is a substantial likelihood that the peremptory challenges are being exercised solely on the basis of race. If the court finds no such likelihood, no inquiry may be made of the person exercising the questioned peremptory challenges. If, on the other hand, the court decides that such a likelihood has been shown to exist, the burden shifts to the complained about party to show that the questioned challenges were not exercised solely because of the prospective jurors' race. *State v Neil*, 457 So 2d 481, 486-87 (Fla 1984). Both the state and the defense may challenge the allegedly improper use of peremptory challenges. *Id* 487.

Although *Wheeler* and *Soares* speak in terms of group bias based on racial, religious, ethnic, sexual, or other grounds, the Florida court in *Neil* limited its decision to racial groups, specifically leaving open the question of its applicability to other groups.

While declining to reject *Swain's* "clear, direct and unequivocal" rule that a defendant may not mount a successful equal protection challenge to the prosecution's racially discriminatory use of challenges solely on the basis of its action in a single case, the Second Circuit has recognized that such use of challenges may violate a state court defendant's Sixth Amendment right to a cross-sectional petit jury. *McCray v Abrams*, 750 F2d 1113, 1124 (2d Cir 1984), US Appeal Pending. Adapting the test established by the Supreme Court in *Duren v Missouri*, 439 US 357 (1979) to determine whether a Sixth Amendment with respect to the venire has occurred, the court held that to establish a prima facia case of discrimination, the defendant

> must show that in his case (1) the group alleged to be excluded is a cognizable group in the community, and (2) there is a substantial likelihood that the challenges leading to this exclusion have been made on the basis of the individual venire person's group affiliation rather than because of any indication of a possible inability to decide the case on the basis of the evidence presented.

McCray v Abrams, 750 F2d 1113, 1131-32 (2d Cir 1984), US App Pending.

If the defendant establishes a prima facia case, the state must rebut the presumption of unconstitutional action. But the court stated:

> In order to rebut the defendant's showing, the prosecutor need not show a reason rising to the level of cause. There are any number of bases in which a party may believe, not unreasonably, that a prospective juror may have some slight bias that would not support a challenge for cause, but that would make excusing him or her desirable. Such reasons, if they appear to be genuine, should be accepted by the court, which will bear the responsibility of assessing the genuineness of the prosecutor's response and of being alert to reasons that are pretextual.

Id 1132.

§17.10   Exclusion of Jurors from Petit Jury and the Death Penalty

Page 287, text, at end of carryover paragraph add:

In *Wainwright v Witt*, 105 S Ct 844 (1985), the Court clarified precisely what *Witherspoon* required, rejecting the view accepted by many lower courts, based upon dicta in *Witherspoon*, that jurors may be excluded for cause only if they make it unmistakably clear that they would automatically vote against capital punishment without regard to the evidence, or that their attitudes toward the death penalty would prevent them from making an impartial decision as to the defendant's guilt. *Witherspoon v Illinois*, 391 US 510, 522 n 21 (1968). In *Wainwright v Witt*, the Court held that a juror may be excluded for cause because of his or her views on capital punishment if the jurors views would "prevent or substantially impair the performance of his duties as a juror in accordance with his instructions and his oath." 105 S Ct at 852.

In *Lockhart v McCree*, 106 S Ct 1758 (1986), however, the United States Supreme Court held that the Constitution does not prohibit the removal for cause, prior to the guilt phase of a bifurcated capital trial, of prospective jurors whose opposition to the death penalty is so strong that it would prevent or substantially impair their performance of their duties as jurors at the sentencing phase of the trial. The Court held that exclusion of "Witherspoon-excludable" jurors does not violate the fair cross-section requirement of the Sixth Amendment since groups defined solely in terms of shared attitudes are not distinctive groups, such as blacks, women, and Hispanics are. Moreover, *death qualification* of a jury does not violate the constitutional right to an impartial jury. The Court noted that *Witherspoon* and *Adams* "dealt with the special context of capital sentencing, where the range of jury discretion necessarily gave rise to far greater concern over the possible effects of an imbalanced jury." *Id* 1769, and "reject[ed] [the defendant's] suggestion that *Witherspoon* and *Adams* have broad applicability outside the special context of capital sentencing." *Id* 1770. *See also Darden v Wainwright*, 106 S Ct 2464 (1986).

§17.11   Prosecutor's Closing Argument

Page 289, note 86, at end of note add:

However, the Court has specifically held that comment on a defendant's failure to testify may be harmless error. United States v Hastings, 461 US 499 (1983).

Page 289, note 89, at end of note add:

The latitude given prosecutors by the federal constitution is illustrated by Darden v Wainwright, 106 S Ct 2464 (1986), in which the Court held that a prosecutor's argument which "deserves the condemnation it has received from every court to review it," *Id* 2471, and during the course of which the prosecutor attempted to place some of the blame for the crime on the department of corrections because the defendant was on weekend furlough from a prison sentence when the crime occured, referred to the defendant as an animal, and implied that the death penalty would be the only guarantee against a future similar act, did not violate the defendant's right to a fair trial.

§17.12   Lesser Included Offense Instruction and the Constitution

Page 291, text, add at end of section:

While adhering to its holding in *Beck v Alabama*, 447 US 625 (1980) in *Hopper v Evans*, 456 US 605 (1982), the Court emphasized that a lesser included offense instruction in a capital case is constitutionally required only when the evidence warrants such an instruction. Where the evidence produced at a capital trial supported a claim of intentional killing, and affirmatively negated any claim that the defendant did not intend to kill the victim, the Court held that an instruction on the lesser included offense of unintentional killing was not warranted nor constitutionally required. *See also Spaziano v Florida,* 104 S Ct 3154 (1984).

§17.14   The *Allen v United States* or Dynamite Charge

Page 293, note 108, at end of note add:

See also People v Cook, 33 Cal 3d 406, 658 P2d 86, 189 Cal Rptr 159 (1983).

§17.15   Interference with Jury When It is Deliberating

Page 294, text, add at end of section:

However, an ex parte conference between the trial judge and a juror may be harmless error. *Rushen v Spain,* 104 S Ct 453 (1983).

18 Sentencing and Release

§18.01A Committal After Finding of Not Guilty By Reason of Insanity (New)

Most jurisdictions allow a defendant in a criminal case to interpose the defense of insanity. If a person is acquitted on that ground, he or she is generally confined to a mental hospital for some period of time. In *Jones v United States*, 463 US 354 (1983), the Court found no constitutional deficiency in the fact that the government had a lower burden of proof in such circumstances than that imposed upon it when it attempts to civilly commit a person.

In *Jones*, the Court considered the District of Columbia Code, which provided that a person may be acquitted by reason of insanity if he or she establishes insanity by a preponderance of the evidence at his or her criminal trial. The insanity-acquitted individual is then confined to a mental hospital, and within 50 days is entitled to a judicial hearing to prove by a preponderance of the evidence that he or she is entitled to release. If confined after the 50-day hearing, the insanity acquittee may be released with court approval, when the hospital chief of services certifies that he or she has recovered. The insanity acquittee is entitled to a judicial hearing every six months at which he or she may establish by a preponderance of the evidence that the acquittee is entitled to release. The Court found no difficulty in distinguishing between insanity-acquitted and civil committees, since the verdict of not guilty by reason of insanity is sufficiently probative of mental illness and dangerousness to justify hospitalization. Proof that the insanity acquittee committed a criminal act as the result of mental illness eliminates the risk that he or she is being committed for mere idiosyncratic behavior, and it is this risk which requires a higher standard of proof in civil commitments. Moreover, because an insanity acquittee is treated and not punished, he or she may be confined in a hospital for an indefinite period if necessary, and is not entitled to release merely because he or she has been hospitalized longer than he or she could have been incarcerated if he or she had been convicted of the act of which he or she was acquitted by reason of insanity.

§18.03 Sentence Pursuant to Separate Legislative Act

Page 300, text, add at end of section:

In *McMillan v Pennsylvania,* 106 S Ct 2411 (1986), the Court considered the question of what facts must be proved beyond a reasonable doubt as an element of the offense and what facts may be found, by a preponderance of the evidence, to enhance punishment. The Court noted that it was unable to lay down any bright line test. This inability "may leave the constitutionality of statutes . . . to depend on differences of degree," *Id* 2419, so the Court held that a Pennsylvania statute, which provided that anyone convicted of certain felonies is subject to a mandatory minimum of five years imprisonment if the sentencing judge finds, by a preponderance of the evidence that the defendant visibly possessed a firearm during the commission of the offense, did not violate the constitutional guarantee of due process.

§18.04 Evidence Which May Be Considered in Sentencing Hearing

Page 301, text, add at end of first paragraph:

In *McMillan v Pennsylvania,* 106 S Ct 2411 (1986), the Court approved a statute which required the sentencing judge to impose a mandatory five-year term on a defendant if the judge found, by a preponderance of the evidence, that the defendant visibly possessed a firearm during the commission of the offense. Justice Rehnquist noted that "sentencing courts have traditionally heard evidence and found facts without any prescribed burden of proof at all," and stated "we see nothing in Pennsylvania's scheme that would warrant constitutionalizing burdens of proof at sentencing." *Id* 2420.

§18.05 Scope of Prohibition of Cruel and Unusual Punishment

Page 302, note 31, at end of note add:

See also Enmund v Florida, 458 US 782 (1982), holding that a punishment of death imposed upon a person convicted of felony murder who neither took life, attempted to take life, or intended to take life violated the Eighth Amendment's prohibition of excessive and disproportionate punishments.

Page 302, note 34, at end of note add:

However, it is settled that the Eighth Amendment's ban on cruel and unusual punishment prohibits a state from inflicting the death penalty upon a condemned prisoner who is insane. Ford v Wainwright, 106 S Ct 2595 (1986).

§18.05A   Restitution (New)

Courts have generally assumed the right to order restitution to a victim of a crime as part of a criminal sentence. In recent years a number of statutes have been enacted which specifically authorize restitution as part of a criminal sentence in certain circumstances. Illustrative of the many statutes is 18 USC §§3579, 3580, the Victim and Witness Protection Act of 1982, which authorizes a sentencing court to order a defendant convicted of enumerated crimes, "in addition to or in lieu of any other penalty authorized by law [to] . . . make restitution to any victim of the offense." 18 USC §3579 (a)(1). Such statutes have begun to engender much litigation. Federal courts have generally rejected claims that civil restitution orders pursuant to the Victim and Witness Protection Act violate the Seventh Amendment right to jury trial in suits at common law, since at the time the Seventh Amendment was adopted, common law judges awarded restitution in larceny cases. *See, e.g., United States v Brown,* 744 F2d 905, 910 (2d Cir), *cert denied,* 105 S Ct 599 (1984); *United States v Florence,* 741 F2d 1066 (8th Cir 1984); *United States v Satterfield,* 743 F2d 827 (11th Cir 1984). The fact of current indigency does not render imposition of a restitution sentence unconstitutional; financial obligations may be imposed upon a defendant who is indigent at the time of sentencing but subsequently acquires the means to discharge his obligations. *United States v Brown,* at 911.

§18.06   Length of Sentence as Violation of Constitutional Prohibition of Cruel and Unusual Punishment

Page 304, text, add at end of section:

Dicta to the effect that the length of a sentence imposed upon a felony conviction is purely a matter of legislative prerogative was flatly rejected in *Solem v Helm,* 463 US 277 (1983). Helm had been convicted of uttering a no-account check for $100, a felony under South Dakota law. He had been convicted of six previous felonies, all of which were characterized by the Court as nonviolent crimes against property. Helm was sentenced to life imprisonment without possibility of parole under South Dakota's recidivist statute because of his six prior convictions. A five-judge majority held that the sentence violated the Eighth Amendment because it was disproportionate to the crime committed. The Court employed a detailed historical analysis to show that the concept of proportionality has always applied to felony prison sentences, relegating to a footnote Justice Rehnquist's dicta in *Rummel* that "one could argue . . . length of sentence . . . is purely a matter of legislative prerogative," and emphasizing that "the Court did not adopt the standard proposed, but merely recognized the argument was possible." *Id* 288.

Justice Powell's majority opinion attempted to establish objective criteria that reviewing courts should apply to determine whether a sentence is constitutionally disproportionate:

> [A] court's proportionality analysis should be guided by objective criteria, including (i) the gravity of the offense and the harshness of the penalty, (ii) the sentences imposed on other criminals in the same jurisdiction and (iii) the sentences imposed for commission of the same crime in other jurisdictions.

Id 292.

The Court recognized that such an analysis requires a reviewing court to make judgments about the seriousness of particular crimes, but concluded:

> [T]here are widely shared views as to the relative seriousness of crimes [citation omitted]. For example, as the criminal laws make clear, non-violent crimes are less serious than crimes marked by violence or by threat of violence.
>
> There are other accepted principles that courts may apply in measuring the harm caused or threatened to the victim or society. The absolute magnitude of the crime may be relevant. Stealing a million dollars is viewed as more serious than stealing a hundred dollars—a point recognized in statutes distinguishing petty theft from grand theft [citation omitted]. Few would dispute that a lesser included offense should not be punished more severely than the greater offense. . . . It is also generally recognized that attempts are less serious than completed crimes [citation omitted]. Similarly, an accessory after the fact should not be subject to a higher penalty than the principal.
>
> Turning to the culpability of the offender, there are again clear distinctions that courts may recognize and apply. . . . Most would

agree that negligent conduct is less serious than intentional
conduct. . . .

This list is by no means exhaustive.

Id 292-93. Applying its analytical framework to the case before it, the
Court held Helm's sentence impermissible. It pointed out that "his
prior offenses, although classified as felonies, were all relatively minor.
All were non-violent, and none was a crime against a person." *Id* 3013.
No other offense in South Dakota was so severely punished for a first
offense, and many very serious crimes were not punished by so severe
a sentence. Finally, a similar sentence under like facts could only have
been imposed in one other state. The Court rejected the state's claim
that the possibility of an executive pardon constituted a possibility of
parole which presumably led the court to find the life sentence imposed
in *Rummel* acceptable.

Most courts have traditionally viewed length of sentence as a matter
entirely within the discretion of the trial judge. The breadth of the
Court's language necessarily suggests that appellate review of sentences must be conducted in a less cursory fashion in the future. Indeed
Chief Justice Burger, dissenting, noted:

> There is a real risk that this holding will flood the appellate
> courts with cases in which equally arbitrary lines must be drawn.
> . . . The vast majority of criminal cases are disposed of by pleas
> of guilty, and ordinarily there is no appellate review in such cases.
> To require appellate review of all sentences of imprisonment—as
> the Court's opinion necessarily does—will administer the coup de
> grace to courts of appeal as we know them.

Id 315 (Burger, CJ, dissenting).

A sentence of life without possibility of parole, imposed upon a
defendant convicted of three felony counts of distribution of a
controlled substance, who had been convicted previously of three
felonies of third-degree burglary, was held disproportionate and
violative of *Solem v Helm*, in *State v Weiker*, 342 NW2d 7 (SD 1983).

§18.09   Death Penalty as Cruel and Unusual
Punishment

Page 306, note 50, at end of note add:

In Enmund v Florida, 458 US 782 (1982), the Court held that
imposition of the death penalty on a person who aided and abetted a
felony, during the course of which a murder was committed, but who
neither "took life, attempted to take life nor intended to take life"
violated the Eighth and Fourteenth Amendments. *Id* 3371. The death

penalty is an unconstitutionally excessive punishment for robbery. *Id* 3377.

It has been held, however, that a sentence of death imposed upon a person 17 years and 8 months old at the time of the offense does not constitute cruel and unusual punishment in violation of the Eighth Amendment in the United States Constitution. Trimble v State, 300 Md 387, 478 A2d 1143 (1984), *cert denied,* 105 S Ct 1231 (1985); Cabana v Bullock, 106 S Ct 689 (1986).

§18.11   Constitutionally Permissible Death Penalty Statutes

Page 310, note 70, at end of note add:

See also Enmund v Florida, 458 US 782 (1982); Barclay v Florida, 463 US 969 (1983).

Page 310, note 75, at end of note add:

The Eighth Amendment does not, for example, require a proportionality review in every death penalty case. In Pulley v Harris, 104 S Ct 871 (1984), the Court held the California capital punishment statute constitutional despite the absence of a statutorily mandated comparative proportionality review.

Page 311, note 78, at end of note add:

Despite the fact that the American Psychiatric Association has concluded that psychiatrists are incompetent to predict with any degree of reliability that a particular criminal will or will not commit other crimes in the future, such testimony may constitutionally be heard and considered by a jury in the penalty phase of a capital case. Barefoot v Estelle, 463 US 880 (1983).

Where the prosecution places before the jury psychiatric testimony on the issue of future dangerousness, due process requires that an indigent defendant be afforded access to a psychiatric examination on relevant issues, the testimony of the psychiatrist, and his assistance in preparation at the sentencing phase. Ake v Oklahoma, 105 S Ct 1087, 1097 (1985).

Exclusion from a sentencing hearing of testimony of jailers and visitors regarding the defendant's good conduct during the seven months he spent in jail awaiting trial was held to have denied the defendant his right to present mitigating evidence before the jury in Skipper v South Carolina, 106 S Ct 1669 (1986).

Page 311, text, add at end of section:

The Court has held that a statutory scheme which allows the sentencing judge to override the jury's recommendation of life imprisonment and impose the death penalty is constitutional. *Spaziano v Florida,* 104 S Ct 3154 (1984).

§18.11A   Instruction on Governor's Right to Commute Death or Life Without Parole Sentence [New]

The Eighth and Fourteenth Amendments do not forbid the jury being instructed, in the penalty phase of a capital murder trial, that it may impose a sentence of death or life without possibility of parole, and that under the applicable law, the governor may commute a sentence of life without possibility of parole to a sentence that includes the possibility of parole. *California v Ramos,* 463 US 992 (1983). Such an instruction does not result in any diminution of the reliability of the sentencing decision, nor deflect the jury's focus from its central task of undertaking an individualized sentencing determination; rather, it simply accurately states a potential sentencing alternative. The fact that the jury is not instructed that a governor may commute a death sentence is not constitutionally required when the jury is instructed on the governor's right to commute life without possibility of parole sentences. Advising the jury that their death sentence is modifiable may well incline them to approach their sentencing decision with less appreciation for the gravity of the sentence to be imposed. *Id.*

On remand from the United States Supreme Court, the California Supreme Court held that the instruction given the jury violated the California Constitution. *People v Ramos,* 37 Cal 3d 136, 689 P2d 430, 207 Cal Rptr 800 (1984). The court reasoned that the challenged instruction was misleading and therefore violative of due process, since the challenged instruction informed the jury only that a sentence of life without possibility of parole may be commuted, while in fact, under the California Constitution, the governor's power of commutation or pardon extends equally to a sentence of death and to a sentence of life without possibility of parole. *Id.* The court stated that even if the instruction were accurate, it would still violate the state constitutional due process guarantee because its reference to the commutation power invites the jury to consider matters that are totally speculative, and should not, in any event, influence the jury's determination. *Id.*

Despite the decision in *Ramos,* in *Caldwell v Mississippi,* 105 S Ct 2633 (1985) a four-judge majority of the Court (Justice O'Connor concurred in the result, Justice Powell did not participate, and three justices dissented) held that it is unconstitutionally impermissible to rest a death sentence on a determination made by a sentencer who has been led to believe that the responsibility for determining the appropriateness of the defendant's death rests elsewhere. In the case before the Court, the prosecutor, in rebuttal to the defendant's closing, sought to minimize the seriousness of the decision before the jury by arguing that the jury's decision on penalty was not the final decision because it was reviewable by an appellate court. Because the Court could "not say that this effort had no effect on the sentencing decision," it held that "that decision does not meet the standard of reliability that the Eighth Amendment requires." *Id* 2646.

§18.12   Appeal by Government in General

Page 312, note 81, at end of note add:

See also Arizona v Rumsey, 104 S Ct 2305 (1984), holding that the government may not appeal and seek imposition of the death penalty where a trial judge, at a capital sentencing hearing at which the judge must make findings of fact, misinterpreted the law and sentenced defendant to life imprisonment.

Page 312, note 83, at end of note add:

See also Pennsylvania v Goldhammer, 106 S Ct 353 (1985), holding that double jeopardy did not bar resentencing of defendant on a count upon which he had received a suspended sentence where on appeal, the count upon which he had been sentenced to imprisonment was dismissed.

§18.13   Parole and Probation in General

Page 312, note 85, at end of note add:

See also Solem v Helm, 463 US 277 (1983).

§18.15   Conditions on Parole or Probation

Page 315, text, add at end of section:

The general obligation to appear before a probation officer and to answer the officer's questions truthfully was held not to convert a probationer's otherwise voluntary statements into compelled ones within the meaning of the Fifth Amendment in *Minnesota v Murphy*, 104 S Ct 1136 (1984). The Court held that a probationer, confronted with questions the answers to which would incriminate him or her, must assert the Fifth Amendment privilege rather than answer if he or she desires not to incriminate himself or herself. Since it was not clear from the record in the case that invocation of the privilege would have resulted in revocation of probation, the Court rejected the defendant's claim that incriminating disclosures to his probation officer were compelled. *Id* 1146.

§18.16 —Payment of Fine

Page 316, text, add at end of section:

In *Bearden v Georgia*, 103 S Ct 2064 (1983), the defendant pleaded guilty to burglary and theft by receiving stolen property, and, pursuant to the Georgia First Offender's Act, he was sentenced to probation and ordered to pay a $500 fine and $250 in restitution. The defendant borrowed $200 and made the first scheduled payment, but was then laid off from his job, and notified the state probation officer that his next payment would be late. The state filed a petition to revoke probation, and after hearing, the defendant was sentenced to a prison term.

The United States Supreme Court held that the revocation of the defendant's probation was unconstitutional, and that to comport with the requirement of fundamental fairness, before revoking probation for failure to pay a fine or restitution, a sentencing court must inquire into the reasons for the failure to pay. If the probationer willfully refuses to pay, or fails to make sufficient bona fide efforts to acquire the resources to pay, a court may revoke probation and sentence the defendant to imprisonment. If a probationer cannot pay despite bona fide efforts to do so, a court must consider alternative methods of punishment other than imprisonment. Only if such measures are not adequate to meet the state's interests in punishment and deterrence may a court imprison a probationer who has made a bona fide effort to pay.

Because the Georgia courts had never considered ability to pay or the effect of alternate sentences, the case before the Supreme Court was remanded.

§18.17 Procedural Requirements for Revocation of Parole or Probation

Page 316, note 108, at end of note add:

See also Bearden v Georgia, 103 S Ct 2064 (1983).

Page 317, text, at end of last paragraph add:

Although *Morrissey* and *Gagnon* outline the minimum procedural safeguards required by due process, the Court has stated that "neither decision purports to restrict the substantive grounds for revoking probation or parole." *Black v Romano,* 105 S Ct 2254 (1985). There is no general requirement that a court state explicitly why it has rejected alternatives to incarceration. *Id.*

An exception to the general rule exists, however, when a court revokes probation for failure to pay a fine. If a probationer cannot pay despite bona fide efforts to do so, a court must consider alternative methods of punishment other than imprisonment. *Bearden v Georgia,* 461 US 660 (1983).

§18.18   Due Process When Credits on Sentence Are Revoked

The due process clause of the Fourteenth Amendment does not require that a prison official's reason's for denying an inmate's witness request appear in the administrative record of the disciplinary hearing. Ponte v Real, 105 S Ct 2192 (1985).

Page 319, text, add at end of section:

The United States Supreme Court has expressly left open the issue of whether due process requires that judicial renew be afforded a prisoner whose time credits have been revoked. *Superintendent v Hill,* 105 S Ct 2768 (1985). Where such review is allowed by law, the Court has held that the requirements of due process are satisfied if some evidence supports the decision by the prison disciplinary board to revoke the good time credits. *Id.*

19

Appeal and Postconviction Remedies

§19.01 Constitutional Right to Appeal

Page 321, text, add at end of section:

While reaffirming the traditional view of *McKane v Durston*, 153 US 684 (1894) that the Constitution does not require the state to grant appeals of right to defendants seeking review of alleged trial court errors, the Court emphasized in *Evitts v Lucey*, 105 S Ct 830 (1985) that if the state establishes an appeal process, "the procedures used in deciding appeals must comport with the demands of the due process clause." *Id* 834. The Court held that the due process clause of the Fourteenth Amendment guarantees a criminal defendant the effective assistance of counsel on his or her first appeal as a matter of right, and that such an appeal "is not adjudicated in accordance with due process of law if the defendant does not have the effective assistance of an attorney." *Id* 836. Thus, in the case before it, where the defendant's appeal had been dismissed for failure of his counsel to comply with local procedural rules, the Court held that the dismissal of the appeal violated the due process clause.

§19.02 Indigent's Right to Appeal

Page 322, note 12, at end of note add:

See also Evitts v Lucey, 105 S Ct 830 (1985).

Page 323, text, add at end of section:

While an indigent has a constitutional right to counsel for at least one appeal, he or she has no right to compel his or her court-appointed attorney to present all the arguments which could be made in his or her behalf, even if the arguments are nonfrivolous, if the attorney as a matter of professional judgment believes pressing those issues would be unwise. *Jones v Barnes*, 463 US 745 (1983).

§19.04   Sentencing on Conviction After Trial De Novo

Page 325, note 25, at end of note add:

See also Thigpen v Roberts, 104 S Ct 2916 (1984) (leaving open question of whether a narrower rule would apply if the new charges were instituted by a different prosecutor).

§19.05   Sentencing on Conviction After Appeal

Page 325, note 26, at end of note add:

The Court has, however, recognized a distinction between reversal by an appellate court due to insufficient evidence, and reversal by an appellate court because the verdict was against the weight of the evidence. In the first instance, the double jeopardy clause bars retrial; in the second it does not, because a reversal on the ground that the verdict was against the weight of the evidence does not mean that acquittal was the only proper verdict. Tibbs v Florida, 457 US 31 (1982). In such a case, the appellate court sits as a *thirteenth juror* and disagrees with the jury's resolution of the conflicting testimony. The appellate court's disagreement no more signifies acquittal than does disagreement among the jurors, and since the Court has consistently held that a deadlocked jury does not result in acquittal barring retrial under the double jeopardy clause, it reasoned that the "appellate court's disagreement with the jurors' weighing of the evidence does not require the special deference accorded verdicts of acquittal." *Id* 42.

Page 325, note 31, at end of note add:

However, there is no occasion for a presumption of vindictiveness when the trial judge sets aside a verdict and grants the defendant's motion for a new trial. Texas v McCollough, 106 S Ct 976, 979 (1986).

Page 326, text, add at end of section:

In *Wasman v United States*, 104 S Ct 3217 (1984), the Court made clear that the presumption of vindictiveness established in *Pearce* can be overcome by competent evidence. In *Wasman*, the defendant was convicted of making false statements in a passport application, and was sentenced to two years of imprisonment with all but six months suspended. At the sentencing hearing, the trial judge stated that he had not considered an outstanding mail fraud indictment. The defendant pleaded guilty to a lesser charge on the mail fraud indictment, and his conviction on the passport charges was reversed. After retrial he was again convicted, and the same judge sentenced him. The court imposed a two-year sentence, based upon the intervening conviction, despite the fact that the conduct which resulted in the intervening conviction had occurred prior to the first trial. Dismissing the defendant's reliance on the language in *Pearce* (cited in the main volume) that reasons for an increased sentence "must be based upon objective information concerning identifiable conduct on the part of the defendant occurring after the time of the original sentencing proceeding," Chief Justice Burger concluded that "any language in *Pearce* suggesting that an intervening conviction for an offense committed prior to the original sentence may not be considered upon sentencing after retrial is inconsistent with the *Pearce* opinion as a whole." *Id* 3225.

§19.06 Sentence of Death Following Appeal of Conviction in Which Death Penalty Was Not Imposed

Page 327, text, add after first paragraph:

Where however, the sentencing judge at the first trial erroneously ruled that a particular aggravating circumstance did not apply to the defendant but ruled that if the circumstance were applicable to the defendant, the evidence would justify imposition of the death penalty, and the ruling that the circumstance was not applicable was reversed on appeal, the double jeopardy clause did not bar imposition of the death penalty, since there was no death penalty acquittal. *Poland v Arizona*, 106 S Ct 1749 (1986).

§19.07 Harmless Constitutional Error

Page 327, note 38, at end of note add:

See also Connecticut v Johnson, 460 US 73 (1983).

Page 327, note 40, at end of note add:

See also United States v Hastings, 461 US 499 (1983).

Page 327, note 42, at end of note add:

Comment on the defendant's failure to produce evidence or testify is not, however, reversible error per se. In United States v Hastings, 461 US 499 (1983), the Court specifically held that such error may be found to have been harmless beyond a reasonable doubt by a reviewing appellate court.

Page 328, text, add at end of section:

In *Connecticut v Johnson,* 460 US 73 (1983), the Court affirmed a decision of the Connecticut Supreme Court which had reversed a conviction obtained in violation of *Sandstrom v Montana,* 442 US 510 (1979) (which held that the due process clause of the Fourteenth Amendment was violated by a jury instruction that "the law presumes that a person intends the ordinary consequences of his voluntary acts"), without discussing whether the violation of *Sandstrom* was harmless error. Four Justices agreed with the state that a violation of *Sandstrom* may, in *rare situations* where the defendant is acquitted of an offense requiring specific intent, and the instruction had no bearing on the offense for which the defendant was convicted, or where the defendant's intent is not an issue, be harmless error, but found that the case before it was not one of those rare situations. Justice Stevens concurred only in the result, believing that the Connecticut decision rested upon adequate state grounds. Justice Powell, joined by three other justices in a vigorous dissent, took the view that violation of *Sandstrom* may be harmless error even if the defendant does not concede intent, if the case against the defendant is strong enough.

Violation of the confrontation clause of the Sixth Amendment by failure to allow cross-examination may, in some circumstances, be harmless error. *Delaware v Van Arsdall,* 106 S Ct 1431 (1986).

§19.08A   Indictment on New Charges After Successful Appeal (New)

A prima facie case of prosecutorial vindictiveness is made when a prosecutor adds a charge following a successful appeal. However, in such circumstances, a prosecutor may offer evidence that his actions in bringing the new charges were not vindictive. The Fifth Circuit has held that the ultimate burden of proving vindictiveness lies with the defendant who is asserting the affirmative defense. *United States v Krezdorn,* 718 F2d 1360 (5th Cir 1983).

§19.09   Pardon

Page 329, note 65, at end of note add:

Solem v Helm, 463 US 277 (1983).

Page 329, text, add at end of section:

The fact that a person sentenced to life without possibility of parole for relatively minor offenses may apply for a pardon does not render the sentence constitutional. The possibility of an "ad hoc exercise of clemency" is fundamentally different from a parole, since a governor may commute, or refuse to commute, any sentence at any time without reference to any standards. *Solem v Helm,* 103 S Ct 3001 (1983).

The Eighth and Fourteenth Amendments do not forbid the jury being instructed, in the penalty phase of a capital murder trial, that it may impose a sentence of death or life without possibility of parole, and that under the applicable law, the possibility of parole, and that under the applicable law, the governor may commute a sentence of life without possibility of parole to a sentence that includes the possibility of parole. *California v Ramos,* 103 S Ct 3446 (1983). Such and instruction does not result in any diminution of the reliability of the sentence, nor deflect the jury's focus from its central task of undertaking an individualized sentencing determination; rather, it simply accurately states a potential sentencing alternative.

The fact that the jury is not instructed that a governor may commute a death sentence is not constitutionally required when the jury is instructed on the governor's right to commute life without possibility of parole sentences. Advising the jury that their death sentence is modifiable may well incline them to approach their sentencing decision with less appreciation for the gravity of the sentence to be imposed. *Id.*

20

Extradition and Interstate Transfer of Persons Resulting from Criminal Prosecutions

§20.11   The Interstate Agreement on Detainers

Page 340, note 64, at end of note add:

The Supreme Court has held that article III of the Interstate Agreement on Detainers does not apply to detainers based on parole violation charges. Carchman v Nash, 105 S Ct 3401 (1985).

Cases

A

Acoff v Absto, 762 F2d 1543 (11th Cir 1985) §4.06

Adamson v. Ricketts, 789 F2d 722 (9th Cir 1986) §12.15

Aguilar v Texas, 378 US 108 (1964) §3.08

Ake v Oklahoma, 105 S Ct 1087 (1985) §§14.04, 18.11

Ake v State, 663 P2d 1 (Okla Crim App 1983) §16.16

Anaya v Hansen, 781 F2d 1 (1st Cir 1986) §17.07

Arizona v Rumsey, 104 S Ct 2305 (1984) §18.12

Associated Press v United States, District Court for Central District, of California 705 F2d 1143 (9th Cir 1983) §15.07

B

Barber v Ponte, 772 F2d 982 (1st Cir 1986) §17.07

Barclay v Flonda, 463 US 939 (1983) §18.11

Barefoot v Estelle, 463 US 880 (1983) §18.11

Barker v Wingo, 407 US 514 (1972) §11.07

Batson v Kentucky, 106 S Ct 1712 (1986) §17.08

Bearden v Georgia, 461 US 660 (1983) §§8.09, 14.01, 18.16, 18.17

Beck v Alabama, 447 US 625 (1980) §17.12

Beemer v Commonwealth, 665 SW2d 912 (Ky 1984) §3.08

Berkemer v McCarty, 104 S Ct 3138 (1984) §§5.08, 5.09

Black v Romano, 105 S Ct 2254 (1985) §18.17

Blackledge v Perry, 417 US 21 (1974) §12.06

Blanks v State, 254 Ga 420, 330 SE2d 575 (1985) §5.03

Bonsness v State, 672 P2d 1291 (Wyo 1983) §3.08

Boyd v United States, 116 US 616 (1886) §3.06

Brewer v Raines, 670 F2d 117 (9th Cir 1982) §13.04

131

N

New Jersey v TLO, 105 S Ct
733 (1985) §§**3.01, 3.02,
3.04, 3.09, 3.27B**

New York v Class, 106 S Ct 960
(1986) §**2.03**

New York v PJ Video, 106 S Ct
1610 (1986) §**3.07**

New York v Quarles, 104 S Ct
2626 (1984) §**5.12**

Nix v Whiteside, 106 S Ct 988
(1986) §**14.10**

Nix v Williams, 104 S Ct 2501
(1984) §**15.05**

O

Ohio v Johnson, 104 S Ct 2536
(1984) §**15.13**

Oliver v United States, 104 S Ct
1735 (1984) §**3.02**

Oregon v Bradshaw, 462 US
1039 (1983) §**5.13**

Oregon v Elstad, 105 S Ct 1285
(1985) §§**5.07, 15.02**

Oregon v Kennedy, 456 US 667
(1982) §**15.17**

P

Patton v Yount, 104 S Ct 2885
(1984) §**17.05**

Payton v New York, 445 US 573
(1980) §§**1.04, 4.04**

Pennsylvania v Goldhammer,
106 S Ct 353 (1986) §**18.12**

People v Bartley, 109 Ill 2d 273,
486 NE2d 880 (1985), *cert
denied sub nom* Bartley v
Illinois, 106 S Ct 1384 (1986)
§**2.04**

People v Bigelow, 66 NY2d 417,
488 NE2d 451, 497 NYS2d
630 (1985) §**3.17A**

People v Carney, 34 Cal 3d 597,
668 P2d 807, 194 Cal Rptr
500 (1983) §**3.25**

People v Chavers, 33 Cal 3d
462, 658 P2d 96, 189 Cal
Rptr 169 (1983) §**3.25**

People v Claudio, 59 NY2d 556,
453 NE2d 500, 466 NYS2d
301 (1983) §**14.02**

People v Cook, 33 Cal 3d 406,
658 P2d 86, 189 Cal Rptr
159 (1983) §**17.14**

People v Davis, 93 Ill 2d 155,
442 NE2d 855 (1982) §**17.08**

People v Fosselman, 33 Cal 3d
572, 659 P2d 1144, 189 Cal
Rptr 159 (1983) §**14.09**

People v Garcia, 109 Ill App 3d
142, 440 NE2d 269 (1982)
§**3.14**

People v Garries, 645 P2d 1306
(Colo 1982) §**10.01**

People v Gokey, 60 NY2d 309,
457 NE2d 723, 469 NYS2d
618 (1983) §**3.26**

People v Hall, 35 Cal 3d 161,
672 P2d 854, 197 Cal Rptr
71 (1983) §**17.08**

People v Jacobs, 158 Cal App
3d 740, 204 Cal Rptr 849
(1984) §**5.18**

People v John BB, 56 NY2d
482, 438 NE2d 864, 453
NYS2d 158 (1982) §**2.04**

People v Johnson, 55 NY2d
398, 488 NE2d 439, 497
NYS2d 618 (1985) §**3.08**

People v Killibrew, 416 Mich
189, 330 NW2d 834 (1982)
§**12.16**

Solem v Helm, 463 US 277
(1983) §§18.06, 18.13, 19.09

Solem v Stumes, 104 S Ct 1338
(1984) §§1.04, 5.13

South Dakota v Neville, 459 US
553 (1983) §§5.06, 5.10, 5.19

Spaziano v Florida, 104 S Ct
3154 (1984) §17.12

Spence v State, 296 Md 416,
463 A2d 808 (1983) §§16.21,
18.11

Spinelli v United States, 393 US
410 (1969) §3.08

State v Abbati, 99 NJ 418, 493
A2d 513 (1985) §15.17

State v Anaya, 456 A2d 1255
(Me 1983) §14.04

State v Anderson, 286 Ark 58,
688 SW2d 947 (1985) §3.17A

State v Arrington, 311 NC 633,
319 SE2d 254 (1984) §3.08

State v Beam, 109 Idaho 616,
710 P2d 526 (1985) §16.06

State v Bruzzese, 94 NJ 210,
463 A2d 320 (1983) §4.02

State v Caraher, 293 Or 741,
653 P2d 942 (1982) §3.26

State v Ching, 67 Hawaii 911,
678 P2d 1088 (1984) §3.03

State v Deskins, 234 Kan 529,
673 P2d 1174 (1983) §2.04

State v Evans, 215 Neb 433,
338 NW2d 788 (1983) §2.03

State v Fort, 101 NJ 123, 501
A2d 140 (1985) §§9.06,
12.03, 13.03

State v Freeman, 307 NC 357,
298 SE2d 331 (1983) §4.02

State v Fusco, 93 NJ 578, 461
A2d 1169 (1983) §14.02

State v Gethers, 197 Conn 369,
497 A2d 408 (1985) §14.06

State v Glosson, 462 So 2d
1085 (Fla 1985) §2.10

State v Grisby, 97 Wash 2d 493,
647 P2d 6 (1982) §5.10

State v Havlatt, 222 Neb 554,
385 NW2d 436 (1986) §3.02

State v Hunt, 91 NJ 338, 450
A2d 952 (1982) §2.09

State v Jackson, 102 Wash 2d
432, 688 P2d 136 (1984)
§3.08

State v Johnson, __P2d__ (Mont
1986) §5.11

State v Jones, 706 P2d 317
(Alaska 1985) §3.08

State v Kennedy, 295 Or 260,
666 P2d 1316 (1983) §15.17

State v Kim, 711 P2d 1291
(Hawaii 1985) §2.03

State v Koppel, 127 NH 286,
499 A2d 995 (1985) §2.04

State v Lang, 105 Idaho 683,
672 P2d 561 (1983) §3.08

State v Marchand, 104 Wash 2d
434, 706 P2d 225 (1985)
§2.04

State v Moriwake, 65 Hawaii 47,
647 P2d 705 (1982) §15.17

State v Myatt, 237 Kan 17, 697
P2d 836 (1985) §13.05A

State v Neil, 457 So 2d 481 (Fla
1984) §17.08

State v Neville, 346 NW2d 425
(SD 1984) §5.19

State v Norgaard, 653 P2d 483
(Mont 1982) §5.03

State v Novembrino, 200 NJ
Super 229, 491 A2d 37
(1985) §3.17A

State v Orr, 375 NW2d 171
(ND 1985) §14.01

Y

Index

A

APPEAL
  indictment on new charges
    after successful appeal
    §19.08A
  retrial after successful appeal
    §15.15
ARREST
  force to effectuate §4.06

C

CONFRONTATION
  contingent plea bargain,
    testimony of witness
    entering into §13.09A
  infant witnesses §13.05A
COUNSEL, RIGHT TO
  defendant's right to testify
    §14.10A

D

DOUBLE JEOPARDY
  retrial after successful appeal
    §15.15
DUE PROCESS
  forfeiture proceedings §11.07

E

ELECTRONIC SURVEILLANCE
  radio transmitter in suspects'
    property §§2.09, 2.09A,
    3.02, 3.25
EXCLUSIONARY RULE
  good faith exception §§3.17A,
    15.05A

F

FORFEITURE PROCEEDINGS
    §11.07

I

IMMUNITY
  compulsion in civil
    proceedings §13.13
INSANITY
  commitment after acquittal by
    reason of §18.01A

Trial Practice Series

CONSTITUTIONAL LIMITATIONS ON CRIMINAL PROCEDURE

Richard B. McNamara
Member of the New Hampshire and Massachusetts Bars

SHEPARD'S/McGRAW-HILL
P.O. Box 1235
Colorado Springs, Colorado 80901

McGRAW-HILL BOOK COMPANY

New York • St. Louis • San Francisco • Colorado Springs • Auckland
Bogota • Hamburg • Johannesburg • London • Madrid • Mexico
Montreal • New Delhi • Panama • Paris • São Paulo • Singapore
Sydney • Tokyo • Toronto

12345678910 SHEN 8921098765432

Library of Congress Cataloging in Publication Data

McNamara, Richard B.
  Constitutional limitations on criminal procedure

  (Trial practice series)
  Bibliography: p.
  Includes indexes.
  1. Criminal procedure—United States.
I. Title. II. Series.
KF9619.M37   1982   345.73'05   82-10559
                        347.3055

ISBN 0-07-045674-7

For Jenny

Preface

The last 30 years have witnessed a virtual revolution in the law governing criminal procedure. During this period of time, the United States Supreme Court, slowly at first and then ever more boldly, began imposing constitutional resrtictions upon police practices, preliminary proceedings, trial, sentencing, and even parole and probation. By 1970, the Court had created a virtual judge-made code of criminal procedure. Policemen all over the United States began carrying small cards containing the warnings required by *Miranda v Arizona*, and consulting with defense attorneys before holding line-ups.

In the early 1970's, the justices of the United States Supreme Court became less inclined toward activism and began to limit some of the more expansive holdings of 1960s. In some areas, procedural protections afforded the accused were restricted. At the same time, state supreme courts, deciding cases based on their state constitutions, began taking a more significant role in imposing procedural requirements at various stages of the criminal process as a matter of state constitutional law. The result has been a constitutional code of criminal procedure which has been established by federal constitutional law, but which varies in some states because of more expansive readings of state constitutions.

The purpose of this book is to delineate precisely what procedures are mandated at every stage of the criminal process as a matter of federal constitutional law. Thus, the chapters of this book track the criminal process from legislation, to search, to arrest, to the decision to charge, to discovery, to jury selection, and through trial, sentence, and parole or pardon. In addition, I have attempted to delineate the trends in state constitutional law wherever possible since well-reasoned state constitutional decisions may be persuasive authority in other jurisdictions. Decisions of the United States Supreme Court have been included through June 1, 1982; later cases will be treated in annual supplements.

Throughout this work, I have tried to set out the present state of the law without elaboration. It is sometimes impossible to predict with confidence what the United States Supreme Court will do when presented with a constitutional issue, no matter how clear the precedent. Despite the fact that decisions of the United States Supreme Court are usually couched in comprehensive citations to historical authority, as Chief Justice Burger recently noted, "We are well reminded that this Court once employed an exhaustive analysis of English and colonial practices regarding the right to counsel to justify the conclusion that it was fundemental to a fair trial, and less than 10 years later, used essentially the same material to conclude it was not." *Faretta v California*, 422 US 806, 843-44 (1975). For the practicing attorney, it is helpful simply to know what is decided, rather than to be provided with predictions which may turn out to be no more accurate than weather forecasts from an almanac. Moreover, there must, in any work of this scope, be space limitations. Volumes on search and seizure alone have been written; virtually every section of this book would be a fit subject for a full law review article, and many sections such as, for example, those concerning the death penalty, could themselves be the subject of a book. In order to cover the entire gamut of criminal procedure in one volume, it is necessary to be succinct. I have attempted to produce a ready reference for the practitioner which will state the law and provide a foundation for more detailed research.

Despite the fact that throughout this work, conflicting views of differing judges are cast in harsh relief, it must be borne in mind that all judicial disagreements are simply that—disagreements within the framework of a legal system that provides an accused perhaps more procedural protection than any other. I have, throughout this work, merely attempted to set forth the views of judges who disagree on a subject, without interjecting my own thoughts. I recognize that no lawyer can ever wholly dispassionate when examining constitutional doctrines which form the basis for our cherished liberties. While I have attempted to be as objective as possible, I rather suspect that this work may be colored by the belief I share with most other American lawyers, that for every *Bleak House*, there have been at least 10 *Ox-Bow Incidents*.

Richard B. McNamara
June, 1982
Manchester, New Hampshire

Acknowledgments

This work would not have been possible without the assistance of my wife, Linda McNamara, who carefully reviewed the various drafts of the manuscript, and prepared the table of cases. My colleagues at Wiggin and Nourie in Manchester, N.H. were most supportive during the many months of preparation. The editorial staff of Shepard's/McGraw-Hill of Colorado Springs, Colorado, carefully and promptly reviewed the manuscript, suggesting many changes which hopefully corrected some of my more turgid prose. Mrs. Janice S. Duso typed the various drafts of the manuscript without ever complaining about my handwritten notes in the margins. Finally, a word of thanks is due to Donald P. McDonald of the Colorado Bar, whose cogent comments about the manuscript served to help me refine the text and put it in its present form.

R. B. M.

Contents

Detailed

3   Search

4   Arrest

5   Rights of Persons in Custody

Right to Counsel

Privilege against Self-Incrimination

6   **Identification Procedures**

7 Institution of Charges

Formalities in Charging an Offense

Grand Juries

13 Witnesses

16 Mode and Conduct of Trial

Duties and Role of Trial Judge

1

The Constitution and Criminal Procedure

Significance of Constitutional Limits

§1.01   Significance of Limits in General

The federal Constitution established and defined the rights and duties of the several states, the federal government, and federal officers. It was amended by the first 10 amendments, called the Bill of Rights, shortly after its adoption in 1789. While it established a mode of government, the Constitution, as written, also contained particular and precise provisions relating to enactment and execution of the criminal laws.

1

The world has changed greatly since 1789, but the words of the Constitution have not. Yet the meaning of the Constitution, and its impact on police practices throughout the country have changed remarkably over the last 50 years, and exponentially over the last 20 years. Beginning about 1950, federal judges, slowly at first and then ever more boldly, began to alter the manner in which the criminal laws were executed and criminal cases were tried, until, by 1970, a virtual judge-made code of criminal procedure had been created. The legal theory by which this was accomplished revolved around the due process clause of the Fourteenth Amendment to the federal Constitution, enacted in 1868. The extent of the applicability of the Bill of Rights to the states, by virtue of the Fourteenth Amendment, had divided the Court since the time of the enactment of the latter.[1] Academicians have long debated the intent of the framers of the amendment; for the purposes of the practicing attorney, it is sufficient to say that within the last 20 years, the Court has explicitly held that the Fourth Amendment,[2] the Fifth Amendment privilege against self-incrimination,[3] the Fifth Amendment prohibition against double jeopardy,[4] and the Sixth Amendment guarantees of the effective assistance of counsel, [5] of a speedy trial,[6] of the right to confrontation[7] and compulsory process,[8] and of the right to jury trial,[9] and the right to be free from cruel and unusual punishment[10] are applicable to the states. It has been assumed that the right to a public trial[11] and the right to bail which is not excessive[12] are applicable to the states. Perhaps even more importantly, the United States Supreme Court has used the concept of fundamental fairness, required by due process, to further regulate police practices and criminal trial procedure.

Most of the radical changes in criminal procedure developed during the 1960s and early 1970s. Since that time, a more conservative United States Supreme

---

[1] *See, e.g.*, Mapp v Ohio, 367 US 643 (1961); Wolf v Colorado, 338 US 25 (1949); Adamson v California, 332 US 46 (1947); Twining v New Jersey, 211 US 78 (1908); Hurtado v California, 110 US 516 (1884).

[2] Mapp v Ohio, 367 US 643 (1961).

[3] Malloy v Hogan, 378 US 1 (1964).

[4] Benton v Maryland, 395 US 784 (1969).

[5] Gideon v Wainwright, 372 US 335 (1963); Scott v Illinois, 440 US 367 (1979).

[6] Klopfer v North Carolina, 386 US 213 (1967).

[7] Pointer v Texas, 380 US 400 (1965).

[8] Washington v Texas, 388 US 14 (1967).

[9] Duncan v Louisiana, 391 US 145 (1968).

[10] Robinson v California, 370 US 660 (1962).

[11] *In re* Oliver, 333 US 257 (1948).

[12] Schilb v Kuebel, 404 US 357 (1971).

Court has been less inclined to dramatically alter constitutional doctrines. State supreme courts in some jurisdictions have, however, tended to take a more activist view toward judicial regulation of criminal procedure, premised on either federal or state constitutional grounds. As a practical matter, in virtually every jurisdiction, the law concerning police practices is judge-made and not always clearly defined. It is the purpose of this work to attempt to clarify a basic framework for the elusive constitutional code of criminal procedure.

§1.02 Interpretation of Constitutional Guarantees

Federal constitutional claims may, of course, be raised in state criminal proceedings since the United States Supreme Court has held so many federal constitutional limitations applicable to the states. In such circumstances, the state court has the duty of interpreting the extent of the particular constitutional guarantee. When a state court interprets the federal Constitution, it is bound by decisions of the United States Supreme Court. While a state court is free to impose greater limitations on police practices or criminal procedure as a matter of its own law, it cannot impose greater restrictions as a matter of federal constitutional law where the United States Supreme Court has expressly refrained from doing so.[13] Where the United States Supreme Court has not ruled on a particular issue, if a state court or lower federal court is interpreting a federal constitutional guarantee, it is the duty of the court to, in effect, predict what the United States Supreme Court would do if faced with the precise issue.

Because the jurisdiction of the United States Supreme Court extends only to cases and controversies, it will not review a judgment of a state court which may rest on adequate state grounds, since, in such a circumstance, the interpretation of federal law may be a mere advisory opinion.[14] State supreme courts which wish to ensure that a liberal construction of a constitutional rule will not be limited on review by the United States Supreme Court are thus able to do so by grounding their decisions on state constitutional guarantees or state law. Indeed, the United States Supreme Court has explicitly approved of this practice.[15]

---

[13] Oregon v Haas, 420 US 714 (1975).

[14] Herb v Pitcairn, 324 US 117 (1945).

[15] *See, e.g.*, Pruneyard Shopping Center v Robbins, 447 US 74 (1980); *see also* Pennsylvania v Minns, 434 US 106, 114 n 3 (1977) (Marshall, J, dissenting); Brennan, *State Constitutions and the Protection of Individual Rights*, 90 Harv L Rev 489 (1977).

§1.03   Remedies to Vindicate Violation of Constitutional Guarantees

Compensation for violation of an individual's federal constitutional rights may be afforded by 42 USC §1983.[16] To the practicing criminal lawyer, however, the significance of violation of constitutional guarantees is not the prospect of money damages, but the possibility that evidence obtained by the police may be suppressed and excluded from trial,[17] or that the entire prosecution may be dismissed.[18]

§1.04   Retroactivity of Constitutional Decisions

The fact that the constitutionalization of criminal procedure in the 1950s through 1970s was an extraordinary change in the law has been explicitly recognized by the decisions of the United States Supreme Court which developed new rules in those years to determine whether a judicial decision should be prospective or retroactive. The concept of retroactive as against nonretroactive judicial decisions did not inspire much judicial or critical commentary prior to the 1960s. The common law rule, of course, was that a judge is "not delegated to pronounce a new law, but to maintain and expound the old one."[19] Traditionally, the United States Supreme Court, like other courts, treated the judge as the discoverer rather than the creator of law, and held that unconstitutional action was a nullity.[20] But this view became less realistic as years passed.[21] In *Linkletter v Walker*[22], the United States Supreme Court faced the issue of whether a decision of the Court, which worked a great change in the law by holding the federal exclusionary rule applicable to the states, should be considered to have retrospective effect. The Court held that the federal Constitution "neither prohibits nor requires" retrospective effect.[23] In the case before it,

---

[16] See generally S. Nahmod, Civil Rights and Civil Liberties Litigation (Shepards/McGraw-Hill 1979.)

[17] See §15.02.

[18] See, e.g. §2.10.

[19] W. Blackstone, Commentaries 69 (U Chi ed 1979).

[20] Norton v Shelby County, 118 US 425, 442 (1886).

[21] *See, e.g.*, Chicot County Drainage Dist v Baxter State Bank, 308 US 371 (1940).

[22] 381 US 618 (1965).

[23] *Id* 629.

the Court held that the 1961 decision of *Mapp v Ohio*[24] would not be applied retrospectively to cases finally decided prior to it. In *Linkletter*, the Court established a framework for deciding whether a new constitutional decision should be applied retroactively. Such a determination requires consideration of (1) the purpose to be served by the new standard, (2) the extent of the reliance by law enforcement authorities on the old standards, and (3) the effect on the administration of justice of a retroactive application of the new standards.[25] Foremost of the factors is the purpose to be served by the new rule.[26] Where a rule is primarily prophylatic in nature, it is much more likely to be applied prospectively only.[27] Retroactive application of mere prophylatic rules could result in a windfall benefit for defendants who have suffered no constitutional deprivation.[28] Thus, for example, the Court has held that the *Miranda* decision, which established procedures to ensure that an arrested person is fully aware of constitutional rights when arrested, is not retroactive.[29]

On the other hand, where the new rule may go to the question of a fair determination of guilt or innocence, the new constitutional rule is likely to be held fully retroactive. Thus, for example, the Court has held that the so-called *Bruton*[30] rule—that where one of multiple defendants makes an admission implicating the codefendant which is used at trial by the government, and the defendant who made the admission does not testify, failure to sever trial of the codefendant is constitutional error because jury instructions are inadequate to protect against denial of confrontation—is fully retroactive, since the constitutional error presents a serious risk that the issue of guilt or innocence may not have been reliably determined.[31]

---

[24] 367 US 643 (1961).

[25] Michigan v Payne, 412 US 47, 51 (1973); Stovall v Denno, 388 US 293, 297 (1967).

[26] Desist v United States, 394 US 244, 248-49 (1969).

[27] *See, e.g.*, Michigan v Payne, 412 US 47 (1973) (requirement that trial judge state explicit reasons for increase of sentence after successful appeal, first required in North Carolina v Pearce, 395 US 711 (1969), not retroactive).

[28] Michigan v Payne, 412 US at 53.

[29] Johnson v New Jersey, 384 US 719 (1966); *see also* Desist v United States, 389 US 244 (1969), holding that Katz v United States, 389 US 347 (1967) was to be prospectively applied only.

[30] Bruton v United States, 391 US 123 (1968).

[31] Roberts v Russell, 392 US 293 (1968). *See also* Ivan v City of New York, 407 US 203 (1972), holding the reasonable doubt requirement in juvenile cases of *In re* Winship, 397 US 358 (1970) retroactive; Berger v California, 393 US 314 (1969), holding Barber v Page, 390 US 719 (1968), which significantly limited prosecution use of a witness's prior testimony in lieu of his live testimony at trial retroactive, and Pickelsheimer v Wainwright, 375 US 2 (1963), holding Gideon v Wainwright, 372 US 335 (1963), requiring that counsel be afforded indigents in felony cases retroactive. State courts considering the retroactivity or nonretroactivity of decisions on state constitutional grounds have taken a similar approach. *See, e.g.*, People v Bustamonte, 30 Cal 3d 88, 634 P2d 927, 177 Cal Rptr 576 (1981).

Constitutional Limits on Legislative Action

§1.05   Limits on Legislation in General

When lawyers consider the impact of the Constitution on criminal procedure, they tend to consider only the impact of constitutional rules on police practices and criminal trials. However, it must be remembered that the Constitution may restrain a legislative body from acting at all. If a criminal statute would punish exercise of a constitutional right, that statute itself is void.[32] Analysis is whether a criminal law, because of its subject matter, is violative of the Constitution is a matter of substantive constitutional law, and is beyond the scope if this work.

There are, however, three kinds of statutes which, regardless of their subject matter, are constitutionally void. These types of statutes are bills of attainder, ex post facto laws, and unconstitutionally vague laws. These kinds of laws are discussed in the following sections.

§1.06   Bills of Attainder

Article 1, §§9 and 10 of the federal Constitution provides that no "Bill of Attainder" may be passed by any state or the Congress. The very term *bill of attainder* has a certain quaintness which would suggest that the concept has little practical relevance. The clause has, however, been considered in connection with legislatures relatively frequently in recent years.

Bills of attainder and bills of pains and penalties were well known to the framers of the Constitution. The English parliament, at the time of the Revolution, had the authority to pass laws *attainting* certain persons of treason or felony, that is, it could inflict pains and penalties beyond or contrary to the common law.[33] The difference between a bill of attainder and a bill of pains and penalties was that the punishment for the former was death while the punishment specified in a bill of pains and penalties was imprisonment, banishment, or refusal to allow a person to engage in some particular trade.[34] During the Revolution, the legislatures of all the 13 colonies passed such statutes directed against the Tories.[35] The framers of the Constitution were revolted by this practice and sought to ensure that it could not take root in the United

---

[32] *See, e.g.,* Roe v Wade, 410 US 113 (1973) holding a Texas statute which punished abortion void because it infringed on a woman's constitutional right to privacy.

[33] 4 W. Blackstone, Commentaries 256 (U Chi ed 1979).

[34] Nixon v Administrator of GSA, 433 US 425, 473-74 (1977).

[35] United States v Brown, 381 US 437, 442 (1965).

States. Since earliest times, the constitutional phrase *bill of attainder* has been held to include bills of pains and penalties.[36]

The purpose of the prohibition of bills of attainder is historically clear; it was intended as "a general provision against arbitrary and tyrannical legislation over existing rights. . . ."[37] Punishment for crime was to be imposed by the courts and not by the legislature.

The United States Supreme Court has, for purposes of determining whether legislation is prohibited by the bill of attainder clause, attempted a functional analysis of the legislation before it.[38] For present purposes, a bill of attainder is considered a legislative act which inflicts punishment on a named individual or on members of an easily ascertainable group without a judicial trial.[39] *Punishment* is not restricted to retribution for past events, but may include deprivations intended to prevent future misconduct.[40] To determine if an act is a bill of attainder a reviewing court must consider whether three elements exist in the statute: (1) specificity in identification, (2) punishment, and (3) lack of a judicial trial.[41]

Application of these rules to the cases decided by the United States Supreme Court has led to relatively consistent results. For example, in *United States v Lovett*,[42] Congress, over the objection of the employing agency, passed a statute providing that no monies should be paid three government employees who had been attacked by several Congressmen as "radical crackpot bureaucrats, unfit to hold office" unless they were, prior to a certain date, appointed to their positions by the President. Despite the fact that the legislation did not prescribe punishment in the usual sense, the United States Supreme Court held that the act was nonetheless a bill of attainder since it was obviously directed at specific individuals, and was obviously intended to punish them without a judicial trial on the issue of their loyalty or disloyalty.[43]

§1.07 Ex Post Facto Laws—Legislative Bodies

Article 1, §§9 and 10, which prohibit Congress and the states from enacting bills of attainder, also prohibit *ex post facto laws*. Like bills of attainder, ex post

---

[36] United States v O'Brien, 391 US 367, 383 n 30 (1968); Fletcher v Peck, 10 US (6 Cranch) 87, 138 (1810).

[37] Ogden v Saunders, 25 US (12 Wheat) 213, 286 (1827); *see also* Chadha v Immigration & Naturalization Serv, 634 F2d 408 (4th Cir 1980).

[38] Nixon v Administrator of GSA, 433 US 425, 475-76 (1977).

[39] *Id* 476 n 40.

[40] United States v O'Brien, 391 US 367, 383 (1968).

[41] *Id.*

[42] 328 US 303 (1946).

[43] *Id* 316. *See also* United States v Brown, 331 US 437 (1965).

facto laws were well known to English lawyers at the time of the American Revolution. Indeed, at the time the Constitution was drafted, the phrase was a term of art; as Justice Chase noted in 1798, "naked and without explanation it is unintelligible and means nothing."[44] Literally, it only means that a law shall not be passed concerning an action done.

Blackstone considered an ex post facto law to exist "when after an action is committed, the legislature then for the first time declares it to have been a crime and inflicts a punishment upon the person who has committed it".[45] This definition was accepted by Justice Chase in *Calder v Bull* [46] in 1798. He considered the prohibition "an additional bulwark in favor of the personal security of the subject, to protect his person from punishment by legislative acts, having a retrospective application."[47] He pointed out that the clause was not a prohibition of retrospective laws, for although every ex post facto law must necessarily be retrospective, every retrospective law is not necessarily ex post facto.[48] In dicta which have been cited over and over again, he enumerated the various kinds of ex post facto laws:

> 1st. Every law that makes an action done before the passing of the law; and which was innocent when done, criminal; and punishes such action. 2d. Every law that aggravates a crime, or makes it greater than it was when committed. 3d. Every law that changes the punishment, and inflicts a greater punishment, than the law annexed to the crime when committed. 4th. Every law that alters the legal rules of evidence, and receives less, or different testimony than the law required at the time of the first offense, in order to convict the offender.[49]

Almost 185 years of judicial accretion have rendered the meaning of the ex post facto clause ever more clear. The first two types of law discussed by Justice Chase are easy to identify. For example, laws passed near the end of the Civil War which required those who wished to engage in certain professions or practice as attorneys in federal courts to swear that they had never taken part in the rebellion against the United States were held to be ex post facto.[50] Similarly, habitual offender statutes, which impose enhanced punishment on persons who previously have been convicted of serious crime,

---

[44] Calder v Bull, 3 US (3 Dall) 386, 390 (1798).

[45] 1 W. Blacksone, Commentaries 46 (U Chi ed 1979).

[46] 3 US (3 Dall) 386 (1798).

[47] *Id* 390.

[48] *Id* 391.

[49] *Id* 390 cited with approval in Dobbert v Florida, 432 US 282, 292 (1977).

[50] Cummings v Missouri, 71 US (4 Wall) 277 (1867); *Ex parte* Garland, 71 US (4 Wall) 333 (1867).

are not ex post facto laws because such laws are not additional punishment for earlier crimes, but a "stiffened penalty for the latest crime which is considered to be an aggravated offense because a repetitive one."[51]

It is similarly relatively easy to identify statutes which enhance the punishment for crime, and it is well settled that a change in the law which is ameliorative does not render the law ex post facto. Indeed, it appears that any change which does not enhance the punishment is permissible.[52] But where the penalty for a crime is aggravated after the act, as by, for example, requiring that the maximum penalty allowed by law for a given offense be given as a sentence, the ex post facto clause is violated.[53] A statute repealing the amount of credit a person may gain on his prison sentence which was in effect at the time of the crime is similarly impermissible.[54]

The fact that at the time a murder is committed the applicable death penalty statute is unconstitutional does not mean that a constitutional, later-drafted statute may not be applied to the murderer, for the later, constitutional statute cannot be considered to have enhanced the applicable punishment on the theory that the prior statute was a nullity.[55] A state which has enacted a death penalty statute for a particular crime, even though the statute is later held unconstitutional, has given fair notice of its intent to potential criminals; such persons cannot complain if, after they act, a more narrowly drawn, constitutional statute is enacted.[56]

Finally, a person has no right to be tried in accordance with the procedures in effect at the time an offense was committed, and purely procedural changes in trial do not violate the ex post facto clause.[57] A statute which merely alters rules of evidence applicable to all litigants cannot reasonably be said to be violative of the ex post facto clause, despite the fact that the alteration may negatively affect a particular person.[58] But a statute which materially affects a person's right to have guilt determined by the law in effect at the time of the act, as by,

---

[51] Gryger v Burke, 334 US 728, 732 (1948); McDonald v Massachusetts, 180 US 311 (1901).

[52] *See, e.g.*, Rooney v North Dakota, 196 US 319 (1905); Malloy v South Carolina, 237 US 180 (1915)(change in punishment from hanging to electrocution not ex post facto).

[53] Lindsey v Washington, 301 US 397 (1937); *see also In re* Medley, 134 US 176 (1890).

[54] Weaver v Graham, 101 S Ct 960 (1981).

[55] Dobbert v Florida, 432 US 282 (1977); *but see* United States v Jackson, US 570 390 (1968).

[56] Dobbert v Florida, 432 US 282 (1977).

[57] *Id*; *see also* Thompson v Missouri, 171 US 380, 386 (1898).

[58] Thompson v Missouri, 171 US 380 (1898) (no violation where state statute, after defendant's murder conviction at first trial was reversed on ground that letters were improperly admitted into evidence, provided that disputed handwriting could be admitted for comparison with that handwriting proved genuine); Hopt v Utah, 110 US 574 (1884) (no violation where, after date of offense, statute removed common law disability of felons, and felon testified against defendant in murder trial).

for example, reducing the number of jurors needed to convict[59] or changing a rule that a plea of guilty to a lesser offense is an acquittal of the greater,[60] is ex post facto.

§1.08 — The Judiciary

By its terms, the ex post facto clause is applicable only to parliamentary bodies. If a common law judge is considered to be merely the discoverer rather than the creator of law, the ex post facto clause can have no application to judicial decisions. As recently as 1961, Justice Harlan could express the traditional view that "the decisions of a court interpreting the acts of a legislature have never been subject to the same limitations which are imposed on legislatures themselves . . . forbidding them to make any ex post facto law. . . ."[61] However, in the last 20 years, an acceleration of the growth of judge-made constitutional law and the mercurial rises and declines of constitutional doctrines, depending on the predilection of a majority of the United States Supreme Court at any given time, have led the United States Supreme Court to apply the same restrictions, used to protect citizens from arbitrary legislative action, to itself and to state courts. On several occasions, the Court has reversed state court convictions because of unforeseeable judicial enlargement of a criminal statute which, applied retroactively, "operates precisely like an ex post facto law."[62] In *Marks v United States*,[63] while noting that the words of the ex post facto clause are directed to the legislature and not the courts, the court held that

> the principle upon which the clause is based—the notion that persons have a right to fair warning of that conduct which will give rise to criminal penalties —is fundamental to our concept of constitutional liberty. As such, that right is protected against judicial action by the Due Process Clause of the Fifth Amendment.[64]

In the case before it, the Court held that a defendant prosecuted for possession of obscene material had a right to have his conduct judged under the more liberal *utterly without redeeming social value* test[65] enunciated by the United States

---

[59] Thompson v Utah, 170 US 343 (1898).

[60] Kring v Missouri, 107 US 221 (1882).

[61] James v United States, 366 US 213, 247 (1961) (Harlan, J, concurring and dissenting); *see also* Franks v Magnum, 237 US 309 (1915) (stating traditional rule).

[62] Bouie v City of Columbia, 378 US 347, 353-54 (1964); *see also* Rabe v Washington, 405 US 313 (1972).

[63] 430 US 188 (1977).

[64] *Id* 191.

[65] Memoirs v Massachusetts, 383 US 413 (1966).

Supreme Court at the time of his act, rather than under the narrower *Miller v California*[66] test of obscenity formulated by the United States Supreme Court after the defendant's alleged criminal conduct had occurred.

§1.09   The Void for Vagueness Doctrine

At common law, courts generally were considered to have the power to impose punishment for actions which contravened statutes or the common law. At present, however, charges of crimes must be based on a statutory offense.[67] Yet despite the evenhandedness of the decision to charge, and the sufficiency of the form of the complaint or indictment presenting the charge, the prosecution may nonetheless be barred if the statute which authorizes it is unconstitutionally vague. The Fourteenth Amendment requirement of due process demands that penal statutes give fair warning of precisely what it is they proscribe. It is often stated, as a sort of shorthand for this rule, that penal statutes must provide notice of what is forbidden, sufficient that persons of reasonable intelligence need not guess at their meaning.[68] In construing a state penal statute, the United States Supreme Court will consider not only the statute itself, but any limiting construction placed on the statute by the state's highest court. Thus, for example, in *Wainwright v Stone*,[69] the Court held that a Florida statute which proscribed the "abominable and detestable crime against nature" was not void for vagueness, since the Florida Supreme Court had construed this statute to forbid copulation per os and per anum.

Considered from a strict notice analysis, the vagueness decisions are difficult to reconcile. The United States Supreme Court has, for example, sustained a statute which forbade the mailing of a firearm "capable of being concealed on a person," stating that "the law is full of instances where a man's fate depends upon his estimating rightly, that is, as the jury subsequently estimates it, in some degree."[70] Moreover, as a practical matter, given the continuing proliferation of malum prohibitum offenses, John Chipman Gray's observation that "practically, in its application to the laity, the law . . . is all ex post facto"[71] seems ever more pertinent. Finally, the United States Supreme Court

---

[66] 413 US 15 (1973).

[67] *See, e.g.*, State v Fletcher, 5 NH 257 (1830). Of course, the nonstatutory offense of criminal contempt is universally recognized. *See, e.g.*, Groppi v Leslie, 404 US 496 (1972); Mayberry v Pennsylvania, 400 US 455 (1971).

[68] Connolly v General Constr Co, 269 US 385 (1926).

[69] 414 US 21 (1973); *see also* Rose v Locke, 423 US 48 (1975).

[70] United States v Powell, 423 US 87 (1975); *see also* Nash v United States, 229 US 373 (1913).

[71] J.C. Gray, The Nature and Sources of Law 100 (1921).

has traditionally held that it would consider limiting instructions on the statute in question made by state courts after the time of the questioned conduct.[72]

But the vagueness doctrine cannot be understood only in terms of notice. An important corollary purpose of the doctrine is to limit the use of arbitrary state laws which afford state officers limitless discretion to prosecute or not to prosecute. As Justice Brennan noted:

> [W]e have never treated claims of unconstitutional statutory vagueness in terms of the statute as written or construed prior to the time of the conduct in question. Instead, we have invariably dealt with the statute as glossed by the courts below at the time of decision here. . . [I]f the vagueness doctrine were fundamentally premised upon a concept of fair notice, such treatment would make no sense: a citizen cannot be expected to forsee subsequent construction of a statute by this or any other court. But if, as I believe, the doctrine of vagueness is premised upon the fundamental notion that due process requires governments to make explicit their choices among competing social policies . . . the inconsistency between theory and practice disappears.[73]

Only when the doctrine is seen as a tool to insure evenhanded law enforcement as well as to provide fair notice may it be understood. For example, in *Papachristou v City of Jacksonville*,[74] the Court held that a Florida ordinance which purported to punish "vagrants" and others was unconstitutional.[75] The Court reasoned that the statute placed standardless discretion in the hands of police officers and that it could be used as a convenient tool for harsh and discriminatory law enforcement against groups deemed to merit police displeasure.[76] Justice Douglas pointed out:

> Another aspect of the void for vagueness doctrine appears when we focus, not on the lack of notice given a potential offender, but on the effect of the unfettered discretion it places in the hands of the Jacksonville police . . . we allow our police to make arrests only on probable cause, a Fourth and Fourteenth Amendment standard applicable to the States as well as to the Federal Government. . . .[A] direction by the legislature to the police

---

[72] Winters v New York, 333 US 507 (1948); *but see* Bouie v City of Columbia, 378 US 347 (1964).

[73] McGautha v California, 402 US 183, 258 (1971) (Brennan, J, dissenting).

[74] 405 US 156 (1972).

[75] *Id* 157 n, 1.

[76] Colacutti v Franklin, 439 US 379 (1979) (anti-abortion statute which "conditions potential criminal liability upon confusing and ambiguous criteria" presented "serious problems of notice, discriminatory application, and chilling effect on the exercise of constitutional rights" and was therefore unconstitutionally vague).

to arrest all "suspicious" persons would not pass constitutional muster. A vagrancy prosecution may be merely the cloak for a conviction which could not be obtained on the real but undisclosed grounds for the arrest.[77]

However, the notice aspect of the doctrine is real, and a narrowing construction of a state statute made after the conduct in question will not be accepted if the construction unforeseeably alters the meaning of the statute. Thus, in *Bouie v City of Columbia*,[78] construction of a state statute which prohibited only "entry on the lands of another . . . after notice from the owner . . . prohibiting such entry," to include the act of remaining on property after being asked to leave, was so unforeseeable as to deprive the defendant of his right to fair warning and thus his right to due process of law. Similarly, in *Douglas v Buder*,[79] the Court stated that if a state court construed a statute which required a probationer to report all arrests to his probation officer to require reporting of traffic citations, the unforeseeable application of that interpretation would violate due process of law.

Because the vagueness doctrine is directed toward moderation of prosecutorial discretion and limiting the effect discretion would have on individual activities, the Court has been particularly strict in construing statutes which threaten to inhibit the exercise of constitutional rights.[80] The vagueness doctrine, then, may properly be considered not merely as a safeguard against careless legislative drafting, but rather as still another judicial safeguard against prosecution which is unfair or improperly motivated.

---

[77] Papachristou v City of Jacksonville, 405 US at 168-69.

[78] 378 US 347 (1964).

[79] 412 US 430 (1973).

[80] Colacutti v Franklin, 439 US 379 (1979) (abortion statute); Smith v Goguen, 415 US 566 (1974) (First Amendment).

2 | Police-Citizen Contact and Extraordinary Investigative Techniques

Police-Citizen Contact

§2.01 Police-Citizen Contact and the Fourth Amendment

An average individual who is approached and questioned by a police officer may feel some trepidation. If the encounter takes place on a crowded city street,

14

the person questioned may also experience some feelings of humiliation. If the encounter occurs when a person is driving an automobile and is precipitated by a police officer who is driving a police cruiser, the encounter may not only be inconvenient, but "may create substantial anxiety."[1] Indeed, there can be no question that any intrusion by police on a citizen's privacy is significant—and is likely to be more significant if the citizen is a law-abiding sort, who infrequently deals with police officers. For this reason, the United States Supreme Court has held that the Fourth Amendment must govern the actions of police officers "whenever a police officer accosts an individual and restrains his freedom to walk away."[2] Even if the actions of the police do not result in arrest, they must be *reasonable*.[3] An unreasonable pat down or *frisk* for evidence will result in exclusion of that evidence as surely as there will be exclusion of evidence obtained pursuant to an arrest made without probable cause.

The precise degree of police intrusion, short of arrest (which, of course, can only be made on probable cause), which will invoke the protection of the Fourth Amendment is presently in question. By and large, in considering the legitimacy of an intrusion, the United States Supreme Court has tended to balance the intrusion on the citizen's privacy against the opposing interests in crime prevention and detection and in police safety.[4] Chief Justice Warren's analysis, in *Terry v Ohio*,[5] of the application of the Fourth Amendment to police conduct which does not result in arrest is perhaps the best and most vital statement of their interrelation:

> In order to assess the reasonableness of [the police] conduct as a general proposition, it is necessary first to focus upon the governmental interest which allegedly justifies official intrusion upon the constitutionally protected interests of the private citizen, for there is no ready test for determining reasonableness other than by balancing the need to search [or seize] against the invasion which the search [or seizure] entails. And in justifying the particular intrusion, the police officer must be able to point to specific and articulable facts which, taken together with rational inferences from those facts, reasonably warrant that intrusion.[6]

Since *Terry* was decided, neither lower courts nor the Supreme Court have departed from the general proposition that police conduct must be considered

---

[1] Delaware v Prouse, 440 US 648, 653 (1979).

[2] Terry v Ohio, 392 US 1, 16 (1968).

[3] *See* United States v Mendenhall, 446 US 544 (1980); Reid v Georgia, 448 US 151 (1980); see also **§2.02**.

[4] Michigan v Summers, 101 S Ct 2587, 2591 (1981).

[5] 392 US 1 (1968).

[6] *Id* 20-21.

in light of the governmental interest involved and the negative effect on the defendant. The central concern has been that an individual's reasonable expectation of privacy not be subject to arbitrary invasion solely at the discretion of an officer in the field.[7] Application of this analytical framework to specific facts has, however, spawned a great deal of case law.

§2.02   Questioning by Police Officers

There has been some disagreement among the justices of the United States Supreme Court over whether mere questioning of a citizen is sufficient to invoke the protections of the Fourth Amendment. The Court has held that a *seizure* occurs when a person's freedom of movement is restrained in some way.[8] But there is no clear holding that mere questioning by police officers is a seizure since, presumably, a citizen "is free to disregard the questions and walk away."[9]

While a citizen may be free to walk away as a matter of law, the subjective anxiety created by the police contact may limit that freedom as a matter of fact. Recognition of this troubling problem has caused the United States Supreme Court to specifically leave the issue of whether questioning alone can ever be a seizure open.[10] It is at least clear, however, that police officers may not seize an individual simply because he has refused to identify himself, when there are no objective circumstances which would warrant a police officer in thinking that inquiry was appropriate. In *Brown v Texas,*[11] police officers stopped a man at 12:45 in the afternoon because they observed him a few feet from another man and they had never seen the individual in the area before. They asked him to identify himself and explain his business, and he refused, asserting the police had no right to stop him. He was arrested and charged with violating a Texas law which made it a crime for a person to refuse to identify himself when "lawfully stopped."[12] Holding that the detention of the defendant was a seizure because the defendant was not free to walk away, the Court passed to the question of whether the seizure was reasonable under the Fourth Amendment by attempting to balance "the gravity of the public concerns served by the seizure, the degree to which the seizure advance[d] the public interest, and the severity of the interference with individual liberty".[13] While recognizing that a brief detention may be based on less than the probable

---

[7] Brown v Texas, 443 US 47, (1979).

[8] *See, e.g.,* Terry v Ohio, 392 US 1, 16-19 (1968); Brown v Texas, 443 US 47 (1979).

[9] United States v Mendenhall, 446 US 544, 554 (1980).

[10] *See* Reid v Georgia, 448 US 151 (1980); United States v Mendenhall, 446 US 544 (1980); Brown v Texas, 443 US 47, 53 n 3 (1979).

[11] 443 US 47 (1979).

[12] *Id* 50.

[13] *Id* 51.

cause required for a full arrest, the Court held that the lack of objective reasons for the intrusion made the brief detention unreasonable within the meaning of the Fourth Amendment.[14]

In later cases, the Court has emphasized that the improper police conduct at issue in *Brown* was the brief detention of the individual and not the mere questioning. Although the issue is presently open, some of the justices presently on the court apparently would hold that a seizure occurs only when detention, however brief, occurs.[15] Such a view does not fully address the question of the defendant's right to refuse to answer a police officer who accosts him or her. If the police may accost anyone, may the person simply ignore the officer? And if so, may the person be arrested?

§2.03 Investigative Stops

While mere questioning by a police officer may not infringe an individual's Fourth Amendment rights, there is no doubt that detention, for however brief a time, does implicate those rights. While the United States Supreme Court will balance the reasonableness of the intrusion against the governmental interest in the stop to determine if the detention is reasonable, the Court has made it plain that no full custodial arrest can ever be reasonable without probable cause.[16] Detention for custodial interrogation intrudes so severely upon the interests protected by the Fourth Amendment as to trigger the traditional safeguards provided by the requirement of probable cause.[17]

The police need not, however, refrain from briefly detaining individuals in all circumstances if they do not have probable cause to arrest. If the police can articulate objective facts which led them to believe that the person stopped is engaging, or is about to engage, in criminal activity, the detention is reasonable. As Chief Justice Burger noted in *United States v Cortez*:[18]

> Courts have used a variety of terms to capture the elusive concept of what cause is sufficient to authorize police to stop a person. Terms like "articulable reasons" and "founded suspicion" are not self-defining; they fall short of providing clear guidance dispositive of the myriad factual situations that arise. But the essence of all that has been written is that totality of the circumstances—the whole picture—must be taken into

---

[14] *Id* 50-51.

[15] *See, e.g.*, Reid v Georgia, 448 US 151 (1980) (Powell, J, concurring); United States v Mendenhall, 446 US 544 (1980).

[16] Dunaway v New York, 442 US 200 (1979).

[17] *Id.*

[18] 101 S Ct 690 (1981).

account. Based upon that whole picture the detaining officers must have a particularized and objective reason for suspecting the particular person stopped of criminal activity.[19]

Of course, an investigative stop of a motor vehicle is proper if the stop is not wholly random but is based upon objective criteria, or is pursuant to a neutral, discretionless plan.[20] If a person is stopped for a traffic violation, the Court has held that it is not unreasonable, within the meaning of the Fourth Amendment, to require the person to step out of the car.[21]

§2.04 Regulatory Checks

The vice which inheres in stops of individuals which are not based on objective criteria is not the delay and inconvenience that such a stop will cause, but rather the fact that such stops may occur in the unbridled discretion of police officers. In *Delaware v Prouse*,[22] the United States Supreme Court held that a random stop of an automobile made by a police officer which results in interference with an individual's travel and privacy at the whim of a police officer was unreasonable under the Fourth Amendment.

However, the Court specifically approved the use of spot checks as long as those spot checks are conducted pursuant to neutral and specific criteria.[23] The Court has specifically stated that questioning of all oncoming traffic at roadblock-type stops is permissible.[24] Similarly, there is no constitutional infirmity in the use of roadside weigh stations and inspection checkpoints at which some vehicles may be subject to further detention for safety and regulatory inspection.[25]

§2.05 Stop and Frisk

The Fourth Amendment requirement of "reasonableness" presents a continuum. A minimal intrusion, such as an investigative stop, requires some objective reason;[26] a full custodial arrest must be based on probable cause.[27]

---

[19] *Id* 695; *see also* United States v Brignoni-Ponce, 422 US 873 (1975).

[20] Delaware v Prouse, 440 US 648 (1979).

[21] Pennsylvania v Mimms, 434 US 106, 111 (1977).

[22] 440 US 648 (1979).

[23] *Id; see also* United States v Ortiz, 422 US 891, 895 (1975).

[24] 440 US at 663.

[25] *Id* 663 n 26.

[26] Delaware v Prouse, 440 US 648 (1979); Brown v Texas, 443 US 47 (1979).

[27] Dunaway v New York, 442 US 200 (1979).

Less intrusive than a full arrest but obviously far more intrusive than the investigative stop is an external search, or, as it is colloquially called, a *frisk*.

The United States Supreme Court first recognized the validity of frisks in the landmark case of *Terry v Ohio*.[28] In that case, an experienced police officer observed three men walking up a street and repeatedly staring into one store window. The officer approached one of the men and identified himself as a police officer. When the man "mumbled something," the officer spun him around, patted him down, and found a weapon.

While recognizing that the officer did not have probable cause to make an arrest, and that the type of intrusion involved was one which could fairly be characterized as "a serious intrusion upon the sanctity of the person which may inflict great indignity and arouse strong resentment",[29] the Court held that on the facts and behavior presented to the officer, a reasonably prudent person would have believed that the defendant was armed and thus presented a danger and that, therefore, the action taken was appropriate.[30] The Court emphasized that reasonableness of a search depends on the police officer's need for protection; and as the Court noted in a companion case, *Sibron v New York*,[31] the officer "must be able to point to particular facts from which he reasonably inferred that the individual was armed and dangerous."

The amount of information needed to support such a search need not be great, although it must be objective and articulable. In determining whether an officer's actions are reasonable, due weight must be given to the inferences the officer is entitled to draw, based on experience from the specific facts.[32] Indeed, even an unverified tip from a known informant, in a high crime area, which would not establish probable cause to search may be sufficient for a *Terry*-type frisk.[33]

Even if an officer has reason to believe that a person is armed, the intrusion, or search, must be related to the officer's attempt to protect himself or herself.[34] The Court has, with surprising consistency, held in the years since *Terry* was decided that it created only a "narrow exception" to the requirement of probable cause, which is applicable only when an officer's safety is involved.[35] Thus, the Court has held that *Terry* does not authorize the police to conduct frisks of

---

[28] 392 US 1 (1968).

[29] *Id* 17.

[30] *Id.*

[31] 392 US 40, 64 (1968).

[32] Terry v Ohio, 392 US 1, 27 (1968).

[33] Adams v Williams, 407 US 143 (1972).

[34] Sibron v New York, 392 US 40, 65 (1968).

[35] Ybarra v Illinois, 444 US 85 (1979).

persons who just happen to be on the premises of a public tavern when it is searched pursuant to warrant.[36]

Extraordinary Investigative Techniques

§2.06   Use of Informers—Before Person Is Charged with Crime

No justice of the United States Supreme Court has ever wholeheartedly embraced the use of informers as a reliable and salutary method of investigating crime. Rather, the practice has been tolerated; even in opinions upholding such practices, they are referred to as "dirty business."[37] Indeed, Justice Frankfurter once condemned the use of informers because "it makes for lazy and not alert law enforcement. It puts a premium on force and fraud, not on imagination and enterprise and professional training."[38]

Despite the continuing judicial dislike for the use of informers, the practice has been accepted by the courts.[39] No Fourth Amendment violation occurs when, for example, an undercover police officer comes to a defendant's house under the guise of purchasing controlled drugs, does so, and later arrests the defendant, for the government is entitled to conceal the identity of its agents.[40] The rationale by which courts uphold the use of informers is straightforward: the Fourth Amendment protects only expectations of privacy;[41] a person conversing with another has no justifiable and constitutionally protected expectation that the person with whom he or she is speaking will not repeat the conversation to the police.[42]

An important distinction must be made between conversations relayed by a paid informer and searches conducted by government informers. While there is no constitutional infirmity in the former, it has long been settled that it is violative of the Fourth Amendment for a private citizen, at the request of the government, to conduct a furtive search of a person's home or other protected area.[43]

---

[36] *Id.* But a person whose home is searched may be detained while the search is conducted. Michigan v Summers, 101 S Ct 2587 (1981).

[37] On Lee v United States, 343 US 747, 757 (1952).

[38] *Id* 761 (Frankfurter, J, dissenting).

[39] *See, e.g.* United States v Henry, 447 US 264 (1980); Hoffa v United States, 385 US 293 (1966); Weatherford v Bursey, 429 US 545 (1977).

[40] Lewis v United States, 385 US 206, 210 (1966). *See also* Osborn v United States, 385 US 323 (1966); Lopez v United States, 373 US 427 (1963); United States v White, 401 US 745 (1971).

[41] Katz v United States, 389 US 347 (1967).

[42] *See, e.g.*, United States v White, 401 US 745, 749 (1971).

[43] *See, e.g.*, Gouled v United States, 255 US 298 (1921).

A different question is presented if the informer does not merely attempt to obtain information from the defendant, but instead provides the opportunity and means to commit a crime. Under some circumstances, the defendant may be able to raise the defense of entrapment.[44] The prevailing view is that the defense of entrapment is not a constitutional one.[45] However, if the conduct of the law enforcement officers is so shocking as to violate *fundamental fairness*, due process may bar the government from proceeding.[46]

§2.07 —After Person Has Been Charged with Crime

The United States Supreme Court has looked askance at the use of informers to elicit admissions of crime from a defendant who has been formally charged and thus has a constitutional right to counsel. In 1964, in *Massiah v United States*,[47] the Court held that the defendant's Sixth Amendment right to counsel was violated when, after the defendant was arraigned and had had counsel appointed, a government informer elicited inculpatory statements from him. The Court reasoned that interrogation by the government after a defendant has retained counsel, without the presence of counsel, renders the guarantee of counsel hollow and thus violates the Sixth Amendment.[48]

Similarly, the Court has held that merely by telling an indicted defendant's cellmate, a paid informant, to "be alert" to any inculpatory statement made by the defendant, the government intentionally created a situation likely to induce the defendant to make incriminating statements without the assistance of counsel, and thus violated his Sixth Amendment rights.[49] This holding calls a common prosecutorial tactic (scouring the jailhouse for a prisoner who has heard a defendant jailed pending trial make a damaging statement, in order to make a deal) into question, for it is common knowledge among experienced prisoners that anything inculpatory a pretrial detainee says may be used to bargain for one's own early release in exchange for testimony.

Of course, it is a different matter entirely if a government informer is not sent by the government to interrogate the defendant, but merely becomes aware of information as a result of the defendant's confidence.[50] Indeed, the United States

---

[44] The classic case of entrapment is Sherman v United States, 356 US 369 (1958); *see also* Sorrells v United States, 287 US 435 (1932).

[45] United States v Russell, 411 US 423, 433 (1973).

[46] *Id* 432; *see also* Hampton v United States, 425 US 484, 491 (1976) (Powell, J, concurring). See §2.10.

[47] 377 US 201 (1964).

[48] *Id* 206.

[49] United States v Henry, 447 US 264 (1980).

[50] Hoffa v United States, 385 US 293 (1966).

Supreme Court has refused to adopt a per se rule that a conviction cannot stand whenever a government informer, taken into confidence by a defendant, attends a meeting with the defendant and his attorney at which they plan trial strategy, where the information is not passed on by the informer to his superiors for use at trial.[51] However, if a government informer were to meet with a defendant and his attorney and then pass on information received to his superiors for use at trial, the Court would be likely to hold that a violation of the Sixth Amendment had occurred.[52]

§2.08 —Notice

One of the traditional requirements of a reasonable search is notice; a defendant whose property is searched must, as a general rule, be afforded notice of the search. The United States Supreme Court has even held a statute authorizing interception of electronic communications invalid, in part, because it did not require that the subject of the search be afforded notice of it.[53] Despite these holdings, the Court has held that there is no constitutional requirement that a defendant be given notice that the government has used an informer to gather evidence against the defendant at any time prior to trial.[54] The Court has reasoned that there is no constitutional right to discovery generally, nor thus to learn the strength of the state's case, even though that knowledge might induce the defendant to begin plea bargaining negotiations, since there is no constitutional right to plea bargain.[55] However true that may be as a matter of constitutional law, most jurisdictions afford defendants substantial discovery rights as a matter of local law, and in most cases, failure to disclose the existence of an informer until the day of trial would violate the defendant's rights under local law. If the defendant learns that the state has used an informer to gather evidence, under some circumstances, the government may be compelled to release the informer's identity.[56]

§2.09 Electronic Surveillance

The United States Supreme Court has approved the use of recording devices or transmitters placed on government informers, since an informer could simply

---

[51] Weatherford v Bursey, 429 US 545, 551 (1977).

[52] *Id* 559. *But see* Hoffa v United States, 385 US 293, 306 n 8 (1966).

[53] Berger v New York, 388 US 41, 60 (1967).

[54] Weatherford v Bursey, 429 US 545, 559 (1977).

[55] *Id* 539-41.

[56] See **§10.02**.

write down or repeat everything said after an encounter with a defendant.[57] No constitutionally protected expectation of privacy is affected when a conversation is recorded with the consent of one party to it, since a person who reposes confidence in another must assume the risk that his confidence has been misplaced.

A different result occurs when a conversation is intercepted without the consent of any party to it, although the recognition that such an interception is *unreasonable* was slow to develop. In 1928, in *Olmstead v United States*,[58] a bare majority of the Supreme Court, over the vigorous dissents of Justices Butler, Brandeis, and Holmes, and Chief Justice Stone, held that wiretapping did not implicate the Fourth Amendment, since it did not involve a search, nor was a conversation a "thing" which could be seized.[59] It was not until 1961 that the Court began to recognize that wiretapping implicated Fourth Amendment rights because it involved government intrusion into a constitutionally protected area.[60] Eventually the Court explicitly recognized that the Fourth Amendment protects individuals' reasonable expectations of privacy and not merely places.[61] With that recognition, it became apparent that a wiretap was a search governed by the Fourth Amendment.[62] In response to the Court's decisions, Congress in 1968 enacted 18 USC §2518 *et seq*, which establishes a complex and comprehensive scheme for judicial approval of electronic surveillance. The statute allows the states to enact statutes more strict, but not less strict, than the federal statute. If a state chooses to enact a more restrictive statute, federal agents in that state are not bound by the state statute in investigating federal crime.[63]

There is no doubt that the federal statute comports with the requirements of the Fourth Amendment, and most of the litigation concerning it has turned on statutory construction rather than constitutional law.[64] Exhaustive analysis of the statute would be far beyond the scope of this work. However, it is settled

---

[57] United States v White, 401 US 745, 750-51 (1971).*White* was decided by a four-judge plurality, but all of the federal courts of appeal have held that surreptitious recording of conversations with the consent of one party is not violative of any part of the Constitution. *See, e.g.*, United States v Wright, 573 F2d 681 (1st Cir), *cert denied*, 436 US 949 (1978); United States v Fuentes, 563 F2d 527 (2d Cir), *cert denied*, 434 US 959 (1977); United States v Horton, 601 F2d 319 (7th Cir), *cert denied*, 444 US 937 (1979); United States v Axselle, 604 F2d 1330 (10th Cir 1979). A few states forbid such conduct by statute. *See, e.g.*, NH Rev State Ann §570-A:9, VIII (1955).

[58] 777 US 438 (1928).

[59] *Id* 466.

[60] Silverman v United States, 365 US 505 (1967).

[61] Katz v United States, 389 US 347, 351 (1967).

[62] *See, e.g.*, Berger v New York, 388 US 41 (1967) (holding a New York law authorizing electronic interception of communications unconstitutional).

[63] *See, e.g.*, United States v Hall, 543 F2d 1729 (9th Cir 1976), *cert denied*, 429 US 1075 (1977); People v McGee, 49 NYS2d 48, 399 NE2d 1177, 424 NYS2d 157 (1979), *cert denied*, 446 US 942 (1980).

[64] *See, e.g.*, Scott v United States, 436 US 128 (1978) (minimization requirement).

that when a judge issues a valid interception order, the Fourth Amendment does not per se bar a covert entry into the defendant's premises to install a transmitter, since such an entry may be a reasonable manner of carrying out the authorized search.[65] Further, the Court has held that use of *pen registers*, which merely record the telephone number dialed and do not intercept conversations, does not constitute a search within the meaning of the Fourth Amendment.[66] Thus, no warrant is required before such devices may be used by law enforcement officers.

§2.10 Government Manufacture of Crime

When a government agent offers a person the opportunity and means to commit a crime, that person, if prosecuted, may be able to assert the defense of entrapment. The prevailing view is that the defense of entrapment is not of constitutional dimension.[67] The entrapment defense focuses on the predisposition of the defendant to commit the crime, rather than on the conduct of the government's agents.[68] Judges have frequently stated in dicta, however, that if the conduct of the law enforcement officers is so shocking as to violate fundamental fairness, due process may bar the government from proceeding.[69]

The validity of this dictum has become highly important in light of the scheme conducted by the Justice Department now widely known as Abscam. At least one court has concluded that the entire scheme was conceived to test the virtue of members of Congress.[70] The facts described in the court's opinion in *United States v Kelly*[71] are bizarre. The FBI persuaded a federal judge to allow one Melvin Weinberg, a swindler, to remain free on probation in exchange for his promise to cooperate in its endeavors against organized crime. The Abscam scheme was conceived by Weinberg, who was paid $3,000 a month while the scheme was in operation. Legislators would be tested by an investment/immigration scheme involving both legal investments in their districts and illegal bribes. Weinberg used his contacts with other criminals to spread the word about the deals, and the FBI had no firsthand knowledge of whether both the legal and the illegal aspects of the deal were presented. An associate of Congressman Kelly was attracted to the scheme. He presented both the legal and the illegal aspects to Kelly, and Kelly rejected the illegal

---

[65] Dalia v United States, 441 US 238 (1979).

[66] Smith v Maryland, 442 US 735 (1979).

[67] United States v Russell, 411 US 423, 437 (1973).

[68] *Id.*

[69] *See, e.g.,* Hampton v United States, 425 US 484, 491 (1976) (Powell, J, concurring).

[70] United States v Kelly, 31 Crim L Rep (BNA) 2149 (DDC May 13, 1982).

[71] *Id.*

aspects. Kelly agreed to meet to discuss the legal aspects of the scheme and, prior to the meeting, his associate pleaded with the government agent not to present a bribe. Kelly then met with the government agent alone, was offered a bribe, and rejected it. The government agent, posing as a sheik, said that the legal aspects of the deal, investments in Kelly's district, could very well be made in another congressman's district. Kelly tried to keep the conversation on legal investments. A government lawyer, monitoring the meeting, called the agent and told him Kelly was being "cute." The agent then persisted, and finally convinced Kelly to accept a bribe.

In holding that fundamental fairness barred the conviction, Judge Bryant placed particular emphasis on the fact that there was no inkling of corruption on the part of Kelly prior to the scheme. The court also held that if the government presents a temptation, it must be "one which the individual is likely to encounter in the ordinary course."[72] Since offering a congressman a bribe is a crime, the court found that continuing to press a bribe, as the government did, would be far removed from reality. Finally, the court placed particular emphasis on the fact that the government persisted after Kelly refused the initial bribes:

> If the government had no knowledge of Kelly doing anything wrong, its continuing role as the third man in a fight between his conscience and temptation rises above the level of mere offensiveness to that of being outrageous. No concept of fundamental fairness can accommodate what happened to Kelly in this case.[73]

The court took the view that once an illegal offer is rejected, the government cannot press on.

The notoriety of the Abscam cases suggests that Judge Bryant's opinion is but the first of many, and that the law in this area will be further defined. While the Abscam cases are sui generis, the principles involved could have application to a wide range of investigative activity.

---

[72] *Id* 2150.
[73] *Id.*

3

Search

§3.01 Search and the Fourth Amendment

The Fourth Amendment to the federal Constitution provides, in relevant part, that:

> The right of the people to be secure in their persons, houses, papers, and effects, against unreasonable searches and seizures, shall not be violated, and no warrants shall issue, but upon probable cause, supported by oath or affirmation, and particularly describing the place to be searched, and the persons or things to be seized.

Of all the 10 amendments in the Bill of Rights, the intent of the framers in enacting the Fourth Amendment is clearest. Fresh in the minds of the drafters of the amendment were the hated writs of assistance which had, prior to the Revolution, given English customs officials blanket authority to search where they pleased for goods imported in violation of the English tax laws.[1] Moreover, the lawyers of the time were acutely aware of the Crown's practice of issuing general warrants, which had been held to violate the common law

---

[1] Stanford v Texas, 379 US 476, 481 (1965); *see also* Boyd v United States, 116 US 616, 625 (1886).

only in 1765.[2] Thus, the framers sought to safeguard the privacy and security of citizens' homes by requiring that the decision to invade that privacy be made by a neutral and detached magistrate, and not by a police officer engaged in the often competitive business of ferreting out crime.[3] The crucial guarantee of the Fourth Amendment is freedom from arbitrary police action; before a citizen's home is to be invaded, a neutral, unbiased person must decide that the invasion is necessary. Except in a few exceptional circumstances, a search without a warrant is per se unreasonable.[4]

The requirements of the Fourth Amendment became even more important in 1914, when the United States Supreme Court, in *Weeks v United States*,[5] held that evidence gathered in violation of a person's Fourth Amendment rights could not be introduced against him in a federal criminal trial. In 1961, in *Mapp v Ohio*,[6] the Court held that the Fourth Amendment was made applicable to the states by the due process clause of the Fourteenth Amendment and that, therefore, evidence obtained in violation of the Fourth Amendment was inadmissible in state criminal trials.[7]

Application of the federal exclusionary rule to the states has resulted in volumes of reported litigation and scholarly writing. Perhaps because the social cost of the exclusionary rule—exclusion of competent evidence - is so high, constitutional decisions relating to the propriety of searches have become ever more explicit. Moreover, as the members of the United States Supreme Court have changed, that Court has become ever less willing to expand the rules regarding unlawful seizures and has, in fact, in several instances legitimized searches which would have been condemned as unlawful only a few years before. The law regarding search, perhaps more than any other aspect of constitutional criminal procedure, has been in flux in the last few years; it is simply ingenuous to pretend that the decisions of the United States Supreme Court regarding search and seizure are all principled. This chapter merely attempts to outline precisely what procedures are lawful.

§3.02   Areas Protected from Government Search

In the early part of this century, in analyzing the lawfulness of a search, the United States Supreme Court would generally begin, and often end, the

---

[2] Entick v Carrington, 19 Howard's State Trials: 1029 (1765).

[3] Johnson v United States, 333 US 10 (1948).

[4] *See, e.g.*, Coolidge v New Hampshire, 403 US 443 (1971).

[5] 232 US 383 (1914).

[6] 367 US 643 (1961).

[7] The exclusionary rule is discussed in **ch 15**.

inquiry by looking to whether any property interest of the defendant had been violated. Thus, in 1928, a majority of the Court was willing to hold that electronic eavesdropping on private conversations was permissible as long as there was no trespass.[8] The idea that property rights could define the scope of constitutional rights gradually lost favor, and by 1967 the United States Supreme Court had made clear that the Fourth Amendment protects a person's reasonable expectation of privacy, not a place.[9] A person may have a constitutionally protected expectation of privacy if that person exhibits a subjective expectation of privacy and if the expectation is one which society will regard as reasonable, regardless of the person's physical location or property interest in that location.[10] Thus, for example, the Court has held that a person having a telephone conversation with another in a public telephone booth has a reasonable expectation that the conversation will not be overheard, which is violated if government agents electronically intercept the conversation.[11]

Analysis of an individual's right to be free from unreasonable search and seizure depending on privacy interest may easily be reconciled with older cases which recognized an exception to the requirement of a search warrant for property found in open fields[12] or outside the curtilage. The *curtilage* was defined as an area of domestic use surrounding a dwelling and usually, but not always, fenced in with the dwelling.[13] Traditionally, an analysis of the area comprising curtilage would require consideration of proximity to the dwelling house, whether an area is within the enclosure surrounding the dwelling, and whether it is used as an adjunct to the domestic economy of the family.[14] In such buildings, a resident of an adjacent home would have a reasonable expectation of privacy.

The concept really makes sense only when applied to rural properties; the curtilage includes those outbuildings, such as barns and silos, which are necessary and convenient and used for domestic purposes and family employment.[15] Courts have, for example, refused to employ the curtilage concept to allow

---

[8] Olmstead v United States, 277 US 438 (1928).

[9] Katz v United States, 389 US 347 (1967).

[10] Smith v Maryland, 442 US 735 (1979).

[11] Katz v United States, 389 US 347 (1967).

[12] Hester v United States, 265 US 57, 59 (1924) (Holmes, J: the Fourth Amendment's protection of persons, houses and papers "is not extended to open fields. The distinction between the latter and the house is as old as the common law"); *see also* Air Pollution Bd Variance Bd v Western Alfalfa Corp, 416 US 861 (1974).

[13] *See, e.g.*, Marullo v United States, 328 F2d 361 (5th Cir), *cert denied*, 379 US 850 (1964).

[14] *See, e.g.*, United States v Minker, 312 F2d 632 (3d Cir 1962), *cert denied*, 372 US 953 (1963). The modern privacy interest approach is represented by United States v Ramapuram, 632 F2d 1149 (4th Cir 1980), *cert denied*, 101 S Ct 1739 (1981).

[15] State v Charette, 98 NH 477, 103 A2d 192 (1954).

a tenant of a multifamily urban dwelling to claim that areas not within his exclusive control, such as common hallways, are part of the curtilage.[16]

§3.03   Abandoned Property

A person has no constitutionally cognizable interest in abandoned property, which may be seized without a warrant.[17] Obviously, having discarded an object, a person has no reasonable expectation of privacy in it.

§3.04   Search by Private Individuals

In 1921, the United States Supreme Court was presented with two cases in which a warrantless and unlawful search by a private individual produced evidence which the government sought to use in a criminal prosecution. In the first, *Gouled v United States*,[18] an acquaintance of the defendant, acting on the instructions of government officers, pretended to make a social call but used the opportunity to rummage through the defendant's papers. The Court did not even consider the fact that the acquaintance was not a regular investigating officer to be significant, holding that a secret taking of the defendant's property without a warrant by a representative of the government was violative of the Fourth Amendment.[19]

Hovever, in *Burdeau v McDowell*,[20] decided the same year, a seven-judge majority of the Court held that unlawful seizure of evidence by a private person, without the connivance or knowledge of any government agent, was not violative of the Fourth Amendment. The Court reasoned that since the government had no part in illegally obtaining the papers, it should not be penalized by not being permitted to use them. Justice Holmes, joined by Justice Brandeis, dissented, pointing out that "respect for law will not be advanced by resort,

---

[16] Commonwealth v Thomas, 358 Mass 771, 267 NE2d 489 (1971); *see also* United States v Cruz Pagan, 537 F2d 554 (1st Cir 1976) (no privacy interest in material stored in condominium garage).

[17] Abel v United States, 362 US 217 (1960).

[18] 255 US 298 (1921).

[19] *Id* 305.

[20] 256 US 465, 476 (1921).

in its enforcement, to means which shock the common man's sense of decency and fair play."[21]

Despite Justice Holmes's dissent, the present state of federal constitutional law is much the same as it was in 1921. The Court has on several occasions since that time held that private persons who do not act as agents of the state are not bound by the strictures of the Fourth Amendment.[22]

In terms of federal constitutional law, the only issue relating to the admissibility of evidence provided by searches by private persons is the degree to which unlawful private conduct insulates later government conduct from Fourth Amendment challenge. In *Walters v United States*,[23] a package of film was misdelivered, and the recipients opened the package and attempted to view the contents, movie film, which contained descriptive labeling suggesting that the film was obscene. They could not do so because they had no projector, but they called the FBI, which did view the film without a warrant. Justice Stevens, in the course of the majority opinion holding the viewing unlawful, suggested that it was an open question whether the government's projection of the films would have infringed the defendant's rights if the private parties had first projected the film.

While the United States Supreme Court has been unwilling to apply the exclusionary rule to private actions, a few states have, based on state constitutional considerations. The California Supreme Court, for example, has recognized the remarkable proliferation of private security forces and the fact that, as a practical matter, the intrusions on privacy by a private security officer may be as great as any inflicted by police. Moreover, private security guards, insofar as their activities are directed toward the same ends as those of law enforcement officers, would be likely to be deterred by application of the exclusionary rule to the fruits of their illegal conduct. Thus, the California Supreme Court has held that, at least in situations where the private security guards act in a public capacity as by, for example, arresting shoplifters, the exclusionary rule is applicable to the fruits of their unlawful conduct.[24] Similar results in other jurisdictions have been reached where the security officer is an off-duty policeman.[25]

---

[21] *Id* 477 (Holmes, J, dissenting).

[22] Walters v United States, 447 US 649 (1980); Irvine v California, 347 US 128, 136 (1954); Coolidge v New Hampshire, 403 US 443, 487 (1971).

[23] 447 US 649 (1980). Justice White in a concurring and dissenting opinion, joined by Justice Brennan, thought that the question was not open since "[T]he notion that private searches insulate from Fourth Amendment scrutiny subsequent government searches of the same or lesser scope is inconsistent with traditional notions of Fourth Amendment principles. Nor does it follow from our recognition in [*Burdeau*] and [*Coolidge*] that the Fourth Amendment proscribes only government action." *Id* 660.

[24] People v Zelinski, 24 Cal 3d 357, 594 P2d 1000, 155 Cal Rptr 575 (1979).

[25] State v Carter, 267 NW2d 385 (Iowa Sup Ct 1978).

§3.05   What May Be Searched For—The Mere Evidence Rule

The law governing the seizure of evidence has not been static. As recently as 1932, Justice Butler could write with assurance that "the decisions of this Court distinguish searches of one's house, office, papers or effects merely to get evidence to convict him of crime from searches such as those made to find stolen goods for return to the owner, to take property that has been forfeited, to discover property concealed . . . and from searches [for contraband]."[26] Courts reasoned that a search for *mere evidence* of crime was a form of compulsion prohibited by the Fifth Amendment. But subsequent judicial construction of the Fifth Amendment as a purely testimonial privilege[27] and interpretation of the Fourth Amendment as protecting a privacy interest eliminated the foundation of the so-called mere evidence rule. In 1967, the Court specifically rejected the mere evidence rule, holding that items of clothing which linked a defendant to a crime could be the proper subject of a search.[28] The Court reasoned that nothing on the face of the Fourth Amendment supports a distinction between searches for evidence and those for contraband, and that privacy is invaded no more by one type of search than by another. Elimination of the mere evidence rule means that a prosecutor may obtain by search warrant documents which a person would be excused from producing on the grounds of Fifth Amendment privilege since, in such a case, no valid Fifth Amendment claim can be asserted because there is no compulsion.[29]

If a search warrant is obtained in order to search for evidence, one additional element of probable cause is required. The supporting affidavit must not only establish probable cause to believe that the evidence sought is in a particular place, but also that it will aid in a particular apprehension or conviction.[30]

§3.06   Subpoenas and the Right to Be Free from Unreasonable Seizures

In numerous instances, the various states and the federal government have cloaked administrative agencies with subpoena power. Obviously, use of such power may result in a seizure of evidence without the neutral judgment of a

---

[26] United States v Lefkowitz, 285 US 452, 464-65 (1932).

[27] *See, e.g.*, Schmerber v California, 384 US 757 (1966).

[28] Warden v Hayden, 387 US 294 (1967); *see also* Zurcher v Stanford Daily, 436 US 547 (1978).

[29] Andreson v Maryland, 427 US 463, 473 (1976).

[30] *Id* 483; Warden v Hayden, 387 US 294, 307 (1967).

magistrate. Nonetheless, such statutory schemes have been routinely upheld by courts.

Perhaps the most familiar and illustrative subpoena power is that given the Internal Revenue Service by 26 USC §7602 which provides, in relevant part:

> For the purpose of ascertaining the correctness of any return, making a return where none has been made, determining the liability of any person for any internal revenue tax or the liability at law or in equity of any transferee or transferror or any fiduciary of any person in respect of any internal revenue tax for collecting such liability, the secretary is authorized . . . (2) to summon the person liable for tax or required to perform the act or any officer or employee or such person or any person having possession, custody or care of books of account containing entries relating to the business or the person liable.

No federal court has ever suggested that the summons procedure creates a system of unreasonable searches. However, courts have generally assumed that use of the summons procedure to gain evidence from a defendant for use in a criminal prosecution would be unconstitutional.[31] Certainly, at least, if a summons were directed at an individual and the documents sought were incriminating, that person would be able to assert a claim of Fifth Amendment privilege, for that privilege may be violated by compelled production of private papers as well as by compelled testimony.[32] Of course, a distinction must be made in those cases in which the individual summoned has placed the documents sought in the hands of a third party, such as an accountant[33] or an attorney;[34] in such cases there is no forbidden compulsion of the individual investigated. Similarly, even if the papers sought remain in the hands of the potential defendant, they must be private papers; papers of a collective entity, such as a partnership, are not private papers within the meaning of the Fifth Amendment.[35]

Probable Cause to Search

---

[31] United States v LaSalle Natl Bank, 437 US 298, 306 (1978); Donaldson v United States, 400 US 517, 537 (1971); Mancusi v Deforte, 392 US 364, 370-71 (1968); Boren v Tucker, 239 F2d 767, 769 (9th Cir 1956).

[32] *See* Andreson v Maryland, 427 US 463, 474 (1976); Bellis v United States, 417 US 85, 87-88 (1974); Couch v United States, 409 US 322 (1973); Boyd v United States, 116 US 616 (1886).

[33] Couch v United States, 409 US 322 (1973).

[34] Fisher v United States, 425 US 391 (1976).

[35] Bellis v United States, 417 US 85 (1974).

§3.07   The Requirement of Probable Cause

The Fourth Amendment specifically states that "no warrants shall issue but upon probable cause," yet nowhere is that term statutorily defined. Probable cause is required before an arrest or search, with or without warrant, is made. While the United States Supreme Court has suggested that there is a preference for searches pursuant to warrant, and that a doubtful search pursuant to warrant might be sustained while a search without warrant on the same facts would fail,[36] there has never been a decision of the Court further explaining the dichotomy.

There is no doubt about the purpose of the requirement, which is to minimize the likelihood of official intrusion into the lives of citizens. If the phrase does not lend itself to precise legal analysis, it may be because the concept itself deals with mere probabilities, which are not technical but are the factual and practical considerations on which reasonable and prudent persons, and not legal technicians, act.[37] The term certainly means less than evidence which would justify condemnation.[38] But perhaps most important, the concept must be considered in concrete terms.[39] It is easier to illustrate than to define.

When a warrant is presented to a magistrate, the magistrate personally must judge the persuasiveness of the facts set forth, and cannot merely accept the conclusion of the person seeking the warrant that the place sought to be searched contains the evidence asserted.[40] The magistrate personally must determine the source of the affiant's belief, and whether the source, be it communications from others or observations, is reliable and credible.[41] Thus, for example, an arrest warrant which merely stated that

> The undersigned complainant . . . being duly sworn states: that on or about July 26, 1956, at Houston, Texas in the Southern District of Texas, [defendant] did receive, conceal, etc., narcotic drugs, to wit, heroin hydrocholoride

---

[36] United States v Ventresca, 380 US 102, 108 (1965) (Goldberg, J):

affidavits for search warrants warrants must be tested and interpreted by magistrates in a common sense and realistic fashion. They are normally drafted by nonlawyers in the midst and haste of a criminal investigation. Technical requirements of elaborate specificity have no proper place in this area. A grudging or negative attitude by reviewing courts toward warrants will tend to discourage police officers from submitting their evidence to a judicial officer before acting.

[37] Brinegar v United States, 338 US 160, 175 (1949).

[38] United States v Ventresca, 380 US 102 (1965).

[39] Id.

[40] Giordenello v United States, 357 US 480, 486 (1958).

[41] Id.

was held by the United States Supreme Court to be invalid.[42]

The validity of the determination of probable cause supporting a search warrant will, of necessity, turn on the facts of each case, and may even turn, in part, on the magistrate's own willingness to draw conclusions. The cases decided by the Supreme Court are instructive, insofar as the affidavits (or fact situations in warrantless searches) illustrate the very limit of what is permissible.[43] The ultimate determination to be made, however, is straightforward; would the evidence presented justify belief by a person of reasonable caution that the evidence sought is where the affiant says it is? If so, probable cause exists; if not, it does not.

§3.08 Information from Informers

Much of the litigation concerning the sufficiency of probable cause to support a search warrant has centered upon the frequently encountered situation where the information which supports the warrant has been obtained from an informer. The United States Supreme Court has long recognized that information obtained from persons not known to be reliable may not establish probable cause.[44] In *Aguilar v Texas*,[45] the Court established rather precise guidelines for determining whether information obtained from an informer establishes probable cause. While the information may be all hearsay, and even the informer's name need not be provided,[46] the magistrate must personally have the opportunity to determine whether the informer is credible, just as he or she must have the opportunity to determine whether the affiant present is credible.[47] Thus, if information is received from an informer, the officer preparing an affidavit supporting a search warrant must include (1) some of the underlying circumstances from which the informer drew a conclusion, and (2) some of the underlying circumstances from which the officer concluded that the informant, whose identity need not be disclosed, was reliable.[48]

The requirements set out in *Aguilar* have come to be known as the *two-prong test*[49] and, as a general rule, any warrant based on information obtained from

---

[42] *Id* 486-87.

[43] *See, e.g.*, Brinegar v United States, 338 US 160 (1949); United States v Ventresca, 380 US 102 (1965); Jones v United States, 362 US 257 (1960); Zurcher v Stanford Daily, 436 US 547 (1978).

[44] Recznik v City of Lorain, 393 US 154, 169 (1968).

[45] 378 US 108 (1964).

[46] Jaben v United States, 381 US 214 (1965).

[47] *See, e.g.*, Giordenello v United States, 357 US 480 (1958).

[48] Aguilar v Texas, 378 US 108 (1964).

[49] *Id* 114; *see also* McCray v Illinois, 386 US 300 (1967).

informers may be judged by it.[50] However, even if the information given by an informant does not satisfy *Aguilar's* standards, the information, when considered in light of other information known to the police, may establish probable cause.[51] If information given by an informant is as trustworthy as a tip which would pass *Aguilar's* tests without independent corroboration, probable cause exists.[52] A classic example of verification by corroborating circumstances is *Draper v United States.*[53] In that case, an informer told a federal officer in one city that Draper was peddling narcotics in the city, and had gone to Chicago by train the day before and was going to bring back three ounces of heroin. The informer gave the officer a detailed description of the clothes Draper was wearing, and said he would be carrying a tan zipper bag and that he "walked real fast."[54] The following day, the officer went to a train station and observed a person with the exact physical attributes and wearing the exact clothing described by the informer, walking quickly from the train carrying a tan zipper bag. In holding the arrest was supported by probable cause, the Court found dispositive the fact that all of the information the informer had given the officer had been verified; it was thus reasonable to assume that the remaining unverified bit of information—that the defendant would have heroin with him—would be true.[55]

A mere allegation that the defendant is "known" to the police officers as a criminal is entitled to some but not great weight.[56] Evidence from a person considered prudent and who admits personal involvement in wrongdoing will be considered highly probative.[57] But in the final analysis, each affidavit offering more than bald conclusions purportedly from informers must stand or fall on its own facts.

§3.09 Probable Cause for Warrantless Search

In a few narrow circumstances, a search may be made without a warrant in conformity with the Fourth Amendment. Such a search must, however, like a search pursuant to warrant, be based on probable cause. Indeed, there is reason

---

[50] The classic example of a search warrant affidavit which sets out information obtained from informers sufficient to establish probable cause is Jones v United States, 362 US 257 (1960).

[51] Spinelli v United States, 393 US 410 (1969).

[52] *Id* 415.

[53] 358 US 307 (1959).

[54] *Id* 309.

[55] *Id* 313.

[56] *Compare* Spinelli v United States, 393 US 410 (1969) *with* United States v Harris, 403 US 573 (1971).

[57] Spinelli v United States, 393 US 410 (1969).

to suspect that the quantum of evidence required to support probable cause in such a circumstance is greater than when a neutral judicial officer approves the search.[58] The circumstances in which warrantless searches are permissible are described in §§3.21-3.31. While a search can never be justified by what it produces,[59] in some cases, information which would not otherwise be credible may, as in the case of search warrant affidavits, be verified by corroborating circumstances known to the police. This rule is particularly applicable to information received from informants.

§3.10   Evidence Which May Be Relied on to Establish Probable Cause

Because probable cause is a concept on the basis of which laypersons and not legal technicians act, the United States Supreme Court has been loath to impose restrictions on the type of evidence which may be considered to establish probable cause. Indeed, an affidavit supporting a search warrant may be based entirely on hearsay.[60] The rules of evidence do not apply in such cases, and normally inadmissible evidence such as a defendant's prior criminal record may be considered.[61] The general rule is that virtually any evidence may be considered, but its relevance depends on the evidence itself; for example, a credible informer's information that he bought heroin from a person six months ago, while it could be considered by a magistrate, would be unlikely to establish probable cause to believe that the named person presently possesses heroin, since the information is stale.

At least one court has, however, held that evidence obtained in violation of *Miranda* cannot be considered in establishing probable cause.[62] Since *Miranda* embodies a prophylactic rule and not a rule which excludes unreliable evidence, such a rule of exclusion, in effect, amounts to an extension of the exclusionary rules. This extension of the exclusionary rule has been rejected by some courts as not constitutionally required and not justifiable on policy grounds.[63]

---

[58] United States v Ventresca, 380 US 102 (1965).

[59] Byars v United States, 273 US 28 (1927).

[60] McCray v Illinois, 386 US 300 (1967); Jones v United States, 362 US 257 (1960).

[61] Brinegar v United States, 338 US 160, 174 (1949).

[62] Commonwealth v White, 374 Mass 132, 381 NE2d 777 (1978), *affd by an equally divided court sub nom* Massachusetts v White, 439 US 280 (1979), holding that evidence obtained in violation of Miranda v Arizona, 384 US 436 (1966), cannot be considered in determining probable cause.

[63] *See, e.g.*, State v Ann Marie C, 407 A2d 715, 723 (Me Sup Ct 1979).

§3.11   Detention of Those Found in Place Where Search Warrant Executed

The mere fact that a person is found in a place generally accessible to members of the public at a time when it is searched pursuant to warrant does not authorize the officers, executing the warrant to search or even frisk the individual.[64] However, a person may be detained while his or her home is searched pursuant to warrant.[65]

Issuance and Execution of Search Warrants

§3.12   Procedure for Issuance of Warrants

Virtually every jurisdiction has established a statutory scheme for the issuance of search warrants. Most statutes require that the applicant for a warrant appear before the judicial officer empowered to issue warrants, and provide an affidavit which sets forth facts from which the magistrate may determine whether probable cause exists. The officer applying for the warrant may present evidence in support of the application for a warrant. However, if the officer does so, the magistrate must make note of the evidence provided.

§3.13   Who May Issue Warrants

The constitutional imperative of judicial impartiality applies with particular force to search warrants
The United States Supreme Court has adopted a per se rule of disqualification; if the magistrate issuing a search warrant is not neutral and detached, the warrant is void, and it is irrelevant that the affidavit on which the warrant was issued so clearly establishes probable cause that any magistrate considering the affidavit would have found probable cause.[66] Thus, a warrant issued by a magistrate who is also a law enforcement officer, such as a prosecutor, is per se void.[67] A magistrate who has a pecuniary interest in issuing search warrants is, like a judge who has a financial stake in a case, not neutral and detached.[68] An otherwise neutral magistrate may, by becoming involved in the search, lose

---

[64] Ybarra v Illinois, 444 US 85 (1979).

[65] Michigan v Summers, 101 S Ct 2587 (1981).

[66] Coolidge v New Hampshire, 403 US 443, 450 (1971).

[67] *Id*; *see also* Mancusi v Deforte, 392 US 364, 371 (1968).

[68] Connally v Georgia, 429 US 245 (1977).

the neutrality essential under the Fourth Amendment. In *Lo-Ji Sales Inc v New York*,[69] a magistrate presented with evidence that obscene materials could be found in a New York bookstore decided to accompany the officers on their search and make an on-the-spot determination of what items were seizable while on the search. The Supreme Court held that the justice, having become, in effect, the leader of a search party, was no longer neutral and detached.

As anyone familiar with law enforcement knows, police frequently find it necessary to obtain warrants late at night or on weekends from "friendly judges." The Court was careful to note in *Lo-Ji Sales* that a magistrate is not rendered partial simply because of having agreed to meet law enforcement officers outside his or her regular office and outside office hours.[70]

The Constitution does not specify the type of person who may issue warrants. The Supreme Court has held that the Constitution does not require that warrants be issued by judges or magistrates of any type, since the substance of the constitutional guarantee of the Fourth Amendment cannot be made to turn on mere labels. What is required is that the person issuing the warrant be neutral and detached, and capable of determining probable cause; he or she need not even be a lawyer.[71] Thus, the Court has held that neutral municipal clerks, who are capable of determining probable cause and who have no connection with law enforcement authorities, may issue warrants.[72] The Court has, however, left open the issue of whether a state can place the warrant authority entirely outside the judicial branch of government.[73]

§3.14   Effect of Misrepresentation in Supporting Affidavit

In 1978, the United States Supreme Court first held that an accused could challenge the truthfulness of factual statements made in an affidavit supporting a search warrant, in *Franks v Delaware*.[74] However, the Court made clear that the circumstances under which such an attack is permissible are narrow indeed. Only when the defendant makes a substantial preliminary showing that a false statement made knowingly or with reckless disregard for the truth was included in the warrant affidavit, and that the allegedly false statement is necessary to the finding of probable cause, does the Fourth Amendment require that a hearing

---

[69] 442 US 319 (1979).

[70] *Id* 328 n 6.

[71] Shadwick v City of Tampa, 407 US 345, 350 (1972).

[72] *Id* 350-52.

[73] *Id* 352.

[74] 438 US 154 (1978).

be held.[75] Allegations of culpable negligence or deliberate falsehood must be accompanied by an offer of proof, pointing out with particularity the portion of the affidavit claimed to be false.[76] Moreover, the deliberate falsity or reckless disregard on the basis of which impeachment is permitted includes only that of the police officer, and not that of any nongovernment informant.[77]

§3.15 Specificity of Description of Evidence Sought

Because of the framers' abhorrence of general warrants, the constitutional requirement that a warrant "particularly describe the place to be searched and the persons or things to be seized" has been given a narrow construction. The obvious purpose of this provision is to limit the discretion and opportunity for arbitrary action of the executing officers.[78] It has been held that the amendment should be liberally construed to guard against general searches.[79]

The inclusion of the above-quoted language in the Constitution was a reflection of the struggle of the English citizenry against the sovereign's use of general warrants, which culminated in Lord Camden's decision in 1765 in *Entick v Carrington*[80] that general warrants were contrary to the common law. Indeed, Blackstone, that same year, felt able to write that "a general warrant, to apprehend all persons suspected, without naming or particularly describing any person in special, is illegal, and void for its uncertainty; for it is the duty of the magistrate and ought not to be left to the officer, to judge the ground of suspicion."[81] To be constitutionally sufficient, a warrant must describe precisely

---

[75] *Id* 155-56; however, some state courts have held, based on state constitutions, that where an affidavit for a search warrant contains intentionally false allegations, the court cannot exclude such allegations and presume the remainder to be true, but must quash the warrant regardless of whether probable cause would exist apart from the false statement. *See, e.g.,* People v Cook, 22 Cal 3d 67, 583 P2d 130, 148 Cal Rptr 605 (1978).

[76] 438 US 154, 171.

[77] *Id.*

[78] Andresen v Maryland, 427 US 463, 480 (1976).

[79] *See, e.g.,* Go-Bart v United States, 282 US 344, 357 (1931).

[80] 19 Howard's State Trials 1029 (1765); *see also* Wilkes v Wood, 19 Howard's State Trials 1153 (1763). The history of the struggle against the Crown's use of general warrants, which apparently began with the Tudors and continued even after the Revolution of 1688, is outlined in Stanford v Texas, 379 US 476, 481-84 (1965) and Marcus v Search Warrant, 361 US 717, 724-29 (1961).

[81] 4 W. Blackstone, Commentaries 287 (U Chi ed 1979).

what is to be taken, so that nothing is left to the discretion of the officer executing the warrant.[82]

Of course, specificity of description varies with the kind of thing to be seized. The requirement that a warrant particularly describe things to be seized is afforded the most scrupulous exactitude when the objects to be seized are books.[83] Mere items of commerce, however, may lawfully be seized if they are sufficiently identified to distinguish them from other objects.[84]

§3.16 Seizure of Items Not Named in Warrant

If evidence not described in the warrant is seized by the police, it will be excluded from evidence if the police were aware of its location when they applied for the warrant.[85] The entire search is not void, however; the evidence described in the warrant may still be introduced.[86]

There is an exception to the general rule that only evidence described in the search warrant may be seized. If, in the course of a lawful search pursuant to a warrant, an officer comes across evidence of another crime, the officer may seize it.[87] The rationale for such a search is really the plain view doctrine; an officer has a right to seize evidence that can be seen from a place the officer has a lawful right to be.[88]

§3.17 Description of Place to Be Searched

As important as the constitutional requirement that the objects to be seized be particularly described in the warrant is the requirement that the place to be searched be particularly described. Again, the purpose of the specificity requirement is merely to ensure that the officers executing the search warrant are not afforded discretion. The United States Supreme Court has, perhaps because there is less likelihood of an officer's stretching an affidavit to search

---

[82] Marron v United States, 275 US 192, 196 (1927); the limit to which the requirement of specificity may be stretched is illustrated by Commonwealth v Postolan, 361 Mass 869, 281 NE2d 588 (1972), in which the Massachusetts Supreme Judicial Court upheld the seizure of a torn green shirt under a warrant authorizing seizure of a green bandanna, since basically the warrant authorized seizure of any cloth capable of being used as a bandanna.

[83] Stanford v Texas, 379 US 476 (1965); Lo-Ji Sales Inc v New York, 442 US 319 (1979).

[84] Steele v United States, 267 US 498 (1925) (cases of whiskey).

[85] Marron v United States, 275 US 192 (1927); but see §3.23.

[86] Id; Scott v United States, 436 US 128 (1978).

[87] See, e.g., Commonwealth v Wojuk, 358 Mass 623, 266 NE2d 645 (1971).

[88] See §3.22.

one place with an affidavit authorizing search of another, than of an officer attempting to conduct a general exploratory search after receiving a narrow warrant, taken a more liberal view of the specificity required of the former. Justice Holmes's pronouncement of 57 years ago is still valid today: "it is enough if the description is such that the officer with a search warrant can, with reasonable effort, ascertain and identify the place intended."[89] More specificity is generally required when the warrant authorizes search of urban rather than rural property, since the risk of misidentification is greater in the former.

Execution of Search Warrant

§3.18   Search of Those on Premises Searched

The fact that a person is lawfully present in a place the police have a warrant to search does not automatically provide authority for the warrantless search of that person. Indeed, the United States Supreme Court has specifically held that a frisk of a patron of a bar which the police had a warrant to search was unreasonable, since there is no reason to assume that a person lawfully in a public place has any connection with unlawful activities which may be occurring there.[90] The Court has specifically rejected the proposition that a person on compact premises subject to search warrant may be searched if the police have a "reasonable belief" that the person is "connected with" drug trafficking, and may be concealing or carrying away the contraband.[91]

However, a different result may obtain when the search is of a dwelling. The Court has held that it is constitutionally reasonable to detain the occupants of a dwelling while a search pursuant to warrant is conducted.[92] Obviously, such detention is no more intrusive than a search of one's possessions, and because the search is in the person's own residence, it could increase only minimally the public stigma associated with the search itself. Moreover, there are important law enforcement interests which tend to weigh heavily against the minimal violation of privacy; the brief detention may prevent flight of potential defendants; it may ensure the safety of the officers by limiting an occupant's frenzied attempt to destroy evidence; and an orderly search may be facilitated if the occupants are available to open locked areas.[93]

---

[89] Steele v United States, 267 US 498, 503 (1925).
[90] Ybarra v Illinois, 444 US 85 (1979).
[91] *Id.*
[92] Michigan v Summers, 101 S Ct 2587 (1981).
[93] *Id.*

§3.19 Notice of Search

Virtually every statute regulating search warrants provides for notice of the search and an inventory of the objects taken to be furnished to the defendant. The United States Supreme Court has strongly suggested that notice of a search is required in order for the search to be considered reasonable under the Fourth Amendment.[94]

§3.20 Persons Against Whom Search Warrants May Issue

The Fourth Amendment does not bar search of property even though its owner is not suspected of crime.[95] There is no requirement that the police first direct a subpoena duces tecum to the owner of the property before resorting to a search warrant in such a case.[96] However, it has been held that a warrant authorizing search of an attorney's offices for his client's records, where the attorney is not suspected of wrongdoing and there is no threat the documents will be destroyed, is unreasonable.[97]

Warrantless Searches

§3.21 Warrantless Searches in General

While the general rule is that searches outside the judicial process are pre se unreasonable, a number of exceptions to the warrant requirement have, over the years, developed.[98] Perhaps no aspect of constitutional criminal procedure is tethered so loosely to precedent; the scope and content of the exceptions to the warrant requirement have changed dramatically over the last 20 years, and in some cases, over the last two or three years.

The traditional exceptions to the warrant requirement number seven. They are the plain view exception, the search incident to arrest exception, the exigent circumstances exception, the hot pursuit exception, the automobile exception, the consent exception, and the border searches exception. Each of these exceptions

---

[94] Berger v New York, 388 US 41, 60 (1967).

[95] Zurcher v Stanford Daily, 436 US 547, 559-60 (1978).

[96] *Id.*

[97] O'Connor v Johnson, 287 NW2d 400 (Minn Sup Ct 1979) (decision based on both Minnesota and United States Constitutions).

[98] Coolidge v New Hampshire, 403 US 443, 454-55 (1971).

is treated separately and, indeed, the body of law which has grown up around the consent exception requires that it be treated in a separate subheading.

While no amount of probable cause can ever justify a warrantless search absent the circumstances outlined in one of the exceptions, it is nonetheless axiomatic that, except for border searches, which are sui generis, warrantless searches cannot be made on less than probable cause.[99] Indeed, there is a distinct judicial preference for searches pursuant to warrant. The United States Supreme Court has specifically stated that in a case of doubtful probable cause, a search pursuant to warrant may be sustained where a search without warrant would not be.[100]

When the government seeks to introduce evidence obtained without a warrant, it has the burden of persuading the court, by a preponderance of the evidence, that one of the exceptions to the warrant requirement is applicable.[101]

§3.22   Exceptions—Plain View

The plain view exception to the warrant requirement is closely related to the idea that the Fourth Amendment protects privacy interests. The plain view doctrine may be simply stated: if a police officer, standing where he or she has a lawful right to be, observes seizable items, they may be seized if the officer is already in the constitutionally protected area. The plain view doctrine usually is applicable when the police are in a dwelling searching for some other object, although it may be applicable in cases in which the property is in an area which is not constitutionally protected.[102] *Plain view* like *exigent circumstances* can never justify a police officer's entering a dwelling because of having probable cause to believe that evidence of crime or contraband will be found inside, unless there is some reason to believe that it will be impossible to obtain a warrant before the evidence is destroyed or concealed.[103]

Plain view may allow the police to seize objects regardless of whether the initial intrusion is the result of a search pursuant to warrant or the result of a

---

[99] *See generally* United States v Almeida-Sanchez, 413 US 266 (1973); United States v 12,200 Ft Reels of Film, 413 US 123 (1973).

[100] United States v Ventresca, 380 US 102 (1965).

[101] Coolidge v New Hampshire, 403 US 443, 455 (1971); United States v Jeffers, 342 US 48, 51 (1951).

[102] *See, e.g.,* Colorado v Bannister, 449 US 1 (1980) (seizable items lying on seat of car which could be observed from outside the vehicle); Harris v United States, 390 US 234 (1968).

[103] Coolidge v New Hampshire, 403 US 443, 468 (1971); *see, e.g.,* Johnson v United States, 333 US 10, 15 (1948); *see also* Rawlings v Kentucky, 448 US 98 (1980).

warrantless search.[104] In either case, whether the initial intrusion is pursuant to warrant or in accordance with an exception to the warrant requirement, a person's privacy has already been lawfully breached. The rationale for the rule is that there is no reason why the police should avert their eyes if they find contraband or evidence inadvertently.

The concept of plain view requires that the object be in plain view—there can be no rummaging about until something incriminating turns up.[105] Extension of the original justification for the intrusion is legitimate only when it is immediately apparent to the police that they have evidence before them; the doctrine may not be used to extend a search from one object to another until something incriminating turns up.[106] The discovery of the evidence must be inadvertent. If the warrant supporting the initial intrusion failed to mention the seized object, although the police were aware of the object's location at the time they applied for the warrant, it may not be seized pursuant to the plain view doctrine because the constitutional requirement of particularity in description has been violated.[107]

What items may be said to have been found in plain view depends on the scope of the search. If, for example, police enter a dwelling without a warrant, pursuant to the exigent circumstances exception, to look for a victim of crime, evidence found in places a police officer could reasonably have searched for a victim will be admitted into evidence, but evidence found in places where the officer could not reasonably have been looking for a victim will be excluded.[108]

§3.23   —Exigent Circumstances

The exigent circumstances exception to the warrant requirement is easily defined. When the police have probable cause to search, but the delay occasioned by getting judicial approval will lead to the destruction or loss of evidence, seizure may take place without prior judicial authorization. As Chief Justice Burger pithily stated, "where there are exigent circumstances in which police action must literally be now or never, to preserve the evidence of the crime, it is reasonable to permit action without prior judicial authorization."[109]

---

[104] Coolidge v New Hampshire, 403 US 443, 465 (1971); *see also* Washington v Chrisman, 102 S Ct 812 (1982) (where officer arrested defendant, and then accompanied him to his room so he could get identification, and while waiting at the door of the room observed marijuana inside, its seizure was lawful pursuant to the plain view exception, since the police officer had a right to remain at the arrestee's side).

[105] Coolidge v New Hampshire, 403 US 443, 465-66 (1971).

[106] *Id* 466.

[107] *Id; see also* Commonwealth v Rand, 363 Mass 554, 296 NE2d 200 (1973).

[108] State v Slade, 116 NH 436, 362 A2d 194 (1976).

[109] Roaden v Kentucky, 413 US 494, 505 (1973).

The exigent circumstances exception was first articulated in *Carroll v United States*[110] in which the United States Supreme Court held that warrantless search of an automobile when probable cause existed to believe it contained contraband could be justified by the automobile's mobility—the car is movable, the occupants are alerted, and the car's contents may never be found again if a warrant must be obtained. Automobile cases are not a good subject for analysis of the exigent circumstances exception, however, since it appears that the Court has, in the last few years, developed a separate but related automobile exception to the warrant requirement. More characteristic of the exigent circumstances exception are cases in which police enter a house to search for a victim[111] or in which the police take fingernail scrapings of one not under arrest before he has an opportunity to wash his hands.[112] Fundamental to the exception is the requirement of an emergency: a fleeing suspect, moving vehicle or vessel, or contraband threatened to be removed.[113] If there is no reason the search must be made without a warrant, it will not be upheld under the exigent circumstances exception no matter how strong the probable cause.[114]

§3.24 Hot Pursuit

Closely akin to, if not the same as, the exigent circumstances exception is the *hot pursuit* exception to the warrant requirement. In *Warden v Hayden*,[115] the United States Supreme Court held that police officers, who had been informed that an armed robbery had taken place and that a suspect had entered a certain house less than five minutes before they reached it, acted reasonably in entering the house and searching the house for the robber and the fruits and instrumentalities of the crime. The Court reasoned that, in the circumstances described, speed was essential and only a thorough search of the entire house for persons and weapons could ensure that the robber was present and was the only person present, and that the police had control of all weapons which might be used against them or to effect an escape.[116]

While some element of a pursuit is probably necessary for invocation of the particular exigent circumstance of hot pursuit, the United States Supreme Court has made clear that there need not be any sort of extended "hue and

---

[110] 267 US 132 (1925).

[111] State v Slade, 116 NH 436, 362 A2d 194 (1976).

[112] Cupp v Murphy, 412 US 291 (1973); *see also* Schmerber v California, 384 US 757 (1966).

[113] Vale v Louisiana, 399 US 30 (1970); Johnson v United States, 333 US 10 (1948).

[114] GM Leasing v United States, 447 US 649 (1980); Arkansas v Sanders, 442 US 753 (1979); United States v Chadwick, 433 US 1 (1977).

[115] 387 US 294 (1967).

[116] *Id* 298-99; *see also* Johnson v United States, 333 US 10, 16 n 7 (1948).

cry" in and about the public streets.[117] The purpose of the exception is to avoid the escape of a criminal and the destruction of implements of crime; once there is a "realistic expectation" that either may occur, the requisites of a hot pursuit exist.[118]

§3.25 Automobile

The exigent circumstances exception waś, until the 1970s, closely related to automobiles. In 1925 in *Carroll v United States*,[119] the United States Supreme Court held that warrantless seizure of an automobile when probable cause exists to believe it contains contraband is proper since the car is movable, the occupants are alerted, and the car's contents may never be found again if a warrant must be obtained. But the fact that automobile searches were somehow different from other searches was first suggested by the Court in 1970, in *Chambers v Moroney*,[120] when it rejected the argument that a car stopped on the highway could simply be immobilized until a warrant was obtained. In so holding, the Court noted:

> Arguably, because of the preference for a magistrate's judgment, only the immobilization of the car should be permitted until a search warrant is obtained; arguably only the lesser intrusion is permissible until the magistrate authorizes the greater. But which is the greater and which is the lesser intrusion is itself a debatable question, and the answer may depend upon a variety of circumstances. For constitutional purposes, we see no difference between on one hand seizing and holding a car before presenting the issue to a magistrate and on the other hand carrying out an immediate search without warrant.[121]

Of course, there would be a great constitutional difference between seizing a piece of luggage and holding it until a warrant could be obtained and opening it immediately.[122] The recognition that automobiles were somehow different from other things developed through the 1970s, as the Court sustained automobile searches which would not have been justifiable on traditional ex-

---

[117] United States v Santana, 427 US 38, 43 (1976).

[118] *Id.*

[119] 267 US 132 (1925).

[120] 399 US 42 (1970).

[121] *Id* 51-52.

[122] *See, e.g.*, Arkansas v Sanders, 442 US 753 (1979).

igent circumstances grounds.[123] In 1981, in *Robbins v California*,[124] a four-judge plurality finally explicitly articulated the basis for a separate automobile exception, holding that such an exception is justified not only by the fact that autos are mobile, but because individuals have a diminished expectation of privacy in automobiles, which are used for transportation and not as residences, travel in plain view, and are highly regulated by the government. The *Robbins* plurality held that automobiles are subject to search whenever a police officer has probable cause to believe they contain contraband, but that objects found within the vehicle, in which an owner has manifested an expectation of privacy, such as closed luggage or even cardboard boxes or paper bags, could not be opened pursuant to the automobile exception.

The practical difficulties which inhere in determining whether individuals held legitimate expectations of privacy in containers within an automobile led a six-judge majority of the Court to discard *Robbins* less than one year later in *United States v Ross*.[125] In that case, the Court held that "the scope of a warrantless automobile search based on probable cause is no narrower — and no broader — than the scope of a search authorized by a warrant supported by probable cause."[126] Thus, if police officers have probable cause to search a vehicle for drugs, they may search any containers found within the vehicle, just as a warrant which authorizes search of a home for weapons provides authority to open closets, chests, drawers, and other containers in which weapons might be found. But the fact that police officers have probable cause for the warrantless search of an automobile does not mean that any container in the automobile may always be opened. Mr. Justice Stevens was careful to point out:

> Just as probable cause to believe that a stolen lawn mower may be found in a garage, will not support a warrant to search an upstairs bedroom, probable cause to believe that undocumented aliens are being transported in a van will not justify warrantless search of a suitcase. Probable cause to believe that a container placed in the trunk of a taxi contains contraband or evidence does not justify a search of the entire cab.[127]

---

[123] *See, e.g.*, Cardwell v Lewis, 417 US 583 (1974) (warrantless examination of paint on exterior of vehicle); Texas v White, 423 US 67 (1975) (if probable cause and exigent circumstances exist at one point, search may be made later and at another place without showing justification for the delay); Colorado v Bannister, 449 US 1 (1980) (officer could seize objects he saw inside car pursuant to plain view doctrine even though at the time neither he nor the driver was inside the vehicle—the "constitutionally protected area"); South Dakota v Opperman, 428 US 364 (1976) (inventory search of seized auto upheld, rejected on remand, as violative of the South Dakota Constitution, in State v Opperman, 247 NW2d 673 (SD 1976)).

[124] 453 US 420 (1981).

[125] 50 USLW 4580 (June 1, 1982).

[126] *Id* 4587.

[127] *Id.*

There is one important caveat. Even though opening containers may be impermissible under the automobile exception, if the driver of the vehicle is arrested, opening containers may be justified by the search incident to arrest exception. The Court also held in 1981 that if the operator of a motor vehicle is arrested, a police officer may, as a search incident to arrest, search the entire passenger compartment of the vehicle, including the glove compartment or consoles, and open any container found therein.[128] Obviously, this expansion of the search incident to arrest exception[129] is predicated upon the peculiar status of automobiles.

§3.26 — Search Incident to Arrest

Like the automobile exception, the search incident to arrest exception to the warrant requirement has undergone a metamorphosis in the last 50 years. In *Marron v United States*,[130] the United States Supreme Court upheld the seizure of a ledger found in a closet where officers were, after the arrest of the defendant and pursuant to warrant, searching for liquor. While the seizure probably could have been upheld under the plain view doctrine, the Court broadly stated that, after a valid arrest, the officers had a right to search without a warrant contemporaneously in order to find and seize the things used to carry on the criminal enterprise.[131] By 1947, the Court sustained a search of a four-room apartment merely because the defendant was arrested there.[132] Such a rule permitted police officers to evade the requirements of the Fourth Amendment by the simple expedient of arresting an individual at home. Thus, in *Chimel v California*,[133] the Court limited the scope of the search incident to arrest exception by holding that when an arrest is made, it is reasonable to search the person arrested in order to remove any weapons that the arrestee may use to resist arrest or escape, and to seize evidence on the arrestee to prevent its concealment or destruction, but that a more intense search is impermissible. The Court also held that a search of the area into which the arrestee might reach to grab a weapon or evidentiary items — the area under the arrestee's immediate control — is also lawful.[134]

---

[128] New York v Belton, 453 US 454 (1981).

[129] Chimel v California, 395 US 752 (1969).

[130] 275 US 192 (1927).

[131] *Id* 199.

[132] Harris v United States, 331 US 145 (1947).

[133] 395 US 752 (1969); *see also* Vale v Louisiana, 399 US 30 (1970); Von Cleef v New Jersey, 395 US 814 (1969).

[134] Chimel v California, 395 US 752, 763 (1969).

There is one exception to the *Chimel* rule, premised on the diminished privacy expectation in automobiles. When a person is arrested while in or just after exiting a vehicle, the officer may lawfully search the passenger compartment, including the glove compartment and console, and open any closed containers therein, as a search incident to arrest.[135]

The Supreme Court has upheld custodial arrests for traffic offenses as long as the arrests are not mere subterfuges.[136] Some courts, however, do not premise the lawfulness of the search on the mere fact of arrest, holding instead that the permissibility of a full body search depends on the degree of danger to the officer, and that, therefore, full body field searches in cases of minor offenses which will be disposed of by mere citation are impermissible.[137]

A person who has been validly arrested and detained may be subjected to physical tests.[138]

§3.27   Border Searches

Border searches are unique because of the interest every sovereign has in ensuring that injurious objects do not enter the country and that the customs laws are not violated. There is no constitutional bar to routine inspections and searches of individuals or conveyances seeking to cross international borders.[139] At a border or its functional equivalent, vehicles may be searched on the slightest suspicion.[140] However, such stops may not be conducted by roving border patrols[141] or at checkpoints far removed from the border.[142]

---

[135] New York v Belton, 453 US 454 (1981). Of course, if there is probable cause to search the automobile, a separate search of the entire vehicle must be justified on that ground. See §3.25.

[136] United States v Robinson, 414 US 218 (1973); *but see* Gustafson v Florida, 414 US 260, 266-67 (1973) ("It seems to me a persuasive case might have been made . . . that the custodial arrest of the defendant for a minor traffic offense violated his rights under the Fourth and Fourteenth Amendments . . .") (Stewart, J concurring).

[137] *See, e.g.,* People v Longwill, 14 Cal 3d 943, 538 P2d 753, 123 Cal Rptr 297 (1975); People v Brisendine, 13 Cal 3d 528, 531 P2d 1099, 119 Cal Rptr 315 (1975).

[138] See §5.20.

[139] Carroll v United States, 267 US 132, 154 (1925), *quoted with approval in* United States v Almeida-Sanchez, 413 US 266 (1973).

[140] United States v Ramsey, 431 US 606 (1977); Carroll v United States, 267 US 132 (1925).

[141] United States v Brignoni-Ponce, 422 US 873 (1975).

[142] United States v Ortiz, 422 US 891 (1975).

Consent Searches

§3.28 Consent Searches In General

Perhaps the most common exception to the warrant requirement is the consent search. Because the issue of a consent search relates to the very crux of the notion of a government of limited powers—the relation between police officers and citizens—it is frequently litigated. But perhaps because consent searches are so heavily relied on by law enforcement authorities, the United States Supreme Court has been unwilling to bring the type of scrutiny to bear on police practices regarding consensual search that it has in, for example, the area of interrogation practices. Certainly, many citizens, particularly if they have had little contact with the police, would regard an officer's request to search as merely a courteous statement of intention. The numerous litigated cases in which consent to search is claimed, the search produces incriminating evidence, and the person who allegedly consented alleges coercion, lead inexorably to an obvious question: if the consenting individual was *not* coerced, why would he or she ever have assented to a search which he or she knew would produce damning evidence?[143] The United States Supreme Court and most other courts have avoided this question, requiring only that searches be "voluntary," and baldly admitting that the test of voluntariness in this area is far different from the test in others, characterizing the word voluntariness, for this constitutional purpose, as an "amphibian."[144]

§3.29 Standard for Valid Consent

The great many decided consent cases provide rather clear standards for determining when consent is valid. First, it is the prosecutor's burden to prove a valid consent.[145] There must be a true consent; mere submission to authority is insufficient.[146] Consent obtained by fraud, as when, for example, the police officer pretends to have a warrant, is invalid;[147] and, of course, the consent must be voluntary. This much is probably applicable to waiver of all other constitutional rights.

---

[143] *See, e.g.*, United States v Mendenhall, 446 US 544 (1980); Washington v Chrisman, 102 S Ct 812 (1982).

[144] Schneckloth v Bustamonte, 412 US 218, 224 (1973), citing Culombe v Connecticut, 367 US 568, 604-05 (1960).

[145] Bumper v North Carolina, 391 US 543 (1968).

[146] *Id; see also* Johnson v United States, 333 US 10 (1948); Amos v United States, 255 US 313 (1921).

[147] Bumper v North Carolina, 391 US 543 (1968); Gouled v United States, 255 US 298 (1921).

What sets consent searches apart is the unwillingness of the United States Supreme Court to apply the traditional criteria for waiver of constitutional rights — "intentional abandonment or relinquishment of a known right or privilege"[148] — to analysis of whether consent to search has occurred. In *Schneckloth v Bustamonte*,[149] the Court reaffirmed the rule that whether a consent had occurred was a question of fact, and specifically held that while knowledge of the ability to refuse consent is one factor in determining whether consent is voluntary, the government need not establish such knowledge as a sine qua non of an effective consent.[150] The Court declined to apply the traditional waiver test to consent searches, reasoning that the waiver concept itself was somewhat amorphous and that, in the past, the concept had only been applied to those rights accorded a criminal defendant to insure the ability to take advantage of every facet of the constitutional model of a fair criminal trial.[151]

In *State v Johnson*,[152] the New Jersey Supreme Court declined to follow *Schneckloth*, and held that the New Jersey constitution requires that when the prosecution seeks to justify a warrantless search, it must show that the consent was *voluntary* in the traditional constitutional sense, since the constitutional right to be free from unreasonable seizure is at issue in such a case. The prosecution must show that the defendant was aware of having the right to refuse consent.

It is difficult to gainsay the logic of the New Jersey Supreme Court. However, few courts have followed *State v Johnson*. Most reason as the Alaska Supreme Court did: "We recognize that good arguments can be made in favor of a stricter consent standard in the Fourth Amendment area. Nevertheless, we find that the *Schneckloth* rule strikes the appropriate balance between the need for effective police work and the need to prevent coerced consent."[153]

§3.30 Factors Bearing on Valid Consent to Search

Because the determination of whether a valid consent to a search has occurred is a factual one, there are no per se rules governing when a consent to search is valid or invalid. But courts have identified numerous factors which will be given great weight in making such a determination.

---

[148] Johnson v Zerbst, 304 US 458, 464 (1938).

[149] 412 US 218 (1973).

[150] In *Schneckloth*, the Court emphasized that the defendant was not in custody at the time of the consent. But the Court followed *Schneckloth* in United States v Watson, 423 US 411 (1976), where the defendant *was* in custody.

[151] Schneckloth v Bustamonte, 412 US 218, 235-46 (1973).

[152] 68 NJ 349, 346 A2d 66 (1975).

[153] Henry v State, 621 P2d 1, 4 n 9 (Alaska 1980); *see also* State v Flores, 280 Or 273, 570 P2d 965 (1977); State v Knauber, 27 Ariz App 53, 550 P2d 1095 (1976).

As a general rule, the fact of custody does not render consent invalid per se, but it is an important factor.[154] Coercive factors, such as the display of weapons or use of handcuffs, may also be important.[155] The age and experience of the person who allegedly consented is relevant; mere submission is not consent.[156] Conduct leading to the consent is important as well; if, for example, the defendant has struggled with the police prior to being arrested and then is asked to consent, courts are unlikely to find waiver.[157] In short, virtually any factor which could affect an individual—for the ultimate question is subjective and not objective; may be relevant.

§3.31 Third-Party Consent

As recently as 60 years ago, the United States Supreme Court questioned whether a wife could consent to search of her husband's property, and thus waiver of his constitutional rights.[158] However, as the view that the protection afforded by the Fourteenth Amendment is protection of reasonable expectations of privacy has developed, it has become clear that a person who has joint control over an object or place may consent to search of it. In *United States v Matlock*,[159] the Court specifically held that the consent of one who possesses common authority over premises or effects is valid as against an absent, nonconsenting person with whom the authority is shared.

As a general rule, courts have upheld searches conducted with the consent of a defendant's spouse.[160] The mere fact that one spouse is incarcerated will not void his or her spouse's consent.[161] But if the spouse has left the family home, he or she cannot consent, because he or she no longer has common authority over the premises.[162] The mere fact that the consent is motivated by antagonism toward the other spouse is generally not sufficient to void consent,[163] but the

---

[154] People v Gonzales, 39 NY2d 122, 347 NE2d 575, 383 NYS2d 215 (1976); see generally Annot, *Validity of Consent to Search Given by One in Custody of Officers*, 9 ALR3d 858.

[155] Hubbard v Tinsley, 350 F2d 397 (10th Cir 1965).

[156] Johnson v United States, 333 US 10 (1948).

[157] People v Gonzales, 39 NY2d 122, 347 NE2d 575, 383 NYS2d 215 (1976).

[158] Amos v United States, 255 US 313 (1921).

[159] 415 US 164 (1974); *see also* Frazier v Cupp, 394 US 731 (1969) (joint owner of bag).

[160] *See, e.g.,* Coolidge v New Hampshire, 403 US 443 (1971); Bruce v State, 268 Ind 180, 375 NE2d 1042 (1978). See generally Annot, *Admissibility of Evidence Discovered in Search of Defendant's Property or Residence Authorized by Defendant's Spouse (Resident or Non-Resident)—State Cases*, 1 ALR4th 616.

[161] Collins v State, 548 SW2d 368 (Tex Crim App 1976), *cert denied*, 430 US 959 (1977).

[162] State v Verhagen, 86 Wis 2d 262, 272 NW2d 105 (1978); Bettuo v Pelton, 260 NW2d 423 (Iowa 1977).

[163] Commonwealth v Martin, 358 Mass 282, 264 NE2d 366 (1970); *but see* State v Gonzalez-Valle, 385 So 2d 681 (Fla Dist Ct App 1980).

police have no authority to search where they know the absent spouse objects to the search.[164] There is some authority for the proposition that not even a spouse may consent to the search of private, personal effects of the other spouse.[165]

Consent by a relative[166] or other resident of the household[167] may also be valid, for the crucial aspect of the inquiry is not the relationship between the defendant and the consenting party, but the consenting party's control over the area or property in question. Courts are generally unwilling to uphold consent to search given by a child, either because a child does not have the same degree of control and dominion over the residence as his or her parent, or because a child is incapable of informed consent.[168] While some courts uphold a parent's right to consent to search of a child's room[169] other courts have recognized that if the area is under the child's exclusive control, his or her expectation of privacy should be constitutionally protected.[170] Those courts have held that a parent cannot consent to search of a child's personal effects.[171]

Finally, a landlord[172] or hotel keeper cannot consent unless the defendant has abandoned the property[173] or been evicted,[174] or the lease has expired.[175]

---

[164] People v Elliot, 77 Cal App 3d 673, 144 Cal Rptr 137 (1978).

[165] State v Evans, 45 Hawaii 622, 372 P2d 365 (1962); State v McCarthy, 260 Ohio St 2d 87, 269 NE2d 424 (1971).

[166] Bumper v North Carolina, 391 US 543 (1968); see generally, Annot, *Admissibility of Evidence Discovered in Search of Property or Residence by Defendant's Adult Relative or Other Than Spouse*, 4 ALR4th 196.

[167] Butler v Commonwealth, 536 SW2d 139 (Ky 1976) (babysitter could give valid consent); see generally Annot, *Admissibility of Evidence Discovered in Search of Defendant's Property or Residence Authorized by Domestic Employee or Servant*, 99 ALR3d 1232.

[168] State v Garcia, 478 Pa 406, 387 A2d 46 (1978); State v Malcolm, 58 Del 1, 203 A2d 270 (1964); see generally Annot, *Admissibility of Evidence Discovered in Search of Defendant's Property or Residence Authorized by Defendant's Minor Child*, 99 ALR3d 598.

[169] *See, e.g.,* State v Kelly, 284 NW2d 236 (Iowa 1979).

[170] *See, e.g.,* People v Flowers, 23 Mich App 523, 179 NW2d 56 (1970).

[171] *In re* K, 24 Cal 3d 395, 595 P2d 105, 155 Cal Rptr 671, *cert denied,* 444 US 973 (1979); see generally, Annot, *Admissibility of Evidence Discovered in Search of Defendant's Property or Residence Authorized by Defendant's Adult Relative Other Than Spouse—State Cases,* 4 ALR4th 196.

[172] Chapman v United States, 365 US 610 (1965); People v Reed, 393 Mich 342, 224 NW2d 867, *cert denied,* 422 US 1044 (1975).

[173] Abel v United States, 362 US 217 (1960); Jones v State, 332 So 2d 615 (Fla 1976).

[174] State v Carrillo, 26 Ariz App 113, 546 P2d 838 (1976).

[175] State v O'Bryan, 96 Idaho 548, 531 P2d 1193 (1976); see generally Annot, *Admissibility of Evidence Discovered in Warrantless Search of Rental Property Authorized by Lessor of Such Property—State Cases,* 2 ALR4th 1173.

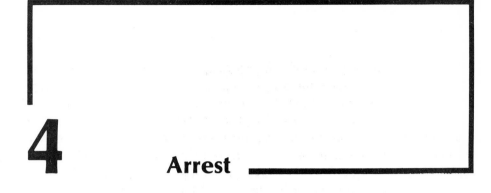

4 Arrest

§4.01 Constitutional Significance of Arrest

No other procedural step in the criminal process has the immediate and direct impact of an arrest. Certainly, an arrest is far more instrusive than an investigative stop, or even a search of one's home.[1] It has been noted that:

Being arrested and held by the police, even if for a few hours, is for most persons, awesome and frightening. Unlike other occasions on which one may be authoritatively required to be somewhere, or do something, an arrest abruptly subjects a person to constraint, and removes him to unfamiliar and threatening surroundings. Moreover, this exercise of control over the person depends not just upon his willingness to comply with an impersonal directive, such as a summons or a subpoena, but on

---

[1] United States v Watson, 423 US 411, 428 (1976) (Powell, J concurring).

an order which a policeman issues on the spot and stands ready then and there to back up with force.[2]

Because of the wholesale deprivation of liberty which occurs when a person is arrested, a discrete body of law has developed which governs precisely when a person may be arrested. Once a person is arrested, a plethora of constitutional rights and, in most jurisdictions, statutory rights attach.[3]

The procedures which govern arrest, and the lawfulness of an arrest, the subject of this chapter, are important for several reasons. First, if a person is arrested unlawfully, evidence gathered pursuant to a search incident to arrest is likely to be excluded from evidence as fruit of the illegal arrest.[4] Physical evidence[5] or oral evidence[6] obtained during an illegal arrest may be excluded. Second, a person who is in custody may not be interrogated unless informed of the rights to remain silent and to have a lawyer.[7]

The traditional rule is that the manner in which a person is brought before a criminal court is no bar to the jurisdiction of the court to try him or her. Thus, a person cannot challenge the right of a court to hear a criminal case merely because the person was illegally arrested.[8] Of course, if a person were brought before a court in a particularly brutal fashion, or in flagrant disregard of civil rights, it is possible that a court could refuse to consider the case on due process grounds.

§4.02   When Arrest Occurs

To the defense lawyer or the prosecutor, the fact of an arrest may be a double-edged sword. Police officers may, if they have obtained valuable evidence without advising a person of *Miranda* rights, take the position that the person interrogated was not "in custody" at the time. On the other hand, if valuable evidence was uncovered at a time the police had probable cause to arrest but no probable cause to search, they may seek to justify the search by claiming that the defendant was under arrest at the time of the search.

State and lower federal courts have frequently framed precise definitions of arrest, requiring (1) an intention to arrest, (2) accompanied by actual or constructive restraint of the person to be arrested, (3) with the understanding of

---

[2] United States v Watson, 423 US 411, 446 (1976) (Marshall, J, dissenting), quoting with approval Model Code of Pre-Arraignment Procedure, commentary at 290-91 (1975).

[3] See generally **ch 5**.

[4] See **ch 15**.

[5] *See e.g.,* Davis v Mississippi, 394 US 721 (1969).

[6] Wong Sun v United States, 371 US 471 (1963).

[7] Miranda v Arizona, 384 US 436 (1966).

[8] *See, e.g.,* State v Keating, 108 NH 402, 326 A2d 684 (1967).

the arrested person that he or she is being arrested.[9] There is no requirement that the word *arrest* be used at all. The conflicting interests of both police officers and defendants have led courts, however, to place little reliance on subjective police perceptions of when an arrest occurs. The validity of an arrest is judged by an objective standard rather than by resort to the personal motives of the police officer.[10] The crucial factor in determining whether an arrest has occurred is the facts, which must be viewed objectively by the reviewing court. A court may find that a person has been arrested even though the police officers did not intend to make the arrest.[11]

The United States Supreme Court has held that a person has been arrested for Fourth Amendment purposes when, in view of all circumstances surrounding the incident, a reasonable person would have believed that he or she was not free to leave.[12] Even though there is no physical restraint, circumstances such as the threatening presence of several officers, the display of a weapon by an officer, or even "the use of language or tone of voice indicating that compliance with the officer's request might be compelled" could constitute an arrest.[13] Thus, for example, the United States Supreme Court has found an arrest to have occurred where four officers surrounded a person's bed at 4:00 a.m. and questioned him.[14]

When an arrest occurs, in sum, generally turns on the facts of each case.

§4.03 Constitutional Necessity for Arrest Warrant—In General

The privacy of a citizen's home may not be invaded by a search conducted by state officers, unless a judicial officer has issued a warrant, except in a few narrow circumstances. Since the Fourth Amendment speaks to both searches and seizures, and since arrest is not only a seizure, but is in fact a far greater intrusion on an individual than a mere search of a home, it seems logical that arrest should not occur, except in extraordinary circumstances, without the imprimatur of a neutral judicial officer.

However, as Justice Powell once noted in discussing this question, "logic sometimes must defer to history and experience".[15] At common law, arrest without a warrant was permitted for all felonies, and for any misdemeanors

---

[9] *See, e.g.*, Commonwealth v Avery, 365 Mass 59, 309 NE2d 497 (1974); State v Hutton, 108 NH 279, 235 A2d 117 (1968).

[10] United States v McCambridge, 551 F2d 865 (1st Cir 1977).

[11] United States v Taylor, 471 F2d 848, 851 (9th Cir 1972), *cert denied*, 409 US 1130 (1973).

[12] United States v Mendenhall, 446 US 544 (1980).

[13] *Id* 554.

[14] Orozco v Texas, 394 US 324 (1969).

[15] United States v Watson, 423 US 411, 428 (1976) (Powell, J, concurring).

which occurred in the presence of the officer which were a breach of the peace.[16] This view was accepted by all the American colonies, and, in fact, is substantially intact in all the 50 states.[17] The fact that a warrant was presumptively required for a less intrusive search, but not for a more intrusive arrest, was recognized by state courts of last resort in the nineteenth century. Illustrative is the opinion of the Massachusetts Supreme Judicial Court in *Rohan v Sawin*:[18]

> It has been sometimes contended that an arrest of this character, without a warrant, was a violation of the great and fundamental principles of our national and state constitutions, forbidding unreasonable searches and arrest, except by warrant founded upon a complaint made under oath. These provisions doubtless had another and different purpose, being in restraint of general warrants to make searches, and requiring warrants to issue only upon a complaint made under oath. They do not conflict with the authority of constables or other peace officers or private persons under proper limitations to arrest without warrant those who have committed felonies. The public safety, and the due apprehension of criminals, charged with heinous offenses, imperiously require that such arrests should be made without warrant by officers of the law.[19]

The rule that the Fourth Amendment did not require that arrests be made with a warrant remained virtually unchallenged until 1976; it was often assumed that the common law rule, allowing warrantless arrest, for a felony or for a breach of peace in the officer's presence, established the constitutional standard.[20] In 1976, in *United States v Watson*,[21] the United States Supreme Court specifically held that while there is a constitutional preference for warrants, there is no constitutional bar to a warrantless arrest for a felony, if the arrest occurs in a public place. The Court reasoned that the universally accepted practice of allowing warrantless arrest, and the possibility of a great volume of litigation should the court hold that arrest without warrant is impermissible, both militated against such a requirement. Justice White, writing for the majority, noted that police officers might "find it wise to seek arrest warrants where practicable . . . [since]their judgments about probable cause may be more readily accepted where backed by a warrant issued by a magistrate.[22]

---

[16] 4 W. Blackstone, Commentaries 289 (U Chi ed 1979).

[17] United States v Watson, 423 US 411, 421-22 (1976).

[18] 59 Mass 281 (1850), *quoted with approval in* United States v Watson, 423 US 411 (1976); *see also* Holley v Mix, 3 Wend 350 (NY Sup Ct 1829); State v Brown, 5 Del (1 Harr) 505 (Ct Gen Sess 1853).

[19] Rohan v Sawin, 59 Mass 281, 284-85 (1850).

[20] *See, e.g.,* Henry v United States, 361 US 98, 100 (1959).

[21] 423 US 411 (1976).

[22] *Id* 423.

The fact that a warrant is not required for routine arrests is illustrated by the general rule that an arrest made pursuant to an invalid warrant is sufficient if the police officer has probable cause to arrest.[23]

§4.04 — Arrest in a Person's Home

While the common law rule permitting warrantless arrest for a felony or for a misdemeanor which occurred in the officer's presence was universally accepted at common law before and after the ratification of the United States Constitution, the question of whether a warrant was needed to arrest a person in his home divided both courts and commentators. Lord Coke thought a warrant was required to effect a forcible arrest for felony in a person's home,[24] while Blackstone thought entry without a warrant under such circumstances was permissible.[25] The law in the various states was in similar disarray until 1980 when the United States Supreme Court held in *Payton v New York*[26] that the Fourth Amendment prohibits the police from making a warrantless and nonconsensual entry into a person's home in order to make a warrantless felony arrest. The Court reasoned that if warrantless search of a home for weapons or contraband is unlawful because of the breach of privacy of the home, a warrantless entry of a home for a *person* must be unlawful since it is inherent in such an entry that a search for the suspect may be required before the suspect can be apprehended.[27] The decision represents a judgment that the need of law enforcement officers to make arrests promptly, while sufficient to allow warrantless arrests in public places, is simply not sufficient to justify breach of the sanctity of the home.

Of course, a person may not evade arrest by simply retreating from a public place where police officers have observed him or her. In such a case, the hot pursuit exception to the warrant requirement allows the police to pursue the person to be arrested into the home.[28] The mere fact that the police have a valid arrest warrant does not mean that they may enter the home of a third party where they suspect the person to be arrested may be.[29] In such circumstances,

---

[23] *See, e.g.*, United States v White, 342 F2d 379 (4th Cir), *cert denied*, 382 US 871 (1965).

[24] E. Coke, Institutes 177 (Brooke ed 1797).

[25] 4 W. Blackstone, Commentaries 289 (U Chi ed 1979):

And, in case of felony actually committed, or a dangerous wounding whereby felony is like to ensue, he may upon probable suspicion arrest the felon; and for that purpose is authorized (as upon a justice's warrant) to break open doors, and even to kill the felon if he cannot otherwise be taken. . .

[26] 445 US 573 (1980),

[27] *Id.*

[28] United States v Santana, 427 US 38, 43 (1976).

[29] Steagald v United States, 101 S Ct 1642 (1981).

the police must have probable cause to believe the person to be arrested is in the place to be searched, and must either obtain a warrant before entering or be prepared to justify their warrantless entry.[30]

§4.05   Probable Cause for Arrest

While the Fourth Amendment's strict requirement that all searches, absent extraordinary circumstances, be conducted with a warrant is not applicable to arrests, the requirement that arrests, like searches, be made only on probable cause is.[31] It is, of course, true that seizures less intrusive than full custodial arrests, such as investigative stops or frisks for weapons, may be made on less than probable cause;[32] but the constitutional requirement of probable cause for arrest has not been weakened by the looseness with which the warrant requirement has been applied to arrests. There is a judicial preference for arrest by warrant, and, as in the area of search, in a doubtful case, an arrest pursuant to warrant may be sustained while a warrantless arrest may fail.[33]

The definition of probable cause for arrest is basically the same as the definition of probable cause for search; it is a standard on the basis of which ordinary people and not legal technicians act.[34] As Justice Powell recently noted, the United States Supreme Court has never attempted a more precise definition of probable cause to arrest than that established in *Carroll v United States*:[35] "facts and circumstances . . . such as to warrant a man of [reasonable] prudence and caution in believing that the offense has been committed, and, of course, that the person to be arrested was the offender."[36] A police officer may, as a general rule, consider any evidence in determining whether probable cause exists. The rules applicable to probable cause established by information received from informers are, of course, applicable to arrest warrants[37] and arrests without warrant[38] as well as to search warrants and searches without warrant. The decisions of courts defining what establishes probable cause for search are equally applicable to probable cause for arrest and, thus, are not treated in detail in this section.[39]

---

[30] *Id.*

[31] *See, e.g.,* Dunaway v New York, 442 US 200 (1979).

[32] See **ch 2**.

[33] United States v Watson, 423 US 411 (1976).

[34] See **§3.07**.

[35] 267 US 132, 161 (1925).

[36] United States v Watson, 423 US 411, 431 n 4 (1976) (Powell, J, concurring).

[37] Whitely v Warden, 401 US 560 (1971).

[38] Draper v United States, 358 US 307 (1959).

[39] The law relating to probable cause is discussed in **§§3.07-3.11**.

A police officer may make a valid arrest if informed by another police officer that the other officer has probable cause or a warrant to arrest. But if the second officer, acting on the first officer's information, makes the arrest, and the first officer either does not have probable cause or the warrant is invalid, the arrest made by the second officer is unlawful.[40] While the first officer's information can provide probable cause for the arresting officer, mere conveyance of information cannot insulate the initial determination of probable cause from judicial scrutiny.

---

[40] Whitely v Warden, 401 US 560, 568 (1971).

5

Right of Persons in Custody

Right to Counsel

§5.01   General Consideration of Right to Counsel

The Sixth Amendment to the United States Constitution provides, in relevant part, "In all criminal prosecutions, the accused shall enjoy . . . the assistance of counsel for his defense." Most state constitutions contain similar provisions.

Over the past 50 years, the United States Supreme Court has gradually expanded the reach of the Sixth and Fourteenth Amendments to ensure that individuals do not face loss of their liberty without being able to properly defend themselves against charges made against them. In 1938, the Court held that the Sixth Amendment required that individuals be provided counsel in all federal criminal cases, regardless of their ability to pay.[1] In 1942, relying on the due process clause of the Fourteenth Amendment, the Court held that counsel had to be afforded state court defendants, whether or not they could afford to pay for counsel, if a failure to provide counsel would lead to a denial of fundamental fairness.[2] In 1963, the Court held that the equal protection clause of the Fourteenth Amendment required states to provide counsel for indigents for at least one appeal.[3] Later that year, the Court held that the Sixth Amendment was applicable to the states, and that, therefore, the states had to afford indigent defendants counsel at least in felony prosecutions.[4] The right to counsel was eventually extended to include all misdemeanor cases which actually result in imprisonment.[5] Some states have constitutionally required that counsel be afforded individuals in all cases which could result in imprisonment.[6] Obviously, the Sixth Amendment right to counsel available to nonindigents is at least as broad as the right available to indigents.[7]

---

[1] Johnson v Zerbst, 304 US 458 (1938).

[2] Betts v Brady, 316 US 455 (1942).

[3] Douglas v California 372 US 353 (1963).

[4] Gideon v Wainwright, 372 US 335 (1963).

[5] Argersinger v Hamlin, 407 US 25 (1972); Scott v Illinois, 440 US 367 (1979).

[6] See, e.g., NH Const pt I, art 15.

[7] See, e.g., Wainwright v Torna, 102 S Ct 1300 (1982).

The first United States Supreme Court cases concerning the right to counsel did not consider a specific time at which the right to counsel attached, but rather were concerned with the right to counsel at the time of trial.[8] Eventually, the Supreme Court adopted a rule that the right to counsel attaches at least "at or after the time judicial proceedings have been instituted against a defendant,"[9] and is applicable at each "critical stage" of the criminal prosecution.[10] But the Court has also held that a right to counsel may exist prior to the institution of judicial proceedings, to ensure that identification procedures are conducted fairly ensure that the defendant's privilege against self-incrimination is fully effectuated.

Federal constitutional decisions in this area have not been consistent, and much litigation concerning the precise time at which the right to counsel attaches has occurred at both the state and federal level.[11]

§5.02   Right to Counsel During Police Investigation of Crime

The concept of a Sixth Amendment right to counsel which existed apart from the traditional adversary process was first suggested by the United States Supreme Court in *Massiah v United States*.[12] In *Massiah*, the defendant was indicted, retained a lawyer, pleaded not guilty, and was released on bail. A codefendant decided to cooperate with the government, and allowed a radio transmitter to be installed in his car. He engaged the defendant in an incriminating conversation which government agents recorded. The Court held that the defendant's Sixth Amendment right to counsel had been violated because the federal agents had deliberately elicited from the defendant incriminating statements without the presence of his counsel. The *Massiah* holding was expanded in *Escobedo v Illinois*,[13] a case in which police officers detained a defendant, interrogated him, and refused to allow him to consult with counsel. The specific holding suggested that a right to counsel attached at the time of interrogation:

> We hold, therefore, that where, as here, the investigation is no longer a general inquiry into an unsolved crime, but has begun to focus on a particular suspect, the suspect has been taken into police custody, the

---

[8] *See, e.g.*, Betts v Brady, 316 US 455 (1942); Gideon v Wainwright, 372 US 335 (1963).
[9] Brewer v Williams, 430 US 387, 398 (1977).
[10] Mempa v Rhay, 398 US 128 (1967).
[11] See §14.02.
[12] 377 US 201 (1964).
[13] 378 US 478 (1964).

police carry out a process of interrogations that lends itself to eliciting incriminating statements, the suspect has requested and been denied an opportunity to consult with his lawyer, and the police have not effectively warned him of his absolute constitutional right to remain silent, the accused has been denied the "Assistance of Counsel," in violation of the Sixth Amendment to the Constitution as "made obligatory on the states by the Fourteenth Amendment," and that no statement elicited by the police during the interrogation may be used against him at a criminal trial.[14]

The *Massiah* and *Escobedo* holdings are not particularly important in present practice, because only two years later, in *Miranda v Arizona*,[15] the United States Supreme Court held that the Fifth Amendment to the federal Constitution affords a criminal defendant an absolute right to remain silent at the time of arrest, and that to fully effectuate this right, the arrested person has a constitutional right to an attorney while undergoing custodial interrogation. Moreover, in the years since *Escobedo* was decided, at least a plurality of the Court has assented to the proposition that *Escobedo* was not decided to vindicate the right to counsel as such, but, like *Miranda*, to guarantee full effectuation of the privilege against self-incrimination.[16] The Court has limited *Escobedo* to its facts.[17]

Nevertheless, the decisions of the Court in recent years concerning when the right to counsel attaches are far from a model of clarity. While Justice Stewart wrote for a five-man majority in *Kirby v Illinois*[18] that the initiation of judicial proceedings "marks the commencement of the criminal prosecutions which alone the explicit guarantees of the Sixth Amendment are applicable," the conflicting rules of law set out in later decisions led him to candidly admit in *Brewer v Williams*[19] that:

There has occasionally been a difference of opinion within the court as to the peripheral scope of this constitutional right. But its basic contours, which are identical in state and federal contexts are too well established to require extensive elaboration here. Whatever else it may mean, the right to counsel guaranteed by the Sixth and Fourteenth Amendments means at least that a person is entitled to the help of a lawyer at or after the time that judicial proceedings have been instituted against him —whether by

[14] *Id* 490-91.
[15] 384 US 436 (1966).
[16] Kirby v Illinois, 406 US 682, 689 (1972).See §14.02.
[17] Kirby v Illinois, 406 US 682, 689 (1972).
[18] 406 US 682,690 (1972).
[19] 430 US 387, 398 (1977).

way of formal charge, preliminary hearing, indictment, information or arraignment.

A number of courts have seized on the language in *Kirby* and *Brewer* to conclude that the Sixth Amendment right to counsel does not attach until the institution of formal criminal proceedings.[20] It is probably more correct to state, however, that as a matter of federal constitutional law, the right to counsel attaches at the time an accused is charged or at the time of custodial detention.[21] A few courts have interpreted their state constitutional guarantees of the right to counsel to provide a right to counsel to persons accused of crime prior to institution of formal charges.[22]

Why does it matter when the right to counsel attaches if the Fifth Amendment provides an accused with a right to have an attorney present before being subjected to interrogation? The answer is that the accused may be subjected to procedures which will make the accused the source of real physical evidence without interrogation. Obviously, since the Fifth Amendment is a testimonial privilege, an accused would have no Fifth Amendment right to refuse to allow himself or herself to become the source of real physical evidence. An attorney may ensure that any tests done are done fairly. The most common situation concerns identification procedures, such as line-ups. Because identification evidence is considered so important by a jury and because it is so inherently unreliable and subject to suggestion, the United States Supreme Court has developed specific and complex rules involving the right to counsel and establishing other prophylactic procedures. Often, too, an attorney may be able to help an accused decide whether to participate in voluntary testing.

---

[20] State v Bourgeois, 388 So 2d 359 (La 1980); State v McDowell, 301 NC 279, 271 SE2d 286 (1980) *cert denied*, 101 S Ct 1731 (1981); State v Delahunt, 401 A2d 1261 (RI 1979).

[21] Hummel v Commonwealth, 219 Va 252, 247 SE2d 385 (1978), *cert denied*, 440 US 935 (1979); United States v Nashataway, 571 F2d 71, 75 (1st Cir 1975); United States v Zazzarra, 626 F2d 135 (9th Cir 1980); *see also* People v Samuels, 49 NY2d 218, 400 NE2d 1344, 424 NYS2d 892 (1980):

The defendant is entitled to counsel at all critical stages of the criminal proceeding. The right to counsel attaches, of course, once the criminal proceeding has commenced. But it may attach at an earlier stage if there has been significant judicial activity. Thus, for example, a court order permitting the police to bring the defendant to the scene of the crime or direct that he appear at a line-up may be sufficient to trigger the right to counsel even though the criminal action may not have finally commenced. See §14.02.

[22] *See, e.g.*, Blue v State, 558 P2d 636 (Alaska 1977); People v Jackson, 391 Mich 323, 217 NW2d 22 (1974). Cases in which state courts have held that state law or a state constitutional guarantee requires that counsel be afforded persons prior to the institution of formal charges are collected at 46 U Mo L Rev 148, 152 n 35 (1977).

§5.03 Waiver of Right to Counsel by Arrestee

Traditionally, the United States Supreme Court has held that the prosecution bears a heavy burden when it asserts that an accused has waived the right to counsel. The Court has never departed from the rule that the prosecution must prove the "intentional relinquishment of a known right or privilege."[23] In determining whether an accused has waived counsel, courts are constitutionally required to indulge in every reasonable presumption against waiver.[24]

The Supreme Court has held that whether a constitutionally acceptable waiver has occurred in a given case depends on the particular facts and circumstances of the case, and that an explicit waiver of counsel by the defendant is not necessary to support a waiver.[25] The *totality of the circumstances* approach is sufficient even if the accused is a juvenile.[26]

The factors considered significant by the United States Supreme Court are illustrated by its decision in *Brewer v United States*.[27] In that case, a defendant was arrested for murder in one city, arraigned, had an attorney appointed, and was then transported to another city. His appointed attorney did not accompany the defendant, who was an escaped mental patient, to the second city, but instructed the transporting police officers not to interrogate the defendant until he had consulted with his attorney in the second city. The police promised that they would not. During the trip, the defendant stated on several occasions that he would tell the police everything once he saw his attorney. Knowing that the defendant was exceedingly religious, and addressing him as "Reverend," one policeman attempted to convince the defendant to tell them where the victim's body was. Since it was snowing and the officers told him the body might never be found and was entitled to a Christian burial, the defendant finally told them. A bare majority of the Court held that there had been no valid waiver of counsel because the defendant's statement that he would tell the police everything after speaking with his attorney was the "clearest expression" that he wished to consult with counsel before interrogation. Moreover, the Court noted that the police did not preface their interrogation by explicitly reminding the defendant of his right to counsel and by obtaining a waiver.

---

[23] Brewer v Williams, 430 US 387 (1977); Johnson v Zerbst, 304 US 458 (1938).

[24] Brewer v Williams, 430 US 387 (1977); Brookhart v Janis, 384 US 1 (1966).

[25] North Carolina v Butler, 441 US 369 (1979). The Pennsylvania Supreme Court has held that the Pennsylvania constitution requires that an in-custody defendant expressly waive the right to counsel, rejecting *North Carolina v Butler*. Commonwealth v Bussey, 486 Pa 221, 404 A2d 1309 (1979).

[26] Fare v Michael C, 442 US 707 (1979).

[27] Brewer v Williams, 430 US 387 (1977); Brookhart v Janis, 384 US 1 (1966).

Brewer was decided by a bare plurality of the Court. Perusal of the majority and dissenting opinions reveals the need to characterize evidence which appears in a cold transcript to reach a result. This at least suggests that the Supreme Court's approach to waiver is flawed by the degree of subjectivity it permits.

The New York Court of Appeals has held, based on the guarantees of counsel and due process of law and the privilege against self-incrimination expressed in the New York constitution, that once a lawyer has entered a criminal proceeding representing a defendant in connection with criminal charges under investigation, the defendant may not waive the right to counsel in the absence of the lawyer.[28] The court has recognized that the presence of counsel is a more effective safeguard against an involuntary waiver of counsel than a mere written or oral warning in the absence of counsel. Perhaps even more importantly, the presence of the lawyer serves to limit the risk of "inaccurate, sometimes false and inevitably incomplete"[29] descriptions of events. As Chief Judge Breitel noted in *People v Hobson*,[30] "Surely the need for and right to a lawyer at an identification line-up is insignificant compared to the need in an ensuing interrogation."

The logic of the New York rule has led to its acceptance by a number of jurisdictions.[31] A few other jurisdictions have, in order to fully effectuate the right to counsel or the privilege against self-incrimination, required that a voluntary express or oral waiver of the right to counsel be obtained once the right is asserted.[32]

§5.04 Effect of Denial of Right to Counsel

If evidence is obtained from a person in violation of a Sixth Amendment right to counsel, the evidence will be excluded from the prosecution's case at trial.[33]

---

[28] People v Hobson, 39 NY2d 479, 348 NE2d 894, 384 NYS2d 419 (1976); *see also* People v Arthur, 22 NY2d 325, 239 NE2d 537, 292 NYS2d 663 (1968).

[29] People v Hobson, 39 NY2d 479, 348 NE2d 894, 384 NYS2d 419 (1976).

[30] 39 NY2d 479, 485, 348 NE2d 894, 899, 384 NYS2d 419, 423 (1976).

[31] *See, e.g.,* Commonwealth v Hilliard, 471 Pa 318, 370 A2d 322 (1977); *but see* Commonwealth v Rigler, 488 Pa 441, 412 A2d 846 (1980); State v Johns, 185 Neb 590, 177 NW2d 580 (1970); State v Marx, 113 Ariz 71, 546 P2d 807 (1976); Shouse v State, 231 Ga 716, 203 SE2d 537 (1974); *cf* United States v Thomas, 474 F2d 110 (10th Cir 1977) (violation of ethics, when defendant questioned without lawyer, but no constitutional violation); State v Haynes, 288 Ore 59, 602 P2d 272 (1979) (refusing to follow New York rule, but holding that police cannot rely on waiver of counsel when they refuse to admit counsel).

[32] *See, e.g.,* State v Nash, 119 NH 728, 407 A2d 365 (1979); Commonwealth v Bussey, 486 Pa 221, 404 A2d 1309 (1979).

[33] Brewer v Williams, 430 US 387 (1977); Escobedo v Illinois, 378 US 478 (1964).

Privilege against Self-Incrimination

§5.05 Nature and Source of Privilege against Self-Incrimination

Perhaps no aspect of Anglo-American criminal jurisprudence is more universally known than the privilege against being compelled to give testimony against oneself. The privilege is deeply rooted in the Anglo-American legal tradition; almost 90 years ago, Justice Brown wrote:

> The maxim nemo tenetur seipsum accusare had its origin in a protest against the inquisitorial and manifestly unjust methods of interrogating accused persons which [have] long obtained in the continental system, and until the expulsion of the Stewarts from the British throne in 1688 and the erection of additional barriers for the people against the exercise of arbitrary power [were] not uncommon even in England. . . . So deeply did the iniquities of the ancient system impress themselves on the minds of the American colonists that the states, with one accord, made a denial of the right to question an accused a part of their fundamental law, so that a maxim, which in England was a mere rule of evidence, became clothed in this country with the impregnability of a constitutional enactment.[34]

The Fifth Amendment to the United States Constitution provides, in relevant part, no person "shall be compelled. . . to be a witness against himself."[35] Virtually every state constitution contains a similar guarantee. The Fifth Amendment was held to be binding on the states in 1964.[36]

It is important to remember that the fundamental purpose of the privilege is as much to protect the integrity of the criminal justice system as to protect the dignity of the individual. Even Dean Wigmore, a critic of judicial expansion of the scope of the privilege, once noted:

> Any system of administration which permits the prosecution to trust habitually to compulsory self-disclosure of a source of proof must itself suffer morally thereby. The inclination develops to rely mainly upon such evidence, and to be satisfied with an incomplete investigation of the

---

[34] Brown v Walker, 161 US 591, 596-97 (1896).

[35] US Const amend V.

[36] Malloy v Hogan, 378 US 1 (1964), overruling Twining v New Jersey, 211 US 78 (1908). Even before the Fifth Amendment was held applicable to the states, federal courts were willing to consider claims by state prisoners that their confessions were involuntarily obtained, and generally held that admission of an involuntary confession violated a defendant's right to due process of law. *See, e.g.*, Brown v Mississippi, 297 US 278 (1936).

other sources. The exercise of the power to extract answers begets the
forgetfulness of the just limit of that power. The simple and peaceful
process of questioning, breeds a readiness to resort to physical force and
torture. If there is a right to an answer, there soon seems to be a right
to the expected answer —that is, to a confession of guilt. Thus, the
legitimate use runs into the unjust abuse. Ultimately, the innocent are
jeopardized by the encroachment of a bad system. Such seems to have
been the course of experience in those legal systems where the privilege
was not recognized.[37]

§5.06   When Privilege against Self-Incrimination Is Applicable

Literally read, the Fifth Amendment prohibition against self-incrimination
would seem to apply only to the physical act of testifying in court.[38] However, as
early as 1897, the United States Supreme Court, considering a federal case in
which the privilege was applicable, held that issues relating to the voluntariness
of an extrajudicial confession were controlled by the Fifth Amendment.[39] The
Court's holding thus suggested that the Fifth Amendment privilege is applicable
when an individual is questioned by a police officer. Whatever doubt existed
was resolved in 1966 in *Miranda v Arizona*[40] when the Court specifically held
that the privilege applies to informal compulsion by law enforcement officers
during in-custody questioning. The Court reasoned that:

We are satisfied that all the principles embodied in the privilege apply
to informal compulsion exerted by law enforcement officers during in-
custody questioning. An individual swept from familiar surroundings,
into police custody, surrounded by antagonistic forces, and subjected to
the techniques of persuasion [of police officers]. . . cannot be otherwise
than under a compulsion to speak. As a practical matter, the compulsion
to speak in the isolated setting of the police station may well be greater than

---

[37] 8 Wigmore on Evidence §309 (3d ed 1940). Indeed, continental law developed in the
seventeenth century an elaborate system to judicially determine when investigation had proceeded
far enough to permit a recalcitrant defendant to be tortured. See A.L. Lowell, The Judicial Use
of Torture, 11 Harv L Rev 220 (1898).

[38] The Fifth Amendment states, in relevant part, "No person . . . shall be compelled in any
criminal case to be a witness against himself."

[39] Bram v United States, 168 US 532 (1897).

[40] 384 US 436 (1966).

in courts or other official investigations, where there are often impartial observers to guard against intimidation or trickery.[41]

However, the Fifth Amendment privilege is a testimonial privilege; the Supreme Court has stated in no uncertain terms that the privilege does not protect an accused from being the source of real physical evidence.[42]

§5.07 Procedural Requirements of *Miranda v Arizona*

Few cases have had the impact on American jurisprudence of *Miranda v Arizona*.[43] In *Miranda*, the United States Supreme Court fully expressed the premise that scholars had long asserted: that the constitutional rights afforded those accused of crime are of very limited value if confined only to the courtroom itself.   The fulcrum of the Court's decision was the secrecy and intrinsic compulsion of police interrogation. The Court reasoned that the process of custodial interrogation itself creates inherently compelling pressures which may undermine a person's will to resist and compel the person to speak when he or she would otherwise not do so. To counteract these pressures, the Court held that an arrested person must be fully apprised of constitutional rights, and that the exercise of those rights must be scrupulously honored. While asserting that it was not purporting to establish rigid requirements which would place the states in a constitutional straitjacket, the Court stated that the following procedures must be observed:

1. A person in custody who is to be subjected to interrogation must first be informed in clear and unequivocal terms of the right to remain silent

2. The warning of the right to remain silent must be accompanied by an explanation that anything said can and will be used in court

---

[41] Id 461.

[42] Schmerber v California, 384 US 757 (1966); *see also* United States v Wade, 388 US 218 (1967) (defendant required to wear disguise and speak words used by perpetrator of crime); Gilbert v California, 388 US 263 (1967) (defendant required to submit to taking of handwriting exemplars); United States v Dionisio, 410 US 19 (1973) (defendant required to provide handwriting exemplars); see §§5.19-5.21.

[43] 384 US 436 (1966).

3. An individual held for interrogation must be clearly informed of the right to consult with a lawyer, and that if the person cannot afford a lawyer, one will be appointed if he or she wishes

Despite the Court's disclaimer that it did not intend to place the states in a constitutional straightjacket, the *Miranda warnings*, generally given using the terms set out by the United States Supreme Court, have been adopted by police departments and law enforcement agencies throughout the country. The Court has specifically held, however, that the warnings need not consist of verbatim repetition of the words of the *Miranda* opinion, as long as the words used are sufficient to advise a person of his or her rights.[44]

In the course of the majority opinion, Chief Justice Warren attempted to set down specific rules for treatment of interrogation which later becomes the subject of further litigation. The Court stated that if the accused indicates prior to or during questioning the wish to remain silent, the interrogation must cease.[45] If interrogation occurs without an attorney after the defendant has been warned of his or her rights, a "heavy burden" rests on the prosecution to show that the defendant knowingly and intelligently waived the right to counsel. The Court stated that any evidence that an accused was tricked or cajoled into a waiver will show that the privilege against self-incrimination was not validly waived. Silence after an accusation made by the police would, of course, not be admissible.

The *Miranda* rules did not displace the body of law holding that a criminal defendant's constitutional rights are violated when a confession is involuntarily obtained.[46] They simply established objective procedures to act as a counterweight to the inherent pressures of interrogation. The fact that the police in interrogating a defendant comply with the dictates of *Miranda* does not automatically mean that a defendant's confession is voluntary and, therefore, admissible. The former inquiry is objective; the latter is subjective, and depends on the individual. For example, a defendant may have his *Miranda* rights fully explained to him, but not understand English.[47] The fact that the warnings were given would not make his statement admissible. While the fact that the *Miranda* warnings have been given a defendant is relevant in determining whether a statement is voluntary, it is never controlling.[48]

---

[44] California v Prysock, 453 US 355 (1981).
[45] Miranda v Arizona, 384 US 436 (1966).
[46] *See, e.g.*, Reck v Pate, 367 US 433 (1961); Davis v North Carolina, 384 US 737 (1966).
[47] Miranda v Arizona, 384 US 436 (1966).
[48] *Id.*

§5.08 When Person Is in Custody within Meaning of *Miranda*

The decision in *Miranda* was explicitly made applicable only to *custodial interrogation*.[49] The United States Supreme Court attempted to define custodial interrogation by stating that a custodial interrogation occurs if the interrogation is at a police station or if it occurs when a person is deprived of freedom in a significant way. A few years after *Miranda* was decided, the Court held in *Orozco v Texas*[50] that a defendant who was questioned in his bedroom by four policemen at 4:00 in the morning had undergone custodial interrogation since he was not free to leave the bedroom.

However, since the decision in *Orozco*, the Court has limited the situations it considers to be custodial interrogation. It has been said to have occurred only in those cases in which there was some actual limitation on a defendant's physical freedom.[51] In *Beckwith v United States*,[52] for example, the Court held that a custodial interrogation requiring *Miranda* warnings did not occur when an individual was interrogated in his home, and then voluntarily drove to his office and was again interrogated by Internal Revenue Service agents who considered him the focus of their investigation. While the Supreme Court has never explicitly so stated, its analysis of whether interrogation is custodial seems to be, like the question of when an arrest occurs, an issue to be determined by an objective standard. It is generally held that a suspect is subjected to custodial interrogation if actually in custody or deprived of freedom in a significant way, or if questioned reasonably believing himself or herself to be so detained.[53] At first blush, a rule that establishes an objective standard for the determination of when interrogation is custodial would seem inimical to the purpose of *Miranda*, which is to provide some counterweight to the coercion of police interrogation. But *Miranda* establishes no more than a prophylactic rule applicable to all cases. While *Miranda* warnings may not be required in a noncustodial interrogation, statements made by an accused may still, depending on the accused's subjective

---

[49] Miranda v Arizona, 384 US 436, 477 (1966).

[50] 394 US 324 (1969).

[51] *See, e.g.*, Oregon v Mathiason, 429 US 492 (1977) (no custodial interrogation where defendant voluntarily came to the police station, was interrogated by the officer with the door to the interrogation room closed, but was allowed to leave after the interview); United States v Mandujano, 425 US 564 (1976) (no custodial interrogation when one who was the focus of an investigation appeared before a grand jury).

[52] 425 US 341 (1976).

[53] People v Arnold, 66 Cal 2d 438, 426 P2d 515, 58 Cal Rptr 115 (1967); People v Rodney P, 21 NY2d 1, 233 NE2d 255, 286 NYS2d 225 (1967); United States v Irion, 482 F2d 1240 (9th Cir), *cert denied*, 414 US 1026 (1973); United States v Del Soccorro Castro, 573 F2d 213 (5th Cir 1976); see generally Annot., *What Constitutes Custodial Interrogation Within Rule of Miranda v Arizona Requiring That Suspect Be Informed of His Federal Constitutional Rights Before Custodial Interrogation*, 31 ALR3d 565.

state of mind, be inadmissible because they are involuntary. As the Court noted in *Beckwith*:

> We recognize, of course, that non-custodial interrogation might possibly, in some situations, by virtue of some special circumstances, be characterized as one where the behavior of . . . law enforcement officials was such as to overbear the defendant's will to resist and bring about confessions not freely self-determined. . . . When such a claim is made, it is the duty of an appellate court, including this court, to examine the entire record and make an independent determination of ultimate issue of voluntariness.[54]

§5.09 Applicability of *Miranda* to Minor Offenses

In the first few years after *Miranda*[55] was decided, numerous state courts, faced with what they perceived as an impossible burden on legitimate law enforcement, developed a rule that *Miranda* is not applicable to minor offenses such as motor vehicle offenses and public drunkenness.[56] The United States Supreme Court has, of course, never countenanced such a position. The decisions of the state courts are best understood in their factual contexts; most of the broad language in these opinions derives from the fact that the questioning challenged occurred when the person had merely been "stopped" and not "arrested," a distinction the United States Supreme Court has explicitly recognized.[57] The true rule appears to be that questioning by a police officer after a limited stop for a traffic offense, or, for that matter, for any offense, does not require that *Miranda* warnings be afforded the persons stopped, since the interrogation is not truly custodial.[58]

---

[54] Beckwith v United States, 425 US 341, 347-48 (1976).

[55] 384 US 436 (1966).

[56] *See, e.g.*, State v Bliss, 238 A2d 848 (Del Super Ct 1968) (*Miranda* does not apply to traffic offenses because there are "practical reasons" why motor vehicle offenses should be treated differently from other offenses); State v Desjardins, 110 NH 511, 272 A2d 599 (1970) (*Miranda* not required when a person is arrested for drunkenness, since prosecution for drunkenness is a sometime thing, such an arrest is as much for the protection of the defendant as for the protection of the public, an arresting officer can release a person arrested for the offense without charging him or her, and traditionally the offense has been considered to be under the jurisdiction of justices of the peace); McCrary v State, 529 SW2d 467, 474 (Mo Ct App 1975) (there is no requirement that *Miranda* warnings be given to individuals who are arrested for traffic offenses); see generally, Annot, *Right of Motorist Stopped by Police Officer for Traffic Offense to be Informed at That Time of His Federal Constitutional Rights Under Miranda v Arizona*, 25 ALR3d 1076.

[57] *See, e.g.*, Dunaway v New York, 442 US 200 (1979); Terry v Ohio 392 US 1 (1968).

[58] *See, e.g.*, United States v Chase, 414 F2d 780 (9th Cir), *cert denied*, 396 US 920 (1969); United States v LeQuire, 424 F2d 341 (5th Cir 1970).

Application of any other rule could lead to results inconsistent, if not with the letter, certainly with the spirit of *Miranda*.[59]

§5.10 When Person Is Interrogated within Meaning of *Miranda*

Chief Justice Warren stated in *Miranda*[60] that an individual must be informed of both the right to counsel and the privilege against self-incrimination before being subjected to custodial interrogation. However, the United States Supreme Court has recognized that the oppressive atmosphere of police custody could well create the same type of pressure on an accused as traditional questioning. In *Rhode Island v Innis*,[61] the Court held that the *Miranda* safeguards come into play whenever a person is "exposed to either express questioning or its functional equivalent."[62] The Court held that a person who was arrested for armed robbery alleged to have been committed with a shotgun was not interrogated when one policeman driving the arrestee from an area near the scene of the crime to the police station stated to a policeman who was traveling with him, in the defendant's hearing, that handicapped children played in the area in which the defendant was arrested, and that it would be too bad if a handicapped child found the gun and hurt herself. The Court established a general rule that interrogation under *Miranda* "refers not only to express questioning, but also to any words or actions on the part of the police (other than those normally attendant to arrest and custody) that the police should know are reasonably likely to elicit an incriminating response from the suspect."[63]

The Court emphasized that by *incriminating response* it meant any response made by a defendant, whether inculpatory or exculpatory, that the prosecution might seek to introduce at trial.[64] Because the thrust of *Miranda* is to establish

---

[59] *See, e.g.*, McCrary v State, 429 SW2d 467 (Mo Ct App 1975), which held *Miranda* not required when defendant interrogated after arrest for traffic offense, even though he was handcuffed at the time of the interrogation, because the interrogation related solely to the traffic offense.

[60] Miranda v Arizona, 384 US 436 (1966).

[61] 446 US 291 (1980).

[62] *Id* 300-01.

[63] *Id* 301.

[64] *Id* 301 n 5. The significance of this aspect of the Court's holding lies in the fact that any statement made by a defendant - inculpatory, exculpatory, or irrelevant - can be damning if shown to be false by the prosecution.

objective standards for reducing the coercion inherent in custody, the intent of the police, while relevant, is not controlling.[65]

On the facts before it in *Innis*, a divided Court held that the statement made by the police officer was not one which the police should have known would be reasonably likely to elicit an incriminating response from the suspect.

§5.11 Interrogation After Invocation of Fifth Amendment Rights

In the course of its decision in *Miranda*,[66] the United States Supreme Court held that, if interrogation continues after an accused is advised of his or her rights, the prosecution bears a "heavy burden" and must show that the defendant knowingly and intelligently waived the privilege against self-incrimination. If the arrested person invokes constitutional rights, and indicates the wish to avoid further interrogation, the Court stated that the right to cut off questioning must be "scrupulously honored." However, the invocation of rights by a defendant does not necessarily prohibit all further questioning. In *Michigan v Mosley*,[67] a person arrested for robbery, after having been advised of his *Miranda* rights, decided he wished to exercise his right to remain silent. The police stopped questioning him. Two hours later, a second policeman, after once again advising the defendant of his rights, began questioning him about an unrelated murder. The Court held that the statements made by the defendant in the second interrogation were admissible. Justice Stewart reasoned that:

> To permit the continuation of custodial interrogation after a momentary cessation would clearly frustrate the purposes of *Miranda* by allowing repeated rounds of questioning to undermine the will of the person being questioned. At the other extreme, a blanket prohibition against the taking of voluntary statements or a permanent immunity from further interrogation regardless of the circumstances, would transform the *Miranda* safeguards into wholly irrational obstacles to legitimate police investigative activity, and deprive suspects of an opportunity to make informed and

---

[65] *See generally* People v Lynes, 49 NY2d 286 401 NE2d 405, 409, 425 NYS2d 295, 299 (1980):

> The test in such situations cannot be whether, through hindsight, the defendant professes to believe the police intended to provoke an incriminating response. Were that so, virtually any police remark, no matter how innocuous, would constitute an interrogation as long as it was followed by an inculpatory statement. Instead, fully sensitive to the defendant's rights, yet using an objective standard, the trial judge must determine whether the defendant's statement can be said to have been triggered by police conduct which should reasonably have been anticipated to evoke a declaration from the defendant.

[66] Miranda v Arizona, 384 US 436 (1966).

[67] 423 US 96 (1976).

> intelligent assessments of their interests. Clearly . . . *Miranda* can [not] be read to create a per se proscription of indefinite duration upon any further questioning by any police officer on any subject once the person in custody has indicated a desire to remain silent.[68]

The Court held that a case-by-case approach would be taken to determine when a waiver was voluntary.

However, the fact that allowing interrogation after a defendant has declined to speak to police officers will doubtless create a pressure to confess, coupled with the uncertainty which the test enunciated by the United States Supreme Court creates, has led the California Supreme Court to fashion a rule based on the California constitution that is more liberal and far easier to apply than *Mosley*. The California Supreme Court has held that once a defendant invokes the privilege against self-incrimination, and determines that he or she wishes no further questioning to occur, the police cannot lawfully subject the suspect to further interrogation even if they give further *Miranda* warnings.[69] The California Supreme Court reasoned that the difficulty in determining whether, in any case coming before a court, a defendant had validly waived Fifth Amendment rights would very likely give rise to a body of law "rivaling that which exists in the area of search and seizure,"[70] and thus waste scarce judicial resources. Moreover, although not specifically mentioned by the California Supreme Court, it seems apparent that the dicta in *Mosley* to the effect that adoption of a per se rule would "deprive suspects of an opportunity to make informed and intelligent assessments of their interests" is without logical foundation; certainly, the police can act on exculpatory information and the accused may introduce exculpatory evidence into court; *Miranda* forbids only use of statements which would not benefit the defendant.

§5.12 Permissible Violation of *Miranda* Rescue Doctrine

Prior to the decision of the United States Supreme Court in *Miranda*,[71] the California Supreme Court had held that where the paramount purpose of interrogation is to save a life, police officers are justified in not impeding their rescue effort by informing a defendant of the right to counsel and the privilege

---

[68] *Id* 102-03.

[69] People v Pettingill, 21 Cal 3d 231, 578 P2d 108, 145 Cal Rptr 861 (1978) (decision based on California constitutional privilege against self-incrimination).

[70] *Id* at 250, 578 P2d at 120, 145 Cal Rptr at 873, *quoting with approval* People v Disbrow, 16 Cal 3d 101, 111, 545 P2d 272, 278, 127 Cal Rptr 360, 366 (1976).

[71] *Miranda v Arizona*, 384 US 436 (1966).

against self-incrimination.[72] Since the *Miranda* decision, intermediate California courts have recognized a *rescue exception* to the requirements of *Miranda*.[73] Those courts hold that the police may interrogate an individual after invocation of *Miranda* if there is an urgent need to save the life of a victim, there is no other way to save the life, and rescue is the primary (although it need not be the only) motive of the police.

California, of course, has declined to follow *Michigan v Mosley*,[74] which held that interrogation after invocation of a person's Fifth Amendment right is permissible in some circumstance, and the cases decided by the California courts would, on their facts, go no further than *Mosley*. Whether the California cases merely represent an exception to the narrow California rule that all interrogation after invocation of Fifth Amendment rights is prohibited[75] or whether the cases stand for a developing exception to *Miranda* is in doubt.

§5.13   Interrogation After Invocation of Right to Counsel

Despite the fact that the United States Supreme Court held in *Michigan v Mosley*[76] that a statement by an arrestee to the effect that he does not wish to speak further with the police does not render inadmissible any voluntary statement he later makes as a result of further interrogation, a different result may obtain if a defendant asserts the right to counsel. As Justice White noted in his concurring opinion in *Mosley:*

> the reasons to keep the lines of communication open between the authorities and the accused when the accused has chosen to make his own decisions are not present when he indicates instead that he wishes legal advice with respect thereto. The authorities may then communicate with him through an attorney. More to the point, the accused having expressed his own view that he is not competent to deal with the authorities without legal advice, a later decision at the authorities' insistence to make a statement without counsel's presence may properly be viewed with skepticism.[77]

---

[72] People v Modesto, 62 Cal 2d 436, 42 Cal Rptr 417, 398 P2d 753 (1965).

[73] See People v Dean, 39 Cal App 3d 875, 114 Cal Rptr 555 (1974); People v Riddle, 83 Cal App 3d 563, 148 Cal Rptr 170 (1978); People v Willis, 104 Cal App 3d 433, 163 Cal Rptr 718, cert denied 101 S Ct 222 (1981). See Annot., *Concern for Possible Victim (Rescue Doctrine) as Justifying Violation of Miranda Requirements*, 9 ALR 4th 595.

[74] 423 US 96 (1976).

[75] People v Pettingill, 21 Cal 3d 231, 145 Cal Rptr 861, 578 P2d 108 (1978).

[76] 423 US 96 (1976).

[77] *Id* 110 n 2 (White, J, concurring).

In *Brewer v Williams*,[78] the Court held that the police had violated a defendant's right to counsel where the defendant stated that he would tell the police "everything" after consulting with an attorney and the police continued to interrogate him before he saw his attorney. Despite the fact that *Williams* was based on the factual circumstances of the waiver, given the disfavor with which the Court views interrogation of an accused who has professed a desire to be represented by counsel, and the logical distinction between interrogation of an accused who does not wish to speak, but does feel the need for an attorney, and an accused who believes he or she cannot proceed at all without the assistance of counsel, a number of courts have held that *Miranda* imposes a per se rule prohibiting the police from interrogating a defendant further once the right to counsel has been invoked until an attorney is provided.[79]

The decisions of the United States Supreme Court do not seem to support quite so broad a rule; but it is clear that a waiver of the right to counsel must be not only voluntary, but knowing and intelligent. The United States Supreme Court has specifically held that an accused who expresses the desire to deal with the police only through counsel "is not subject to further interrogation until counsel has been made available to him, unless the accused himself initiates further communications, exchanges or conversations with the police."[80]

§5.14 Use at Trial of Statement Obtained in Violation of *Miranda*

If a person is subjected to custodial interrogation without being afforded the warnings required by *Miranda v Arizona*,[81] the prosecution will not be able to introduce those statements in its case-in-chief. However, in *Harris v New York*,[82] the United States Supreme Court held that if a defendant testifies in a way inconsistent with the statement given to the police before being advised of *Miranda* rights, the prior statement may, if its truthworthiness satisfies traditional legal standards, be admitted for impeachment purposes. The Court reasoned that a defendant who testifies should be expected to undergo the usual techniques used in the adversary process to determine the truth: "The shield provided by *Miranda* cannot be perverted into a license to use perjury by way of a defense, free from the risk of confrontation with prior inconsistent

---

[78] Brewer v Williams, 430 US 398 (1977). See §5.03.

[79] People v Grant, 45 NY2d 358, 380 NE2d 257, 408 NYS2d 429 (1978); Ochoa v State, 573 SW2d 796 (Tex Crim App 1978): we read this language in Miranda literally; where a defendant indicates in any way that he desires to invoke his right to counsel, interrogation must cease.

[80] Edwards v Arizona, 451 US 477, 484-85 (1981).

[81] Miranda v Arizona, 384 US 436 (1966).

[82] 401 US 222 (1971).

utterances."[83] But the Court has also held that any statement introduced by the government, whether in its case-in-chief or for impeachment purposes, must be voluntary,[84] since any use by the government of an involuntary statement would constitute a denial of due process of law.

The *Harris* rationale was expanded in *Oregon v Hass.* [85]   In that case, the defendant was afforded his *Miranda* rights, requested an attorney and had his request denied, and was further questioned. He made statements which were inconsistent with his statements at trial. Reasoning again that the Fifth Amendment did not provide a license for perjury, the Court held that the statements made by the defendant were admissible for impeachment purposes.

Harris v New York and its progeny have been the subjects of much negative comment.[86] Commentators have pointed out the obvious inability of a jury to distinguish evidence admitted for impeachment purposes only and the burden placed on the exercise of the right to testify by the fact that, if the right is exercised, the government will be permitted to exploit its own illegality.[87] A few courts have, on state constitutional grounds, refused to follow *Harris.*[88] Perhaps the most carefully reasoned opinion of a court declining to follow *Harris* is that of the California Supreme Court in *People v Disbrow.*[89] In rejecting the use of evidence obtained in violation of *Miranda* for impeachment purposes, Justice Mosk recognized that a jury would be likely to view the prior inculpatory statement as evidence of guilt and not merely as evidence which would impeach the defendant, even with a limiting instruction. More importantly, the Court recognized that "to permit admission leaves little or no incentive for police to comply with *Miranda* requirements."[90] Obviously, a cynical police officer could even advise a defendant that anything said while not advised of rights is inadmissible, and encourage the defendant to speak. The California Court

---

[83] *Id* 226.

[84] Mincey v Arizona, 437 US 385 (1978). *See also* Estelle v Smith, 451 US 454 (1981) (statements made to psychiatrist at court ordered competency examination, before defendant was advised of his right to remain silent, could not be used by prosecution in penalty phase of murder trial.)

[85] 420 US 714 (1975).

[86] See, e.g., Dershowitz & Ely, *Harris v New York: Some Anxious Observations on the Candor of the Emerging Nixon Majority*, 80 Yale LJ 1198 (1971).

[87] *See, e.g.*, Commonwealth v Woods, 455 Pa 1, 7, 312 A2d 357, 360 (1973) (*Harris*-type use of constitutionally infirm confessions forces on an accused a Hobson's choice, since either an accused must forgo the right to testify, or the accused must risk the sure and devastating prejudice occasioned by the prosecution's use of impermissibly obtained evidence at the critical rebuttal state).

[88] People v Disbrow, 16 Cal 3d 101, 545 P2d 272, 127 Cal Rptr 360 (1976); State v Santiago, 53 Hawaii 254, 492 P2d 657 (1971); Commonwealth v Tripplitt, 462 Pa 244, 341 A2d 62 (1975).

[89] 16 Cal 3d 101, 545 P2d 272, 127 Cal Rptr 360 (1976).

[90] *Id* at 113, 545 P2d at 279, 127 Cal Rptr at 1367.

reasoned that admission of the evidence could make the court a party in a lawless venture.

§5.15 Retrospective Application of *Miranda*

The decision of the United States Supreme Court in *Miranda v Arizona*[91] is applicable only to cases tried after the date of that decision.[92]

§5.16 Requirement That Confessions Be Voluntarily Made

Miranda[93] simply establishes a broad prophylactic rule: a defendant who is arrested must be advised of federal constitutional rights. If the defendant is not advised of federal constitutional rights, any incriminating statement made cannot be introduced against him or her.

The fact that a defendant has been advised of rights, however, does not automatically make an admission admissible. While the *Miranda* warnings are evidence that a defendant knowingly and voluntarily waived the constitutional privilege against self-incrimination, they are not conclusive.[94] No statement made by a criminal defendant may be admitted against him or her for any purpose unless the statement was "voluntarily" made.

At common law, involuntary confessions were generally excluded on evidentiary grounds; it was believed that the confessions were so unreliable that the jury should not consider them.[95] The United States Supreme Court slowly recognized that an involuntary confession violated a federal defendant's Fifth Amendment privilege against self-incrimination,[96] and a state court defendant's right to due process of law.[97] Eventually, of course, the Fifth Amendment was held applicable to the states.[98]

The standard of whether a confession is voluntary is easily quantified:

---

[91] 384 US 436 (1966).

[92] Johnson v New Jersey, 384 US 719 (1966).

[93] Miranda v Arizona, 384 US 436 (1966).

[94] Brown v Illinois, 422 US 590 (1975).

[95] *See, e.g.*, State v Howard, 17 NH 171, 182 (1845):

Confessions, obtained in the hope of favor, or by the fear of punishment, are inadmissible. . . . The evidence is rejected because the inducement may have led to a false statement, and the confession is, therefore, not entitled to credit; and not because the public faith is pledged by means of the promise.

[96] Bram v United States, 168 US 532 (1897).

[97] Brown v Mississippi, 297 US 278 (1936).

[98] Malloy v Hogan, 378 US 1 (1964).

The ultimate test remains that which has been the only clearly established test in Anglo Saxon law for over 200 years: the test of voluntariness. Is the confession a product of an essentially free and unconstrained choice by its maker? If it is, if he has willed to confess, it may be used against him. If it is not, if his will has been overborne, and his capacity for self-determination critically impaired, the use of his confession offends due process.[99]

In determining whether a statement is voluntary, a court must make an independent determination of the disputed facts.[100]

§5.17 —Proof

While the standard by which the voluntariness of a confession is judged is easily stated, whether a particular confession is voluntary is not so easily determined. The question of whether a confession is voluntarily made must be answered on the facts of each case. No single fact is dispositive. Determination of whether a statement is involuntarily made "requires more than a mere color matching of cases."[101] Whether a waiver of Fifth Amendment rights has occurred is determined on the basis of the totality of the circumstances surrounding the waiver.[102] Any number of factors may bear on an alleged involuntary confession, including: an illegal arrest,[103] whether the defendant has been abused,[104] threatened,[105] or held incommunicado;[106] the accused's age;[107] and the accused's physical condition.[108] More important than the type of proof, however, is the quantum required to prove a confession voluntary. In *Lego v Twomey*,[109] the United States Supreme Court held that the Fifth Amendment required only that the states prove a confession, alleged to be involuntary

---

[99] Columbe v Connecticut, 367 US 568, 602 (1961); Mincey v Arizona, 437 US 385 (1978); Beecher v Alabama, 408 US 234 (1972); Brooks v Florida, 389 US 413 (1967); Davis v North Carolina, 384 US 737 (1966); Reck v Pate, 367 US 433 (1961).

[100] Mincey v Arizona, 437 US 385 (1978); *see also* Stroble v California, 343 US 181 (1952).

[101] Mincey v Arizona, 437 US 385, 401 (1978), citing Reck v Pate, 367 US 433, 442 (1961).

[102] North Carolina v Butler, 441 US 369 (1979).

[103] Mincey v Arizona, 437 US 385 (1978).

[104] Lee v Mississippi, 332 US 742 (1948).

[105] Payne v Arkansas, 356 US 560 (1958).

[106] David v North Carolina, 384 US 737 (1966).

[107] Crooker v California, 357 US 433 (1958).

[108] Jackson v Denno, 378 US 368 (1964).

[109] 404 US 477 (1972).

by a defendant, to be voluntary by a preponderance of the evidence. The Court specifically noted that the states could, if they wished, adopt a higher standard based on their own law. In the years since *Lego* was decided, a substantial minority of jurisdictions have accepted the United States Supreme Court's invitation, and held that when a defendant claims that a confession was involuntarily made, the government must prove its voluntariness beyond a reasonable doubt.[110] The reasoning of these jurisdictions is well expressed by the New Hampshire Supreme Court:

> [The reasonable doubt standard] was the standard adopted by the Supreme Court of the United States in *Bram* v *United States*.
>
> The danger of admitting involuntary confessions is as great now as it was then and the policy considerations for excluding confessions which are involuntary are as compelling now as they ever were. There is always the danger that a defendant's involuntary confession will be admitted against him. The preponderance test does not provide a sufficient safeguard against that danger. The adoption of the preponderance standard would amount to a determination that it is no more serious for an involuntary confession to be admitted than it is for a voluntary one to be excluded.
>
> A confession is a special type of evidence. Its acceptance basically amounts to conviction. . . . The stakes are too high, and the risk of error are too great to permit a determination of admissibility to be decided by a balance of probabilities.[111]

Even courts which accept the mere preponderance standard often establish particular rules which make it difficult for the prosecution to prove a confession voluntary. Several jurisdictions have held that at a hearing on a motion to suppress a confession as involuntary, all material witnesses must be called by the state or their absence satisfactorily explained in order for the state to meet its burden.[112]

---

[110] *See, e.g.*, Priest v State, 386 NE2d 686 (Ind 1979); State v Tanguay, 388 A2d 913 (Me 1978); State v Phinney, 117 NH 145, 370 A2d 1153 (1977); State v Kelley, 61 NJ 283, 294 A2d 41 (1972); People v Valerius, 31 NY2d 51, 286 NE2d 254, 334 NYS2d 871 (1972); State v Stumes, 90 SD 382, 241 NW2d 587 (1976); *cf* State v Espinosa, 109 RI 221, 283 A2d 465 (1971) (clear and convincing evidence required); People v Jiminez, 21 Cal 3d 595, 580 P2d 672, 147 Cal Rptr 172 (1978).

[111] State v Phinney, 117 NH 145, 146-47, 370 A2d 1153, 1154 (1977).

[112] Smith v State, 256 Ark 67, 505 SW2d 504 (1974); Stevens v State, 228 So 2d 888 (Fla 1969); People v Armstrong, 51 Ill 2d 471, 282 NE2d 575 (1972); Mercer v State, 237 Md 479, 206 A2d 797 (1965); *see also* Farr v State, 519 SW2d 876 (Tex Crim App 1975).

§5.18 Comment on Silence of Defendant

If a defendant is arrested and advised of his rights in accordance with *Miranda v Arizona* [113] and then remains silent, due process forbids cross-examination on the silence of the defendant if he testifies at trial.[114] In *Doyle v Ohio*,[115] for example, the defendants were arrested and advised of their rights and said nothing. At trial, both defendants testified, and their testimony suggested that they had been innocent victims of circumstances when arrested in a compromising position. The United States Supreme Court held that due process forbade cross-examining the defendants about the fact that they had not told the arresting officers the exculpatory story to which they had testified. Mr. Justice Powell, writing for a six-judge majority, reasoned that:

> Silence in the wake of these [*Miranda*] warnings may be no more than the arrestee's exercise of these *Miranda* rights. Thus, every post-arrest silence is insolubly ambiguous because of what the state is required to advise the person arrested. Moreover, while it is true that the *Miranda* warnings contain no express assurance that silence will carry no penalty, such assurance is implicit to any person who receives the warnings. In such circumstances, it would be fundamentally unfair and a deprivation of due process to allow the arrested person's silence to be used to impeach an explanation subsequently offered at trial.[116]

Of course, failure to speak in circumstances prior to a person's being taken into custody may be admissible.[117] Thus, where an individual stabbed another, killing him, and ran from the scene, and testified at trial that he had stabbed the victim but acted in self-defense, the United States Supreme Court held that there was no constitutional violation when the prosecutor cross-examined the defendant on his failure to report the stabbing or advance his exculpatory explanation to the arresting officers. The Court emphasized that, "in the absence of the sort of affirmative assurances embodied in *Miranda*, we do not believe it violates due process of law for a state to permit cross-examination as to post-arrest silence when a defendant chooses to take the stand."[118]

---

[113] 384 US 436 (1966).

[114] United States v Hale, 422 US 171, 180 (1975) (based on supervisory power over federal courts); *see also* Doyle v Ohio, 426 US 610 (1976).

[115] 426 US 610 (1976).

[116] *Id* 617-18.

[117] Jenkins v Anderson, 447 US 231 (1980); Anderson v Charles, 447 US 404 (1980).

[118] Fletcher v Weir, 102 S Ct 1309, 1312 (1982).

Physical Tests of Arrested Persons

§5.19 Physical Testing and Privilege against Self-Incrimination

Dean Wigmore believed that the Fifth Amendment privilege against self-incrimination barred the government only from compelling the accused to provide evidence from his own lips.[119] While not taking quite so narrow a view, the United States Supreme Court as well as state courts have generally held that the Fifth Amendment offers no protection against compulsion to submit to fingerprinting, blood tests,[120] physical exhibition,[121] or being required to provide handwriting[122] or voice exemplars.[123] The accused may even be required to speak words spoken by a criminal if the purpose of the speech is merely voice identification and not communication.[124] The United States Supreme Court has explicitly held, "The privilege is a bar against compelling communications or testimony, but that compulsion which makes an accused the source of real physical evidence does not violate it."[125]

However, the Court has also recognized that no precise formulation could ever encompass all the possibilities which exist. The Court has been careful to note that if the test seemingly directed to obtaining physical evidence, such as a polygraph test which measures changes in body function during interrogation, is actually directed toward eliciting responses which are essentially testimonial, the evidence will be excluded if the defendant invokes the Fifth Amendment privilege.[126]

§5.20 Right to Counsel During Physical Testing

While the right to counsel may attach when one is arrested or charged,[127] it is settled that a person has the right to counsel only during critical stages

---

[119] 8 Wigmore on Evidence §2263 (McNaughton rev 1940).

[120] Schmerber v California, 384 US 757 (1966); State v Arsenault, 115 NH 109, 336 A2d 244 (1975).

[121] Gilbert v California, 388 US 263 (1967).

[122] *Id.*

[123] United States v Dionisio, 410 US 19 (1973).

[124] United States v Wade, 388 US 218 (1967).

[125] Schmerber v California, 384 US 757 (1966).

[126] *Id.*

[127] See §14.02.

of the prosecution.[128] A *critical stage* of the prosecution has been defined by the United States Supreme Court as a stage of the prosecution at which the accused's rights may be affected.[129] In general, the Supreme Court has been loath to hold that an accused has the right to counsel's presence during physical testing, since there is no lawyer's decision to be made; an accused has no legal right to refuse the physical test and the presence of an attorney will not affect the fairness of the physical test, since the test can be easily reproduced. Thus, the Court has held that a person is not entitled to the presence of counsel at the time of the taking of a handwriting exemplar since: "If for some reason an unrepresentative exemplar is taken, this can be brought out and corrected through the adversary process process at trial, since the accused can make an unlimited number of additional exemplars for analysis by government and defense handwriting experts."[130]

There are two important exceptions to the rule that the right to counsel is not implicated when an accused is subjected to physical testing. The first and most important concerns the viewing of an accused for purposes of identification by victims of or witnesses to a crime. Because identification procedures can easily be manipulated, purposely or unintentionally, by the police, the United States Supreme Court has established a complex thicket of rules concerning when line-ups may be conducted with or without counsel.[131]

A second and somewhat less important exception to the general rule concerns a defendant's right to counsel when requested to submit to a physical test to determine the amount of alcohol in his or her system, usually pursuant to a state's *implied consent law* which requires a defendant to take the test or face automobile operator's license revocation.[132] The majority of jurisdictions which have dealt with the issue have concluded that a person is not entitled to consult with an attorney prior to taking the test, either because the decision to be made is not a lawyer's decision,[133] or because the license revocation proceedings will

---

[128] Mempa v Rhay, 389 US 128 (1967).

[129] *Id.*

[130] Gilbert v California, 388 US 263, 267 (1967); *see also* United States v Dionisio, 410 US 19 (1973).

[131] See **ch 6**.

[132] Such statutes, which exist in most American jurisdictions, generally provide that a person who operates a motor vehicle on the highways of the state is deemed to have consented to chemical tests to determine the amount of drugs or alcohol in the person's blood. If the person refuses to take such a test, his or her license to operate a motor vehicle is revoked for a stated period of time. See generally Annot, *Suspension or Revocation of Driver's License for Refusal to Take Sobriety Test*, 88 ALR2d 1064.

[133] *See, e.g.*, Harlan v State, 113 NH 194, 308 A2d 856 (1973).

be civil and not criminal and, therefore, the decision to take the test cannot be a critical stage of a criminal proceeding.[134]

However, a growing number of jurisdictions have recognized that the severe penalty for refusal to take the test, loss of an operator's license, makes the proceeding quasi-criminal in nature, and more importantly, that the test itself may be introduced in evidence in a criminal trial. Such courts have, for these reasons, held that a person should be entitled to consult with counsel once arrested, prior to making the decision whether to take the test.[135] Because alcohol dissipates rapidly in the human body, the privilege to consult with counsel cannot extend so far as to palpably impair or nullify the procedure requiring a driver to take the test or lose the license;[136] if the arrested person cannot reach his or her attorney within a few hours of arrest, such courts hold that the person must make the decision alone.[137]

§5.21   Physical Testing and Right of Person Arrested to Be Free from Unreasonable Searches

Undeniably, once arrested and taken into official custody, an individual's reasonable expectation of privacy, and thus his or her Fourth Amendment rights, shrink dramatically. The United States Supreme Court has held, for example, that once arrested for even a traffic offense, an individual may be lawfully subjected to a full search.[138] But while an arrested person's Fourth Amendment rights may diminish after arrest, they do not disappear. The mere fact that a person has been arrested does not mean that he or she may be forced to submit to any search a police officer desires.[139] The Supreme Court has pointed out that the propriety of a particular law enforcement practice is judged by balancing its intrusion on the individual's Fourth Amendment

---

[134] *See, e.g.,* Campbell v State, 106 Ariz 542, 479 P2d 685 (1971); Deaner v Commonwealth, 210 Va 285, 170 SE2d 199 (1969); the cases are collected in Annot, *Chemical Sobriety Tests - Right to Counsel,* 97 ALR3d 852.

[135] *See, e.g.,* People v Gursey, 22 NY2d 224, 239 NE2d 351, 292 NYS2d 416 (1968); Prideaux v State Dept of Pub Safety, 310 Minn 405, 247 NW2d 385 (1976) (but not based on constitutional grounds); State v Fitzsimmons, 93 Wash 2d 436, 610 P2d 893 (1980); State v Welch, 135 Vt 316, 376 A2d 351 (1976); Hall v Secretary of State, 60 Mich App 431, 231 NW2d 396 (1975); *see also* Peterson v Dorius, 547 P2d 693 (Utah 1976), *legislatively overruled,* Beck v Cox, 597 P2d 1335 (Utah 1979); State v Bieter, 261 NW2d 828 (Iowa 1978); Sieguned v Curry, 40 Ohio App 2d 313, 319 NE2d 381 (1974).

[136] Hunter v Dorius, 23 Utah 2d 122, 458 P2d 877 (1969).

[137] *See, e.g.,* State v Braunsreither, 276 NW2d 139 (SD 1979).

[138] United States v Robinson, 414 US 218 (1973); *but compare* People v Longwill, 14 Cal 943, 538 P2d 753, 123 Cal Rptr 297, 753 (1975).

[139] United States v Mills, 472 F2d 1231 (DC Cir 1972).

interests against its promotion of legitimate governmental interests.[140] Even a person arrested and held in custody has some Fourth Amendment protection against an unreasonable governmental search.

Thus, courts have held that strip searches of prisoners arrested for noncriminal offenses are unreasonable,[141] and that even incarcerated prisoners cannot be subjected to body cavity searches after visits without some objective reason for the intrusion unless the search is pursuant to a neutral administrative plan.[142] The courts of appeal have developed strict and specific rules concerning when particularly intrusive searches at a border are permissible[143] despite the fact that warrantless border searches are permissible on the slightest suspicion.[144] Courts have recognized that blood tests and other physical tests implicate an arrested person's Fourth Amendment rights. The majority of recent reported cases concerning the manner in which an in-custody test is done relate to the manner of the test. Before the Fourth Amendment to the federal Constitution was held applicable to the states in 1961,[145] the United States Supreme Court held that a search which was so brutal as to shock the conscience violated a state court defendant's right to due process of law,[146] and occasionally, cases are still decided on that basis.[147] Since the Fourth Amendment's protection of a defendant against unreasonable search and seizure is far broader than that of the due process clause of the Fourteenth Amendment, most recent decisions have turned on the "reasonableness" of the search of the person under the Fourth Amendment.

A few general rules have developed. A test which does not involve an intrusion into a person's body, such as fingernail scrapings or taking hair samples, is generally considered so minimal as to be a reasonable search within the meaning

---

[140] Delaware v Prouse, 440 US 648 (1979).

[141] *See, e.g.*, Pinatti v White, 620 F2d 160 (7th Cir 1980).

[142] Bell v Wolfish, 441 US 520 (1979).

[143] *See, e.g.*, United States v Himmelwright, 551 F2d 991 (5th Cir 1977); *see also* United States v Guadalupe-Garza, 421 F2d 876 (9th Cir 1970) (government must have "real suspicion of criminal activity" in border search before strip search is permissible); United States v Sosa, 469 F2d 271 (9th Cir) *cert denied*, 410 US 910 (1972) (*clear indication of criminal conduct* required before body search is permissible at border).

[144] United States v Ramsey, 431 US 606 (1977); United States v Almeida-Sanchez, 413 US 266 (1973).

[145] *See* Mapp v Ohio, 367 US 643 (1961).

[146] Rochin v California, 342 US 165 (1952) (police saw defendant swallow capsules, jumped on him, unsuccessfully tried to extract capsules, then took him to hospital to have stomach pumped involuntarily). See generally, Annot, *Requiring Submission to Physical Examination and Tests as Violative of Constitutional Rights*, 25 ALR2d 1407; *but see* Hernandez v State, 548 SW2d 904 (Tex Crim App 1974) (while one officer held arrested defendant, other choked him to force him to spit out drugs; no constitutional violation since an officer has the authority to take "reasonable measures to make sure evidence is not destroyed").

[147] *See, e.g.*, State v Williams, 16 Wash App 2d 868, 560 P2d 1160 (1977) (defendant choked by two policemen attempting to obtain drugs from his mouth).

of the Fourth Amendment, with or without a warrant.[148] However, a search of a person's body must be conducted carefully and properly, or evidence obtained thereby will be excluded. In *Schmerber v California*,[149] the United States Supreme Court held that the extraction of blood from a defendant arrested and accused of crime was proper because the blood was taken in a medically proper way. The Court reasoned that a blood sample involves little risk of disease or pain, and is a type of procedure commonly experienced by most members of society. The Court noted that in the case before it, the defendant did not claim that he had any religious scruples against blood samples, and held that since blood alcohol levels diminish rapidly over time, such a warrantless intrusion was permissible.

By and large, courts have looked askance at warrantless searches of other parts of a person's body absent an emergency.[150] Illustrative is the opinion of the California Supreme Court in *People v Bracamonte*.[151] In that case, a police officer who had a search warrant for a defendant's person for violation of the narcotics laws saw her swallow two balloons shortly before her arrest. The defendant then remained with the officer while he searched her apartment pursuant to warrant. She was taken to a hospital, where the officer required that her stomach be pumped. The defendant refused to cooperate, or to drink an emetic. She was strapped to a table, and a tube was forced down her nasal passage as she struggled. After five minutes, the defendant agreed to drink the emetic solution because of the pain. She then vomited for a period of time. In holding that the search was unreasonable, the court was careful to point out that it did not countenance police-citizen struggles, but that there was no allegation of medical emergency and no reason why the police could not have obtained a warrant.

The true rule appears to be that a defendant has no right to destroy evidence and the fact of having secreted evidence in body cavities will not allow the defendant to keep it from the authorities. If the police obtain a warrant, a search of a defendant's body cavities by a physician, under proper medical conditions, is permissible.[152]

---

[148] *See, e.g.*, Cupp v Murphy, 412 US 291 (1973).

[149] 384 US 757 (1966).

[150] *See, e.g.*, State v Reynolds, 298 NC 380, 259 SE2d 843 (1979), *cert denied*, 446 US 941 (1980); Commonwealth v Tarver, 369 Mass 302, 345 NE2d 671 (1975); *cf* Cupp v Murphy, 412 US 291 (1973) (taking of fingernail scrapings proper even though no formal arrest).

[151] 15 Cal 3d 394, 540 P2d 624, 124 Cal Rptr 528 (1975).

[152] *See, e.g.*, State v Magress, 115 Ariz 317, 565 P2d 194 (1977) (anal search).

6

Identification Procedures

§6.01 Introduction

Exhibition of an accused for identification by a witness to or a victim of a crime has been repeatedly held not to violate the individual's Fifth Amendment privilege against self-incrimination because exhibition of an accused's person or measurement of unalterable physical characteristics is not a *communication* the privilege protects.[1] Yet, both the United States Supreme Court and state courts of last resort have spent a great deal of time and energy defining the manner and circumstances under which exhibition of an accused's person or likeness may occur. Relying on both the Sixth Amendment right to counsel[2] and the requirement of due process embodied in the Fourteenth Amendment to the United States Constitution,[3] the United States Supreme Court has fashioned a complex of rules which govern the manner and circumstances under which physical exhibition of an accused may occur. State courts have further modified and refined these rules, and in some circumstances, established more restrictive rules.

There are a number of reasons why courts have seen fit to impose constitutional strictures on identification procedures that they have not imposed on all other physical tests. The most important, perhaps, is the unreliability of such evidence. There is a vast reservoir of scholarly writing, much of it based on empirical evidence, which illustrates the unreliability of such evidence.[4] Yet, despite the fact that such evidence is objectively unreliable, it is common experience that jurors give great weight to it—that they frequently attach the same degree of weight to an eyewitness identification as to a confession. Indeed, medieval continental jurists developed a rule that a person could not be convicted of a capital crime unless his guilt was "clear as the noonday sun"—unless there were two eyewitnesses to the crime or a confession.

The consequences of error in identification are grave indeed. In addition to the obvious fact that an innocent person may be convicted, courts have pointed out that if an error is made at an identification proceeding, the real outlaw will remain at large.[5] Moreover, line-ups and other identification procedures traditionally occur in the privacy of a police station where an accused is alone and unable to control the manner in which the line-up is conducted, or to later reconstruct it. Unlike scientific tests, there is a human factor in such proceedings. While the Supreme Court has specifically stated in announcing the constitutionalization of identification procedures that it did not act because it believed that the risks of misidentifications are the result of intentional police

---

[1] *See, e.g.*, United States v Dionisio, 410 US 1, 9 (1973); Gilbert v California, 388 US 263 (1967); United States v Wade, 388 US 218 (1967) (accused may be required to exhibit himself wearing a disguise worn by the perpetrator of a crime, and may also be required to speak the words spoken by the perpetrator); Schmerber v California, 384 US 757 (1966).

[2] *See, e.g.*, United States v Wade, 388 US 218 (1967).

[3] *See, e.g.*, Manson v Brathwaite, 432 US 98 (1977).

[4] See, e.g., E. Loftus, Eyewitness Testimony 237, 247 (1979), *cited in*, Watkins v Sowders, 449 US 341 (1981) (Brennan, J, dissenting).

[5] *See, e.g.*, State v LeClair, 118 NH 214, 385 A2d 831 (1978).

misconduct, it has recognized that in the absence of legislative rules, there is no neutral way to conduct an identification procedure as there is to conduct, for example, a blood test for the presence of alcohol, and that identification procedures are inherently fraught with suggestiveness.[6]

The United States Supreme Court has relied on both the Sixth Amendment right to counsel and the Fourteenth Amendment guarantee of due process of law in attempting to eliminate some of the potential for unfairness in identification proceedings. The Fourteenth Amendment guarantee of due process in this context, as in other contexts, provides an "outer limit" beyond which the police may not go.

The primary safeguard established by the United States Supreme Court is the Sixth Amendment right to counsel. The Court has, in applying the right to counsel to such proceedings, reasoned that the business of prosecuting crime at present is far different from the way it was in colonial times, since the type of organized professional police force which exists today simply did not exist at that time. While in colonial times a defendant usually faced the witnesses and evidence against him for the first time at trial, modern law enforcement machinery establishes pretrial confrontations which may reduce the trial itself to a mere formality.[7] Moreover, the concept of a public prosecutor who has state officials at his or her command is a product of the continental system and was unknown to the English common law.[8] Under such circumstances, the attorney is as necessary at the identification proceeding as at the trial; as Justice Brennan pointed out:

> where so many variables and pitfalls exist, the first line of defense must be the prevention of unfairness and the lessening of hazards of eyewitness identification at the line-up itself. The trial which might determine the accused's fate may well not be that in the courtroom but that at the pretrial confrontation, with the State aligned against the accused, the witness the sole jury, and the accused unprotected against the overreaching, intentional or unintentional, and with little or no effective appeal from the judgment there rendered by the witness — "that's the man".[9]

---

[6] United States v Wade, 388 US 218, 235 (1967).
[7] Id.
[8] United States v Ash, 413 US 300 (1973).
[9] United States v Wade, 388 US 218, 235-236 (1967).

Corporeal Identification After Formal Charges Are Brought

§6.02   Identification After Charges in General

In a trilogy of cases decided in June, 1967, the United States Supreme Court first intimated that the suggestive nature of a pretrial identification proceeding was anything more than an issue to be argued to the jury. *United States v Wade*[10] and *Gilbert v California*[11] concerned line-ups conducted by the police after the defendant had been arrested and charged, and after the defendant had had counsel appointed, without notice to that counsel. In *Stovall v Denno*,[12] the police simply took a person they had arrested and whom they suspected of committing a crime to a hospital where the victim of the crime had been taken.

The Court established a general rule in *Wade* that a postindictment line-up is a *critical stage* of a criminal prosecution at which an accused is entitled to counsel. The Court reasoned that the Bill of Rights envisioned a far broader role for counsel than had existed in England at the time of the Revolution, and that at the time the Constitution was ratified, no *confrontation* would take place until trial, since there were no organized police forces or public prosecutors.[13] Thus, it was historically supportable to expand the right to counsel to pretrial proceedings which might well, given the propensity of juries to accept eyewitness testimony, be dispositive of the entire criminal proceeding. The Court also pointed out that while an identification procedure does not implicate a defendant's Fifth Amendment rights as interrogation does, since nothing of a testimonial nature can be compelled from an accused who is subjected to exhibition, the proceeding cannot be analogized to a scientific test like fingerprinting or blood tests. Unlike such scientific tests, identification procedures involve a peculiarly human factor, and there is no established means by which one can ensure a neutral identification has been conducted. Finally, an accused who is alone in a police station may be unable to reconstruct the manner in which the identification procedure was conducted and may be unaware of abuses which occur.

Because the right to counsel announced in *Wade* constituted such a significant departure from prior practice, the Court held that the *Wade* rule would only apply to line-ups conducted after the date of the decision June 12, 1967.[14] Thus, in *Stovall v Denno*, a federal habeas corpus proceeding, the Court held that the fact that a defendant had not been provided counsel at the time of a line-up would not entitle him to relief on habeas corpus, since his conviction was final

---

[10] 388 US 218 (1967).
[11] 388 US 263 (1967).
[12] 388 US 293 (1967).
[13] United States v Wade, 388 US 218 (1967).
[14] See §6.05.

at the time of the Court's ruling in *Wade* and *Gilbert*.[15] The Court did, however, establish a constitutional standard of admissibility of evidence of identification proceedings apart from the right to counsel. The Court held in *Stoval* that an identification procedure could be so suggestive as to violate a person's right to due process of law guaranteed by the Fourteenth Amendment. The rule, which in effect guarantees that a jury will not hear evidence unless that evidence has "some aspects of reliability,"[16] amounts to a virtual constitutional rule of evidence.[17]

In the first few years after *Wade* and *Gilbert* were decided, the impact of *Stovall* seemed historically limited, since it was generally assumed that the right to counsel was applicable at all post-*Wade* identification proceedings. However, the limitation on the broad right to counsel rule established in *Wade* and *Gilbert* by *Kirby v Illinois*[18] has led to application of the *Stovall* due process test in numerous circumstances, and in recent years, the Court has expanded and refined its due process standard.[19]

§6.03 Proceedings Sufficiently Adversarial to Require Counsel

Wade and *Gilbert* involved identification proceedings in which the accused had been formally charged with a crime. In those cases, the United States Supreme Court did not specifically hold that the right to counsel was applicable in identification proceedings which took place prior to the lodging of a formal charge against an accused. In the wake of *Wade* and *Gilbert*, the majority of state courts and every federal court of appeal considering the question held that the Sixth Amendment right to counsel was applicable at both pre- and postindictment identification proceedings.[20] However, in *Kirby v Illinois*[21] the Supreme Court limited the impact of *Wade* and *Gilbert* by holding that the Sixth Amendment right to counsel did not attach until at or after the institution of formal judicial proceedings against an accused.[22] Identification proceedings

---

[15] The Court held that the rules announced in *Wade* and *Gilbert* would not be applied to judgments not yet final because the rules were so novel and unanticipated, and held the rules would only apply to identification proceedings conducted after June 12, 1967, the date of the decision. See §6.05.

[16] Manson v Braithwaite, 432 US 98, 112 (1977).

[17] *Id.*

[18] 406 US 682 (1972).

[19] See §6.08.

[20] The cases are set out in Kirby v Illinois, 406 US 682, 704, n 14 (1972) (Brennan, J, dissenting).

[21] *Id.*

[22] Moore v Illinois, 434 US 220 (1977).

conducted prior to that time are, under the federal Constitution, constrained only by the due process standard established in *Stovall* and its progeny.[23]

Commentators have been generally critical of *Kirby* because there is no reason to assume that any of the reasons the Court found persuasive in holding the right to counsel applicable in *Wade* to postindictment identifications are not applicable in preindictment identification proceedings.[24] However, several of the 13 states which had, prior to the decision in *Kirby*, held that the right to counsel was applicable at any pretrial identification proceeding promptly, and without much discussion, disapproved their prior holdings and followed *Kirby*.[25] Many courts which had not considered the question prior to *Kirby* simply followed it.[26] Of course, the United States Supreme Court has recognized that the states are free to impose more rigid restrictions on identification proceedings based on their own constitutions if they wish,[27] and a few states have carefully considered arguments favoring a less restrictive grant of the right to counsel before following *Kirby*.[28] For example, while holding that a New York criminal defendant may have a broader right to counsel under the New York constitution than under the federal Constitution, because the New York right may attach at an earlier stage, the New York Court of Appeals has declined to require counsel at all identification proceedings since speedy procedures without counsel, may benefit both the state and the accused in that they may be more accurate and may lead to prompt release of the not guilty, and decisions about the manner of identification procedures are best left to legislative judgment.[29] In its decision, the New York court cited New York Police Department rules concerning the manner in which line-ups are to be conducted, and it may fairly be assumed

---

[23] *See, e.g.*, Moore v Illinois, 434 US 220 (1977); United States v Ash, 413 US 300 (1973); Kirby v Illinois, 406 US 682 (1972).

[24] *See, e.g.*, Comment, *Kirby v Illinois: A New Approach to Right to Counsel*, 58 Iowa L Rev 404 (1972).

[25] *See, e.g.*, State v Johnson, 327 So 2d 388 (La 1976) *overruling* State v Singleton, 253 La 18, 215 So 2d 838 (1968); Commonwealth v Lopes, 362 Mass 448, 287 NE2d 118 (1972), *overruling* Commonwealth v Guillory, 356 Mass 591, 254 NE2d 427 (1970); Reed v Warden, 89 Nev 141, 508 P2d 2 (1973), *overruling* Thompson v State, 85 Nev 134, 451 P2d 704 (1969); State v Sheardon, 31 Ohio St 2d 20, 285 NE2d 335 (1972), *overruling* State v Issacs, 24 Ohio App 2d 115, 265 NE2d 327 (1970); State v Delahunt, 401 A2d 1261 (RI 1979), *overruling In re* Holley, 107 RI 615, 268 A2d 723 (1970); Nichols v State, 511 SW2d 269 (Tex Crim App 1973), *overruling* Martinez v State, 437 SW2d 842 (Tex Crim App 1969).

[26] People v Lowe, 184 Colo 182, 519 P2d 344 (1974); State v Easthope, 29 Utah 2d 400, 510 P2d 933 (1973).

[27] Manson v Braithwaite, 432 US 98 (1977) (Stevens, J concurring).

[28] *See* Foster v State, 272 Md 273, 323 A2d 419 (1974); State v Taylor, 60 Wisc 2d 506, 210 NW2d 873 (1973).

[29] People v Blake, 35 NY2d 331, 361 NYS2d 881, 320 NE2d 625 (1974); *see also* People v Chojinacky, 8 Cal 3d 759, 505 P2d 530, 196 Cal Rptr 106 (1973) seemingly adopting a *Kirby* rule in California; *but compare* the majority opinion of Beach, J, *with* the dissenting opinion of Roth, J in People v Johnson, 149 Cal App 30, 149 Cal Rptr 661 (1978).

that the existence of such regulations, which ameliorate a defendant's inability to reconstruct the identification procedure, influenced the court.

Some courts have, however, explicitly rejected *Kirby* on the basis of their state constitutions and held that the right to counsel is applicable at all identification proceedings absent exigent circumstances.[30] Reasoning that the same risks of misidentification exist at both pre- and postindictment identification proceedings, other courts have held that *Kirby* requires the presence of counsel at identification proceedings at earlier stages than the institution of formal charges. Illustrative is the opinion of Justice Nix of the Pennsylvania Supreme Court in *Commonwealth v Richman*:[31]

> *Kirby* does not establish an all inclusive rule. Rather the line to be drawn depends upon the procedure, employed by each state. . . We are convinced that it would be artificial to attach conclusory significance to the indictment of Pennsylvania. Rather, we hold that *Commonwealth v Whiting* appropriately draws the line for determining the initiation of judicial proceedings in Pennsylvania at the arrest.[32]

§6.04   Effect of Failure to Provide Counsel

In *Wade*[33] and *Gilbert*,[34] the United States Supreme Court attempted to fashion a rule which would require police officers and prosecutors to observe the standards it had established to govern identification proceedings. The Court decided that the only effective way to deter government officials from illegal acts would be, in this as in other instances, to ensure that government officials could not exploit their illegal activity. The Court thus held in *Gilbert v California*[35] that if a defendant is not afforded counsel at a postindictment corporeal identification proceeding, evidence of the out-of-court identification will not be admissible at trial. Justice Brennan stated that "only a per se exclusionary rule as to such testimony can be an effective sanction to ensure that law enforcement authorities will respect the accused's constitutional right to his counsel at the critical line-

---

[30] *See, e.g.*, Blue v State, 558 P2d 636 (Alaska 1977); People v Bustamonte, 30 Cal 3d 88, 634 P2d 927, 177 Cal Rptr 576 (1981); People v Jackson, 391 Mich 323, 217 NW2d 22 (1974); People v Anderson, 389 Mich 155, 205 NW2d 461 (1973).

[31] 458 Pa 167, 320 A2d 351 (1974).

[32] Id at 171, 320 A2d at 353. *See also* State v Butler, 117 NH 888, 379 A2d 827 (1977); State v Keeling, 89 SD 436, 233 NW2d 586 (1975).

[33] United States v Wade, 388 US 218 (1967).

[34] Gilbert v California, 388 US 263 (1967).

[35] *Id.*

influence on a jury, is crucial.[77] Perhaps an even more unfortunate aspect of the adoption of the totality test by the United States Supreme Court is that the ultimate constitutional decision in such cases depends on facts which must be gleaned from a cold record. The risk of subjectivity in the Supreme Court's approach is illustrated by *Neil v Biggers*[78] and *Biggers v Tennessee*[79] The same defendant's claim that the identification procedure used by the police to allow him to be identified by a witness was considered in 1968 on direct appeal from the Tennessee Supreme Court and in 1972 on federal habeas corpus. In the 1968 case, an equally divided Supreme Court affirmed the judgment of the Tennessee Supreme Court which had held that a one-man show-up at a police station did not violate the defendant's right to due process of law. Justice Douglas, in a dissenting opinion, wrote that he felt Biggers had been denied due process, and pointed out that the victim had little opportunity to view her assailant because "there was no light in the hall where Mrs. Beamer was first assaulted; from that hall, the assailant took her out of the house through a kitchen, where there was 'no light' and the railroad track where the rape occurred was illuminated only by the moon."[80]

In contrast, in 1972, in holding that the identification of Biggers had not violated his right to due process of law, Justice Powell, writing for a divided Court, found that the identification had aspects of reliability, because the victim "[W]as with him [the defendant] under adequate artificial light in her house and under a full moon outdoors."[81] While the difference in "facts" found by the Supreme Court on direct review and on habeas corpus could be partially explained by the additional facts determined in the postconviction evidentiary hearing, it is obvious that the difference could also be explained by the personal predilections of the judges on the Court. Indeed, the potential for subjectivity which exists is further illustrated by Justice Powell's statement that the district court's holding that the identification was not reliable was clearly erroneous in part because the witness had been "the victim of one of the most personally humiliating of all crimes," rape.[82]

The Supreme Court has held that the ultimate question of the constitutionality of a pretrial identification is a mixed question of law and fact not governed by the habeas corpus statute.[83] A federal court must accept the facts found by a

---

[77] See, e.g., Pulaski, *Neil v Biggers; The Supreme Court Dismantles the Wade Trilogy's Due Process Protections*, 26 Stan L Rev 1097, 1111-14 (1977).

[78] 409 US 188 (1972).

[79] 390 US 404 (1968).

[80] 407-08 (1968) (Douglas, J, dissenting).

[81] Neil v Biggers, 409 US 188, 200 (1972).

[82] *Id* 200.

[83] Sumner v Mata, 102 S Ct 1303 (1982).

state court, but may give different weight to them in determining the question of the lawfulness of the identification procedure.[84]

§6.11 —Application of Due Process Test

The United States Supreme Court has been loathe to reverse convictions on the grounds that an identification was so suggestive as to violate the defendant's right to due process of law. A one-man show-up in which the defendant, a black man, was taken to the hospital room of the victim handcuffed to a white policeman was held admissible in *Stovall v Denno*[85] because the suggestive identification procedure was necessary given the witness's hospital confinement. The Court held that no error had been committed when a Tennessee court permitted evidence of a one-man show-up in *Neil v Biggers*[86] because the victim had had a substantial opportunity to view the perpetrator of the crime and was able to recognize his distinct voice, and because she had been subjected to a rape. While the Court held in 1969, in *Foster v California*,[87] that a line-up procedure in which the defendant was much taller than the other participants was impermissible, more recent decisions have suggested that the Court will, in a close case, allow the issue of the identification to go to the jury. In *Manson v Braithwaite*,[88] the Court pointed out that its holdings protect only an evidentiary interest, and that interest is limited in an adversary system.

Manson itself illustrates the narrowness of the Supreme Court's rules at present. In *Manson*, an undercover police officer went to the hallway of an apartment building illuminated only by natural light at twilight. He knocked on the door and the door opened 12 to 18 inches. The officer asked for "2 things"; the man behind the door held his hand out and the officer gave him money. The door closed, and opened a short time later. The man inside handed the officer two bags of narcotics. The officer left and drove to police headquarters where he gave a description of the seller as "a colored man approximately 5' 11" tall, dark complexion, black hair, short Afro style and having high cheekbones and a heavy build." Another officer, to whom the description was given, suspected the defendant, obtained a single photograph, and showed it to the first officer two days later. The first officer identified the defendant's photograph as representing the person who had sold him narcotics. The officer testified at trial that he had identified the photograph and also made an in-court identification of the defendant. The United States Supreme Court held that

---

[84] *Id.*
[85] 388 US 293 (1967).
[86] 409 US 188 (1972).
[87] 394 US 440 (1969).
[88] 432 US 98 (1977).

the identification was suggestive and that it was unnecessarily suggestive since there were no emergency or exigent circumstances which precluded a line-up or photographic array. However, looking to the five factors first established in *Neil v Biggers*,[89] the Court held that the identification was admissible. The Court noted that the witness had a good opportunity to view the seller because he had stood within two feet of him for two or three minutes, and that the officer, a trained undercover policeman, was paying "scrupulous" attention to detail. The Court found the description given accurate, and seemed satisfied, on the basis of the officer's transcribed testimony, of his certainty. Finally, the Court reasoned that the two-day delay in the officer's viewing was not significant. Weighing the corrupting effect of the identification procedure against the circumstances of the case, the Court held that evidence of the identification was admissible.

Manson represents, at the very least, the farthest edge of a permissible identification. Lower federal and state courts have, in general, been less willing to admit evidence of such suggestive identifications.

---

[89] 409 US 188 (1972).

7

Institution of Charges

Formalities in Charging an Offense

§7.01   Decision to Charge a Crime

American courts have traditionally devoted little of their resources to considering the constitutional implications of the institution of criminal charges. In

whether it contains the elements of the offense intended to be charged, and sufficiently apprises the defendant of what he must be prepared to meet and in case any other proceedings are taken against him for a similar offense, whether the record shows with accuracy, to what extent he may plead a formal acquittal or conviction.[25]

These principles of law have never varied over the years.[26] Both state and federal courts have frequently been faced with constitutional claims that a particular complaint or indictment is defective. In each case, the reviewing court must undertake a functional analysis of the challenged complaint or indictment. The court must determine first whether the complaint or indictment provides proper notice of the crime which it alleges the defendant has committed, and second, whether the allegations are specific enough to ensure that the defendant cannot be forced to trial again because of the same act.[27] If the particular jurisdiction provides a procedural mechanism to allow a defendant to request a more specific statement of the offense with which he or she is charged, such as a bill of particulars or even amendment by the prosecution, the availability of specification will be considered in determining whether the charge is constitutionally sufficient.[28] A subtle difference must be recognized, however, between felony prosecutions in federal courts, which must be prosecuted by indictment in accordance with the Fifth Amendment, and misdemeanor prosecutions and prosecutions in states which do not require that felonies be prosecuted by grand jury indictment. The United States Supreme Court has held on many occasions that a bill of particulars cannot cure a defective indictment.[29] The reason for this rule is that a bill of particulars, or amendment, may charge an offense which the grand jury never considered. Since the Fifth Amendment to the federal Constitution requires that all federal felony prosecutions proceed by grand jury indictment, it follows that such an amendment or bill would vitiate the independent Fifth Amendment right not to be tried on an infamous offense except on the indictment of a grand jury.[30] The distinction recognized is not premised on due process grounds and is not applicable to the states.

It must be remembered that the notice required by the Constitution is fair notice. Amendment of indictments, even in a state prosecution, must occur at a time which will give the defendant a reasonable chance to prepare to rebut

---

[25] Hagner v United States, 285 US 427,431 (1932).

[26] Sanabria v United States, 437 US 54 (1978); Hamling v United States, 418 US 87 (1974), *rehearing denied*, 419 US 885 (1975).

[27] Of course, a defendant may rely on other parts of the record beside the indictment for protection from prosecution for the same offense. Bartel v United States, 227 US 427 (1913).

[28] United States v Debrow, 346 US 374 (1953); Hodgson v Vermont, 168 US 262 (1897).

[29] *See, e.g.*, Russell v United States, 369 US 749 (1962).

[30] *Id. See also* Stirone v United States, 361 US 212 (1960); *see also Ex parte* Bain, 121 US 1 (1887) (indictments may be amended in matters of form, and not in substance).

the prosecution's case. It has been held that allowing the prosecutor to amend an indictment at trial and seek conviction on a crime not charged by the grand jury constitutes a denial of due process by not giving the defendant fair notice of the charges faced.[31]

Cases concerning the specificity of indictments, of necessity, tend to turn on their own facts and the particular statute involved. A few specific rules of general application have developed. The means used to commit a crime need not be specifically alleged unless the means constitute an element of the offense.[32] Courts generally hold that a prosecutor may charge that the same crime was committed in several different ways in order to meet the evidence at trial.[33] If the defendant is prejudiced by the allegations in alternative counts, a court has the authority to require the prosecution to elect to proceed on one particular charge.[34] The indictment must set out the specific offense coming under the general description of conduct with which the defendant is charged.[35] The reason for this rule is not only to provide the defendant with fair notice of the charge, but to inform the court of the facts alleged so that it may decide if they are sufficient in law to support a conviction.[36] Thus, in *Russell v United States*,[37] the Supreme Court held that indictments for refusal to answer a question when summoned before a Senate subcommittee were defective, despite the fact that the indictments recited the time and place at which the refusal occurred, because they did not recite what the subject under inquiry was at the time of the refusal to answer. The relevant statute made it an offense to refuse to answer questions pertinent to the matter under inquiry, and the indictment simply recited that the question was "pertinent to the matter under inquiry" by the committee. The Court held the indictments were obviously defective, since the lack of specificity left the prosecution free to "roam at large —to shift its theory of criminality so as to take advantage of each passing vicissitude of the trial and appeal."[38] The Court stated that the corollary purpose of the specificity requirement, to inform the Court of the facts alleged so that it may decide whether they are sufficient in law to support the conviction if one should be had,[39] was designed not only for the benefit of the defendant, but for the

---

[31] Watson v Jago, 558 F2d 330 (6th Cir 1977).

[32] State v Greenwood, 113 NH 625, 312 A2d 695 (1973); Anderson v State, 479 SW2d 57 (Tex Crim App 1972).

[33] State v Nelson, 103 NH 478, 175 A2d 814 (1961), *cert denied*, 369 US 879, 369 US 881 (1962).

[34] *Id; see also* United States v Olson, 504 F2d 1222 (9th Cir 1974); State v Moore, 131 Vt 149, 303 A2d 141 (1973).

[35] Russell v United States, 369 US 749 (1962); United States v Cruikshank, 92 US 542 (1875).

[36] *Id.*

[37] Russell v United States, 369 US 749 (1962).

[38] *Id* 768.

[39] *Id* (citing United States v Cruikshank, 92 US 542 (1875)).

proceeded by information and whose judges were the sole judge of laws, facts, and penalty.[50]

The institution of the grand jury was included in the American Bill of Rights to provide the same protection from an oppressive executive. In fact, however, the history of American law does not reflect an antagonism between an executive and the populace similar to that in the England of a few centuries ago. As early as 1887, the United States Supreme Court noted that "[i]t has been said that since there is no danger to the citizenry from the oppression of a monarch, or of any form of executive power, there is no longer need of a grand jury."[51] And the grand jury was abolished in England in 1933. The United States Supreme Court held in *Hurtado v California*[52] that the Fifth Amendment requirement that felonies be prosecuted by grand jury is not binding on the states, and it has never deviated from that view.[53] But where the right to a grand jury exists, implicit within it is the right to an unbiased jury.[54]

In order to fully understand the role of the grand jury in modern practice, it must be remembered that the grand jury is not merely an investigatory body but an accusatory body. In American jurisdictions, this function of the grand jury has become preeminent. Justice Powell, discoursing on the modern role of the grand jury, recently wrote:

> Traditionally, the grand jury has been accorded wide latitude to inquire into violations of criminal law. No judge presides to monitor its proceedings. It deliberates in secret and may determine alone the course of its inquiry. The grand jury may compel the production of evidence or the testimony of witnesses as it considers appropriate, and its operation generally is unrestrained by the technical procedural and evidentiary rules governing the conduct of criminal trials. "It is a grand inquest, a body with powers of investigation and inquisition, the scope of whose inquiries is not to be limited narrowly by questions of propriety or forecasts of the probable result of the investigation, or by doubts whether any particular individual will be found properly subject to an accusation of crime."[55]

That the role of the grand jury in the United States is far different than that in England is illustrated by the fact that at the time of the adoption of the Constitution, the English practice was to have private individuals prefer charges to the grand jury, who, if satisfied charges should be brought, requested the

---

[50] 4 W. Blackstone, Commentaries 310 (U Chi ed 1979).

[51] *Ex parte* Bain, 121 US 1, 12 (1887).

[52] 110 US 516 (1884).

[53] Castanada v Partida, 430 US 482 (1977).

[54] United States v Gold, 470 F Supp 1336 (ND Ill 1979).

[55] United States v Calandra, 414 US 338, 343 (1974).

court to draw up the charges.[56] As a practical matter, at present, grand juries are subject to the de facto control of the prosecutor. In many jurisdictions, a busy prosecutor simply has a police officer tell the jury briefly about a case, and the grand jury returns an indictment. In the federal system, and in many states, the prosecution will often convene investigative grand juries which will meet over the course of several months to inquire into courses of conduct the prosecutor believes may have involved criminal activity. Any attorney who has served as a prosecutor in states in which grand juries exist will readily admit that grand jurors do not generally view the prosecutor as an adversary. Prosecutors, using the grand jury, are able to compel the attendance of witnesses, compel their testimony, and require the production of documents which they could not obtain by warrant. For this reason, the United States Supreme Court has imposed certain limitations on the manner in which grand juries may function. The potential for prosecutorial abuse of grand juries and the increase of cases of actual prosecutorial abuse has led to a number of legislative proposals to afford targets of prosecutorial action greater procedural protection.

§7.04 Invocation of the Fifth Amendment in the Grand Jury Room

A grand jury has extraordinary powers.

> It is a grand inquest, a body with powers of investigation and inquisition, the scope of whose inquiries is not to be limited narrowly by questions of propriety or forecasts of the probable result of the investigation, or by doubts whether any particular individual will be found properly subject to an accusation of crime.[57]

The grand jury typically may issue subpoenas add testificandum and subpoenas duces tecum.[58] The Fourth Amendment provides protection against subpoenae duces tecum too broad to be reasonable.[59]

Because of their vast powers and perhaps because grand juries at present must fairly be characterized as tools of the prosecution, rather than bulwarks against governmental oppression, the United States Supreme Court has been ever more ready to regulate their conduct. The greatest counterweight to the broad investigative power of the grand jury is the Fifth Amendment privilege

---

[56] 4 W. Blackstone, Commentaries 300 (U Chi ed 1979); *see* State v Freeman, 13 NH 488, 489-90 (1843) (comparing the difference between the English and early American practices).

[57] Blair v United States, 250 US 273, 282 (1919).

[58] *See, e.g.*, Branzberg v Hayes, 408 US 665 (1972).

[59] *Id; see also* Hale v Henkel, 201 US 43 (1906).

against self-incrimination. A witness may not be compelled to incriminate himself or herself by testimony before a grand jury.[60] But the United States Supreme Court has held that testimony can be compelled from an unwilling witness over a claim of Fifth Amendment privilege, if the witness is afforded immunity from use of the compelled testimony and evidence derived therefrom in subsequent criminal proceedings.[61] This type of immunity is called *use immunity* because it requires only that the prosecutor not be permitted to make use of the compelled testimony. Some states require that a grant of immunity from prosecution for the transaction is necessary to overcome the state constitutional claim of the self-incrimination privilege.[62]

The scope of the Fifth Amendment privilege in the grand jury room is the same as it is in court. Since Chief Justice Marshall's time, it has been recognized that the privilege may not be construed to merely provide an accused with the right to refuse to admit to a crime:

> If the question be of such a description that an answer to it may or may not incriminate the witness . . . it must rest with himself; who alone can tell what the answer would be, whether to answer the question or not. . . . Many links frequently compose the chain which is necessary to convict an individual of crime. It appears to the court to be the true sense of the rule that no witness is compellable to furnish any of them against himself.[63]

The scope of the privilege is the same in both state and federal proceedings. The privilege is purely testimonial, and a person cannot refuse to provide handwriting exemplars or voice exemplars to a grand jury.[64] Of course, the question of whether testimony, if given, would incriminate the witness is ultimately for the court, and not for the witness.[65] As a practical matter in most cases, a witness's assertion of a Fifth Amendment privilege will not be challenged by a court.[66] As Justice Clark noted:

> The privilege afforded not only extends to answers that would in themselves support a conviction . . . but likewise embraces those which would

---

[60] Kastigar v United States, 406 US 441 (1972). Of course, the privilege is only a testimonial privilege; an accused may be required to submit to tests which would make him the source of real physical evidence; *see, e.g.*, United States v Dionisio, 410 US 1 (1973).

[61] *Id.* Immunity is discussed in §13.11.

[62] *See, e.g.*, NH Rev Stat Ann §516:34 (1955).

[63] United States v Burr, 25 F Cas 38, 40 (CC Va 1807).

[64] United States v Dionisio, 410 US 1 (1973).

[65] *Id.*

[66] See generally, Annot., *Sufficiency of Witness' Claim of Privilege Against Self-Incrimination*, 51 ALR2d 1178.

furnish a link in the chain of evidence needed to prosecute. . . . But this protection must be confined to instances where the witness had reasonable cause to apprehend danger from a direct answer. The witness is not exonerated from answering merely because he declares that in doing so he would incriminate himself—his say-so does not of itself establish the hazard of incrimination. It is for the court to say whether his silence is justified, and to require him to answer if it clearly appears to the court that he is mistaken. However, if the witness, upon interposing his claim, were required to prove the hazard in the sense in which a claim is usually required to be established in court, he would be compelled to surrender the very protection which the privilege is designed to guarantee. To sustain the privilege, it need only be evident from the implication of the question, in the setting in which it is asked, that a responsive answer to the question or an explanation of why it cannot be answered might be dangerous because injurious disclosure could result. The trial judge, in appraising the claim, must be governed as much by his peculiar perception of the peculiarities of the case as by the facts actually in evidence.[67]

There is authority for the proposition that the Fifth Amendment may be invoked where there is a real and palpable danger of a foreign prosecution.[68] It is only in the rare case, as when a witness declines to answer questions before a grand jury because he fears his statements may be at odds with his prior sworn testimony and thus subject him to a perjury prosecution, that a court will find the privilege unavailable.[69]

A proper grant of immunity, which is discussed in Chapter 13, will require the witness to answer or be held in contempt. However, even a witness given immunity need not answer a question if the source of the inquiry is illegal electronic surveillance.[70] Testimony given after a grant of immunity may not be used to impeach a witness if he testifies differently at trial.[71]

There is authority for the proposition that a person cannot be punished for invocation of Fifth Amendment rights before a grand jury.[72] Refusal to answer a question before a grand jury, without a valid assertion of the Fifth Amendment or other privilege, is punishable as a contempt.

---

[67] Hoffman v United States, 341 US 479, 486-87 (1951).

[68] *In re* Quinn, 525 F2d 222 (1st Cir 1975) The United States Supreme Court has explicitly left the question open. *See* Zicarelli v New Jersey Investigation Comm, 406 US 472 (1972).

[69] *In re* Boiardo, 34 NJ 599, 170 A2d 816 (1961).

[70] Gelbard v United States, 408 US 41 (1972).

[71] New Jersey v Portash, 440 US 450, 459-60 (1979).

[72] *See, e.g.,* Spevack v Klein, 384 US 511 (1967); Uniformed Sanitation Men's Assn v Commissioner of Sanitation, 342 US 280 (1968).

§7.05   Invocation of Privileges Other Than the Fifth Amendment Before a Grand Jury

A grand jury has no right to pierce any privilege of a witness, whether created by statute, the Constitution, or common law. What statutory or common law privileges are available to witnesses depend, of course, on the law of the particular jurisdiction where the grand jury sits.[73]

Apart from the evidentiary privileges available in the law of the particular jurisdiction, federal constitutional privileges other than the Fifth Amendment privilege may be invoked. Perhaps the most commonly invoked of these other privileges are those found in the First Amendment. In *Branzburg v Hayes*,[74] a journalist had refused to testify before a grand jury, asserting that the First Amendment created a journalist's privilege which allowed him to withhold the identity of his sources. A sharply divided Supreme Court held that requiring the reporter to appear and testify did not violate the First Amendment to the United States Constitution. The four-judge majority was joined in a separate concurring opinion by Justice Powell, who seemingly recognized some limited First Amendment privilege in reporters to withhold information from the grand jury.[75] A number of jurisdictions have resolved the problem by enacting journalist shield laws. Analysis in other jurisdictions has tended to turn upon the reviewing court's interpretation of the opinion of the United States Supreme Court in *Branzburg*. Undoubtedly, further litigation in the United States Supreme Court will resolve the matter.

First Amendment claims made by clergy who assert that being required to testify will harm their ministry and thus affect their First Amendment rights have generally been unsuccessful.[76] There is, however, authority which suggests that interrogation into protected First Amendment areas—religious beliefs, political beliefs, and the like—is forbidden.[77] A lawyer called before a grand jury to testify about a client's affairs would be able to assert an attorney-client privilege based, in part, on the Sixth Amendment.[78] Even if the lawyer waives the privilege by filing an affidavit summarizing the results of his investigation into the reasons

---

[73] *See, e.g.*, Keenan v Gigante, 47 NY2d 160, 390 NE2d 1151, 417 NYS2d 226 (1979) (no priest-penitent privilege available to witness under New York law); State v Smith, 237 Ga 647, 229 SE2d 443 (1976) (where Georgia law provided that husband and wife are not compellable to give evidence for or against each other in any criminal proceeding not committed on the person of the other, wife could invoke privilege when husband was the subject of the grand jury's investigation).

[74] 408 US 665 (1972).

[75] *Id* (Powell, J, concurring).

[76] Keenan v Gigante, 47 NY2d 160, 390 NE2d 1151, 417 NYS2d 226 (1979).

[77] Baggett v Bullitt, 377 US 360 (1964); *see also* NAACP v Button, 371 US 415 (1963).

[78] *In re* Grand Jury Subpoena, 438 F Supp 1176 (SDNY 1977).

for his client's inability to produce documents subpoenaed by the grand jury, at least one court has held that he may not be subpoenaed to testify about his investigation, since his testimony would relate to protected work product.[79]

§7.06   Evidence Which May Be Considered by a Grand Jury

While the grand jury may not violate a valid privilege, whether established by the Constitution, statutes, or common law, it may base its indictment on hearsay, incompetent evidence,[80] and evidence obtained in violation of a person's Fourth[81] or Fifth[82] Amendment rights. The United States Supreme Court's reasoning in refusing to apply the exclusionary rule to grand jury proceedings has been that extending the exclusionary rule to the grand jury would seriously impair its function:

> Because the grand jury does not finally adjudicate guilt or innocence, it has traditionally been allowed to pursue its investigatory and accusatory functions unimpeded by the evidentiary and procedural restrictions applicable to a criminal trial. Permitting witnesses to invoke the exclusionary rule before the grand jury would precipitate adjudication of issues hitherto reserved for the trial on the merits and would delay and disrupt grand jury proceedings.[83]

Since the grand jury only decides to charge, the Supreme Court has held it may consider tips, common rumors, evidence proffered by the prosecution, or the personal knowledge of the grand jurors.[84]

The grand jurors, as a practical matter, may hear only what the prosecutor wishes them to hear, by selective subpoenaing of witnesses. Thus, at least one court has held that where the extent of incompetent and irrelevant evidence is such that it is unreasonable to expect that the grand jury could limit its consideration to relevant, admissible evidence, the defendant has been denied due process of law.[85] And while the vast majority of courts hold that an indictment is not vitiated by the fact that the jury considered inadmissible evidence, it is

---

[79] *Id.*

[80] Costello v United States, 350 US 359 (1956).

[81] United States v Calandra, 414 US 339 (1974).

[82] Lawn v United States, 355 US 339 (1958); United States v Blue, 384 US 251 (1966).

[83] United States v Calandra, 414 US 339, 349 (1974); *see also* United States v Dionisio, 410 US 19 (1973).

[84] Costello v United States, 350 US 359 (1956).

[85] People v Backus, 23 Cal 3d 360, 590 P2d 837, 152 Cal Rptr 710 (1979).

8

Bail and Pretrial Restraint

§8.01   Nature of Bail

The criminal process may begin with ex parte judicial proceedings which result in a judicial command to peace officers to arrest and detain an individual, or it may begin with an arrest without prior judicial authorization. In either case, the most important and obvious purpose for the arrest is to take an alleged offender before a court in which guilt or innocence may be determined and a sentence, if the defendant is found guilty, imposed. Because a trial cannot be had, nor a defense prepared, summarily, it is obviously sometimes necessary that an accused person be detained for some period of time to ensure availability to answer charges.

The deleterious effects such detention has on an accused are obvious. In addition to the physical unpleasantness of confinement in a jail or prison, the accused may be unable to prepare a defense or continue employment, and may suffer severe strains in family relationships.[1] For that reason, the common law early developed the concept of bail. However, bail at common was quite different from bail as we know it today. Rather than requiring an individual to post a sum of money to ensure his appearance, the common law allowed an accused person to remain in the custody of his friends. Thus, Blackstone wrote that bail is "a delivery or bailment of a person to his sureties, upon their giving, together with himself, sufficient security for his appearance; he being supposed to continue in their friendly custody instead of going to jail."[2] The defendant's sureties were considered to be his jailers. While the sureties could allow an accused to go beyond the limits of the jurisdiction in which the accused was to answer, they were liable for his nonreturn.[3] The sureties could, at any time, discharge their burden by seizing the principal and delivering him to the court.[4]

By the time of the American Revolution, the idea of posting property as surety had been accepted. Indeed, the bail clause of the Eighth Amendment to the federal Constitution was lifted with slight changes from the English Bill of Rights Act.[5] Similar provisions were inserted in many state constitutions.[6] The last 100 years have seen the rise and very recently the near demise of bail bondsmen who post cash surety for a fee.[7] In a curious way, the law has seemingly come almost full circle; the thrust of modern legislation has been to allow release in as many circumstances as possible by imposing conditions which require the accused to meet with a probation officer while on bail, or by personal recognizance—the promise of an individual to forfeit a certain sum if that person does not appear as promised for trial.[8] The effect of such legislation is to make the probation officer or the accused his or her own jailer. Modern statutes usually provide that one released on personal recognizance will be civilly and usually criminally[9] liable for nonappearance.

---

[1] *See, e.g.,* Gerstein v Pugh, 420 US 103 (1975).

[2] 4 W. Blackstone, Commentaries 294 (U Chi ed 1979).

[3] *See, e.g.,* Taylor v Tainter, 83 US (16 Wall) 366 (1872).

[4] *Id.*

[5] Carlson v Landon, 342 US 524, 545 (1952).

[6] *See, e.g.,* Ill Const art I, §9.

[7] *See, e.g.,* Schilb v Kuebel, 404 US 357 (1971).

[8] *Id.*

[9] *See, e.g.,* NH Rev Stat Ann §597:14-a (1955).

§8.02   Constitutional Necessity for Bail

There was never a right to bail in all cases at common law. There were a number of crimes for which the accused "could have no other sureties but the four walls of the prison."[10] The Eighth Amendment to the federal Constitution, which was adopted virtually word for word from the English Bill of Rights, provides in relevant part that "excessive bail shall not be required." The amendment does not say that bail must be afforded in all circumstances. The United States Supreme Court has stated that bail is fundamental to our system of criminal justice and that the Eighth Amendment's prohibition of excessive bail is applicable to the states through the due process clause of the Fourteenth Amendment.[11] It has never held, however, that there is a right to bail in all cases. In 1894, before the Eighth Amendment prohibition of excessive bail had been held applicable to the states by the Fourteenth Amendment, the Court held that denial of bail pending appeal offended neither the due process clause of the Fourteenth Amendment nor the privileges and immunities clause of the federal Constitution.[12]

While doubts as to whether bail ought be granted should always be resolved in favor of the accused,[13] it is nonetheless true that state courts have generally held that in some circumstances bail may constitutionally be denied. Such courts frequently deny bail where the court is satisfied that an accused will not appear for trial regardless of the amount or conditions of bail.[14] Bail is generally denied in very serious cases, such as first-degree murder,[15] or when bail is sought pending a frivolous appeal.[16] Dicta in *Stack v Boyle*[17] to the effect that unless the right to freedom before conviction of crime is honored, the presumption of innocence would lose its meaning, has led commentators to question the propriety of denial of bail.

Denial of bail merely because charges are pending is difficult to reconcile with the presumption of innocence. The United States Supreme Court has held that the mere fact that an accusation is pending against a person found incompetent to stand trial does not allow the state to confine him to a mental institution without the procedural due process given to those who are civilly committed.[18]

---

[10] 4 W. Blackstone, Commentaries 295 (U Chi ed 1979).

[11] Schib v Kuebel, 404 US 357, 365 (1971).

[12] McKane v Durston, 153 US 684, 687 (1894).

[13] *See, e.g.*, Sellers v United States, 89 S Ct 36 (1968) (Black, Circuit Justice); Herzog v United States, 75 S Ct 349 (1955) (Douglas, Circuit Justice).

[14] *See, e.g.*, People *ex rel* Hemingway v Elrod, 60 Ill 2d 74, 322 NE2d 837 (1975).

[15] Commonwealth v Marshall, 373 Mass 65, 364 NE7d 1237 (1977).

[16] Hamilton v New Mexico, 479 F2d 343 (10th Cir 1973).

[17] 342 US 1, 3 (1951).

[18] Jackson v Indiana, 406 US 715 (1972); *see also* Hunt v Roth 648 F2d 1148 (8th Cir 1981) *dismissed at moot* Murphy v Hunt, 102 S Ct 1181 (1982).

It could reasonably be argued that the mere fact that serious unproven charges are pending against a person does not justify denying that person liberty, when other persons against whom charges are pending are afforded bail.

But even if the right to deny bail altogether is assumed, as Justice Douglas once noted, "there is a constitutional issue that lurks in every bail case."[19] It has been stated that the prohibition against excessive bail means that an individual may not be "capriciously" held[20] without bail. It is the unreasoned denial of bail that the Constitution condemns.[21] Since an unreasoned denial of bail is subject to judicial review, it may be said that the Constitution sets an outer limit on even the power to deny a person bail altogether.

§8.03 Constitutional Limitations on Pretrial Incarceration

Distinct from and yet related to the constitutional right to bail is the right to a judicial determination of probable cause to believe that an accused has committed a crime before the accused's liberty is limited. Because the federal requirement that felony prosecutions be instituted by indictment is not binding on the states,[22] and because arrests are commonly made without a warrant, it is quite possible for an individual to be detained and incarcerated without there ever having been a judicial determination of probable cause to believe that person has committed a crime. While such an individual may apply for bail, even if it is granted, he or she is in a less favorable position than a person never charged with a crime.

In *Gerstein v Pugh*,[23] the United States Supreme Court held that the Fourth Amendment requires a judicial determination of probable cause before a person is subjected to an extended deprivation of liberty. The Court recognized that maximum protection of individual rights could be assured by requiring a magistrate's review of arrest prior to any actual arrest, but that such a requirement would hamstring legitimate law enforcement because summary action is often needed to prevent crime or apprehend criminals. But once the need for summary action subsides, the correlative need for a judicial determination of probable cause increases. In the case before it in *Gerstein*, the Court held that the Fourth Amendment required some sort of a judicial determination of probable cause, which might be ex parte by a judicial officer, before an

---

[19] Carlson v Landon, 73 S Ct 1179, 1182 (1953) (Douglas, Circuit Justice).
[20] Carlson v Landon, 342 US 524, 548 (1952) (Burton, dissenting).
[21] Carlson v Landon, 73 S Ct 1179, 1182 (1953) (Douglas, Circuit Justice).
[22] See §7.03.
[23] 420 US 103 (1975).

individual could be detained based on a mere complaint; a determination by a prosecutor or policeman that probable cause existed was insufficient.[24]

The Court was careful to point out that it would not impose any particular type of procedure on the states. While recognizing that the procedure it outlined bore a resemblance to probable cause hearings held in states with grand juries, when a person accused of a felony is arrested before indictment, to determine if there is probable cause to hold the individual until the grand jury meets, the Court emphasized that it was not requiring the creation of such a procedure in all states. The Court specifically held that a full adversary hearing to determine probable cause is not necessary, since such a determination is traditionally made on an ex parte basis without notice or hearing, by grand juries and magistrates determining sufficiency of arrest warrants.

§8.04 Excessive Bail

The Eighth Amendment provides, in relevant part, that "excessive bail shall not be required," and most state constitutions contain similar guarantees.[25] *Excessive bail* is, at least superficially, easy to define; it is, as Justice Butler stated in 1926, bail set at a figure higher than an amount reasonably calculated to ensure the presence of the accused.[26] Because bail in an amount greater than that required to ensure the defendant's appearance constitutes excessive bail within the meaning of the Eighth Amendment, it has been held that an order allowing release on $100,000 bail as long as $30,000 of the bail is applied to payment of a fine is excessive, since the bail would serve a purpose not intended.[27] In some cases, the United States Supreme Court has been willing to countenance no bail.[28]

In cases in which bail is permitted, the determination of what bail is excessive must, of necessity, turn on the facts of the particular case. The reported cases generally find the nature of the crime charged crucial. The applicant's ties in the community, family relationships, physical condition, prior criminal record, and prior record of appearances after having been bailed are also relevant.[29] Obviously, an individual with close family and social ties to a particular community is less likely to abscond than a stranger. The evidence against

---

[24] *Id.*

[25] *See, e.g.*, Ill Const art I, §9: "All persons shall be bailable by sufficient sureties, except for capital offenses where the proof is evident or the presumption great."

[26] United States v Motlow, 10 F2d 657 (7th Cir 1926) (Butler, Circuit Justice); Stack v Boyle, 342 US 1, 5 (1951).

[27] Cohen v United States, 82 S Ct 526 (1962) (Douglas, Circuit Justice).

[28] *See, e.g.*, Carlson v Landon, 342 US 524 (1952); See **§8.02**.

[29] Chambers v Mississippi, 405 US 1205, 1206 (1972) (Powell, Circuit Justice); Sica v United States, 82 S Ct 669 (1962) (Douglas, Circuit Justice).

the accused may also be relevant. Indeed, many states provide that there is to be no bail in first-degree murder cases where the proof is evident or the presumption great.[30] The stage of the proceedings is also relevant, as greater bail may be required pending appeal of a conviction.

Moreover, the defendant's personal financial resources may be highly relevant. In *Mecom v United States*,[31] for example, Justice Powell, as Circuit Justice, held that bail pending appeal of $750,000 was not excessive for a defendant convicted of possession of marijuana with intent to distribute. While the defendant could show that he had substantial roots in the community and local business interests, and that he had never before been charged with a criminal offense, Justice Powell found persuasive the fact that the government had introduced evidence at trial that he was engaged in large-scale marijuana smuggling, that his wife, a co-indictee, was a fugitive in Mexico, and that he was known to carry large amounts of cash. At a bail hearing, there was evidence that the defendant had paid $100,000 for the murder—unsuccessfully attempted—of an associate suspected of cooperating with the government. The combination of the defendant's motive to leave the community and his access to large amounts of bail money makes the decision explicable.

More difficult to comprehend, however, is the thread which seems to run through many of the bail cases and which is suggested by Justice Powell's reference to Mecom's attempt to intimidate a witness. Traditionally, courts have considered the propensity of the defendant before them to commit crime in granting or denying bail. Even Justice Douglas once wrote that if "the safety of the community would be jeopardized, it would be irresponsible judicial action to grant bail. . ."[32] Indeed, it has been suggested that, while bail of $500,000 would be excessive for an insane person, denial of bail would be proper.[33] There is authority for the proposition that a defendant may be denied bail to render fruitless attempts to intimidate witnesses or jurors.[34]

While judges have only recently explicitly and candidly discussed the potential for harm to the community if an accused is released pending trial or appeal, there can be no doubt that American judges have long tacitly considered the potential harm to the community in release on bail. The new judicial candor has led to a spate of law review articles and opinions concerning preventive detention.[35]

---

[30] *See, e.g.*, People v District Court, 187 Colo 164, 529 P2d 1335 (1974).

[31] 98 S Ct 19 (1977) (Powell, Circuit Justice).

[32] Carbo v United States, 82 S Ct 662, 666 (1962).

[33] Rehman v California, 85 S Ct 8, 9 (1964) (Douglas, Circuit Justice).

[34] Fernandez v United States, 81 S Ct 643 (1961) (Harlan, Circuit Justice).

[35] See §8.05.

constitutional.[65] Despite the fact that modern legislation has ameliorated some of the worst abuses of the bail bondsman system, the fact remains that a bail system which relies on property for security discriminates between rich and poor.

The problem was first articulated by Justice Douglas in *Bandy v United States*.[66] While not holding that the equal protection clause of the Fourteenth Amendment was violated when bail was set at $5,000 and the defendant made a showing that he did not have $5,000, Justice Douglas noted that "to continue to demand a substantial bond . . . raises considerable problems for the equal administration of the law."[67] There is a line of United States Supreme Court cases which seems to forbid discrimination between rich and poor in the context of the criminal process.[68]

In *Tate v Short*,[69] the Court held that, where a state had legislated a fines-only system for certain classes of offenses, indigents could not be incarcerated to work off their offenses at a certain amount per day. A few courts have reasoned that distinctions between indigents and nonindigents are as invidious in the context of bail as in sentencing. In *Pugh v Rainwater*,[70] the Fifth Circuit held that incarceration of an indigent whose presence at trial could be assured by other means would constitute imposition of excessive bail, and would violate the equal protection and due process clauses of the Fourteenth Amendment.[71] Like the law concerning preventive detention, the impact of bail on indigents seems likely to provide grist for the judicial mill in the 1980s.

§8.10 Testimony at Bail Hearing

In most state systems and in the federal system, evidence is usually taken at some point to establish the facts necessary to allow a judicial officer to make an informed decision on bail. Most American courts have assumed, without much discussion, that statements made by an accused at a bail hearing, if the accused is adequately warned of his or her rights, are admissible against the accused in subsequent proceedings.[72] Thus, a defendant who seeks to exercise

---

[65] *Id.*

[66] 81 S Ct 197 (1960) (Douglas, Circuit Justice).

[67] *Id.*

[68] *See, e.g.,* Scott v Illinois, 440 US 367 (1979); Mayer v City of Chicago, 404 US 189 (1971); Rinaldi v Yeager, 384 US 305 (1966); Douglas v California, 372 US 353 (1963); Griffin v Illinois, 351 US 12 (1956).

[69] 401 US 395 (1971).

[70] 572 F2d 1053 (5th Cir 1978) (en banc).

[71] *See also* United States v Gaines, 449 F2d 143 (2d Cir 1971).

[72] *See, e.g.,* Raffield v State, 333 So 2d 534 (Fla Dist Ct App 1976); State v Van Wert, 294 Minn 464, 199 NW2d 514 (1972).

the right to nonexcessive bail by testifying at a bail hearing takes the risk that statements made may be later used at trial. Obviously, a tension is created between the Fifth Amendment right against self-incrimination and the Eighth Amendment right to nonexcessive bail.

In 1955, Justice Harlan recognized the problem in an application for bail made to him by a defendant who had been indicted under the Smith Act and who invoked the privilege against self-incrimination when asked about his whereabouts during the three preceding years at a bail hearing.[73] While recognizing that the defendant's whereabouts could be relevant to a court considering whether to grant bail, Justice Harlan wrote that "it would seem that, in fixing bail, as in a criminal trial, an unfavorable inference should not be drawn from the mere fact that the Fifth Amendment has been invoked."[74]

A firm constitutional footing for Justice Harlan's dicta was established in *Simmons v United States*[75] in 1968. In *Simmons*, the United States Supreme Court held that testimony given by an accused in a suppression hearing to establish standing to challenge a violation of Fourth Amendment rights could not be used against the accused at trial. The Court reasoned that to allow the government to do so would require a defendant who seeks to vindicate the Fourth Amendment right to have evidence excluded from trial which was illegally seized, but who must testify in a manner which would incriminate him or her to establish standing, to either waive the Fifth Amendment privilege to remain silent, or to waive Fourth Amendment rights. Justice Harlan, writing for a six-man majority, found it "intolerable that one constitutional right should have to be surrendered to assert another."[76] The *Simmons* rationale has led lower federal courts to state that a defendant's testimony at a competency hearing could not be used against him at a trial on the merits,[77] and that a prosecutor's comment that a defendant's ability to produce cash bail was evidence of his guilt would violate the defendant's constitutional rights.[78] The logical application of *Simmons* would seen to require exclusion of testimony given by an accused at a bail hearing, if the testimony was given in an attempt to obtain nonexcessive bail. A few judges have been willing to accept this view, but they are a distinct minority.[79]

---

[73] Noto v United States, 76 S Ct 255 (1955).

[74] *Id* 257.

[75] 390 US 377 (1968).

[76] *Id* 394.

[77] Pedrero v Wainwright, 590 F2d 1383, 1388 n 3 (5th Cir 1979).

[78] United States v Vargas, 582 F2d 380, 388 (7th Cir 1978).

[79] *See, e.g.,* State v Williams, 115 NH 437, 343 A2d 29 (1975) (Grimes, J, dissenting). The majority view is, of course, that such statements are admissible. *See, e.g.,* Raffield v State, 333 So 2d 534 (Fla Dist Ct App 1976) (bond reduction hearing); State v Haggard, 94 Idaho 249, 486 P2d 260 (1971); State v Van Wert, 294 Minn 464, 199 NW2d 514 (1972).

even though new evidence relating to the credibility of witnesses would not be grounds for a new trial in most state systems and in the federal system.[11] When a defendant shows that false evidence has been presented to a jury, the conviction must be reversed if the false evidence "could . . . in any reasonable likelihood have affected the judgment of the jury."[12]

Because the strict rules relating to false testimony are designed to protect the public and not to punish the prosecutor, it is irrelevant that the particular prosecutor who appears in court when false testimony is presented believes it to be true.[13] Because it is the right to a fair trial and not the prosecutor's state of mind which is at issue, promises of leniency to a witness made by one government agent are attributed to the prosecutor's office as a whole.[14] For similar reasons, the fact that a prosecutor or police officer had no authority to make the promises made to the witness is irrelevant in determining whether a defendant's rights were violated by the witness's testimony.[15]

If a defendant alleges, on habeas corpus, that false testimony was used to convict, a reviewing federal court will make an independent examination of the record before it, and the federal court will not be bound by a state court's findings of fact.[16] The breadth of the standard of review, and the fact that federal courts may make independent judgments about the effect of testimony at trials held years earlier, has resulted in the granting of a writ of habeas corpus in numerous cases where the defendant could make any reasonable showing that false testimony was presented at trial.[17]

§9.03 *False Testimony* **Which May Not Be Presented to a Jury**

The rule which requires reversal if the government has allowed false testimony to be presented to the trier of fact depends, of necessity, on the definition of false testimony. Perhaps because of the nature of the deprivation which occurs when perjured testimony is introduced against an accused in a criminal case, courts have not been inclined to adopt a technical definition of the word *false*. Rather, courts have generally held that if testimony would be misleading to a

---

[11] Giglio v United States, 405 US 150 (1972); Napue v Illinois, 360 US 264 (1959); Giles v Maryland, 386 US 66 (1967).

[12] Giglio v United States, 405 US 150, 154 (1972); United States v Agurs, 427 US 97, 103 (1976).

[13] Commonwealth v Halewell, 477 Pa 232, 383 A2d 909 (1978).

[14] *Id*; Giglio v United States, 405 US 150, 154 (1972).

[15] Giglio v United States, 405 US 150, 154 (1972).

[16] Napue v Illinois, 360 US 264, 271 (1959).

[17] *See, e.g.*, Imbler v Craven, 299 F Supp 795, 812 (CD Cal 1969), noted in Imbler v Pachtman, 424 US 409, 414 (1976).

jury, even though technically not perjurious, the court must analyze the case in the same fashion as it would have if the prosecutor had knowingly introduced perjured testimony.[18] Illustrative is the Fifth Circuit's opinion in *Blankenship v Estelle*.[19] In that case, the habeas corpus petitioner alleged that, at his trial, the prosecutor asked two witnesses who had participated in the robbery for which he was being tried whether they were "under indictment" for the same crime, and they responded affirmatively. One witness denied on cross-examination that he had changed his story and testified against the defendant to "get himself off the hook." The petitioner alleged that there had been a tacit understanding that if the witnesses testified against the petitioner, the charges against them would be dismissed. The court held that if those allegations were true, the petitioner's rights would have been violated. The court noted that a course of conduct such as testifying could be "voluntary" although motivated by legally coercive considerations such as testifying or facing criminal prosecution.[20]

The principles outlined in *Blankenship* should be borne in mind by any attorney considering review of a file after conviction. In some states, it is still the practice of prosecutors to tell witnesses facing criminal charges that no formal promises will be made until after the trial in which they must testify.[21] Even if the statement is truthful, if both the prosecution and the witness understand that the witness will receive a benefit by testifying, it would appear that the witness's testimony that "no promises have been made" would be considered to be false, and the rule of *Mooney v Holohan*[22] invoked.[23]

§9.04 Duty to Provide Exculpatory Evidence — Upon Request

In *Brady v Maryland*,[24] the United States Supreme Court held that the suppression of evidence favorable to an accused after the accused's request violates due process when the evidence is material to guilt or punishment, irrespective of the good faith or bad faith of the prosecution. Perhaps because

---

[18] Dupart v United States, 541 F2d 1148 (5th Cir 1976); United States v Harris, 498 F2d 1164 (3d Cir), *cert denied*, 419 US 1069 (1974); *but see* Commonwealth v Gilday, 415 NE2d 797 (Mass 1980).

[19] 545 F2d 510 (5th Cir 1977).

[20] *Id* 514.

[21] *See, e.g.*, Commonwealth v Gilday, 1980 Mass Adv Sh 2551, 415 NE2d 797 (Mass 1980).

[22] 294 US 103 (1935).

[23] *Cf Franklin v State*, 97 Nev 220, 577 P2d 860 (Nev 1978) (prosecutor plea bargained with alleged accomplice of defendant by using his testimony at preliminary hearing, but would not allow him to plead guilty until after testifying; held, use of the testimony at trial violated defendant's due process rights).

[24] 373 US 83 (1963).

failure to provide exculpatory evidence on request is not as egregious as the use of false evidence, the Court has fashioned a separate standard to determine when a conviction must be reversed because of the prosecution's failure to provide exculpatory evidence. While a defendant seeking reversal of a conviction on the grounds that the prosecution knowingly used false testimony need only show the existence of any reasonable likelihood that the false testimony could have affected the judgment of the jury, the defendant alleging that the prosecution did not provide exculpatory evidence on request must show that the evidence was "material" to either guilt or punishment.[25] If the defendant makes no request for exculpatory evidence, or only a generalized request, a new trial will not be ordered unless the evidence creates a reasonable doubt which did not exist before.[26]

Because of the great difference between the showing a person must make to obtain a new trial when the allegation concerns denial of access to exculpatory evidence after a specific request, and when the allegation concerns denial of exculpatory evidence after a nonspecific request, a substantial number of courts have wrestled with the issue of what constitutes a *specific* production request. Federal courts have been willing to consider even requests which appear general on their face in the context of the litigation, to determine whether the request was specific or nonspecific and whether the defendant is entitled to have the court review the evidence at trial pursuant to the stricter standard of review.[27] The Eighth Circuit has pointed out that specificity cannot be determined in a vacuum, and that to determine whether a request is specific, the court must decide whether the prosecutor had reasonable notice of what it was that the defendant was seeking.[28] Thus, the literal language of the defense request, the reasonableness of the explanation of the failure to provide the evidence, and the statements of counsel at motion hearings may all be relevant.[29] In *Scurr v Niccum*,[30] the Eighth Circuit held, for example, that a request for "all statements exculpatory in nature" was, considering the context of the case, a specific request for evidence regarding other suspects, since in the course of one of the motion hearings, defense counsel had stated that he assumed exculpatory evidence would include evidence that "someone else did it."

In a major criminal investigation, police officers often develop leads in more than one direction before they become convinced of the guilt of one particular individual and concentrate their efforts on proof of that individual's guilt. Such

---

[25] United States v Agurs, 427 US 97, 104 (1976).

[26] *Id.*

[27] *See, e.g.*, Scurr v Niccum, 620 F2d 186 (8th Cir 1980); United States v McCrane, 547 F2d 204 (3d Cir 1976).

[28] Scurr v Niccum, 620 F2d 186 (8th Cir 1980); see §9.05.

[29] Scurr v Niccum, 620 F2d 186 (8th Cir 1980).

[30] 620 F2d 186 (8th Cir 1980).

parts of an investigative file become less important as the investigation progresses and may even be culled from the working file. In any case, it behooves a defendant's attorney to make a specific request for all evidence which suggests that any individual other than the defendant committed the crime charged so that even if the evidence is not produced, if a conviction results, the defendant may bear a far lighter burden in seeking a new trial.

§9.05 — When No Request for Exculpatory Evidence or a Nonspecific Request Is Made by the Defendant

In *United States v Agurs*,[31] the United States Supreme Court held that when the prosecutor has, in good faith, failed to provide a defendant with exculpatory evidence, but no specific request was made for the evidence, a heavy burden rests on the defendant who seeks a new trial. Distinguishing the cases in which the prosecutor knowingly uses false evidence (in which case the defendant need only show that the false evidence could, in any reasonable likelihood, have affected the judgment of the jury[32]) and the cases in which the prosecution does not provide exculpatory evidence after it has been specifically requested to do so (in which case the defendant must show that the evidence suppressed was *material* to the finding of guilt or innocence or the degree of punishment to be inflicted[33]), the Court held that when a defendant has made no request for exculpatory evidence, or a nonspecific request, and the government has not provided the defendant with exculpatory evidence, a new trial need not be granted unless "the omitted evidence creates a reasonable doubt that did not otherwise exist."[34]

The issues created by *Agurs*, in the words of Justice Kaplan of the Massachusetts Supreme Judicial Court, "have become a lively problem for the federal courts."[35] In addition to litigation over whether a particular request is specific or general,[36] there has been some conflict over whether the evidence must create a reasonable doubt in the mind of the reviewing court,[37] or whether the evidence must create a reasonable doubt in the mind of a rational juror.[38]

---

[31] 427 US 97 (1976).

[32] Mooney v Holohan, 294 US 103 (1935).

[33] Brady v Maryland, 373 US 83 (1963).

[34] United States v Agurs, 427 US 97, 112 (1976).

[35] Commonwealth v Ellison, 376 Mass 1, 15, 379 NE2d 560, 572 (1978).

[36] See §9.04.

[37] *See, e.g.*, United States v Gordon, 570 F2d 397, 402 (1st Cir 1978) (*doubt in mind of court* standard applied).

[38] Cannon v Alabama, 558 F2d 1211, 1214 n 11 (5th Cir 1977), *cert denied*, 434 US 841 (1978) (*doubt in mind of trial factfinder* standard applied).

for truth. A number of courts have suggested that, as a matter of state law, sanctions should be imposed on a prosecutor who violates state law.[53] But there are constitutional considerations which must be addressed in any case in which prosecutorial misconduct has occurred. First, the United States Supreme Court has suggested that if prosecution or police conduct is so shocking as to outrage the court, due process may bar the state from proceeding.[54] More fundamentally, the action of the prosecutor may affect the fairness of the trial itself, or a particular right of the defendant.[55] It has been held, for example, that when a prosecutor refuses to provide the address of a witness, as ordered by the court, so that the defendant may investigate his background and assess his veracity as a witness, the court may exclude the witness's testimony because to allow it would violate the defendant's Sixth Amendment right to confront the witnesses against him.[56] Similarly, it has been held that where the prosecution failed to comply with discovery orders on several occasions, and succeeded in having the matter continued to give it time to comply but did not comply even then, dismissal for violation of the defendant's speedy trial right was proper.[57] The lodestone is prejudice; the defendant who can show that improper action of the police or prosecutor has affected any of his or her rights may be able to obtain relief from the courts; otherwise, the remedy will be sanctions against the prosecutor, or the prosecutor's office, as an attorney.[58]

§9.08 Liability of Prosecutors for Violation of a Defendant's Constitutional Rights

A person whose constitutional rights have been infringed by the actions of a prosecutor may bring a civil action to recover damages for violation of his or her civil rights pursuant to 42 USC §1983.[59] If police officers have violated the civil rights of an individual, an action may be brought against them as well.

---

[53] *See, e.g.*, State v Smothers, 605 SW2d 128 (Mo 1980); State v Arthur, 118 NH 561, 391 A2d 884 (1978).

[54] Hampton v United States, 425 US 484, 495 n 7 (1976) (Powell, J, concurring); United States v Kelly, 31 Crim L Rep (BNA) 2149 (DDC May 31, 1982).

[55] Griffin v California, 380 US 609 (1965) (comment on failure of defendant to testify).

[56] State v Burgoon, 4 Kan App 485, 609 P2d 194 (1980).

[57] Commonwealth v Silvia, 413 NE2d 349 (Mass App Ct 1980).

[58] *See, e.g.*, State v High Elk, 298 NW2d 87, 90 (SD 1980) (prosecution comment to news media regarding defendant's prior record of felony conviction improper, but no violation of defendant's rights where jury did not hear the evidence).

[59] See generally, S. Nahmod, Civil Rights and Civil Liberties §§1.01-1.21 (Shepard's/McGraw-Hill 1979).

The United States Supreme Court has explicitly held that liability pursuant to 42 USC §1983 must be considered against a broad background of tort principles.[60] Thus, the Court has extended the common law immunity from tort liability to §1983 actions. The reason for immunity is not that the law presumes that prosecutors will always act in good faith, but rather that the societal interest in providing such public officials with the maximum ability to deal fearlessly and impartially with the public at large has long been recognized as an acceptable justification for official immunity.[61]

Thus, a prosecutor enjoys the same immunity from §1983 actions that prosecutors enjoyed from tort actions at common law.[62] A prosecutor is immune from civil liability for actions taken in the traditional role as a prosecutor, such as initiating a prosecution and presenting the state's case.[63] While the Supreme Court has expressly left the issue open, lower courts have generally held that when a prosecutor who acts outside the traditional role of a prosecutor and performs investigative functions he shares the good faith immunity afforded police officers.[64]

However, prosecutorial misconduct does not per se void a criminal conviction, no matter how egregious the misconduct; such misconduct may be harmless error.[65] The aim of due process is not punishment of society for the misdeeds of the prosecutor, but avoidance of an unfair trial to the accused.[66]

---

[60] Tenney v Brandhove, 341 US 367 (1951).

[61] Ferri v Ackerman, 444 US 193 (1979).

[62] Imbler v Pachtman, 424 US 409, 427 (1976).

[63] *Id* 431.

[64] Guerro v Mulhearn, 498 F2d 1249, 1256 (1st Cir 1974); see generally, S. Nahmod, Civil Rights and Civil Liberties §§7.10-7.11 (Shepard's/McGraw-Hill 1979).

[65] Smith v Phillips, 102 S Ct 940 (1982).

[66] *Id.*

privileges which have been invalidated are perhaps of lesser social significance. An individual suffering from an illness will probably see a physician, even if what the patient says might be used against him or her at some later date in court, but no individual would ever tell an attorney about having committed a crime if there were an expectation that the attorney might testify against the client in a subsequent proceeding.

In any event, no privilege will be cast aside merely because evidence produced thereby might be relevant. Generally, courts require the defendant to make a showing that the evidence sought is necessary to allow the defendant to adequately cross-examine the witness for the purpose of showing unreliability or bias.[39] The rule has been well stated by Judge Fuchsberg of the New York Court of Appeals in outlining the analysis to be applied in such cases. In the case before the court, a defendant sought discovery of police department personnel records of two police officers who were the chief government witnesses against the defendant:

> Granting, however, that the constitutional roots of the guarantee of compulsory process and confrontation may entitle these to a categorical primacy over the state's interest in safeguarding the confidentiality of police personnel records, it is not to be assumed that, in striking the balance between the two, police confidentiality must always yield to the demands of the defendant in a criminal case. The circumstances which support such demands may vary greatly. And, although an accused must be afforded access to otherwise confidential data relevant and material to the determination of guilt or innocence, as, for example, when a request for access is directed towards revealing specific biases, prejudices, or ulterior motives of the witnesses as they may relate directly to issues or personalities in the case at hand, or when it involves other information which, if known to the trier of fact could very well affect the outcome of the trial, there is no such compulsion when requests to examine records are motivated by nothing more than impeachment of witnesses' general credibility. In such cases, the defendant's rights have generally been canalized within the bound of the evidentiary rule that governs the introduction of extrinsic proof of matters collateral to the issues at trial, i.e., its availability rests largely on the exercise of a sound discretion by the trial court.[40]

When a defendant seeks privileged information and has made a showing which would tend to show an entitlement to the material, many courts hold

---

[39] *See, e.g.*, State v Farrow, 116 NH 731, 366 A2d 1177 (1976).

[40] People v Gissendanner, 48 NY2d 543, 545, 399 NE2d 924, 927, 423 NYS2d 893, 396 (1979).

that the presumptively privileged material should be examined by the trial court in camera to determine whether it should be turned over to the defendant.[41]

§10.04 Defendant's Constitutional Right to Obtain and Use Evidence of Rape Victim's Sexual History

Virtually all American jurisdictions have, within the last few years, enacted statutes which limit the introduction of evidence about a rape victim's sexual history.[42] These statutes differ among themselves in some degree, but they generally exclude evidence of the complainant's reputation for unchastity or prior sexual activity with persons other than the defendant. Their purpose is to limit the degree of embarrassment a rape complainant may be subjected to at trial. These laws have represented a new development in an area of the law which has been slow to reflect societal changes. Chief Justice Hale's famous dictum, that rape "is an accusation easily to be made . . . and harder to be defended by the party accused tho never so innocent,"[43] has been given as part of the jury instruction in rape cases in many American jurisdictions for many years.

The common law theory which permitted evidence of the rape complainant's reputation for prior sexual activity was that an unchaste woman was more likely to consent to sexual intercourse than a chaste woman. Some courts also admitted evidence of prior specific sexual activity on the same general theory.[44] This view of relevancy has been severely critized by commentators.[45]

Modern rape shield laws, in effect, create a statutory privilege to bar evidence of the complainant's prior sexual conduct at trial. While the privilege created is statutory and not constitutional, it is somewhat different from the other purely statutory privileges in that it protects what the United State Supreme Court has intimated is a constitutionally protected right—the right to engage in sexual intercourse.[46] Nonetheless, courts have been willing to set aside this "privilege"

---

[41] United States v Nixon, 418 US 638, 713-14 (1974); State v Farrow, 116 NH 731, 732, 366 A2d 1177, 1179 (1976); People v Gissendanner, 48 NY2d 543, 399 NE2d 924, 423 NYS2d 893 (1979).

[42] Tanford & Bocchino, *Rape Shield Laws and the Sixth Amendment*, 128 U Pa L Rev 544 (1980); a good example of these laws is Fed R Evid 412.

[43] 1 M Hale, Pleas of the Crown 634 (1st Am ed 1874).

[44] See generally, Annot, *Modern Status of Admissibility in Forcible Rape Prosecution, of Complaining Witnesses' Reputation for Unchastity*, 95 ALR3d 1181.

[45] One of the best and most cogent of the many criticisms appears in Berger, *Man's Trial, Woman's Tribulation: Rape Cases in the Courtroom*, 77 Colum L Rev 1, 15-22 (1977).

[46] Skinner v Oklahoma, 316 US 535, 541-42 (1942); *see also* Roe v Wade, 410 US 113 (1973).

there to be no constitutional basis to news reporters' claims of privilege. Such courts hold that when a defendant's fundamental constitutional right to a fair trial and the journalist's privilege collide, the reporter's privilege must yield.[56] In such circumstances, the journalist must generally provide the information sought or be incarcerated.[57] The majority of courts, however, regard the news reporter's privilege as constitutional in nature.[58] Thus, the reporter's First Amendment rights and the defendant's constitutional rights must be balanced. The approach taken by most courts, balancing the defendant's need for the information against the public interest in maintaining confidentiality, is similar to the approach used to determine whether the government should be permitted to keep the identity of a government informant confidential because the public interests in the free flow of information to the police and to journalists are so similar. The majority view has been well expressed by Chief Justice Barney of the Vermont Supreme Court:

> When a newsgatherer . . . objects to inquiries put to him in a deposition proceeding conducted in a criminal case on the ground of . . . privilege, he is entitled to refuse to answer unless the interrogator can demonstrate to the judicial officer appealed to that there is no other adequately available source of information, and that it is relevant and material on the issue of guilt or innocence.[59]

When courts determine that a journalist's privilege should not be sustained, they usually simply require the journalist to provide the information requested.[60] Frequently the reporters refuse and are held in contempt.[61] Commentators have pointed out the possibility of other remedies, such as dismissal of the prosecution or permitting the jury to draw an inference from invocation of a privilege,[62] but the practical operation of such procedures would seem difficult at best.

---

[56] *See, e.g., In re* Farber, 78 NJ 259, 394 A2d 330, 334, *cert denied,* 439 US 997 (1978).

[57] *Id.*

[58] *See, e.g.,* Bursey v United States, 466 F2d 1059, 1083 (9th Cir 1972); Hammarly v Superior Court, 89 Cal App 3d 388, 153 Cal Rptr 608 (1979); State v St Peter, 132 Vt 266, 315 A2d 254 (1974); Brown v Commonwealth, 214 Va 755, 204 SE2d 429 (1974); Zelenka v State, 83 Wisc 2d 601, 266 NW2d 279 (1979).

[59] State v St Peter, 132 Vt 266, 271, 315 A2d 254, 256 (1974).

[60] *See, e.g.,* Rosato v Superior Court, 51 Cal App 3d 190, 124 Cal Rptr 427 (1975), *cert denied,* 427 US 912 (1976); *In re* Farber, 78 NJ 259, 394 A2d 330, *cert denied,* 439 US 997 (1978).

[61] *Id.*

[62] See, e.g., Hill, *Testimonial Privilege and Fair Trial,* 80 Colum L Rev 1173 (1980).

§10.06 Defendant's Right to Discover and Use Information Which Another Person Claims May Incriminate Him or Her

When a defendant seeks to obtain information which another person claims may incriminate him or her, the defendant's constitutional right to a fair trial and the other individual's Fifth Amendment privilege to be free from testimonial compulsion collide. Under these circumstances, courts have invariably and uniformly held that the Fifth Amendment privilege must prevail.[63] However, under certain circumstances, the requirements of due process of law may force the prosecutor to grant immunity to defense witnesses or discontinue the prosecution.[64]

§10.07 Defendant's Right to Compel Prosecution Witnesses to Submit to Psychiatric Evaluation

Dean Wigmore suggested in 1940 that "no judge should ever let a sex offense charge go to the jury unless the female complainant's social history and mental makeup have been examined and testified to by a qualified physician."[65] This dictum has not been popular with feminists or most courts.[66] However, the law has generally recognized that in any sort of prosecution, a psychiatric evaluation of an important prosecution witness may be relevant and indeed crucial to the defense.[67] Obviously, such an evaluation has a substantial impact on the witness because the examination infringes on the witness's right to privacy and may well be used by a defendant to harass the witness.[68] Indeed, the possibility that

---

[63] *See, e.g.,* United States v Alessio, 528 F2d 1079, 1082 (9th Cir), *cert denied,* 426 US 948 (1976); Myers v Frye, 401 F2d 18, 20-21 (7th Cir 1968); State v Sims, 170 Conn 206, 209, 365 A2d 821, 823-24, *cert denied,* 428 US 954 (1976); People v Sapia, 41 NY2d 160, 164-65, 359 NE2d 688, 691, 391 NYS2d 93, 96 (1976).

[64] See §13.14.

[65] 3 Wigmore on Evidence §924(a) (Chadbourne rev 1970)

[66] *See, e.g.,* Forbes v State, 559 SW2d 318 (Tenn 1977); People v Davis, 91 Mich App 434, 282 NW2d 768 (1979).

[67] *See, e.g.,* State v Butler, 27 NJ 560, 143 A2d 530 (1958) (court-ordered psychiatric evaluation of chief government witness in murder case); *cf* United States v Hiss, 88 F Supp 559 (SDNY 1950) (the famous Alger Hiss perjury trial, in which the court held that psychiatric testimony concerning the government's chief witness, Whittaker Chambers, would be admissible); see generally Annot, *Necessity and Admissibility of Expert Testimony as to Credibility of Witness,* 20 ALR3d 684.

[68] United States v Benn, 476 F2d 1127, 1137 (DC Cir 1973).

a witness who complains of a crime may be required to submit to such an examination may deter the person from complaining about the crime.[69] Yet some courts have held that the defendant's need for information which can only be obtained by a psychiatric evaluation of a defendant may be elevated to the status of a constitutional right.[70] In finding a constitutional right to have a witness examined, courts have relied on the Sixth Amendment guarantee of the effective assistance of counsel[71] and on the Fourteenth Amendment guarantee of due process.[72] It would also seem that the defendant's Sixth Amendment right to compulsory process and to confront witnesses would support the right.

No court has ever, however, held that a defendant has the right to have a prosecution witness examined by a psychiatrist in all circumstances. Rather, courts generally hold that an examination should only be ordered in a few particular circumstances.[73] Many courts have stated that the defendant seeking the evaluation must present *compelling* reasons why it should be ordered.[74] Generally, courts require the defendant to produce substantial and convincing evidence at a pretrial hearing which impugns the psychiatric stability and testimonial credibility of the witness before ordering an examination.[75]

It would be impossible to catalog all of the reasons which would require such an evaluation. Certainly, if the witness is the only witness to a crime, and he or she has a history of mental illness which could cause hallucinations, an examination would seem necessary to safeguard the defendant's constitutional rights.[76] Most of the reported cases concern sex crimes. Psychiatrists have postulated, and some courts have accepted, the proposition that "a woman or girl may falsely accuse a person of a sex crime as a result of a mental condition that transforms into fantasy, a wishful biological urge."[77] Certainly a defendant who makes such a claim should, at a minimum be required to produce substantial evidence to support the claim, since the trauma of a sexual assault itself may be sharply increased by the indignity of a psychiatric examination.[78]

---

[69] *Id*; Forbes v State, 559 SW2d 318, 320 (Tenn 1977).

[70] *See, e.g.*, Ledbetter v United States, 350 A2d 379 (DC App 1976); State v Boisvert, 119 NH 174, 400 A2d 48 (1979).

[71] Ledbetter v United States, 350 A2d 379 (DC App 1976).

[72] State v Boisvert, 119 NH 174, 400 A2d 48 (1979).

[73] *See, e.g.*, State v Kahiru, 53 Hawaii 536, 498 P2d 635 (1972), *cert denied*, 409 US 1126 (1973); State v Miller, 35 Wis 2d 454, 157 NW2d 157 (1967).

[74] Ballard v Superior Court, 64 Cal 2d 159, 410 P2d 838, 49 Cal Rptr 302 (1966); State v Boisvert, 119 NH 174, 400 A2d 48 (1979); State v Kleuber, 132 NW2d 847 (SD 1965); *see also* Forbes v State, 559 SW2d 318, 320 (Tenn 1977) (examination should be ordered "only for the most compelling of reasons, all of which must be documented in the record").

[75] *See, e.g.*, State v Boisvert, 119 NH 174, 400 A2d 48 (1979).

[76] State v Butler, 27 NJ 560, 143 A2d 530 (1958); *cf* State v Farrow, 116 NH 731, 366 A2d 1177 (1976).

[77] Ballard v Superior Court, 64 Cal 2d 159, 410 P2d 838, 49 Cal Rptr 302 (1966).

[78] United States v Benn, 476 F2d 1127, 1137 (DC Cir 1973).

Of course, a witness may simply refuse to submit to a psychiatric examination despite the fact that a court has ordered him or her to do so. Particularly in cases where the witness is a victim of an alleged sexual assault, courts have not seen fit to hold the witness in contempt if he or she refuses to submit to an evaluation, but have allowed evidence of the witness's refusal to participate in such an examination to be presented to the jury.[79]

Right of Government to Discover Defendant's Case

§10.08 Government Discovery Right in General

Courts have approved the extension of discovery to the defendant, reasoning that increased discovery allows both the government and the defendant to more reasonably assess their cases and enchances the likelihood of a just verdict. Discovery, however, can be a two-way street, and courts have sometimes required that defendants provide information to the prosecutor in exchange for information received. State trial judges frequently require the defense and prosecution to exchange expert witness reports if expert testimony is anticipated.

It is settled that such discovery orders do not violate the defendant's Fifth Amendment rights as long as they do not require the defendant to testify and produce private papers. In *United States v Nobles*,[80] the United States Supreme Court held that a trial judge did not err in ordering that reports prepared for a defense attorney be produced and provided for examination and discovery by the prosecution when the defendant's attorney cross-examined two witnesses on the basis of statements allegedly given to the investigator by the witnesses. The court recognized that the work product doctrine[81] applies in criminal cases and that it could bar discovery in some cases. But even more significantly, the court held that the trial court's discovery order did not violate the Fifth Amendment.[82] The court reasoned that the Fifth Amendment privilege is primarily an "intimate and personal one" which protects "individual feeling and thought."[83] Production

---

[79] Ballard v Superior Court, 64 Cal 2d 159, 410 P2d 838, 49 Cal Rptr 302 (1966).
[80] 422 US 225 (1975).
[81] *See* Hickman v Taylor, 329 US 495 (1947).
[82] United States v Nobles, 422 US 225, 234 (1975).
[83] Couch v United States, 409 US 322, 327 (1973).

of an investigator's materials would not "compel" the defendant to be a witness against himself or herself or extract communication from the defendant.[84]

Discovery from the defendant does, however, implicate the defendant's right to due process of law. Appellate courts have scrupulously construed trial courts' discovery orders to ensure that the prosecution is not given any unfair advantage. The United States Supreme Court has noted that "the state's inherent information gathering advantages suggests that if there is to be any imbalance in discovery rights, it should work in the defendant's favor."[85] Illustrative is the decision of the Massachusetts Supreme Judicial Court in *Commonwealth v Hanger*,[86] in which the trial court, after trial had begun, granted the government's motion to discover whether the defendant intended to rely on an alibi defense, and if so, where the defendant was, and to discover the witnesses he planned to call, and granted the government's motion for copies of the statements the witnesses had made. The Supreme Judicial Court held that the discovery order violated due process, even though the commonwealth had supplied the defendant with written statements of all of its witnesses, grand jury minutes, and all the photos in its possession, because the order did not require the prosecutor to notify the defendant of the witnesses it intended to rely on in rebuttal.[87]

§10.09 Right of Prosecution to Discover Defendant's Alibi

The fairness aspect of discovery from the defendant has been considered most frequently in cases in which a statute or court rule requires the defendant to give notice of an alibi defense. The United States Supreme Court has generally approved of the purpose of such statutes, which is to make trial less of a sporting proposition and more a search for truth. As Justice White noted, the adversary system of trial "is not yet a poker game in which players enjoy an absolute right always to conceal their cards until played".[88] Requiring a defendant to give notice of an alibi defense does not violate the defendant's Fifth Amendment

---

[84] United States v Nobles, 422 US 225, 234 (1975); *see also* Fisher v United States, 425 US 391, 397 (1976) (suggesting that records otherwise privileged would not be privileged when placed in the hands of a third party, an attorney); Williams v Florida, 399 US 78, 82-84 (1970) (requiring defendant to get notice of alibi does not violate Fifth Amendment because the defendant is not "compelled" to raise an alibi defense).

[85] Wardius v Oregon, 412 US 470, 475 n 9 (1973).

[86] 377 Mass 503, 386 NE2d 1262 (1979).

[87] *Id.*

[88] Williams v Florida, 399 US 78, 82 (1970).

privilege against self-incrimination because the defendant is not "compelled" to raise the alibi defense.[89]

However, in *Wardius v Oregon*,[90] the court held that the due process clause of the Fourteenth Amendment forbade enforcement of rules excluding alibi evidence unless notice is given, except where reciprocal discovery rights are given the defendant. Courts have applied *Wardius* retroactively, so that if a defendant can show preclusion from raising an alibi defense because of the operation of a state notice of alibi rule, the defendant may be able to obtain postconviction relief.[91]

---

[89] *Id* 85.

[90] 412 US 470 (1973).

[91] *See, e.g.,* United States *ex rel* Hairston v Warden, 597 F2d 604, 609 (7th Cir 1979).

federal court] scrupulously review the record."[8] For example, the Court has held that a defendant who asserted his right to counsel when informed that he would be tried pursuant to a habitual offender statute, but who was denied a continuance in order to obtain counsel was denied his right to due process of law.[9]

There are no mechanical tests which may be applied to determine when a denial of a request for a continuance is so arbitrary and capricious as to violate a defendant's right to due process of law. Rather, the answer must be found in the facts of each case, with particular emphasis on the facts presented to the trial judge.[10] A defendant who alleges denial of due process because of a court's failure to grant a continuance must be prepared to show that he or she has been diligent. While it has been held to be violative of due process to refuse to allow an attorney a continuance to prepare for cross examination of a witness the attorney could not have reasonably anticipated would testify,[11] it has been held that denial of a continuance so that a defendant could have a psychiatric evaluation performed on him was not error, when the defendant had been indicted three months earlier and could have obtained an examination anytime during that period.[12] Courts have even upheld denial of continuances when a defendant runs out of witnesses because trial proceeds more quickly than the defendant anticipated and defense witnesses were not under subpoena or on notice.[13]

While the principles embodied in the decisions of the United States Supreme Court have remained immutable over the years, there is little doubt that time has rendered the factual aspects of some decisions meaningless as standards against which the grant or denial of a continuance may be measured.[14]

Speedy Trial

§11.02 Constitutional Right to Speedy Trial

The Sixth Amendment to the United States Constitution provides, in relevant

---

[8] *Id* 447.

[9] Chandler v Fretag, 348 US 3, 10 (1954).

[10] Ungar v Sarafite, 376 US 575, 589 (1964).

[11] People v Wilson, 397 Mich 76, 243 NW2d 257 (1976).

[12] Noble v Black, 539 F2d 586 (6th Cir 1976), *cert denied*, 429 US 1105 (1977).

[13] *Compare* O'Connor v United States, 399 A2d 1, 8 (DC 1979); *with* Shirley v North Carolina, 528 F2d 819, 822 (4th Cir 1975) (denial of due process where defense witness on way to testify was arrested by army officers for being AWOL, and the court would not grant a continuance until the witness, whose testimony was crucial, would be available).

[14] *See, e.g.,* Avery v Alabama, 308 US 444, 446-47 (1940) (held no error in denial of continuance where attorneys appointed three days before first-degree murder trial (which resulted in conviction and death sentence) began, even though appointed counsel was busy with other cases and claimed more time was needed to prepare a proper insanity defense).

part, that "in all criminal prosecutions, the accused shall enjoy the right to a speedy and public trial."[15] The importance of the right has long been recognized in Anglo-American jurisprudence. Sir Edward Coke interpreted the words of Magna Carta, "we will not deny or defer to any man either justice or right" to mean that "every subject . . . may take his remedy by the course of the law and have justice, and right for the injury done to him, freely without sale, fully without any denial, and speedily without delay."[16] Pointing out that the concept of a speedy trial stretches back even earlier than the time of Magna Carta, the United States Supreme Court has held that the right is a "fundamental right" and that it is applicable to state prosecutions.[17]

The Supreme Court has long been willing to consider claims that a speedy trial was denied.[18] The reasons for the pre-eminent position of the right are self-evident: a speedy trial ensures that the accused will not be subjected to oppressive pretrial delay; it serves to minimize the anxiety attendant on a public accusation; and it limits the possibility that the accused's opportunity to prepare a defense will be impaired.[19] Yet the right is said to be one of orderly expedition and not mere speed, for without the time to prepare a defense, all the other procedural guarantees afforded a criminal defendant would be meaningless.[20] Moreover, the right to a speedy trial is unique among all other constitutional rights because its denial can work to an accused's advantage. It is no secret among experienced criminal lawyers that time is the greatest cocounsel in the world. Witnesses' memories may fade or they may disappear.[21] Staff in a prosecutor's office may change and an old case may come to be regarded as a chestnut. The possibility of a viable speedy trial claim may convince the most tenacious prosecutor to consider a plea bargain.

In addition to the effect of denial of the right on the defendant and the prosecution, there is a palpable effect on the public at large. While awaiting trial on bail, a defendant may commit other crimes or jump bail.[22] Moreover, the delay between arrest and prosecution may have an untoward effect on the public perception of justice.

The importance of a speedy trial to both the participants and the public has led many jurisdictions, and the federal government, to enact speedy trial

---

[15] US Const, amend VI.

[16] E. Coke, Institutes 55 (Brooke ed 1797), *quoted in* Klopfer v North Carolina, 386 US 213, 224 (1967).

[17] Klopfer v North Carolina, 386 US 213, 223 (1967); moreover, each of the 50 states provides a similar guarantee to its citizens. *Id* 226.

[18] *See, e.g.*, Beavers v Haubert, 198 US 77 (1905).

[19] Smith v Hooey, 393 US 374, 377-78 (1969).

[20] Smith v United States, 360 US 1, 10 (1959).

[21] Barker v Wingo, 407 US 514, 519 (1972).

[22] *Id* 519.

laws[23] which provide that a case must be tried within a specific time frame or be dismissed. Such acts, where they exist, have rendered the constitutional litigation concerning speedy trial nugatory.

§11.03 When Right to Speedy Trial Attaches

In *United States v Marion*,[24] the defendants alleged that their Sixth Amendment right to speedy trial had been denied because charges were not instituted against them until three years after the government had gathered all of the information which enabled it to prosecute, and a three-year delay was so inherently prejudicial as to require dismissal. The United States Supreme Court rejected the defendants' claim and held that the Sixth Amendment speedy trial provision has no application until the putative defendant "becomes an accused," which occurred in the case before the Court when the defendants were indicted.[25] The Court made clear that there was no magic in the act of indictment in *Dillingham v United States*.[26] In that case, the court held that a defendant becomes an accused and the right to speedy trial attaches when the defendant is arrested, even if the defendant is not formally charged with a crime until after arrest. A few courts have suggested that there may be situations in which provisions of the Sixth Amendment guarantee to speedy trial are activated by *public charges* that fall short of the arrest or indictment specified in *Marion*.[27] It has also been suggested that a delay in bringing a federal indictment after dismissal of state charges based on the same transaction could be violative of the defendant's speedy trial rights.[28]

While most courts take the position that a defendant's Sixth Amendment right to speedy trial cannot be violated by prearrest or preindictment delay, the

---

[23] *See, e.g.*, 18 USC §§3161-3174.

[24] 404 US 307 (1971).

[25] *Id* 313. *See also* United States v MacDonald, 102 S Ct 1497 (1982).

[26] 423 US 64 (1975).

[27] *See, e.g.*, United States v Elsbery, 602 F2d 1054, 1059 (2d Cir 1979); United States v Vispi, 545 F2d 328, 331-32 n 2 (2d Cir 1976). Such a rule is suggested by Justice Douglas's concurring opinion in United States v Marion, 404 US 307 (1971); *but see* United States v MacDonald, 102 S Ct 1497 (1982).

[28] United State v Elsbery, 602 F2d 1054 (2d Cir 1979); United States v Lai Ming Tanu, 589 F2d 82, 88-89 (2d Cir 1978); *id* 90-91 (Oakes, J, concurring); United States v Mejias, 552 F2d 435, 443 (2d Cir), *cert denied*, 434 US 847 (1977); *but compare* United States v Shaw, 555 F2d 1295, 1298 (5th Cir 1977) ("Since we are considering pre-arrest and pre-indictment delay, the speedy trial clause of the Sixth Amendment is irrelevant to our analysis").

Fourteenth Amendment right to due process of law may be violated by such delay.[29]

§11.04 Effect of Delay in Bringing Charges

While the Sixth Amendment right to a speedy trial does not attach until a person is formally arrested or charged with a crime, it has long been recognized that a substantial delay in bringing charges may be as devastating to a person's right to a fair trial as delay after formal charges are brought. As early as 1844 Baron Alderson, in a much-quoted opinion, held that a charge of bestiality, made two years after the alleged crime, could not be prosecuted:

> It is monstrous to put a man on trial after such a lapse of time. How can he account for his conduct so far back? If you accuse a man of a crime the next day, he may be enable to bring forward his servants and family to say where he was and what he was about at the time; but if the charge be not preferred for a year or more, how can he clear himself? No man's life would be safe if such a prosecution were permitted. It would be very unjust to put him on his trial.[30]

The United States Supreme Court first suggested a due process limit on oppressive pretrial delay in *United States v Marion*,[31] noting in dicta that the government conceded that due process would require dismissal of an indictment if it were shown that the preindictment delay was an intentional device to obtain a tactical advantage over an accused.

A defendant who alleges that a pretrial delay has violated the right to due process of law must make a showing of prejudice.[32] But prejudice to the accused is not dispositive; a court must give equal weight to the reasons for the delay. There is no constitutional requirement that a prosecutor bring charges as soon as there is probable cause to do so; the prosecutor is free to delay instituting charges to see if other individuals may be implicated. Indeed, in *United States v Lovasco*,[33] the United States Supreme Court held that no constitutional violation

---

[29] See §11.04.

[30] Regina v Robbins, 1 Cox's Crim Cases (Somerset Assizes 1844).

[31] 404 US 307, 324 (1971).

[32] United States v Lovasco, 431 US 783, *rehearing denied*, 434 US 881 (1977); United States v MacDonald, 102 S Ct 1497 (1982).

[33] United States v Lovasco, 431 US 783, *rehearing denied*, 434 US 881 (1977).

had occurred where the prosecution delayed bringing charges for 17 months after having probable cause to do so, even though two potential defense witnesses died during the 17-month delay, since the prosecution's delay was caused by its desire to determine whether the defendant's son was also implicated in the crime. Apart from the obvious public interest in allowing prosecutors to delay the decision to charge, the Court recognized that the delay could benefit an accused, since insisting that prosecutors charge as soon as they have probable cause to do so would very likely pressure prosecutors into resolving doubtful cases in favor of early prosecution, and would not give the government a full opportunity to consider not charging the defendant.[34]

While establishing a broad due process rule, the Court has explicitly left to the lower courts the task of applying the principles it has established to particular cases.[35] Those courts have been remarkably unsympathetic to claims of preaccusation delay. Courts usually require a defendant alleging that due process rights were violated by such delay to show that the delay has caused *substantial prejudice* to the defendant's case. A showing that time has dimmed the memory of defense witnesses is usually not sufficient.[36] Delay until the defendant has been convicted of another crime, which could be used to impeach him or her is likewise insufficient.[37] Moreover, a showing of substantial prejudice alone is insufficient; the reasons for the delay must be examined.[38] It is only when the government has an "ulterior motive for the delay" that a violation of due process may be said to occur.[39]

Courts are divided regarding the burden of showing the government's bad faith. Some courts hold that, once a defendant shows prejudice resulting from a pretrial delay, the burden is on the government to show a legitimate reason for the delay.[40] Other courts require the defendant to prove both the prejudicial effect of the delay and the government's ulterior motive for the delay.[41]

---

[34] *Id* 793. *See also* United States v MacDonald, 102 S Ct 1497 (1982) (no violation of due process where murder on military base occurred in 1970, Army Criminal Investigation Division completed report in 1972 and, following evaluation of the reports, the Justice Department presented the case to a grand jury in 1974, obtaining an indictment in 1975).

[35] United States v Lovasco, 431 US 783, 797, *rehearing denied*, 434 US 881 (1977).

[36] United States v MacDonald, 102 S Ct 1497, 1509 (1982) (Marshall, J, dissenting); United States v Elsbery, 602 F2d 1054, 1059 (2d Cir 1979); United States v King, 560 F2d 121, 131 (2d Cir), *cert denied*, 434 US 925 (1977).

[37] United States v Krasn, 614 F2d 1229, 1235 (9th Cir 1980); United States Pallon, 571 F2d 497, 499 (9th Cir), *cert denied*, 436 US 911 (1978).

[38] United States v Packer, 586 F2d 422, 431, *rehearing denied*, 590 F2d 333 (5th Cir 1978), *cert denied*, 441 US 962 (1979).

[39] United States v Francesco, 575 F2d 815, 817 (10th Cir 1978).

[40] *See, e.g.*, United States v King, 593 F2d 269, 272 (7th Cir 1979); United States v Brand, 556 F2d 1312, 1317 n 2 (5th Cir 1977), *cert denied*, 434 US 1063 (1978).

[41] United States v Francesco, 575 F2d 815, 817 (10th Cir 1978).

§11.05 Standard for Determining When Right to Speedy Trial Has Been Denied

Because the right to speedy trial is fundamental, but deprivation of it may not always work to the disadvantage of an accused and may in fact work to the accused's advantage, the United States Supreme Court has held that the issue of speedy trial cannot be dealt with in absolute terms. There is no specific time at which a defendant's right to speedy trial must be said to have been violated, nor is there a quantifiable degree of prejudice which must accrue to a defendant before the right to a speedy trial must be considered to have been denied. Moreover, the length of delay between arrest and trial which is appropriate can vary, depending on the nature of the crime charged. Obviously, it takes longer to prepare a defense to a charge of homicide than to a charge of driving a motor vehicle while under the influence of an intoxicant.

For these reasons, the Supreme Court has held that a court considering a claim that a defendant has been denied the right to a speedy trial cannot adopt an inflexible rule, but must balance the conduct of the defendant against that of the prosecutor. In *Barker v Wingo*,[42] the Court held that a trial court must approach speedy trial claims on an ad hoc basis and must specifically consider four factors: the length of the delay; the reason for the delay; the defendant's assertion of the right; and the prejudice caused to the defendant.[43] No particular factor is pre-eminent although some courts stress the latter two factors. Indeed, the Court has specifically held that a defendant need not show prejudice to establish a violation of the right to a speedy trial.[44] Unintentional delay resulting from prosecutorial neglect or crowded trial dockets is to weigh less heavily against the prosecution than intentional delay.[45] Moreover, while a defendant must assert the right to a speedy trial, because it is a fundamental right, waiver cannot be presumed from a silent record.[46] In deciding that a reviewing court must, at a minimum, balance the four factors referred to above in determining whether a denial of the right to speedy trial has occurred, the Supreme Court was careful to note that it did not bar state courts from adopting a presumptive rule, in the exercise of their supervisory powers, to establish a fixed time period by the end of which cases must be tried or dismissed. A number of courts have done so.[47]

---

[42] 407 US 514 (1972).

[43] *Id* 530.

[44] Moore v United States, 414 US 25, 26 (1973).

[45] Strunk v United States, 412 US 434, 436 (1973).

[46] Barker v Wingo, 407 US 514, 526 (1972).

[47] *See, e.g.*, State v Hobson, 99 Idaho 200, 579 P2d 697 (1978)

§11.06 Effect of Denial of Right to Speedy Trial

Because of the important policies which underlie the constitutional right to a speedy trial, the United States Supreme Court has held that dismissal of charges is the only remedy for its violation.[48]

---

[48] Strunk v United States, 412 US 434, 436 (1973).

12

Guilty Plea

§12.18 Right to Withdraw Guilty Plea

§12.01 Effect of Guilty Plea

A plea of guilty is far more than a mere admission; it is itself a conviction.[1] Like the verdict of a jury, it is conclusive; all that remains for the court to do is to impose sentence.[2] For this reason, courts have long taken care to protect defendants from improvident pleas. Indeed, in 1765, Blackstone wrote:

> Upon a simple and plain confession, the court hath nothing to do but award judgment; but it is usually very backward in receiving and recording such confession, out of tenderness to the life of the subject, and will generally advise the prisoner to retract it and plead to the indictment.[3]

In addition to an admission of guilt, a plea of guilty also constitutes a waiver of an accused's federal constitutional right to be free from self-incrimination, to jury trial, and to confront prosecution witnesses. A valid guilty plea may be considered akin to a waiver of the right to challenge deprivation of constitutional rights which antedated the plea, where this deprivation does not stand in the way of establishment of factual guilt.[4] A valid plea of guilty does not, however, waive a claim that the charge made is one which the state may not prosecute. Thus, the United States Supreme Court has held that a counseled plea of guilty does not constitute a waiver of the defendant's right to challenge the prosecution on double jeopardy grounds.[5]

Because a guilty plea constitutes a waiver of a defendant's constitutional rights, federal standards must govern the validity of the plea, whether in state or federal court.[6] The Supreme Court has established a firm and unyielding rule: to be constitutionally valid, a plea of guilty must be voluntarily and intelligently made.[7] Moreover, apart from the substantive requirement that the plea be intelligently and voluntarily made, the Court has seemingly imposed a two-tier level of analysis on validity of guilty pleas, not unlike the two-tier analysis imposed on confessions by *Miranda*[8] and its progeny. Whether a plea

---

[1] Kercheval v United States, 274 US 220, 223 (1927).

[2] *Id* 223-24.

[3] 4 W. Blackstone, Commentaries 324 (U Chi ed 1979).

[4] *See, e.g.*, Tollett v Henderson, 411 US 258, 267 (1973). Of course under some circumstances a defendant may enter a so-called *conditional guilty plea*, pleading guilty conditionally but reserving the right to challenge portions of the prosecution's case.

[5] Menna v New York, 423 US 61, 62 (1975).

[6] *See, e.g.*, Boykin v Alabama, 395 US 238 (1969).

[7] *See, e.g.*, Brady v United States, 397 US 742 (1970).

[8] Miranda v Arizona, 384 US 436 (1966); see §5.16.

is intelligently and voluntarily made or not, a defendant has a constitutional right to withdraw it if the record does not *affirmatively show* that the plea was intelligently and voluntarily made.[9] For that reason, both state and federal courts generally hold detailed and complex hearings before allowing a defendant to enter a guilty plea to a serious charge.

There is, however, no constitutional right to have a guilty plea accepted by a court.[10]

Plea Bargaining

§12.02 Definition of Plea Bargain

A relatively small percentage of individuals accused of crimes stand trial. Instead they plead guilty pursuant to a plea bargain. A plea bargain is a simple arrangement: a defendant agrees to plead guilty to certain charges in exchange for the prosecutor's agreement to drop other charges, not to bring other charges, to recommend a specific sentence, or any one or combination of those things. The manner in which plea bargaining is conducted differs from one jurisdiction to another; for example, in some jurisdictions judges take an active role in plea bargaining, while in others their participation is strictly limited.[11]

The existence of plea bargaining had, prior to the rapid constitutionalization of criminal procedure in the 1960s, attracted the attention of federal courts on few occasions.[12] Indeed, for decades, it was "sub rosa practice, shrouded in secrecy and deliberately concealed by participating defendants, defense lawyers, prosecutors, and even judges."[13] But as the constitutional rights applicable to criminal defendants in state prosecutions were expanded, it became ever more

---

[9] *See, e.g.*, Boykin v Alabama, 395 US 238 (1969). McCarthy v United States, 394 US 459 (1969) which details the procedures followed in federal courts pursuant to Fed R Civ P 11. *See also* United States v Timmreck, 441 US 780 (1979).

[10] *See, e.g.*, North Carolina v Alford, 400 US 25 (1970); *see also* United States v David E Thompson, Inc, 621 F2d 1147, 1150-51 (1st Cir 1980) (no right of defendant to plead nolo to criminal antitrust violation, where effect of plea would have been to deprive injured persons of benefit of government's investigation).

[11] State v Chalaire, 375 So 2d 107, 108 n 1 (La 1979); Kisamore v State, 286 Md 654, 409 A2d 719 (1980).

[12] *See, e.g.*, Smith v O'Grady, 312 US 329 (1941); Kercheval v United States, 274 US 220 (1927).

[13] Blackledge v Allison, 431 US 63, 76 (1977).

clear that the practice of plea bargaining actually involved a negotiated waiver of constitutional rights. Thus, from 1970 or thereabouts, the United States Supreme Court, lower federal courts, and state courts of last resort have paid ever more attention to the manner in which plea bargaining is conducted.

The Supreme Court has expressly indicated its approval of the practice on numerous occasions. In *Santobello v New York*,[14] Chief Justice Burger noted that:

> The disposition of criminal charges by agreement between the prosecutor and the accused, sometimes loosely called plea bargaining, is an essential component of the administration of justice. Properly administered, it is to be encouraged. If every criminal charge were subject to a full scale trial, the States and the Federal Government would need to multiply by many times the number of judges and court facilities.[15]

The salutary effects of plea bargaining are palpable. First, the defendant may avoid extended pretrial incarceration and the anxieties and uncertainties of a trial. He or she gains a speedy disposition of the case, and the chance to acknowledge guilt and promptly begin the task of rehabilitation.[16] In addition to conservation of judicial and prosecutorial resources, the public is protected by limiting the period of time those guilty of crime are free on bail.[17]

The negative effects of plea bargaining are perhaps less palpable, but no less real. Obviously, a criminal defendant runs a risk of being overreached by the prosecutor, and cannot possibly be considered to have a similar bargaining position. Moreover, as a practical matter, the defendant will usually be responding to prosecution offers, and not initiating bargaining with any real hope of success. Certainly, the defendant facing incarceration is subjected to far more mental pressure than is a prosecutor facing the prospect of a trial instead of a plea. The defendant will always be less comfortable with the legal system than will an experienced prosecutor.

For these reasons, courts have begun to impose rather precise limits on the manner in which plea negotiations may be conducted. The United States Supreme Court has attempted to mitigate the defendant's natural and expected confusion by establishing procedures to ensure awareness of the existence of the rights being waived.

---

[14] 404 US 257 (1971).

[15] *Id* 260.

[16] Blackledge v Allison, 431 US 63, 71 (1977).

[17] *Id.*

Despite the fact that a defendant may receive a real advantage from plea bargaining, the Supreme Court has held that, as there is no constitutional right to plead guilty[18] there is no right to engage in plea bargaining.[19]

§12.03 Interpretation and Enforcement of Plea Bargain Agreements

There is a natural tendency among lawyers to consider a plea bargain as a kind of contract. Certainly, a plea bargain contains all of the traditional earmarks of a contract. The criminal defendant offers a benefit to the state by waiving trial, while the state offers the defendant a benefit by promising to recommend more lenient treatment.[20] Courts and lawyers have been encouraged to think of plea bargains as contracts by decisions of the United States Supreme Court holding that a prosecutor's plea bargain may be enforceable.[21]

There is no doubt that the concept of a plea bargain as a kind of contract is helpful in some circumstances. Indeed, some courts have flatly stated that plea bargaining disputes should be resolved by resort to contract law.[22] But the general rules of contract law cannot provide the only standards by which to interpret agreements between the government and a defendant who may be deprived of liberty. The Supreme Court has never looked favorably on attempts to engraft civil doctrines onto the branches of constitutional law.[23] While analysis of a plea bargain in contract terms will usually provide a reliable inclusive test for the existence of constitutional rights and violations, it may not provide an equally reliable exclusive test.[24] The obviously unequal bargaining positions of the defendant and the government, as well as the interest the courts have in ensuring that the prosecutor acts fairly, constrain the government from engaging in activity that would be accepted commercial practice.[25]

---

[18] North Carolina v Alford, 400 US 25 (1970); United States v David E Thompson Inc, 621 F2d 1147, 1150-51 (1st Cir 1980).

[19] Weatherford v Bursey, 429 US 545 (1977).

[20] Brady v United States, 397 US 742, 753 (1970).

[21] *See, e.g.*, Santobello v New York, 404 US 257 (1971).

[22] *See, e.g.*, United States v Krasn, 614 F2d 1229, 1233 (9th Cir 1980).

[23] *See, e.g.*, Brewer v Williams, 430 US 387, 401 n 8 (1977) ("We deal here not with notions of offer, acceptance, consideration, or other concepts of the law of contracts . . . but with constitutional law in deciding whether a prosecutor's promise to interrogate was enforceable"); Katz v United States, 389 US 347, 353 (1967) ("The premise that property interests control the right of the government to search and seize has been discredited"); Stoner v California, 376 US 483, 488 (1964) (rights protected by Fourth Amendment not to be eroded by strict application of the law of agency or by unrealistic application of apparent authority); Jones v United States, 362 US 257, 266 (1960) ("unnecessary and ill advised to import into 4th Amendment law . . . subtle distinctions of private property").

[24] *See, e.g.*, Cooper v United States, 594 F2d 12, 16-17, (4th Cir 1979).

[25] *Id.*

It must be remembered that a plea must be voluntary to be valid. Thus, while plea bargains may be specifically enforceable against the prosecution,[26] they are never specifically enforceable against a defendant.[27] While a certain degree of coercion by the prosecutor is permitted,[28] a great deal of law has developed concerning precisely what amount of coercion is permissible.

The distinction between contract law and the law of plea bargaining is illustrated by the use of the concept of promissory estoppel in plea bargaining. Some courts have held that if the prosecution makes a plea offer, it may be bound to it, without regard to whether the defendant has "detrimentally relied" on the offer, a traditional requirement for promissory estoppel.[29] Such courts have reasoned that the fairness required of a prosecutor is much greater than that required of a party in a commercial transaction.[30]

Requirements of Valid Plea

§12.04 General Requirements of Plea

Because a plea is conclusive, it is a final waiver of several important constitutional rights, including the right to jury trial, the privilege against self-incrimination, and the right to confront one's accusers. Even before such constitutional rights were held applicable to the states, the United States Supreme Court reviewed records of state pleas to determine whether the plea had been coerced or if circumstances of the plea violated the Fourteenth Amendment requirement of due process.[31] Since the application of federal constitutional rights to state court defendants, the United States Supreme Court has considered the records of plea hearings to determine whether the defendant knowingly waived all constitutional rights.[32]

The general rule is that, to be valid, a guilty plea must be *voluntarily and intelligently* made.[33] Much litigation has concerned the precise factors which

---

[26] Santobello v New York, 404 US 257, 262 (1971), *See also* Lane v Williams, 102 S Ct 1322 (1982).

[27] Kisamore v State, 286 Md 654, 409 A2d 719, 720-21 (1980); State v LaRoche, 117 NH 127, 131-32, 370 A2d 631, 634 (1977); see **§12.15.**

[28] See **§12.07.**

[29] *See e.g.*, Cooper v United States, 594 F2d 12, 16-17 (4th Cir 1979).

[30] *Id. But see* United States v Krasn, 614 F2d 1229, 1233 (9th Cir 1980); Commonwealth v Tirrell, 416 NE2d 1357, 1362 (Mass 1981); Government of VI v Scotland, 614 F2d 360, 365 (3d Cir 1980).

[31] *See, e.g.*, Pennsylvania v Claudy, 350 US 116, 118 (1956).

[32] *See, e.g.*, McMann v Richardson, 397 US 759, 764 (1970).

[33] *See, e.g.*, Brady v United States, 397 US 742, 748 (1970).

tend to render a plea involuntary, and these specific factors are considered in the following sections. The general rule can be stated as follows: a plea of guilty entered by one fully aware of the direct consequences, including the actual value of any commitments made to the defendant by the court, the prosecutor, or the defendant's own counsel, is voluntary, unless induced by threats, promises to discontinue improper harassment, misrepresentation, or promises that are by their nature improper.[34] The plea is voluntary if it represents a free and rational choice to plead rather than go to trial.[35] Similarly, in order for a guilty plea to be intelligent, the defendant must be aware of the significance of the plea.[36] Obviously, the inquiry to determine whether a plea is voluntarily and intelligently made is subjective in nature; it depends on the intellectual capacity and physical condition of the defendant.

Even if a plea is voluntarily and intelligently made, however, the defendant may have a federal constitutional right to withdraw the plea if the record of the plea hearing does not affirmatively show that the plea was voluntarily and intelligently made.[37] Such an affirmative showing is required because a guilty plea is a waiver of federal constitutional rights, and waiver may not be presumed from a silent record.[38]

Defense counsel bears much of the responsibility for ensuring that a client is aware of all of the consequences of a plea of guilty, as well as the alternatives to such a plea. Before allowing a client to plead guilty, most experienced attorneys send a client a letter detailing the elements of the crime charged, the plea bargain offer, a list of the rights being waived by such a plea, and the lawyer's recommended course of action. Many attorneys require the client to sign the letter, and then keep it in their files for their own protection.

§12.05 Voluntariness Requirement

Because the determination of whether a plea is voluntary depends on the subjective intent of the person pleading guilty, the circumstances surrounding the plea must be examined to determine whether a plea has been voluntarily made. The circumstances which can cause a plea to be involuntary are many. A defendant may plead guilty because of coercion, the threat of mob violence, fear, or out of a desire to simply "get it over with," and if so, the plea may be involuntary.[39] Of course, no defendant pleads guilty *voluntarily* as he or she

---

[34] *Id* 755.

[35] North Carolina v Alford, 400 US 25, 31 (1970).

[36] Henderson v Morgon, 426 US 637 (1976).

[37] Boykin v Alabama, 395 US 238, 242-43 (1969).

[38] *Id* 242.

[39] State *ex rel* White v Gray, 57 Wis 2d 17, 203 NW2d 638 (1973).

may voluntarily drink a glass of water. But what is required is not that the defendant's decision reflect a "wholly unrestrained will," but that it constitute an intelligent choice between available alternatives.[40] The voluntariness of any plea must be determined in light of all the surrounding circumstances.[41] Moreover, the government is not constitutionally permitted to inject some factors in the decision-making process.[42]

Innumerable factors may render a plea involuntary. For example, a decision to plead guilty because one's counsel is unprepared for trial will render the plea involuntary,[43] but erroneous advice from an attorney will not render the plea involuntary unless the attorney is incompetent.[44] The defendant's mental condition, use of intoxicants, and experience with criminal proceedings may all be relevant. While the ultimate inquiry in every case is subjective, enough litigation has concerned certain circumstances that it is helpful to discuss, in a general way, their impact.

§12.06 — Threat by Prosecutor to Charge a More Serious Crime

There is more obvious example of a practice which could render a defendant's plea of guilty involuntary, in the lay sense, than the threat to charge a more serious crime. Yet, the United States Supreme Court has explicitly held that a prosecutor may legitimately threaten a defendant with more severe charges if he or she does not plead guilty to the crime charged. The Court explicitly recognized in *Bordenkircher v Hayes*[45] that prosecutorial conduct which does no more than openly present the defendant with the unpleasant alternatives to a plea of going to trial or facing charges on which the defendant is plainly subject to prosecution does not violate the due process clause.[46]

However, a distinction must be made between plea negotiation and prosecutorial vindictiveness. It is a due process violation to punish a person for exercising rights. The Court has strongly suggested that a prosecutor cannot, without notice, bring a new and more serious charge based on a particular incident, where plea negotiations concerning a lesser charge stemming from the same incident have ended with the defendant insisting on pleading not

---

[40] Rosado v Civiletti, 621 F2d 1179, 1191 (2d Cir 1980).

[41] Brady v United States, 397 US 742, 749 (1970).

[42] Parker v North Carolina, 397 US 790, 802 (1970) (Brennan J, dissenting).

[43] Colson v Smith, 438 F2d 1075 (5th Cir 1971).

[44] McMann v Richardson, 397 US 759 (1970).

[45] 434 US 357 (1978).

[46] *See also* Platte v State, 600 SW2d 803 (Tex Crim App 1980).

guilty.[47] Moreover, while a prosecutor may legitimately bargain over the sentence to be imposed, if, after plea, the sentencing judge does not follow the agreed-on recommendation but instead determines to impose a lesser sentence, the prosecutor may not bring other charges based on the same incident unless the defendant knew or should have known that the plea was not intended to dispose of all charges arising out of the transaction.[48]

§12.07 — Threat to Impose a More Serious Penalty

Obviously, because the whole point of plea bargaining is, at least from the defendant's perspective, to ameliorate the punishment received, a prosecutor is not barred from encouraging pleas of guilty by offers of leniency or by threats of a greater sentence if the defendant proceeds to trial.[49]

There is no specific penalty which is so great that the threat of it renders a guilty plea *per se* involuntary. Indeed, in *Brady v United States*,[50] the United States Supreme Court held that the fact that the defendant was threatened with the death penalty if he did not plead guilty did not render his plea involuntary as a matter of law. The Court was careful to note, however, that if a showing could be made that the defendant's plea was made while he was "so gripped by fear of the death penalty or hope of leniency that he did not or could not, with the help of counsel, rationally weigh the advantages of going to trial against the advantages of pleading guilty," a different result might obtain.[51] In *North Carolina v Alford*,[52] the Court held that, under some circumstances, a defendant could plead guilty to avoid imposition of the death penalty if he was found guilty, even though he protested his innocence at the time of the plea. Such a plea is permissible, as long as there is a strong factual basis for the plea demonstrated by the state which substantially negates the defendant's claim of innocence and provides a means by which the trial judge can test whether the plea is intelligent.[53]

---

[47] Bordenkircher v Hayes, 434 US 357, 361 (1978).

[48] *See e.g.*, State v Lordan, 116 NH 479, 363 A2d 201 (1976).

[49] Bordenkircher v Hayes, 434 US 357, 365 (1978); Chaffin v Stynchcombe, 412 US 17, 30 (1973); Brady v United States, 397 US 742, 750 (1970).

[50] 397 US 742 (1970); *see also* North Carolina v Alford, 400 US 25 (1970).

[51] Brady v United States, 397 US 742, 750 (1970).

[52] 400 US 25 (1970).

[53] *Id* 37-38.

However, a defendant has no constitutional right to plead guilty, and a court may reject a plea in the belief that the public interest will not be satisfied by less than an explicit acknowledgment of guilt by the defendant.[54]

§12.08 —Statutory Requirement of Enhanced Penalty If Defendant Goes to Trial

Under some circumstances, the very existence of a statutory scheme which punishes exercise of a defendant's trial right may be unconstitutional. In *United States v Jackson*,[55] the United States Supreme Court held that the sentencing portion of the federal kidnapping statute was unconstitutional because it provided that the maximum penalty for a defendant who pled guilty was life imprisonment, while the maximum penalty for a defendant found guilty after jury trial was death. The Court reasoned that Congress could not "needlessly" chill the exercise by a defendant of the right to jury trial, a constitutional right.[56] The evil the Court found in the statute was "not that it necessarily coerces guilty pleas and jury waivers but that it needlessly encourages them."[57] The Court also found significant the fact that a defendant had no right to plead guilty and that a court could refuse to accept any plea of guilty.[58]

Obviously, any judicial system which allows and even encourages plea bargains, as does ours, must permit some encouragement of guilty pleas by statute as well as by prosecuting attorneys. The precise permissible amount of such coercion is open to some dispute.

In *State v Corbitt*,[59] the New Jersey Supreme Court held that the New Jersey statutory scheme which punished those accused of murder was not unconstitutional simply because under the New Jersey scheme, if a verdict of guilty to first-degree murder is returned by a jury, a mandatory sentence of life imprisonment must be imposed while a defendant pleading non vult may receive a sentence less than life imprisonment. The New Jersey court reasoned that the *Jackson* rationale was applicable only in cases where the plea avoided the possibility of the death penalty. In affirming, the United States Supreme Court noted in *Corbitt v New Jersey*[60] that while it "need not agree with the New Jersey court that the *Jackson* rationale is limited to those cases where a plea avoids any possibility of the death penalty's being imposed," it did

---

[54] *See, e.g.*, United States v Jackson, 390 US 570, 584 (1968); United States v David E Thompson, Inc, 621 F2d 1147, 1150-51 (1st Cir 1980).

[55] 390 US 570 (1968).

[56] *Id* 582.

[57] *Id* 583.

[58] *Id* 584.

[59] 74 NJ 379, 378 A2d 235 (1977).

[60] 439 US 212, 217 (1978).

consider the fact that the punishment to be avoided by a plea of non vult is life imprisonment, not death, which is "unique in its severity and irrevocability."[61] The Court emphasized its view that encouraging a defendant to make choices which waive constitutional rights was necessary in a system that encourages plea bargaining and pointed out that the gravamen of its holding was that the New Jersey statutory scheme did not create such a "powerful influence to coerce inaccurate pleas non vult" that it should be deemed constitutionally suspect.[62] The Court also recognized that the statutory scheme did not violate the Fourteenth Amendment right to equal protection by penalizing the exercise of a constitutional right.[63]

Justice Stewart, who had authored *Jackson*, concurring in the judgment, emphasized the important interests protected by the right to trial and suggested that a legislature could not, for example, provide that the penalty for every criminal defendant who pleads guilty is one-half that of a defendant convicted of the same offense after a jury trial.[64] Yet certainly there is no reason a prosecutor cannot constitutionally offer a defendant half the sentence which will be recommended if the defendant is convicted after trial. The majority in *Corbitt* seemed to make a distinction between the offers which could be made by a prosecutor and those which could be made by the legislature. It may be pointed out that a plea bargain offer made under a statute could be considered fairer than that made by a prosecutor, insofar as the limit on discretion equally limits the possibility of prosecutorial vindictiveness. Undoubtedly, further constitutional litigation will clarify the matter.

§12.09 — Offers of Leniency to or Threats to Relatives

Police and prosecutors may tacitly or openly threaten an accused's relatives in the face of the accused's intransigence, or offer them leniency as an inducement for a plea of guilty. Despite the repellant nature of such conduct, courts have been relatively slow to condemn the practice. While suggesting that making of threats or promises of leniency to a defendant's family or loved ones who are facing criminal liability themselves is certainly not desirable, the United States Supreme Court has left open the question of whether the practice renders a guilty plea involuntary per se.[65] The prevailing rule in most courts which have considered the issue appears to be that a threat or offer of leniency to a relative

---

[61] Gregg v Georgia, 428 US 153, 187 (1976).
[62] Corbitt v New Jersey, 439 US 212, 225 (1978).
[63] *Id* 226.
[64] *Id* 227 (Stewart, J, concurring).
[65] Bordenkircher v Hayes, 434 US 357, 363 n 8 (1978).

does not render a guilty plea involuntary as a matter of law, but may render the plea involuntary as a matter of fact.[66] The Wisconsin Supreme Court has noted that "a plea bargain which contemplates special concessions to another —especially a sibling or loved one —bears particular scrutiny by a trial or reviewing court conscious of the psychological pressures upon an accused in such a situation".[67]

§12.10 —Requirement That Defendant Understand Charge

A plea cannot be voluntary in the constitutional sense unless the defendant understands the crime to which he or she is pleading guilty. A defendant must have "actual notice of the charge against him," the first and most universal requirement of due process.[68] Thus, in *Henderson v Morgan*,[69] the United States Supreme Court held that a guilty plea was *involuntary* in the constitutional sense because the defendant's lawyers had not explained one element of the offense—that the murder of which the defendant was accused had to have been willful. In so holding, the Court assumed that the prosecutor had overwhelming evidence of guilt available, that the advice given by defense counsel to plead guilty was wise, and that the defendant, had he been apprised of the element, would have pled guilty anyway. The Court nonetheless held that intent was such a crucial element of the offense that without its exposition, a plea could never be voluntary in the constitutional sense of constituting an intelligent admission of the crime charged.[70] The Court left open the question of whether due process always requires a description of every element of the offense, assuming it did not.[71]

Lower courts have held that due process does not always require an explanation of every element of a charge or a showing that the defendant understood every element of a charge. The First Circuit, for example, has held that a defendant who lacked the intellectual capacity to understand all of the elements of a complex burglary statute, but nonetheless rationally chose to rely on his

---

[66] *See, e.g.,*Crow v United States, 397 F2d 284 (10th Cir 1968); Blinken v State, 46 Md App 579, 420 A2d 497 (1980); People v James, 393 Mich 807, 225 NW2d 520 (1975); State *ex rel* White v Gray, 57 Wis 2d 17, 203 NW2d 638 (1973).

[67] State *ex rel* White v Gray, 57 Wis 2d 17, 23, 203 NW2d 638, 644 (1973).

[68] Henderson v Morgan, 426 US 637, 644 (1976); the Court has assumed, without deciding that failure to advise a defendant of a mandatory parole requirement prior to accepting the defendants guilt plea would render the plea void. Lane v Williams, 102 S Ct 1322, 1326 n 9 (1982).

[69] 426 US 637 (1976).

[70] *Id* 647.

[71] *Id* 647 n 18.

competent counsel's advice to plead guilty, pled *voluntarily* in the constitutional sense.[72]

§12.11 Requirement That Guilty Plea Be Intelligent

An intelligent guilty plea is, in the constitutional sense, a plea that is knowingly made. A plea is intelligent if it is a voluntary and rational choice among the alternative courses of action open to the defendant.[73] The defendant must understand the charges faced, although the defendant need not have a lawyer's understanding of those charges.[74]

That a guilty plea is *intelligently* made does not mean that the advice given to a defendant by a lawyer to plead guilty is, in retrospect, correct. Waiving trial entails the risk that the evaluations of one's attorneys may not have been correct. In *McMann v Richardson*,[75] the United States Supreme Court held that a defendant who pleads guilty based on "reasonably competent" legal advice has entered an intelligent plea, not open to attack on the ground that counsel may have misjudged the admissibility of the defendant's confession. To show that a plea was not intelligent, the defendant must show that counsel's advice was outside the realm of competence required of attorneys in a criminal case, and thus, that the defendant was denied the effective assistance of counsel.[76] Similarly, even though a lawyer representing a defendant may have a gross conflict of interest, if that conflict does not affect the defendant's choice to plead guilty, the defendant's plea may not be considered unintelligent.[77]

§12.12 Competency to Plead Guilty

Because a plea of guilty is a waiver of important federal constitutional rights, it is tautological to say that a defendant cannot voluntarily plead guilty unless competent to do so. If a defendant is incompetent at the time of pleading guilty,

---

[72] Allard v Helgemoe, 572 F2d 1 (1st Cir), *cert denied*, 439 US 858 (1978).

[73] North Carolina v Alford, 400 US 25, 31 (197U); *see also* Lane v Williams 102 S Ct 1322, 1326 n 9 (1982) assuming, but not deciding a plea entered without knowledge of a mandatory parole term relating to sentences for the particular crime would be void.

[74] See §12.10.

[75] 397 US 759, 770 (1970).

[76] *Id* 770-71; see §14.09.

[77] Dukes v Warden, 406 US 250, 257 (1972) (even though attorney representing defendant had a conflict of interest, since that conflict of interest did not affect his decision to plead guilty, the conflict did not render his plea unintelligent); *but see* Holloway v Arkansas, 435 US 475, 489 (1978) (right to counsel is so basic that its violation can never be harmless error).

whether due to mental illness, intoxication, or the use of drugs, the plea will be constitutionally invalid.

A more difficult issue is the definition of competency. Traditionally, competency to stand trial has been considered a rather broad term. The standard of competency to stand trial was defined by the United States Supreme Court in 1960 as "whether the defendant has sufficient present rational ability to consult with his lawyer with a reasonable degree of rational understanding —and whether he has a rational as well as factual understanding of the proceedings against him."[78] Competency evaluations done by psychiatrists may be somewhat cursory; a defendant may be suffering from a mental disease and still satisfy the standard of competency to stand trial.

Most courts have assumed that the degrees of competency needed to stand trial and to plead guilty are the same.[79] A few courts have held that the degree of competency required to plead guilty is greater than the degree of competency required to stand trial because a plea of guilty constitutes a waiver of important federal constitutional rights.[80]

The difficulty with the position taken by those courts which hold that a higher standard of competency is necessary to plead guilty is that it may force some less competent defendants to forgo the advantages of plea bargaining.[81] Such a view raises serious equal protection questions. It seems likely that further litigation will concern this issue.

§12.13 Duty of Prosecutor When Plea Bargain Is Made

The law is settled that when a defendant pleads guilty in exchange for a specific sentence recommendation from the government, the government may not breach its part of the plea bargain under any circumstances. In *Santobello v New York*,[82] the United States Supreme Court held that where a defendant

---

[78] Dusky v United States, 362 US 402 (1960).

[79] *See, e.g.*, Allard v Helgemoe, 572 F2d 1 (1st Cir), *cert denied*, 439 US 858 (1978); United States *ex rel* McGough v Hewitt, 528 F2d 339 (3d Cir 1975); Malinvaskas v United States, 505 F2d 694 (5th Cir 1975); Wolf v United States, 430 F2d 443 (10th Cir 1970). See generally, Annot, *Compliance With Federal Constitutional Requirement that Guilty Pleas Be Made Voluntarily and Understandingly in Cases Involving Incompetent State Convicts*, 38 ALR Fed 238.

[80] *See, e.g.*, Seiling v Eyeman, 478 F2d 211, 215 (9th Cir 1973) (decision to plead guilty is a waiver of important constitutional rights, and the competency to waive those rights must be assessed "with specific reference to the gravity of the decision with which the defendant is faced"); United States v Moore, 599 F2d 310, 313 (9th Cir 1979); United States v Mattes, 539 F2d 721 (DC Cir 1976).

[81] Allard v Helgemoe, 572 F2d 1, 5 (1st Cir), *cert denied*, 439 US 858 (1978); *see also* United States *ex rel* Cybert v Rowe, 638 F2d 1100, 1103 n 8 (7th Cir 1981).

[82] 404 US 257 (1971).

had pled guilty in reliance on an agreement that a certain sentence would be recommended but, through inadvertence, a different sentence was recommended by the prosecutor, the judgment had to be vacated and the case remanded to the lower court for proper relief. That the sentencing judge had stated at the sentencing hearing that he would not consider the prosecutor's recommendation anyway was held irrelevant, since allowing the prosecutor's office to breach the plea bargain was inconsistent with the "interests of justice" and the "appropriate recognition of the duties of the prosecutor."[83]

That a prosecutor's office should be required to live up to its plea bargaining agreement seems obvious from a lawyer's basic grounding in contract law. But that very same grounding in contract law has led to some confusion over when the bargain that the prosecutor must live up to is made. Many courts have considered that a plea bargain can be considered to have been made when the traditional elements of the contract—offer and acceptance—are established.[84] For that reason, it is frequently held that the fact that the prosecutor has made an offer does not make the offer binding unless the defendant accepts the offer by pleading in reliance on the offer, unless there is a promissory estoppel.[85]

However, a strictly contractual analysis, or the creation of a doctrine of *constitutional promissory estoppel,* stands on a weak footing. The United States Supreme Court has been notoriously dubious about importing concepts of property law and contract law into the jurisprudence of fundamental constitutional rights.[86] The Fourth Circuit has held that merely because the elements of a promissory estoppel cannot be found in the actions of the prosecutor and the defendant does not mean a plea bargain should not be considered to have been created, since contract law, unlike the law concerning plea bargains, is not primarily concerned with fairness.[87] Once a prosecuting officer makes an offer, the prosecutor should be bound, because to hold otherwise creates the possibility of abuse by the prosecutor and harassment of the defendant.[88] Certainly, the prosecutor's action in offering and then withdrawing a plea bargain could lead to serious mental strain on the defendant,[89] and perhaps even more importantly, undermine the defendant's confidence in counsel.[90]

---

[83] *Id* 262.

[84] *See, e.g.,* United States v McIntosh, 612 F2d 835, 837 (4th Cir 1979); Commonwealth v Tirrell, 416 NE2d 1357 (Mass 1981).

[85] *See, e.g.,* Commonwealth v Tirrell, 416 NE2d 1357, 1361 (Mass 1981); Government of VI v Scotland, 614 F2d 360, 365 (3d Cir 1980); *cf* United States v Krasn, 614 F2d 1229, 1243 (9th Cir 1980).

[86] *See, e.g.,* Brewer v Williams, 430 US 387, 401 n 8 (1977); Katz v United States, 389 US 347, 352-53 (1967); Jones v United States, 362 US 257, 266 (1960).

[87] Cooper v United States, 594 F2d 12, 17 (4th Cir 1979).

[88] *Id.*

[89] Commonwealth v Tirrell, 416 NE2d 1357 (Mass 1981).

[90] Government of VI v Scotland, 614 F2d 360 (3d Cir 1980).

The fact that the trial judge imposes a lesser sentence on the defendant than the one recommended does not allow the prosecutor to prefer additional charges, arising out of the same incident, in order to obtain the sentence originally recommended.[91] Like the defendant in most jurisdictions, the prosecutor takes a chance in agreeing to a plea bargain, and the fact of disappointment with its outcome does not afford the prosecutor the right to try once again to inflict further punishment on the defendant.[92]

§12.14 Remedy for Prosecutor's Failure to Comply with Plea Bargain

There is no specific remedy to be afforded in all circumstances when the prosecution breaches a plea bargain agreement. In *Santobello v New York*,[93] a case in which the prosecutor at a sentencing hearing, through inadvertence, failed to recommend the sentence bargained for, the United States Supreme Court held that the judgment would be vacated and that the ultimate relief to be afforded Santobello would be left to the state courts. The Court made clear that the state courts could order specific proof of the plea bargain, which would require resentencing the defendant before a different judge, or could order that the defendant be permitted to withdraw his plea of guilty and proceed to trial.[94]

§12.15 Remedy for Breach of Plea Bargain by Defendant

Because a plea of guilty is a waiver of constitutional rights, the plea must be voluntary in the lay sense as well as in the constitutional sense. Thus, courts have generally held that the prosecutor is never entitled to specific performance of a plea bargain.[95]

---

[91] State v Lordan, 116 NH 479, 363 A2d 201 (1976).

[92] *Id* at 483, 363 A2d at 203; *but cf* United States v Krasn, 614 F2d 1229, 1234 (9th Cir 1980).

[93] 404 US 257 (1971).

[94] *Id* 263; *see also* Government of VI v Scotland, 614 F2d 360 (3d Cir 1980); Lane v Williams, 102 S Ct 1322 (1982).

[95] *See, e.g.*, Kisamore v State, 286 Md 654, 409 A2d 719 (1980); State v LaRoche, 117 NH 127, 131-32, 370 A2d 631, 634 (1977).

§12.16 Duty of Court When Plea Bargain Is Made

In some jurisdictions, judges are permitted to take part in plea negotiations. Such participation is often criticized because it may create an impression in the mind of the defendant that the judge wants him or her to plead guilty, and because the defendant may therefore, fear that if he or she goes to trial, a greater sentence will be imposed. Participation in the plea bargain may make it difficult for the judge to objectively assess the voluntariness of the plea. In those jurisdictions which permit such judicial participation, plea bargaining must be scrupulously honored.[96]

In most jurisdictions and under the Federal Rules of Criminal Procedure,[97] courts hold that a judge need not follow a prosecutor's recommendation made pursuant to a plea bargain and that the defendant has no right to withdraw a plea, as long as he or she was aware when entering the plea that the court was not required to follow the recommendation.[98] Indeed, the Illinois Supreme Court has held that a defendant is not entitled to withdraw a plea because of receiving a harsher sentence than bargained for even though the trial judge before sentencing had informed the defendant's counsel that he followed plea bargaining recommendations 90 to 95 per cent of the time, and in fact had in 50 cases only twice imposed a more severe sentence than that recommended, although he had imposed a more lenient sentence on several occasions.[99]

It cannot be disputed that, if a defendant is told by the court that if he or she pleads guilty, the court is not bound to follow the plea bargain, the defendant who nonetheless pleads guilty must, strictly speaking, be considered to have decided to assume the risk of a greater sentence. But as a practical matter, in most cases, judges do follow plea bargains. The defendant is encouraged to believe that the judge will do so by both the prosecutor and his or her own lawyer; a defendant who did not believe that the judge would follow the recommendation, would never, in most cases, plead guilty. Finally, and most importantly, a defendant who pleads guilty only to have the court impose a much more severe sentence than expected may, with some justification, feel taken advantage of. For that reason, a number of courts have begun to hold

---

[96] *See, e.g.,* State v Chalaire, 375 So 2d 107 (La 1979). See Alschuler, *Plea Bargaining,* 76 Colum L Rev 1059 (1978).

[97] *See* Fed R Crim P 11.

[98] *See, e.g.,* Miles v Parrott, 543 F2d 638 (8th Cir 1976); State v Adams, 342 So 2d 818 (Fla 1977); State v Ramos, 85 NM 438, 512 P2d 1274 (1973).

[99] People v Lambreuts, 69 Ill 2d 544, 372 NE2d 641 (1977). Of course, a plea may be rendered involuntary if a defendant is led to believe that a judge must impose the sentence recommended when that is not the law. *See, e.g.,* Miles v Parrott, 543 F2d 638 (8th Cir 1976); People v Frederick, 45 NY2d 520, 382 NE2d 1332, 410 NYS2d 555 (1978).

that, as a matter of fundamental fairness, a court should afford a defendant the opportunity to withdraw a plea of guilty if the court does not intend to follow the prosecutor's bargained-for recommendation.[100]

Withdrawal of Guilty Plea

§12.17 Requirement That Record of Plea Hearing Affirmatively Show That Plea Is Voluntarily and Intelligently Made

Because a plea of guilty is a waiver of important federal constitutional rights and because presuming waiver from a silent record is impermissible, the United States Supreme Court held in *Boykin v Alabama*[101] that the record of a plea of guilty must "affirmatively show" that the plea was intelligently and voluntarily made. If the record does not contain such a showing, the defendant has the right to withdraw the plea as a matter of federal constitutional law. For this reason, in felony cases in most jurisdictions, rather elaborate plea hearings are held and the proceedings are transcribed. Federal courts, in addition to requiring a virtual litany of questions, usually call the defendant directly to the judge's bench, so that the judge may observe the defendant's demeanor, and tape record, and also have the court reporter transcribe, the proceedings.[102] If the validity of the plea is questioned, the government has the burden of showing that the plea was voluntary and intelligently made.[103]

Boykin is applicable only to pleas entered after June 2, 1969, the date of the decision.

§12.18 —Right to Withdraw Guilty Plea

If the record of the plea hearing does show that the plea was intelligently and voluntarily made, the defendant does not have the right to withdraw the plea

---

[100] Schillert v State, 569 SW2d 735 (Mo 1978) (en banc); State v Goodrich, 116 NH 477, 363 A2d 425 (1976). Other Jurisdictions have established a similar rule by statute, People v Johnson, 10 Cal 3d 868, 519 P2d 604, 112 Cal Rptr 556 (1974), or court rule, Commonwealth v Evans, 434 Pa 52,252 A2d 689 (1969), thus eliminating the need for constitutional litigation. See generally Annot, *Right to Withdraw Guilty Plea in State Criminal Proceeding Where Court Refuses to Grant Concession Contemplated by Plea Bargain*, 66 ALR3d 902.

[101] 395 US 238, 242-43 (1969).

[102] *See* Fed R Crim P 11; McCarthy v United States, 394 US 459 (1969).

[103] Boykin v Alabama, 395 US 238 (1969).

as a matter of constitutional law.   Neither, however, is the defendant bound by the plea under all circumstances; he or she has the right to show that as a matter of fact the plea was involuntarily made, but bears the burden of making such a showing.[104]

If there are no constitutional aspects to the desire to withdraw the defendant's plea, the matter is usually, under state law, said to be within the court's discretion.

---

[104] *See, e.g.*, Blackledge v Allison, 431 US 63, 73-74 (1977); Tollett v Henderson, 411 US 258, 267 (1973).

13 Witnesses

Defendant's Right to Compel Attendance of Witnesses

§13.01 Nature and Source of Right to
Compel Attendance

The Sixth Amendment to the federal Constitution provides, in relevant part, that "[i]n all criminal prosecutions, the accused shall enjoy the right . . . to have compulsory process for obtaining witnesses in his favor."[1] Although the United States Supreme Court had held that the right to offer testimony was a basic ingredient of due process of law,[2] the Sixth Amendment guarantee of compulsory process was not held applicable to the states until 1967.[3]

Justice Story wrote in 1833 that the right to compulsory process was included in the Bill of Rights in reaction to the common law rule that, in cases of treason or felony, the accused was not allowed to introduce witnesses in his defense at all.[4] However, the common law rule forbidding the accused to call witnesses in felony cases had been abolished in England in the reign of Mary I and, by Blackstone's time, was regarded as an anachronism.[5] Of course, at the time of the adoption of the Constitution, the defendant was incompetent as a witness, as were his codefendants.[6] Given the somewhat ambiguous history on the point, the Supreme Court has not been content to be "bound by the dead hand of 1789," but has long been willing to consider the spirit as well as the letter of the Sixth Amendment in interpreting it.[7]

§13.02 Scope of Right to Compel
Attendance

The Sixth Amendment right to compel the attendance of witnesses encompasses the rights to present a defense and to present witnesses to the jury so that it may determine the truth. Perhaps because the nature of the right is so obvious and its value so universally recognized, the United States Supreme Court has considered it on relatively few occasions. In *Washington v Texas*,[8] the Court held that a Texas statute which barred a codefendant from testifying

---

[1] US Const amend VI

[2] *In re* Oliver, 333 US 257, 273 (1948).

[3] Washington v Texas, 388 US 14, 19 (1967).

[4] 3 Story, Comment on the Constitution of the United States §§7786-7787 (1st ed 1833), *cited in* Washington v Texas, 388 US 14, 20 n 12 (1967).

[5] 4 W. Blackstone, Commentaries 352-53 (U Chi ed 1979).

[6] United States v Reid, 53 US (12 How) 361 (1852).

[7] Rosen v United States, 245 US 467, 471 (1918).

[8] 388 US 14 (1967).

on behalf of the defendant violated the defendant's Sixth Amendment right to confrontation. The Court pointed out that the law was arbitrary because the accused accomplice could testify on behalf of the prosecution, when he would have had a great motive to fabricate his testimony, or if acquitted, when he could freely incriminate himself.[9] The Court held that the Texas statute violated the defendant's Sixth Amendment right to compulsory process because it arbitrarily denied him the right to put on the stand a witness who was physically and mentally capable of testifying to events that he had personally observed, and whose testimony would have been relevant and material to the defense.[10]

Chief Justice Warren, the author of the opinion, was careful to point out that nothing in the opinion should be construed as disapproving testimonial privileges, such as the privilege against self-incrimination or the husband-wife privilege, which are based on entirely different considerations from those underlying the common law disqualification for interest.[11] He further noted that the Court did not deal with state statutes or procedural rules which disqualify as witnesses persons who, because of mental incapacity or infancy, are unable to accurately observe events or testify about them.[12]

Thus, while lower courts have been willing to allow testimonial privileges to be pierced to afford a defendant the right to confrontation, at least in some circumstances,[13] they have not, as a general rule, been somewhat less willing to allow a criminal defendant to pierce a witness's testimonial or constitutional privilege to obtain evidence.[14] As Judge Jones of the New York Court of Appeals recently noted, the right to compel the attendance of witnesses is not absolute:

> The right exists only to the extent that witnesses may otherwise be compelled to attend and so testify; the Constitution mandates no more. Thus, there is manifestly no constitutional right to obtain the attendance of a witness who has disappeared or is otherwise unavailable. Similarly, the defendant has no right to compel testimony over a claim of recognized privilege such as that of attorney-client or of penitent-priest. Nor may testimony be extracted from a witness who appears but persistently refuses to testify despite the sanction of punishment for contempt. Furthermore, in none of such instances do courts accord a broader meaning to the Sixth Amendment by holding ·that where the desired testimony may not be

---

[9] *Id* 20-21.

[10] *Id* 23.

[11] *Id* 23 n 21.

[12] *Id.*

[13] See §13.08.

[14] *See e.g. Roznovsky v Estelle,* 546 F2d 1185, 1187 (5th Cir 1977); *State v Taylor,* 118 NH 859, 359 A2d 1239 (1978); see §10.03.

compelled, due process requires that the conviction of the defendant be set aside.[15]

There is, however, one exception to the rule that testimony may not be compelled over a witness's claim of constitutional privilege. Under some circumstances, if the government has interfered with the defendant's right to compel the attendance of witnesses, due process may require that the witness be afforded immunity for his or her testimony.[16]

§13.03 Infringement by Government Right to Compel Attendance

The United States Supreme Court has explicitly recognized that conduct by a judge or prosecutor which may make a witness less willing to testify for the defendant may in that way violate the defendant's right to due process of law. In *Webb v Texas*,[17] the defendant called as his sole witness a person who was serving a prison sentence. Before he testified, the trial judge admonished him about his duty to tell the truth and stated that if he lied, the "court would personally see that he was prosecuted."[18] The witness then declined to testify. Despite the fact that the defendant was available and could have, presumably, been required to take the witness stand, the Court held that the judge's threatening remarks, directed only at the single witness of the defendant, effectively drove that witness off the witness stand and thus deprived the defendant of due process of law. The Court tacitly recognized that there is a difference between the free and open testimony of a voluntary witness and the "perhaps guarded testimony of a witness who is willing to testify only at the command of a court."[19]

Lower courts have recognized that a prosecutor, as well as a judge, may infringe a defendant's right to compulsory process. For example, in *United States v Morrison*,[20] where the prosecuting attorney on several occasions "lectured" the defense witness in his office on the duty to testify truthfully and, as result of this lecture, the witness took the Fifth Amendment at the defendant's jury

---

[15] People v Sapia, 41 NY2d 160, 164-65, 359 NE2d 688, 691, 391 NYS2d 93, 96 cert denied, (1976), 434 US 823 (1977); *see also* State v Farrow, 118 NH 296, 386 A2d 808 (1978).

[16] See **§13.09.**

[17] 409 US 95 (1972).

[18] *Id* 98; *see also* United States v Thomas, 488 F2d 334 (6th Cir 1973).

[19] United States v Thomas, 488 F2d 334 (6th Cir 1973).

[20] 535 F2d 223 (3d Cir 1976).

trial, the Third Circuit held that the defendant's right to compulsory process had been violated.[21]

In *Webb v Texas*, the United States Supreme Court did not fashion any specific remedy for the Sixth Amendment violation other than reversal of the defendant's conviction. Lower courts have, however, recognized that mere reversal of a conviction may not be sufficient to remove the chilling effect of the unconstitutional action. A growing number of courts have held that only if immunity is given to the threatened witnesses may the violation be remedied.[22]

There is substantial authority for the proposition that a violation of a defendant's right to compulsory process can never be harmless error.[23]

Right to Confront Witnesses

§13.04 Nature and Source of Right to Confront

The Sixth Amendment provides, in relevant part, that "in all criminal prosecutions, the accused shall enjoy the right . . . to be confronted with the witnesses against him." The Supreme Court has long taken the view that the primary object of the provision is to prevent depositions and ex parte affidavits from being used against a defendant in lieu of personal examination and cross-examination.[24] The right ensures that the accused not only has the opportunity of testing the recollection of the witness, and "sifting the conscience of the witness, but of compelling him to stand face to face with the jury in order that they may look at him and judge by his demeanor upon the stand and the manner in which he gives his testimony whether he is worthy of belief."[25] The actual historical reason for the amendment is the subject of some scholarly dispute.[26] Whatever the historical nature of the right, and despite the occasional comment

---

[21] *See also* People v Shapiro, 50 NY2d 747, 409 NE2d 897, 431 NYS2d 422 (1980) (holding that the defendant's right to due process of law was violated when the prosecutor told a potential defense witness that "he would be subjecting himself to prosecution for perjury if he gets on the stand and tells a different story than he told before the grand jury"); *see also* United States v Hammond, 598 F2d 1008, 1013 (5th Cir 1979).

[22] People v Shapiro, 50 NY2d 747, 409 NE2d 897, 431 NYS2d 422 (1980); United States v Thomas, 488 F2d 334 (6th Cir 1973); *see also* United States v Herman, 589 F2d 1191, 1200 (3d Cir), *cert denied*, 441 US 913 (1978).

[23] United States v Hammond, 598 F2d 1008, 1013 (5th Cir 1979); *see also* United States v Morrison, 535 F2d 223 (3d Cir 1976); United States v Thomas, 488 F2d 334 (6th Cir 1973).

[24] Mattox v United States, 156 US 237, 242-43 (1895).

[25] *Id*, *quoted in* Barber v Page, 390 US 719, 721 (1968); *see also* Ohio v Roberts, 448 US 56 (1980).

[26] California v Green, 399 US 149, 177-78 (1970) (Harlan, J, concurring, discussing the views of Wigmore and other scholars).

that the right only preserves the right of confrontation as it existed at common law,[27] a review of the United States Supreme Court decisions interpreting the right discloses a specific body of law which has, over the years, gradually been refined and expanded.

The right was first held applicable to the states in 1965.[28] The right is fundamental; if, for example, a witness who has testified on direct examination invokes the Fifth Amendment on a material aspect of cross-examination, the witness's direct testimony will be stricken.[29] The precise contours of the right are explored in the following sections.

§13.05 Hearsay and the Confrontation Clause

There has traditionally been a tension between the constitutional right to confront the witnesses against one and the concept of hearsay. If the language of the Sixth Amendment were read literally, it would require, on objection, the exclusion of any testimony by a declarant not present at trial.[30] It has never been so applied. In contrast to the interpretations given to the Sixth Amendment right to compulsory process, the United States Supreme Court has looked beyond the form of evidentiary rules to determine whether a defendant's right to confrontation is violated by the substance of an arbitrary or unreasonable evidentiary rule. In a series of cases, the Court has considered a number of hearsay exceptions and their application to a defendant's case to determine whether the application of the hearsay exception violates the defendant's rights. The process has been a gradual one, in the common law tradition. While the Court has held that admission of prior testimony,[31] or of a prior inconsistent statement of a witness as substantive evidence,[32] or of a coconspirator's statement made after the conspiracy would have been considered over in most states, but not under the law of the state concerned,[33] does not violate the right, the Court has

---

[27] *See, e.g.*, Salinger v United States, 272 US 542, 548 (1926).

[28] Pointer v Texas, 380 US 400, 405 (1965).

[29] *See, e.g.*, United States v Cardillo, 316 F2d 606 (2d Cir), *cert denied*, 375 US 822 (1963); §13.09.

[30] Ohio v Roberts, 448 US 56 (1980).

[31] Mattox v United States, 156 US 237, 242-43 (1895).

[32] California v Green, 399 US 149, 161 (1970).

[33] Dutton v Evans, 400 US 74, 83 (1970). The peculiar confrontation problems created by admission of statements of a codefendant who does not testify at a joint trial are discussed in §16.04.

not hesitated to set aside convictions obtained when an archaic rule of evidence has caused fundamentally unfair results. Thus, where a statute allowed persons accused of the same crime to testify for the state but not for each other and thus barred the defendant from producing relevant evidence,[34] or when a state's *voucher rule* barred a defendant from cross-examining a witness who had given devastating evidence against him,[35] the Court found constitutional error.

The Sixth Amendment right to confront witnesses is not absolute, but relative; when a denial of the right to confrontation is claimed, courts will closely examine the competing evidentiary interests to determine whether the ultimate integrity of the fact-finding process has been called into question.[36]

In the course of holding that testimony at a prior hearing could be admitted at trial, Justice Blackmun reviewed the confrontation decisions and formulated a general framework of analysis, in *Ohio v Roberts*.[37] He noted that the Sixth Amendment established a rule of necessity, which means that the prosecution must either produce or demonstrate the unavailability of the declarant whose evidence it wishes to use against the accused. Once the witness is shown to be unavailable, the prosecutor must show that the hearsay to be placed before the jury has "indicia of reliability which have been widely viewed" as determinative of whether an out-of-court statement may be admitted.[38] Rejecting the criticisms of the many commentators who have written on the play between the confrontation clause and the admission of hearsay and urged the Court to take a new approach,[39] he noted:

> The Court has applied this indicia of reliability requirement principally by concluding that certain hearsay exceptions rest upon such solid foundations that admission of virtually any evidence within them comports with the substance of the constitutional protection. This reflects the truism that "hearsay rules and the confrontation clause are generally designed to protect similar values" and "stem from the same roots." It also responds to the need for certainty in the workaday world of conducting criminal trials.[40]

---

[34] Pointer v Texas, 380 US 400, 407 (1965).

[35] Chambers v Mississippi, 410 US 284, 299-302 (1973).

[36] *Id* 298; *see also* Mancusi v Stubbs, 408 US 204, 213 (1972) ("The focus of the court's concern has been to ensure that there are indicia of reliability which have been widely regarded as determinative and to afford the trier of fact a satisfactory basis for evaluating the truth of the prior statement").

[37] 448 US 56 (1980).

[38] *Id* 65 (quoting Mancusi v Stubbs, 408 US 204, 213 (1972)).

[39] 448 US at 66 n 9.

[40] *Id* 66.

§13.06 Prior Testimony of Witnesses

A significant number of cases have arisen concerning the effect of the confrontation clause on testimony given by a witness at a former trial. The traditional rule was that testimony given by a witness at a former trial, who was cross-examined by the defendant, could be admitted against a defendant in a subsequent trial if the witness had died by the time of the second trial.[41] Such testimony is admissible because the witness is unavailable and the testimony has indicia of reliability, i.e., the cross-examination by the defendant.

The United States Supreme Court has made clear that, in order for prior testimony to be admitted, the witness must truly be unavailable. In *Barber v Page*,[42] the Court held that testimony of a prospective witness who had testified at a former trial could not be admitted against the defendant at a subsequent trial merely because the state could show that the witness was incarcerated in another jurisdiction. The Court held a witness is not unavailable within the meaning of the exception to the confrontation clause unless the prosecution has made a good faith effort to obtain his or her presence.[43] Where a good faith effort to secure the attendance of the witness has been made, however, the prior testimony will be admissible if it meets the second prong of the standard for judging the admissibility of such testimony, indicia of reliability.[44]

The indicia of reliability depend on the circumstances of the case and the sufficiency of the opportunity to confront the witness. The Court has specifically left open the question of whether the opportunity to cross-examine, without actual examination, satisfies the confrontation clause.[45] Much depends on the circumstances of the prior testimony; for example, counsel examining at a probable cause hearing may proceed, and usually does proceed, very differently than he or she would at trial. A lawyer at a probable cause hearing may simply be attempting to learn as much as possible about the case. For that reason, he or she may ask questions to obtain information instead of asking questions he or she knows the answer to to highlight inconsistencies in the witness's testimony, as he or she would at trial. Moreover, in federal practice, and in many states, motions to suppress illegally obtained evidence may not be made at probable cause hearings. Recognizing these facts, the United States Supreme Court has held that cross-examination at a probable cause hearing is not necessarily sufficiently reliable to allow admissibility of the testimony if the witness becomes unavailable.[46]

---

[41] Mattox v United States, 156 US 237, 242-43 (1895).

[42] 390 US 719 (1968).

[43] *Id* 724-25; Ohio v Roberts, 448 US 56 (1980).

[44] *See, e.g.,* Mancusi v Stubbs, 408 US 204, 212-13 (1972).

[45] Ohio v Roberts, 448 US 56 (1980).

[46] Barber v Page, 390 US 719, 725 (1968); *see also* Pointer v Texas, 380 US 400 (1965).

Of course, in a federal system, each procedure and the circumstances of each case must be examined to determine if the confrontation bears indicia of reliability. In *Ohio v Roberts*,[47] the Court held that testimony of a witness at a Ohio probable cause hearing could be admitted at trial, where defense counsel's cross-examination of the witness was obviously a prepared cross-examination in form, replete with leading questions, and his examination satisfied the purposes of cross-examination.

§13.07 Extent of Cross-Examination

The right of confrontation would be meaningless if the extent of questioning of an accused allowed were narrowly circumscribed. Yet the entire trial process would be rendered nugatory if a trial judge could not control the bounds of cross-examination. Accommodation of these conflicting interests has led the United States Supreme Court to require that trial judges in criminal cases give broad latitude to an examiner on cross-examination, but also to hold that the right to cross-examine is a right to reasonably cross-examine.[48] In *Alfred v United States*,[49] for example, the Court held that the defendant's right to a fair trial was infringed when the trial judge refused to allow the defendant's attorney to ask a prosecution witness about his current address, although the defendant's attorney believed that the witness's address would show that he was in federal custody. In reversing the defendant's conviction, the Court established a general standard by which to judge the propriety of a line of cross-examination:

> Counsel often cannot know in advance what pertinent facts may be elicited on cross-examination. For that reason, it is necessarily exploratory; and the rule that the examiner must indicate the purpose of his inquiry does not, in general, apply. It is the essence of a fair trial that reasonable latitude be given the cross-examiner, even though he is unable to state to the court what facts a reasonable cross-examination might develop. . . . The extent of cross-examination with respect to an appropriate subject of inquiry is within the sound discretion of the trial court. It may exercise a reasonable judgment in determining when the subject is exhausted. But no obligation is imposed on the court, such as that suggested below to protect a witness from being discredited on cross-examination, short of an

---

[47] 448 US 56 (1980).

[48] Cheek v Bates, 615 F2d 559, 562 (1st Cir), *cert denied*, 446 US 944 (1980); United States v Ramirez, 622 F2d 898, 899 (5th Cir 1980); Smith v State 388 NE2d 484, 486 (Ind 1979).

[49] 282 US 687 (1931).

attempted invasion of his constitutional privilege from self-incrimination, properly invoked.[50]

Although not decided on constitutional grounds in 1931, it has become clear that the decision in *Alfred* is of constitutional dimension.[51] Perhaps because of the obviously crucial nature of cross-examination, few cases concerning the scope of cross-examination have reached the United States Supreme Court. Absent an evidentiary or statutory privilege in the witness, few judges are ever willing to cut off a defendant's questioning of the witness. In *Smith v Illinois*,[52] the Court held that a trial court's refusal to allow a defendant to obtain a government witness's real name and address violated the defendant's rights under the Sixth and Fourteenth Amendments. The Court made clear, however, that there had been no claim that release of the witness's name would have violated his Fifth Amendment privilege against self-incrimination.

§13.08 —Evidentiary Privileges of Witnesses

The traditional rule was that an evidentiary privilege rendered the testimony of a witness *unavailable* so that no constitutional issue was raised by the inability of a defendant to procure evidence or cross-examine.[53] However, in 1974, the Supreme Court held that an Alaska statute which forbade disclosure of a juvenile's record violated a defendant's constitutional right to confrontation, when the defendant was forbidden to examine the witness about his record, even though the record showed a strong motive to lie.[54] The same year, in the famous *United States v Nixon*[55] case, the Court held that the constitutional executive privilege must be "balanced" against the need for a fair trial when privileged materials are subpoenaed. These cases, and the resulting critical commentary, have led to a virtual explosion of law concerning what privileges must yield to the right to confront and to compulsory process. Because the right to present evidence and cross-examine cannot, in modern practice, be separated from the right to obtain access to information, these subjects are treated in Chapter 10 on discovery.

---

[50] *Id* 692-94.

[51] Smith v Illinois, 390 US 129, 133 (1968); State v Hassberger, 350 So2d 1 (Fla 1977); *see also* Cloud v State, 567 SW2d 801 (Tex Crim App 1978) (en banc).

[52] 390 US 129 (1968).

[53] *See, e.g.*, Washington v Texas, 388 US 14, 23 n 21 (1967).

[54] David v Alaska, 415 US 308 (1974).

[55] 418 US 683 (1974).

§13.09 —Witness's Invocation of Fifth Amendment Privilege

While a witness has an absolute right to invoke Fifth Amendment protection when called as a witness unless the witness is afforded immunity, courts have been vigilant to ensure that a defendant cannot be prejudiced by the witness's acts. In *Douglas v Alabama*,[56] a defendant and his codefendant were tried separately. The codefendant, who had been tried first, decided to appeal his conviction, and when the government called him in the defendant's trial, he invoked his Fifth Amendment privilege. The prosecutor, under the guise of refreshing his recollection, read his confession to him, which, of course, the defendant could not cross-examine the witness about. The Supreme Court held that the defendant's right of confrontation was violated by this procedure.

Such a procedure is, obviously, extraordinary. Far more common is the invocation of the Fifth Amendment privilege on cross-examination by a witness after having testified on behalf of the government. While the United States Supreme Court has never spoken to this issue, virtually all of the federal courts considering the issue have adopted the Second Circuit rule first enunciated in *United States v Cardillo*:[57]

> Where the privilege has been invoked as to purely collateral matters, there is little danger of prejudice to the defendant, and therefore the witness' testimony may be used against him. On the other hand, if the witness' invoking the privilege precludes inquiry into the details of his direct testimony, there may be a substantial danger of prejudice because the defense is deprived of the right to test the truth of his direct testimony and therefore that witness' testimony should be stricken in whole or in part.[58]

While application of the *Cardillo* test must turn on the facts of the particular case, a few specific rules have emerged. Generally, invocation of a Fifth Amendment privilege when the witness is asked about past crimes or pending

---

[56] 380 US 415 (1965).

[57] 316 F2d 606 (2d Cir), *cert denied*, 375 US 822 (1963); *see* United States v LaRoche, 549 F2d 1088 (6th Cir), *cert denied*, 430 US 987 (1977); United States v Newman, 490 F2d 139 (3d Cir 1974); Wisconsin v Gagnon, 497 F2d 139 (7th Cir 1974); United States v Ginn, 455 F2d 980 (5th Cir 1972); United States v Norman, 402 F2d 73 (9th Cir 1969), *cert denied*, 397 US 938 (1970); United States v Smith, 342 F2d 525 (4th Cir), *cert denied*, 381 US 913 (1965); Coil v United States, 343 F2d 573 (8th Cir), *cert denied*, 382 US 82 (1965); *see also* Dunbar v Harris, 612 F2d 690, 692 (2d Cir 1979).

[58] United States v Cardillo, 316 F2d 606, 611 (2d Cir), *cert denied*, 375 US 822 (1963); Dunbar v Harris, 612 F2d 690, 692 (2d Cir 1979).

charges does not require that direct testimony be stricken.[59] Testimony which involves the facts of the crime charged will, however, not be held collateral. For example, in *Cardillo*, the government witness who claimed he had given the defendant $5,000 for stolen furs refused to say where he got the $5,000. The Court held that his testimony was not collateral and held that his direct testimony should have been stricken.[60]

Immunity

§13.10 Privilege against Self-Incrimination and Immunity

The privilege against self-incrimination afforded by the federal Constitution is broad; since Chief Justice Marshall's time, it has been recognized that the privilege may not be construed to merely provide an accused with the right to refuse to admit to a crime:

> If the question be of such a description that an answer to it may or may not incriminate the witness . . . it must rest with himself; who alone can tell what the answer would be, whether to answer the question or not. . . . many links frequently compose the chain which is necessary to convict an individual of a crime. It appears to the court to be the true sense of the rule that no witness is compellable to furnish any of them against himself. . . .[61]

The breadth of the Fifth Amendment and of the correlative guarantees contained in most state constitutions has led to a proliferation of immunity statutes. These statutes generally authorize a prosecutor to give immunity from either the use of the testimony or prosecution for the crime in exchange for a person's testimony about the crime.[62]

The use of such statutes has been widespread. In 1972, the United States Supreme Court noted that every state in the Union had an immunity statute in force, and that there were 50 different federal immunity statutes.[63] In the past few years, there has been a flurry of cases dealing with abuse of the statutory

---

[59] *Id* 693-94; United States v Norman, 402 F2d 73, 76-77 (9th Cir 1969), *cert denied*, 397 US 938 (1970); United States v Ginn, 455 F2d 980 (5th Cir 1972).

[60] *See also* United States v Newman, 490 F2d 139 (3d Cir 1974).

[61] United States v Burr, 25 F Cas 38 40 (CC Va 1807) (No 14,692e).

[62] See generally Annot, *Prosecutor's Power to Grant Prosecution Witness Immunity From Prosecution*, 4 ALR4th 1221.

[63] Kastigar v United States, 406 US 441, 447 (1972).

immunity power. While the law is doubtless evolving an explicit scheme for protecting defendants from abuse of the immunity power, it must be remembered that prosecutors also have vast power to grant de facto immunity by simply not choosing to prosecute or by striking very fair plea bargains. Because use of immunized testimony may make a case more difficult to prosecute, immunity is granted in a relatively small percentage of cases in some jurisdictions.

§13.11 When Witness May Claim Privilege against Self-Incrimination

It was early suggested that an actual witness would be the only one who could determine what testimony would incriminate him or her.[64] Obviously, a rule which would place in the witness the power to determine whether to answer questions would be unsatisfactory, since the privilege protects only disclosures which would incriminate the witness, and not disclosures which might merely humiliate or embarrass. Thus, it has been generally held that it is for the court to say whether a witness's claim of privilege is justified.[65] On raising a claim of privilege, the witness need not prove the claim because this would compel the witness to surrender the protection afforded by the privilege. The United States Supreme Court has said:

> To sustain the privilege, it need only be evident from the implications of the question, in the setting in which it is asked, that a responsive answer to the question might be dangerous because injurious disclosure could result. The trial judge in appraising the claim must be governed as much by his personal perception of the peculiarities of the case as by the facts actually in evidence.[66]

The scope of the privilege is the same in both state and federal cases. The privilege is purely testimonial, and cannot be asserted to avoid compliance with a court order that a person produce a voice exemplar or a handwriting exemplar.[67]

Although, as a matter of law, the question of whether testimony would violate the privilege is for the court, as a matter of fact, in most instances, such an assertion by a witness will be honored. It is only in the extraordinary case, as where, for example, a witness refuses to give any testimony before a grand jury because of fear that testimony given may be at odds with the same witness's

---

[64] United States v Burr, 25 F Cas 38 (CC Va 1807) (Chief Justice Marshall).
[65] Rogers v United States, 340 US 367 (1951).
[66] Hoffman v United States, 341 US 479, 486-87 (1951).
[67] United States v Dionisio, 410 US 19 (1973).

prior statement, thus subjecting him or her to a perjury prosecution, that a court will find the privilege unavailable.[68] There is authority for the proposition that a witness may invoke the privilege where there is a real and palpable threat of a foreign prosecution.[69]

§13.12 Scope of Immunity Required by Constitution

Considering an immunity statute for the first time in 1895, the United States Supreme Court held that the Fifth Amendment privilege was broad and afforded a witness a privilege from being compelled to disclose the circumstances of his offense, or even the "sources from which, or the means by which, evidence of its commission, or his connection with it, may be obtained, or made effectual. . . ."[70] In dicta, the Court stated that no immunity can have the effect of supplementing the privilege unless it affords "absolute immunity against future prosecution for the offense to which the question related."[71] This type of immunity is referred to as *transactional immunity*—the witness who is given immunity is afforded immunity from prosecution for crimes arising out of the transaction.

Until 1970, federal statutes authorizing the grant of immunity purported to afford a witness transactional immunity. In 1970, however, Congress enacted 18 USC §6002, which provided authority for compulsion of testimony over a grant of immunity, and provided in relevant part that "no testimony or other information compelled under the order or any information directly or indirectly derived from such testimony or other information may be used against a witness in a criminal case, except a prosecution for perjury, giving a false statement, or otherwise failing to comply with the order."

This statute provided what is called *use and derivative use immunity*. A witness afforded such immunity is not immune from prosecution for the transaction about which he testified, but the prosecutor may not use the compelled testimony as evidence or as an investigative lead.[72] The prosecuting attorney may not even use any evidence obtained by focusing investigation on a witness as a result of compelled disclosures.[73] Indeed, once a person testifies under a grant of use immunity, if the person is later prosecuted, the government bears the burden of

---

[68] *In re* Boiardo, 34 NJ 599, 170 A2d 816 (1961). The propriety of a witness's claim of the Fifth Amendment privilege is discussed in greater detail in §7.04.

[69] *In re* Quinn, 525 F2d 222 (1st Cir 1975); The United States Supreme Court has explicitly left the question open. *See* Zicarelli v New Jersey Investigation Commn, 406 US 472 (1972).

[70] Counselman v Hitchcock, 142 US 547, 585 (1892).

[71] *Id* 586.

[72] Kastigar v United States, 406 US 441, 460 (1972).

[73] *Id* .

showing its evidence is not tainted, by establishing that it had an independent, legitimate source for the evidence objected to.[74] In *Kastigar v United States*,[75] the United States Supreme Court held that the statute providing use and derivative use immunity was constitutional. The Court reasoned that use and derivative use immunity leaves the government and the witness in the same position as if the witness had claimed the privilege.[76]

State courts and legislatures are free to provide broader immunity based on state constitutional privileges.[77] Of course, in a federal system, a single act may be a crime under both state and federal law. If a state grants a witness immunity from use of the testimony which would incriminate him or her under state law, federal prosecutors may not use the testimony to prosecute the individual for a federal offense, even if the testimony would incriminate the witness under federal law.[78] If the federal government intends to prosecute a witness for a crime about which the witness testified pursuant to a state grant of immunity, the federal prosecutors must, as in the case where a witness is prosecuted by federal authority for an offense about which the witness testified pursuant to a federal grant of immunity, show that their evidence is not tainted by establishing that they had an independent, legitimate source for the disputed evidence.[79]

§13.13 Permitted Use of Testimony Given under a Grant of Immunity

Virtually all immunity statutes provide that testimony given pursuant to a grant of immunity may be used in a prosecution for perjury based on false swearing. The United States Supreme Court has long held that there is no constitutional infirmity in such provisions.[80] In *United States v Apfelbaum*,[81] the Court held that a witness's *truthful* testimony, given under a grant of immunity, may be admitted at trial for false swearing to show the *falsity* of other statements made by the witness.

---

[74] *Id*.

[75] *Id*.

[76] *Id* 458-59.

[77] *See, e.g.*, NH Rev Stat Ann §516:34 (1955).

[78] Murphy v Waterfront Commn, 378 US 52, 79 (1964).

[79] *Id* 79 n 18. A witness need not answer questions put to him, despite a constitutionally sufficient grant of immunity if the source of the questioning is unlawful electronic surveillance. Gelbard v United States, 408 US 41 (1972).

[80] *See, e.g.*, United States v Mandujano, 425 US 564, 584-85 (1977); Bryson v United States, 396 US 64, 72 (1969); United States v Knox, 396 US 77, 82 (1969); Glicksteen v United States, 222 US 139, 142 (1911).

[81] 445 US 115 (1980).

However, if a person is tried for an offense about which he or she was questioned after a grant of immunity, statements made pursuant to the grant may not be admitted to impeach the person if he or she testifies differently at trial than at the proceedings at which the immunized testimony was given.[82] In such a case, the witness's prior statements cannot be used because they are compelled and therefore involuntary as a matter of law. In so holding in New Jersey v Portash[83] the Court found the rationale of *Harris v New York*,[84] inapplicable because, in that case, the need to deter unlawful police conduct collided with the need to prevent perjury. Justice Stewart wrote: "Here, by contrast, we deal with the constitutional privilege against self-incrimination in its most pristine form. Balancing therefore is not simply unnecessary. It is impermissible."[85]

§13.14 Right to Have Immunity Granted to Defense Witnesses

Doubtless the most unsettled aspect of the law of immunity is the defendant's right to immunized testimony. Traditionally, immunity has been a tool of the prosecutor.[86] But within the past 10 years, a number of state and federal courts have held or implied that due process may require that witnesses for the defense be afforded immunity.[87] Different courts have reached different conclusions about when due process would require immunity to be granted to defense witnesses.

Of course, a number of courts have rejected the theory that the Constitution requires that immunity be granted to defense witnesses in any circumstances.[88] A number of courts have pointed out the difficult separation of powers problem a court-ordered grant of immunity to a defense witness creates.[89]

---

[82] New Jersey v Portash, 440 US 450, 459 (1979).

[83] *Id.*

[84] 401 US 222 (1971).

[85] New Jersey v Portash, 440 US 450, 459 (1979).

[86] See, e.g., Annot, *Prosecutor's Power to Grant Prosecution Witnesses Immunity From Prosecution*, 4 ALR4th 1221 (1981).

[87] Grouchulski v Henderson, 637 F2d 50 (2d Cir 1980), *cert denied*, 101 S Ct 1383 (1981); United States v Carman, 577 F2d 556 (9th Cir 1978); United States v Morrison, 535 F2d 223 (3d Cir 1976); State v Farrow, 116 NH 731, 366 A2d 1177 (1976); People v Shapiro, 50 NY2d 747, 409 NE2d 897, 431 NYS2d 422 (1980); State v Broady, 41 Ohio App 17, 321 NE2d 890 (1974).

[88] *See, e.g.*, State v Swinborne, 116 Ariz 403, 569 P2d 833 (1977); Hebel v State, 60 Wis 2d 325, 210 NW2d 695 (1973).

[89] *See, e.g.*, United States v Herman, 589 F2d 1191, 1203 (3d Cir), *cert denied*, 441 US 913 (1978); *see also* People v Shapiro, 50 NY2d 747, 405 NE2d 897, 431 NYs2d 422 (1980).

Judicial immunity is most frequently considered an appropriate remedy when the government has intentionally attempted to interfere with the defendant's right to present evidence on his or her own behalf.[90] In *United States v Morrison*,[91] for example, the prosecutor repeatedly called a defense witness to his office and "lectured" the witness on her rights so that she refused to testify that she and not the defendant was guilty of the offense charged and invoked her Fifth Amendment right. The Third Circuit held that due process required that, on retrial, the witness be afforded immunity. In *United States v Herman*, the Third Circuit quantified the standard established in *Morrison*, holding that a defendant seeking judicial immunity for a witness must be prepared to show that the government's actions were taken "with the deliberate intention of distorting the judicial factfinding process."[92]

Some courts have held that immunity may constitutionally be required even if the prosecution has not attempted to deliberately distort the fact-finding process. The Third Circuit has held,[93] and other courts have suggested,[94] that due process requires immunity to be granted to a defense witness where immunity is the only way in which clearly exculpatory evidence can be presented to a jury. The Third Circuit has created a procedure whereby a witness who seeks immunity must make a showing specifying the particulars of the witness's testimony, and that it is clearly exculpatory, not cumulative, and does not relate merely to credibility.[95] Once the defendant satisfies this threshold burden, the state's countervailing interests must be considered.[96]

While this view is favored by some commentators,[97] well-reasoned opinions have held that immunity cannot be given witnesses merely because it seems fair to grant it.[98] Undoubtedly, the ultimate resolution of the issue of a defendant's due process right to immunity will be in the United States Supreme Court.

---

[90] *See, e.g.*, United States v Turkish, 623 F2d 769, 771-79 (1979); United States v Morrison, 535 F2d 223 (3d Cir 1976).

[91] *See, e.g.*, United States v Herman, 589 F2d 1191, 1203 (3d Cir), Witcert denied, 441 US 913 (1978); Witsee also People v Shapiro, 50 NY2d 747, 409 NE2d 897, 431 NYS2d 422 (1980).

[92] 589 F2d 1191, 1204 (3d Cir), *cert denied*, 441 US 913 (1978).

[93] Government of VI v Smith, 615 F2d 964, 970-74 (3d Cir 1980).

[94] United States v Alessio, 528 F2d 1079 (9th Cir), *cert denied*, 429 US 873 (19769.

[95] Government of VI v Smith, 615 F2d 964, 970-74 (3d Cir 1980).

[96] *Id.*

[97] See, e.g., Westen, *The Compulsory Process Clause*, 73 Mich L Rev 73 (1974).

[98] Grochulski v Henderson, 637 F2d 50 (2d Cir 1980), *cert denied*, 101 S Ct 1383 (1981).

14 Right to Counsel

Right of Indigent Persons to Counsel

§14.01 Nature and Source of Right of Indigents

The Sixth Amendment to the federal Constitution provides, in pertinent part, that "in all criminal prosecutions, the accused shall enjoy the right . . . to have the assistance of counsel for his defense."

The Sixth Amendment has, over recent years, been interpreted to provide that an indigent person may not be jailed without being represented by counsel. The evolution of the right to counsel began in 1932, when the United States Supreme Court first held that denial of counsel could constitute denial of due process of law in some circumstances.[1] In 1938, the Court held that the Sixth Amendment strips federal courts of all power to deprive individuals of their life or liberty unless they are afforded, or voluntarily waive, counsel.[2] In 1942, the Court held that due process required that counsel be appointed in state cases whenever the failure to do so would result in a denial of *fundamental fairness*.[3]

The dichotomy between state and federal courts diminished in 1963 when the United States Supreme Court held in *Gideon v Wainwright*[4] that the Sixth Amendment was applicable to the states and that, therefore, indigent state felony defendants had to be afforded counsel at state expense. Eventually the Court held that counsel must be afforded in all misdemeanor cases, state or federal, which actually result in imprisonment.[5] A misdemeanor conviction obtained without counsel which does not result in imprisonment, although not constitutionally defective, may not be used to enhance a second misdemeanor to a felony.[6]

Litigation over the right to counsel in the abstract is rare; the law concerning the existence of the right is unquestioned. There are, however, significant areas of litigation which concern when the right to counsel is applicable and when the attorney afforded a defendant is constitutionally sufficient. It is these areas which this chapter discusses.

Courts have begun to examine the quantity and quality of legal services required. The United States Supreme Court has held that an indigent need not be afforded all the services a person with unlimited resources could bring to bear to avoid conviction of crime. In *Ross v Moffitt*,[7] for example, the Court held that the Fourteenth Amendment did not require that counsel be afforded indigents for discretionary appeals to North Carolina courts, considering the North Carolina statutory scheme. The Court made plain that the states need

---

[1] Powell v Alabama, 287 US 45, 71 (1932).
[2] Johnson v Zerbst, 304 US 458 (1938).
[3] Betts v Brady, 316 US 455 (1942).
[4] 372 US 335 (1963).
[5] Scott v Illinois, 440 US 367 (1979); Argersinger v Hamlin, 407 US 25 (1972).
[6] Baldasar v Illinois, 446 US 222 (1980) (per curiam).
[7] 417 US 600, 610 (1974); *see also* Wainwright v Torna, 102 S Ct 1300 (1982).

"not duplicate the legal arsenal that may be privately retained by a criminal defendant."[8]

§14.02 When Right Attaches

The right to counsel cannot be considered apart from the right to be free from self-incrimination. In *Miranda v Arizona*,[9] the United States Supreme Court held that a person who is arrested has a right to an attorney in order to be informed of, and fully effectuate the Fifth Amendment privilege to be free from compulsory self-crimination. The right to counsel guaranteed by the Sixth Amendment has a different reach. In a number of decisions, the United States Supreme Court has held it applicable or inapplicable, depending on whether the particular stage of the proceedings may affect substantial rights of the accused.[10]

The decisions of the Court have not been uniform. In *Kirby v Illinois*,[11] it held that the right to counsel extended only to postindictment identification proceedings. Justice Stewart acknowledged that the Court's decisions concerning the right to counsel had established no specific rationale, but noted that all involved points "at or after the initiation of adversary judicial criminal proceedings —whether by way of formal charge, preliminary hearing, indictment, information, or arraignment".[12] There are obviously few proceedings after the institution of formal judicial proceedings in which an accused's rights could not be affected. Still, Justice Stewart's dictum cannot serve as an inclusive test for the right to counsel, for the Court has considered cases after the institution of charges where counsel is not required. The Court has held that the right to counsel is applicable at preliminary hearings, which occur in some states which retain grand juries, because discoverable information may be obtained from those prosecution witnesses who testify, and because a record may be made of their testimony which may be used for impeachment at trial.[13] But an important distinction must be made between those types of hearings at which witnesses must testify under oath and where the right to confrontation exists, and the narrower type of hearing required by the Supreme Court's decision in

---

[8] *Id* 616.

[9] 384 US 436 (1966); *see also* Escobedo v Illinois, 378 US 478 (1964).

[10] Mempa v Rhay, 389 US 128 (1967).

[11] 406 US 682 (1972).

[12] *Id* 689. Some state courts have taken a more liberal view. See §5.02.

[13] Coleman v Alabama, 399 US 1 (1970).

Gerstein v Pugh.[14] In *Gerstein*, the Court held that an individual could not be incarcerated for an extended period of time under a prosecutor's information without an impartial judicial determination of probable cause, whether by a magistrate's arrest warrant or by a grand jury indictment or hearing. Such hearings are not adversary hearings, and despite the fact that they occur after the institution of formal judicial charges, an indigent defendant is not entitled to counsel.[15]

The Court has held that counsel is required at arraignment if the defendant seeks to enter a guilty plea.[16] If the arraignment consists only of charges being read to the defendant, and the defendant is not allowed to enter a plea, counsel is not necessarily required. Whether defendant is entitled to counsel as a matter of constitutional law if summoned before a grand jury is questionable, although it is settled that counsel may not accompany the defendant inside the grand jury room.[17] Neither a defendant nor counsel has any right to be present if not summoned, even if the defendant knows the grand jury is considering his or her case.[18] A defendant is entitled to counsel at all stages of trial[19] and at sentencing.[20] The Fourteenth Amendment guarantee of equal protection of the laws requires that an indigent be afforded counsel for at least one appeal from a conviction.[21] Counsel need not be afforded at state expense for discretionary appeals.[22]

In sum, whether counsel is required depends on the nature of the proceeding and whether counsel can aid the defendant. If there is any way counsel can aid a defendant at a proceeding after formal judicial charges have been instituted, counsel's presence will be considered constitutionally required; if not, counsel's presence will not be considered constitutionally required.

§14.03 Proceedings in Which Right Is Applicable

The United States Supreme Court has explicitly held that the Sixth Amendment right to counsel is applicable at every stage of criminal proceedings

---

[14] 420 US 103 (1975).

[15] *Id* 122.

[16] White v Maryland, 373 US 59 (1963).

[17] United States v Mandujano, 425 US 564 (1976); *compare* plurality and dissenting opinion of Justice Brennan; *see also* United States v Cannesa, 644 F2d 61 (1st Cir 1981); **§7.08.**

[18] Gerstein v Pugh, 420 US 103 (1975).

[19] Geders v United States, 425 US 80 (1976).

[20] Mempa v Rhay, 389 US 128 (1967).

[21] Ross v Moffitt, 417 US 600 (1974); Douglas v California, 372 US 353 (1963).

[22] Ross v Moffitt, 417 US 600 (1974); *see also* Wainwright v Torna, 102 S Ct 1300 (1982).

where substantial rights of an accused may be affected.[23] The Court has tended to construe the term *criminal proceeding* somewhat narrowly, to include only procedures involving investigation of crime, proof of crime, and sentencing. Thus, while the Court has held that counsel must be afforded indigents in criminal cases when their probation is revoked and a deferred sentence is imposed.[24] there is no Sixth Amendment right to counsel in a probation revocation hearing where the sentence has already been imposed.[25] Similarly, because a parole revocation hearing[26] or a prison disciplinary hearing[27] cannot be considered part of the criminal process, there is no Sixth Amendment right to counsel for indigents at such hearings.

The Sixth Amendment, however, is not the only constitutional guarantee which may afford a criminal defendant protection. An individual who faces loss of liberty, whether the proceedings are denominated civil or criminal, must be afforded due process of law. The process due depends on the circumstances; if the hearing an individual faces is complex, or if self-representation is impossible, the due process clause of the Fourteenth Amendment may require that he or she afforded counsel. The Court has held that the decision must be made on a case-by-case basis; the Court must consider whether the facts involved in the hearing are complex or difficult to develop, and whether the defendant appears capable of speaking for himself or herself.[28] Because juveniles are presumed to be incapable of speaking for themselves, the due process clause of the Fourteenth Amendment requires counsel at "civil" juvenile delinquency hearings which may be result in a loss of liberty.[29]

§14.04 Indigent's Right to Expert Services

The focus of litigation concerning an indigent's right to counsel has shifted away from the right to counsel, which is firmly established, to the right to effective assistance of counsel. Perhaps the clearest example of this shift is the flood of litigation concerning an indigent's right to obtain expert services.

No attorney who has ever tried a serious criminal case can doubt the efficacy and, in some cases, the necessity of expert assistance. Though a defendant has a valid insanity defense, it may be impossible to effectively present it to

---

[23] Mempa v Rhay, 389 US 128, 134 (1967).

[24] *Id.*

[25] Gagnon v Scarpelli, 411 US 778, 782 (1973).

[26] Morrissey v Brewer, 408 US 471 (1972).

[27] Wolff v McDonnell, 418 US 539 (1974); *see also* Baxter v Palmigiano, 425 US 308 (1976).

[28] Gagnon v Scarpelli, 411 US 778,791 (1973); *see also* Morrissey v Brewer, 408 US 471 (1972) (parole revocation); *cf* Wolff v McDonnell, 418 US 539 (1974) (prison disciplinary hearing).

[29] *In re* Gault, 387 US 1 (1967).

a jury unless the defendant's attorney has the opportunity to consult with a psychiatrist who will help the attorney understand and effectively cross-examine the government's psychiatric expert. In a case involving many witnesses, or in one which has been investigated intensively by the government, the sheer number of potential witnesses may require that a defendant's attorney be afforded the services of an investigator.

While it is still possible to find courts which reject a constitutional right to expert services out of hand,[30] by far the majority of courts have begun to recognize a defendant's constitutional right to expert services.[31] Courts generally premise the indigent's right not on the Sixth Amendment right to counsel, but on the Fourteenth Amendment's guarantees of fundamental fairness and equal protection.[32] No court has ever held that an investigative expert is constitutionally required in all circumstances. Rather, relying on the United States Supreme Court's decision in *Ross v Moffitt*,[33] that due process requires that indigents be furnished counsel for one appeal (but not for discretionary appeals) because the single appeal allows them to fairly present their claims, courts have generally held that expert services must be furnished a defendant whenever failure to do so would deny the defendant's right to fundamental fairness.[34] The need for expert services must be determined, of course, on the facts and circumstances of each case.[35] The defendant has the burden of convincing the court that the grant of expert services is necessary.[36]

Courts have recognized that it may be difficult, in advance of trial, for counsel representing an accused to demonstrate a need for such services. The Ninth Circuit has stated:

> [Counsel] can at least advise the court as to the general lines of inquiry he wishes to pursue, being as specific as possible. He should advise the court why it is not practical for counsel himself to make the investigation, with or without the allowance of out of pocket expenses. If a reasonable showing of this kind is made, the trial court should probably view with liberality a motion for pre-trial assistance.[37]

---

[30] *See, e.g.*, Hoback v State, 338 So 2d 439 (Ala Crim App) *cert denied*, 338 So 2d 444 (Ala 1976); State v Glass, 283 So 2d 696, 697 (La 1976).

[31] Mason v Arizona, 504 F2d 1345, 1351 (9th Cir 1974), *cert denied*, 420 US 936 (1975); *See, e.g.*, State v Lee, 221 Kan 109, 558 P2d 1096 (1976); see generally Annot, *Right of Indigent Defendant in Criminal Case to Aid of State by Appointing of Investigator or Expert*, 34 ALR3d 1256.

[32] *Id. See also* Ruff v State, 65 Wis 2d 713, 223 NW2d 445 (1973).

[33] 417 US 600 (1974).

[34] United States v Charis, 486 F2d 1290 (DC Cir 1973); State v Lee, 221 Kan 109, 558 P2d 1096, 1100-01 (1976); Graham v State, 547 SW2d 531 (Tenn 1977).

[35] Mason v Arizona, 504 F2d 1345, 1352 (9th Cir 1974), *cert denied*, 420 US 936 (1975).

[36] *Id.*

[37] *Id* 1352.

Courts have also recognized that the government may improperly gain information about defense strategy if allowed to attend a hearing on a defendant's request for expert services. Where a defendant objects to the government's presence at such a hearing, failure to exclude the government is error.[38]

If a court fails to appoint an investigator or expert at a defendant's request, it is generally held on appeal that the defendant must show substantial prejudice by clear and convincing evidence.[39]

One common area of litigation merits special attention. While statutes and court rules granting defendants the right to experts are of relatively recent vintage, most jurisdictions have long had statutes providing for examination of those accused of crime and thought to be mentally ill.[40] Under such statutory schemes, the defendant is usually sent to a government facility and a report is made to the court.[41] Much litigation has concerned whether this type of examination is constitutionally sufficient. Most courts have assumed that such a statutory scheme meets the due process standard of allowing the defendant the opportunity to fairly present the claim in the context of the state's procedure,[42] and that the defendant has no constitutional right to an independent psychiatric evaluation, although the trial court may have discretion to appoint an independent psychiatrist.[43]

§14.05 Indigent's Right to Choose Appointed Counsel

Most American jurisdictions have established public defender systems to meet the needs of indigents. Even in jurisdictions in which members of a public defender's office rather than the private bar are expected to handle substantially all of the indigents charged with crime, private attorneys must be appointed in

---

[38] *See, e.g.,* United States v Sutton, 464 F2d 552 (5th Cir 1972); Marshall v United States, 423 F2d 1315 (10th Cir 1970). However, the defendant must make a showing of prejudice. Mason v Arizona, 504 F2d 1345, 1353 (9th Cir 1974), *cert denied,* 420 US 936 (1975).

[39] United States v Eagle, 586 F2d 1193 (8th Cir 1978); Mason v Arizona, 504 F2d 1345, 1154-55 (9th Cir 1974), *cert denied,* 420 US 936 (1975); *see also* United States v Harris, 524 F2d 1283, 1315 (7th Cir 1977).

[40] See generally Annot, *Right of Indigent Defendant to Aid of State by Appointing of Investigator or Expert Services,* 34 ALR3d 1256.

[41] *See, e.g.,* 18 USC §4244, which provides that a court may, on motion, appoint a psychiatrist to examine the defendant and report back to it, and 18 USC §3006(A)(e), which authorizes the court to appoint experts to aid an indigent defendant.

[42] Ross v Moffitt, 417 US 600 (1974).

[43] United States v Oliver, 626 F2d 254 (2d Cir 1980); United States v Charis, 486 F2d 1290, 1292 (DC Cir 1973); State v Lee, 221 Kan 109, 558 P2d 1096 (1976); State v Thomas, 310 So 2d 517 (La 1975); Commonwealth v Silvia, 371 Mass 819, 359 NE2d 942 (1977); Graham v State, 547 SW2d 531 (Tenn 1977). *See also* State v Downs, 51 Ohio St 2d 47, 364 NE2d 1140 (1977).

some cases, because codefendants may have conflicting interests and the public defender's office may not be able to represent all of the individuals involved in a particular transaction.

Nothing is more common in criminal courts than to hear an indigent excoriate the public defender's office and request that a private attorney be appointed to handle a case. Courts have, however, uniformly held that an indigent has no constitutional right to choose the particular attorney who will represent him or her.[44] Courts generally reason that allowing an indigent to choose the particular attorney desired would create impossible problems in administration, because every defendant would want a Clarence Darrow and yet a defendant may be ill-equipped to choose an attorney.[45] Moreover, allowing the defendant to choose an attorney could, quite obviously, lead to dilatory tactics and delay.[46]

The general rule that a defendant may not choose an attorney must, however, yield when a defendant and his or her lawyer have a disagreement as to tactics affecting some fundamental right which is of sufficient magnitude to jeopardize the defendant's right to effective assistance of counsel.[47] A common example of such a breakdown in the attorney-client relationship is the decision to testify; while the decision whether a defendant should testify is within the realm of a defendant's attorney, the right to testify at one's trial is a fundamental one.[48] A court must give close attention to a defendant's motion to substitute counsel based on the disagreement between attorney and defendant about the defendant's testifying.[49] Refusal by a court to substitute counsel where a defendant's attorney refused to call a defendant as a witness, and the defendant asserted a wish to exercise the right to testify, would raise troubling constitutional questions.

§14.06 Waiver of Counsel and Right to Proceed Pro Se

While the United States Supreme Court has been jealous of a defendant's right to counsel and has been unwilling to assume waiver of counsel from

---

[44] See, e.g., Brown v Graven, 424 F2d 1160, 1170 (9th Cir 1970); Drumgo v Superior Court, 8 Cal 3d 830, 506 P2d 1007, 106 Cal Rptr 631 (1973) (en banc), cert denied, 414 US 979 (1974); Costarelli v Municipal Court, 367 Mass 35, 323 NE2d 859 (1975); Commonwealth v Chumley, 482 Pa 626, 394 A2d 497 (1978), cert denied, 440 US 966 (1979); see generally Annot, Indigent's Right to Choose Participating Counsel Appointed to Represent Him, 66 ALR3d 966, but see Tague, An Indigent's Right to the Attorney of His Choice, 27 Stan L Rev 73 (1974).

[45] Costarelli v Municipal Court, 367 Mass 35, 323 NE2d 859 (1975).

[46] Id.

[47] Drumgo v Superior Court, 8 Cal 3d 930, 506 P2d 1007, 106 Cal Rptr 631, cert denied, 414 US 979 (1974); see also Commonwealth v Tyler, 468 Pa 193, 360 A2d 617 (1976).

[48] People v Robles, 2 Cal 2d 205, 215, 466 P2d 710, 85 Cal Rptr 166 (1970).

[49] Id.

a silent record,[50] the Court has never suggested that defendants who wish to represent themselves must be represented by counsel. But defendants who do so must bear the consequences of their actions.

In 1943, the Court reversed a holding of the Second Circuit that a defendant in a federal criminal case could not waive his right to jury trial unless he had counsel, since waiving his Sixth Amendment right demanded a free and voluntary waiver.[51] The Court reasoned that "there is nothing in the Constitution to prevent an accused from following the guidance of his own wisdom and not that of a lawyer."[52] In *Faretta v California*,[53] the Court squarely held that a defendant has a constitutional right to represent himself or herself without the services of a lawyer. A defendant may waive counsel, because the language and spirit of the Sixth Amendment contemplate that counsel "shall be an aid to a willing defendant, not an organ of the state interposed between an unwilling defendant and his right to defend himself personally."[54]

A defendant who waives counsel also waives the right to complain of ineffective representation.[55] For that reason, the United States Supreme Court has suggested that *standby* counsel be appointed to assist the accused if, at any point in the trial, he or she desires assistance.[56]

Right of Effective Assistance of Counsel

§14.07 Effective Assistance in General

The Sixth Amendment guarantee of the assistance of counsel does not state that an individual must be afforded a skilled attorney who is experienced in defending criminal cases. But the United States Supreme Court has long recognized that the fact that an accused is represented by an attorney does not necessarily mean that the attorney will be able to properly represent him or

---

[50] *See, e.g.,* Boyd v Dutton, 405 US 1, 2-3 (1972): ("A person charged with a felony in a state court has an unconditional and absolute constitutional right to a lawyer. This right . . . may be waived only by voluntary and knowing action . . . waiver will not be lightly presumed, and a judge must indulge every reasonable presumption against waiver".

[51] Adams v United States *ex rel* McCann, 317 US 269 (1943); *see also* Moore v Michigan, 355 US 155, 161 (1957).

[52] Adams v United States *ex rel* McCann, 317 US 269, 275 (1943).

[53] 422 US 806 (1975).

[54] *Id* 820.

[55] *Id* 836.

[56] *Id; see also* Mayberry v Pennsylvania, 400 US 455, 467-68 (1971) ("When a defendant refused counsel, as he did here, or seeks to discharge him, a trial judge is well advised —as so many do—to have such standby counsel to perform all the services a trained adviser would perform ordinarily by examining and cross-examining of witnesses . . . ").

her. In *Avery v Alabama*,[57] the Court stated that the denial of an opportunity for appointed counsel to consult with the accused and to prepare his defense could convert the appointment of counsel "into a sham" and into nothing more than a formal compliance with the constitutional requirement that a person be given the assistance of counsel. Perhaps because of the oft-voiced concerns by members of the judiciary that the attorneys who appeared before them were not prepared to properly try criminal cases, and because criminal cases themselves became more complex and difficult to try as criminal procedure was revolutionized by the constitutionalization of criminal procedure in the 1960s and early 1970s, a trickle of cases concerning competence of counsel began reaching the United States Supreme Court.[58] The trickle has become a torrent in lower courts[59] as few convicted defendants are entirely pleased with their attorneys. It is the rare appellate court which does not regularly consider claims of ineffective assistance.

A defendant has a right to effective counsel at all stages of a criminal proceeding at which there is a right to counsel. Thus, litigation concerning the attorney's role in plea bargaining techniques, investigation, and appeals, as well as trial techniques, has been considered by courts.

§14.08 Effective Assistance of Retained and Appointed Counsel

In *Cuyler v Sullivan*,[60] the United States Supreme Court rejected the theory that a nonindigent defendant who had selected an attorney to represent him could not be deprived of his Sixth Amendment right to the effective assistance of counsel by his attorney's inadequate performance. The Court reasoned that "the vital guarantee of the Sixth Amendment would stand for little if the often uninformed decision to retain a particular lawyer could reduce or forfeit the defendant's entitlement to constitutional protection."[61]

---

[57] 308 US 444, 446 (1940).

[58] *See, e.g.*, Parker v North Carolina, 397 US 790 (1970); McMann v Richardson, 397 US 759 (1970); Anders v California, 386 US 738 (1967); Nowakowski v Maroney, 386 US 542 (1967).

[59] *See, e.g.*, Annot, *Modern Status of Rules and Standards in Test in State Courts of Effective Representation by Counsel*, 2 ALR4th 27; Annot, *Modern Status of Rule as to Test in Federal Court of Effective Representation by Counsel*, 26 ALR Fed 218.

[60] 446 US 335 (1980).

[61] *Id* 344; *see also* Wainwright v Torna, 102 S Ct 1300 (1982).

§14.09 Standard for Determining When Defendant Has Been Deprived of Counsel

In determining the standard to be applied when a defendant claimed that his right to counsel had been violated by the ineffective performance of his attorney, the District of Columbia Court of Appeals formulated a standard which was applied by most courts for a quarter of a century, and is still applied in many courts—that relief would be given when counsel was so ineffective that the trial was a farce, or a mockery of justice, or was shocking to the conscience of the court, or where the purported representation was only perfunctory, in bad faith, a sham, a pretense, or without adequate opportunity for conference and preparation.[62] In 1970, in *McMann v Richardson*,[63] the United States Supreme Court considered a claim by a defendant who alleged that his plea of guilty was involuntary because his attorney had erroneously advised him that his confession was admissible. While not establishing a broad rule regarding the competency of counsel, the Court seemingly adopted a standard of *reasonable competence* by which advice given by an attorney should be judged. The Court seemed primarily concerned with the possibility of increased litigation if every criminal lawyer's decision were subject to close postconviction scrutiny. Justice White wrote:

> That a guilty plea must be intelligently made is not a requirement that all advice offered by a defendant's lawyer withstand retrospective examination in a post-conviction hearing. Courts continue to have serious difficulties among themselves on the admissibility of evidence both with respect to the proper standard by which facts are to be judged and with respect to the application of that standard to particular facts. That this Court might hold a defendant's confession inadmissible in evidence, possibly by a divided vote, hardly justifies a conclusion that the defendant's attorney was incompetent or ineffective when he thought the admissibility of the confession sufficiently probable to advise a plea of guilty.

> In our view, a defendant's plea of guilty based upon reasonably competent advice is not open to attack on the ground that counsel may have misjudged the admissibility of the defendant's confession.[64]

---

[62] Diggs v Welch, 148 F2d 667 (DC Cir), *cert denied*, 325 US 889 (1945).
[63] 397 US 759 (1970).
[64] *Id* 770.

The Court has adhered to its holding in *McMann* with little elaboration.[65] Because no explicit rule regarding the standard to be applied to determine if counsel has been ineffective has been established, lower courts are split over the proper standard to be applied. The clear trend, however, is toward a rejection of the *sham and mockery test* and establishment of a standard requiring *reasonably competent representation*. All of the courts of appeal (including the District of Columbia Circuit, which originated the test) except for the Second Circuit have rejected the *sham and mockery* rule.[66] A number of well-reasoned state court opinions have abandoned the sham and mockery test in favor of a *reasonably competent* test,[67] although some retain it.[68] A few courts have articulated the reasonable competence test in other terms.[69]

The tests which have been adopted by courts abandoning the sham and mockery test may vary slightly, but such courts generally provide that an accused must be afforded counsel "reasonably likely to render and reasonably rendering effective assistance."[70] Almost all courts require the defendant to bear the burden of showing prejudice.[71] The permutations are many, and resolution into legal groupings is not particularly helpful because each case must stand on its own facts. It has been suggested that the nebulous nature of the assistance of counsel rule may increase the efficacy of the Sixth Amendment guarantee

---

[65] *See, e.g.*, Cuyler v Sullivan, 446 US 335, 344 (1980).

[66] Gustave v United States, 627 F2d 901, 904 (9th Cir 1980); Lovell v Florida, 627 F2d 706 (5th Cir 1980); United States v Porterfield, 624 F2d 122 (10th Cir 1980); United States v Bosch, 584 F2d 1113, 1121 (1st Cir 1978); United States *ex rel* Williams v Turmey, 510 F2d 634 (7th Cir 1975), *cert denied*, 423 US 876 (1976) (not explicitly rejecting test, but interpreting it to require that counsel conform to expected professional standards and exercise the customary skills and diligence of a reasonably competent attorney); Beasley v United States, 491 F2d 687, 697 (4th Cir 1974); Coles v Peyton, 389 F2d 224 (4th Cir), *cert denied*, 393 US 849 (1968). Even the Second Circuit seems likely to abandon the rule in the near future. Brinkley v Lefevre, 621 F2d 45 (2d Cir 1980) (Weinstein, J, dissenting). See generally, Annot, *Modern Status of Rule as to Test in Federal Court of Effective Representation by Counsel*, 26 ALR Fed 218.

[67] *See, e.g.*, Risher v State, 523 P2d 421 (Alaska Sup 1974); People v Pope, 23 Cal 3d 412, 152 Cal Rptr 732, 590 P2d 859 (1979); State v Tucker, 97 Idaho 4, 539 P2d 556 (1976); Commonwealth v Safarian, 366 Mass 89, 315 NE2d 878 (1974); People v Garcia, 398 Mich 250, 247 NW2d 547 (1976); State v Thomas, 203 SE2d 445 (W Va Sup 1974); State v Harper, 57 Wisc 2d 543, 205 NW2d 1 (1973). See generally, Annot, *Modern Status of Rules and Standards in State Courts as to Adequacy of Defense Counsel's Representation of Criminal Client*, 2 ALR4th 27.

[68] *See, e.g.*, Smith v State, 383 NE2d 324 (1978); Slayton v Weinberger, 213 Va 690, 194 SE2d 703 (1973); Annot, *Modern Status of Rules and Standards In State Courts as to Adequacy of Defense Counsel's Representation of Criminal Clients*, 2 ALR4th 27.

[69] *See, e.g.*, State v Hesler, 45 Ohio St 2d 71, 341 NE2d 304 (1976).

[70] *See, e.q.*, Lovell v Florida, 627 F2d 706, 708 (5th Cir 1980).

[71] *See, e.g.*, Gustave v United States, 627 F2d 901, 904 (9th Cir 1980); see also Strazella, *Ineffective Assistance of Counsel Claims: New Uses, New Problems*, 19 Ariz L Rev 443 (1977)

because courts could not formulate rigid rules to meet all circumstances even if they tried.[72]

However, before a court considers whether a person has been denied the constitutional right to the effective assistance of counsel, the court must determine that the person has a constitutional right to counsel. In *Wainwright v Torna*,[73] the defendant's conviction was affirmed by a Florida Court of Appeal, but his retained attorney did not timely file his petition for certiorari to the Florida Supreme Court. The United States Supreme Court held that the defendant's right to the effective assistance of counsel had not been denied, since he had no constitutional right to retained or appointed counsel to pursue discretionary appeals.

§14.10 Denial of Effective Assistance of Counsel

Despite the imprecise nature of the standards by which ineffective assistance is judged, it is possible to suggest some factors which may lead a court to conclude that a defendant has been denied the effective assistance of counsel. Apart from conflicting interests,[74] cases alleging the denial of effective assistance may generally be broken into two groups; cases in which the attorney did not use due diligence, and cases which the attorney was not competent to handle. Courts have, generally speaking, listened more sympathetically to claims of lack of due diligence than to claims of incompetence. The two most crucial aspects of a defendant's representation are investigation and consultation. Courts have no hesitation in holding that the attorney must investigate both the facts and the law concerning the case,[75] and that the attorney must consult with the client about the case.[76] An unexplained failure to interview defense witnesses[77] or undertake plea bargaining[78] is likely to lead to a finding of ineffective assistance.

Courts will not second-guess a trial tactic, even if the tactic was unwise. If a defense attorney makes an error in judgment, that will not necessarily require a finding of ineffective assistance. Courts will grant relief however, where an attorney has prejudicially blundered for no reason at all. For example,

---

[72] Strazella, In*effective Assistance of Counsel Claims: New Uses, New Problems*, 19 Ariz L Rev 443 (1977).

[73] Wainwright v Torna, 102 S Ct 1300 (1982).

[74] See §14.11.

[75] People v Pope, 23 Cal 3d 412, 590 P2d 859, 150 Cal Rptr 732 (1979).

[76] *See, e.g.*, Geders v United States, 425 US 80 (1976).

[77] *See, e.g.*, United States v Fosterfield, 624 F2d 122 (10th Cir 1980).

[78] Reynolds v Mabry, 574 F2d 978 (8th Cir 1978); see generally Annot, *Assistance of Counsel—Plea Bargaining*, 8 ALR4th 660.

where a defense attorney's closing argument does not make sense,[79] or where a defendant does not raise a speedy trial claim even though six years have elapsed since indictment because the prosecution misplaced the file,[80] a reviewing court may well find a denial of the right to effective assistance.

Even more illustrative is the common circumstance of an attorney miscalculating the admissibility of evidence or deliberately not objecting to inadmissible evidence as a trial tactic. The United States Supreme Court has specifically held that the fact that an individual pleads guilty on erroneous legal advice does not mean that the person has been denied the effective assistance of counsel.[81] But acquiescence in the admission of clearly inadmissible evidence where there is no possible reason for a competent attorney to allow the evidence to come in may be a different matter. In *Commonwealth v Witherspoon*,[82] the Pennsylvania Supreme Court held that a defendant had been denied the effective assistance of counsel when his attorney failed to object to hearsay evidence which implicated him in a murder. The Court reasoned that the only possible advantage the defendant could have received from the admission of the evidence was that it tended to show that the murder was not intentional—which was not relevant, since the defendant was charged with felony murder.

Most courts require that a defendant who alleges denial of effective assistance show prejudice as a result of the alleged incompetence of counsel. For that reason, virtually any circumstance from defense counsel's illness[83] to failure to convey a plea offer[84] may result in a denial of effective assistance.[85]

A defendant may, of course, waive the right to effective assistance of counsel, as long as the waiver is voluntary and knowing.[86] Most commonly, such waivers occur when defendants represent themselves, but courts have held that a defendant who has advised that the counsel selected is incompetent, but who

---

[79] Oesby v United States, 398 A2d 1 (DC 1978); see Annot, *Adequacy of Defense Counsel's Representation of Criminal Client Regarding Argument*, 6 ALR4th 16.

[80] Commonwealth v Roundtree, 469 Pa 241, 364 A2d 1359 (1976); see Annot, *Adequacy of Defense Counsel's Representation of Criminal Client Regarding Speedy Trial and Related Matters*, 6 ALR4th 1208.

[81] McMann v Richardson, 397 US 759 (1970); Tollett v Henderson, 411 US 258 (1973); Annot, *Adequacy of Defense Counsel's Representation of Criminal Client Regarding Speedy Trial and Related Matters*, 6 ALR4th 1208.

[82] 481 Pa 321, 392 A2d 1313 (1978).

[83] Thorton v State, 369 So 2d 505 (Miss 1979); *Ex parte* Love, 468 SW2d 836 (Tex Crim App. 1971).

[84] *Ex parte* Bratchett, 513 SW2d 851 (Tex Crim App 1974).

[85] See generally Annot, *Assistance of Counsel—Plea Bargaining*, 8 ALR4th 660; Annot, *Adequacy of Defense Counsel's Representation Regarding Venue and Recusal Matters*, 7 ALR4th 942.

[86] Faretta v California, 422 US 806 (1975).

still elects to go to trial with that counsel, waives the right to the effective assistance of counsel.[87]

§14.11 Joint Representation of Defendants

More than one person accused of a crime may be represented by a single attorney. Few experienced defense attorneys encourage retention by multiple clients accused of the same crime because there is always a potential for conflict; at any time an attorney may be approached by a prosecutor who has an attractive plea bargain for one client, on the condition of testifying against the other client. Obviously, the assistance of counsel guaranteed by the Sixth Amendment contemplates that the assistance be untainted by conflicting interests.[88] Yet despite the obvious potential for prejudice in every case of joint representation, the United States Supreme Court has never held that joint representation is, in all circumstances, improper.[89] The Court has held that trial judges must be solicitous of a defendant's right to have an attorney who fully represents the defendant's interests.

In *Holloway v Arkansas*,[90] the Supreme Court held that when an attorney, as an officer of the court, announces the existence of a conflict of interest in representing more than one defendant and seeks to withdraw, the court must grant the attorney's request. The Court reasoned that the attorney representing the accused is in the best position to determine whether a conflict exists and that defense attorneys have an ethical obligation to inform the court of any conflict of interest. Finally, attorneys are officers of the court, under an obligation not to mislead the court. A trial court may impose sanctions against an attorney who seeks permission to withdraw for dilatory purposes, and the court may make inquiries to explore the reason for the conflict, short of piercing the attorney-client privilege.[91] If an attorney is improperly forced to represent a defendant with conflicting interest over the attorney's objection, the resulting impairment of the right to counsel can never be harmless error.[92]

A different result obtains when the defense attorney does not bring an alleged conflict to the attention of the court. Absent special circumstances, a trial

---

[87] People v Johnson, 75 Ill 2d 180, 387 NE2d 688 (1979); see Annot, *Waiver or Estoppel in Incompetent Legal Representation Cases*, 2ALR4th 807.

[88] Glasser v United States, 315 US 60, 70 (1942); *see also* People v Blalock, 197 Colo 320, 592 P2d 406 (1979) (conflict of interest requiring reversal where defense attorney had had sexual relations with complaining witness in sexual assault case).

[89] Holloway v Arkansas, 435 US 475, 482 (1978); *see also* Glasser v United States, 315 US 60 (1942).

[90] Holloway v Arkansas, 435 US 475, 485 (1978).

[91] *Id* 485.

[92] *Id* 487.

judge may assume that when multiple defendants appear, represented by one attorney, and no claim of conflict is made, either no conflict exists or the defendants knowingly accept the risk of whatever conflict there is.[93] Moreover, if a defendant who raised no objection to joint representation at trial alleges after conviction that Sixth Amendment rights were violated by the joint representation, the Court has held that the defendant must demonstrate an actual conflict of interest that adversely affected the lawyer's performance.[94] The defendant need not, however, show prejudice, since a violation of the Sixth Amendment can never be harmless error;[95] it is only necessary to establish an actual conflict.

---

[93] Cuyler v Sullivan, 446 US 335 (1980); circumstances requiring inquiry by the court were held to exist in Wood v Georgia, 450 US 261 (1981) where the court knew that the attorney representing the defendants in an obscenity prosecution was paid by the defendants' employer and did not make any arguments for leniency on behalf of his clients, but only challenged the constitutionality of the statute under which they were charged.

[94] Cuyler v Sullivan, 446 US 335 (1980); *see also* Dukes v Warden, 406 US 250 (1972).

[95] Cuyler v Sullivan, 446 US 335 (1980); *but see* United States v Morrison, 449 US 361 (1981).

15

Motions to Suppress Evidence or Bar Prosecution

Devices to Exclude Evidence at Trial

§15.01 Motion to Suppress

Perhaps the most important part of preparation for any trial is the determination of what evidence will be admitted and what evidence will be excluded. It is only after an attorney can judge what evidence is likely to be produced and admitted that it is possible to predict what will happen at trial and advise a client. The lawyer preparing a criminal case faces a doubly complex task; in addition to considering the evidentiary issues, the lawyer must consider whether evidence may be excluded because it was obtained in violation of the client's constitutional rights. While evidentiary issues are usually dealt with at trial, exclusion of evidence on constitutional grounds is considered in advance of trial in most jurisdictions. Indeed, the courts have even treated pretrial consideration of the lawfulness of evidence as a constitutional necessity in some circumstances.[1] The most commonly used procedural device to vindicate constitutional rights is the motion to suppress evidence. Procedural rules in most jurisdictions govern the time periods during which such motions must be filed. What an attorney may, as a matter of constitutional law, achieve by filing such a motion is the subject of this chapter.

§15.02 What Evidence May Be Suppressed

The origin of the so-called exclusionary rule in the federal courts is often said to be in *Boyd v United States*,[2] in which the United States Supreme Court held that evidence obtained in violation of the Fifth Amendment could not be admitted in evidence because it was "compelled." In 1914, in *Weeks v United States*,[3] the Court first held that evidence obtained in violation of a person's Fourth Amendment rights had to be excluded from evidence in federal cases. In 1961, the Court expanded *Weeks* and held that evidence obtained in violation of a person's Fourth Amendment rights could not be introduced in state courts.[4]

---

[1] Jackson v Denno, 378 US 368 (1964); see §15.06.

[2] 116 US 616 (1886).

[3] 232 US 383, 398 (1914).

[4] Mapp v Ohio, 307 US 643 (1961).

The Court has also held that evidence obtained in violation of due process of law[5] and of a person's Sixth Amendment rights[6] must be suppressed under some circumstances.

The purpose of the exclusionary rule is basic—it exists to protect citizens by detering police from acting unlawfully[7] and to protect judicial integrity.[8] Obviously, the rule often leads to the keeping of relevant and even crucial evidence from the finder of fact. To analyze all of the competing interests and policies would be impossible; it is sufficient to say that the wisdom of the exclusionary rule had divided perhaps the greatest American jurists.[9]

At present the rule is alive and well, although its health seemingly waxes and wanes with each addition to and departure from the United States Supreme Court. Given the fluctuating support of the rule, it is perhaps easiest to deal with it in purely precedential terms. Predictably, in recent years the Court has, on the whole, been disinclined to expand the rule, and in fact has been willing to place some limits on its operation.

First and foremost, the rule prohibits introduction at trial of illegally seized evidence. The Court has specifically held that illegally obtained evidence may be considered by grand juries.[10] For that reason, it has generally been held that illegally seized evidence may be considered by magistrates in preliminary examinations,[11] and, of course, may be considered by magistrates determining whether to issue warrants.

Under some circumstances, the Supreme Court has held that illegally seized evidence may even be admissible at trial. The Court has taken the position that, while the exclusionary rule bars the use of illegally obtained evidence by the prosecution in its case-in-chief, such evidence may be used by the prosecution if the defendant testifies falsely and the evidence obtained illegally would show the falsity of the defendant's testimony.[12] The Court has reasoned that the Fourth and Fifth Amendments do not afford a defendant a privilege to commit perjury. Thus, in *Walder v United States*,[13] the Court held that

---

[5] Rochin v California, 342 US 165 (1952).

[6] United States v Wade, 388 US 218 (1967).

[7] Linkletter v Walker, 381 US 618 (1965).

[8] Terry v Ohio, 392 US 1, 12-13 (1968).

[9] *Compare* People v Defore, 242 NY 13, 21, 150 NE 585, 587 (1926) (Cardozo, J) ("the criminal is to go free because the constable blundered"); *with* Olmstead v United States, 277 US 438, 470 (1928) (Holmes, J, dissenting) ("We have to choose,, and for my part, I think it a less evil that some criminals should escape than that the government should play an ignorable part".

[10] United States v Calandra, 414 US 338 (1974).

[11] *See* Fed R Crim P 5.1(a).

[12] Walder v United States, 347 US 62 (1954) (Fourth Amendment); Harris v New York, 401 US 222 (1971) (Fifth Amendment).

[13] 347 US 62 (1954).

narcotics seized illegally from the defendant could be introduced to impeach him when he testified that he had never seen narcotics before. Of course, the prosecutor may never ask the defendant questions which the prosecutor knows will require the defendant to either admit incriminating facts or lie, just so that the defendant may be impeached with illegally obtained evidence. The fact that the false statement is made on cross-examination will not, however, prohibit the prosecutor from impeaching the defendant with illegally obtained evidence in all circumstances. Illustrative is *United States v Havens*,[14] in which a defendant charged with narcotics smuggling was arrested with a codefendant at an airport. The codefendant was wearing an undershirt on which pockets had been sewn, and the pockets contained drugs. An illegal search of the defendant's luggage disclosed cloth which matched that from which the pockets were sewn. The codefendant testified at trial that the defendant was involved in smuggling. The defendant denied it, and on cross-examination denied that he had helped the codefendant cut pockets for his T-shirt. The Court held that admission of the illegally seized cloth for impeachment was permissible, because the questioning of the defendant was reasonable and proper. The Court refused to impose a per se rule that only statements made on direct examination would be proper bases for impeachment admissibility. The Court's decision requires that an attorney who has succeeded in suppressing illegally obtained evidence carefully consider what questions will be proper on cross-examination if the defendant testifies.

There is one important caveat to the rules governing use of legally obtained evidence. A number of state courts have held, based on their own state constitutions, that evidence obtained in violation of *Miranda* may not be used to impeach a defendant.[15] The United States Supreme Court has held that the states, while free to interpret their own constitutions more strictly than they interpret the federal Constitution, may not interpret the federal Constitution more strictly than the United States Supreme Court does.[16] The United States Supreme Court has held, however, that a confession which was obtained involuntarily cannot be used to impeach a defendant because use of an involuntary confession would violate the Fourteenth Amendment right to due process of law.[17]

In addition to the use of illegally seized evidence at trial, mere possession of the information may provide the government with a substantial advantage. The government may use the evidence as an investigative lead, or to obtain other evidence. The United States Supreme Court has developed a number of special rules to deal with this problem.

---

[14] 446 US 620 (1980).

[15] See §5.13.

[16] Oregon v Haas, 420 US 714 (1975).

[17] Mincey v Arizona, 437 US 385 (1978).

§15.03 Exceptions to Exclusionary Rule — Independent Source

While the United States Supreme Court recognized in *Silverthorne Lumber Co v United States* [18] that illegally seized evidence may not be used at all, it also noted that the facts thus uncovered do not become "sacred and inadmissible." If knowledge of the facts is obtained from an independent source, the evidence is admissible. [19]

The Court has never engaged in extended discussion of the independent source exception. It has held that the government bears the ultimate burden of showing that evidence was lawfully obtained. [20] It is generally conceded that where illegal government activity is concerned, the defendant is entitled to access to the government's investigative file to determine whether the evidence does, in fact, have an independent source. [21]

§15.04 — Purged Taint

While the United States Supreme Court has forbidden the government to exploit illegally obtained evidence, it has also recognized that the degree of exploitation may be so minimal as to render irrelevant the illegality. A very specific set of rules has developed concerning when the illegal action is so far removed that it will not bar the use of the evidence. The classic statement of this exception to the exclusionary rule, which is called the purged taint exception, was stated by Justice Brennan in *Wong Sun v United States*: [22]

> We need not hold that all evidence is "fruit of the poisonous tree" simply because it would not have come to light but for the illegal actions of the police. Rather, the more apt question in such a case is "whether, granting establishment of the primary illegality, the evidence to which instant objection is made has been come at by expoitation of that illegality or instead by means sufficiently distinguishable to be purged of the primary taint." [23]

---

[18] 251 US 385, 392 (1920).

[19] *Id*; *see also* United States v Crews, 445 US 463 (1980); Costello v United States, 365 US 265, 280 (1961).

[20] Harrison v United States, 392 US 219, 225 (1968); Nardone v United States, 308 US 338, 341 (1939).

[21] *See, e.g.*, Alderman v United States, 394 US 165, 182 (1969).

[22] 371 US 471 (1963).

[23] *Id* 487-88.

The facts of *Wong Sun* illustrate the workings of the rule. Police officers illegally arrested one Toy, who told the police officers they should arrest Yee. When they arrested Yee, the police found narcotics in his possession and he implicated Wong Sun. Wong Sun was arrested, arraigned, and released. Four days later, he returned voluntarily to the police and made a voluntary statement. The Court held that the statements made and the narcotics seized from Yee were *fruits of the poisonous tree* and could not be admitted into evidence. The Court held that the statement made by Wong Sun four days after the arrest was admissible, because "the connection between the arrest and the statement had become so attenuated as to dissipate the taint."[24]

In the years since *Wong Sun* was decided, the United States Supreme Court has further refined the purged taint rules. The Court has stated that the question of causal connection between the illegal activity and the evidence obtained "is not to be determined solely through the kind of analysis which would be applicable in the physical sciences."[25] The issue of causation in the constitutional sense cannot be determined by logic alone. In *United States v Ceccolini*,[26] for example, a police officer, lawfully in a flower shop, observed an envelope behind the counter, searched it, and discovered policy slips. The cashier stated that the envelope belonged to her manager. An FBI agent later visited the cashier at home, and she agreed to testify for the government to a grand jury. Despite the fact that, logically, the government would never have obtained the cashier's testimony unless the officer had uncovered the policy slips, the Court held that the testimony of the cashier did not have to be suppressed. The Court distinguished between physical evidence and the testimony of a live witness, because a live witness may be willing to testify freely even if discovered as a result of unlawful conduct, and to perpetually disable the witness would impose too great a cost on the criminal justice system.[27] Since the police officer had almost inadvertently committed the illegal seizure, and since a substantial period of time elapsed between the illegal search and the initial contact by the police with the cashier and between the contact and testimony at trial, and since the witness was willing to testify and her relationship with the defendant had been known to the police prior to the discovery of the policy slips, the Court held that the taint had been so attenuated as not to require suppression of the evidence.[28]

Particular rules have also developed concerning confessions. In *Wong Sun*, the Court recognized that the pressures of an illegal arrest could result in a subsequent confession being held to be a fruit of the illegal arrest, but that

---

[24] *Id* 491.

[25] United States v Ceccolini, 435 US 268, 274 (1977).

[26] *Id.*

[27] *Id* 276-79.

[28] *Id* 279-80.

events subsequent to the arrest could eliminate those pressures and free the confession from the taint of the illegal arrest. In *Brown v Illinois*,[29] the Court held that the fact that an individual who was illegally arrested was given the *Miranda* warnings before he was interrogated would not, as a matter of law, purge the taint of the illegal arrest. The Court pointed out that, in order for the chain of taint to be broken, the statement must not only meet Fifth Amendment standards of voluntariness, but must be sufficiently an act of free will to purge the primary taint.[30] While recognizing that giving a person *Miranda*[31] rights is a relevant consideration in determining whether the confession is a product of free will, the Court held that all of the circumstances surrounding the confession must be considered:

> The question whether a confession is the product of a free will under *Wong Sun* must be answered on the facts of each case. No single fact is dispositive. The workings of the human mind are too complex, and the possibilities of misconduct too diverse to permit protection of the Fourth Amendment to turn on such a talismanic test. The *Miranda* warnings are an important factor, to be sure, in determining whether the confession is obtained by exploitation of an illegal arrest. But they are not the only factors to be considered. The temporal proximity of the arrest and the confession, the presence of intervening circumstances, and particularly, the purpose and flagrancy of the official misconduct are all relevant.[32]

In *Brown*, the Court held that the statement made by the defendant was tainted because it was made two hours after he was arrested by the police "for questioning" without probable cause. Cases decided since *Brown* suggest that, at least in this narrow area, the Court has considered that the crucial factor in determining whether the evidence will be considered tainted is the good faith of the police officers; if, for example, the police arrest a defendant without probable cause hoping that something turns up, and no intervening circumstance breaks the chain between the arrest and the confession, the confession will be held inadmissible.[33] If, on the other hand, the police act illegally, but in a manner which is, if *unreasonable* within the Fourth Amendment, at least understandable, by, for example, searching the persons of occupants of a house for which they have obtained a search warrant, a confession they obtain as a result of the arrest will be held admissible.[34]

---

[29] 422 US 590 (1975).

[30] *Id* 602.

[31] Miranda v Arizona, 384 US 436 (1966).

[32] 422 US at 603-04.

[33] *See, e.g.*, Dunaway v New York, 422 US 200 (1979).

[34] *See, e.g.*, Rawlings v Kentucky, 448 US 98 (1980).

§15.05 —Inevitable Discovery

A third exception to the rule that evidence come at by exploitation of illegality will be suppressed is the *inevitable discovery rule*. The rule is easily explained: if the government can show that illegally obtained evidence would inevitably have been discovered by the police acting lawfully, the same evidence, although illegally obtained, will not be excluded from trial since the government has not gained any benefit from the illegal activity.[35] Commentators have pointed out, however, that the independent discovery rule diminishes the sanction imposed on the government for illegal activity and this encourages lawless conduct.[36]

While the United States Supreme Court has never explicitly held the inevitable discovery rule constitutional, it has, in dicta, referred to it approvingly as "one of the three commonly advanced exceptions to the exclusionary rule."[37]

The workings of the inevitable discovery rule are illustrated by the decision of the New Hampshire Supreme Court in *State v Beede*.[38] In that case, the court held that the fruits of an illegal search of an apartment, a corpse, would not be suppressed because the body had already begun to decay, and, when it decayed further, the smell would have attracted attention and provided probable cause for the search.

§15.06 Suppression Hearings Right to Have Held Out of Jury's Presence

Virtually every jurisdiction makes provision for pretrial hearings on motions to suppress evidence. Indeed, in some jurisdictions, the right to suppress evidence may be lost if the suppression motion is not filed within a specific time.[39]

Holding suppression hearings prior to trial can benefit both the prosecution and the defendant; it is a statistical fact that most criminal cases are disposed of by negotiation, and certainly knowing what evidence will or will not be admitted can only help each side more realistically assess the prospect of success at trial, thus expediting plea bargaining.

---

[35] *See, e.g.*, United States *ex rel* Owens v Twomey, 508 F2d 858 (7th Cir 1974); United States v Seohnlein, 423 F2d 1051 (4th Cir), *cert denied*, 399 US 913 (1970); Somer v United States, 138 F2d 790 (2d Cir 1943); Lockridge v Superior Court, 3 Cal 3d 166, 474 P2d 683, 89 Cal Rptr 731, *cert denied*, 395 US 969 (1969); State v Williams, 285 NW2d 248 (Iowa 1979); see generally Annot, *Fruit of the Poisonous Tree Doctrine Excluding Evidence Obtained From Information Gain in Illegal Search*, 43 ALR3d 385 §9(a).

[36] See, e.g., Pitler, *The Fruit of the Poisonous Tree*, 56 Cal L Rev 579 (1968).

[37] United States v Crews, 445 US 463, (1980); *see also* United States v Ceccolini, 435 US 268, 273 (1977).

[38] 119 NH 620, 406 A2d 125 (1979).

[39] *See, e.g.*, Fed R Crim P 12.

Probably because the prevailing practice has been to consider suppression motions out of the hearing of the jury, the United States Supreme Court has considered the constitutional necessity that such hearings be held out of the jury's presence in relatively few cases. However, in *Jackson v Denno*,[40] the Court held that, as a matter of federal constitutional law, if a defendant challenges the voluntariness of a confession, a hearing on its voluntariness must be held outside the jury's presence. The Court reasoned that if the issue of voluntariness were simply submitted to the jury, a defendant on appeal could never know if the jury had accepted it, and that a jury probably could not entirely ignore the confession in its deliberations.[41] Although there is no constitutional right to have the issue of voluntariness resubmitted to the jury if the court finds a confession voluntary,[42] many appellate courts require a trial judge to do so.[43]

In *Watkins v Sowders*,[44] the Court made clear that *Jackson v Denno* must be considered sui generis, as it dealt with the "peculiar problems the issue of voluntariness of a confession presents. . . ."[45] While recognizing that the "prudence" of holding suppression hearings outside of the presence of the jury "has been emphasized by many decisions in the Courts of Appeals, most of which have . . . admonished lower trial courts to use that procedure,"[46] the Court held that there was no constitutional reason why hearings on the admissibility of identification evidence must be held outside the presence of the jury.[47] The Court recognized, however, that in some circumstances, the Constitution might require that suppression hearings be held outside the jury's presence.[48]

§15.07 —Exclusion of Press

The presence of the press at a pretrial suppression hearing may raise formidable difficulties for the attorney attempting to obtain a fair trial for his or her client. If, for example, the defendant moves to suppress a confession and the press carries stories about the hearing, the jury panel may become aware of the confession even if it is suppressed.

---

[40] 378 US 368 (1964).
[41] *Id* 389.
[42] Lego v Twomey, 404 US 477 (1978).
[43] *See, e.g.*, Commonwealth v Preece, 140 Mass 276, 5 NE 494 (1885).
[44] 101 S Ct 654 (1981).
[45] *Id* 658.
[46] *Id* 657.
[47] *Id* 658-59.
[48] *Id.*

In *Gannett v DePasquale*,[49] the United States Supreme Court, recognizing the detrimental effect that pretrial suppression hearings could have on a fair trial, severely limited the access of the press to such proceedings in circumstances in which the defendant seeks that the press be barred. The Court reasoned that the Sixth Amendment exists for the benefit of the defendant, who may waive it. Even more significantly, the plurality held that, while there may be a Sixth Amendment right of the public to attend trials, there is no Sixth Amendment right to attend pretrial proceedings.[50] The Court assumed that there was a First Amendment right of the public to attend trials,[51] but that this right must be balanced against the defendant's right to a fair trial. The Court found the procedure employed by the state judge, in the case before it, who found that the defendant's rights to a fair trial would be imperiled if the press were allowed to attend the proceedings, adequate.

§15.08 Use at Trial of Defendant's Testimony at Suppression Hearing

A voluntary statement made by a defendant in a criminal case is, under evidentiary rules in all jurisdictions, admissible as an admission. A different rule obtains, however, when the defendant makes statements at a pretrial suppression hearing in which the defendant must testify to vindicate constitutional rights. In such a circumstance, if the testimony could be used against him or her at trial, the defendant must waive one constitutional right, the Fifth Amendment right against self-incrimination, to vindicate another. Thus, in *Simmons v United States*,[52] the United States Supreme Court held that when a defendant testifies to establish standing to challenge a Fourth Amendment violation, the defendant's statement may not thereafter be used against the defendant at trial over his or her objection.

Courts have generally held that testimony given at a suppression hearing to vindicate any constitutional right may not be used against a defendant.[53] However, most courts considering the issue have held that such statements

---

[49] 443 US 368 (1979).

[50] *Id* 387.

[51] This right was seemingly established in Richmond Newspapers, Inc v Virginia, 448 US 555 (1980).

[52] 390 US 377 (1968).

[53] Woody v United States, 379 F2d 130, 131-32 (DC Cir) (Burger, J), *cert denied*, 389 US 961 (1967); People v Douglas, 66 Cal App 3d 998, 136 Cal Rptr 358 (1977); People v Sturgis, 37 Ill 2d 299, 317 NE2d 545 (1974), *cert denied*, 420 US 936 (1975); Gray v State, 43 Md App 238, 403 A2d 853 (1979); People v Walker, 374 Mich 87, 132 NW2d 87 (1965).

may be used for impeachment purposes if the defendant testifies at trial.[54] In *United States v Salvucci*,[55] the Court noted that it had never specifically decided whether *Simmons v United States* precludes the use of a defendant's testimony at a suppression hearing for impeachment at trial. The Court noted, however, that most lower courts considering the issue had held the testimony admissible for impeachment purposes, and pointedly noted that "this Court has held that the protective shield of *Simmons* is not to be converted into a license for false representations."[56] It seems likely that if the issue were squarely presented to it, the Supreme Court would hold that a defendant's statements made at a pretrial suppression hearing could be used at trial for impeachment purposes, as long as the statements were not involuntary.

Standing to Object to Illegal Search

§15.09 Constitutional Requirement of Standing

The fact that unlawful government action which violated a person's Fourth Amendment rights has resulted in the prosecution's obtaining evidence does not always mean that the evidence must be excluded from trial. It is well established that suppression of evidence because it was obtained in violation of the Fourth Amendment can only be urged by those whose rights were violated by the search, and not by those who are aggrieved solely by introduction of damaging testimony.[57] This rule follows from the general proposition that constitutional rights are personal and may not be asserted vicariously.[58] The rule also presents a policy judgment that the additional deterrent effect which would be gained by extending the exclusionary rule would not be justified by the social cost of excluding competent, relevant evidence. As a general proposition, the issue of standing involves two inquiries; first, whether the proponent of a particular legal right has alleged injury in fact; and second, whether the proponent is asserting his or her own legal right and interests, rather than merely basing a claim for relief on the rights of another.[59] The person asserting a Fourth

---

[54] *See, e.g.*, People v Sturgis, 37 Ill 2d 299, 317 NE2d 545 (1974), *cert denied*, 420 US 936 (1975).

[55] 448 US 83, 93-94 (1980).

[56] *Id* 94 n 9 (citing United States v Kahn, 415 US 239, 243 (1975)).

[57] Alderman v United States, 394 US 165, 174 (1969).

[58] Broadrick v Oklahoma, 413 US 601, 610 (1973).

[59] Rakas v Illinois, 439 US 128, 139 (1978).

Amendment violation bears the burden of showing that his or her rights were violated.

The rules governing standing have been in flux over the last 30 years. At the beginning of that period, as in other aspects of Fourth Amendment jurisprudence in considering the application of the Fourth Amendment, courts considered first the property interest of the defendant.[60] The United States Supreme Court, by 1960, began to specifically recognize that property law distinctions "often only of gossamer strength," ought not to be determinative in "fashioning procedures ultimately referable to constitutional safeguards,"[61] and began to emphasize the expectation of privacy that a person enjoyed in the place searched, rather than the person's property right in it.

It is now plain that, to determine whether a person has standing to object to a search, the appropriate inquiry is whether a person has a reasonable expectation of privacy in the place or property searched. Thus, while a person who is given a key to another's apartment, and who is allowed to use it for several days, has a constitutionally protected privacy interest in the apartment and may complain of an illegal search of it,[62] a person has no standing to complain of an illegal search of another's apartment, in which the person does not reside or have any reasonable expectation of privacy.[63] Similarly, if a person gives another, on only a few days' acquaintance, drugs to keep in her purse, and he has no right to exclude others from the purse, he has no reasonable expectation of privacy in it and may not, therefore, complain of an unlawful search of it.[64] While dicta from earlier decisions suggested that "anyone legitimately on premises" may challenge a search of those premises, the Supreme Court has specifically held that the term *anyone legitimately on the premises* [65] is "too broad a gauge for the measurement of Fourth Amendment rights"[66] and has required a showing of a reasonable expectation of privacy in the premises of a person challenging a search.

Of course, the states are free to impose more liberal requirements of standing in cases arising under state constitutions.[67] The California Supreme Court, for example, has specifically held as a matter of state law that the legality of a

---

[60] *See* the cases cited in Jones v United States, 362 US 257, 265-66 (1960).

[61] *Id* 266.

[62] *Id.*; (defendant had standing to complain of search of apartment which was leased by friend, who had given him the key and allowed him to stay there for at least one night while his friend was away).

[63] United States v Salvucci, 448 US 83 (1980); *but see* Simmons v United States, 390 US 377, 389-94 (1968).

[64] Rawlings v Kentucky, 448 US 98 (1980).

[65] Jones v United States, 362 US 257, 267 (1960).

[66] Rakas v Illinois, 439 US 128, 141-42 (1978).

[67] Alderman v United States, 394 US 165, 175 (1969).

search and seizure may be challenged by anyone against whom such evidence is used.[68]

§15.10 Automatic Standing

In *Jones v United States*,[69] the United States Supreme Court held that a person charged with an offense which consists of the possession of certain items automatically has standing to object to the introduction of items as evidence. The Court reasoned that to require that defendant to testify that he owned the property before allowing him to challenge the seizure of the property would be impermissible because the defendant would be forced to choose between asserting his Fourth Amendment rights and his Fifth Amendment right to remain silent.

The rationale for the automatic standing rule was eliminated in *Simmons v United States*[70] in which the Court specifically held that testimony given to establish standing at a motion to suppress could not be used against the defendant at trial. Regarded as an anachronism by lower courts after *Simmons* was decided, the automatic standing rule was explicitly rejected by the United States Supreme Court in 1980.[71]

A few states have, however, *revived* the automatic standing rule as a matter of state constitutional law, reasoning that the *automatic standing* doctrine provides for greater protection of individual rights, and that the *legitimate expectation of privacy* analysis favored by the United States Supreme Court introduces yet another flexible determination to be pondered by police and litigated in courts.[72]

§15.11 Use of Testimony Given by Defendant to Establish Standing at Suppression Hearing

In *Simmons v United States*,[73] the United States Supreme Court specifically held that testimony given by a person to establish standing to object to a Fourth

---

[68] Kaplan v Superior Court, 6 Cal 3d 150, 491 P2d 1, 98 Cal Rptr 649 (1971). A similar result has been reached in a few other states, as a matter of state law. *See State v Gibson*, 391 So 2d 421 (La 1980); *State v Alston*, 87 NJ 531, 436 A2d 81 (1981); *State v Settle*, 122 NH, ___, ___ A2d ___ (Mar 10, 1982).

[69] 362 US 257 (1960).

[70] 390 US 377, 394 (1968).

[71] United States v Salvucci, 448 US 83 (1980).

[72] State v Settle, 122 NH ___, ___ A2d ___ (Mar 10, 1982); State v Gibson, 391 So 2d 421 (La 1980); State v Alston, 87 NJ 531, 436 A2d 81 (1981).

[73] 390 US 377 (1968).

Amendment violation could not be introduced against him or her at trial. While the issue of whether testimony given by a defendant who testifies differently at trial than at a suppression hearing was explicitly left open in *United States v Salvucci*,[74] the Court noted in the course of its opinion that it had previously "noted that the protective shield of *Simmons* is not to be converted into a license for false representation."[75] Justice Marshall, in dissent, noted that the majority had "broadly hint[ed]"[76] that such testimony could be used to impeach a defendant who testifies differently at trial, and there is no doubt that he is correct. Assuming that such testimony could be used to impeach a defendant, it is likely that the general rules which specifically relate to use for impeachment purposes of evidence obtained illegally would be applicable to it.[77]

Burden of Proof

§15.12 Burden of Proof on Motion to Suppress

When unlawful government activity has occurred and the prosecution seeks to introduce evidence which is the product of that unlawful activity, it has the ultimate burden of showing that its evidence is untainted.[78] At the same time, however, those asserting that the prosecution's evidence is tainted must produce some evidence of taint.[79] Perhaps even more significantly, the defendant must establish standing to complain of the illegal activity.[80]

The burden of proof which the government must meet in order to prove challenged evidence admissible may vary depending on the type of evidence sought to be introduced and the particular jurisdiction. The United States Supreme Court has held that the prosecution must establish the lawfulness of a search[81] and the voluntariness of a confession[82] by a preponderance of the evidence. Some states have, however, imposed greater burdens of proof

---

[74] 448 US 83 (1980).

[75] United States v Salvucci, 448 US 83, 87 n 9 (1980) (citing United States v Kahn, 415 US 239 (1974)).

[76] *Id* (Marshall, J, dissenting).

[77] See §15.02.

[78] *See, e.g.*, United States v Jeffers, 342 US 48, 51 (1951); *see also* Nardone v United States, 308 US 338, 341 (1939).

[79] Alderman v United States, 394 US 165, 183 (1969).

[80] See §15.09.

[81] *See, e.g.*, United States v Jeffers, 342 US 48 (1972); Bumper v North Carolina, 391 US 543 (1968).

[82] Lego v Twomey, 404 US 477 (1972).

based on their own constitutions.[83] Finally, if the prosecution seeks to have a witness, who identified a defendant at an illegal identification procedure prior to trial, identify the defendant at trial, it must first show by clear and convincing evidence that the in-court identification is not tainted by the illegal pretrial identification procedure, but has an independent source.[84]

Double Jeopardy

§15.13 Constitutional Prohibition against Double Jeopardy

The Fifth Amendment to the federal Constitution provides, in relevant part, "nor shall any person be subject for the same offense to be twice put in jeopardy of life or limb."

The prohibition is not merely against double punishment; it forbids the state's "mak[ing] repeated attempts to convict a person for an alleged offense, thereby subjecting him to embarrassment, expense and ordeal and compelling him to live in a continual state of anxiety and insecurity as well as enhancing the possibility that even though innocent, he may be found guilty."[85] The Fifth Amendment prohibition was not held applicable to the states until 1969.[86] However, virtually all state constitutions contain some form of the protection, the origins of which are often said to be found in Greek and Roman law.[87] By Blackstone's time, the English courts recognized four pleas in bar which embrace the concept; autrefois acquit or former acquit; autrefois convict or former convict; autrefois attaint or former attaint; and pardon.[88] The very words of the Fifth Amendment are found in Blackstone's explanation for the doctrine of autrefois acquit and autrefois convict: "that no man ought to be twice brought in danger of his life for one and the same crime.[89]

It might be assumed that the fundamental nature and universal recognition of the doctrine would have led to the development of a relatively ordered body of law. However, as Justice Rehnquist has candidly noted, the United States Supreme Court's holdings could "hardly be characterized as models of

---

[83] See §3.28 (consent searches); and §5.17 (voluntariness of confession).

[84] United States v Wade, 388 US 218 (1967); see §6.04.

[85] Green v United States, 355 US 184, 187-88 (1957).

[86] Benton v Maryland, 395 US 784 (1969).

[87] Id 795.

[88] 4 W. Blackstone, Commentaries 329-31 (U Chi ed 1979).

[89] Id 330.

consistency and clarity."[90] In fact, the Court's opinions have frequently been flatly contradictory.[91]

The core of the double jeopardy rule is fixed. The same act may constitute more than one crime; but to determine whether one offense is different from another, a court must determine whether one requires proof of a fact that the other does not.[92] The two offenses for which the defendant is prosecuted cannot be the same in law and fact.

The proliferation of criminal laws, and, particularly, the frequency of conspiracy prosecutions, have led to a significant amount of litigation about the kinds of prosecution barred by the Fifth Amendment. Some judges have proposed that once a defendant has been prosecuted for a crime arising from a transaction, the Fifth Amendment should protect that defendant from further prosecution; the Supreme Court has never adopted that position.[93] But in *Brown v Ohio*,[94] the Court specifically held that a defendant cannot be successively prosecuted for a greater offense after successful prosecution of a lesser included offense unless there was some reason why the prosecution could not proceed on the more serious charge at the outset,[95] or unless the defendant requests separate trials.[96]

A prosecutor could, of course, harass a defendant by dividing a crime into discrete elements—as, for example, by prosecuting a person for separate crimes of bigamy for each day he lives with two wives.[97] The Supreme Court has held that the double jeopardy clause "is not such a fragile guarantee that prosecutors can avoid its limitations by the simple expedient of dividing a simple crime into a series of temporal or spatial units,"[98] and has uniformly rejected such attempts.[99] Thus, the Court has held that a defendant could not be prosecuted for the greater and lesser offenses of theft and joyriding under Ohio law, during different parts of a nine-day transaction.[100] The double jeopardy clause does not, however, bar the government from prosecuting a person for a substantive offense and for conspiracy to commit that same offense.[101] Despite the fact that a person may not be criminally prosecuted a second time for the same offense,

---

[90] Whalen v United States, 445 US 684 (1980) (Rehnquist, J, dissenting).

[91] *See, e.g.*, United States v Scott, 437 US 82 (1978) (overruling United States v Jenkins, 420 US 258 (1975)).

[92] Brown v Ohio, 431 US 161 (1977).

[93] Ashe v Swenson, 397 US 436, 448 (1970) (Brennan, J, concurring).

[94] 431 US 161 (1977).

[95] *See, also* Jeffers v United States, 432 US 137, 150-52 (1977).

[96] *Id.*

[97] *See, e.g., In re* Neilson, 131 US 176 (1889).

[98] Brown v Ohio, 431 US 161, 169 (1977).

[99] *Id.*

[100] *Id.*

[101] Ianelli v United States, 420 US 770 (1975).

an acquittal in a criminal case does not bar the government from litigating the same issue in a civil case.[102]

The Court has not been receptive to the argument that a defendant has waived the right to be free from double jeopardy if acquitted of a crime. A defendant convicted of a lesser included offense who appeals cannot, on retrial, be prosecuted for the greater offense, since the defendant has once been acquitted of the greater offense by the jury's action in convicting of the lesser included offense; there is no waiver of a plea in bar by appealing conviction of the lesser included offense.[103] A defendant may, however, validly waive the right to plead autrefois convict, as when, for example, a person convicted of a crime in a nonjury court exercises a statutory right of appeal for trial de novo by jury.[104]

Violations of a person's right to be free from twice being placed in jeopardy can never be harmless error, because the risk of trial, and not conviction, is the right that the constitutional guarantee safeguards.[105]

§15.14 When Jeopardy Attaches

One of the few areas clarified by the United States Supreme Court is the time at which the right to raise the defense of double jeopardy is said to *attach*. Until jeopardy attaches, a prosecutor may dismiss a pending prosecution and revive it at a later date. Jeopardy attaches in a jury trial when the jury is sworn[106] and in a bench trial, when the judge begins to hear evidence.[107] Once jeopardy has attached, a mistrial over the defendant's objection will bar retrial of the defendant unless there is a "manifest necessity for the retrial."[108]

§15.15 Appeal by Government

The unsettled nature of the law of double jeopardy is perhaps more understandable when its application to criminal appeals is considered. Criminal appeals are a relatively recent invention. Indeed, in federal practice, the right of a criminal defendant to appeal was not recognized until 1896.[109] The estab-

---

[102] One Lot Stones v United States, 409 US 232 (1972).
[103] Price v Georgia, 398 US 323 (1970); *but see* Jeffers v United States, 432 US 137 (1977).
[104] Ludwig v Massachusetts, 427 US 618 (1976).
[105] Price v Georgia, 398 US 323 (1970).
[106] Crist v Bretz, 437 US 28 (1978).
[107] Serfass v United States, 420 US 377 (1975).
[108] See §15.17.
[109] United States v Ball, 163 US 662 (1896).

lishment of a government right to appeal created a certain tension between the right to be free from double jeopardy and the right of the government to appeal. This tension was exacerbated by the 1970 Criminal Appeals Act,[110] which has been copied in many jurisdictions. Congress, in the Criminal Appeals Act, attempted to give the government the right to appeal to the full extent permitted by the Constitution. Thus, the litigation engendered by that act in the United States Supreme Court is highly relevant in all jurisdictions.

In broad terms, the relationship between the government's right to appeal and double jeopardy may be simply explained: the government may appeal if its appeal would not result in the retrial of a defendant, but may not appeal where a retrial would be the government's remedy.[111] The successful appeal by a defendant of a conviction on any grounds except insufficiency of evidence would not bar further prosecution.[112] But the Court has steadfastly held that an acquittal, whether by court or by jury, cannot be appealed, however mistaken the acquittal may have been.[113] Where a defendant moves to dismiss a charge on a ground unrelated to factual guilt or innocence, however, there is no bar to the government's appeal.[114]

§15.16 Constitutional Collateral Estoppel

Implicit in the Fifth Amendment prohibition of double jeopardy is the doctrine of constitutional collateral estoppel. The United States Supreme Court first explicitly recognized the doctrine in 1970 in *Ashe v Swenson*,[115] when it held that a defendant who had been acquitted of the robbery of one person playing poker with five others could not be prosecuted for robbery of any of the remaining five poker players, where his defense at trial was based in the prosecutor's failure to establish his identification. In a series of cases since *Ashe*, the Court has reaffirmed and applied the doctrine.[116]

When a defendant raises the defense of constitutional collateral estoppel, its application is a matter of constitutional fact.[117] When a previous judgment

---

[110] 18 USC §3731.

[111] *See, e.g.*, United States v Wilson, 420 US 332 (1975); *see also* Kepner v United States, 195 US 100 (1904).

[112] Burks v United States, 437 US 1 (1978).

[113] United States v Scott, 437 US 82 (1978); Sanabria v United States, 437 US 54 (1978).

[114] United States v Scott, 437 US 82, 98-99 (1978).

[115] 397 US 436 (1970).

[116] *See, e.g.*, Turner v Arkansas, 407 US 366 (1972); Harris v Washington, 404 US 55 (1971); Simpson v Florida, 403 US 384 (1971); Standefer v United States, 447 US 10 (1980)

[117] Ashe v Swenson, 397 US 436, 444 (1970).

of acquittal was based on a general verdict, a reviewing court must review the entire record and conclude whether a rational jury could have founded its verdict on an issue other than the one the defendant seeks to foreclose from consideration.[118] The straightforward nature of the collateral estoppel doctrine has meant that there has been little confusion in its application. The United States Supreme Court has held, however, that the fact that a defendant has been successful in a criminal prosecution does not bar the government from attempting to prove the same fact on which a jury found in the defendant's favor in a civil proceeding.[119] The Court has recognized that the difference in burden of proof in civil and criminal cases and the possibility that relevant evidence will be excluded from criminal proceedings on grounds not applicable in civil proceedings militate against application of the doctrine in such circumstances. Thus, the Court has permitted the government to prosecute civil forfeiture proceedings against items it alleged were smuggled into the country despite the fact that the owner of the items was acquitted of smuggling.[120]

While the Court has recognized the doctrine of nonmutual collateral estoppel in cases in which the government has had a full and fair opportunity to litigate,[121] it has specifically held that the acquittal of a principal in one trial does not bar trial of his accomplice in another.[122] The Court reasoned that the government is often without a full and fair opportunity to litigate in a criminal proceeding, that its discovery rights are limited, and that it may not appeal or obtain judgment n.o.v.[123] Further, the vagaries of exclusionary rules may make evidence admissible against one defendant inadmissible against another.[124] Finally, the Court recognized an important independent interest in enforcement of criminal law which would be defeated by application of the doctrine.[125]

The doctrine of constitutional collateral estoppel may never be applied against a defendant.[126]

---

[118] *Id* 444.

[119] One Lot Stones v United States, 409 US 232 (1972).

[120] *Id.*

[121] *See, e.g.*, Parkline Hosiery Co v Shane, 439 US 322 (1979) (holding that a defendant who had a full and fair opportunity to litigate in a civil proceeding brought by the Securities and Exchange Commission could be estopped from relitigating those issues in a civil proceeding brought by a private party).

[122] Standefer v United States, 447 US 10 (1980).

[123] *Id* 22.

[124] *Id* 23.

[125] *Id* 24-25.

[126] Simpson v Florida, 403 US 384 (1971).

§15.17 Retrial After Mistrial

The law governing the propriety of trial after a mistrial has not significantly changed since Justice Story's pronouncement in 1824:

> We think, that in all cases of this nature, the law has invested courts of justice with the authority to discharge a jury from giving any verdict, whenever, in their opinion, taking all the circumstances into consideration, there is a manifest necessity for the act, or the ends of public justice would otherwise be defeated. They are to exercise a sound discretion on the subject; and it is impossible to define all the circumstances which would render it proper to interfere.[127]

In dealing with the issue of when retrial after mistrial would be proper, the United States Supreme Court has "explicitly declined the invitation of litigants to formulate rules based on categories of circumstances which will permit or preclude retrial."[128] The Court has spoken many times of the importance of the right to have a particular tribunal pass on one's guilt or innocence, pointing out that a second trial constitutes a severe emotional and financial strain and may even enhance the chance of conviction.[129]

The decided cases tend to establish a continuum. First, it is clear that if a mistrial is caused by, or the defendant is required to request a mistrial as the result of, the bad faith actions of the judge or prosecutor, retrial will be barred.[130] At the opposite end of the spectrum, if the defendant causes a mistrial by clearly improper conduct and there is no remedy other than a mistrial, retrial will not be barred.[131] If mistrial is based on the premise that the jury is unable to agree on a verdict, "long considered the classic basis for a proper mistrial," retrial is not barred.[132] The difficulty arises in determining which of the many problems which may arise at any trial could require mistrial over a defendant's objection. Review of the Supreme Court's decisions suggests that the Court will give great deference to the trial judge's decision.[133] Thus, in a variety of

---

[127] United States v Perez, 22 US (9 Wheat) 579, 580 (1824).

[128] United States v Jorn, 400 US 470, 480 (1971); Gori v United States, 367 US 364, 369 (1961).

[129] Arizona v Washington, 434 US 497, 503-04 (1978).

[130] *See, e.g.*, United States v Dinitz, 424 US 600, 611 (1976); *see also* Arizona v Washington, 434 US 497 (1978); Downum v United States, 372 US 734 (1963); see generally, Annot, *Double Jeopardy as Bar to Retrial After Grant of Defendant's Motion for Mistrial*, 98 ALR3d 997.

[131] *See, e.g.*, Lee v United States, 432 US 23 (1977).

[132] Arizona v Washington, 434 US 497, 509 (1978); *See* Logan v United States, 144 US 263 (1892).

[133] Arizona v Washington, 434 US 497, 510 (1978).

situations, the Court has upheld a trial judge's determination that mistrial was the only way to eliminate prejudice and ensure a fair trial.[134]

There is no constitutional requirement that a trial court declaring a mistrial make findings of fact, although the Supreme Court has suggested that such findings facilitate review.[135] If a mistrial is declared over an attorney's objection, he or she would be well advised to request findings and rulings, if such requests can be made in that particular forum, to bolster an appeal.

§15.18 Prosecution by Two Sovereigns for Same Act

Just as one act may constitute more than one crime in a single jurisdiction, one act can offend two sovereigns, the state and federal government. When that occurs, the individual committing the act is subject to two prosecutions. In *Bartkus v Illinois*,[136] the United States Supreme Court, held that such multiple prosecution is not a violation of the double jeopardy clause. The multiple prosecutions must, in fact, commence at the behest of two sovereigns, such as the state or federal governments.[137] A state may not create two sovereigns by

---

[134] *See, e.g.*, Arizona v Washington, 434 US 497 (1978) (mistrial where defense attorney made improper opening statement no bar to retrial); United States v Dinitz, 424 US 600 (1976) (mistrial when defense counsel barred for improper conduct no bar to retrial); Illinois v Somerville, 410 US 458 (1973) (mistrial because indictment defective no bar to later trial); United States v Jorn, 400 US 470 (1971) (mistrial ordered by trial judge so government witnesses could consult with attorney where there was no showing this was necessary barred retrial); Downum v United States, 372 US 734 (1963) (mistrial at government's request because its witnesses were not available barred retrial); Gori v United States, 367 US 364 (1961) (mistrial because judge, apparently erroneously, believed prosecution was engaging in improper and prejudicial questioning of witness did not bar retrial); Wade v Hunter, 336 US 684 (1949) (retrial not barred where military court discharged defendant due to tactical necessities in the field); Thompson v United States, 155 US 271 (1894) (retrial not barred where mistrial declared because one juror served on grand jury which indicated defendant); Simmons v United States, 142 US 148 (1891) (retrial not barred where mistrial declared because letter published in newspaper rendered jury's impartiality doubtful). See generally, Annot, *Double Jeopardy as Bar to Retrial After Grant of Defendant's Motion for Mistrial*, 98 ALR3d 997; Annot, *Propriety of Trial Court's Declaration of Mistrial or Discharge of Jury; Without Accused's Consent, on Ground of Prosecutor's Disclosure of Prejudicial Matter, or Making Prejudicial Remarks in Presence of Jury*, 77 ALR3d 1143.

[135] Arizona v Washington, 434 US 497, 517 (1978).

[136] 359 US 121 (1959); *see also* United States v Wheeler, 435 US 313 (1978); Lavon v State, 586 SW2d 112 (Tenn 1979); State v Castonguay, 240 A2d 747 (Me 1968); State v Cooper, 54 NJ 330, 255 A2d 232 (1969); State v Rogers, 90 NM 604, 566 P2d 1142 (1977); State v West, 260 NW2d 215 (SD 1977); Lavon v State, 586 SW2d 112 (Tenn 1979); see generally Annot, *Conviction or Acquittal in Federal Court as a Bar to Prosecution in State Court for State Offense Barred on Same Facts*, 6 ALR4th 802.

[137] *See, e.g.*, United States v Wheeler, 435 US 313 (1978) (holding that Indian tribes are sovereigns, so that a person may lawfully be prosecuted by both federal government and the Navaho Tribe for multiple crimes arising out of one act).

establishing state and municipal courts. Successive prosecutions in state and municipal courts of the same state are forbidden by the Constitution.[138]

Obviously, multiple prosecution can be vindictive, and can result in unfairness. Since 1960, as a result of the *Bartkus* decision, the Justice Department has followed the *Petite*[139] policy. Under that policy, a federal trial after a state prosecution for the same act is barred unless the reasons are compelling. A United States attorney contemplating a prosecution in these circumstances is required to obtain authorization from an assistant attorney general.[140] The *Petite* policy recognizes that there is little difference between, for example, the crimes of robbing a bank and robbing a federally insured bank.

Perhaps as a result of the common sense recognition that multiple prosecutions for the same act by two sovereigns offend the values protected by the double jeopardy clause, a number of states have enacted statutes which provide that prior acquittal or conviction in another jurisdiction of a crime arising out of the same transaction is a proper plea in bar.[141] A number of states have also found prosecution after acquittal or conviction in a prior proceeding in another jurisdiction to be barred as a matter of state constitutional law. Illustrative is the decision of the Michigan Supreme Court in *People v Cooper*,[142] in which the court held that a prior conviction in federal court for robbing a federally insured bank barred a subsequent prosecution in state court. The court reasoned that the interests of both the state and federal government were satisfied by the federal prosecution, and thus further prosecution was impermissible. This analysis has been applied by a number of other courts.[143] Most of these courts take the view that if the difference between the two crimes is merely jurisdictional, as, for example, where the offense is robbery of a federally insured bank, the second prosecution should be barred.[144] At least one court has fashioned a similar rule as a matter of nonconstitutional state law.[145] Most courts which follow *Bartkus v Illinois* have rejected the argument that a defendant acquitted

---

[138] Waller v Florida, 397 US 387 (1970).

[139] Petite v United States, 361 US 529, 530 (1960).

[140] *Id* 530-31. Violation of the *Petite* policy by the government can be grounds for dismissal. *See generally* Rinaldi v United States, 434 US 22 (1977).

[141] *See e.g.*, Luke v State, 373 So 2d 1228 (Ala Crim App), *cert denied*, 373 So 2d 1230 (Ala 1979); Journey v State, 261 Ark 259, 547 SW2d 433 (1977); People v Belcher, 11 Cal 3d 91, 520 P2d 385, 113 Cal Rptr 1 (1974); Dorsey v State, 237 Ga 876, 230 SE2d 307 (1976); Wilson v State, 383 NE2d 304 (Ind 1978); Abraham v Justices of NY Supreme Court, 37 NY2d 560, 338 NE2d 597, 376 NYS2d 79 (1975).

[142] 398 Mich 450, 247 NW2d 866 (1976).

[143] *See, e.g.*, People v Gray, 407 Mich 681, 289 NW2d 651 (1980); State v LeCoure, 158 Mont 340, 491 P2d 1228 (1971); State v Heinz, 119 NH 717, 407 A2d 814 (1979); Commonwealth v Grazier, 481 Pa 622, 393 A2d 335 (1978).

[144] State v Hogg, 118 NH 262, 266, 385 A2d 844 (1978); *but see* State v Heinz, 119 NH 717, 407 A2d 814 (1979); Commonwealth v Grazier, 481 Pa 622, 393 A2d 335 (1978).

[145] Commonwealth v Cepulonis, 374 Mass 487, 373 NE2d 1136 (1978).

in a prior proceeding for a different crime arising from the same act may raise the defense of constitutional collateral estoppel.[146]

---

[146] *See, e.g.*, Martin v Rose, 481 F2d 658 (6th Cir 1973), *cert denied*, 414 US 876 (1974); State v Rogers, 90 NM 604, 566 P2d 1142 (1977).

16

Mode and Conduct of Trial

Duties and Role of Trial Judge

§16.01 Right to an Impartial Judge

Judges have differing roles in the federal and state systems. In the former, the judge may be an active participant in the trial, while in the majority of states, the trial judge is akin to an impartial referee. In all jurisdictions, however, the court bears the responsibility for determining the law of the case and for protecting the defendant's constitutional rights.[1] In most jurisdictions, the trial judge may, in the normal course, be the finder of fact, at the preliminary stage at least; in some jurisdictions, the judge may be the finder of fact if the defendant waives the right to trial by jury. In such circumstances, a defendant has the same interest in having his or her case heard by an impartial judge as in having an impartial jury hear the case. But even if the judge is not the finder of fact, the defendant has a vital interest in ensuring the fairness of the trial judge who will rule on the law of the case and control the course of the trial.

The United States Supreme Court has never distinguished between the impartiality required of a judge sitting merely as a judge and the impartiality required of a judge sitting as a finder of fact.[2] The Court has emphatically held that a fair trial in a fair tribunal is a basic element of due process.[3] Thus it has held that where a judge acts as complainant, prosecutor, judge, and finder of fact, the conviction obtained violates due process.[4] Moreover, even if the judge sits merely as a trial judge, if the judge's overbearing conduct could influence the jury, a violation of the defendant's rights occurs.[5] Of course, actions by the court which unfairly prejudice the defendant's case as, for example, threatening

---

[1] Lakeside v Oregon, 435 US 333, 341-42 (1978).

[2] *Compare, e.g.,* Ungar v Sarafite, 376 US 575 (1964) *with* Connally v Georgia, 429 US 245 (1977).

[3] *In re* Murcheson, 349 US 133, 136 (1955).

[4] *Id.*

[5] Offut v United States, 348 US 11, 16 (1954).

defense witnesses, violate a defendant's constitutional rights.[6] The Constitution requires not only that the defendant *be* afforded a fair trial, but that the trial *appear* fair, for the appearance of justice is as necessary as the fact.[7]

Most of the cases concerning this issue which have been decided in the United States Supreme Court in the last 20 years have involved a claim by an attorney that the trial judge who cited him or her for contempt is biased, and should not sit on trial of the contempt charges. There is no per se constitutional rule that a judge who cites a person for contempt during a trial recuse himself or herself when the contempt charges are tried.[8] It is only when the trial judge becomes personally embroiled with the defendant that a new judge is required to hear the contempt charges.[9] But where the trial judge has been reviled by the alleged contemner, whether or not the judge responds in kind, the Court has held that the judge must recuse himself or herself from the contempt trial since "no one so cruelly slandered is likely to maintain that calm detachment necessary for fair adjudication."[10]

One other situation deserves mention. In many states, judges are elected. The United States Supreme Court has specifically held that a defendant has no constitutional right to be tried by a trial judge with life tenure;[11] but a defendant may not, particularly in notorious cases, be subjected to the vicissitudes of the electoral process. If a particularly notorious criminal case were to come to trial shortly before a judges' election, the Court has suggested that continuance of the trial might be constitutionally required.[12]

§16.02 Court's Interest in Outcome of Case as Constituting Prejudice

The United States Supreme Court has long recognized that the due process guarantee that a defendant be afforded a fair trial in a fair tribunal is offended when a judicial officer sitting on it has an interest in the proceedings. In 1927, the Court held that an Ohio statutory scheme which established village courts in which liquor offenses could be prosecuted and which provided that the mayor of the village could recover a fee if the defendant were convicted but not if he were acquitted violated due process.[13] The Court emphasized that all questions

---

[6] Webb v Texas, 409 US 95 (1972).

[7] *In re* Murchison, 349 US 133, 136 (1955); Tumey v Ohio, 273 US 510, 532 (1927).

[8] Ungar v Sarafite, 376 US 575 (1964).

[9] Mayberry v Pennsylvania, 400 US 455, 465 (1971).

[10] *Id. See also* Bloom v Illinois, 391 US 194 (1968).

[11] Palmore v United States, 411 US 389, 390-91 (1973).

[12] Sheppard v Maxwell, 384 US 333, 354 n 9 (1966).

[13] Tumey v Ohio, 273 US 510, 523 (1927).

of judicial qualification did not rise to a constitutional level, but that the "direct, personal, substantial pecuniary interest in reaching a conclusion against" the defendant was a violation of due process.[14] The Court emphasized that the fact that the procedure employed by Ohio did not lead to abuse was irrelevant; Chief Justice Taft wrote:

> Every procedure which would offer a possible temptation to the average man to forget the burden of proof required to convict the defendant, or which might lead him not to hold the balance nice, clear and true between the state and the accused denies the latter due process of law.[15]

The Court has remained adamant that any pecuniary interest in a case held by a judge, no matter how small, violates a defendant's right to due process. In *Ward v City of Monroeville*,[16] the Court held that a defendant's right to due process was violated when he was forced to trial in a municipal court the fines from which provided a substantial portion of the municipality's funds, where the presiding judicial officer was the mayor of the municipality who had responsibility for the municipality's finances. The Court reasoned that the mayor's responsibility for finances might make him partisan to maintain the level of contribution from fines from the court.[17]

§16.03 Right to Be Tried Before a Lawyer Judge

In many jurisdictions, traffic courts and other courts of inferior jurisdiction are not staffed by lawyer judges. Obviously, the spectacle of a nonlawyer judge ruling on the exclusion or admission of evidence or on the proper seating of jurors, or hearing the motions to suppress which could be raised in any routine misdemeanor case is not a pleasant one. The most skilled advocate can have little effect on a judge who does not understand the lawyers' arguments.

For that reason, 1974, the California Supreme Court held, in *Gordon v Justice Court*,[18] that allowing a nonlawyer judge to preside in cases which could result in the defendant's imprisonment constituted a violation of due process of law. The court pointed out that Magna Carta had provided in 1215: "We will not

---

[14] *Id* 523.

[15] *Id* 532.

[16] 409 US 57 (1972).

[17] *Id* 60; *see also* Connally v Georgia, 429 US 245 (1977).

[18] 12 Cal 3d 323, 525 P2d 72, 115 Cal Rptr 551 (1974), *cert denied*, 420 US 938 (1975).

make men justices, sheriffs or bailiffs unless they are such as know the law of the realm and are minded to observe it rightly."[19]

A mere two years later, the United States Supreme Court held, in *North v Russell*,[20] that an accused was not denied due process of law where he was tried for an offense which could result in imprisonment before a nonlawyer judge, where the defendant could vacate the conviction and obtain a trial de novo by appealing. The Court did not reach the issue decided by the California Supreme Court in *Gordon*, holding that that issue was not before it, since the conviction in *North* would in no way be final.

State Courts have generally considered *North* to stand for the proposition that a defendant cannot be put to trial, for an offense punishable by imprisonment, by a nonlawyer magistrate, unless the defendant is afforded an alternative to the trial before the magistrate.[21] The issue of whether due process forbids trial for an imprisonable offense before a nonlawyer judge is, narrowly speaking, still open, and state courts of last resort have reached differing conclusions.[22] It is quite likely, however, that if the issue were squarely presented to the United States Supreme Court, it would now hold, as did the Florida Supreme Court in *Trieman v State*,[23] that due process does not require that a judge who hears a criminal case which could result in imprisonment be a member of the bar, but that due process does require that the judge be able to understand the legal issues presented. The Florida Supreme Court reasoned that the United States Supreme Court had held in *Shadwick v City of Tampa*[24] that the Constitution does not require that warrants be issued by magistrates or even judicial officers, and that warrants could be issued by city clerks as long as the clerks were capable of understanding the concept of probable cause. Since Florida had established a complex and comprehensive judicial training program, which required that a nonlawyer judge attend a three-year judicial training program which included 600 hours of classroom instruction, there was no constitutional prohibition against allowing trained nonlawyer judges to try criminal cases which could result in imprisonment.[25]

---

[19] *Id.*

[20] 427 US 328 (1976).

[21] *See, e.g.* People v Skynski, 42 NY2d 218, 366 NE2d 797, 397 NYS2d 707 (1977).

[22] *See, e.g.*, Re Judicial Interpretation of 1975 Senate Enrolled Act 441, 263 Ind 350, 332 NE2d 97 (1975) (due process requires judge presiding in criminal case to have qualifications of attorney); *Ex parte* Ross, 522 SW2d 214 (Tex Crim App 1975) (duty of judge is to decide fairly and impartially, and this does not require legal training); see generally Annot, *Constitutional Restrictions on Non-Attorney Acting as Judge in a Criminal Proceeding*, 71 ALR3d 562.

[23] 343 So 2d 819 (Fla 1977).

[24] 407 US 345 (1972).

[25] Trieman v State, 343 So 2d 819, 823-24 (Fla 1977).

Joint Trials

§16.04 Trial of Defendants Jointly

The prosecution generally has a strong interest in trying defendants accused of committing a crime together jointly. Obviously, one trial rather than two, minimizes expenses and delay. It is easier to gather all the witnesses needed for a trial once, rather than twice; and if the same witnesses must testify twice, defense counsel may be able to obtain a transcript of the first trial with which to cross-examine. Counsel will almost certainly learn a great deal about the government's trial strategy.

A defendant may be placed at a substantial disadvantage in a joint trial. Crucial evidence, technically admissible against only one defendant, may be admitted with a limiting instruction to the jury that may or may not be effective. Two defendants may have antagonistic defenses, each blaming the other. A jury may be confused by the complexity of a case or impressed by a strong case against one defendant, and convict a codefendant against whom the prosecution has a weak case.

The law governing joinder and severance of defendants is primarily local and not constitutional. Illustrative are Federal Rules of Criminal Procedure 8 and 14.[26]   Courts generally hold that cases should be tried together[27] and that the decision to sever is within the discretion of the trial court.[28] The 1980 version of the American Bar Association Standards for Criminal Justice

---

[26] Fed R Crim P 8 provides:

> Rule 8. Joinder of Offenses and of Defendants
>
> (a) Joinder of Offenses. Two or more offenses may be charged in the same indictment or information in a separate count for each offense if the offenses charged, whether felonies or misdemeanors or both, are of the same or similar character or are based on the same act or transaction or on two or more acts or transactions connected together or constituting parts of a common scheme or plan.
>
> (b) Joinder of Defendants. Two or more defendants may be charged in the same indictment or information if they are alleged to have participated in the same act or transaction or in the same series of acts or transactions constituting an offense or offenses. Such defendants may be charged in one or more counts together or separately and all of the defendants need not be charged in each count.

Fed R Crim P 14 provides, in relevant part, "If it appears that a defendant or the government is prejudiced by a joinder of offenses or defendants . . . the court may order an election or separate trials of counts, grant a severance of defendants or provide whatever relief justice requires."

[27] United States v Crawford, 581 F2d 489 (5th Cir 1978).

[28] United States v Ocanas, 628 F2d 353 (5th Cir 1980).

establishes explicit guidelines for use by trial courts.[29] As in other aspects of criminal procedure, however, even the discretionary joinder and severance of a defendant's case can affect the fundamental fairness of the trial required by the due process clause of the Fourteenth Amendment. Thus, for example, a claim that joinder of a relatively minor actor's case with the case of a co-defendant against whom the government's case was overwhelming violated his right to a fair trial may be of constitutional magnitude.[30] A few specific constitutional rules concerning joint trials have developed, and they are discussed in the following sections.

§16.05 Rule of *Bruton v United States*

The most significant constitutional limit on joint trials applies to the situation where a defendant and codefendant are tried jointly, and the codefendant has made an admission which inculpates the defendant. The traditional rule, in both state and federal courts prior to 1968, was that the statement of the codefendant would be admitted, but that the jury would be instructed that the evidence should be considered only against the defendant who made the

---

[29] Standard 13-3.2. Severance of defendants

(a) When a defendant moves for severance because an out-of-court statement of a codefendant makes reference to, but is not admissible against, the moving defendant, the court should determine whether the prosecution intends to offer the statement in evidence as part of its case in chief. If so, the court should require the prosecuting attorney to elect one of the following courses:

(i) a joint trial at which the statement is not admitted into evidence;

(ii) a joint trial at which the statement is admitted into evidence only after all references to the moving defendant have been deleted, provided that, as deleted, the statement will not prejudice the moving defendant; or

(iii) severance of the moving defendant.

(b) The court, on application of the prosecuting attorney, or on application of the defendant other than under paragraph (a), should grant a severance of defendants:

(i) before trial, whenever the defendants are not joinablent pursuant to standard 13-2.2(a), or whenever severance is deemed appropriate to promote a fair determination of the guilt or innocence of one or more defendants; or

(ii) during trial, whenever, upon consent of the defendant to be severed or upon a finding of manifest necessity, severance is deemed necessary to achieve a fair determination of the guilt or innocence of one or more defendants.

(c) When evaluating whether severance is "appropriate to promote" or "necessary to achieve" a fair determination of one or more defendants' guilt or innocence for each offense, the court should consider among other factors whether, in view of the number of offenses and defendants charged and the complexity of the evidence to be offered, the trier of fact will be able to distinguish the evidence and apply the law intelligently as to each offense and as to each defendant.

[30] Woodcock v Amaral, 511 F2d 985 (1st Cir 1974).

statement.[31] In *Bruton v United States*,[32] the United States Supreme Court held that the conviction of a defendant, had at a joint trial, must be reversed because an admission of a codefendant which inculpated the defendant was admitted at trial and the codefendant did not testify. Although the jury had been instructed not to consider the codefendant's statement against Bruton, the Court recognized the practical difficulties which inhere in such an instruction. The Court held that the risk that the jury might not have disregarded the instruction, coupled with the fact that the defendant did not testify, violated the defendant's Sixth Amendment right to confront the witnesses against him. Although a federal case, *Bruton* was held retroactive and fully applicable to the states in *Roberts v Russell*.[33]

That *Bruton* was primarily based on a denial of confrontation, and not the risk of prejudice because a codefendant made admissions which were admitted into evidence although hearsay, was made absolutely clear a few years after *Bruton* was decided in *Nelson v O'Neil*.[34] In that case, two individuals were tried jointly for robbery, and an admission made by O'Neil's codefendant, which implicated O'Neil, was admitted into evidence. The codefendant testified, denied making the statement, and O'Neil's attorney had the opportunity to cross-examine him. In holding that no constitutional violation had occurred, Justice Stewart emphasized that "the Constitution, as construed in *Bruton* . . . is violated *only* where the out of court hearsay statement is that of a declarant who is unavailable at trial for full and effective cross-examination"[35] (emphasis in original).

While the meaning of *Bruton* is reasonably clear, there is some question about its applicability when a defendant has made an admission which "interlocks" with the admission of a codefendant. In *Parker v Randolph*,[36] four judges of the United States Supreme Court held that *Bruton* is simply not applicable when a defendant makes a statement which interlocks with a statement of a codefendant. The four judges reasoned that when a defendant's own confession is properly before the jury, the possible prejudice resulting from the failure of the jury to follow the trial court's instructions is not so vital as to require departure from the general rule allowing admission of evidence, properly admissible against only one defendant, at a joint trial, with a limiting instruction on the evidence

---

[31] Delli Paoli v United States, 352 US 232 (1957).

[32] 391 US 123 (1968).

[33] 392 US 293 (1968).

[34] 402 US 622 (1971).

[35] *Id* 627; *see also* Dutton v Evans, 400 US 74 (1970) (held, fact that coconspirator's hearsay statement was admitted under peculiar Georgia evidentiary rule which allowed statements of coconspirators to be admitted even if the statements were made after the object of the conspiracy was accomplished, did not violate the defendant's Sixth Amendment confrontation rights).

[36] 442 US 62 (1979).

given the jury.[37] Justice Blackmun concurred in the result on the ground that the violation of *Bruton* in the case before the Court was harmless error, but explicitly rejected the plurality's per se rule of inapplicability.[38] Justice Stevens, joined by Justices Brennan and Marshall, explicitly rejected the plurality's per se rule because the per se rule assumes the jury's ability to disregard a prejudicial confession is increased by the existence of a corroborating statement by the defendant, and it assumes that all admissions are equally reliable.[39] Justice Powell did not participate.

The lack of a definition of an *interlocking confession*, as well as the division of opinion on the Supreme Court, has led some courts to conclude that *Parker* is of no precedential value whatsoever.[40] Lower courts are badly split on the issue of whether a per se rule of inapplicability exists when an interlocking confession is available, and it appears that the United States Supreme Court will be required to refine its holdings in the near future.[41]

§16.06 Alternatives to Severance

If a codefendant has made a statement which the prosecution intends to introduce at trial, and which inculpates the defendant, and the codefendant will not testify at trial, the trial court generally has the alternative of agreeing to a severance of the trials of the two defendants, or requiring that all references to the defendant against whom the statement is not admissible be excised.[42] Obviously, the references to a codefendant in some statements cannot be excised without distorting the statement. But one of these two procedures is the usual fashion in which *Bruton* problems are resolved.

However, other alternatives do exist. The Sixth Circuit, while expressing doubt about the practice, affirmed a conviction following a joint trial, in which the jury heard the statements of the codefendant only after reaching a verdict with respect to the defendant who made no statement.[43] A few courts have affirmed convictions held after trial before two separate juries, where the two juries

---

[37] *Id* 75.

[38] *Id* 77.

[39] *Id* 81.

[40] *See, e.g.,* Earhart v State, 48 Md App 695, 429 A2d 557 (1981).

[41] *Compare* Hodges v Rose, 570 F2d 643 (6th Cir 1978); United States v DiGilio, 538 F2d 977 (3d Cir 1976), *cert denied,* 429 US 1038 (1977), *and* Ignacio v Cram, 397 F2d 513 (9th Cir 1969), *cert denied,* 397 US 943 (1970), all rejecting a per se rule that *Bruton* is inapplicable, *with* Mack v Maggio, 538 F2d 1139 (5th Cir 1976); United States v Spinks, 470 F2d 64 (7th Cir), *cert denied,* 409 US 1011 (1972). *See also* People v Moll, 26 NY2d 1, 256 NE2d 175, 307 NYS2d 876, *cert denied,* 398 US 911 (1970) *and* People v Rosochacki, 41 Ill 2d 483, 244 NE2d 136 (1969).

[42] Bruton v United States, 391 US 123, 134 n 10 (1968).

[43] United States v Crane, 499 F2d 1385 (6th Cir 1974), *cert denied,* 419 US 1002 (1975).

heard different opening and closing statements, and both heard the evidence admissible against both defendants, and one jury would be withdrawn when evidence inadmissible against the defendant whose case the jury would consider was admitted.[44] However, as the New Jersey Supreme Court recently noted in reluctantly affirming such a conviction, the reasons for lack of widespread adoption of this trial technique would appear to be the belief that application of the appropriate safeguards necessary to protect the rights of individuals involved in the trials would be more time-consuming than if separate trials were ordered, and the belief that the possibility of error in such a complicated procedure is enhanced.[45] In the case before it, the New Jersey Court held only that the procedure used, which had been suggested by defense counsel and agreed on by the prosecutor, was not "plain error," but stated that it did not recommend the procedure because of the substantial risks of prejudice to a defendant's right to a fair trial, and suggested that if used at all, the procedure should be used only in relatively uncomplicated situations which will not involve excessive moving of juries.[46]

§16.07 Antagonistic Defenses

If two defendants are tried jointly and each attempts to exculpate himself or herself by blaming the other, there exists a perceptible risk that a jury will simply convict both. As a general proposition, the fact that two codefendants have antagonistic defenses may raise a question as to whether joint trial is proper as a matter of local law, but does not raise an issue of constitutional magnitude.[47] However, some courts have held that the existance of antagonistic defenses can render a fair trial impossible. In *United States v Crawford*,[48] the Fifth Circuit held that the defendant had been denied a fair trial because the trial judge had refused to sever his trial for possession of an unregistered sawed-off shotgun from his codefendant's trial, where the sole defense of each defendant was the guilt of the other. In holding that the defendant had been denied a fair trial, Judge Vance reasoned:

> Each defendant had to confront not only hostile witnesses presented by the government, but also hostile witnesses presented by his codefendant.

---

[44] *See, e.g.*, United States v Rimar, 558 F2d 1271 (6th Cir 1977), *cert denied*, 434 US 984 (1978); United States v Sidman, 470 F2d 1158 (9th Cir 1972), *cert denied*, 409 US 1127 (1973); People v Brooks, 92 Mich App 393, 285 NW2d 307 (1979).

[45] State v Corsi, 86 NJ 172, 430 A2d 210 (1981).

[46] *Id.*

[47] See generally, Annot, *Antagonistic Defenses as Ground for Separate Trials of Co-Defendants in Criminal Case*, 82 ALR 3d 245.

[48] 581 F2d 489 (5th Cir 1978).

Witnesses against each defendant were thus examined by one adversary, and cross-examined by another adversary. A fair trial was impossible under these inherently prejudicial conditions.[49]

§16.08 Comment on Codefendant's Silence

If two defendants are tried jointly and one testifies and one does not, the prosecution may not, of course, comment on the failure of the defendant who did not testify to do so. But may the defendant who testified comment on the codefendant's failure to testify? In *DeLuna v United States*,[50] Judge Wisdom of the Fifth Circuit carefully considered the history of the privilege and held that while the defendant who did not testify had a right to remain silent and have no inference drawn from his failure to testify, the defendant who did testify had a right to have his attorney comment on the failure of the codefendant to testify. In the case before it, the court reversed the conviction and ordered separate trials.

Although the United States Supreme Court has never specifically decided the issue, most courts considering the issue have similarly held that a testifying defendant does have the right to comment on a codefendant's failure to testify.[51] Thus, a defendant who expects not to testify and expects a codefendant to testify antagonistically to him or her may be in a strong position to assert a constitutional right to a severance.

§16.09 Exculpatory Testimony by Codefendant

A number of courts have held that a defendant has a right to a severance on showing that a codefendant will exculpate the defendant by testimony, but will not testify at a joint trial because the codefendant will inculpate himself or herself.[52] Courts generally require a defendant who makes such a claim to make some showing that the testimony of the codefendant will, in fact, be forthcoming if severance is granted.[53]

---

[49] *Id* 492.

[50] 308 F2d 140 (5th Cir 1962).

[51] *See, e.g.*, Eder v People, 179 Colo 22, 498 P2d 945 (1972).

[52] United States v Shuford, 454 F2d 722 (4th Cir 1971).

[53] United States v Martinez, 486 F2d 15 (3d Cir 1973); United States v Echeles, 352 F2d 892 (7th Cir 1965).

§16.10 Identification of Codefendant

An identification of a codefendant would certainly be thought to be prejudicial by an attorney for a codefendant accused of the same crime at a joint trial. However, the prevailing view appears to be that the prejudice caused by an identification of a codefendant does not entitle the defendant who has not been identified to a severance as a matter of law.[54]

Trial Publicity

§16.11 Right to a Public Trial

The right to a public trial is a fundamental right, guaranteed by the due process clause of the Fourteenth Amendment as well as by the explicit guarantee of a public trial in the Sixth Amendment to the federal Constitution. As early as 1928, long before the Sixth Amendment was held fully applicable to the states in 1968,[55] the United States Supreme Court suggested in dicta that exclusion of the public from a criminal trial would violate due process.[56] In 1948, in *In re Oliver*,[57] the Court explicitly held that a secret trial was violative of the defendant's right to due process of law. Emphasizing the fundamental nature of the right to a public trial, the Court pointed out that it had been unable to find any instance of a criminal trial conducted in secret in either the United States or England since abolition of the Court of Star Chamber, and pointed out that "whether that court ever convicted people secretly is in dispute."[58]

The purpose of the guarantee is obvious: the contemporaneous review of the judge's actions in the forum of public opinion is an effective restraint on possible abuse of judicial power.[59]

The guarantee of a public trial does not, of course, mean that disruptive or unruly members of the public must be allowed to remain during a trial. Moreover, while the guarantee is directed toward the right of the friends and relatives of the accused to attend a trial, there is no question that a court has the authority to sequester witnesses.[60]

---

[54] People v Robles, 182 Colo 4, 514 P2d 630 (1973).

[55] Duncan v Louisiana, 391 US 145 (1968).

[56] Gaines v Washington, 277 US 81, 86 (1928).

[57] 333 US 257 (1948).

[58] *Id* 266; *see also* People v Jones, 47 NY2d 409, 391 NE2d 1335, 418 NYS2d 359 (1979) (judge's grant of prosecutor's motion to close courtroom when undercover police officer was testifying constituted a violation of the defendant's right to a public trial).

[59] *In re* Oliver, 333 US 257, 270 (1948).

[60] *See, e.g.*, Richmond Newspaper Inc v Virginia, 448 US 555 (1980).

§16.12 Role of Press at Trial

In addition to the defendant's interest in a public trial, the United States Supreme Court has recognized that the public has a palpable interest in open judicial proceedings.[61] Thus, the fact that the Sixth Amendment affords a defendant the right to a public trial does not give the defendant the right to insist on the opposite, a closed trial.[62] Because criminal trials have always been open, the Court has held that the public has a right of access to criminal trials which is protected by the Constitution.[63] During much of the nation's history, criminal trials were peculiarly local affairs, and individuals frequently went to the local courthouse to pass the time. That day is long gone, however, in most parts of this country, and the information most people obtain about criminal trials comes from newspapers or from television or radio. For that reason, the United States Supreme Court has recognized that the press acts as a surrogate for the public at large and may reasonably be afforded preferential treatment.[64] Frequently, in important criminal trials, the trial court will allow reporters special seating, sometimes within the bar of the court, to ensure that they are able to obtain accurate information. The United States Supreme Court has held that the right of the press to attend a criminal trial is protected by the First Amendment to the federal Constitution.[65]

The right to attend a trial is not, however, absolute. When a defendant seeks closure of a trial on the grounds that trial publicity may impair the right to a fair trial, the court must balance the public's First Amendment right against the defendant's right to a fair trial. The Supreme Court has stated that, "absent an overriding interest, articulated in findings, the trial of a criminal case must be open to the public."[66] Before closing a trial, a court must be satisfied that alternative solutions, such as sequestration of witnesses or the jury or change of venue, would not be effective.[67]

§16.13 — Violation of Defendant's Right to a Fair Trial

The presence of the press at trial can cause unfairness which violates a defendant's right to due process of law. At one extreme are the cases in which

[61] Gannett v DePasquale, 443 US 368 (1979).
[62] Id.
[63] Richmond Newspapers, Inc v Virginia, 448 US 555 (1980).
[64] Id 573.
[65] Id; of course, there is no First Amendment right to attend pretrial proceedings. See §15.06.
[66] Id 581.
[67] Id. See also Nebraska Press Assn v Stewart, 427 US 539 (1976).

the extraordinary and pervasive press coverage results in "such a probability prejudice will result that it is deemed inherently lacking in due process."[68] The few cases in which the United States Supreme Court has applied its per se rule are extraordinary and probably sui generis.[69] In recent years, the Court has tended to look carefully at the facts of each case before determining whether publicity was prejudicial. For example, in 1965, in *Estes v Texas*,[70] the Court held that the defendant had been denied due process of law because his trial had been televised without requiring a particularized showing of prejudice. However, in 1981, the Court held that televising of criminal trials is not an inherent violation of due process, despite the fact that televising a trial may make a cocky witness more cocky and a reluctant witness more reluctant, and may cause the judge, lawyers and jury to role play instead of performing their proper functions.[71] Recognizing that televising trials not only could violate due process, but also could be a form of punishment, the Court held that whether a constitutional violation has occurred must be decided on a case-by-case basis.[72]

In recent years, the Court has not looked favorably on a defendant's claim that pretrial publicity violated the right to due process of law. Most recent cases have concerned claims that prejudice has caused bias in the jury panel.[73] Such a claim is difficult to maintain since the Court has held that, while entitled to an impartial jury, a defendant is not deprived of that right if a juror has knowledge of the case, as long as the juror is willing to lay any opinion formed aside and base a verdict totally on the evidence received in court.[74] Since the Court has recognized the constitutional right of the press to gather news and attend criminal trials and has strongly urged that, rather than excluding the press,[75] judges should sequester jurors if press coverage of the trial becomes extensive, it does not appear that the Court will establish further rules for excluding the press or vitiating verdicts.

---

[68] Estes v Texas, 381 US 532, 542-43 (1965).

[69] Sheppard v Maxwell, 384 US 333 (1966) (trial of physician for murder of wife, which had attracted national attention); Estes v Texas, 381 US 532 (1965) (televised trial of former associate of United States president); Rideau v Louisiana, 373 US 723, 726 (1963) (defendant's confession, given to sheriff, telecast before trial) *but see* Beck v Washington, 369 US 541, 556-57 (1962) (per se rule not applied, even though defendant was prominent union official and much publicity had been given to investigation of defendant).

[70] 381 US 532 (1965).

[71] Chandler v Florida, 449 US 560 (1981).

[72] *Id.*

[73] Dobbert v Florida, 432 US 282 (1977).

[74] Murphy v Florida, 471 US 794 (1975). The rule in the federal courts, however, and in most state courts is that a juror who has formed an opinion is incompetent. Marshall v United States, 360 US 310 (1959).

[75] See §16.12.

Presence of Defendant at Trial

§16.14 Source of Right to Be Present

One of the most basic of the rights guaranteed by the confrontation clause of the Constitution is the right to be present at one's own trial.[76] The Sixth Amendment right to confront the witnesses against one would be meaningless if one were not allowed to be present at trial. A defendant in a criminal case, in either state or federal court, enjoys an absolute Sixth Amendment right to be present at his or her trial.[77]

A defendant may waive the right to be present at trial, as a defendant may waive any other constitutional right. However, waivers of federal constitutional rights are not presumed. A court must indulge every reasonable presumption against waiver.[78] Few reported cases consider the effect of a rational (if such a decision can be rational) decision to simply forgo attendance at trial. Rather, the reported cases generally concern whether a defendant's actions may be considered a waiver of the right to be present.

The cases generally fall into one of two categories involving either waiver as a result of voluntary absence from trial or waiver as a result of the defendant's unruly conduct.

§16.15 Waiver of Defendant's Right to Attend Trial—Voluntary Absence

Courts have never considered the governmental prerogative to proceed with a trial to be subject to the willingness of the defendant to attend. The United States Supreme Court has long held that, at least in noncapital cases, if a defendant is voluntarily absent after trial has begun, this does not nullify the proceedings or prevent completion of the trial, but rather operates as a waiver of the right to be present.[79] The Court has further held that there is no constitutional right to be warned that a trial will continue if one absents oneself, and that voluntary absence is a sufficient intentional relinquishment of a known right to constitute waiver.[80] When a defendant voluntarily absents himself or herself, most courts require clear evidence that the defendant was aware of the trial and of the right

---

[76] Lewis v United States, 146 US 370 (1892).

[77] Illinois v Allen, 397 US 337, 338 (1970).

[78] Johnson v Zerbst, 304 US 458 (1938).

[79] Diaz v United States, 223 US 442, 445 (1912).

[80] Taylor v United States, 414 US 17, 19 (1973).

and obligation to be present, and that the defendant had no sound reason for staying a away.[81]

It has been held that proceedings have *commenced*, so that the trial may continue in the defendant's absence, when the defendant absents himself or herself during jury selection.[82]

§16.16 —Disruptive Conduct

Just as defendants cannot stop the government from proceeding with their trials, by absenting themselves, they also cannot stop trials by engaging in disruptive behavior. In *Illinois v Allen*,[83] the United States Supreme Court held that, while courts must indulge in every reasonable presumption against waiver of constitutional rights, a defendant can lose the right to be present at trial if, after having been warned by the judge that he or she will be removed if disruptive behavior continues, the defendant does continue. The type of disruptive behavior engaged in must be something more than a mere contempt; it must make continuation of the trial a practical impossibility. Once lost, the right to be present may be regained as soon as the defendant is willing to behave in a proper manner.

The Court has held that there are three constitutionally permissible ways to deal with a recalcitrant defendant. First, of course, the court may cite the defendant for contempt.[84] Second, the court may bind and gag the defendant.[85] Third, the court may have the defendant removed.[86]

Binding and gagging a defendant in a courtroom, no matter how deserved, strikes most lawyers as basically unfair, and few courts have been willing to countenance the practice. The United States Supreme Court has specifically disapproved authority to the effect that a defendant must be allowed to attend his or her trial regardless of how disruptive the defendant's behavior and that the only constitutional remedy for the disruption is to bind and gag the defendant.[87]

---

[81] *See, e.g.*, Cureton v United States, 396 F2d 671 (DC Cir 1968).

[82] *See, e.g.*, State v Lister, 119 NH 713, 406 A2d 969 (1979).

[83] 397 US 337 (1970).

[84] Id 343-44.

[85] *Id.*

[86] *Id.*

[87] *Id* (disapproving Allen v Illinois, 413 F2d 232 (7th Cir 1969)).

Presumptions and Burden of Proof

§16.17 Proof Beyond a Reasonable Doubt

The requirement that a person's guilt vel non of a crime be proved beyond a reasonable doubt has been universally accepted in common law jurisdictions. The government must prove each element of a crime beyond a reasonable doubt, although it need only prove evidentiary facts by a preponderance of the evidence. It was not, however, until 1970 that the United States Supreme Court held that the reasonable doubt standard was required by the due process clause of the Fourteenth Amendment in *In re Winship*.[88] That case concerned a juvenile court proceeding. The Court found the reasonable doubt standard to be required because juvenile delinquency proceedings are the functional equivalent of criminal proceedings.[89] The reasonable doubt rule exists primarily because the basis of our criminal justice system is that it is far worse to sentence the innocent than not to convict the guilty.[90]

Because the reasonable doubt standard is so universally accepted, relatively little litigation has concerned whether it must be applied. However, in the last few years the Court has begun to consider the applicability of legal presumptions and their effect on the reasonable doubt rule. In *Mullaney v Wilbur*,[91] the Court seemingly established a broad rule that every element of a crime must be proved by the government, and that it is, therefore, unconstitutional to require a defendant to bear any burden of showing the absence of a requisite mental state. *Mullaney* concerned a Maine statutory scheme that provided that absent justification or excuse, all killing was presumed to be felonious homicide, but that the killing might be manslaughter if the defendant proved action in a sudden heat of passion. In holding that the statutory scheme violated due process, the Court noted:

> Maine has chosen to distinguish those who kill in the heat of passion from those who kill in the absence of that factor. . . . By drawing this distinction, while refusing to require the prosecution to establish beyond a reasonable doubt the fact upon which it turns, Maine denigrates the interests found critical in *Winship*.[92]

---

[88] 397 US 358 (1970). *See also* Richmond Newspapers, Inc v Virginia, 448 US 555 (1980).

[89] *In re* Winship, 397 US 358, 365-66 (1970). Because of the important interests protected by the reasonable doubt standard, the Court has held the rule retroactive. IvanV. v City of New York, 407 US 203 (1972).

[90] *In re* Winship, 397 US 358, 363 (1970).

[91] 421 US 684, 703 (1975).

[92] *Id* 698. *Mullaney* has been held retroactive because it affects the integrity of the fact-finding process. Harkenson v North Carolina, 432 US 233 (1977).

The scope of the Court's holding in *Mullaney* has, however, been significantly narrowed in later decisions. In *Patterson v New York*,[93] the Court sustained a New York statutory scheme which provided that the crime of murder has two elements, the intent to cause the death of another and causing the death of another, but also provided that a defendant could raise and prove the affirmative defense that he acted under the influence of extreme emotional disturbance for which there was reasonable explanation or excuse. In sustaining the statutory scheme, the Court took a somewhat rigid view of the statutes, holding that New York was entitled to treat all intentional killing as murder, unless the defendant could provide an excuse for his act.[94] Reasoning that *Mullaney* had merely held "that a state must prove every ingredient of an offense beyond a reasonable doubt" doubt",[95] the Court found no infirmity in the New York statute since the elements of murder must in all cases be proved by the prosecution.

The Court recognized that its analysis, which looks to the statute itself and not to the practical effect of the statute, could lead to difficulty if legislatures attempt to draft statutes to unfairly assist prosecutors.[96] While the present state of the law is that the legislatures may constitutionally require defendants to prove as affirmative defenses matters which go to mental state, there must be a rational nexus between the definition of the crime and the affirmative defense.[97]

§16.18 Proof Beyond a Reasonable Doubt and Use of Presumptions

The same considerations which forbid a legislature from placing a burden of proof on a defendant by presuming mens rea from the commission of certain acts[98] forbid a trial judge from presuming, or instructing a jury that it can presume, the mens rea required for a crime from an act. The United States Supreme Court has been disinclined to approve instructions by trial judges that "the law presumes that a person intends the natural consequences of his acts" when the intent with which the act was done will establish the crime.[99] A conclusive presumption would, of course, effectively eliminate intent as an element of the offense,[100] and would obviously violate both the presumption

---

[93] 432 US 197 (1977).

[94] *Id* 206.

[95] *Id* 215.

[96] *Id* 210.

[97] *See, e.g.*, Leland v Oregon, 343 US 790 (1952) (government may place burden of proving insanity defense on defendant).

[98] See §16.17.

[99] Sandstrom v Montana, 442 US 510 (1979); United States v United States Gypsum, 438 US 422 (1978).

[100] Morrissette v United States, 342 US 246, 274-75 (1952).

of innocence and the defendant's right to be found guilty by proof beyond a reasonable doubt. Thus, the Court has been concerned that language such as *the law presumes* in jury instructions could lead a juror to assume that the proposed inference is mandatory.[101] Moreover, such an instruction may allow the jury to make an assumption which all of the evidence does not logically support.[102] In short, it would not seem prudent for a trial judge to give such an instruction.

§16.19 Presumption of Innocence

The presumption of innocence is a basic component of a fair trial under our system of criminal justice.[103] However, an instruction on the presumption of innocence, although certainly helpful, need not as a matter of federal constitutional law be given in every case.[104] A trial judge takes a grave risk in refusing to give such an instruction, however, since, if the other instructions do not adequately explain the state's burden of proof, but create a danger that the jury may convict the defendant on extraneous considerations, the defendant's rights have been violated.[105]

§16.20 — Trial of Defendant in Prison Garb

The right to a fair trial is a fundamental liberty secured by the due process clause of the Fourteenth Amendment. A basic component of a fair American trial is the presumption of innocence. It has been uniformly held a denial of due process of law to compel a defendant to go to trial in prison clothes because "of the possible impairment of the presumption so basic to the adversary system."[106] However, a defendant must object to being tried in jail clothes just as he or she must invoke or abandon other rights, and a defendant who does not do so, and is convicted, has waived the right to have the issue considered.[107]

---

[101] Sandstrom v Montana, 442 US 510 (1979).

[102] United States v United States Gypsum, 438 US 422 (1978).

[103] Estelle v Williams, 425 US 501, 503 (1976).

[104] Kentucky v Whorton, 441 US 786 (1979).

[105] Kentucky v Taylor, 436 US 478 (1978).

[106] Estelle v Williams, 425 US 501, 504 (1976); *see also* State v Brown, 368 So 2d 961 (La 1979); People v Shaw, 381 Mich 467, 164 NW2d 7 (1969).

[107] Estelle v Williams, 425 US 501, 512-13 (1976).

Right of Counsel to Argue

§16.21 Constitutional Nature of Right to Argue

The right to counsel is basic to a fair trial. Even the greatest advocate can be of no value to an accused if silenced. Thus, the United States Supreme Court has held that a total denial of the right to final argument, in a jury or nonjury case, is a violation of the right to effective assistance of counsel.[108] However, a defense lawyer does not have the right to filibuster in the courtroom. The judge may limit counsel to a reasonable time, and terminate the argument when it becomes repetitive, if necessary.[109]

Verdict

§16.22 Verdict

At the close of a trial, the jury or the judge, if the defendant has waived jury, will make a finding of guilty or not guilty, unless the trial is to a jury, and the jury states it is unable to agree upon a verdict. While there are occasions when due process requires that a statement of reasons for a decision be given,[110] one of those occasions is not a criminal trial.[111] It has long been settled that an inconsistent jury verdict, as by, for example, finding a person guilty of maintaining a common nuisance by keeping at a certain place intoxicating liquor for sale but not guilty of possessing intoxicating liquor, is not unconstitutional as long as there is evidence to support the conviction.[112] As long as there is evidence to support guilt, the acquittal is interpreted as the jury's assumption of the "power which they had no right to exercise, but to which they were disposed through lenity;"[113] the assumption of its unreviewable power to return a verdict of not guilty for impermissible reasons. As Justice Holmes noted: "That the verdict may have been the result of compromise, or of a mistake on the part of the jury is possible. But verdicts cannot be upset by speculation or inquiry into such matters."[114] For similar reasons, the United States Supreme

---

[108] Herring v New York, 422 US 853, 864-65 (1975).

[109] *Id* 862.

[110] *See, e.g.*, Morrissey v Brewer, 408 US 471 (1972); Wolff v McDonnell, 418 US 539 (1974).

[111] Harris v Rivera, 102 S Ct 460 (1981).

[112] Dunn v United States, 284 US 390, 393 (1932).

[113] *Id* 393; *see also* Hamling v United States, 418 US 87 (1974).

[114] Dunn v United States, 284 US 390, 394 (1932).

Court has been unwilling to examine jury verdicts which are inconsistent as to two defendants in a joint trial.[115]

In *Harris v Rivera*,[116] the Court held that inconsistency in a judge's verdict after a bench trial of joint defendants is not sufficient reason to set it aside. The Court reasoned that even the unlikely possibility that the acquittal of one defendant was the product of a lenity that judges are free to exercise at sentencing, but not at trial, would not create a constitutional violation since there is nothing in the federal Constitution which would prevent a state from empowering its judges to render verdicts of acquittal whenever they are convinced that no sentence should be imposed for reasons unrelated to guilt or innocence.[117] The Court emphasized that the relevant issue is whether the defendant had a fair trial, and found no constitutional violation where the record contained adequate evidence of his guilt.[118]

---

[115] United States v Dotterweich, 320 US 270, 279 (1943).
[116] 102 S Ct 460 (1981).
[117] *Id.*
[118] *Id.*

17

Trial by Jury

§17.01 Introduction

The fundamental distinguishing factor in the Anglo-American legal system is the right to jury trial. It was secured to Englishmen by Magna Carta. Even before the United States Supreme Court began to constitutionalize the requirement of trial by jury, it was taken for granted in virtually all jurisdictions as a matter of state law.[1] The reasons which have sustained the institution since its beginnings before Runnymede were cogently stated by Blackstone in 1765:

> Our law has therefore wisely placed this strong and twofold barrier, of a presentment and a trial by jury, between the liberties of the people and the prerogative of the crown. It was necessary, for preserving the admirable balance of our constitution, to vest the executive power of the laws in the prince: and yet this power might be dangerous and destructive to that very constitution, if exerted without check or control by justices of oyer and terminer occasionally named by the crown; who might then, as in France or Turkey, imprison, dispatch, or exile any man that was obnoxious to the government, by an instant declaration that such is their will and pleasure. . . . So that the liberties of England cannot but subsist, so long as this palladium remains sacred and inviolate, not only from all open attacks (which none will be so hardy as to make) but also from all secret machinations, which may sap and undermine it; by introducing new and arbitrary methods of trial, by justices of the peace, commissioner of revenue, and courts of conscience. And however convenient these may appear at first (as doubtless all arbitrary powers, well executed are the most convenient), yet let it be again remembered, that delays, and little inconveniences in the forms of justice, are the price that all free nations must pay for their liberty in more substantial matters. . . .[2]

No lawyer who has tried many cases can doubt that jury trials can be long, complex and more difficult in many ways than bench trials. Still, in many cases, lawyers rely on the jury to perform the task Blackstone envisioned for it—to serve as a check against the exercise of arbitrary government powers.

Yet there are dramatic differences between Blackstone's time and ours. There is no American king whose subjects view him with suspicion. Moreover, the American criminal defendant is cloaked with numerous procedural rights, including the right to testify and the right to cross-examine and produce witnesses, which were nonexistent or not fully developed in Blackstone's time.

---

[1] Duncan v Louisiana, 391 US 145 (1968).
[2] 4 W. Blackstone, Commentaries 343-44 (U Chi ed 1979).

Finally, in Blackstone's England, there were no racial animosities like those which exist so widely today.

As legal proceedings have become more complex, there has been an ever greater need to ensure that the jury is not confused by procedures and can function as a fact-finder. To the extent that the jury may be biased against a defendant because of race, or even because of the jury's predilections, courts have attempted to create new procedures to overcome the problems.

Right to Jury Trial

§17.02 Right Guaranteed by United States Constitution

Because jury trial in criminal cases was traditionally afforded in all the states for serious offenses, it was not until 1968 that the United States Supreme Court held that the Fourteenth Amendment guaranteed a right to jury trial in criminal cases in state courts in the same circumstances in which the Sixth Amendment would guarantee a federal criminal defendant the right to jury trial.[3] The Court reasoned that the universal use of jury trial made it *fundamental* to the American scheme of justice.[4]

In holding that jury trial was required by the Fourteenth Amendment in all criminal cases, the Court specifically included the offense of criminal contempt,[5] if the potential sentence was severe enough.[6] The right is not, however, applicable in civil proceedings brought to determine whether an item is obscene.[7] Despite the fact that most of the other procedural rights afforded adult criminal defendants as a matter of federal constitutional law have been afforded juveniles charged with juvenile delinquency under nominally "civil" state statutory schemes, the United States Supreme Court has held that there is no federal constitutional right to a jury in such proceedings.[8]

A number of states, principally in the East, retain a statutory scheme whereby an individual accused of a minor criminal offense to which the constitutional right to a jury trial is applicable must be first tried by a judge without a jury. If the defendant is acquitted, the matter ends. If the defendant is convicted, however, the defendant may appeal for a trial de novo before a jury. The

---

[3] Duncan v Louisiana, 391 US 145, 149 (1968).

[4] *Id.* The Court held, however, that its decision was not to be applied retrospectively. DeStefano v Woods, 392 US 631 (1968).

[5] Codispoti v Pennsylvania, 418 US 506 (1974); Bloom v Illinois, 391 US 194 (1968).

[6] See §17.03.

[7] Alexander v Virginia, 413 US 836 (1973).

[8] McKeiver v Pennsylvania, 403 US 528 (1971).

appeal vacates the prior conviction and any sentence, but adverse collateral consequences, such as loss of a motor vehicle operator's license, may be imposed pending appeal.

In *Ludwig v Massachusetts*,[9] the United States Supreme Court held that such statutory schemes did not violate the federal guarantee of jury trial, despite the fact that the second trial imposes an increased financial and emotional cost on the defendant, and may subject the defendant (at least under Massachusetts law) to a harsher sentence if the de novo trial ends in conviction. In the case before it, the Court noted that there was no evidence that the defendant's jury trial was unreasonably delayed by the two-tier procedure.[10] The Court found that the Massachusetts system was "fair and not unduly burdensome."[11] State courts in states which retain such a system have been disinclined to find any constitutional infirmity in it.[12]

§17.03 Cases in Which Jury Trial Is Constitutionally Required

In holding that the Fourteenth Amendment guarantee of due process required that the Sixth Amendment right to jury trial be held applicable to state criminal proceedings, the United States Supreme Court did not suggest that there was a right to jury trial in all criminal proceedings. Rather, the Court held that the right to jury trial was guaranteed only to the extent that it existed at common law —that it was applicable to "non-petty offenses."[13] In *Duncan v Louisiana*,[14] the case in which the Court first held that there was a federal constitutional right to jury trial in state proceedings, the Court did not attempt to define *petty* offenses, but noted that, under federal law, petty offenses were those punishable by no more than six months imprisonment and a $500 fine. The Court merely held, however, that the crime before it, which was punishable by two years imprisonment, was not a petty offense. Two years later, in *Baldwin v New York*,[15] the Court held that a crime punishable by one year imprisonment was not a petty offense which could be tried without a jury. Reasoning that the potential penalty is the most obvious criterion by which to judge the seriousness of an offense, the Court established a flat rule that any offense punishable by

---

[9] 427 US 618 (1976).

[10] *Id* 628-29.

[11] *Id* 630. The Court also held that the prior conviction and appeal did not implicate the defendant's double jeopardy rights since it is the defendant's decision to appeal and to obtain a new trial. *Id* 631-32.

[12] *See, e.g.*, Jenkins v Canaan Mun Court, 116 NH 616, 366 A2d 208 (1976).

[13] Duncan v Louisiana, 391 US 145, 161-62 (1968).

[14] *Id* 161-62.

[15] 399 US 66 (1970).

more than six months imprisonment is not a petty offense, and a jury trial must be afforded the defendant.[16]

Because criminal contempt is a nonstatutory offense which may be punishable by a sentence imposed in the court's discretion, it presents a particular problem. The Court has held that while a court may summarily try a person for contempt, no sentence may be imposed greater than six months.[17] If a judge proposes to inflict a greater sentence, the contemnor must be informed at the beginning of the proceedings and awarded a right to jury trial.[18] Moreover, even if more than one contemporaneous offense occurred during a trial, a judge may not try them as separate petty offenses, and impose consecutive sentences for each petty offense which will aggregate more than six months imprisonment.[19]

§17.04 Right to a Nonjury Trial

Every experienced defense lawyer is aware that there are cases in which it is highly desirable to waive a jury. Such cases are generally those in which a lawyer represents an unpopular client or a client charged with a heinous crime, or where a lawyer must present a technical defense which a jury may not understand, or worse, may simply choose to ignore. However, there is an important governmental interest in insuring that the public perceives that justice is done, and that perception may not exist if trial is to the court alone.

The United States Supreme Court has uniformly held that the ability to waive a constitutional right does not give one the right to insist on the opposite of that right.[20] Thus, just as a defendant has no constitutional right to plead guilty,[21] he or she has no constitutional right to waive a jury and be tried before a court.[22] The Court has specifically held that the government has a "legitimate interest in seeing that cases in which it believes conviction is warranted are tried before the tribunal most likely to produce a fair result."[23] Some states, as a matter of state law, allow a defendant to waive a jury as a matter of right.[24]

However, the Supreme Court has suggested that even in the federal system and in state systems in which a defendant may not waive a jury without

---

[16] *Id* 69.

[17] Codispoti v Pennsylvania, 418 US 506, 514 (1974).

[18] *See, e.g.*, State v Linsky, 117 NH 866, 379 A2d 813 (1977).

[19] Codispoti v Pennsylvania, 418 US 506, 517 (1974).

[20] Singer v United States, 380 US 24, 34-35 (1965).

[21] United States v Jackson, 390 US 570 (1968).

[22] Singer v United States, 380 US 24 (1965)

[23] *Id* 36.

[24] *See, e.g.*, NH Rev Stat Ann §606:7 (1955).

the prosecution's assent, there are circumstances which would, as a matter of fundamental fairness, require trial to the court. The Court has suggested that trial to the court may be constitutionally required if public feeling runs so high that an impartial jury could not be impaneled.[25]

Selection and Composition of Petit Jury

§17.05 Constitutional Requirement of a Fair Tribunal

A fair trial in a fair tribunal was held to be a requirement of the due process clause before the United States Supreme Court held that the right to jury trial was constitutionally required.[26] Thus, apart from the constitutional right to a jury, a defendant in a criminal case has a right to an impartial jury.[27] For that reason, a defendant may not be forced to trial before a jury which believes the defendant guilty or is biased against him or her.

Cases concerning impartiality of the jury which have reached the United States Supreme Court generally concern the effect of publicity on a jury, or the likelihood that the jury is biased against a particular defendant because of race.

The difficulty caused by publicity of a particular crime and the possible effect that knowledge about the crime might have on a jury have absorbed ever more of the Court's attention. The Supreme Court has held that a juror is not necessarily partial, and, therefore, constitutionally unfit to sit merely because of having formed an opinion about a case.[28] The Court has reasoned that, in these days of widespread modern communication, "scarcely any of those best qualified to serve as jurors will not have formed some impression or opinion as to the merits of the case."[29] The Court has held that "it is sufficient if the juror can lay aside his impression, or opinion, and render a verdict based upon the evidence presented in court."[30] The federal rule that a juror who has learned about a case from newspapers or magazines is presumptively prejudiced is not of constitutional magnitude.[31]

---

[25] Singer v United States, 380 US 24, 38 (1965).
[26] See, e.g., *In re* Murchaison, 349 US 133, 136 (1955).
[27] Irvin v Dowd, 366 US 717, 722 (1961); *see also* Smith v Phillips, 102 S Ct 940 (1982).
[28] Irvin v Dowd, 366 US 717 (1961).
[29] *Id* 722.
[30] *Id* 723.
[31] Murphy v Florida, 421 US 794, 498 (1975).

Whether a juror is impartial is a mixed question of law and fact.[32] The burden of showing partiality is on the party who asserts the juror is biased.[33] Unless that party shows the actual existence of such an opinion in the mind of the juror as will raise the presumption of partiality, the juror need not be set aside.[34]

Obviously, the burden established by the Court is a heavy one because in most cases, the voir dire—the process of questioning the jurors to determine whether they have any opinions on a given subject—is done by the court and not by counsel. Frequently, the judge in both state and federal courts simply addresses questions to the panel as a whole. Only if a juror responds to the judge's questions need further inquiry take place. Moreover, a claim of impartiality may be asserted by a juror who has, in fact, made up his or her mind about the case the juror will be called on to decide.

Perhaps for this reason, the Court has been willing to set aside convictions where the record of the jury selection process establishes that a large percentage of the jurors were biased. In *Irvin v Dowd*,[35] for example, the Court held that the defendant's right to a fair trial was violated when the area in which the trial was held was saturated with unfavorable publicity, and two-thirds of the jurors examined stated that they had an opinion as to the defendant's guilt. The Court reasoned that in a community in which most members will admit a disqualifying prejudice, the reliability of the others' protestations may be called into question, for it is then more probable that they are part of a community deeply hostile to the accused, and it is more likely that they have been unwillingly influenced by it.[36] Moreover, the lengths to which the court must go to ensure an impartial panel is relevant.[37]

The mere fact that there has been extensive pretrial publicity does not, however, necessarily mean that a defendant will be able to challenge a jury panel which a court has found to be impartial.[38] The decided cases suggest that it is only in the extraordinary case that a denial of due process will be held to have occurred.

---

[32] *Id; see also* Smith v Phillips, 102 S Ct 940 (1982) (no due process violation where juror, during trial, submitted application for employment as criminal investigator to prosecutor's office, where trial judge found beyond a reasonable doubt that the juror's conduct did not impair his ability to render an impartial verdict).

[33] *Id.*

[34] *Id;* Smith v Phillips, 102 S Ct 940 (1982).

[35] 366 US 717 (1961).

[36] Murphy v Florida, 421 US 794 (1975).

[37] *Id* 802-03.

[38] Dobbert v Florida, 432 US 282 (1977).

§17.06 Constitutionally Required Voir Dire

Voir dire is the method generally employed to determine whether or not a juror is indifferent. In cases in which counsel for each side conduct voir dire by examining each prospective juror, a lawyer may inquire into anything he or she believes may prejudice the potential juror and may observe the juror's reactions to questions. Most lawyers consider individual voir dire to be the most efficacious way to discover biases of jurors.[39] It may also be a useful way to find jurors who may be predisposed to find in a defendant's favor.

Individual voir dire is most time-consuming, however, and is generally reserved, in most jurisdictions, for extraordinarily serious crimes or for cases which have attracted an inordinate amount of publicity. It is not required by the Constitution. In the usual case, voir dire is simply conducted by the trial judge, who reads questions required by statute, which relate to the panel's impartiality, to the panel at large.[40] The judge will, in most states and in federal practice, accept questions from lawyers for either side to be asked to the panel.

Under state law, the judge's discretion in deciding whether to ask a particular question is great, but it is not wholly unfettered by the federal Constitution. In *Ham v South Carolina*,[41] the defendant was a young bearded black man who was well known as a civil rights activist. Ham claimed he had been framed because of his civil rights activities. The defendant's counsel asked the trial judge to ask the jury four questions in addition to the usual questions relating to bias. The first two questions related to racial prejudice, the third related to beards, and the fourth dealt with pretrial publicity. The United States Supreme Court held that, in the peculiar circumstances of the case, the failure to voir dire on racial prejudice was reversible error since a principal purpose of the Fourteenth Amendment was to prohibit the states from individiously discriminating on the basis of race. But the Court held that the court did not violate the defendant's constitutional rights when it refused to voir dire on beards, since it was unable to "distinguish possible prejudice against beards from a host of other possible similar prejudices."[42]

In later cases, the Court has made clear that *Ham* stands on its own peculiar facts and that the fact that the victim of a violent crime is of a different race than the accused does not require voir dire on racial prejudice as a matter of

---

[39] W. Jordan, Jury Selection (Shepard's/McGraw-Hill 1980).

[40] *See, e.g.*, Mass Gen Laws Ann ch 234 §28 (1981). Where a court reasonably believes jurors may be threatened by the defendant, their names and addresses need *not* be disclosed on voir dire. United States v Barnes, 604 F2d 121 (2d Cir 1979).

[41] 409 US 524 (1973).

[42] *Id* 529.

constitutional law.[43] The Court has distinguished later cases by noting that, in *Ham*, the defense that he had been framed because of his civil rights activities would tend to exacerbate even limited prejudices. The general rule appears to be that only when there are substantial indications of the likelihood of racial or ethnic prejudice affecting the jurors in a particular case does the trial court's denial of a request to probe the matter rise to a constitutional level.[44]

§17.07 Fair Cross-Section of the Community Requirement

When the United States Supreme Court held in 1968 that the Fourteenth Amendment requirement of due process of law required that juries be afforded defendants in state criminal trials for all nonpetty offenses, the Court imposed on the states a requirement that the jury comprise a fair cross-section of the community. Prior to the Supreme Court's having so held, the composition of the petit jury was reviewable on constitutional grounds only if members of one race had been excluded from it in violation of the Fourteenth Amendment to the federal Constitution.[45] This standard of review, which is of historical interest only insofar as petit juries are concerned, is the same one still applied to determine the constitutionality of the composition of state grand juries.[46]

As in other areas of criminal procedure, the United States Supreme Court has been willing to allow the states much latitude in the methods used to achieve the desired result, as long as the result, a jury which is selected from a group which constitutes a fair cross-section of the community,[47] is achieved. Thus, the Court has been willing to countenance virtually any sort of jury selection system, looking primarily at the result achieved by operation of the system.[48]

Because the right to a jury panel comprising individuals representing a fair sample of the racial composition of the population is so well settled, most of the cases considered by the United States Supreme Court in the last 10 years have concerned exclusion from juror panels of members of other cognizable groups.

---

[43] Ristiano v Ross, 424 US 589 (1976). Such inquiry is required, however, as a matter of federal common law. Rosales-Lopez v United States, 101 S Ct 1629 (1981).

[44] Rosales-Lopez v United States, 101 S Ct 1629 (1981).

[45] Peters v Kiff, 407 US 493 (1972).

[46] See §7.11.

[47] Taylor v Louisiana, 419 US 522, 529 (1975).

[48] *See, e.g.* Carter v Jury Commrs, 396 US 320 (1970) (Alabama statute which required jury commissioners to select for jury service those persons who are "generally reputed to be honest and intelligent and . . . esteemed in the community for their integrity, good character and sound judgment"); Turner v Foucher, 396 US 346 (1970) (provision of Georgia law allowing superior court judge to exclude any member of panel the judge does not deem "discreet" not invalid on its face, but provision requiring jurors to be owners of real property invalid).

In *Hamling v United States*,[49] the defendant claimed that the jury selection plan which allowed a jury to be drawn from a jury which was refilled with the names of newly eligible jurors every four years violated his right to a fair cross-segment of the community because the youngest possible jurors at the time of his trial (just before the wheel was refilled) would be four years above the age of majority. The Court explicitly left open the question of whether the young are a cognizable group in the sense that a racial group is, but held that the evidence presented did not show that the defendant had established a prima facie case of discrimination which would require the government to produce evidence to overcome it.[50]

More successful have been claims that women have been purposely excluded from a jury panel. In *Taylor v Louisiana*,[51] the Court held that a Louisiana statute, which did not disqualify women for jury service but provided that they did not have to serve unless they filed a written declaration of their desire to be subject to jury service, violated the defendant's rights because the panel from which the defendant's jury was drawn contained only 10 per cent women, while the county population was 53 per cent women. While holding that the *fair cross-section of the community* doctrine must have much leeway in application," the Court held that the obvious exclusion of women from the panel rendered the male defendant's trial unfair.[52]

The Court expanded its holding in *Taylor* in *Duren v Missouri*,[53] holding that a defendant was denied a fair cross-section of the community by a Missouri statute which granted exemption from jury service to women automatically on request, where the defendant showed that the population of the county was 53 per cent women, but the percentage of women on the panel his jury was drawn from was 26.7 per cent, and 14.5 per cent of the persons in the weekly venues were women. Once again, the Court emphasized that the result, that is, the composition of the jury, was far more significant than the facial aspects of the statutes themselves. The Court established a general rule that to establish a prima facie violation of the fair cross-section of the community requirement, the defendant must show that (1) the group alleged to be excluded is a distinctive group, (2) that the representation of this group in venues from which juries are drawn is not fair and reasonable in relation to the number of such persons in the community, and (3) that the underrepresentation is due to systematic exclusion of the group in the jury selection process.[54] Once a defendant makes such a showing, the State cannot justify the exclusion on merely rational grounds, but must show

---

[49] 418 US 87 (1974), *rehearing denied*, 419 US 885 (1975).
[50] *Id* 139.
[51] 419 US 522 (1975).
[52] *Id* 531. The *Taylor* decision is not retroactive. Daniel v Louisiana, 419 US 31 (1975).
[53] 439 US 357 (1979).
[54] *Id* 364.

that the disproportionality is caused by a "significant state interest."[55] In the case before it, the Court found a constitutional violation because "exempting all women because of the preclusive domestic responsibilities of some women is insufficient justification for their disproportionate exclusion on jury venues."[56]

§17.08 Use of Peremptory Challenges to Exclude Members of a Minority Group

The right to a fair cross-section of the community relates to the jury panel and not to the particular petit jury which tries the defendant. A defendant has no constitutional right to be tried by a jury which mirrors the makeup of the community. Moreover, traditionally, both parties to a criminal case are able to challenge witnesses peremptorily as well as for cause. A peremptory challenge allows a defendant to remove jurors without making a showing of bias, and without stating a reason for so doing. The number of peremptory challenges afforded a party usually depends on the seriousness of the offense. As a general rule, a party need give no reason for exercising a peremptory challenge and thus removing a juror.

What happens when a prosecutor peremptorily strikes all the members of a minority group from the defendant's petit jury? In *Swain v Alabama*,[57] the United States Supreme Court held such activity did not violate the defendant's right to equal protection of the laws. Because members of all races and creeds are subject to exclusion in this fashion, the Court reasoned that in light of the purpose of the peremptory challenge in a pluralistic society, the Constitution would not require an examination of the prosecutor's motives in exercising his challenges.[58]

A few state courts have, however, interpreted their own constitutions more strictly. The seminal case is *People v Wheeler*,[59] in which the California Supreme Court held that the use of peremptory challenges to exclude members of a racial group violated the defendant's right to an impartial jury under the California Constitution. In *Commonwealth v Soares*,[60] the Massachusetts Supreme Judicial

---

[55] *Id* 367.

[56] *Id* 369.

[57] 380 US 202 (1965).

[58] *Id* 221-22.

[59] 22 Cal 3d 258, 583 P2d 748, 148 Cal Rptr 890 (1978); *see also* State v Eames, 365 So 2d 1361 (La 1968); People v Kagan, 101 Misc 2d 274, 420 NYS2d 987 (Sup Ct 1979). A more expansive reading of state constitutions has, however, been rejected in some cases. *See, e.g.,* People v Fleming, 91 Ill App 3d 99, 413 NE2d 133 (1980); State v Stewart, 225 Kan 410, 591 P2d 166 (1979); State v Grady, 93 Wis 2d 1, 286 NW2d 607 (1979).

[60] 377 Mass 461, 387 NE2d 499 (1979).

Court established a precise scheme for determining when a defendant's state constitutional rights were violated by the use of peremptory challenges. The Massachusetts court begins with a presumption of proper use of peremptory challenges. That presumption may be rebutted by either the defendant or the government on a showing that (1) a pattern of conduct has developed whereby several prospective jurors who have been excluded are members of a discrete group, and (2) there is a likelihood that they are being excluded merely because of their group membership. Once the trial judge draws such an inference, the burden shifts to the offending party to show that the members of the group were not stricken because of their group affiliations. A court which finds that the burden of justification is not sustained must conclude the jury will not be representative and dismiss it.

§17.09 Number of Petit Jurors Required

Although the United States Supreme Court held in 1968[61] that the federal Constitution required that trial by jury be afforded for all nonpetty criminal offenses, the Court did not specify the number of persons who must sit on the petit jury. Two years later, in *Williams v Florida,*[62] the Court specifically held that the traditional twelve person jury panel is not a necessary ingredient of due process of law, and that, therefore, Florida could constitutionally force a defendant to trial in a criminal case before a six-person jury. After a searching historical analysis, the Court determined that the jury at common law consisted of twelve persons, but that that fact is a "historical accident, unnecessary to effect the purposes of the jury system, and wholly without significance, except to mystics."[63] The Court reasoned that the function of a jury is the interposition between the accused and the state of the common sense judgment of a group of lay people, and saw no relation between the jury's function and the particular number of persons in the body that makes up the jury. The Court rejected the argument that a twelve-person jury might be advantageous to a defendant because one juror out of twelve may disagree and force a hung jury, stating that there was no empirical evidence to support this theory, and added in a footnote that it regarded a hung jury as something that "might be thought to result in minimal advantage for the defendant."[64]

Of course, any lawyer who has actually tried a number of criminal cases knows that a hung jury provides an accused with far more than a minimal advantage. After the holding in *Williams,* a number of studies of the effect of

---

[61] Duncan v Louisiana, 391 US 145 (1968).

[62] 399 US 78, 86 (1970).

[63] *Id* 102.

[64] *Id* 101 n 47.

smaller juries were undertaken. These studies obviously influenced the Court in 1978 when it held, in *Ballew v Georgia*,[65] that the purpose and functioning of a jury are impaired to a constitutional extent when a jury is reduced below six persons. Drawing on empirical research since *Williams* had been decided, the plurality opinion noted that progressively smaller juries were less likely to foster effective group deliberation, that there might be some question about the reliability of fact finding in smaller groups, and that in smaller panels, minority groups are less likely to be represented, regardless of the fairness of selection procedures.[66] Three concurring judges simply found the five-person jury unfair.[67]

The *Ballew* decision is of relatively little significance insofar as, at the time of the decision, only Georgia and Virginia allowed trials with fewer than six jurors.[68] But the Court rejected Georgia's claim that its requirement that a jury return a unanimous verdict satisfied the constitutional problem, holding that the jury reduced in size below six would not be able to engage in "meaningful deliberation."[69]

§17.10 Exclusion of Jurors from Petit Jury and the Death Penalty

Prior to 1968, in most American jurisdictions which permitted capital punishment, as a matter of state law the trial judge had the duty, in a capital case, to examine the prospective jurors about their feelings on capital punishment and exclude those who were opposed to it.[70] However, in 1968 in *Witherspoon v Illinois*,[71] the United States Supreme Court imposed a constitutional limitation on such state rules by holding that due process forbade imposition of the death penalty when jurors who had expressed general conscientious or religious scruples against the death penalty were excluded from the panel. In so holding, the Court noted that a defendant might assert that a person tried by such a panel could claim not to have been tried by a fair tribunal, and thus challenge the conviction.[72] The Court found the empirical studies offered by the defendant too tentative and fragmented to establish the broad conclusion that exclusion of

---

[65] 435 US 223 (1978).

[66] *Id* 232.

[67] *Id* 246.

[68] *Id* 244.

[69] *Id* 241.

[70] *See, e.g.*, State v Comery, 78 NH 6, 95 A 670 (1915).

[71] 391 US 510, 522 (1968).

[72] *Id* 520 n 18.

jurors with scruples against capital punishment results in an unrepresentative jury on the issue of guilt or substantially increases the risk of conviction.

However, in recent years, compelling empirical evidence has been produced to show that jurors excluded because of *specific* conscientious scruples against the death penalty which would exclude them from a jury in accordance with *Witherspoon* are less likely to convict than jurors who do not have such scruples. Such studies raise a serious question about the *Witherspoon* rule which allows exclusion of jurors who are unequivocally opposed to the death penalty, but who are fair and impartial in determining guilt or innocence.[73]

In holding that the exclusion of jurors who had conscientious scruples against the death penalty violated due process, the Court placed much weight on what it perceived to be broad opposition to the death penalty in the community. Justice Stewart wrote:

> in a nation less than half of whose people believe in the death penalty, a jury composed exclusively of such people cannot speak for the community. Culled of all who harbor doubts about the wisdom of capital punishment —of all who would be reluctant to pronounce the extreme penalty —such a jury can speak only for a distinct and dwindling minority.[74]

The firestorm of controversy surrounding capital punishment has, if anything, intensified in recent years, and even Justice Stewart was forced to admit in 1976 that legislative developments in the 1970s made evident the fact that "a large proportion of American society continues to regard [the death penalty]as an appropriate and necessary criminal sanction."[75] Yet the Court has never retreated from the *Witherspoon* rule, apparently holding in 1976 that violation of the rule can never be harmless error and that if even one juror is impaneled in violation of *Witherspoon*, the death penalty may not be imposed,[76] and affirming the vitality of the rule on several other occasions.[77] In *Adams v Texas*,[78] the Court held that *Witherspoon* was applicable to the Texas bifurcated procedure in which a jury first considers guilt, and only then deliberates on punishment. The Court held that a Texas statute which required that a prospective juror take an oath that the mandatory penalty of life imprisonment or death could not affect that juror's deliberation on any issue of fact was unconstitutional. The Court rejected Texas's argument that the statute was neutral in that it

---

[73] Hovey v Superior Court, 28 Cal 3d 1, 616 P2d 1301, 168 Cal Rptr 128 (1980); Bumper v North Carolina, 391 US 543, 545 (1968); *but see* Lockett v Ohio, 438 US 586, 595 (1978).

[74] Witherspoon v Illinois, 391 US 510, 520 (1968).

[75] Gregg v Georgia, 428 US 153, 179 (1976).

[76] Davis v Georgia, 429 US 122, 123 (1977).

[77] Adams v Texas, 448 US 38 (1980); Lockett v Ohio, 438 US 586, 594-96 (1978).

[78] 448 US 38 (1980).

would obviously exclude those so in favor of capital punishment that it would incline them to convict, as well as those so opposed that they would not convict, since such favorable jurors are few.[79]

Argument and Charge

§17.11 Prosecutor's Closing Argument

One of the most important differences between jury trial and trial to the court is the closing argument to the jury. While the right to closing argument even in a nonjury case is so fundamental that its denial has been held to be a violation of the constitutional right to the assistance of counsel,[80] most lawyers regard the closing argument in a jury case as even more crucial, and spend substantial time in preparation for it. Judges have been willing to grant mistrials or reverse convictions on appeal where a prosecutor exceeded the bounds of legitimate advocacy in closing argument and violated the defendant's constitutional rights.

Error of constitutional magnitude from the prosecutor's closing argument generally arises in two areas. The first is comment by the prosecutor on the defendant's failure to testify, and the second is use of inflammatory language or otherwise improper argument by the prosecutor which allegedly renders the trial unfair.

The law concerning the former is more developed than that concerning the latter. In *Griffin v California*,[81] the United States Supreme Court held that the prosecutor's reference to the defendant's failure to testify, by telling the jury in closing argument that the defendant "ha[d] not seen fit to take the stand and deny or explain" the prosecution's evidence against him, and that his failure to do so should be construed as an admission of guilt, violated the defendant's rights.[82] The Court reasoned that comment on the refusal to testify "is a remnant of the inquisitorial system of criminal justice" and is thus forbidden by the Fifth Amendment.[83] Since the law is so clear on this point, most of the reported litigation concerns what constitutes a comment on the defendant's failure to testify. The commonest situation arises when a prosecutor in closing refers to the government's evidence as *uncontradicted*—a phrase certainly susceptible of

---

[79] *Id.*

[80] Herring v New York, 422 US 853 (1975).

[81] 380 US 609 (1965).

[82] *Id* 611.

[83] *Id* 613-14. The Court expressly reserved the question of whether a defendant had a constitutional right to require a trial judge to instruct the jury that no inference might be drawn from his silence, a question answered affirmatively in Carter v Kentucky, 450 US 288 (1981). But such comment may be harmless error. Chapman v California, 386 US 18 (1967).

more than one meaning. In general, courts have, as the United States Supreme Court did in *Lockett v Ohio*,[84] looked to the circumstances of the particular trial to determine, considering all of the circumstances of the case, whether a constitutional violation has occurred. As a general rule, if the evidence characterized as uncontradicted is such that only the actual defendant could contradict it, an improper reference has been made, but otherwise, there is no constitutional error.[85]

Comment on a defendant's failure to testify is perhaps the most egregious of all prosecutorial misconduct because the only remedy a defendant has after such a reference is to request the court to instruct or reinstruct the jury that it may draw no inference from the defendant's failure to testify. Such a charge by the court can only serve to emphasize the fact that the defendant has not testified.[86]

For argument to result in a violation of a defendant's right to due process of law, apart from comment on the defendant's failure to testify, the error must be extraordinary. In *Donnelly v DeChristoforo*,[87] the Court emphasized the difference between the kind of error which rises to a constitutional level and ordinary trial error, finding that comment by the prosecutor which would have required reversal had the case been a federal one did not constitute a violation of the defendant's right to due process of law.[88] While the federal courts will take "special care" to ensure that misconduct does not prejudice a specific right, such as the privilege against self-incrimination, claims that the prosecutor's argument rendered a state trial unfair have met with little success in the federal courts.[89]

§17.12 Lesser Included Offense Instruction and the Constitution

A lesser included offense is an offense which contains some but not all of the elements of the greater offense. The lesser included offenses doctrine, which permits a court to instruct the jury that it may find the defendant guilty of a lesser

---

[84] 438 US 586, 595 (1978).

[85] See generally Annot, *Comment or Argument by Court or Counsel that Evidence is Uncontradicted as Amounting to Improper Reference to Accused's Failure to Testify*, 14 ALR3d 723.

[86] *Cf* Lakeside v Oregon, 435 US 333 (1978) (seven-judge majority of Court held that defendant's privilege against self-incrimination was not violated when the trial judge instructed the jury over the defendant's objection (and without any precipitating prosecutorial misconduct) that the jury was not to draw any adverse inference from the defendant's decision not to testify).

[87] 416 US 637 (1974).

[88] The prosecutor expressed his personal opinion of the defendant's guilt and argued that "they [the defense]said they hope you find him not guilty. I quite frankly think they hope you find him guilty of something a little less than first degree murder." *Id* 640.

[89] *Id* 643-44.

included offense, even if the prosecution's evidence is insufficient to sustain the crime charged, was developed as an aid to the prosecution.[90] However, such an instruction may also aid a defendant because a jury, for a variety of reasons, may decided to convict a defendant of a less serious crime rather than a more serious crime, despite overwhelming evidence of guilt.

In virtually all jurisdictions, state law provides that lesser included offense instructions should be given whenever they are compatible with the evidence or when there is any evidence to support such an instruction.[91] In most jurisdictions, some variant of common law robbery is a lesser included offense of the more serious offense of armed robbery. Thus, for example, a defendant charged with armed robbery would not be entitled to a lesser included offense instruction on robbery, where the defense at trial was that of nonparticipation in the robbery.

Because of the willingness of courts to give such instructions, few constitutional decisions on point exist. In *Keeble v United States*,[92] Justice Brennan noted in dicta that construction of the federal Major Crimes Act to preclude such instructions would raise serious constitutional questions.

In the only major decision dealing specifically with the lesser included offense doctrine, *Beck v Alabama*,[93] a six-judge majority of the United States Supreme Court held that a defendant could not be put to death when convicted pursuant to a somewhat unusual Alabama statutory scheme which provided in capital murder cases that a judge was not permitted to give the jury a lesser included offense instruction even when the instruction was supported by the evidence. The Court rejected Alabama's claim that the failure to give a lesser included offense instruction increased the reliability of the fact-finding process insofar as it would probably require the jury to acquit rather than, in effect, send a defendant to death in a doubtful case. The Court reasoned that not providing the jury with the option of convicting on the lesser included offense allowed the jury to acquit or convict on extraneous factors, that is, the jury's feeling about the propriety of the death penalty.[94] The Court held that this level of uncertainty was impermissible in a capital case.[95] While expressly leaving open the question of whether the due process clause requires giving lesser included offense instructions in appropriate circumstances in a noncapital case,[96] the Court pointedly noted that the lesser included offense rule "ensures that the jury will accord the defendant the full benefit of the reasonable doubt rule."[97]

---

[90] Keeble v United States, 412 US 205, 208 (1973).

[91] *See* the cases collected in Beck v Alabama, 447 US 625, 636 n 12 (1980).

[92] 412 US 205, 213 (1973).

[93] 447 US 625 (1980); *see also* Roberts v Louisiana, 428 US 325 (1976).

[94] Beck v Alabama, 447 US 625, 637-38 (1980).

[95] *Id.*

[96] *Id* 638 n 14.

[97] *Id* 634; *see also* Keeble v United States, 412 US 205, 212-13 (1973).

In light of the universal acceptance of the doctrine in American law, and the fundamental nature of the reasonable doubt standard in any criminal case, it seems likely that the Court would, if the question were squarely presented, hold that due process requires that a lesser included offense instruction be given at the defendant's request in appropriate circumstances.

§17.13 Instruction That a Defendant Need Not Testify and That No Inference May Be Drawn as a Result of Failure to Do So

Although in most jurisdictions, a trial court has great discretion in framing jury instructions, there would seem little reason for a court to refuse to instruct the jury that a defendant need not testify and that no inference may be drawn if the defendant fails to do so. Indeed, the United States Supreme Court has held that failure to grant such an instruction on a defendant's request is constitutional error.[98]

A more difficult question arises if the defendant objects to the instruction. Many experienced defense counsel believe that such an instruction only emphasizes the defendant's failure to testify and encourages the jury to draw a negative inference despite the court's instructions. In *Lakeside v Oregon*,[99] the Court refused to make such assumptions and held that giving such an instruction over a defendant's objection is not constitutional error. A few jurisdictions, both before and after *Lakeside*, have held that giving such an instruction over the defendant's objection is error as a matter of state law.[100]

The decision in *Lakeside* is probably a necessity in any system that relies on a jury's following basic instructions. However, whether such an instruction is helpful or harmful must depend on the particular facts of each case. It is difficult to believe that there is any legitimate reason why a court should give such an instruction over a competent attorney's request that it not do so.

---

[98] Carter v Kentucky, 450 US 288 (1981).

[99] 435 US 333 (1978).

[100] *See, e.g.*, People v Molono, 253 Cal App 2d 691, 61 Cal Rptr 821 (1967); see generally Annot, *Propriety Under Griffin v California and Prejudicial Effect of Instruction That No Inferences Against Accused Should be Drawn From his Failure to Testify*, 18 ALR3d 1335.

§17.14 The *Allen v United States* or Dynamite Charge

In 1896 in *Allen v United States*,[101] the United States Supreme Court approved a charge calculated to urge a divided jury to agree, given by the trial judge after the jury announced it was deadlocked. As the Court noted in its opinion, the charge given by the trial judge had first been approved by the Massachusetts Supreme Judicial Court in *Commonwealth v Tuey*.[102] The trial court had charged the jury, in substance, that:

> In a large proportion of cases absolute certainty could not be expected; that although the verdict must be the verdict of each individual juror, and not a mere acquiescence in the conclusion of his fellows, yet they should examine the question submitted with candor and with a proper regard to and deference to the opinions of each other; that it was their duty to decide the case if they could conscientiously do so; that they should listen, with a disposition to be convinced, to each other's arguments; that if much the larger number were for conviction, a dissenting juror should consider whether his doubt was a reasonable one which made no impression on the minds of so many men, equally honest, equally intelligent with himself. If, upon the other hand, the majority was for acquittal, the minority ought to ask themselves whether they might not reasonably doubt the correctness of a judgment which was not concurred in by the majority.[103]

No attorney had appeared on behalf of Allen, the appellant, and the Supreme Court approved the use of the charge in a single paragraph, reasoning that "the very object of the jury system is to secure unanimity by a comparison of views, and by arguments among the jurors themselves."[104] The charge is commonly known as the "dynamite" charge, presumably because it is intended to "put a stick of dynamite" under a deadlocked jury.

The *Allen* charge has been the subject of much criticism. Indeed, Judge Aldisert of the Third Circuit once characterized it as "not so much an object of commendation as it is a product of toleration."[105] In recent years, some federal courts have prohibited its use absolutely,[106] while others have allowed

---

[101] 164 US 492 (1896).

[102] 62 Mass (8 Cush) 1 (1851).

[103] Allen v United States, 164 US 492, 501 (1896).

[104] *Id.*

[105] United States v Fioravanti, 412 F2d 407 (3d Cir), *cert denied*, 396 US 837 (1969).

[106] *Id* 420.

it in certain cases.[107] As a matter of state law, most state courts have either completely eliminated or restricted use of the charge.[108] A number of courts have suggested use of the modified charge recommended by the American Bar Association.[109]

There have been many different criticisms of the charge. Perhaps the most basic is that no matter how the charge is phrased, it is directed at jurors who are not satisfied of the defendant's guilt. Any experienced defense lawyer knows that jurors do not hold out for conviction; they are far more likely to hold out for acquittal. Certainly the charge affects the defendant's constitutional right to be found guilty only by a reasonable doubt standard.

Recognition that the *Allen* charge could coerce the jury into not giving the defendant the full benefit of the reasonable doubt doctrine has led some courts to hold use of the charge violative of state and federal constitutions.[110] The United States Supreme Court has never squarely held that use of the *Allen* instruction is constitutionally impermissible.[111]

---

[107] *See, e.g.*, United States v Smith, 635 F2d 716 (8th Cir 1980); see generally Annot, *Modern Status of Rule that Court May Instruct Dissenting Jurors in Federal Criminal Case to Give Due Consideration to Opinion of Majority*, 44 ALR Fed 468.

[108] *See, e.g.*, People v Prim, 53 Ill 2d 62, 289 NE2d 601 (1972), *cert denied*, 412 US 918 (1973). See generally Annot, *Instructions Urging Dissenting Jurors in State Criminal Case to Give Due Consideration to Opinion of Majority (Allen Charge) - Modern Cases*, 97 ALR3d 96.

[109] ABA STANDARDS FOR CRIMINAL JUSTICE, Trial by Jury, §5.4 provides:

(a) Before the jury retires for deliberation, the court may give an instruction which informs the jury:

(i) that in order to return a verdict, each juror must agree thereto:

(ii) that jurors have a duty to consult with one another and to deliberate with a view to reaching an agreement, if it can be done without violance to individual judgment;

(iii) that each juror must decide the case for himself, but only after an impartial consideration of the evidence with his fellow jurors;

(iv) that in the course of deliberations, a juror should not hesitate to reexamine his own views and change his opinion if convinced it is erroneous; and

(v) that no juror should surrender his honest conviction as to the weight or effect of the evidence solely of because of the opinion of his fellow jurors, or for the mere purpose of returning a verdict.

(b) If it appears to the court that the jury has been unable to agree, the court may require the jury to continue their deliberations and may give or repeat an instruction as provided in sub-section (a). The court shall not require or threaten to require the jury to deliberate for an unreasonable length of time or for unreasonable intervals.

(c) The jury may be discharged without without having agreed upon a verdict if it appears that there is no reasonable probability of agreement.

[110] *See, e.g.*, Fields v State, 487 P2d 831 (Alaska 1971); People v Gainer, 19 Cal 3d 835, 566 P2d 997, 139 Cal Rptr 861 (1977); State v Martin, 297 Minn 359, 211 NW2d 765 (1973); State v Garza, 185 Neb 445, 176 NW2d 664 (1970); Commonwealth v Spencer, 442 Pa 328, 275 A2d 299 (1971).

[111] *See, e.g.*, United States v United States Gympsum, 438 US 422 (1978) (use of modified *Allen* charge by lower court not commented on).

Deliberation and Verdict

§17.15 Interference with Jury When It is Deliberating

Because a defendant has a right to trial by an impartial tribunal,[112] it is evident that interference with a jury will violate a defendant's constitutional rights. Most modern decisions have concerned apparently inadvertent interference with the defendant's rights. In *Turner v Louisiana*,[113] for example, the United States Supreme Court held that the defendant's right to an impartial tribunal was violated when two deputy sheriffs who were key witnesses at the defendant's trial had the jury in custody during the defendant's trial. Even though the two deputies had testified that they had never communicated with the jury about the merits of the case, the Court recognized that allowing the jury to engage in "a continuous and intimate association throughout a three day trial"[114] created an impermissible degree of prejudice. In *Gonzales v Beto*,[115] the Court found a due process violation where the sheriff who was in charge of the non-sequestered jury, and thus called them in and out of court and performed administrative tasks such as getting the jurors soft drinks, was a key prosecution witness. The Court emphasized that the court must appear neutral and found error in having a court officer act as a part of the prosecution team.

The importance of the neutrality of the court is illustrated by *United States v United States Gypsum Co*,[116] where, after allowing a jury to deliberate for five days the trial judge gave a modified *Allen* charge, and on the seventh day agreed to meet with the foreman after having received a note suggesting that the jury was deadlocked. In holding that the trial court had committed reversible error of constitutional magnitude, the Court pointed out that the absence of counsel increased the chance of erroneous information being inadvertently conveyed to the foreman and that communication with the foreman alone enhanced the chance that a misapprehension of law or fact by the foreman would be conveyed to other jurors. In short, it seems quite apparent that meetings between the trial judge and jury foreman, without the presence of counsel, may be the most egregious form of interference with the jury's deliberations.

---

[112] *See, e.g.*, Irvin v Dowd, 366 US 717 (1961).

[113] 379 US 466 (1965); *see also* State v Rothburn, 287 Ore 421, 600 P2d 392 (1970).

[114] Turner v Louisiana, 379 US 466, 473 (1965).

[115] 405 US 1052 (1972).

[116] 438 US 422 (1978).

§17.16 Requirement of Unanimity

In *Johnson v Louisiana*,[117] the United States Supreme Court sustained, as consistent with due process, a statutory scheme which required cases in which the punishment might not be imprisonment at hard labor to be tried by a jury of five, all of the members of which had to agree to convict, and more serious cases to be tried by a twelve-person jury, nine of the members of which had to agree to convict. In *Apodaca v Oregon*,[118] the Court held that the Oregon statutory scheme, which allowed conviction by a vote of 10-2, did not violate the Sixth Amendment right to jury trial. The Court reasoned that the purpose of a jury is simply to provide a layer of community judgment between a defendant and the decision to convict, and that a requirement of unanimity did not materially contribute to the exercise of this community judgment.[119]

However, the Court has held that allowing a nonunanimous verdict by a six-person jury to suffice for conviction would violate a defendant's constitutional right to trial by jury.[120] In so holding, the Court explicitly recognized that it was making a value judgment, and has stated that it

> Do[es] not pretend the ability to discern a priori a bright line below which the number of jurors participating in a trial or the verdict would not permit the jury to function. . . . But having already departed from the strictly historical requirements of jury trial, it is inevitable that lines must be drawn somewhere if the jury trial right is to be preserved.[121]

---

[117] 406 US 356 (1972). Five-person juries were later held unconstitutional in Ballew v Georgia, 435 US 323 (1978).

[118] 406 US 404 (1972).

[119] *Id* 410.

[120] Burch v Louisiana, 441 US 130 (1979).

[121] *Id at* 137.

18

Sentencing and Release

§18.01 Constitutional Rules Relating to Sentencing and Discretionary Release

A person convicted of a crime will receive a sentence, which constitutes the judgment in a criminal case.[1] Every state provides penalties for each distinct crime, which are imposed by the sentencing judge. While at common law all felonies were punished by death, the concept of longterm imprisonment for crime developed around the time of the American Revolution, and with it, the idea of sentencing to rehabilitate, as well as to incapacitate and punish. With the idea of rehabilitation eventually came the indeterminate sentence and the concept that punishment should be individualized.[2] By 1949, Justice Black could write without fear of contradiction:

> Undoubtedly the New York statutes emphasize a prevalent modern philosophy of penalogy that the punishment should fit the offender and not merely the crime. The belief no longer prevails that every offense in a like legal category calls for an identical punishment without regard to the past life and habits of a particular offender. . . . Today's philosophy of individualizing sentences makes sharp distinctions for example between first and repeated offenders. Indeterminate sentences, the ultimate termination of which are sometimes decided by non-judicial agencies, have to a large extent taken the place of the rigidly fixed punishments . . . . Retribution is no longer the dominant objective of the criminal law. Reformation and rehabilitation of offenders have become important goals of criminal jurisprudence.[3]

Decisions of the United States Supreme Court concerning sentence still reflect the view that an important aspect of the sentencing process is the defendant's

---

[1] Bradley v United States, 410 US 605, 609 (1973).

[2] *See, e.g.*, Lockett v Ohio, 438 US 586, 602 (1978) ("We begin by recognizing that the concept of individualized sentencing, in criminal cases generally, although not constitutionally required, has long been accepted in this country").

[3] Williams v New York, 337 US 241, 247-48 (1949).

amenability to "rehabilitation."[4] Certainly there are decisions premised upon the view that an inappropriate sentence may impede a defendant's rehabilitation, which may be of value to an attorney attempting to protect his or her client's rights.[5] But the traditional view of sentencing has its critics, who have become more and more vocal every year. The indeterminate sentence frequently results in two people convicted of the same crime suffering very different sentences. It may force prison inmates to undergo schooling they detest, or counseling they do not want, to convince parole boards they have "reformed." The unfairness inherent in such situations has traditionally been justified by the shibboleth of rehabilitation. There is some dispute, though, among scholars about whether there is, in fact, any such thing as rehabilitation. If rehabilitation does not exist, there may be no legitimate reason for imposing drastically different sentences on people who have committed the same crime and, in fact, there may be a great risk, since the touchstone of American law has never been an amorphous absolute called *justice*, but rather, equal treatment under law. Moreover, to incarcerate a person for a longer time because of refusal to rehabilitate — or, depending upon one's point of view, accept the values of the majority — obviously presents a grave risk of abuse.

It is not, of course, the purpose of this book to consider the merits of any penological theory. But it should be noted that some states have begun to reject the rehabilitation model of penology and adopt a model reflecting goals only of retribution and incapacitation.[6] The impact of the state and federal constitutions on such statutory schemes has only begun to be delineated, and will doubtless lead to much litigation in the coming years.

Sentencing: Procedural Requirements

§18.02 Right to a Hearing

By statute or court rule, in most jurisdictions, a person is afforded a hearing before being sentenced. Indeed, in a jurisdiction which has adopted a

---

[4] *See, e.g.*, Roberts v United States, 445 US 552 (1980) (trial judge could impose heavier sentence on defendant who refused to cooperate with the authorities, since his failure to cooperate without good reason could show unwillingness to rehabilitate).

[5] *See, e.g., In re* Grant, 18 Cal 3d 1, 553 P2d 590, 132 Cal Rptr 430, (1976) (mandatory minimum sentences for narcotics offenses do not permit the kind of "individualized consideration of the offender" required by the California constitution).

[6] *See, e.g.*, Me Rev Stat Ann tit 17-A, §1252, abolishing indeterminate sentencing, and requiring sentencing judges to set a definite term of imprisonment, which must be served in full, less credits earned for good conduct or for pretrial imprisonment and the like. *See* Me Rev Stat Ann tit 17-A, §1253.

rehabilitative penological model, a hearing seems necessary in order that the judge may consider the information relevant to fix an appropriate sentence.

However, there is no constitutional requirement that a separate hearing on sentencing be held at all.[7] Proceeding on the theory that the rehabilitative model of sentencing allows a judge to consider all relevant information about a defendant, the United States Supreme Court has specifically held that a sentencing judge may, before sentencing, consider evidence gathered by a probation officer and not allow a defendant to participate in hearings on sentence.[8] Moreover, the Court has upheld the practice of having the jury sentence the offender in noncapital cases, a practice which still exists in a small minority of states.[9] In most cases, courts have upheld mandatory noncapital sentences which, of course, may be imposed without a hearing.[10]

Despite the lack of a constitutional requirement for such a hearing, most courts do require that a sentencing hearing be held before sentence is imposed. If the law of a jurisdiction provides for such a hearing, the defendant has a constitutional right to be represented by counsel at the hearing.[11] While the rules of evidence do not apply at a sentencing hearing, a number of constitutional procedural rules have delineated the considerations which may be taken into account by the sentencing judge.

§18.03 Sentence Pursuant to Separate Legislative Act

The rule that there is no constitutional right to a sentencing hearing has one important caveat. If the sentence to be imposed requires new findings which were not at issue in the criminal trial, a separate hearing must be held and the defendant must be afforded the full panoply of rights before sentence is imposed.[12] Illustrative is *Specht v Patterson*,[13] in which the defendant, convicted of a sexual assault crime involving a maximum punishment of 10 years, was subjected to sentencing to an indeterminate term of one day to life pursuant to the Colorado Sex Offenders Act. Such a sentence was permissible under the act on a finding that the defendant "constituted a threat of bodily harm to members of the public, or [was] a habitual offender and mentally ill."[14] In

---

[7] Specht v Patterson, 386 US 605 (1967); Williams v New York, 337 US 241 (1949).

[8] Williams v New York, 337 US 241 (1949). *But see* Gardner v Florida, 430 US 349 (1977); **§18.04.**

[9] Chaffin v Stynchcombe, 412 US 17 (1973).

[10] See **§18.07.**

[11] Mempa v Rhay, 389 US 128 (1967).

[12] Oyler v Boles, 368 US 448 (1962).

[13] 386 US 605 (1967).

[14] *Id.*

holding that the defendant was entitled to the procedural protections of the due process clause, Justice Douglas noted:

> The Sex Offenders Act does not make the commission of a specific crime the basis for sentencing. It makes one conviction the basis for commencing another proceeding under another Act to determine whether a person constitutes a threat of bodily harm to the public, or is a habitual offender and mentally ill. That is a new finding of fact that was not an ingredient of the offense charged.[15]

The process due in such circumstances includes the rights to be present with counsel, to be heard, to be confronted with the witnesses against one, and to cross-examine and present evidence.[16] Findings adequate to make any appeal allowed meaningful must also be made.[17]

§18.04 Evidence Which May Be Considered in Sentencing Hearing

If a sentencing scheme is premised on a view that a sentence must fit the offender, then obviously the sentencing judge will wish to know as much as possible about the defendant. In such systems, which exist throughout the country, it is generally held that a person who commits the same crime as another cannot complain that his or her sentence is heavier than that of another who committed the same crime because even if the crimes are identical, the defendants may not be.[18]

Relying on the rehabilitative model, the United States Supreme Court has endorsed the use of presentence reports—ex parte investigative reports prepared by probation officers—by sentencing judges.[19] Such reports may contain information bearing no relation to the crime with which the defendant has been charged, and may rest in whole or in part on hearsay.[20] At least when a defendant is facing the death penalty, however, if a judge intends to rely on information obtained in a presentence report, the information must be disclosed to the defendant so that the defendant may challenge inaccuracies in it.[21]

---

[15] *Id* 608.

[16] *Id* 610.

[17] *Id.*

[18] *See, e.g.*, State v Church, 115 NH 537, 345 A2d 392 (1975), *cert denied*, 424 US 955 (1976).

[19] Gregg v United States, 394 US 489 (1969); Williams v New York, 337 US 241 (1949).

[20] Gregg v United States, 394 US 489 (1969).

[21] Gardner v Florida, 430 US 349, 362 (1977).

Because of possible concern about the defendant's amenability to rehabilitation, a sentencing judge may consider his or her own belief that the defendant lied on the witness stand in imposing a heavier sentence.[22] Similarly, a judge may take the refusal, without apparent justification on the grounds of fear for safety or self-incrimination, of a defendant to cooperate with the government in investigating other crimes, as indicia of nonamenability to rehabilitation, and impose a heavier term.[23]

However, a judge may not consider criminal convictions obtained in violation of the defendant's right to counsel.[24]

There is some question about whether evidence obtained in violation of a defendant's Fourth Amendment rights may be considered in a sentencing hearing. The majority of courts follow the reasoning of the Second Circuit in *United States v Schipani*,[25] holding such evidence admissible because application of the exclusionary rule for a second time would not add in any significant way to the deterrent effect of the rule, since it is unlikely that law enforcement officers would conduct illegal searches to obtain evidence they knew would be inadmissible at trial but admissible at sentencing. Other courts have taken a contrary view.[26] There is, of course, a due process right to be sentenced only on reliable information,[27] and for that reason, unreliable evidence, such as an involuntary confession, could not be considered in sentencing by any court.

Constitutional Prohibition of Cruel and Unusual Punishment

§18.05 Scope of Prohibition of Cruel and Unusual Punishment

The Eighth Amendment to the United States Constitution provides, in relevant part, that "[e]xcessive bail shall not be required, nor excessive fines imposed, nor cruel and unusual punishments inflicted." The very language of the Eighth

---

[22] United States v Grayson, 438 US 41 (1978).

[23] Roberts v United States, 445 US 552 (1980).

[24] United States v Tucker, 404 US 443 (1972).

[25] 435 F2d 26 (2d Cir 1970); *see also* United States v Lee, 540 F2d 1205 (4th Cir), *cert denied*, 429 US 894 (1976).

[26] Verdugo v United States, 402 F2d 599 (9th Cir 1968); see generally Annot, *Consideration in Connection With Sentencing in Federal Criminal Case of Evidence Inadmissible at Trial Because Illegally Obtained*, 22 ALR Fed 856.

[27] United States v Lee, 540 F2d 1205 (4th Cir), *cert denied*, 429 US 894 (1976).

Amendment was taken from the English Bill of Rights of 1689, and similar provisions exist in virtually every state constitution.[28]

Early holdings of the United States Supreme Court apparently assumed that the amendment's prohibition of cruel and unusual punishment was applicable to the states, but that it prohibited only cruel methods of inflicting the death penalty.[29] The Eighth Amendment was specifically held applicable to the states in 1962,[30] and since that time, the scope of the protection afforded by the right has been further refined.

The import of the Eighth Amendment has greatly expanded in recent years. It is now settled that a sentence may violate the constitutional prohibition against cruel and unusual punishment if it is grossly disproportionate to the crime charged, or if the punishment is not acceptable according to contemporary standards of dignity.[31] The concept of cruel and unusual punishment is not static, but draws its meaning from evolving standards of decency.[32] Moreover, the conditions of imprisonment under which a lawful sentence must be served may themselves violate the Eighth Amendment.[33]

Perhaps no subject has evoked more judicial discourse on cruel and unusual punishment than the death penalty. In 1972, a bare plurality of the Court held that the death penalty, under the circumstances in which it was inflicted in the United States, was violative of the Eighth Amendment. Subsequent legislation remedied the defects the Court found in 1972, and it is now clear that the death penalty is not per se violative of the Eighth Amendment.[34] Because of the unique rules which have developed concerning the death penalty, it is treated separately.

---

[28] Rummel v Estelle, 445 US 263 (1980) (Stewart, J, concurring).

[29] *See, e.g.*, United States *ex rel* Francis v Resweber, 329 US 459 (1947) (imposition of death penalty after first attempt at electrocution had failed due to mechanical problems); *In re* Kemmler, 136 US 436 (1890) (electrocution as means of inflicting death penalty); Wilkeson v Utah, 99 US 130 (1878) (shooting as means of inflicting death penalty); *cf* O'Neil v Vermont 144 US 323 (1892) (lengthy sentence not violative of 8th Amendment).

[30] Robinson v California, 370 US 660 (1962) (holding that California law which punished the offense of being a narcotics addict violated the prohibition of cruel and unusual punishment).

[31] *See, e.g.*, Trop v Dulles, 356 US 86 (1958).

[32] Gregg v Georgia, 428 US 153, 173 (1976). For example, while it was once generally held that statutes requiring sterilization of repeated offenders were constitutional, there is little doubt that such statutes would not be sustained today. *See, e.g.*, Skinner v Oklahoma, 316 US 535 (1942); Mickle v Nevada, 262 F 687 (D Nev 1918); see generally Annot, *Validity of Statutes Authorizing Asexualization of Sterilization of Criminals or Mental Defectives*, 53 ALR3d 960.

[33] *See, e.g.*, Hutto v Finney, 437 US 678 (1978).

[34] Furman v Georgia, 408 US 238 (1972); Gregg v Georgia, 428 US 153 (1976); see §18.09.

§18.06 Length of Sentence as Violation of Constitutional Prohibition of Cruel and Unusual Punishment

While the United States Supreme Court has, on numerous occasions, stated that the Eighth Amendment prohibition of cruel and unusual punishment prohibits sentences grossly disproportionate to the crime, the Court has been unwilling in recent years to set aside noncapital sentences on that ground. Indeed, in *Rummel v Estelle*,[35] the Court noted that the only noncapital case in which it had ever held a penalty grossly disproportionate to a crime was in a 1910 case which involved an unusual civil law punishment under Philippine law known as cadena temporal. In holding that a Texas law which provided for life imprisonment on conviction of three felonies did not violate the Eighth Amendment, Justice Rehnquist noted that, given the unique nature of the punishment imposed in the death penalty and Philippine Island cases, "one could argue without fear of contradiction by any decision of this Court that for crimes concededly classified and classifiable as felonies, that is, punishable by significant terms of imprisonment in a state penitentiary, the length of the sentence imposed is purely a matter of legislative prerogative."[36]

In *Hutto v Davis*,[37] a bare majority of the Court held that a sentence of 40 years imprisonment and a $20,000 fine on conviction of possession of nine ounces of marijuana with intent to distribute and distribution of marijuana did not violate the Eighth Amendment prohibition of cruel and unusual punishment. Justice Powell concurred in the judgment only, "reluctant[ly] conclud[ing]" that *Rummel* was controlling, and expressing concern over the fact that the sentence imposed was disproportionate to the sentences generally imposed on others for like offenses, and that after the defendant's conviction, the Virginia legislature had reduced the maximum penalty for the defendant's offense to 10 years on each count, regardless of the aggravating circumstances. He pointed out the "seriousness of the disparity in sentencing that may distinguish our system of justice from other mature systems," urging that "effort[s] to minimize this . . . . certainly should be continued."[38] Justice Powell's opinion suggests that the federal Constitution places some limits on the noncapital penalties a particular jurisdiction may affix to a crime, and that the criteria for determining whether a sentence is grossly disproportionate depends not as much on the particular crime and the particular sentence, but on how the crime is treated in other

---

[35] 445 US 263 (1980), *citing* Weems v United States, 217 US 349 (1910).

[36] Rummel v Estelle, 445 US 263, 274 (1980); *see also* O'Neil v Vermont, 144 US 323 (1892).

[37] Hutto v Davis, 102 S Ct 703 (1982).

[38] *Id* 708 (Powell, J, concurring).

jurisdictions. Given the lack of unanimity on the Court, it seems reasonable to expect that further litigation will define the effect of the Eighth Amendment on noncapital sentences.

While Justice Rehnquist's dictum in *Rummel* to the effect that length of sentence is purely a matter of legislative prerogative could very likely be applied to the majority of state courts of last resort interpreting correlative state constitutional guarantees,[39] a few courts have taken a more expansive view. For example, in *Workman v State*,[40] the Kentucky Court of Appeals held that a sentence of life without parole imposed on two 14-year-old boys who had committed rape and robbery on an 81-year-old woman violated the Kentucky constitutional prohibition against cruel and unusual punishment, since such a severe term was intended to punish incorrigibles, and 14-year-old boys could not reasonably be considered incorrigibles.

§18.07 Mandatory Noncapital Sentences

In many jurisdictions, mandatory sentencing statutes have been enacted to deal with crimes the legislature views with particular concern. Such statutes frequently concern drug or firearms offenses. The statutes themselves usually include language to the effect that no part of the mandatory sentence may be suspended nor may the defendant be paroled from the sentence. Courts have, generally speaking, upheld mandatory sentences against claims that such sentences violate the defendant's right to equal protection of the laws or that they are an unwarranted legislative intrusion into the judicial power or constitute cruel and unusual punishment.[41] While the United States Supreme Court has been disinclined to uphold mandatory death penalty statutes, it has recognized that the cases dealing with the death penalty are *sui generis*, and that decisions holding such statutes unconstitutional are not applicable to statutes setting mandatory noncapital sentences.[42] The prevailing view is that the legislature is "paramount in the field of public safety" and may set mandatory sentences for particular crimes.[43]

The California Supreme Court has, however, held certain mandatory sentences violative of the constitutional prohibition of cruel and unusual punish-

---

[39] *See, e.g.,* Annot, *Length of Sentences as Violative of Constitutional Provisions Prohibiting Cruel and Unusual Punishment*, 33 ALR3d 335.

[40] 429 SW2d 374 (Ky Ct App 1968).

[41] *See, e.g.,* McQuaid v Smith, 556 F2d 595 (1st Cir 1977); State v Williams, 115 Ariz 288, 564 P2d 1255 (1975); Owens v State, 316 So 2d 537 (Fla 1975); State v Freeman, 223 Kan 362, 574 P2d 950 (1978); *see also* Annot, *Validity of State Statute Imposing Mandatory Sentence or Prohibiting Granting of Probation or Suspension of Sentence for Narcotics Offenses*, 81 ALR3d 1192.

[42] Lockett v Ohio, 438 US 586, 605 n 13 (1978).

[43] State v King, 330 A2d 124 (Me 1977).

ments because mandatory sentencing statutes do not permit the "individualized consideration" necessary if the purposes of sentences are to be fulfilled.[44] Such a position is premised on the consideration that the punishment should fit the offender which is, in turn, founded on the rehabilitative model of sentencing. In a jurisdiction which had abandoned the rehabilitation model of sentencing and had established a system of fixed sentences, such an analysis would be inappropriate.

§18.08 Constitutional Right to Rehabilitation

Perhaps because of the questions which have been raised about the rehabilitative model of corrections, it has been generally held that there is no constitutional right to rehabilitation.[45]

Death Penalty

§18.09 Death Penalty as Cruel and Unusual Punishment

At common law every felony was punishable by death. Since the time of the American revolution, the numbers of crimes punishable by death and of actual executions have sharply decreased. Within the last 15 years, challenges to the imposition of the death penalty on constitutional grounds have dramatically increased. No subject in the law has inspired such impassioned feelings among lawyers and judges as the death penalty. To weigh or even repeat all the arguments for and against the penalty would be far beyond the scope of this work, and doubtless a fit subject for several separate volumes.

Most of the litigation concerning the death penalty over the last 10 years has related to whether the death penalty violates the constitutional prohibition of cruel and unusual punishment. The application of the Eighth Amendment to death penalty cases must, however, be considered apart from all other punishments for, as Justice Stewart noted:

> The penalty of death differs from all other forms of criminal punishment, not in degree but in kind. It is unique in its total irrevocability. It is unique in its rejection of rehabilitation of the convict as a basic purpose

---

[44] *In re* Grant, 18 Cal 3d 1, 553 P2d 590, 132 Cal Rptr 944, (1976).

[45] Newman v Alabama, 559 F2d 283 (5th Cir 1977), *cert denied*, 438 US 915 (1978); see generally Gobert & Cohen, Rights of Prisoners §11.11 (Shepard's/McGraw-Hill 1981).

of criminal justice. And it is unique, finally, in its absolute renunciation of all that is embodied in our concept of humanity.[46]

In 1972 in *Furman v Georgia*,[47] the United States Supreme Court, in a brief per curiam opinion, held that imposition of the death penalty in the three cases before it constituted cruel and unusual punishment in violation of the Eighth and Fourteenth Amendments to the United States Constitution. The statutes the Court addressed provided, as did most statutes at the time, that the penalty for first-degree murder was to be life imprisonment or death as the jury might determine. Each of the justices then on the Court wrote separate opinions; five concurred with the per curiam, and four dissented. Justices Marshall and Brennan took the position that the death penalty constituted cruel and unusual punishment in all cases. However, the narrowest ground on which Justices Stewart, White, and Douglas concurred was that the discretion afforded juries under the death penalty statutes at bar enabled juries and judges to selectively apply the penalty, and thus allowed it to be "wantonly and freakishly imposed."[48]

In the years since 1972, the United States Supreme Court has declined to invalidate all post-*Furman* death penalty statutes, but also has not formulated a test generally accepted by all of the members of the Court. Justices Marshall and Brennan are apparently committed to vote against the death penalty regardless of how the statute authorizing the penalty is drafted, believing that the death penalty constitutes cruel and unusual punishment in all cases.[49] At least four justices of the Court have, however, accepted the proposition that the penalty of death for the crime of rape of an adult woman is grossly disproportionate and excessive, and thus violative of the Eighth Amendment.[50] Beyond that, the cases turn on particular statutes and application of general principles. Of course, the death penalty may violate state constitutional guarantees as well as federal guarantees.[51]

While litigation involving the death penalty drags on, and on, and the United States Supreme Court has held numerous death penalty statutes constitutional, the stark fact remains that in the 10 years after *Furman*, only three individuals were executed in the United States—and two of these did not challenge their sentence, but were, in the words of Justice Marshall, permitted to commit "state-administered suicide."[52] As he recently noted, "The task of eliminating

---

[46] Furman v Georgia, 408 US 238, 306 (1972) (Stewart, J, concurring).

[47] *Id*.

[48] *Id* 310 (Stewart, J, concurring); *see also* Eddings v Oklahoma, 102 S C+Ct 869 (1982).

[49] *See, e.g.*, Godfrey v Georgia, 446 US 420 (1980) (Brennan, J, concurring; Marshall, J, concurring).

[50] Coker v Georgia, 433 US 584 (1977).

[51] *See, e.g.*, People v Anderson, 6 Cal 3d 628, 493 P2d 880, 100 Cal Rptr 152, *cert denied*, 406 US 958 (1972).

[52] *Godrey v Georgia*, 446 US 420, 439 (1980) (Marshall, J, concurring).

arbitrariness in the infliction of capital punishment is proving to be one which our criminal justice system — and perhaps any criminal justice system — is unable to perform."[53] Each day which passes without an execution necessarily renders imposition of the death penalty more "freakish," and impresses an observer with the cogency of Justice Marshall's observation.

§18.10 Mandatory Death Sentences

Interpreting the decisions of the United States Supreme Court which deal with the death penalty is no easy task. First, it is extremely rare to find an explicit majority holding; rather, the Court's holding must be discerned from reading the concurring opinions, and finding the narrowest common ground in them.[54] It is possible, however, to make some general comments.

Because the thrust of the plurality's concurring opinions holding the death penalty unconstitutional in the cases before it in *Furman v Georgia*,[55] was that the death penalty, when inflicted pursuant to statutes which left the jury without standards to guide its discretion, and when inflicted freakishly, violated the Eighth Amendment, numerous jurisdictions enacted mandatory death penalty statutes in that case's wake. These statutes have met with little favor in the United States Supreme Court. In *Woodson v North Carolina*,[56] for example, a four-judge plurality held that a North Carolina statute which set a mandatory death sentence in all first-degree murder cases violated the Eighth and Fourteenth Amendments because it departed markedly from contemporary standards respecting the imposition of the death penalty.[57] Justice Stewart, writing for the plurality, also found a deficiency of constitutional magnitude in the fact that a jury, being aware of the enormity of the punishment for first-degree murder, could simply refuse to convict on that charge for whatever reason it chose. Thus, the North Carolina mandatory death penalty did not fulfill the basic requirement of *Furman* that arbitrary and wanton jury discretion be replaced with objective standards to guide, regularize and make rationally reviewable the process for imposing a sentence of death.[58] Finally, and perhaps most significantly, the unique nature of the death penalty requires that there be particularized consideration of all relevant aspects of the character

---

[53] *Id* 440.

[54] Marks v United States, 430 US 188 (1977).

[55] 408 US 238 (1972).

[56] Woodson v North Carolina, 428 US 280 (1976) (Justices Marshall and Brennan concurred in the judgment on the ground that the death penalty is violative of the Eighth Amendment in all circumstances).

[57] *Id* 301.

[58] *Id* 303.

of each defendant before the penalty is imposed.[59] While recognizing that "the prevailing practice of individualized sentencing determinations generally reflects simply enlightened policy rather than a constitutional imperative,"[60] Justice Stewart found capital cases to be unique. Similar results have been reached in the other cases involving mandatory death penalties which have come before the United States Supreme Court.[61]

However, while the Court has been disinclined to uphold mandatory death sentences, it has not suggested that all mandatory death penalties are per se unconstitutional. In *Lockett v Ohio*,[62] the Court specifically left open the question of whether the need to deter certain types of homicide would justify mandatory sentences for extreme crimes, such as murder committed by one serving a life term.[63] Furthermore, the Court has noted that its decisions dealing with mandatory sentences in death cases are not necessarily applicable to state or federal statutes dealing with mandatory sentences for noncapital crimes, since sentencing in noncapital cases does not present the same problems which inhere in death penalty cases.[64]

§18.11 Constitutionally Permissible Death Penalty Statutes

The basis premise on which all the death penalty cases turn is that the death penalty, if inflicted by a jury or court which is not given explicit standards to guide it, will or may be inflicted so arbitrarily and freakishly as to constitute cruel and unusual punishment. In *Furman v Georgia*,[65] the United States Supreme Court considered the traditional type of statute which allowed the jury or judge unbridled discretion in deciding whether the punishment should be inflicted.

---

[59] *Id* 304.

[60] *Id.*

[61] *See, e.g.*, Roberts v Louisiana, 428 US 280 (1976) (six justices held Louisiana mandatory death penalty statute unconstitutional, while four justices found that Louisiana responsive verdict procedure, whereby the jury, in a potential death penalty case, was instructed on lesser included offenses even if there was no evidence to sustain the charges, violated *Furman* 's prohibition of standardless jury discretion in imposing the death penalty); Roberts v Louisiana, 431 US 633 (1977) (five justices found Louisiana statute requiring death for killing a police officer constitutionally infirm, and the plurality held that the capital sentencing decision had to allow for consideration of whatever mitigating circumstances might be relevant to either the particular offender or the particular offense). *Cf* Beck v Alabama, 447 US 625 (1980) (Alabama statute which imposed death penalty for murder but prohibited judge from giving jury option of convicting of the lesser included offense unconstitutional).

[62] 438 US 586 (1978).

[63] *Id* 604 n 11 (1978).

[64] *Id* 605 n 13.

[65] 408 US 238 (1972).

While these statutes have received a cold reception in the Supreme Court,[66] a few statutes which provide explicit standards governing the imposition of the death penalty have been upheld. As in the cases dealing with mandatory death sentences, most of the United States Supreme Court decisions upholding such statutes are plurality opinions.

In *Gregg v Georgia*,[67] six justices of the United States Supreme Court upheld a Georgia statute which ensures that the sentencing authority is given adequate information about the factors relevant to imposition of the death penalty, where the authority is provided with objective standards to govern the use of that information. Justice Stewart, writing for the Court in an opinion in which Justices Powell and Stevens concurred, outlined the contours of a constitutional sentencing procedure. He recognized that jury sentencing has long been desirable in capital cases because it maintains a link with the penal system and contemporary community values. But because much of the information relevant to sentencing would be inadmissible or prejudicial at trial, a bifurcated procedure, in which the question of sentence is not determined until after guilt is determined, is necessary. Moreover, the jury, which is inexperienced in such matters, must be given guidance regarding those factors relating to the crime and the defendant that the state, representing organized society, deems particularly relevant to the sentencing decision. He noted, however, that he did not suggest that only the procedures outlined would satisfy *Furman*, or that any sentencing system constructed along these general lines would necessarily satisfy *Furman*, but that each distinct system must be considered on its own.[68]

In the case before it, the Court considered a Georgia statute which allows the death penalty to be inflicted on a defendant if the jury specifies one of ten statutorily aggravating circumstances, which must be found to exist beyond a reasonable doubt before a death penalty can be imposed. The jury is authorized under the statute to consider other mitigating or aggravating factors as well. The jury is not required to find any mitigating circumstance in order not to impose death. It must find a statutory aggravating circumstance before recommending a sentence of death, however. The Georgia Supreme Court automatically reviews all death sentences to determine whether the sentence was imposed under the influence of passion or prejudice, whether the evidence supports the jury's finding of an aggravating circumstance, and whether the sentence is disproportionate, considering the penalties imposed in similar cases. In holding the statute constitutional, Justice Stewart's opinion suggested that the fact that all possibility of caprice was not eliminated from infliction of the death penalty did not render it unconstitutional since all possibility of caprice could never be removed from any system. The Court rejected the argument that

---

[66] See §18.10, on mandatory death sentences.

[67] 428 US 153 (1976).

[68] *Id* 195.

a jury might arbitrarily dispense mercy or return a verdict on a lesser included offense not punishable by death because "the isolated decision of a jury to afford mercy does not render unconstitutional death sentences imposed on defendants who were sentenced under a system that does not create a substantial risk of arbitrariness or caprice."[69]

A similar statutory scheme was upheld in *Proffitt v Florida*[70] and *Jurek v Texas*.[71] The Florida statute requires the sentencing authority to find mitigating and aggravating factors before the death penalty can be imposed, and requires appellate review to determine whether the punishment is too great. The Texas statute allows the death penalty to be imposed only if the jury finds three aggravating factors by a standard of beyond a reasonable doubt, but does not expressly provide for a finding of mitigating factors.[72]

In *Gregg*, *Proffitt*, and *Jurek*, the defendants challenged the definition of mitigating and aggravating factors as being unconstitutionally vague and thus allowing a jury to act arbitrarily. The Supreme Court applied the analysis used when any criminal statute is alleged to be void for vagueness.[73] Although all the challenged statutes contained broad language,[74] the Court held that the narrowing constructions given by state courts rendered them facially valid. The plurality concluded that the statutes did not create a "substantial risk that . . . . [the] capital sentencing system, when viewed in its entity, will result in the capricious or arbitrary imposition of the death penalty."[75]

However, in *Godfrey v Georgia*,[76] the Court was forced to consider the validity of a case in which the death penalty was imposed because the defendant killed his wife and mother-in-law by shooting them, seriatim, in the head with a shotgun. A Georgia jury imposed a death sentence on the defendant, specifying that the aggravating circumstance it found was that the offense was "outrageously or wantonly vile, horrible and inhuman." A four-judge plurality of the Court held that, by affirming the conviction, the Georgia Supreme Court

---

[69] *Id* 203.

[70] 428 US 242 (1976).

[71] 428 US 262 (1976).

[72] *Id* 269.

[73] See §1.09, on the void for vagueness doctrine.

[74] The Texas statute required the jury to determine "whether there is a probability that the defendant would commit criminal acts of violence that would constitute a continuing threat to society," Jurek v Texas, 428 US 262, 269 (1976); the Georgia statute required the jury to consider "whether the offense . . . was outrageously or wantonly vile, horrible or inhuman in that it involved torture, depravity of mind or an aggravated battery to the victim," Gregg v Georgia, 428 US 153, 164 n 9 (1976); the Florida statute required the jury to determine "whether the capital felony was especially heinous, atrocious or cruel," Proffitt v Florida, 428 US 242, 248 n 9 (1976).

[75] Proffitt v Florida, 428 US 242, 254 n 11 (1976); Gregg v Georgia, 428 US 153, 201 n 51 (1976).

[76] 446 US 420 (1980).

unconstitutionally failed to limit the broad language of the statute, and remanded to the Georgia Supreme Court with instructions to reverse the death sentence. Justice Marshall, while adhering to his view that the death penalty is in all circumstances cruel and unusual punishment, noted in a cogent concurring opinion that he believed that

> it is not enough for a reviewing court to apply a narrowing construction to otherwise ambiguous statutory language. The jury must be instructed on the proper, narrow construction of the statute. The Court's cases make clear that it is the sentencer's discretion that must be channelled and guided by clear, objective and specific standards. To give the jury an instruction in the form of the bare words of the statute — words that are hopelessly ambiguous and could be understood to apply to any murder — would effectively grant it unbridled discretion to impose the death penalty. Such a defect could not be cured by the post hoc narrowing construction of an appellate court. The reviewing court can determine only whether a rational jury might have imposed the death penalty if it had been properly instructed; it is impossible for it to say whether a particular jury would have so exercised its discretion if it had known the law.[77]

The states are not wholly free to arbitrarily fix the aggravating and mitigating factors which may be considered before the death penalty is imposed. In *Lockett v Ohio*,[78] the plurality of the Court invalidated an Ohio statute because the mitigating circumstances which could be considered by the judge were very narrow, and did not include the defendant's age, or her role in the offense. The plurality concluded that in "all but the rarest kind of capital cases," the sentencing authority may not be precluded from considering as a mitigating factor any aspect of a defendant's character or record or any of the circumstances of the offense that the defendant proffers as a basis for a sentence less than death.

Appeal of Sentence by Government

§18.12 Appeal by Government in General

The United States Supreme Court has long rejected the proposition that the Fifth Amendment prohibition of double jeopardy is applicable to sentencing proceedings. The prevailing rule is that a federal judge may recall a defendant

---

[77] *Id* (Marshall, J, concurring); *compare* Godfrey v Georgia, 446 US 420 (1980) *with* Winters v New York, 333 US 507 (1948); see **§1.09**.

[78] 428 US 586 (1978); *see also* Eddings v Oklahoma, 102 S Ct 869 (1982).

and increase a sentence before the defendant has begun serving it.[79]   Of course, a defendant may receive a greater sentence after having appealed and being reconvicted.   Although a number of rules have developed to ensure that an enhanced sentence following appeal by the defendant is not the result of prosecutorial vindictiveness,[80] the Court has declined to apply the Fifth Amendment to the usual sentencing proceeding.[81] Pronouncement of a sentence, although the judgment in a criminal case, "does not have the qualities of constitutional finality that attend an acquittal,"[82] and the double jeopardy clause does not require that a sentence be given a degree of finality that prevents its later increase.[83] Thus, if a statute authorizes an appeal by the government of a sentence imposed to correct a mistake of law, abuse of discretion, or clearly erroneous findings, it does not violate the constitutional prohibition against double jeopardy.[84]

Parole and Probation

§18.13 Parole and Probation in General

Probation and parole are common to virtually every state system. A sentence of probation generally allows an individual to remain at large as long as he or she complies with conditions set by the court. A sentence may be imposed and suspended and the defendant placed on probation, in which case the defendant is subject to serve the sentence only on violating probation. In some jurisdictions, a defendant may be placed on probation and imposition of an actual sentence may be delayed until such time as the defendant violates the conditions of probation.

Parole, on the other hand, can only occur when a defendant has served part of a sentence of imprisonment. Parole is a form of early release, which is granted subject to certain conditions. The purpose of parole is often said to be "to help individuals reintegrate into society as constructive individuals as soon as they are able, without being confined for the full term of the sentence imposed."[85] It might also be observed that the institution of parole allows judges to sentence

---

[79] Bozza v United States, 330 US 160 (1947); United States v DiLorenzo, 429 F2d 216 (2d Cir 1970), *cert denied*, 402 US 950 (1971); Vincent v United States, 337 F2d 891 (8th Cir 1964), *cert denied*, 380 US 988 (1965).

[80] See §§19.04-.06.

[81] One notable exception, however, is death penalty cases. *See* Bullington v Missouri, 451 US 430 (1981); §19.05.

[82] United States v DeFrancesco, 449 US 17 (1980).

[83] *Id.*

[84] *Id.*

[85] Morrissey v Brewer, 408 US 471, 477 (1972).

criminals to extraordinarily long terms, presumably deterring others, while allowing the criminal to be imprisoned only for a reasonable amount of time.

Both parole and probation traditionally were considered mere matters of grace. Thus, courts reasoned that a person granted the "privilege" of parole or probation could not complain of the conditions on which it was granted, nor of its summary termination. The United State Supreme Court's decision in the early 1970s to reject "the concept that constitutional rights turn upon whether a governmental benefit is characterized as a right or a privilege"[86] has led to an explosion of law defining the procedures required in granting or revoking parole and probation. For constitutional purposes, parolees and probationers stand in similar positions: they both have qualified interests in their liberty.[87] The United States Supreme Court has, for example, considered the same process to be due when either parole or probation is revoked.[88]

§18.14 Right to Procedural Due Process on Seeking Parole

While abandoning the right-privilege distinction in constitutional law as a test for determining whether the traditional elements of procedural due process are necessary in a given situation, the United States Supreme Court has carefully marked out its view of a liberty interest which is of constitutional magnitude. Simply stated, the rule is as follows: in order for procedural due process to attach, a person must have some legal claim of entitlement to the interest or be in actual possession of the interest. Thus, while entitled to a hearing before parole is revoked, a person has no constitutional right to a hearing on whether he or she should be granted parole, if the statute authorizing parole holds out no more than the mere possibility of parole.[89] But a right to a hearing may be created by the language of the parole statute in question. The United States Supreme Court has held that whether a particular statute creates such a right depends on the statute itself, and must be decided on a case-by-case basis.[90] The use of mandatory language in statutes relating to parole or credits on sentence has seemed crucial.[91] Moreover, a constitutional entitlement cannot be created

---

[86] Graham v Richardson, 403 US 365, 374 (1971).

[87] *See, e.g.*, Gagnon v Scarpelli, 411 US 778, 782 (1973).

[88] *Id.*

[89] Greenholtz v Inmates of Neb Penal & Correctional Complex, 442 US 1 (1979); Connecticut Bd of Pardons v Dumschat, 101 S Ct 2460, 2464 (1981).

[90] Greenholtz v Inmates of Neb Penal & Correctional Complex, 442 US 1 (1979) (constitutional right to a statement of reasons for denial of parole where applicable Nebraska statute provided that inmates "shall" be released unless one of four specified conditions met).

[91] Greenholtz v Inmates of Neb Penal & Correctional Complex, 442 US 1 (1979); Wolff v McDonnell, 418 US 539 (1974).

314 SENTENCING & RELEASE

by estoppel merely because a wholly discretionary benefit has been extended generously in the past. Thus, the Court has held that where a board of pardons had wholly discretionary authority to reduce sentences of inmates sentenced to life to allow them earlier parole eligibility, the fact that it had done so in at least 75 per cent of the cases before it gave the defendant no right to a hearing or statement of reasons when his application was denied.[92]

§18.15 Conditions on Parole or Probation

A person placed on parole or probation is generally supervised by a state official. As a condition of parole or probation, the parolee generally agrees to abide by certain terms and conditions. Such conditions may be onerous; as the United States Supreme Court pointed out in *Morrissey v Brewer*:[93]

> Typically, parolees are forbidden to use liquor or to have associations or correspondence with certain categories of undesirable persons. Typically, they must seek permission from their parole officers before engaging in specified activities, such as changing employment or living quarters, marrying or acquiring or operating a motor vehicle, traveling outside the community, and incurring substantial indebtedness. Additionally, parolees must regularly report to the parole officer to whom they are assigned and sometimes they must make periodic written reports of their activities.[94]

Obviously, such conditions constitute a limitation on important federal constitutional rights. The waiver implicit in probation or parole did not, for many years, trouble courts, which reasoned that parole or probation was a matter of grace and that therefore even unconstitutional conditions could be attached to it. Such courts generally required that the challenged condition bear only a reasonable relation to the goals of criminal justice since probation is not a right, but a mere privilege.[95]

---

[92] Connecticut Bd of Pardons v Dumschat, 101 S Ct 2460 (1981); *see also* Jago v Van Curen, 102 S Ct 31 (1981) (no right to hearing when parole board, after granting parole, learned parolee had not been truthful during interview and summarily and without hearing, denied parole).

[93] 408 US 471 (1972).

[94] *Id* 478.

[95] *See, e.g.*, Edwards v State, 74 Wis 2d 79, 246 NW2d 109 (1976) (holding probation on the condition that the female defendant stay away from the codefendant she had helped escape from prison, and whom she wished to marry, valid because the condition was reasonable and parole is not a matter of right, but a mere privilege); *see also* the bizarre decision in Malone v United States, 502 F2d 554 (9th Cir 1974), *cert denied*, 419 US 1124 (1975).

However, the Supreme Court has explicitly rejected the concept that whether due process protects the loss of entitlement depends on whether the entitlement is characterized as a right or a privilege,[96] and for that reason, some courts have attempted to better articulate the basis for limiting constitutional rights in such circumstances.

The California courts have adopted a rule permitting curtailment of constitutional rights as a condition of probation when: (1) the conditions reasonably relate to the purposes sought by the legislation which confers the benefit; (2) the value of the condition to the public outweighs any impairment of the defendant's constitutional rights; and (3) there is no alternative means of achieving the governmental objective less subversive of constitutional rights.[97] Thus, California courts have upheld as a condition of probation, imposed on a person convicted of crimes which occurred during participation in violent demonstrations, that the defendant not participate in any further demonstrations,[98] but have refused to uphold a condition that the defendant neither become a member of an organization which engages in such activities nor write or publish articles for such organizations.[99] A similar approach has been adopted by the Ninth Circuit, which first considers whether the purposes for which the judge imposed the conditions are permissible, then determines whether, if permissible, the conditions are reasonably related to their purpose, and finally, whether the impact of the conditions is substantially greater than is necessary to carry out their purposes.[100]

Courts are most reluctant to completely limit a person's right to associate with another related person,[101] except, of course, where the relative was the victim of the crime.[102] It has been held that a condition of probation that the probationer consent to search at any time is invalid.[103]

---

[96] *See, e.g.*, Graham v Richardson, 403 US 365, 374 (1971); see generally Van Alstyne, *The Demise of the Right-Privilege Distinction in Constitutional Law*, 81 Harv L Rev 1439 (1968).

[97] *In re* Mannino, 14 Cal App 3d 953, 92 Cal Rptr 880 (1971).

[98] People v King, 267 Cal App 3d 814, 73 Cal Rptr 440 (1969), *cert denied*, 396 US 1028 (1970).

[99] *In re* Mannino, 14 Cal App 3d 953, 92 Cal Rptr 880 (1971).

[100] Hidgon v United States, 627 F2d 888, 898 (9th Cir 1980); see generally Annot, *Propriety of Conditioning Probation or Suspended Sentence on a Defendant's Refraining From Political Activity, Protest or the Like*, 45 ALR3d 1022.

[101] State v Martin, 282 Or 583, 580 P2d 536 (1978).

[102] State v Credeur, 328 So 2d 59 (La 1976) (father prohibited from associating with his 11-year-old child who he was convicted of sexually assaulting). See generally Annot, *Propriety of Conditioning Probation on Defendant's Not Associating With Particular Person*, 99 ALR3d 967.

[103] Grubbs v Stater, 373 So 2d 905 (Fla 1979).

§18.16 —Payment of Fine

Most states provide that crime may be punished by fine or imprisonment, and authorize commitment in lieu of payment of the fine to allow the offender to "work off" the fine. In *Tate v Short*,[104] the United States Supreme Court held that where Texas had mandated a fines-only system for traffic offenses, the Fourteenth Amendment forbade requiring indigents to work off the fines by imprisonment, since to do so would make the maximum punishment for crime greater for indigents than for nonindigents. While the Court has disclaimed the notion that its decisions prohibit the "familiar pattern" of a sentence of "30 days or 30 dollars,"[105] most lower courts have taken the position that an indigent given the alternative of fine or imprisonment must be afforded a reasonable opportunity consistent with his or her means to pay the fine.[106]

§18.17 Procedural Requirements for Revocation of Parole or Probation

Neither parole nor probation revocation is part of a *criminal proceeding* in the sense the term is used by the United States Supreme Court. Thus, the Court has held that the full panoply of rights available to a person facing loss of liberty through criminal charges—including the right to counsel and the right to confrontation—is not applicable to parole and probation revocation hearings.[107] However, a person at liberty on either probation or parole certainly has a legal interest in retaining that liberty, and would suffer *grievous loss* if he or she were to lose it. The Court has, therefore, held that the qualified liberty interest a parolee or probationer has in retaining his or her liberty is of a magnitude sufficient to be protected by the due process clause of the Fourteenth Amendment to the federal Constitution.[108] Termination of a parolee or probationer's liberty interest requires at least an informal hearing to assure that the finding of a parole violation is based on verified facts.

In *Morrissey v Brewer*,[109] the Court outlined the constitutional minima before parole or probation could be revoked. The Court held that a hearing must be held at or near the place of the alleged parole violation or arrest. The

---

[104] 401 US 395 (1971).

[105] Williams v Illinois, 399 US 235, 243 (1970).

[106] United States v Boswell, 605 F2d 171 (5th Cir 1979); United States v Williams, 469 F2d 368 (2d Cir 1972). See generally Annot, *Ability to Pay as a Necessary Condition in Conditioning Probation or Suspended Sentence Upon Reparation or Restitution*, 73 ALR3d 1240.

[107] Gagnon v Scarpelli, 411 US 778, 782 (1973); Morrissey v Brewer, 408 US 471, 480 (1972).

[108] Morrissey v Brewer, 408 US 471 (1972).

[109] *Id* 487.

Court has characterized such an inquiry as a *preliminary hearing* to determine whether there is probable cause or reasonable ground to believe that the arrested parolee has committed acts that would constitute a violation of parole conditions. This determination must be made by someone not directly involved in the case, and may not be made by the defendant's parole officer, although it may be made by another officer not involved in the case. At the preliminary hearing, the defendant must be given notice of the charges and the notice must state particularly what parole violations have been alleged. At the preliminary hearing, the parolee must be permitted to speak and produce evidence, and must be permitted to question the person giving information on which the revocation is based, unless the hearing officer determines that an informant would be subject to a risk of harm if his or her identity were disclosed, in which case identity need not be disclosed.[110] The hearing officer must make a summary of what occurred at the hearing, and must then determine whether there is probable cause to hold the parolee for the decision of the full parole board on revocation.[111]

There must also be a full hearing, if the parolee wishes it, before parole is finally revoked. Such a hearing must be held within a reasonable time after the first hearing; the Court has suggested that a lapse of two months would not be unreasonable.[112] The minimum requirements of a final hearing include:

(a) written notice of the claimed violations of parole; (b) disclosure to the parolee of evidence against him; (c) opportunity to be heard in person and to present witnesses and documentary evidence; (d) the right to confront and cross-examine adverse witnesses (unless the hearing officer finds good cause for not allowing confrontation); (e) a neutral and detached hearing body such as a traditional parole board, members of which need not be judicial officers or lawyers; and (f) a written statement by the factfinders as to the evidence relied upon and reasons for revoking parole.[113]

The Court stated that the hearing process should be flexible enough to include evidence such as letters and affidavits which would not ordinarily be admissible in a criminal case.[114] Lower courts are divided on the issue of whether illegally obtained evidence may be considered at such a hearing.[115]

---

[110] *Id.*

[111] *Id* 488.

[112] *Id* 489.

[113] *Id* 489.

[114] *Id.*

[115] *Compare* United States v Winsett, 518 F2d 51 (9th Cir 1975) *with* United States v Workman, 585 F2d 1207 (4th Cir 1978); see generally Annot, *Admissibility in Federal Probation Revocation Hearing of Evidence Obtained Through Unreasonable Search or Seizure or in Violation of Miranda*, 30 ALR Fed 824.

Although it has not required that counsel be afforded indigents in all probation or parole revocation hearings, the United States Supreme Court has held that counsel must be appointed whenever *fundamental fairness* would require it.[116] The decision must be made on a case-by-case basis. The Court stated that, presumptively, counsel should be appointed in cases where, after being informed of the right to request counsel, the parolee or probationer makes a timely request based on a colorable claim either that he has not committed the alleged violation of the parole or probation conditions, or that, even if the violation is a matter of public record, there are substantial reasons which justified or mitigated the violation and make revocation inappropriate, and that the reasons are complex or otherwise difficult to develop.[117] In doubtful cases, the court must consider whether defendants appear capable of speaking for themselves.[118]

Finally, the fundamental fairness requirement of the due process clause of the Fourteenth Amendment forbids a state to institute revocation proceedings against a person after the state has manifested a *gross disinterest* in the parolee over a period of time.[119] What constitutes gross disinterest depends on the facts of each case.[120]

§18.18 Due Process When Credits on Sentence Are Revoked

Most state penal systems provide that a convict may earn credit on his or her sentence by good conduct. Such credit is not a mere expectancy, once it is earned, but is a legally protected interest. Yet, because of the circumscribed liberty interests of prisoners and the institutional needs of prisons, the process due before such credits can be taken away is even more rudimentary than that required to revoke parole or probation.[121]

Before such credits may be taken away, a person must be afforded a hearing. The prisoner must have written notice of the charges and must be afforded at least 24 hours to prepare a defense.[122] The prisoner must be allowed to call witnesses and present documentary evidence when to do so will not be unduly hazardous to institutional safety or correctional goals.[123] Cross-examination of

---

[116] Gagnon v Scarpelli, 411 US 778, 790 (1973). An example of such a case is Wood v Georgia, 101 S Ct 1097 (1981).

[117] Gagnon v Scarpelli, 411 US 778, 791 (1973).

[118] *Id.*

[119] Shields v Beto, 370 F2d 1003 (5th Cir 1967); State v Sheehy, 115 NH 175, 337 A2d 348 (1975).

[120] Shields v Beto, 370 F2d 1003 (5th Cir 1967).

[121] Wolff v McDonnell, 418 US 539, 560 (1974).

[122] *Id* 564.

[123] *Id* 566.

the administration witnesses is not required.[124] A written statement by the fact-finders of the evidence relied on and reasons for the administrative action must be made.[125] There is no right to retained or appointed counsel at such hearings, but where an illiterate inmate is involved, or where the complexity of the case makes it unlikely that the inmate will be able to call and present the evidence necessary for an adequate consideration of the case, the inmate must be allowed to seek the aid of a fellow prisoner or member of the prison staff.[126]

---

[124] *Id* 567-69.
[125] *Id* 564.
[126] *Id* 570.

19

Appeal and Postconviction Remedies

In General

§19.01 Constitutional Right to Appeal

Every state provides a defendant a method of challenging a criminal conviction by appeal. Moreover, in most states, habeas corpus, a civil proceeding in which the sufficiency of the criminal conviction may be examined, is available. Other proceedings such as coram nobis may also be available.[1] Finally, the federal habeas corpus statute is available to allow a person convicted of a crime to challenge the constitutionality of his or her conviction.[2] Frequently, statutory remedies such as motions for new trial or vacation of sentence are provided.

Because of the multitude of means provided a defendant to attack a conviction in state and federal courts, most constitutional litigation concerning appeal has concerned the rights which must be afforded indigents who wish to take advantage of the avenues afforded by the state to challenge their convictions. What avenues a state chooses to provide however, seems to be a matter which is wholly within the state's discretion.

In 1894, the first Justice Harlan rejected the contention that the right to an appeal of a criminal conviction was required by the privileges and immunities clause or any other provision of the federal Constitution:

> An appeal from a judgment of conviction is not a matter of absolute right, independently of statutory or constitutional provisions allowing such appeal. A review by an appellate court of the final judgment in a criminal case, however grave the offense of which the accused was convicted, was not at common law, and is not now, a necessary element of due process of law. It is wholly within the discretion of the state to allow or not allow such a review.[3]

The United States Supreme Court has stated in dicta in recent years that there is no federal constitutional requirement that any appeal at all be afforded criminal defendants.[4] This fact is more a matter of curiosity than of relevance to modern criminal practice.

§19.02 Indigent's Right to Appeal

In a series of cases, beginning in 1956 with *Griffin v Illinois*,[5] the United States Supreme Court invalidated state statutes which restricted an indigent's ability to appeal because he could not afford to purchase a transcript of his trial,

---

[1] *See, e.g.*, Lane v Brown, 372 US 477 (1963).

[2] *See, e.g.*, Sumner v Mata, 449 US 539 (1981); Wainwright v Sykes, 433 US 72 (1977); Stone v Powell, 428 US 465 (1976); Johnson v Zerbst, 304 US 458 (1938).

[3] McKane v Durston, 153 US 684, 687 (1894).

[4] *See, e.g.*, United States v MacCollum, 426 US 317, 324-25 (1976); Ross v Moffitt, 417 US 600, 606 (1974).

[5] Griffin v Illinois, 351 US 12 (1956); Draper v Washington, 372 US 487 (1963); an alternative to a full transcript is permissible, if the state can show that the alternative will suffice, Mayer v City of Chicago, 404 US 189 (1971).

or could not afford the filing fee necessary to appeal[6] or could not afford an attorney.[7] Relying on the Fourteenth Amendment guarantee of equal protection of the laws, and drawing support from the Fourteenth Amendment guarantee of due process, the Court seemingly rejected the concept that any distinction between indigents and nonindigents who were deprived of their liberty and who wished to challenge their convictions could be made. In *Smith v Bennett*,[8] for example, the Court held that an Iowa statute which required a filing fee to process habeas corpus petitions, as applied to indigents, violated the Fourteenth Amendment. In *Lane v Brown*,[9] the Court held that an Indiana statute which provided that only a public defender could request a free copy of a transcript of a defendant's trial to obtain coram nobis review violated the Fourteenth Amendment, even though Indiana law provided for appointment of counsel for indigents on direct appeal. Justice Stewart stated:

> The present case falls clearly within the area staked out by the court's decision in *Griffin* [and the other cases discussed in this section]. To be sure this case does not involve . . . a direct appeal from a criminal conviction, but . . . the *Griffin* principle also applies to state collateral proceedings, and . . . the principle applies even though the State has already provided one review on the merits.[10]

While *Lane* has not been expressly overruled, the United States Supreme Court severely limited its impact in *Ross v Moffitt*,[11] in which the Court held that no provision of the federal Constitution required that counsel be afforded an indigent for discretionary appeals to either the North Carolina Supreme Court or the United States Supreme Court after he had been afforded free counsel on appeal to the North Carolina Court of Appeals. The Court stated that the "precise rationale" for the *Griffin-Douglas* line of cases had "never been explicitly stated," and suggested that neither the equal protection clause nor the due process clause of the Fourteenth Amendment alone could account for the result reached.[12] In establishing a rationale for what was required by the federal Constitution, Justice Rehnquist wrote for a six-man majority:

---

[6] Burns v Ohio, 360 US 252 ability to appeal because he could not afford to purchase a transcript of his trial, or (1959).

[7] Douglas v California, 372 US 353 (1963). Of course, the defendant's counsel must act as an advocate. Entsminger v Iowa, 386 US 748 (1967). But an indigent has no constitutional right to have an attorney prosecute a frivolous appeal. Polk County v Dodson 102 S Ct 445, 452 (1981).

[8] 365 US 708 (1961).

[9] 372 US 477 (1963).

[10] *Id* 484-85.

[11] 417 US 600 (1974).

[12] *Id* 608-09.

[T]he fact that a particular service might be of benefit to an indigent defendant does not mean that the service is constitutionally required. The duty of the state under our cases is not to duplicate the legal arsenal that may be privately retained by a criminal defendant in a continuing effort to reverse his conviction, but only to assure the indigent defendant an adequate opportunity to present his claims fairly in the context of the State's appellate process.[13]

Since *Ross*, while not overruling *Lane*, the Supreme Court has given *Lane* a much narrower reading. In *United States v MacCollum*,[14] for example, a four-judge plurality of the Court held that there was no constitutional requirement that an indigent who sought vacation of his sentence pursuant to 28 USC §2255 be afforded a free transcript of his trial, even though he had not appealed his conviction. The plurality held that since the defendant could have had an appeal if he had desired, and the district judge had statutory authority to require a transcript to be made if he believed the defendant's suit was not frivolous or if the transcript was needed to decide the issue presented, the defendant had "an adequate opportunity to attack his conviction."[15]

§19.03 Waiver of Appeal

Although there is no federal constitutional right to appeal per se, courts are reluctant to find a waiver of the right to appeal has occurred. Since an indigent defendant has a constitutional right to counsel for at least a single appeal from a judgment of conviction, if the state affords appeal rights to nonindigents, waiver of appeal may not be inferred from silence; rather, there must be an intentional abandonment or relinquishment of a known right.[16] But the United States Supreme Court has sustained statutes which provide that an appeal is automatically dismissed if the defendant escapes from confinement pending appeal,[17] even if the defendant is recaptured before the appeal is scheduled to be heard.[18]

---

[13] *Id* 616.

[14] 426 US 317 (1976).

[15] *Id* 328. *See also* Wainwright v Torna, 102 S Ct 1300 (1982) (no 6th Amendment right to counsel for discretionary appeals to the Florida Supreme Court exists, if a defendant has been afforded counsel for an appeal to an intermediate Florida court).

[16] Swenson v Bosler, 386 US 258 (1967).

[17] Molinaro v New Jersey, 396 US 365, 366 (1970).

[18] Estelle v Dorrough, 420 US 534, 542 (1975).

Sentencing on Conviction Following Successful Appeal

§19.04 Sentencing on Conviction After Trial De Novo

Almost half the states have a two-tier system of adjudicating less serious criminal cases.[19] In such jurisdictions, a less serious criminal charge, usually a misdemeanor, is tried first to an inferior court. If the defendant is found not guilty, the matter ends but a defendant who is convicted may appeal for a trial de novo. If the defendant appeals for a trial de novo in a court of general jurisdiction, the judgment and sentence below are vacated, and the parties stand as if the first proceeding had never occurred. In some of the state systems, there is no right to a jury in the inferior court; the United States Supreme Court has held that even in those circumstances, the de novo procedure is not violative of a defendant's federal constitutional rights.[20]

Of course, because the parties stand on trial de novo as if there had been no proceeding below, the judge at the second trial may logically impose a greater sentence than the judge imposed in the first case if the defendant is convicted. Distinguishing those cases in which a defendant is reconvicted of the same crime after a successful appeal, the United States Supreme Court has held that there is no constitutional bar to such increased sentences, as a general rule. In *Colten v Kentucky*,[21] the Court distinguished *North Carolina v Pearce*,[22] which held that due process bars the imposition of a heavier sentence on a defendant convicted of the same crime after appeal to an appellate court, unless that sentence is based on conduct of the defendant since the first trial, because allowing courts to increase sentences without additional reasons to do so could deter a defendant from appealing or collaterally attacking a conviction. The Court stated, "we see no reason, and none is offered, to assume that the *de novo* court will deal any more strictly with those who insist on a trial in the superior court after conviction in [an inferior court]."[23]

Attorneys who practice in a jurisdiction where a de novo system exists can, however, think of many reasons why a superior court might deal more strictly with those appealing from inferior courts, particularly in those jurisdictions where jury trial is only available on appeal. Perhaps the most obvious motive for increase of sentence would be to deter appeal to avoid the expense of jury trial for relatively minor cases. This concern is so real that a number of courts,

---

[19] The jurisdictions retaining such a system are set out in Colten v Kentucky, 407 US 104, 112 n 4 (1972).

[20] Ludwig v Massachusetts, 427 US 618 (1976).

[21] 407 US 104 (1972).

[22] 395 US 711 (1969).

[23] Colten v Kentucky, 407 US 104, 117 (1972).

in states where a trial de novo system exists, have held as a matter of state constitutional law that an increase in sentence following conviction after appeal for trial de novo is impermissible unless the judge makes findings setting out the reasons for the increased sentence.[24]

The United States Supreme Court has held, however, that a prosecutor may not initiate a felony charge after a defendant appeals for trial de novo from a misdemeanor based on the same conduct unless the prosecutor can show that it was impossible to proceed on a felony charge at the outset.[25]

§19.05 Sentencing on Conviction After Appeal

A defendant who is successful on appeal may be retried for the same offense unless the reversal was obtained on the grounds that the evidence was insufficient to convict.[26] If the defendant is retried for the same offense and is convicted, a second sentence is imposed. The United States Supreme Court has held that the constitutional prohibition against multiple punishments for the same offense requires that punishment exacted on the first conviction must be credited in imposing sentence on the new conviction for the same offense.[27]

Of course, a judge may vitiate the effect of any credit on the second sentence by simply increasing the sentence imposed on the second conviction, except, obviously, in cases in which the maximum sentence was imposed for the first conviction. In *North Carolina v Pearce*,[28] the Supreme Court held that neither the equal protection nor the due process clause of the Fourteenth Amendment bars imposition of a more severe sentence on reconviction, since events subsequent to the first conviction may have thrown "new light on the defendant's life, health, habits, conduct and mental and moral propensities."[29] Such a view is premised on the rehabilitative model of sentencing.[30]

However, the Court did recognize in *Pearce* that the potential for a heavier sentence on retrial could deter a defendant from exercising the right to appeal. Thus, the Court established as a matter of federal constitutional law that whenever a judge imposes a more severe sentence on a defendant after a new trial, the reasons for doing so must affirmatively appear in the record.[31] The

---

[24] *See e.g.*, State v Wheeler, 120 NH 496, 416 A2d 1384 (1980).

[25] Blackledge v Perry, 417 US 21 (1974).

[26] Burks v United States, 437 US 1 (1978).

[27] North Carolina v Pearce, 395 US 711, 718-19 (1969).

[28] *Id*.

[29] *Id* 723.

[30] *See* §18.01.

[31] North Carolina v Pearce, 395 US 711, 726 (1969). The holding in *Pearce* is not retroactive. Michigan v Payne, 412 US 47 (1973).

reasons "must be based upon objective information concerning identifiable conduct on the part of the defendant occurring after the time of the original sentencing proceeding."[32] Moreover, the factual data must be made a part of the record so that the constitutional legitimacy of the increased sentence may be fully reviewed on appeal.[33] A few states permit juries to sentence defendants in noncapital cases. The United States Supreme Court has held that *Pearce* has no application to such systems, as long as the jury is not informed of the prior sentence and the sentence is not otherwise a product of vindictiveness.[34]

§19.06 Sentence of Death Following Appeal of Conviction in Which Death Penalty Was Not Imposed

While adhering to the view taken in *North Carolina v Pearce*[35] that the imposition of a particular sentence is not regarded as an "acquittal" of a more severe sentence within the meaning of the double jeopardy clause, the United States Supreme Court has established a different view in cases involving the death penalty, in which the state is required to prove specific facts to convince the jury it should impose the death penalty. In *Bullington v Missouri*[36] the defendant had been convicted of murder, and then, pursuant to the Missouri penalty statute, a separate hearing was held in which evidence in mitigation and aggravation of the offense was admitted. Under Missouri law, the prosecution was required to prove the existence of aggravating circumstances by a standard of beyond a reasonable doubt before the death penalty could be imposed, and the jury was required to specify in writing the aggravating circumstances it found beyond a reasonable doubt. At the defendant's sentencing hearing, the jury fixed a sentence of life imprisonment. His conviction was reversed, and on retrial, the state gave notice that it intended to seek the death penalty.

The United States Supreme Court held that the double jeopardy clause of the Fifth Amendment barred the state from seeking the death penalty on retrial. The Court reasoned that the state had, by enacting a sentencing proceeding that is like a trial on the issue of guilt and innocence, and which required the jury to determine whether the prosecution had "proved its case," created a system different from mere sentencing. The Court held that the sentence of imprisonment was, in effect, akin to an acquittal of the death penalty and that the jury's determination was absolutely final, and the states could not seek the

---

[32] North Carolina v Pearce, 395 US 711, 726 (1969).
[33] *Id* 726.
[34] Chaffin v Stynchcombe, 412 US 17 (1973).
[35] 395 US 711 (1969).
[36] 451 US 430 (1981).

death penalty, based on the same aggravating circumstances, in a second trial, consistent with the double jeopardy clause.[37]

Arguments on Appeal

§19.07 Harmless Constitutional Error

Even if an error of constitutional magnitude has been committed at a person's trial, the prosecutor may, on appeal, argue that the error was harmless. In *Chapman v California*,[38] the United States Supreme Court rejected the proposition that any violation of a defendant's constitutional rights in the course of criminal proceedings which resulted in a conviction requires that the conviction be reversed. The Court noted that harmless error rules and statutes exist in every state, and that such rules and statutes serve an important purpose in avoiding reversal of convictions on grounds which have little likelihood of changing the result of a trial.[39] However, a prosecutor who alleges that error was harmless bears a great burden. He or she must demonstrate beyond a reasonable doubt that the error did not affect the verdict.[40] This requires the reviewing appellate court to make a de novo assessment of the entire trial record.[41]

In the case before it in *Chapman*, the Court held that a California prosecutor's comment on the defendant's failure to testify was not harmless error.[42] The Court made clear that there were certain types of constitutional error which could never be harmless.[43] It is generally held that admission of a coerced confession,[44] violation of the right to counsel,[45] use of an invalid prior conviction,[46] or trial before a partial judge,[47] can never be harmless error. Virtually every other aspect of criminal procedure, including illegal search or seizure,[48] violation of the constitutional rules relating to identification proceedings,[49] and violation of the rule of *Bruton v United States*[50] (which forbids admissions of one defendant

---

[37] *Id.*

[38] 386 US 18 (1967).

[39] *Id* 22.

[40] *Id* 26; *see also* Fahy v Connecticut, 375 US 85, 86-87 (1963).

[41] Chapman v California, 386 US 18, 56 (1967) (Harlan, J, dissenting).

[42] *Id* 26.

[43] *Id* 23 n 6.

[44] Payne v Arkansas, 356 US 560 (1958).

[45] Holloway v Arkansas, 435 US 475 (1978). *But see* United States v Morrison, 101 S Ct 665, 668 (1981).

[46] Burgett v Texas, 389 US 109 (1967).

[47] Tumey v Ohio, 273 US 510 (1927).

[48] Bumper v North Carolina, 391 US 543 (1968).

[49] Moore v Illinois, 434 US 220 (1977); Foster v California, 394 US 440 (1969).

[50] 391 US 123 (1968).

to be admitted at a trial of the defendant and a codefendant), may in some circumstances be harmless error.[51]

Postappeal Remedies

§19.08 Habeas Corpus

Habeas corpus is perhaps the most commonly misused term in modern criminal practice. Habeas corpus is a generic term, and includes many species of the writ, including the *habeas corpus ad prosequendum*, used at common law to remove a prisoner in order to prosecute him in the proper jurisdiction in which his offense was committed,[52] and the *habeas corpus ad testificandum*, which was issued at common law when it was necessary to bring a prisoner forward to have him testify.[53] But the term habeas corpus has been generally used in the last 50 years not in speaking of a writ, but in speaking of a civil action which may be brought to obtain the release of a person convicted of crime. This function of habeas corpus involves the writ of *habeas corpus ad subjiciendum*. It is this writ which is referred to in the Constitution, and which Chief Justice Marshall referred to as the *great writ*.[54] Most state constitutions contain provisions, like the one in the federal Constitution, providing that the writ may not be suspended.

Habeas corpus was created in England to protect individuals from incarceration without trial. Thus, at common law, the inquiry on habeas corpus was narrow; a court on habeas corpus would inquire only into whether the court pronouncing sentence had jurisdiction to do so.

The United States Supreme Court has for over 100 years, however, allowed habeas corpus, pursuant to the federal habeas corpus statute,[55] to be used to attack constitutional errors made at trial.[56] Indeed, by 1938, the Court rationalized the expanded scope of habeas corpus by reasoning that a court which acts in violation of a person's constitutional rights divests itself of jurisdiction. In *Johnson v Zerbst*,[57] the Court noted:

> Congress has expanded the rights of a petitioner for habeas corpus, and the . . . effect is to substitute for the bare legal review that seems to have been the limit of judicial authority at common law practice, and under the

---

[51] Parker v Randolph, 442 US 62 (1979) (Blackmun, J, concurring); Schneble v Florida, 405 US 427 (1972).

[52] *See, e.g., Ex parte* Bollman, 8 US (4 Cranch 75 (1807).

[53] The various forms of the writ at common law are set out in 3 *W. Blackstone Commentaries*, (U Chi ed 1979).

[54] *Ex parte* Bollman, 8 US (4 Cranch) 75,95 (1807).

[55] 28 USC §2254.

[56] *See, e.g., Ex parte* Neilson, 131 US 176 (1889).

[57] 304 US 458 (1938).

act of 31 Car. II, chap. 2, a more searching investigation, in which the applicant is put on his oath to set forth the truth of the matter respecting the cause of his detention, and the court, upon determing the actual facts, is to dispose of the party as law and justice require.[58]

The modern scope of relief available on habeas corpus is a matter of federal statutory law, rather than constitutional law, and is beyond the scope of this work. While federal habeas corpus may be a valuable vehicle by which to assert constitutional rights, it is not merely a method by which an out-of-time appeal may be obtained; in some circumstances, it may not be available to a defendant.[59]

§19.09 Pardon

The federal Constitution,[60] as do most state constitutions, vests the pardoning power in the executive. While in 1867 the United States Supreme Court held that a pardon reaches both the punishment and the guilt of a person, "so that in the eye of the law the offender is as innocent as if he had never committed the offense,"[61] state courts have questioned this pronouncement.[62]

The scope and effect of the pardoning power is seldom litigated. However, in 1974 in *Schick v Reed*,[63] the Court held that the federal pardoning power flows from the Constitution alone, and that a pardon from a death penalty conditioned on a sentence of imprisonment for life without parole granted in 1960 was not violative of the recipient's constitutional rights despite the fact that, in 1972, the United States Supreme Court held retroactively that the death penalty was unconstitutional as then imposed. The Court held that the pardoning power is an enumerated power, and that its limitations, if any, must be found in the Constitution itself.[64] It thus appears that a pardon may be offered a defendant on any condition the executive believes proper, and the defendant who accepts the pardon is bound.[65]

---

[58] *Id* 466.

[59] *See e.g.*, Stone v Powell, 428 US 465 (1976) (Fourth Amendment claims may not be litigated on habeas corpus, if the defendant has been afforded fair and full opportunity for litigation of the claim at trial); Wainwright v Sykes, 433 US 72 (1977) (habeas corpus may not be available where defendant deliberately bypassed state procedures absent an adequate showing of cause and prejudice).

[60] US Const art II, §2.

[61] *Ex parte* Garland, 71 US (4 Wall) 333, 380 (1867).

[62] See generally S. Williston, *Does a Pardon Blot Out Guilt*, 28 Harv L Rev 647 (1915).

[63] 419 US 256 (1974).

[64] *Id* 267.

[65] *Id* 266; *see also Ex parte* Wells, 59 US (18 How) 307 (1856).

20 Extradition and Interstate Transfer of Persons Resulting from Criminal Prosecutions

§20.01 Interstate Transfer in General

In a country made up of 50 sovereign states and several territories, it is inevitable that defendants and witnesses whose presence is sought in one state may be found in another. The Constitution itself provides a mandate that the several states are to cooperate in returning fugitives from one state to another.[1] Most of the states have entered into compacts to facilitate the involuntary transfer of persons who may be needed as witnesses in other states.[2] Similarly, a number of states and the federal government have entered into the Interstate Agreement on Detainers, which facilitates the transfer of prisoners held in one jurisdiction to another jurisdiction to face charges against them.[3]

While extradition is, of course, a constitutional matter, virtually all of the states have enacted uniform laws to govern the proceedings. Construction of the Interstate Agreement on Detainers has been held to be matter of federal law,[4] and it may well be that the construction of other acts related to interstate transfer of prisoners must be considered a matter of federal law.[5]

It is not the purpose of this chapter to provide an exhaustive analysis of the statutory schemes relating to these procedures, but rather to simply highlight the impact and effect of constitutional decisions on them.

Extradition

§20.02 Constitutional Basis for Extradition

Article IV, §2, cl 2 of the federal Constitution specifically requires that persons sought by one state as fugitives who flee to another state must be delivered to the first state upon request:

> The citizens of each state shall be entitled to the privileges and immunities of citizens in the several states.
>
> A person charged in any state with treason, felony, or other crime who shall flee from justice, and be found in another state, shall, on demand of

---

[1] US Const art IV, ch 2, §2; *see also* Uniform Criminal Extradition Act, 11 ULA 94 (1974).

[2] *See* Uniform Act to Secure the Attendance of Witnesses From Without a State in Criminal Cases, 11 ULA 1 (1974) (enacted in 54 jurisdictions); *see also* Uniform Rendition of Prisoners as Witnesses in Criminal Proceedings Act, 11 ULA 547 (1974).

[3] *See, e.g.*, United States v Mauro, 436 US 340 (1978).

[4] Cuyler v Adams, 449 US 433 (1981).

[5] *Id* 450 (Rehnquist J, dissenting).

the executive authority of the state from which he fled, be delivered up, to be removed to the state having jurisdiction of the crime.

No person held to service or labor in one state, under the laws thereof, escaping into another, shall, in consequence of any law or regulation therein, be discharged from such service or labor, but shall be delivered up on the claim of the party to whom such service or labor may be due.

The extradition clause was enacted to enable each of the states to bring offenders to trial in the state where the alleged offense was committed.[6] Chief Justice Burger recently noted that:

The purpose of the clause was to preclude any state from becoming a sanctuary for fugitives from another state, and thus "balkanize" the administration of criminal justice among the several states. It articulated, in mandatory language, the concepts of comity and full faith and credit, found in the immediately preceding clause of Article IV.[7]

For that reason, interstate rendition has always been characterized as a "summary and mandatory executive proceeding."[8] Extradition is said to be a constitutional duty, and a person may be extradited for any crime, including misdemeanors, known to the demanding state.[9]

While in earlier years extradition cases occupied a significant amount of the time of the United States Supreme Court, recent years have seen a drastic drop in the number of such decisions. The likely reason for the reduction in litigation has been the adoption in most jurisdictions of the Uniform Criminal Extradition Act,[10] which specifically delineates the steps to be followed in extradition proceedings.[11] There are, however, a number of specific issues which have been the subject of constitutional litigation, and these are further discussed in this chapter.

§20.03 Extradition Between Countries

Quite apart from extradition between the several states is extradition between countries. There is no constitutional right or duty on the part of the executive

---

[6] Biddinger v Commissioner of Police, 245 US 128, 132-33 (1917).

[7] Michigan v Doran, 439 US 282, 287-88 (1978).

[8] *Id* 288; *see also In re* Strauss, 197 US 324, 332 (1905). Congress has also acted to implement the extradition clause. *See* 18 USC §3182.

[9] *See, e.g.*, Appleyard v Massachusetts, 203 US 222, 226 (1906). As a practical matter, however, those accused of misdemeanors are rarely extradited.

[10] 11 ULA 51 (1974).

[11] See §20.04.

of any of the states to deliver up a fugitive to a foreign country. Indeed, it has generally been assumed as a matter of international law that, apart from treaty, there is no obligation on one country to deliver up a fugitive to another country, and that where such a delivery is made, it is made on principles of comity.[12]

Perhaps because so few legal systems afford an accused as many procedural protections as ours, American judges have, as a general rule, been most reluctant to countenance extradition of a person in the United States by a foreign sovereign. It has been uniformly held that there is no right to extradition apart from treaty.[13] Moreover, while the power to provide for extradition to a foreign state is a national one, it is not confided to the sovereign in the absence of specific authority by treaty.[14] Courts have reasoned that extradition must be confined to specific offenses enumerated in treaties, since a sovereign might be "very willing to deliver up offenders against such laws essential to the protection of life, liberty and person, while it would not be willing to do this on account of minor misdemeanors, or of a certain class of political offenses in which it would have no interest or sympathy."[15]

In sum, extradition to a foreign country is far different from extradition from one of the several states to another, and does not stand on so firm a constitutional footing.

§20.04 Mechanics of Extradition

The Uniform Criminal Extradition Law, where enacted, is an attempt to comply with the constitutional mandate of Article IV, Section 2, cl 2, and 18 USC §3182. It provides that it is the duty of the governor of an enacting state to have arrested and delivered up to the executive authority of any other state any person charged in that state with treason, felony, or other crime.[16] Extradition may be begun by a formal demand by the executive of a foreign state on the governor of the asylum state, or by arrest on oath of a credible person. However, no demand for extradition need be complied with, unless it is in writing and alleges that the accused was in the state at that time of the

---

[12] United States v Rauscher, 119 US 407, 412 (1886).

[13] *See, e.g.,* Factor v Laubenheimer, 290 US 276, 287 (1933); *see also* United States v Rauscher, 119 US 407 (1886).

[14] Valentine v United States, 299 US 5, 8 (1936).

[15] United States v Rauscher, 119 US 407, 420 (1886). However, there is authority for the proposition that extradition treaties are not to be strictly construed. Factor v Laubenheimer, 290 US 276, 293-94 (1933).

[16] Uniform Criminal Extradition Act §2, 11 ULA 51 (1974).

commission of the alleged crime and thereafter fled from the state.[17] The demand must contain an indictment found in the demanding state, or an information supported by affidavit, or a copy of an affidavit made before a magistrate, with a copy of any warrant issued in that state, or a copy of a judgment of conviction or sentence in that state, with a statement of the executive that the person had escaped from confinement.[18] The indictment, information, or affidavit must charge the defendant with a crime under the law of the demanding state, and it must be authenticated by the demanding state's executive.[19]

In the usual case, a demand is made on the governor of the asylum state by the governor of the demanding state. Once a demand is received, the asylum state's governor may "investigate" to determine "whether (the defendant) ought be surrendered."[20] But except as it relates to identity, the defendant's guilt or innocence may not be inquired into.[21] On deciding to comply with the request, the governor issues a warrant, which is known as a *governor's warrant*, directing the arrest of the defendant.[22] A person arrested on a governor's warrant may not be surrendered to the officers of the demanding state until after having been taken before a judge of a court of record, who must inform the accused of the demand made, of the crime of which he is charged, and that he has the right to legal counsel.[23] If the defendant seeks to test the validity of the extradition, the judge must fix a reasonable time for application for a writ of habeas corpus.[24]

The Uniform Act also provides for arrest in cases in which the governor of the asylum state has not yet issued a warrant. Whenever a credible person charges on oath before a magistrate of the asylum state that the defendant is a fugitive from justice within the meaning of the act, the judge may issue a warrant for the person's arrest.[25] A warrantless arrest for a felony is proper, but the defendant must be taken before a magistrate "with all practicable speed" and a proper complaint on oath must be made.[26] If on examination, the judge finds that the defendant is the person charged and that he or she has fled from justice, the judge

---

[17] *Id* §3.

[18] *Id.*

[19] *Id.*

[20] *Id* §4.

[21] *Id* §20.

[22] *Id* §7.

[23] *Id* §10.

[24] *Id.*

[25] *Id* §13. A warrant may also be issued if, though not present in the demanding state at the time of the offense, the person intentionally committed an act which resulted in a crime in the state the executive authority of which is making the demand. *Id* 612:6.

[26] *Id* §14.

must commit the defendant to jail for 30 days to enable the governor to issue the warrant.[27] Pending action by the governor, the defendant may be admitted to bail unless the offense is punishable by death or life imprisonment.[28] If the governor does not act within 30 days, the court may discharge the defendant or recommit the defendant for up to 60 days.[29] Of course, a person may waive extradition.[30]

The provisions of the Uniform Act, by and large, expressly reflect earlier decisions of the United States Supreme Court. In the past few years, however, litigation has begun to center on the impact of arrest pursuant to extradition and the arrestee's Fourth Amendment rights, and the duty of the governor and courts of the asylum state to return the arrested person to the demanding state.

§20.05 Duty to Surrender Fugitive to Demanding State—Executive

The language of both Article IV, §2, cl 2, and 18 USC §3182 is mandatory; both seemingly require the executive of a state to surrender a fugitive on demand to another state. Yet that appears never to have been the law. The Uniform Act itself provides that when a demand is made by the executive of another state, the executive of the asylum state may direct the attorney general or other prosecuting officer "to investigate or assist in investigating the demand, and to report to him the situation and circumstances of the person so demanded, and whether he ought be surrendered."[31] While there is some early authority for the proposition that the governor's duty to return a fugitive is merely ministerial,[32] the generally accepted view today is that the governor's duty is not "absolute or unqualified," but is "dependent upon the circumstances of each case."[33] The United States Supreme Court has explicitly left open the question of the scope of an executive's discretion.[34]

---

[27] *Id* §15.

[28] *Id* §16.

[29] *Id* §17.

[30] *Id* §25.

[31] Uniform Criminal Extradition Act §6, 11 ULA 51 (1974).

[32] *See, e.g.*, Kentucky v Dennison, 65 US (24 How) 66 (1861); *but see* Marbles v Creecy, 215 US 63, 68 (1909).

[33] Hill v Houck, 195 NW2d 692, 695 (Iowa 1972).

[34] Michigan v Doran, 439 US 282, 288 (1978).

§20.06 —Courts of Asylum State

Chief Justice Burger recently noted in dicta that "whatever the scope of discretion vested in the governor of an asylum state the courts of an asylum state are bound by Art IV §2."[35] The United States Supreme Court has been unwilling to approve the practice of allowing a fugitive to challenge return to the demanding state on the ground that constitutional rights will be violated in the demanding state, but has required that the fugitive litigate such a claim in the demanding state.[36] In *Pacileo v Walker*,[37] for example, the Court held that California courts cannot inquire into prison conditions in the demanding state to determine if those prisons operate in conformity with the Eighth Amendment to the United States Constitution. Since extradition was intended as a mandatory, executive proceeding, the Court reasoned that claims of constitutional defect may be heard in the demanding state as well as in the asylum state, and that "to allow plenary review in the asylum state of issues that can be litigated in the asylum state would defeat the plain purposes of the summary and mandatory procedures authorized by Article IV §2."[38]

A distinction has been recognized by some courts in cases in which the process of extradition itself is alleged to be violative of the accused's rights. For example, the Illinois Supreme Court held in *People ex rel Bowman v Woods*[39] that the constitutional requirement of fundamental fairness barred the extradition of the defendant who had escaped from a long sentence in Alabama for a relatively minor offense in 1951, and had had other extradition proceedings brought against him in 1955, 1957 and 1968, which were later dropped. Since the defendant had been imprisoned three times pending disposition of the extradition proceedings, the Illinois court felt compelled to grant relief. The result in *Bowman* may be reconciled with *Pacileo* and earlier cases by considering that the claim made in it—that of fundamentally unfair harassment by extradition after an unreasonable delay—could not be considered in the demanding state since the extradition which was itself the improper practice would have already occurred.

---

[35] Michigan v Doran, 439 US 282, 288 (1978).
[36] *See, e.g.*, Sweeney v Woodall, 344 US 86, 90 (1952); Pacileo v Walker, 449 US 86 (1980).
[37] 449 US 86 (1980).
[38] *Id* 88 (quoting Michigan v Doran, 439 US 282, 290 (1978)).
[39] 46 Ill 2d 572, 264 NE2d 151 (1970).

§20.07 Issues Which May Be Inquired into by a Court on Habeas Corpus

The Uniform Criminal Extradition Law provides that a person arrested on a governor's warrant may challenge the arrest on habeas corpus.[40] A person who is not satisfied with the relief afforded by state courts may, of course, invoke the habeas corpus jurisdiction of the federal courts.[41]

The issues which will be considered on habeas corpus are, however, narrow. They have traditionally been stated as follows:

(1) Whether the extradition documents on their face are in order

(2) Whether the petitioner has been charged with a crime in the demanding state

(3) Whether the petitioner is, in fact, the person named in the request for extradition

(4) Whether the petitioner is a fugitive[42]

As used in the act, the word *crime* embraces any offense known to the demanding state, including misdemeanors.[43] The sufficiency of the indictment or complaint under the law of the demanding jurisdiction may not be inquired into on habeas corpus.[44]

The word *fugitive*, as used in the act, is a word of art. A person is a fugitive within the meaning of the act if, at the time of the alleged offense, he or she was in the demanding state, and if, at the time of arrest, he or she is in the asylum state; there is no requirement that the accused consciously have fled from the demanding state in order to be considered a fugitive.[45]

In the wake of the United States Supreme Court's holding in *Gerstein v Pugh*[46] that the Fourth Amendment requires a judicial determination of probable cause as a prerequisite to extend restraint of liberty following arrest, a number of courts have wrestled with the impact of *Gerstein* on extradition proceedings. In *Michigan v Doran*,[47] the United States Supreme Court assumed, without

---

[40] Uniform Criminal Extradition Act §10, 11 ULA 51 (1974).

[41] *See, e.g.*, Sweeney v Woodall, 344 US 86 (1952).

[42] Michigan v Doran, 439 US 282, 289 (1978).

[43] Hogan v O'Neil, 255 US 552, 555 (1921).

[44] Munsey v Clough, 196 US 364, 372 (1905).

[45] Appleyard v Massachusetts, 203 US 222, 226 (1906).

[46] 420 US 103 (1975).

[47] 439 US 282 (1978).

deciding, that the Fourth Amendment requirements of *Gerstein* are applicable to extradition proceedings, and held that Article IV §2 requires the courts of the asylum state to accept the demanding state's determination of probable cause. It thus appears that, on habeas corpus, a petitioner seeking to avoid extradition may, at a minimum, assert that the extradition papers are insufficient if they do not facially reflect a judicial finding of probable cause in the demanding state.[48]

§20.08 Successive Extradition Proceedings

It has long been settled that the principle of double jeopardy has no application to either interstate[49] or international[50] extradition. The Fifth Amendment prohibition of double jeopardy is not applicable because extradition is merely a preliminary step in the criminal proceedings.[51]

A number of courts have considered the effect of collateral estoppel on extradition proceedings as well. Most courts have taken the position that the doctrine is not applicable to extradition proceedings at all,[52] reasoning that extradition is an even more preliminary step in a criminal proceeding than the institution of criminal charges, which may be filed and abated and then refiled at the prosecutor's discretion. Thus, for example, the California Supreme Court has held that a second extradition proceeding is not barred by principles of res judicata where habeas corpus was granted in the first extradition proceeding after an express finding that the defendant was not a fugitive. Even in jurisdictions holding that the doctrine of res judicata would be applicable in such circumstances, the prosecution may move to reopen the original proceeding to present additional evidence.[53] A few courts hold that res judicata would bar subsequent extradition proceedings after a court has made a decision favorable to the defendant, where the subsequent extradition proceeding is based on precisely the same evidence as the former proceedings.[54]

Even in the jurisdictions which do not recognize any bar to successive extradition proceedings, it has been said that the due process requirement of

---

[48] *Id* 297-98 (Blackmun, J, concurring).

[49] Bassing v Cady, 208 US 386 (1908).

[50] Collins v Loisel, 262 US 426 (1923).

[51] *Id* 429; *see also In re* Russell, 12 Cal 3d 229, 524 P2d 1295, 115 Cal Rptr 511 (1974).

[52] *See, e.g., In re* Russell, 12 Cal 3d 229, 524 P2d 1295, 115 Cal Rptr 511 (1974); *In re* Maldonado, 364 Mass 359, 304 NE2d 419 (1973).

[53] Wells v Sheriff, Carter County, 442 P2d 535 (Okla Crim App 1968).

[54] Boyd v Cleave, 180 Colo 403, 505 P2d 1305 (1973); Stack v State, 333 So 2d 509 (Fla Dist Ct App 1976).

fundamental fairness may require release of a defendant who has been unduly harassed by successive petitions.[55]

Detainers

§20.09 Definition of Detainers

Although the term *detainer* is commonly used by attorneys conversant in criminal procedure, there is no single, explicit definition of a detainer. Rather, a detainer is generally considered to be a notification of any kind filed with an institution in which a prisoner is serving a sentence, advising that the prisoner is wanted to face pending criminal charges in another jurisdiction.[56] Commonly, a detainer is filed by state or federal authorities on an inmate imprisoned in some other state. The filing of a detainer at an institution may have serious consequences for the prisoner. In many systems, prisoners who have detainers lodged against them are not permitted to take part in prison programs aimed at rehabilitation.[57] Moreover, the presence of a detainer obviously may create in the inmate the same sort of anxiety created by the experience of awaiting trial; indeed, the anxiety may be exacerbated because the prisoner may not be able to contest the charges or prepare a defense if they have been brought in another jurisdiction. For that reason, certain constitutional doctrines and the Interstate Agreement on Detainers have been created to ameliorate some of the problems inherent in a federal system.

§20.10 Constitutional Right to Be Brought to Trial on a Detainer

When charges remain outstanding against an individual, his or her Sixth Amendment right to a speedy trial is implicated.[58] That a defendant against whom charges have been lodged is confined in another jurisdiction and cannot voluntarily return to the jurisdiction in which charges are pending does not render the denial of the right to a speedy trial any less serious. Indeed, the abilities of persons confined in prison to defend themselves are markedly decreased when they are confined in institutions which may be far from the place

---

[55] *In re* Maldonado, 364 Mass 359, 304 NE2d 419, (1973).
[56] United States v Mauro, 436 US 340, 359 (1978).
[57] *Id.*
[58] Smith v Hooey, 393 US 374 (1969).

of a crime. An accused may be unable to confer with potential defense witnesses, investigate the case, or even keep track of potential defense witnesses.[59] For that reason, the United States Supreme Court held in *Smith v Hooey*[60] that the Sixth Amendment requires that when a person who is incarcerated makes a demand for trial on the jurisdiction which has filed a detainer, that jurisdiction has a constitutional duty to make a diligent good faith effort to bring the defendant before the court in which the charges are pending for trial, even if there is no statutory right to compel the incarcerated prisoner's presence.

The holding in *Smith v Hooey* is of limited practical importance at present, since almost all American jurisdictions and the federal government have enacted the Interstate Agreement on Detainers[61] which establishes a method by which prisoners held in one jurisdiction may be transferred for trial in another jurisdiction, and provides for dismissal of charges if such a request is made by a prisoner and not honored.

§20.11 The Interstate Agreement on Detainers

The Interstate Agreement on Detainers had, by 1981, been adopted by 48 states, the District of Columbia, and the federal government.[62] The act explicitly recognizes the detrimental effect of outstanding criminal charges on prisoners, and provides that its purpose is to facilitate the disposition of such charges and to provide cooperative procedures among member states to facilitate such disposition.[63] In furtherance of its objectives, the act permits prisoners against whom a detainer has been filed to demand trial. It provides, in substance, that the warden of the institution in which the prisoner is incarcerated must inform the prisoner promptly of the detainer and of the right to request final disposition of the charges.[64] If the prisoner does make such a request, the jurisdiction that filed the detainer must bring him or her to trial within 180 days, although the court having jurisdiction of the matter may, for good cause shown in open court, with the prisoner and counsel present, grant any necessary or reasonable continuance.[65] The prisoner's request operates as a request for disposition of

---

[59] *Id.*

[60] *Id* 384.

[61] *See* 11 ULA 323 (1974); Cuyler v Adams, 449 US 433 (1981).

[62] Cuyler v Adams, 449 US 433, 437 n 1 (1981).

[63] Interstate Agreement on Detainers art I, 11 ULA 323 (1974).

[64] *Id* art III(c); United States v Mauro, 436 US 340, 351 (1978).

[65] Interstate Agreement on Detainers, 11 ULA 323 (1974). art II(a).

all untried charges underlying the detainer filed against that prisoner by the same jurisdiction, and is deemed to be a waiver of extradition.[66]

A prosecuting attorney may also use the act to secure the presence of a defendant who is incarcerated in another jurisdiction. Once a detainer has been filed, a prosecutor can obtain the presence of the defendant by presenting a written request to the officials in the state in which the defendant is incarcerated for the prisoner's temporary custody.[67] Trial must be had within 120 days, unless the court, for good cause shown, in open court with the prisoner present, grants a continuance.[68] If trial is not had on any indictment prior to the defendant's return to the original place of imprisonment, the indictment is of no further force and effect.[69]

However, enactment of the Interstate Agreement on Detainers was not intended to deprive prisoners of the safeguards of the extradition process. The United States Supreme Court has held, as a matter of statutory construction, that prisoners transferred pursuant to the agreement at a prosecutor's request have the same rights that a person whose extradition is sought has to challenge extradition.[70] Thus, in jurisdictions which have enacted the Uniform Criminal Extradition Law, an incarcerated person whose presence is sought by a prosecutor in the demanding state has the right to bring a habeas corpus petition to challenge the transfer.[71]

Because the Interstate Agreement was adopted by the states with Congress's consent, its interpretation is a matter of federal law.[72]

Securing Attendance of Out-of-State Witnesses

§20.12 Uniform Act to Secure the Attendance of Witnesses From Without a State in Criminal Cases

The ability of the several states to obtain jurisdiction over defendants who have taken refuge in other states would mean little if witnesses could put themselves beyond the reach of a court by simply going to another jurisdiction.

---

[66] *Id* art III(d), (e).

[67] *Id* art VI(a).

[68] *Id* art IV(c).

[69] *Id* art IV(e).

[70] Cuyler v Adams, 449 US 433 (1981).

[71] The issues open to a person in such a hearing are discussed in **§20.07**.

[72] Cuyler v Adams, 449 US 433, 442 (1981).

In recognition of this fact, 54 jurisdictions have enacted the Uniform Act to Secure the Attendance of Witnesses From Without a State in Criminal Cases.[73]

The act is operative only in states which have enacted similar legislation. A judge in a requesting state may file in any court of record in the asylum state a certificate stating the necessity for the appearance of the witness in a criminal prosecution or grand jury investigation in the demanding state, and how long the witness will be required to attend. On receipt of such certificate, a hearing is held by the court in which it is filed. At the hearing, the judge in the asylum state must determine whether an order to attend the prosecution or grand jury investigation would comply with the statutory requirements that the witness be material and necessary, that the trip not be an undue hardship on the witness, and that the laws of the requesting state and states through which the witness must pass grant immunity from service of process.[74] The witness must also be paid travel expenses and witness fees.

The asylum state may simply issue a summons, directing the witness to testify in the demanding state, or, if the certificate of the requesting state so recommends and the recommendation is found desirable, the court may immediately deliver the witness to an officer of the demanding state.[75] Further, if such a recommendation is made by the demanding state, a judge in the asylum state may, on receipt of the certificate, immediately take the witness into custody.[76]

The United States Supreme Court has specifically held that the Uniform Act does not violate the privileges and immunities clause [77] of the Constitution, and does not infringe the constitutional right to travel.[78] The Court has also held that the Constitution does not preclude the states from entry into such cooperative compacts to facilitate interstate transfer of witnesses in furtherance of the interests of criminal justice. However, since the subject matter of the act is one on which Congress could have chosen to legislate, it may be that interpretation of the Uniform Act, when enacted by a state, is a matter of federal law.[79]

---

[73] 11 ULA 1 (1974); 13 states have enacted the similar Uniform Rendition of Prisoners as Witnesses in Criminal Proceedings Act, 11 ULA 547 (1974).

[74] Uniform Act §2 II; *see also* New York v O'Neill, 359 US 1, 4 (1959).

[75] New York v O'Neill, 359 US 1, 5 (1959).

[76] *Id.*

[77] US Const art IV, §2.

[78] New York v O'Neill, 359 US 1 (1959).

[79] Cuyler v Adams, 449 US 433, 450 (1981) (Rehnquist, J, dissenting).

U.S. Constitution & Amendments

Constitution of the United States of America of 1787 and Amendments

Article I.
§1. Legislative powers.
§2. House of Representatives; how constituted; power of impeachment.
§3. The Senate; how constituted; impeachment trials.
§4. Election of Senators and representatives.
§5. Quorum; journals; meetings adjournments.
§6. Compensation; privileges; disabilities.
§7. Procedure in passing bills and resolutions.
§8. Powers of Congress.
§9. Limitations upon powers of Congress.
§10. Restrictions upon powers of states.

Article II.
§1. President and Vice President.
§2. Powers of the President.
§3. Messages to Congress; additional powers and duties.
§4. Impeachment.

Article III.
§1. Judicial power; tenure of office.
§2. Jurisdiction.
§3. Treason; proof and punishment.

Article IV.
§1. Full faith and credit among states.
§2. Privileges and immunities; fugitives.
§3. Admission of new states; power over territory and other property.
§4. Guarantee of republican form of government.

Article V.
Amendment of the Constitution.

Article VI.
Debts; supremacy; oath.

Article VII.
Ratification and establishment.

Amendments

Article I.
Freedom of religion, of speech and of the press.

Article II.
Right to keep and bear arms.

Article III.
Quartering of soldiers.

Article IV.
Searches and seizures.

Article V.
Rights of accused in criminal proceedings; due process; eminent domain.

Article VI.
Right to speedy trial, witnesses, etc.

Article VII.
Trial by jury in civil cases.

Article VIII.
Bail, fines and punishments.

Article IX.

Reservation of rights of the people.

Article X.

Powers reserved to states or people.

Article XI.

Restriction of judicial power.

Article XII.

Election of President and Vice President.

Article XIII.

§1. Slavery abolished.

§2. Enforcement.

Article XIV.

§1. Citizenship rights not to be abridged by states.

§2. Apportionment of representatives in Congress.

§3. Persons disqualified from holding office.

§4. What public debts are void.

§5. Power to enforce article.

Article XV.

§1. Right to vote not to be abridged.

§2. Power to enforce article.

Article XVI.

Income tax.

Article XVII.

Election of Senators.

Article XVIII.

§1. National liquor prohibition.

§2. Power to enforce article.

§3. Ratification within seven years.

Article XIX.

Woman suffrage.

Article XX.

§1. Terms of office.

§2. Time of convening Congress.

§3. Death of President elect.

§4. Election of the President.

§5. Effective date of sections 1 and 2.

§6. Ratification within seven years.

Article XXI.
§1. National liquor prohibition repealed.
§2. Transportation of liquor into "dry" state.
§3. Ratification within seven years.

Article XXII.
§1. Terms of office of the President.
§2. Ratification within seven years.

Article XXIII.
§1. Presidential electors for District of Columbia.
§2. Power to enforce article.

Article XXIV.
§1. Payment of poll and other taxes as prerequisite to voting in federal elections prohibited.
§2. Power to enforce article.

Article XXV.
§1. Succession to Presidency.
§2. Succession to Vice Presidency.
§3. Disability of President; declaration by President.
§4. Disability of President; declaration by Vice President and majority of officers of executive departments; removal of disability.

Preamble

WE THE PEOPLE of the United States, in order to form a more perfect Union, establish justice, insure domestic tranquility, provide for the common defence, promote the general welfare, and secure the blessing of liberty to ourselves and our posterity, do ordain and establish this CONSTITUTION for the United States of America.

Article I

§1. Legislative powers.
All legislative powers herein granted shall be vested in a Congress of the United States, which shall consist of a Senate and House of Representatives.

§2. House of Representatives; how constituted; power of impeachment.
The House of Representatives shall be composed of members chosen every second year by the people of the several states, and the electors in each state

shall have the qualifications requisite for electors of the most numerous branch of the state legislature.

No person shall be a representative who shall not have attained to the age of twenty-five years, and been seven years a citizen of the United States, and who shall not, when elected, be an inhabitant of that state in which he shall be chosen.

[Representatives and direct taxes shall be apportioned among the several states which may be included within this Union, according to their respective numbers, which shall be determined by adding to the whole number of free persons, including those bound to service for a term of years, and excluding Indians not taxed, three fifths of all other persons.] The actual enumeration shall be made within three years after the first meeting of the Congress of the United States, and within every subsequent term of ten years, in such manner as they shall by law direct. The number of representatives shall not exceed one for every thirty thousand, but each state shall have at least one representative; and until such enumeration shall be made, the State of New Hampshire shall be entitled to choose three, Massachusetts eight, Rhode Island and Providence Plantations one, Connecticut five, New York six, New Jersey four, Pennsylvania eight, Delaware one, Maryland six, Virginia ten, North Carolina five, South Carolina five and Georgia three.

When vacancies happen in the representation from any state, the executive authority thereof shall issue writs of election to fill such vacancies.

The House of Representatives shall choose their speaker and other officers; and shall have the sole power of impeachment.

§3. The Senate; how constituted; impeachment trials.

[The Senate of the United States shall be composed of two Senators from each State, chosen by the legislature thereof, for six years; and each Senator shall have one vote.]

Immediately after they shall be assembled in consequence of the first election, they shall be divided as equally as may be into three classes. The seats of the Senators of the first class shall be vacated at the expiration of the second year, of the second class at the expiration of the fourth year, and of the third class at the expiration of the sixth year, so that one third may be chosen every second year; [and if vacancies happen by resignation, or otherwise, during the recess of the Legislature of ahy State, the executive thereof may make temporary appointments until the next meeting of the legislature, which shall then fill such vacancies.]

No person shall be a Senator who shall not have attained to the age of thirty years, and been nine years a citizen of the United States, and who shall not, when elected, be an inhabitant of that state for which he shall be chosen.

The Vice President of the United States shall be president of the Senate, but shall have no vote, unless they be equally divided.

The Senate shall choose their other officers, and also a president pro tempore, in the absence of the Vice President, or when he shall exercise the office of President of the United States.

The Senate shall have the sole power to try all impeachments. When sitting for that purpose, they shall be on oath or affirmation. When the President of the United States is tried, the Chief Justice shall preside: And no person shall be convicted without the concurrence of two thirds of the members present.

Judgment in cases of impeachment shall not extend further than to removal from office, and disqualification to hold and enjoy any office of honor, trust or profit under the United States; but the party convicted shall nevertheless be liable and subject to indictment, trial judgment and punishment, according to law.

§4. Election of Senators and representatives.

The times, places and manner of holding elections for Senators and representatives, shall be prescribed in each state by the leqislature thereof; but the Congress may at any time by law make or alter such regulations, except as to the places of choosing Senators.

The Congress shall assemble at least once in every year, and such meeting shall be on the first Monday in December, unless they shall by law appoint a different day.

§5. Quorum; journals; meetings; adjournments.

Each house shall be the judge of the elections, returns and qualifications of its own members, and a majority of each shall constitute a quorum to do business; but a smaller number may adjourn from day to day, and may be authorized to compel the attendance of absent members, in such manner and under such penalties as each house may provide.

Each house may determine the rules of its proceedings, punish its members for disorderly behavior, and, with the concurrence of two thirds, expel a member.

Each house shall keep a journal of its proceedings, and from time to time publish the same, excepting such parts as may in their judgment require secrecy; and the yeas and nays of the members of either house on any question shall, at the desire of one fifth of those present, be entered on the journal.

Neither house, during the session of Congress, shall without the consent of the other, adjourn for more than three days, nor to any other place than that in which the two houses shall be sitting.

§6. Compensation; privileges; disabilities.

The Senators and representatives shall receive a compensation for their services, to be ascertained by law, and paid out of the treasury of the United States. They shall in all cases, except treason, felony and breach of the peace, be privileged from arrest during their attendance at the session of their respective houses, and in going and returning from the same; and for any speech or debate in either house, they shall not be questioned in any other place.

No Senator or representative shall, duringthe time for which he was elected, be appointed to any civil office under the authority of the United States, which shall have been created, or the emoluments whereof shall have been increased during such time; and no person holding any office under the United States shall be a member of either house during his continuance in office.

§7. Procedure in passing bills and resolutions.

All bills for raising revenue shall originate in the House of Representatives; but the Senate may propose or concur with amendments as on other bills.

Every bill which shall have passed the House of Representatives and the Senate, shall, before it become a law, be presented to the President of the United States; if he approve he shall sign it, but if not he shall return it, with his objections to that house in which it shall have originated, who shall enter the objections at large on their journal, and proceed to reconsider it. If after such reconsideration two thirds of that house shall agree to pass the bill, it shall be sent, together with the obJections, to the other house, by which it shall likewise be reconsidered, and if approved by two thirds of that house, it shall become a law. But in all such cases the votes of both houses shall be determined by yeas and nays, and the names of the persons' voting for and against the bill shall be entered on the journal of each house respectively. If any bill shall not be returned by the President within ten days (Sundays excepted) after it shall have been presented to him, the same shall be a law, in like manner as if he had signed it, unless the Congress by their adjournment prevent its return, in which case it shall not be a law.

Every order, resolution, or vote to which the concurrence of the Senate and House of Representatives may be necessary (except on a question of adjournment) shall be presented to the President of the United States; and before the same shall take effect, shall be approved by him, or being disapproved by him, shall be repassed by two thirds of the Senate and House of Representatives, according to the rules and limitations prescribed in the case of a bill.

§8. Powers of Congress.

The Congress shall have power to lay and collect taxes, duties, imposts and excises, to pay the debts and provide for the common defense and general welfare of the United States; but all duties, imposts, and excises shall be uniform throughout the United States; To borrow money on the credit of the United States; To regulate commerce with foreign nations, and among the several states, and with the Indian tribes; To establish an uniform rule of naturalization, and uniform laws on the subject of bankruptcies throughout the United States.

To coin money, regulate the value thereof, and of foreign coin, and fix the standard of weights and measures; To provide for the punishment of counterfeiting the securities and current coin of the United States; To establish post offices and post roads; To promote the progress of science and useful arts, by securing for limited times to authors and inventors the exclusive right to their respective writings and discoveries; To constitute tribunals inferior to the Supreme Court; To define and punish piracies and felonies committed on the high seas, and offenses against the law of nations; To declare war, grant letters of marque and reprisal, and make rules concerning captures on land and water; To raise and support armies, but no appropriation of money to that use shall be for a longer term than two years; To provide and maintain a navy; To make rules for the government and regulation of the land and naval forces; To provide for calling forth the militia to execute the laws of the Union, suppress insurrections and repel invasions; To provide for organizing, arming and disciplining the militia, and for governing such part of them as may be employed in the service of the United States, reserving to the states respectively, the appointment of the officers, and the authority of training the militia according to the discipline prescribed by Congress; To exercise exclusive legislation in all cases whatsoever, over such district (not exceeding ten miles square), as may, by cession of particular states, and the acceptance of Congress, become the seat of the government of the United States, and to exercise like authority over all places purchased by the consent of the legislature of the state in which the same shall be, for the erection of forts, magazines and arsenals, dock yards, and other needful buildings; —And To make all laws which shall be necessary and proper for carrying into execution the foregoing powers, and all other powers vested by this Constitution in the government of the United States, or in any department or officer thereof.

§9. Limitations upon powers of Congress.

The migration or importation of such persons as any of the states now existing shall think proper to admit, shall not be prohibited by the Congress prior to the year one thousand eight hundred and eight, but a tax or duty may be imposed on such importation, not exceeding ten dollars for each person.

The privilege of the writ of habeas corpus shall not be suspended, unless when in cases of rebellion or invasion the public safety may require it.

No bill of attainder or ex post facto law shall be passed.

No capitation, or other direct, tax shall be laid, unless in proportion to the census or enumeration hereinbefore directed to be taken.

No tax or duty shall be laid on articles exported from any state.

No preference shall be given by any regulation of commerce or revenue to the ports of one state over those of another; nor shall vessels bound to, or from, one state, be obliged to enter, clear, or pay duties in another.

No money shall be drawn from the treasury, but in consequence of appropriations made by law; and a regular statement and account of the recepits and expenditures of all public money shall be published from time to time.

No title of nobility shall be granted by the United States: and no person holding any office of profit or trust under them, shall without the consent of the Congress, accept of any present, emolument, office, or title of any kind whatever from any king, prince or foreign state.

§10. Restrictions upon powers of state.

No state shall enter into any treaty, alliance or confederation; grant letters of marque and reprisal; coin money; emit bills of credit; make any thing but gold and silver coin a tender in payment of debts; pass any bill of attainder, ex post facto law or law impairing the obligation of contracts, or grant any title of nobility.

No state shall, without the consent of the Congress, lay any imposts or duties on imports or exports, except what may be absolutely necessary for executing its inspection laws; and the net produce of all duties and imposts, laid by any state on imports or exports, shall be for the use of the treasury of the United States; and all such laws shall be subject to the revision and control of the Congress.

No state shall, without the consent of Congress, lay any duty of tonnage, keep troops, or ships of war in time of peace, enter into any agreement or compact with another state, or with a foreign power, or engage in war, unless actually invaded, or in such imminent danger as will not admit of delay.

Article II

§1. President and Vice President.

The executive power shall be vested in a President of the United States of America. He shall hold his office during the term of four years, and, together with the Vice President, chosen for the same term, be elected as follows.

Each state shall appoint, in such manner as the legislature thereof may direct, a number of electors, equal to the whole number of Senators and representatives to which the state may be entitled in the Congress; but no Senator or representative, or person holding an office of trust or profit under the United States, shall be appointed an elector.

[The electors shall meet in their respective states, and vote by ballot for two persons, of whom one at least shall not be an inhabitant of the same state with themselves. And they shall make a list of all the persons voted for, and of the number of votes for each; which list they shall sign and certify, and transmit sealed to the seat of the government of the United States, directed to the President of the Senate. The President of the Senate shall, in the presence of the Senate and House of Representatives, open all the certificates, and the votes shall then be counted. The person having the greatest number of votes shall be the President, if such number be a majority of the whole number of electors appointed; and if there be more than one who have such majority, and have an equal number of votes, then the House of Representatives shall immediately choose by ballot one of them for President; and if no person have a majority, then from the five highest on the list the said house shall in like manner choose the President. But in choosing the President, the votes shall be taken by states, the representation from each state having one vote; a quorum for this purpose shall consist of a member or members from two thirds of the states, and a majority of all the states shall be necessary to a choice. In every case, after the choice of the President, the person having the greatest number of votes of the electors shall be the Vice President. But if there should remain two or more who have equal votes, the Senate shall choose from them by ballot the Vice President.]

The Congress may determine the time of choosing the electors, and the day on which they shall give their votes; which day shall be the same throughout the United States.

No person except a natural born citizen, or a citizen of the United States, at the time of the adoption of this Constitution, shall be eligible to the office of President; neither shall any person be eligible to that office who shall not have attained to the age of thirty-five years, and been fourteen years a resident within the United States.

In case of the removal of the President from office, or of his death, resignation, or inability to discharge the powers and duties of the said office the same shall devolve on the Vice President, and the Congress may by law provide for the case of removal, death, resignation or inability, both of the President and Vice President, declaring what officer shall then act as President, and such officer shall act accordingly, until the disability be removed, or a President shall be elected.

The President shall, at stated times, receive for his services, a compensation, which shall neither be increased nor diminished during the period for which he shall have been elected, and he shall not receive within that period any other emolument from the United States, or any of them.

Before he enter on the execution of his office, he shall take the following oath or affirmation: — "I do solemnly swear (or affirm) that I will faithfully execute the office of President of the United States and will to the best of my ability, preserve, protect and defend the Constitution of the United States."

§2. Powers of the President.

The President shall be commander-in-chief of the Army and Navy of the United States, and of the militia of the several states, when called into the actual service of the United States; he may require the opinion, in writing, of the principal officer in each of the executive departments, upon any subject relating to the duties of their respective offices, and he shall have power to grant reprieves and pardons for offenses against the United States, except in cases of impeachment.

He shall have power, by and with the advice and consent of the Senate, to make treaties, provided two thirds of the Senators present concur; and he shall nominate, and by and with the advice and consent of the Senate, shall appoint ambassadors, other public ministers and counsuls, judges of the Supreme Court, and all other officers of the United States, whose appointments are not herein otherwise provided for, and which shall be established by law: but the Congress may by law vest the appointment of such inferior officers, as they think proper, in the President alone, in the courts of law, or in the heads of departments.

The President shall have power to fill up all vacancies that may happen during the recess of the Senate, by granting commissions which shall expire at the end of their next session.

§3. Messages to Congress; additional powers and duties.

He shall from time to time give to the Congress information of the state of the Union, and recommend to their consideration such measures as he shall judge necessary and expedient; he may, on extraordinary occasions, convene both houses, or either of them and in case of disagreement between them, with respect to the time of adjournment, he may adjourn them to such time as he shall think proper; he shall receive ambassadors and other public ministers; he shall take care that the laws be faithfully executed, and shall commission all the officers of the United States.

§4. Impeachment.

The President, Vice President and all civil officers of the United States, shall be removed from office on impeachment for, and conviction of, treason, bribery, or other high crimes and misdemeanors.

Article III

§1. Judicial power; tenure of office.

The judicial power of the United States, shall be vested in one Supreme Court, and in such inferior courts as the Congress may from time to time ordain and establish. The judges, both of the Supreme and inferior courts, shall hold their offices during good behavior, and shall, at stated times, receive for their services, a compensation, which shall not be diminished during their continuance in office.

§2. Jurisdiction.

The judicial power shall extend to all cases, in law and equity, arising under this Constitution, the laws of the United States, and treaties made, or which shall be made, under their authority; —to all cases affecting ambassadors, other public ministers and consuls; —to all cases of admiralty and maritime jurisdiction; —to controversies to which the United States shall be a party; —to controversies between two or more states; —between a state and citizens of another state; —between citizens of different states, —between citizens of the same state, claiming lands under grants of different states, and between a state, or the citizens thereof, and foreign states, citizens or subjects.

In all cases affecting ambassadors, other public ministers and consuls, and those in which a state shall be a party, the Supreme Court shall have original jurisdictions. In all the other cases before mentioned, the Supreme Court shall have appellate jurisdiction, both as to law and fact, with such exceptions, and under such circumstances as the Congress shall make.

The trial of all crimes, except in cases of impeachment, shall be by jury; and such trial shall be held in the state where the said crimes shall have been committed; but when not committed within any state, the trial shall be at such place or places as the Congress may by law have directed.

§3. Treason; proof and punishment.

Treason against the United States, shall consist only in levying war against them, or in adhering to their enemies, giving them aid and comfort. No person shall be convicted of treason unless on the testimony of two witnesses to the same overt act, or on confession in open court.

The Congress shall have power to declare the punishment of treason, but no attainder of treason shall work corruption of blood, or forfeiture except during the life of the person attained.

Article IV

§1. Full faith and credit among states.

Full faith and credit shall be given in each state to the public acts, records and judicial proceedings of every other state. And the Congress may by general laws prescribe the manner in which such acts, records and proceedings shall be proved, and the effect thereof.

§2. Privileges and immunities; fugitives.

The citizens of each state shall be entitled to all privileges and immunities of citizens in the several states.

A person charged in any state with treason, felony, or other crimes, who shall flee from justice, and be found in another state, shall on demand of the executive authority of the state from which he fled, be delivered up, to be removed to the state having jurisdiction of the crime.

No person held to service or labor in one state, under the laws thereof, escaping into another, shall, in consequence of any law or regulation therein, be discharged from such service or labor, but shall be delivered up on claim of the party to whom such service or labor may be due.

§3. Admission of new states; power over territory and other property.

New states may be admitted by the Congress into this Union; but no new state shall be formed or erected within the jurisdiction of any other state; nor any state be formed by the junction of two or more states, or parts of states, without the consent of the legislatures of the states concerned as well as of the Congress.

The Congress shall have power to dispose of and make all needful rules and regulations respecting the territory or other property belonging to the United States; and nothing in this Constitution shall be so construed as to prejudice any claims of the United States, or of any particular state.

§4. Guarantee of republican form of government.

The United States shall guarantee to every state in this Union a republican form of government, and shall protect each of them against invasion; and on application of the legislature, or of the executive (when the legislature cannot be convened) against domestic violence.

Article V

Amendment of the Constitution.

The Congress, whenever two thirds of both houses shall deem it necessary, shall propose amendments to this Constitution, or, on the application of the legislatures of two thirds of the several states, shall call a convention for proposing amendments, which, in either case, shall be valid to all intents and purposes, as part of this Constitution, when ratified by the legislatures of three fourths of the several states, or by conventions in three fourths thereof, as the one or the other mode of ratification may be proposed by the Congress: Provided that no amendment which may be made prior to the year one thousand eight hundred and eight shall in any manner affect the first and fourth clauses in the ninth section of the first article; and that no state, without its consent, shall be deprived of its equal suffrage in the Senate.

Article VI

Debts; supremacy; oath.

All debts contracted and engagements entered into, before the adopticn of this Constitution, shall be as valid against the United States under this Constitution, as under the Confederation.

This Constitution, and the laws of the United States which shall be made in pursuance thereof; and all treaties made, or which shall be made, under the authority of the United States, shall be the supreme law of the land; and the judges in every state shall be bound thereby, anything in the Constitution or laws of any state to the contrary notwithstanding.

The Senators and representatives before mentioned, and the members of the several state legislatures, and all executive and judicial officers, both of the United States and of the several states, shall be bound by oath or affirmation, to support this Constitution; but no religious tests shall ever be required as a qualification to any office or public trust under the United States.

Article VII

Ratification and establishment.

The ratification of the conventions of nine states, shall be sufficient for the establishment of this Constitution between the states so ratifying the same.

Done in Convention by the unanimous consent of the States present the seventeenth day of September in the year of our Lord one thousand seven hundred and eighty-seven and of the Independence of the United States of America the Twelfth. In Witness whereof we have hereunto subscribed our names.

Amendments to the Constitution

Article I

Freedom of religion, of speech and of the press.

Congress shall make no law respecting an establishment of religion, or prohibiting the free exercise thereof; or abridging the freedom of speech, or of the press; or the right of the people peaceably to assemble, and to petition the government for a redress of grievances.

Article II

Right to keep and bear arms.

A well regulated militia, being necessary to the security of a free state, the right of the people to keep and bear arms, shall not be infringed.

Article III

Quartering of soldiers.

No soldier shall, in time of peace be quartered in any house, without the consent of the owner, nor in time of war, but in a manner to be prescribed by law.

Article IV

Searches and seizures.

The right of the people to be secure in their persons, houses, papers, and effects, against unreasonable searches and seizures, shall not be violated, and no warrants shall issue, but upon probable cause, supported by oath or affirmation, and particularly describing the place to be searched, and the persons or things to be seized.

Article V

Rights of accused in criminal proceedings; due process; eminent domain.

No person shall be held to answer for a capital, or otherwise infamous crime, unless on a presentment or indictment of a grand jury, except in cases arising in the land or naval forces, or in the militia, when in actual service in time of war or public danger; nor shall any person be subject for the same offence to be twice put in jeopardy of life or limb; nor shall be compelled in any criminal case to be a witness against himself, nor be deprived of life, liberty, or property, without due process of law; nor shall private property be taken for public use, without just compensation.

Article VI

Right to speedy trial, witnesses, etc.

In all criminal prosecutions, the accused shall enjoy the right to a speedy and public trial, by an impartial jury of the state and district wherein the crime shall have been committed, which district shall have been previously ascertained by law, and to be informed of the nature and cause of the accusation; to be confronted with the witnesses against him; to have compulsory process for obtaining witnesses in his favor, and to have the assistance of counsel for his defense.

Article VII

Trial by jury in civil cases.

In suits at common law, where the value in controversy shall exceed twenty dollars, the right of trial by jury shall be preserved, and no fact tried by a jury shall be otherwise re-examined in any court of the United States, than according to the rules of the common law.

Article VIII

Bails, fines and punishments.

Excessive bail shall not be required, nor excessive fines imposed, nor cruel and unusual punishments inflicted.

Article IX

Reservation of rights of the people.

The enumeration in the Constitution, of certain rights, shall not be construed to deny or disparage other retained by the people.

Article X

Powers reserved to states or people.

The powers not delegated to the United States by the Constitution, nor prohibited by it to the states, are reserved to the states respectively, or to the people.

Article XI

Restriction of judicial power.

The judicial power of the United States shall not be construed to extend to any suit in law or equity, commenced or prosecuted against one of the United States by citizens of another state, or by citizens or subjects of any foreign state.

Article XII

Election of President and Vice President.

The electors shall meet in their respective states, and vote by ballot for President and Vice President, one of whom, at least, shall not be an ihhabitant of the same state with themselves; they shall name in their ballots the person voted for as President, and in distinct ballots the person voted for as Vice President, and they shall make distinct lists of all persons voted for as President, and of all persons voted for as Vice President, and of the number of votes for each, which lists they shall sign and certify, and transmit sealed to the seat of the government of the United States, directed to the President of the Senate; —The President of the Senate shall, in presence of the Senate and House of Representatives, open all the certificates and the votes shall then be counted; —The person having the greatest number of votes for President, shall be the President, if such number be a majority of the whole number of electors appointed; and if no person have such majority, then from the persons having the highest numbers not exceeding three on the list of those voted for as President, the House of Representatives shall choose immediately, by ballot, the President. But in choosing the President, the votes shall be taken by states, the representation from each state having one vote; a quorum for this purpose shall consist of a member or members from two thirds of the states, and a majority of all the states shall be necessary to a choice. And if the House of Representatives shall not choose a President whenever the right of choice shall devolve upon them, before the fourth day of March next following, then the Vice President shall act as President, as in the case of the death or other constitutional disability of the President. The person having the greatest number of votes as Vice President, shall be the Vice President, if such number be a majority of the whole number of electors appointed, and if no person have a majority, then from the two highest numbers on the list, the Senate shall choose the Vice President; a quorum for the purpose shall consist of two-thirds of the whole number of Senators, and a majority of the whole number shall be necessary to a choice. But no person constitutionally ineligible to the office of President should be eligible to that of Vice President of the United States.

Article XIII

§1. Slavery abolished.

Neither slavery nor involuntary servitude, except as a punishment for crime whereof the party shall have been duly convicted, shall exist within the United States, or any place subject to their jurisdiction.

§2. Enforcement.

Congress shall have power to enforce this article by appropriate legislation.

Article XIV

§1. Citizenship rights not to be abridged by states.

All persons born or naturalized in the United States, and subject to the Jurisdiction thereof, are citizens of the United States and of the state wherein they reside. No state shall make or enforce any law which shall abridge the privileges or immunities of citizens of the United States; nor shall any state deprive any person of life, liberty, or property, without due process of law; nor deny to any person within its jurisdiction the equal protection of the laws.

§2. Apportionment of representatives in Congress.

Representatives shall be apportioned among the several states according to their respective numbers, counting the whole number of persons in each state, excluding Indians not taxed. But when the right to vote at any election for the choice of electors for President and Vice President of the United States, representatives in Congress, the executive and judicial officers of a state, or the members of the legislature thereof, is denied to any of the male inhabitants of such state, being twenty-one years of age, and citizens of the United States, or in any way abridged, except for participation in rebellion, or other crime, the basis of representation therein shall be reduced in the proportion which the number of such male citizens shall bear to the whole number of male citizens twenty-one years of age in such state.

§3. Persons disqualified from holding office.

No person shall be a Senator or representative in Congress, or elector of President and Vice President, or hold any office, civil or military, under the United States, or under any state, who having previously taken an oath, as a member of Congress, or as an officer of the United States, or as a member of any state legislature, or as an executive or judicial officer of any state, to support the Constitution of the United States, shall have engaged in insurrection or rebellion against the same, or given aid or comfort to the enemies thereof. But Congress may by a vote of two thirds of each house, remove such disability.

§4. What public debts are void.

The validity of public debt of the United States, authorized by law, including debts incurred for payment of pensions and bounties for services in suppressing insurrection or rebellion, shall not be questioned. But neither the United States nor any state shall assume or pay any debt or obligation incurred in aid of insurrection or rebellion against the United States, or any claim for the loss or emancipation of any slave; but all such debts, obligations and claims shall be held illegal and void.

§5. Power to enforce article.

The Congress shall have power to enforce by appropriate legislation, the provisions of this article.

Article XV

§1. Right to vote not to be abridged.

The right of citizens of the United States to vote shall not be denied or abridged by the United States or by any state on account of race, color, or previous condition of servitude.

§2. Power to enforce article.

The Congress shall have power to enforce this article by appropriate legislation.

Article XVI

Income tax.

The Congress shall have power to levy and collect taxes on incomes, from whatever source derived, without apportionment among the several states, and without regard to any census or enumerations.

Article XVII

Election of Senators.

The Senate of the United States shall be composed of two Senators from each state, elected by the people thereof, for six years; and each Senator shall have one vote. The electors in each state shall have the qualifications requisite for electors of the most numerous branch of the state legislatures.

When vacancies happen in the representation of any state in the Senate, the executive authority of such state shall issue writs of election to fill such vacancies: Provided, That the legislature of any state may empower the executive thereof to make temporary appointment until the people fill the vacancies by election as the legislature may direct.

This amendment shall not be so construed as to affect the election or term of any Senator chosen before it becomes valid as part of the Constitution.

Article XVIII

§1. National liquor prohibition.

After one year from the ratification of this article the manufacture, sale, or transportation of intoxicating liquors within, the importation thereof into, or the exportation thereof from the United States and all territory subject to the jurisdiction thereof for beverage purposes is hereby prohibited.

§2. Power to enforce article.

The Congress and the several states shall have concurrent power to enforce this article by appropriate legislation.

§3. Ratification within seven years.

This article shall be inoperative unless it shall have been ratified as an amendment to the Constitution by the legislatures of the several states, as provided in the Constitution, within seven years from the date of the submission hereof to the states by the Congress.

Article XIX

Woman suffrage.

The right of citizens of the United States to vote shall not be denied or abridged by the United States or by any state on account of sex.

Congress shall have power to enforce the provisions of this article by appropriate legislation.

Article XX

§1. Terms of office.

The terms of the President and Vice President shall end at noon on the 20th day of January, and the terms of Senators and representatives at noon on the 3rd day of January, of the years in which such terms would have ended if this article had not been ratified; and the terms of their successors shall then begin.

§2. Time of convening Congress.

The Congress shall assemble at least once in every year, and such meeting shall begin at noon on the 3rd day of January, unless they shall by law appoint a different day.

§3. Death of President elect.

If, at the time fixed for the beginning of the term of the President, the President elect shall have died, the Vice President elect shall become President. If a President shall not have been chosen before the time fixed for the beginning of his term, or if the President elect shall have filed to qualify, then the Vice President elect shall act as President until a President shall have qualified; and the Congress may by law provide for the case wherein neither a President elect nor a Vice President elect shall have qualified, declaring who shall then act as President, or the manner in which one who is to act shall be selected, and such person shall act accordingly until a President or Vice President shall have qualified.

§4. Election of the President.

The Congress may by law provide for the case of death of any of the persons from whom the House of Representatives may choose a President whenever the right of choice shall have devolved upon them, and for the case of the death of any of the persons from whom the Senate may choose a Vice President whenever the right of choice shall have devolved upon them.

§5. Effective date of sections 1 and 2.

Sections 1 and 2 shall take effect on the 15th day of October following the ratification of this article.

§6. Ratification within seven years.

This article shall be inoperative unless it shall have been ratified as an amendment to the Constitution by the legislatures of three fourths of the several states within seven years from the date of its submission.

Article XXI

§1. National liquor prohibition repealed.

The eighteenth article of amendment to the Constitution of the United States is hereby repealed.

§2. Transportation of liquor into "dry" state.

The transportation or importation into any state, territory, or possession of the United States for delivery or use therein of intoxicating liquors, in violation of the laws thereof, is hereby prohibited.

§3. Ratification within seven years.

This article shall be inoperative unless it shall have been ratified as an amendment to the Constitution by conventions in the several states, as provided in the Constitution, within seven years from the date of the submission hereof to the states by the Congress.

Article XXII

§1. Terms of office of the President.

No person shall be elected to the office of the President more than twice, and no person who has held the office of President, or acted as President, for more than two years of a term to which some other person was elected President shall be elected to the office of the President more than once. But this article shall not apply to any person holding the office of President when this Article was proposed by the Congress, and shall not prevent any person who may be holding the office of President, or acting as President, during the term within which this article becomes operative from holding the office of President during the remainder of such term.

§2. Ratification within seven years.

This article shall be inoperative unless it shall have been ratified as an amendment to the Constitution by the legislatures of three fourths of the several states within seven years from the date of its submission to the states by the Congress.

Article XXIII

§1. Presidential electors for District of Columbia.

The District constituting the seat of Government of the United States shall appoint in such manner as the Congress may direct: A number of electors of President and Vice President equal to the whole number of Senators and Representatives in Congress to which the District would be entitled if it were a State, but in no event more than the least populous State; they shall be in addition to those appointed by the States, but they shall be considered, for the purposes of the election of President and Vice President, to be electors appointed by a State; and they shall meet in the District and perform such duties as provided by the twelfth article of amendment.

§2. Power to enforce article.

The Congress shall have power to enforce this article by appropriate legislation.

Article XXIV

§1. Payment of poll and other taxes as prerequisite to voting in federal elections prohibited.

The right of citizens of the United States to vote in any primary or other election for President or Vice President, for electors for President or Vice President, or for Senator or Representative in Congress, shall not be denied or abridged by the United States or any State by reason of failure to pay any poll tax or other tax.

§2. Power to enforce article.

The Congress shall have power to enforce this article by appropriate legislation.

Article XXV

§1. Succession to Presidency.

In case of the removal of the President from office or of his death or resignation, the Vice President shall become President.

§2. Succession to Vice Presidency.

Whenever there is a vacancy in the office of the Vice President, the President shall nominate a Vice President who shall take office upon confirmation by a majority vote of both House of Congress.

§3. Disability of President; declaration by President.

Whenever the President transmits to the President pro tempore of the Senate and the Speaker of the House of Representatives his written declaration that he is unable to discharge the powers and duties of his office, and until he transmits to them a written declaration to the contrary, such powers and duties shall be discharged by the Vice President as Acting President.

§4. Disability of President; declaration by Vice President and majority of officers of executive departments; removal of disability.

Whenever the Vice President and a majority of either the principal officers of the executive departments or of such body as Congress may by law provide, transmit to the President pro tempore of the Senate and the Speaker of the House of Representatives their written declaration that the President is unable to discharge the powers and duties of his office, the Vice President shall immediately assume the powers and duties of the office as Acting President.

Thereafter, when the President transmits to the President pro tempore of the Senate and the Speaker of the House of Representatives his written declaration that no inability exists, he shall resume the powers and duties of his office unless the Vice President and a majority of either the principal officers of the executive department or of such other body as Congress may by law provide, transmit within four days to the President pro tempore of the Senate and the Speaker of the House of Representative their written declaration that the President is unable to discharge the powers and duties of his office. Thereupon Congress shall decide the issue, assembling within forty-eight hours for that purpose if not in session. If the Congress, within twenty-one days after receipt of the latter written declaration, or, if Congress is not in session, within twenty-one days after Congress is required to assemble, determines by two-thirds vote of both Houses that the President is unable to discharge the powers and duties of his office, the Vice President shall continue to discharge the same as Acting President; otherwise, the President shall resume the powers and duties of his office.

Cases

A

K

(1976) §5.03

People v Jackson, 391 Mich 323,
217 NW2d 22 (1974) **§§5.02,
6.03**

People v James, 393 Mich 807, 225
NW2d 520 (1975) **§12.09**

People v Jiminez, 21 Cal 3d 595,
580 P2d 672, 147 Cal Rptr 172
(1978) **§5.17**

People v Johnson, 75 Ill 2d 180, 387
NE2d 688 (1979) **§14.10**

People v Johnson, 149 Cal App 30,
149 Cal Rptr 661 (1978) **§6.03**

People v Johnson, 10 Cal 3d 868,
519 P2d 604, 112 Cal Rptr 556
(1974) §12.16

People v Jones, 47 NY2d 409, 391
NE2d 1335, 418 NYS2d 359
(1979) **§16.11**

People v Kagan, 101 Misc 2d 274,
420 NYS2d 987 (Sup Ct 1979)
§17.08

People v King, 267 Cal App 814, 73
Cal Rptr 440 (1969), *cert denied*,
396 US 1028 (1970) **§18.15**

People v Lambreuts, 69 Ill 2d 544,
372 NE2d 641 (1977) **§12.16**

People v Longwill, 14 Cal 3d 943,
538 P2d 753, 123 Cal Rptr 297
(1975) **§§3.26, 5.21**

People v Lowe, 184 Colo 182, 519
P2d 344 (1974) **§6.03**

People v Lynes, 49 NY2d 286,
401 NE2d 405, 425 NYS2d 295
(1980) **§5.10**

People v McGee, 49 NY2d 48,
399 NE2d 1177, 424 NYS2d 157
(1979), *cert denied*, 446 US 942
(1980) **§2.09**

People v McKenna, 196 Colo 367,
585 P2d 275 (1978) **§10.04**

People v Modesto, 62 Cal 2d 436,
42 Cal Rptr 417, 398 P2d 753

(1965) §5.12

People v Moll, 26 NY2d 1, 256
NE2d 175, 307 NYS2d 876, *cert
denied*, 398 US 911 (1970) **§16.05**

People v Molono, 253 Cal App 2d
691, 61 Cal Rptr 821 (1967)
§17.13

People v Pettingill, 21 Cal 3d 231,
578 P2d 108, 145 Cal Rptr 861
(1978) **§§5.11, 5.12**

People v Polk, 2 Ill 2d 594, 174
NE2d 393 (1961) **§7.03**

People v Pope, 23 Cal 3d 412, 590
P2d 859, 152 Cal Rptr 732 (1979)
§§14.09, 14.10

People v Prim, 53 Ill 2d 62, 289
NE2d 601 (1972), *cert denied*, 412
US 918 (1973) **§17.14**

People v Reed, 393 Mich 342, 224
NW2d 867, *cert denied*, 422 US
1044 (1975) **§3.31**

People v Reyes, 12 Cal 3d 486, 526
P2d 225, 116 Cal Rptr 217 (1974)
§9.07

People v Riddle, 83 Cal App 3d 563,
148 Cal Rptr 170 (1978) **§5.12**

People v Robles, 182 Colo 4, 514
P2d 630 (1973) **§16.10**

People v Robles, 2 Cal 2d 205, 466
P2d 710, 85 Cal Rptr 166 (1970)
§14.05

People v Rodney P, 21 NY2d 1,
233 NE2d 255, 286 NYS2d 225
(1967) **§5.08**

People v Rosochacki, 41 Ill 2d 483,
244 NE2d 136 (1969) §16.05

People v Samuels, 49 NY 2d 218,
400 NE2d 1344, 424 NYS2d 892
(1980) **§5.02**

People v Sapia, 41 NY2d 160,
359 NE2d 688, 391 NYS2d 93
(1976), *cert denied*, 434 US 823
(1977) **§§10.03, 10.06, 13.02**

Q

Y

Z

Statutes

Uniform Acts

Interstate Agreement on Detainers, 11 ULA 323 (1974) §20.11

Uniform Act to Secure the Attendance of Witnesses From Without a State in Criminal Cases, 11 ULA 1, §§20.01, 20.12

Uniform Criminal Extradition Act, 11 ULA 94 (1974) §§20.01, 20.02, 20.04, 20.05, 20.07

Uniform Rendition of Prisoners as Witnesses in Criminal Proceedings Act, 11 ULA 547 (1974) §§20.01, 20.12

United States Constitution

US Const amend IV §§3.01, 3.15, 7.04, 15.04

US Const amend V §§5.05, 5.06, 7.03, 13.10, 15.13

US Const amend VI §§5.01, 10.03, 11.02, 13.01, 14.03

US Const Amend VIII §§8.01, 8.02, 8.04

US Const art 1, §10 §§1.06, 1.07
US Const art 1 §9 §§1.06, 1.07
US Const art II, §2 §19.09
US Const art IV, §2 §§20.01, 20.02
US Const art IV, §2, cl 2 §§20.04, 20.05, 20.06, 20.12

United States Code

18 USC §2518 §2.09
18 USC §3006(a)(e) §14.04
18 USC §3041 §8.07
18 USC §3161 §§11.01, 11.02
18 USC §3182 §§20.02, 20.04, 20.05
18 USC §3731 §15.15
18 USC §4244 §14.04
18 USC §6002 §13.12
26 USC §7602 §3.06
28 USC §1983 §1.03
28 USC §2254 §19.08
42 USC §1983 §9.08

Authorities

ABA Standards for Criminal Justice, Severance of Defendants, §13-3.2 (1980) **§16.04**

ABA Standards for Criminal Justice, Discovery and Procedure Before Trial, §11-1.1 (1980) **§10.01**

ABA Standards, The Prosecution Function §3-3.6(b)(1980) **§7.12**

Alschuler, *Plea Bargaining*, 76 Colum L Rev 1059 (1978) **§12.16**

Berger, *Man's Trial, Woman's Tribulation: Rape Cases in the Courtroom*, 77 Colum L Rev 1 (1977) **§10.04**

1 W. Blackstone, Commentaries (U Chi ed 1979) **§§1.04, 1.07**

3 W. Blackstone, Commentaries (U Chi ed 1979) **§19.08**

4 W. Blackstone, Commentaries (U Chi ed 1979) **§§1.06, 3.15, 4.03, 4.04, 7.03, 8.01, 8.02, 8.11, 12.01, 13.01, 15.13, 17.01**

Borman, *The Selling of Preventive Detention 1970*, 65 N UL Rev 879 (1971) **§8.05**

Brennan, *State Constitutions and the Protection of Individual Rights*, 90 Harv L Rev 489 (1977) **§1.02**

E Coke, Institutes 177 (Brooke ed 1797) **§§4.04, 11.02**

Comment, ABA Standards—Pretrial Release §10.59 (1980) **§8.05**

Comment, *Kirby v Illinois: A New Approach to Right to Counsel*, 58 Iowa L Rev 404 (1972) **§6.03**

Derschowitz & Ely, *Harris v New York: Some Anxious Observations on the Candor of the Emerging Nixon Majority*, 80 Yale LJ 1198 (1971) **§5.14**

Foote, *The Coming Constitutional Crisis in Bail*, 113 U Pa L Rev 959 (1965) **§8.05**

Gobert & Cohen, Rights of Prisoners (Shepard's/McGraw-Hill 1981) **§18.08**

J.C. Gray, The Nature and Sources of Law 100 (1921) **§1.09**

1 M. Hale, Pleas of the Crown 634 (1st ed Am 1874) (1st ed London 1736) **§10.04**

Hickey, *Preventive Detention and the Crime of Being Dangerous*, 58 Geo LJ 287 (1969) **§8.05**

Hill, *Testimonial Privilege and Fair Trial*, 80 Colum L Rev 1173 (1980) **§§10.03, 10.05**

W. Jordan, Jury Selection (Shepards/McGraw-Hill 1980) **§17.06**

E. Loftus, Eyewitness Testimony (1979) **§6.01**

A.L. Lowell, The Judicial Use of Torture, 11 Harv L Rev 220 (1898) **§5.05**

Model Code of Pre-Arraignment Procedure, commentary at 290-91 (1975) **§4.01**

S. Nahmod, Civil Rights and Civil Liberties Litigation (Shepard's/McGraw-Hill 1979) **§§1.03, 9.08**

Pitler, *The Fruit of the Poisonous Tree*, 56 Cal L Rev 579 (1968) **§15.05**

Pulaski, *Neil v Biggers; The Supreme Court Dismantles the Wade Trilogy's Due Process Protections*, 26 Stan L Rev 1097 (1977) **§6.10**

3 Story, Comment on the Constitution of the United States §§7786-7787 (1st ed 1833) **§13.01**

Strazella, *Ineffective Assistance of Counsel Claims: New Uses, New Problems* 19 Ariz L Rev 443 (1977) **§14.09**

Tague, *An Indigent's Right to the Attorney of His Choice*, 27 Stan L Rev 73 (1974) **§14.05**

Tague, *Multiple Representation of Targets and Witnesses During a Grand Jury*, 17 Am Crim L Rev 301 (1980) **§7.08**

Tanford & Bocchino, *Rape Shield Laws and the Sixth Amendment*, 128 U Pa L Rev 544 (1980) **§10.04**

Tribe, *An Ounce of Detention: Preventive Justice in the World of John Mitchell*, 56 Va L Rev 371 (1970) **§8.05**

Van Alstyne, *The Demise of the Right-Privilege Distinction in Constitutional Law*, 82 Harv L Rev 1439 (1968) **§18.15p**

Westen, *The Compulsory Process Clause*, 73 Mich L Rev 73 (1974) **§13.14**

3 Wigmore on Evidence, §924(a) (Chadbourne rev 1970) **§10.07**

8 Wigmore on Evidence §309 (3d ed 1940) **§5.05**

8 Wigmore on Evidence §2263 (McNaughton rev 1940) **§5.19**

Willard, *The Seventeenth Century Indictment*, 24 Harv L Rev 290 (1911) **§7.02**

S. Williston, *Does a Pardon Blot Out Guilt*, 28 Harv L Rev 647 (1915) **§19.09**

Index

A